GENDER IN CROSS-CULTURAL PERSPECTIVE

- 3 D

-8 M

B. Brettell

F. Sargent

ethodist University

PRENTICE HALL

Library of Congress Cataloging-in-Publication Data

Gender in cross-cultural perspective / edited by Caroline B. Brettell,
   Carolyn F. Sargent.
     p. cm.
    Includes bibliographical references.
    ISBN 0–13–352048–X
     1. Sex role—Cross-cultural studies.   I. Brettell, Caroline B.
II. Sargent, Carolyn Fishel, 1947–
HQ1075.G4634   1993
305.3—dc20   92–11029
                                                        CIP

Acquisitions editor: Nancy Roberts
Editorial assistant: Pat Naturale
Editorial/production supervision and interior design: Joan Powers
Copy editor: Ellen Falk
Cover design: Carol Ceraldi
Prepress buyer: Kelly Behr
Manufacturing buyer: Mary Ann Gloriande

© 1993 by Prentice-Hall, Inc.
A Simon & Schuster Company
Englewood Cliffs, New Jersey 07632

Printed in the United States of America
10   9   8   7   6   5   4   3

ISBN 0-13-352048-X

Prentice-Hall International (UK) Limited, *London*
Prentice-Hall of Australia Pty. Limited, *Sydney*
Prentice-Hall Canada Inc., *Toronto*
Prentice-Hall Hispanoamericana, S.A., *Mexico*
Prentice-Hall of India Private Limited, *New Delhi*
Prentice-Hall of Japan, Inc., *Tokyo*
Simon & Schuster Asia Pte. Ltd., *Singapore*
Editora Prentice-Hall do Brasil, Ltda., *Rio de Janeiro*

Contents

Preface

The initial idea for this reader came from the experience of teaching undergraduate courses in gender and anthropology. In reviewing the textbooks available for an introductory course, we came to the conclusion that there was a need for a readable text that built on the classic contributions of the 1970s while also incorporating the more recent and diverse literature on gender roles and ideology around the world. Although a number of sophisticated theoretical works devoted to this subject existed, we felt there was a dearth of classroom material available in one volume and appropriate for less advanced students, whether undergraduates or beginning graduate students.

In selecting materials, we attempted to accomplish five goals. First, we wanted to introduce students to the most significant topics in the field of the anthropology of gender. These include the study of men and women in prehistory; the relationship between biology and culture; the cultural construction of masculinity, femininity, and sexuality; variations in the sexual division of labor and economic organization; women's involvement in ritual and religion; and the impact on gender issues of various forces of change such as colonialism, the rise of the state, and economic development.

Second, we hoped to provide broad cross-cultural coverage to encourage comparative analysis of the themes under discussion and to encompass studies addressing issues of gender in industrial society as well as in developing societies. Third, we wanted to complement research on women's lives with some articles that dealt with masculinity and male gender roles. Because feminist theory has only recently been applied to the study of men, a truly balanced reader is not yet possible; however, we tried to incorporate some of the most exciting new research in this domain.

Fourth, we were committed to combining theoretical and ethnographically based articles in each section of the book. We hope that we have compiled a volume that can stand alone or, if the instructor so desires, be complemented by the use of full ethnographies. Fifth, we wanted to include introductions to each section that would review as clearly as possible some of the significant issues debated in particular subject areas in the anthropology of gender. These introductions are intended to orient students to the articles in the section and to provide a context in which readers can more fully understand each article. Each introduction concludes with a list of references that can be used by teachers and students to examine further the questions raised in that section.

We do not expect all instructors to assign the sections in the order that they appear in the text. This order makes sense to us, but our ultimate goal is to provide for maximum flexibility in teaching. We also have no intention of imposing a particular theoretical perspective, although our own predilections may be apparent to some readers. We have tried to include readings that reflect a variety of theoretical orientations to enable instructors to emphasize their own approach to the subject.

The text concludes with a list of recommended films that is organized by section. We have previewed most of these films, and we hope that all of them will successfully complement the readings in the text.

Acknowledgments

Many people have contributed substantially to the preparation and development of this volume. Andrew Webb provided invaluable clerical and organizational assistance. The undergraduate students in Professor Sargent's Sex Roles course during the fall semester of 1990 read and critiqued most of the articles in this volume. Their opinions influenced us enormously in the final selection process. John Phinney acted as an invaluable library of knowledge for obscure references. We also thank the reviewers of our manuscript, who offered numerous suggestions about what has become a vast literature in the anthropological study of gender and provided ideas regarding the format of the text. Finally, we thank Nancy Roberts for her confidence in our judgment and her constant support of this project from its inception.

C.B.B.
C.F.S.

I.
Biology, Gender, and Human Evolution

What is the role of biology in human behavior? To what extent are differences between men and women explained by biology, by culture, or by an interaction between the two? Is there a biological basis for the sexual division of labor? These questions are hotly debated in the United States as we struggle with such issues as why men dominate the fields of math and science, whether women are equipped for war and combat, and the implications for child development of female participation in the labor force. When issues of gender are considered in a cross-cultural context, we explore whether women are universally subordinated to men and to what extent biological differences explain the allocation of roles and responsibilities between men and women.

The relative importance of biology, or nature, versus culture, or nurture, is an enduring dilemma. This issue was addressed by Margaret Mead several decades ago. Using cross-cultural data drawn from her fieldwork in Samoa and New Guinea, Mead (1928, 1935) set out to es-tablish the significance of culture or environment in molding gender differences. She wanted to offer an alternative to the powerful intellectual principles of biological determinism and eugenics (biological engineering) that dominated academic circles in the 1920s. She also hoped to demonstrate to North American women that a range of possibilities was open to them and that the social roles of housework and childrearing were not their inevitable lot. In her view, anatomy was not destiny.

Mead's work was challenged in the 1980s by Derek Freeman (1983). Freeman accused Mead of cultural determinism (that is, giving priority to culture over biology) and opened a lively debate within academic and nonacademic circles (Rensberger 1983; Scheper-Hughes 1987; Schneider 1983). For some, Freeman's book was taken (erroneously) as new support for the sociobiological approach to an understanding of human behavior, an approach formulated by Edward Wilson (1975) that contends that there is a genetic basis for all social behavior.

1

Although few people deny the anatomical and hormonal differences between men and women, they disagree about the importance of these differences for gender roles and personality attributes. Recent research, most of it conducted by psychologists, suggests that male and female infants cannot be significantly distinguished by their degree of dependence on parents, their visual and verbal abilities, or their aggression as measured by activity level (Fausto-Sterling 1985; Renzetti and Curran 1989). These characteristics tend to emerge later in the development process, indicating the importance of environment. A current controversy centers on how the brain is organized and to what extent brain lateralization is related to sex differences. One position holds that women are left-brain dominant, giving them superior verbal skills, while men are right-brain dominant, giving them superior visual-spatial skills. While research on variations in the structure and development of male and female brains continues, Renzetti and Curran (1989:33) contend that to date "there is little evidence indicating that the sexual differentiation of the brain, if it occurs in humans, consequently predisposes males and females to behave in gender-specific ways" (see also Fausto-Sterling 1985:44–53).

Within anthropology the role of biology in explaining differences between men and women, including social behaviors such as the division of labor and the tendency for women to be subordinated to men, has been explored within an evolutionary framework. Evolutionary theories fall roughly into four categories: male strength hypotheses, male bonding hypotheses, male aggression hypotheses, and women's childbearing hypotheses. Male strength hypotheses argue that men are physically stronger than women and this gives them superiority. They are larger, and they have stronger muscles and less fat, a pelvis better adapted for sprinting, larger hearts and lungs, and so forth. These physical differences between the males and females of a species are referred to as sexual dimorphism.

Through comparisons drawn with nonhuman primates, Leibowitz (in this book) explores the origins of sexual dimorphism and, by analogy, sexual asymmetry and the sexual division of labor. Her discussion fits into a large body of literature that uses animals as models for understanding human behavior. She challenges the tendency to link sexual dimorphism to particular sex-role patterns by demonstrating enormous variations among different species of primates. Rather than explaining greater male size and strength solely as an adaptation to the roles of protection and provisioning associated with hunting, Leibowitz urges us to consider as well the reproductive advantage to women to the cessation of growth soon after sexual maturity is reached. In the process, she asks us to reconsider what we mean by strength.

Leibowitz particularly cautions that our stereotypes of human male attributes have been drawn from one species of primate, the plains baboon. As Sperling has recently observed, "this use of the baboon troop as model for ancestral human populations was very influential in forming both sexist and anthropomorphic views of monkeys in popular culture" (Sperling 1991:210). Sperling, Fedigan (1986), and Leibowitz have emphasized the inappropriateness of the "baboonization" of early human life, given the distant relationship between humans and baboons. If we are going to draw comparisons with nonhuman primates, it would be preferable to draw analogies with the great apes, particularly the chimpanzees.

A second body of evolutionary theory that explains male domination emphasizes the greater ability of men to form social bonds among themselves (Tiger 1969). This ability is supposedly genetically programmed and associated with the evolutionary adaptation to hunting. Women, conversely, are thought to lack the genetic code for bonding and are therefore unsuited to the kinds of cooperative and political endeavors that give men power and prestige.

Ehrenberg (in this book) explores this bonding issue in its relation to the development of the sexual division of labor among early humans. She suggests that women were often the social center of groups. They fostered sociability and sharing. Ehrenberg also addresses a much wider debate about the relative contributions of men and women to human evolution. She provides an alternative to what has been labeled the coattails theory of biological evolution—"Traits are selected for in males and women evolve by clinging to the men's coattails" (Fedigan 1986:29). The male bias reflected in this approach has been equally evident in analyses of cultural development, especially in the emphasis on hunting, a male activity, as the distinctive human activity (Lee and DeVore 1968). In her reevaluation of a discussion that essentially omitted half of humanity from the story of evolution, Ehrenberg suggests that hunting probably evolved from the physical, technological, and social innovations associated with gathering (a female activity).

A third line of argument attempts to explain male dominance with reference to the biological basis of aggression. Many studies of aggression contend that men are more aggressive than women (Wilson 1975; see Fedigan 1982:87 for a critique of this position), and often link this difference to levels of male hormones (testosterone). According to Fausto-Sterling (1985:126), "many societies, including our own, have tested this belief by castrating men who have a history of violent or antisocial behavior." Scientific research has demonstrated that there is no connection between castration and aggression.

It has also been argued that male aggressive tendencies are an adaptation to the male role in defense (Martin and Voorhies 1975) among both human and nonhuman primates. The problem with any line of argument that links male dominance or male social roles to male aggression is that it ignores the wide variation in behaviors and personalities not only between the sexes, but also within them (Renzetti and Curran 1989:38). In addition, cross-cultural data indicate that human societies differ in culturally appropriate levels of aggression expressed by men and women.

Lee's study of conflict and violence among the !Kung San (in this book), a relatively egalitarian and peace-loving people, addresses the issue of aggression among men and women. Lee lends support to the argument that both men and women are aggressive in different ways. !Kung women engage in verbal abuse, but homicides are disproportionately committed by men. Lee compares trends in !Kung violence to that in several other societies. Although his statistics are from the 1950s and 1960s, more recent research indicates that the patterns remain similar. For example, although the percentage of recorded offenses of "violence against the person" committed by women in England and Wales increased by 58% between 1975 and 1985, the increase in such crimes by men was 40%; the absolute number of crimes committed by men in 1985 remained much higher than that for women, and the male-to-female ratio for violent crimes was 9:1 (Morris 1987:35). Similarly, research on criminal activity in the United States indicates that violent offenses by women have increased but are still predominantly committed by men (Morris 1987:35). A comparison between the !Kung and modern industrial societies suggests that the reasons for gender differences in aggressive behavior are complex. In addition to biological factors, access to weapons, culturally approved expressions of hostility, and the role of the state in the evolution of social control should also be considered.

Among the !Kung the victims of violent crimes tend to be other men, a finding that supports Maccoby and Jacklin's (1974) observation that primate males in general demonstrate more aggression against one another than against females. Dominance of men over women through aggression is thereby brought into question, as is the concept of aggression itself. As Fedigan (1982:89) suggests, aggression "is such a heterogeneous category of behaviors and interactions that 'amount of aggression' is not a very useful concept." Fausto-Sterling (1985:129) concurs and points to the fact that no studies on hormone levels and aggression use female subjects or compare men and women. She raises fundamental questions regarding the causal relationship between testosterone levels and aggression.

A fourth body of theory deals with the absence of women from cooperative and political activity in the nondomestic sphere (hence their subordination) and finds an explanation in the fact that women are biologically adapted for reproduction. A corollary of this argument is the idea that women possess a maternal instinct. The fact that women bear children and lactate has been the basis of assertions that women innately experience an attachment to their children that forms the foundation of effective mothering, while men lack a similar capacity to nurture (Peterson 1983; Rossi 1977, 1978). This attachment may be the result of such factors as hormone levels (O'Kelly 1980:30) or of the experiences of pregnancy, labor, and nursing (Whitbeck 1983:186). In contrast, Collier and Rosaldo (1981:315) argue that "there are *no* facts about human sexual biology that, in and of themselves, have immediate social meanings or institutional consequences. Mothering is a social relation, much like fathering, judging, or ruling, whose meaning and organization must be understood with reference to a particular configuration of relationships within a complex social whole."

The articles by Etienne and by Scheper-Hughes (in this book) illustrate this assertion. Etienne's case study focuses on the adoption of children by urban Baule women in the Ivory Coast, West Africa. Etienne shows that to be without children is considered a regrettable fate, but rights of children are not determined by reproductive capacity alone. While all women are supposed to desire children, the Baule recognize unequal distribution of talent for motherhood. Thus, some women receive many children to adopt because of their childrearing skills, while others give their children to kin because they do not like raising children. Emotional ties to adoptive parents tend to be strong, although children remain in contact with their birth parents. Etienne's research contests the assumption that paternity is inherently social, while maternity is essentially natural.

Similarly, Scheper-Hughes examines the inevitability of maternal-infant attachment among mothers in the shantytowns of northeast Brazil. In an environment of poverty, chronic hunger, and economic exploitation, Scheper-Hughes (1987) finds that mothers adopt a strategy of delayed attachment and neglect of weaker children thought unlikely to survive. Such attitudes of resignation and fatalism toward the death of children are documented in historical studies of other cultures as well; for example, Ransel's account of child abandonment in Russia relates the passive attitude toward childhood death to child death rates in the 50 percent range (Ransel 1988:273; see also Boswell 1988). Parental attitudes are reflected in an entire category of lullabies with the motif of wishing death on babies; women sang these lullabies to infants who were sickly, weak, or crippled (Ransel 1988:273). Thus, mother love seems less a "natural and universal maternal script" than a luxury reserved for the strongest and healthiest children. In the context of frequent infant death, maternal attachment means grief, and mother love emerges as culturally and socially constructed, rather than as an innate emotion.

Research on nonhuman primates has shown that role variability and plasticity are deeply rooted in the evolutionary history of primates. Cross-cultural data suggest a similar plasticity among humans. The evidence from this section should support the argument that biology merely sets the parameters for a broad range of human behaviors. Thus, biological differences between men and women have no uniform and universal implication for social roles and relations. As Rosaldo and Lamphere (1974:4) contend, biology, for humans, takes on meaning as it is interpreted in human culture and society.

REFERENCES

Boswell, John. 1988. *The Kindness of Strangers. The Abandonment of Children in Western Europe from Late Antiquity to the Renaissance.* New York: Pantheon Books.

Collier, Jane F. and Michelle Z. Rosaldo. 1981. The Politics of Gender in Simple Societies. In Sherry B. Ortner and Harriet Whiteheads (eds.). *Sexual Meanings,* pp. 275–330. Cambridge: Cambridge University Press.

Fausto-Sterling, A. 1985. *Myths of Gender.* New York: Basic Books.

Fedigan, Linda Marie. 1982. *Primate Paradigms. Sex Roles and Social Bonds.* Montreal: Eden Press.

———. 1986. The Changing Role of Women in Models of Human Evolution. *Annual Review of Anthropology* 15: 25–66.

Freeman, Derek. 1983. *Margaret Mead and Samoa: The Making and Unmaking of an Anthropological Myth.* Cambridge: Harvard University Press.

Lee, Richard B. and Irven DeVore (eds.). 1968. *Man the Hunter.* New York: Aldine.

Maccoby, E. E. and C. N. Jacklin. 1974. *The Psychology of Sex Differences.* Stanford: Stanford University Press.

Martin, M. Kay and Barbara Voorhies. 1975. *Female of the Species.* New York: Columbia University Press.

Mead, Margaret. 1928. *Coming of Age in Samoa.* New York: Dell.

———. 1935. *Sex and Temperament in Three Primitive Societies.* New York: Dell.

Morris, Allison. 1987. *Women, Crime and Criminal Justice.* Oxford: Basil Blackwell.

O'Kelly, Charlotte. 1980. *Women and Men in Society.* New York: D. Van Nostrand Co.

Peterson, Susan Rae. 1983. Against 'Parenting.' In Joyce Trebilcot (ed.). *Mothering: Essays in Feminist Theory,* pp. 41–62. Totowa, NJ: Rowman and Allanheld.

Ransel, David L. 1988. *Mothers of Misery: Child Abandonment in Russia.* Princeton: Princeton University Press.

Rensberger, Boyce. 1983. Margaret Mead: The Nature-Nurture Debate: From Samoa to Sociobiology. *Science 83:* 28–46.

Renzetti, Clair M. and Daniel J. Curran. 1989. *Women, Culture and Society.* Stanford: Stanford University Press.

Rosaldo, Michelle Z. 1974. Theoretical Overview. In Michelle Z. Rosaldo and Louise Lamphere (eds.). *Woman, Culture, and Society,* pp. 17–48. Stanford: Stanford University Press.

Rosaldo, Michelle Z. and Louise Lamphere (eds.). 1974. *Woman, Culture, and Society.* Stanford: Stanford University Press.

Rossi, Alice. 1977. A Biosocial Perspective on Parenting. *Daedalus 106:* 1–31.

———. 1978. The Biosocial Side of Parenthood. *Human Nature 1:* 72–79.

Scheper-Hughes, Nancy. 1987. The Margaret Mead Controversy: Culture, Biology and Anthropological Inquiry. In Herbert Applebaum (ed.). *Perspectives in Cultural Anthropology,* pp. 443–454. Albany: State University of New York Press.

Schneider, David. 1983. The Coming of a Sage to Samoa. *Natural History* 92(6): 4–10.

Sperling, Susan. 1991. Baboons with Briefcases vs. Langurs in Lipstick. Feminism and Functionalism in Primate Studies. In Micaela di Leonardo (ed.). *Gender at the Crossroads of Knowledge: Feminist Anthropology in the Postmodern Era,* pp. 204–234. Berkeley: University of California Press.

Tiger, Lionel. 1969. *Men in Groups.* New York: Random House.

Trebilcot, Joyce (ed.). 1983. *Mothering: Essays in Feminist Theory.* Totowa, NJ: Rowman and Allanheld.

Whitbeck, Caroline. 1983. The Maternal Instinct (1972). In Joyce Trebilcot (ed.). *Mothering: Essays in Feminist Theory,* pp. 185–192. Totowa, NJ: Rowman and Allenheld.

Wilson, Edward O. 1975. *Sociobiology: The New Synthesis.* Cambridge: Harvard University Press.

Perspectives on the Evolution of Sex Differences

Lila Leibowitz

There are very real physical differences between men and women. They differ not only in the appearance of their external genitalia,

From Rayna R. Reiter (ed.), *Toward an Anthropology of Women* (New York: Monthly Review, 1975), pp. 20–35. Copyright © 1975 by Rayna R. Reiter. Reprinted by permission of Monthly Review Foundation. This is a revised version of a paper presented at the American Anthropological Association Meeting in New Orleans, December 1973.

but in other respects as well. Men are generally bigger, have more facial and body hair, narrower hips, flatter buttocks, and a tendency to greater body mass. Women generally have more fatty tissue on their breasts and buttocks. These anatomical differences were for a long time viewed as intimately related to differences in emotional and intellectual capacities, as well as to differences in physical abilities. The tasks and roles assigned to men and women in our own cultural tradition were assumed to be correlated highly with anatomically based aptitudes. It is still a commonplace belief that anatomy is destiny.

In the era between the late 1930s and the mid-1960s this notion was challenged. Research into the behavior of the sexes in other cultures forced some changes in thinking. Cross-cultural data on the sexual division of labor very quickly dispelled the idea that men (or women) are unable to do some of the tasks assigned women (or men) in our culture. Knitting, weaving, and cooking sometimes fall into the male province, while such things as pearl diving, canoe handling, and housebuilding turn out to be women's work in some settings. Mead's pioneering research on sex roles and personality styles raised some doubts about the biological basis of psychological attributes, for she reported on cultures in which men display such "feminine" emotional qualities as sensitivity, affection, and volatile emotionality, while females are aggressive and calculating. Outside of anthropology, the works of Karen Horney and Viola Klein provided support to the proposition that both men and women are behaviorally flexible, and that the way men and women behave in any particular social setting is a result of circumstances rather than anatomy. Masters and Johnson's startling studies contributed to this view and further undermined many academically propagated assumptions about the workings of the human female's body and psyche. So for a while the main thrust of the respected academic literature on human sexual behavior and social roles challenged the notion that anatomy is destiny, arguing that cultural forces work on the behavioral plasticity of both males and females, shaping their behavior and the roles they assume in society.

Despite the implications of such studies, the issue of men's and women's roles and whether or how to change them was not a significant one at the time these works were appearing. The college women who read Margaret Mead's *Male and Female* in the late 1940s and early 1950s, who admired the highly publicized Yugoslav and Russian army

and guerrilla heroines, and who saw Rosie the Riveter in the United States pulling down the same pay as her male co-workers did not agitate for change. They became the ideal *McCalls* magazine mothers of the 1950s. Unaffected by their college readings, they turned to Spock's handbook on child care, gourmet cooking, and interesting arts and crafts hobbies as they pursued the traditional tasks of being wives and mothers. In the early 1960s, an attack on the "feminine mystique" (Friedan, 1963) by a housewife who felt herself cheated attracted a wide audience among them. But the issue of women's roles and whether they are based on genetic capacities or on cultural forces did not emerge onto the political and intellectual scene out of books but out of the Civil Rights struggle. From the precepts of that struggle grew the women's liberation movement and the conviction that anatomy is not destiny.

When women's liberation finally surfaced as an independent entity, it was supported by some academics (like Matina Horner) but opposed by those who felt that physical differences between the sexes are based on and lead to social-role differences. Since the mid-1960s there has been a vigorous revival of the view that social-role and intellectual differences between men and women, and girls and boys, are physiologically based, substantiated by a plethora of books and articles by psychologists and neurophysiologists. Anthropologists and sociologists have picked up on these views and tied them to renewed investigations of biosocial evolution. Interestingly, these academic investigations into sex differences come at a time of a revival of notions of innate differences in intellectual capacities between blacks and whites; both, it would seem, are reactions to efforts at implementing the liberal, nonbiogenetic social-role perspectives that gained respectability during and after World War II.

On the whole, academics no longer hold the position that particular roles or tasks universally belong to either men or women because of simple differences in bones, muscles, and sex organs. The newer arguments for a biogenetic basis in role behavior have acquired a statistical framework, an evolutionary rationale, and sophisticated physiological models of perception and behavior; researchers work with rats, apes, and babies as often as they work with adult human beings. Yet the argument still boils down to the view that because men and women are obviously different physically, they also have different intellectual and emotional capacities. Whether the traits or capacities investigated are shared by a few or many men or women is often considered "statistically insignificant," if not downright irrelevant. In overall characterizations, men, it is argued, are suitable for certain kinds of roles, women for others.

Because men are larger than the females of their species, it is held that they are naturally "dominant" over women. "Dominance," an unclear term at best, may take several forms: having priority of access to food resources, or acting as a provider; fulfilling a leadership position (among nonhuman primates, this means setting the direction and/or pace of group movement); acting as protector of the females and young; taking the initiative in sexual intercourse; or simply getting others to move out of the way. Women—smaller, softer, and fattier tissued—are supposed to be eminently better equipped to be nurturant, affective, docile followers. Dominance and large size (as well as threatening teeth, bony crests, and other male physical characteristics) supposedly go together in nonhuman dimorphised primate species. In fact, it is argued, the reason that men are larger, bonier, and more muscular than women is that these features, and "dominance" in its various expressions, are intrinsically related to one another and gave those males who had them reproductive advantage. By virtue of being leaders, providers, protectors, and sexually aggressive, larger males are more likely to father stronger babies. They are also better able to help their offspring survive than smaller and presumably less dominant males, who are therefore at a reproductive disadvantage. In short, the argument traces physical differences between the sexes (which are supposed to shape contemporary social-role differences) back to social-role differences among our supposed ancestors. Contemporary physical differences are seen as the result of ancient social-role differences, and contemporary social-role differences are treated as the result of physical differences that became established in early human and prehuman populations.

Since we have no way of observing the social arrangements of our ancestors, the social adaptations of living nonhuman primates provide the models from which this theory is drawn because what living primates do as they adapt to the various environments in which they live should, in theory, throw some light on the social behavior of our ancestors. While researchers have tended to pick the one nonhuman primate they consider to be relevant to understanding dimorphism among humans, favoring some species over others, this paper focuses on the behavior and social adaptations of several species in order to examine whether and how their social-role arrangements are related to the presence or absence of sexual dimorphism.

I will first deal briefly with a nondimorphic species, the gibbons, who are found living in the upper reaches of the forest canopies of Southeast Asia, and then touch on the social adaptations of their close neighbors, the extremely dimorphic orangutans. I will look at our closer relations, the African Great Apes: the very dimorphic gorillas and the much less sexually differentiated chimpanzees, who spend much of their time on the ground. Finally, I will examine in somewhat greater detail the adaptations of terrestrial baboons which, despite being rather distantly related to us, have been the most frequent models for speculative reconstructions of early human adaptations.

This brief overview will demonstrate that the sex-role adaptations of the sexually dimorphic nonhuman primate species do not in fact conform to the models used in current explanations of how and why dimorphism developed among humans. In fact, sexual dimorphism cannot easily be equated with sex-role patterns. The data will show, however, that dimorphic primate species do have one thing in common: they all live under environmental conditions that encourage males to range more widely than females. Thus although the data points up the inadequacy of current theory on the sources of physical sex differentiations, it suggests another.

In the closing section, I will examine the possibility that sexual dimorphism is generated not out of selection favoring animals with a predisposition to particular social-role behavior, but is the result of pressures favoring those animals that have growth and maturation rates which give them a reproductive advantage in environments which permit or encourage males to range more widely than females. Thus I am suggesting that while sexual dimorphism is the outcome of sex differences in growth and maturation rates that lead to different body conformations in adults of each sex, sexual dimorphism is at the same time perfectly compatible with a wide variety of sex-role patterns, and even compatible with the ability to adapt to a variety of social-role patterns.

Gibbons, the first of the primates we will consider, are not dimorphic. Males and females look alike; there are no significant characteristics, aside from genitals, that distinguish them. Members of both sexes take the same length of time to achieve full growth and end up in the same size range (13–16 pounds). In the wild, gibbons live in the high trees in pair groups which include an adult male, an adult female, and the immature young of one or both adults. This pair-centered group occupies a relatively fixed range from which adolescent children move off, sometimes with an opposite sexed sibling and at other times with an opposite sexed adolescent from a nearby group. A pair-centered group forages as a unit in its own arboreal niche, and intruders are driven off by either the adult male or the adult female, neither of whom travels far afield from the range the group occupies (Carpenter, 1948). Pairs mate only when females are neither pregnant or nursing, usually at two- or three-year intervals. In some pairs the male tends to give way to the female; in others the reverse is true.

Orangutans are close neighbors of the gibbons, also living in the high trees. Unlike gibbons, orangutans exhibit a marked degree of sexual dimorphism. Males weigh about 160 pounds, females 80 pounds. Males have goiterous-looking throat sacs which lend volume to their voices. They also have much larger canine teeth than do females and heavier bony prominences around their faces. Females reach sexual maturity and full growth at around age nine; males produce viable sperm at that age, but do not stop growing until several years later. An orang female and her young occupy a stable range which may overlap that of another female and her young. Where mothers and daughters with young live in adjacent areas, they sometimes join together temporarily to make a multifemale group.

Adult males travel alone, moving back and forth across a wide area that cuts across the ranges of several female groups; sometimes they visit, accompany, or follow these groups for awhile. Although these visits do not necessarily involve sexual activity, males mate when they can. Females are rarely receptive, since nursing is quite prolonged. One obvious rape episode was observed by David Horr, but uninterested females usually avoid and rarely excite males, rejecting them without difficulty. Vocalizations appear to help the animals locate one another in dense foliage and males vocalize fairly frequently. They are assiduous in avoiding one another. The large orangutan male is rarely involved in aggressive interactions and has even less opportunity to function as a leader or protector than the male gibbon, but unlike the gibbon he is a traveler and ranges much more widely than the females of his species.*

Gorillas are the largest of the apes: up to 600 pounds for males and 400 or so for females. Adult males differ from females in that they sometimes develop flaring sagital crests, have furry backs that turn silvery at maturity, and usually have larger canine teeth. Gorillas are ground-browsing vegetarians who build

---

* An informal presentation by David Horr to a class at Northeastern University is the source of this information on orangs.

tree nests each night, and adult females are always found in groups in which there is at least one, and usually more, silver-backed males, whose presence is a deterrent to predators. Direction-setting leadership is assumed by a silver-back. Males, especially black-backed adolescents, are not infrequently found outside such groups, evidently joining and leaving them with ease. Females never travel alone. They become pregnant almost immediately on reaching sexual maturity and are nursing an infant or pregnant nearly all their adult lives. Among female gorillas sexual receptivity is rare indeed. In a full year's observation of several groups, Schaller saw only two episodes of intercourse, and neither involved a silver-backed leader. In one case a silver-back approached a copulating pair, displacing the younger male, who ran off. The female displayed no interest whatsoever in the silver-back, who finally left the scene. The female then turned back to her preferred partner, an "outsider" who had just joined, and soon left, the group (Schaller, 1964).

Chimpanzee males weigh around 150 pounds; females weigh about 130, but there are small males as well as big females (in the 140-pound range). Aside from a tendency to larger canine teeth, males develop no marked secondary sexual characteristics, but adolescent females develop perineal sexual skins which swell and recede periodically in conjunction with the changing hormonal balance of the estrus cycle. Chimpanzees in the wild are found in several habitats: gallery forests, a mosaic of plain and forest, and on cultivated plantations or near stocked feeding stations. Although there are local variations in social organization which include troop-like arrangements, semi-stable nursery groups of mothers and children, mixed adolescent groups, all-male groups, and general assemblages, all these are essentially fluid. Groups dissolve, change personnel, and in so doing change form. The "nursery group" of mothers and their young occurs in a variety of environments, including stocked feeding station situations. Like orangutans, gibbons, and gorillas, chimpanzee females in the wild are infrequently free from pregnancy and nursing.

Chimpanzee females are rather more lively than gorillas, however, when they are in estrus. Males mate with interested females wherever and whenever they find them and wait side by side, without friction or competitive scrambling (Goodall, 1965).

Before going on to describe sex differences and social behavior among baboons, let me point out how the social arrangements among gibbons, orangutans, gorillas, and chimpanzees do not confirm current popular and academic theories which associate sex-role behaviors with physical sex differences and then use these associations to account for the evolution of human sex differences. Popular notions about the kinds of sex roles that lead to dimorphism, and about how dimorphism leads to sex roles, are far too simplistic. Sex-related differences among humans, particularly the possession by females of breasts and buttocks, have been tied to pair bonding, a pair bonding in which males are protectors, aggressors, and leaders. Yet pair bonding shows up only among gibbons, who lack any significant sex differentiation either physically or with respect to social roles. Chimp, gorilla, and orangutan populations lack pair bonding but *are* dimorphic.

The sex differences typical of these species—the males are larger, stronger, hairier, and have more formidable dentition—have in turn been tied to a certain kind of social-role pattern: large males are supposed to be the protectors and leaders of the young and female members of the group, and are therefore supposed to have a sexual advantage over smaller males. Females, according to this theory, are more passive, sexually and otherwise. Similarly, the lack of dimorphism among gibbons has been attributed to an adaptation in which males do not play particularly distinctive roles as leaders, protectors, or aggressors. But orangutan males show a similar lack of leadership, and orangutans are dimorphic. And what do we find in the field? Among the dimorphic primate species, the sexes play different roles in different circumstances. Gorillas are the only dimorphic apes to live in groups stable enough to have leaders. Yet while the silver-backed males may set the direction of troop movement, they are mild mannered. Schaller's observations indicate that silver-backed males have no sexual prerogatives, have no pre-emptive rights over food, and can protect others only while they are within the safety of the group.

Further, while many reporters describe chimpanzee dominance hierarchies as being based on who "gives way" to whom, the largest male around is not necessarily dominant. In fluid chimpanzee aggregates, "leadership"—in terms of direction-setting—is temporary and unstable. There is no evidence that some males have sexual prerogatives denied others; nor does a dominant male have special access to vegetable food or in hunting small game. Even when begging meat from animals (male or female) who have taken game, a dominant male does not receive any special or exorbitant quantity of food (Teleki, 1973). Furthermore, chimpanzee and gorilla males do not go in for fights in which big canines are used. Orangutan males are neither group leaders nor protectors, for they do not live with groups. Since orangutan males generally avoid each other, they rarely get into fights. Predators are not significant threats to any of these animals as long as they can escape into trees or remain in large enough groupings to scare them off. Thus the sexual dimorphism in these primate species is not tied to the social-role arrangements that are often cited as the basis of sexual dimorphism among humans.

The physical traits discussed above continue to be attributed to such role patterns largely because of the behavior of certain baboons, who fit our cultural model of our primate past. Baboons live in the kind of terrestrial plains environment early humans apparently became adapted to. They obviously do not and did not compete directly with humans for the same econiche; if they had, they probably would not have survived. Presumably, however, they now face problems similar to those faced by our early ancestors. Baboon males are much bigger than females, and have heavier mantles and bigger canine teeth, which they display quite often.

Males and females are both very volatile in temperament.

The plains-living populations of baboons first described in the anthropological literature by DeVore and Washburn (1961) are called cynocephalous baboons (Buettner-Janusch in Rowell, 1972:45). Cynocephalous baboons also live in forest and "farming" settings. The forest and farm adaptations have been described by Rowell and Maples respectively (Rowell, 1972; Maples,1971). DeVore and Washburn's early study of plains adaptations in "protected" reserves reported that baboons live in large, peaceful, and rather stable groups. Active adolescent males circulate around the periphery of the closed moving troop, while females with infants stick to the central area and cluster around subgroups of "alpha," or dominant, males. Alpha male subgroups involve alliances between several, mostly older, males, who reportedly rush to place themselves between threatening situations and the troop. Alpha males are chosen as sexual consorts by females at the height of estrus, displace other males and compete with or threaten them when they are offered delectable foods in limited quantities, and seem to set the direction of troop movements. In short, early studies of plains-living social adaptations among baboons provide a neat model which nicely correlates sex-role behavior and physical sex differences, corroborating the theory outlined above.

Forest-living cynocephalous baboons behave differently (Rowell, 1972), as do baboons who raid farms and garden plots (Maples, 1971). Groups travel in a linear pattern, with a male in the front and one at the rear. Old females "choose" and set the direction of daily movement. Adult and young males change groups rather frequently. (In at least one instance, some young adult females also changed groups.) When danger threatens males usually issue warning barks and station themselves near the threat and along an escape route; one may stay behind until the others disappear. But if danger is imminent, the first animals into the safety of the trees are those unencumbered by infants—the males.

Rowell observed no patterned preferences for particular consorts by females. Females initiate intercourse, even at the height of estrus, with various males.

Hamadryas baboons live in the dry Ethiopian highlands. They congregate in large assemblages at night and disperse during the day in what has been called—erroneously—one-male groups (Kummer, 1968). Characterized by some authors as "harem" groups, one-male groups often include a junior male, as well as an older male who herds or guides one or several females with or without young. As they age, senior males spend less and less time with the group and the younger males take over herding and mating. These quasi-"family" arrangements provide substantial support for the notion that male-female role differences are related to physical sex differences; in addition, they suggest that a propensity to harem and nuclear "family" arrangements is innate.

Yet an interesting change occurred in one generation in an artificially created colony of hamadryas baboons. An elderly female took over herding-type activities when all the older males born in the wild died off and and colony-reared males failed to fulfill the herder role. Behavioral plasticity and sex-role adaptability, it seems, are part of baboon behavioral capacities, since not only do we see a change of social patterning in one short generation in a group of hamadryas that was shifted from one ecological setting to another, but we encounter, as already noted, social patterns among cynocephalous baboons that vary from one setting to another.

The hamadryas one-male group pattern may not mean quite what current theorists argue for yet another reason. It is doubtful that hamadryas are a distinct species of baboon since they have mated successfully with cynocephalous types, both in the wild and in captivity (Rowell, 1972). If they are not a separate species, then their particular social adaptations may represent local adaptations, one of several alternatives available to them. In any case, when we consider all the baboon adaptations side by side—plains, forest, farm, and Ethiopian upland—we are once again left with no neat and inevitable tie between sex-role behavior and physical sex differences. The baboons join the orangutans, chimpanzees, and gorillas in what appears to be, at best, a loose correlation between sex-role behavior patterning and physical form.

Given that sex-role specializations are but weakly demonstrated in these higher primates, how can we account for the existence of such physical sex differences? Since sex dimorphism among primates is not clearly associated with or attributable to any particular set of sex-role patterns, we need another hypothesis as to the origins and functions of sexual dimorphism. The crucial physical differences boil down to elaborations of a single difference in dimorphic primate species: males continue to grow for some time past the age when females have ceased to grow and have begun to have offspring; sex differences in size and body form begin to become marked only after the age at which both males and females are reproductively mature. If differences in pubertal growth rates are the key to understanding the physical differentiation of the sexes, it seems sensible to ask what factors give a reproductive advantage to females who stop growing shortly after they achieve sexual maturity and to males who continue to grow after they develop viable sperm. In the social adaptations of orangutans, chimps, baboons, and gorillas there is one sex-differentiated behavioral common denominator: for a while males move around more actively than females. It is not that they are more aggressive—they may or may not be—but that they are more *mobile*. I therefore propose that in ecological settings in which mature males are enabled or forced to forage more widely than females, males who continue to grow after reaching sexual maturity have a reproductive advantage over males who do not.

Primate species, as species, vary in size according to the econiche to which they are adapted. For the female of any species, ceasing to grow after becoming pregnant has obvious survival advantages for the female and for her offspring. Eating for two, whether the infant is *in utero* or at breast, requires less intake and less activity for a female who stops growing than for one who continues to grow. Anything that insures a female's efficient reproductive energy allocation will be selectively favored, whether her social group is large or small, open or closed, whether she has one mate or several, or lives in the trees or on the ground.

The optimal size for females is the same as that of males in the vast majority of *arboreal* primate species, for dimorphism is rare among them. This correlates with the fact that in most arboreal primate species males and females have similar foraging patterns and are equally free from predation. Orangutans, who are unusually large when compared to other arboreal primates, also do not conform to the standard arboreal troop or pair arrangements. They are not only markedly dimorphic, but the forage ranges of males are far larger than those of females. Orangutan food resources are strained by these large animals and dispersal is a necessity. Males forage as individuals, roaming widely. A mother and her young forage together in a small area, occasionally joined by another mother and her young. Though orangutans are pre-eminently arboreal, in some ways this adaptation resembles that of ground-living primate species.

Partially or completely terrestrially adapted primates are more readily subject to predation than arboreal species, and immature animals and infant-carrying females are safe only when in a good-sized group. Mother-young groups, like those of the orangutans, simply could not survive on the ground. Ground-living species are group foragers and the core of the group is made up of immature animals and females with young. The only isolated males that are large enough to travel safely on the ground for any length of time are gorillas. Food resources at the center of a ground-foraging group are under some pressure, and there is thus an impetus for mature unencumbered animals to move toward the periphery of the group, and even to eventually leave and join another. Those males that continue to grow after reaching sexual maturity are peculiarly well adapted to foraging on the margins of a group. For one thing, they do not experience either the decline in activity level that accompanies the cessation of growth, or the decline in activity level that affects pregnant and nursing females. They tend to remain active and exploratory longer than males who stop growing, so they are ready and able to exploit resources on the margins of the group. (Sometimes they even eat foods that other members of the species don't encounter, which may explain some secondary sexual developments in the chewing equipment and head structures of males.) Furthermore, the bigger they become, the safer they are from predators in their edge locations. But most significant of all, the more mobile they become, the greater are their reproductive advantages over less mobile males.

From what does this reproductive advantage derive? Male reproductive success is linked to the number of mating opportunities a male can take advantage of. Since primate females are infrequently in estrus, males who move around on the edges of groups, and from group to group, are more likely to find fertile females than those who are bound to their own small groups all their lives, or who stay in the center with nursing mothers all the time. This means that a delayed cessation of growth can afford a male reproductive advantages whether or not he engages in active sexual competition with other males, and whether or not he becomes a leader or a protector. If he is living in a setting where predation is significant, the size he achieves may help him survive, and this of course also contributes to his reproductive success. (Since predation hardly affects orangutans at all, however, protection seems to be less a cause than a result of size increments, which are tied to mobility.)

For the mobile male the particular role he plays in the groups he encounters often changes from situation to situation. He may or may not become a dominant male capable of getting others to move out of his way, but even if he does settle down to a life of "dominance" in a particular group, the number of offspring he fathers will not be increased by his ability to displace others, since "dominance" is not particularly correlated with any special sexual prerogatives. Indeed, his reproductive success rate may be reduced as his mobility diminishes, even though he has achieved full size. If he settles down to a life of subdominance, the same holds true. The role he plays in a group seems to be less significant than how much he moves around among groups.

The hypothesis I am proposing therefore argues that in ecological settings which encourage males to forage more widely than females, reproductive advantages have fallen to those males who are active enough to move around, large enough to do so safely, and versatile enough to exploit alternative food resources and social situations. At the same time, reproductive advantage falls to those females who stop growing at pubescence and are efficient in using their limited food intakes for reproduction and nursing. This hypothesis provides a way to account for the evolution of physical differences without viewing sex roles, past or present, rigidly. (I might add, briefly and by way of support for some of the ideas incorporated into this hypothesis, that when a female baboon was prevented from becoming pregnant she continued to grow and remained active longer than her compeers.)

This hypothesis is a response to the recent spate of evolutionary theories which stress that our sex-role destiny along with our sexual anatomy, was settled a long time ago. A number of theorists have revived the view that sexual dimorphism among humans is tied to sex-role patterns that are current or idealized in our own culture. New data on nonhuman primate behavior has provided source materials for such theories: without too much difficulty, theorists have been able to find one or another population of nonhuman primates that conforms to their cultural model of how things were, are, or ought to be. Unfortunately for such theories, humans and nonhuman primates utilize a variety of social forms in which females and males play a variety of roles. Explaining human sexual dimorphism

in terms which postulate that the sexes are each suited to only certain kinds of role behavior runs contrary to the accumulated evidence. Until we have an explanation that accounts both for the evolution of physical sex differences and for the existence of role plasticity, the belief that anatomy is destiny will linger on. We must familiarize ourselves with the data and deal with it in a sophisticated framework that accounts for its variability. If we don't, the growing body of evidence that role variability and role plasticity run rather deep in the primate heritage will continue to be ignored or distorted.

REFERENCES

Buettner-Janusch, J. 1966. *Folia Primatologica 4;* cited in Thelma Rowell, *Social Behavior of Monkeys.* Baltimore: Penguin Books, 1972.

Carpenter, C. R. 1948. "Life in the Trees: The Behavior and Social Relations of Man's Closest Kin." In *A Reader in General Anthropology,* edited by C. Coon. New York: Henry Holt.

DeVore, I., and Washburn, S. L. 1961. "Social Behavior of Baboons and Early Man." In *Social Life of Early Man,* edited by S. L. Washburn. Chicago: Aldine.

Freidan, Betty. 1963. *The Feminine Mystique.* New York: W. W. Norton.

Goodall, Jane Van Lawick. 1965. "Chimpanzees of the Gombe Steam Reserve." In *Primate Behavior,* edited by I. DeVore. New York: Holt, Rinehart and Winston.

Horney, Karen. 1973. "The Denial of the Vagina." In *Feminine Psychology,* edited by Harold Kelman. New York: W. W. Norton.

Kummer, Hans. 1968. *Social Organization Hamadryas Baboons.* Chicago: University of Chicago Press.

Maples, William R. 1971. "Farming Baboons." Paper presented at the 1971 Meeting of the American Association of Physical Anthropologists, Boston, Mass.

Mead, Margaret. 1950. *Male and Female: A Study of the Sexes in a Changing World.* New York: Morrow.

Rowell, Thelma. 1972. *Social Behavior of Monkeys.* Baltimore: Penguin Books.

Schaller, George B. 1964. *The Year of the Gorilla.* Chicago: University of Chicago Press.

The Role of Women in Human Evolution

Margaret Ehrenberg

Human evolution has traditionally been discussed in terms of the role which 'Man the Hunter' played in devising weapons and tools for catching and slaughtering animals for food, how he needed to walk upright on two feet to see his prey above the tall savanna grass, and how he was more successful than other species in his hunting exploits because he teamed up with other men and learnt the value of co-operation. And what of 'woman', meanwhile? Was she sitting at home, twiddling her thumbs, waiting for 'man' to feed her and increase his brain capacity and abilities until he became *'Homo sapiens sapiens'*? The argument went that as human evolution progressed, more and more time was needed to look after infants, so females no longer had time to hunt, and male co-operative hunting became essential in order that the men could bring enough food home to feed the family. As a result, male-female bonding in monogamous unions was an essential and a very early development. While most accounts of human evolution have assumed that all the advances in human physical and cultural development were led by men, a number of recent studies suggest alternative possibilities and have pointed out the vital role which must have been played by women.

Research into the earliest stages of human evolution is based on three strands of evidence. Physical anthropologists study the remains of early human skeletons, to assess the way in which they developed. For example, it is possible to tell from the structure of the legs and back whether an individual would have walked upright on two legs, or used the fore-arms for balance. Changes in the size of the skull through time give an indication of brain capacity. Secondly, the study of the behaviour of other animals, and especially primates, particularly those species closest to humans such as apes and chimpanzees, reveals some patterns which may have been shared by the earliest humans before cultural norms began to play an overriding part. For example, chimpanzees may be studied to see if males and females eat or collect different foods, or to find out whether they share any of the differences in child-care practices seen in human women and men. Thirdly, archaeological evidence for tools, settlements, environment and diet sheds light on the social and cultural development of the earliest humans.

Some scholars within all these three areas have turned away from the traditional male-dominated view of evolution and have begun to formulate an alternative model, allowing that female primates and hominids have played an important part, if not the key role, in the development of human behaviour. Different authors have stressed different factors in this development. Adrienne Zihlman[1] argues that changes in the environment were crucial in necessitating social and economic changes in human populations in order to exploit this environment efficiently. Sally Slocum[2] points out that the only division of labour by sex amongst other primates is that females take primary care of their young, while males tend to dominate in protecting the group. She argues that a division of labour in food collecting is therefore unlikely to have been a key feature of early human behaviour. Other feminist writers[3] suggest that the female's choice of a co-operative and gentle mate was a critical factor in human evolution, as the chances of survival were improved by caring more closely for near relatives; in all mammals, and especially in primates, this is much more a female task or trait.

Among the physical changes which took place in the early stages of human evolution were increases in the size of the brain and the teeth; a decrease in sexual dimorphism (difference in size between males and females); increased hairlessness over the body; and bipedalism, or walking on two feet, rather than using the forelimbs for support, as chimpanzees and apes do. While an infant chimpanzee can cling to its mother's cover of body hair, leaving her hands free for walking or carrying food, a young human or early hairless hominid would need to be carried by the mother: this seems a much more likely stimulus both to bipedalism and to the invention of tools for carrying the infant as well as food than is the need to see prey animals over tall savanna grass and to throw simple weapons at them, which has been the traditional explanation for these changes.

A key aspect of the debate about the evolution of sex-role behaviour centres on food collection, and the way in which females and males may have foraged for different foods. Many discussions, including those written by some feminist anthropologists, assume that from a very early stage in evolution females primarily gathered plant foods, while males mainly hunted animals, the pattern usual in modern hunter-gatherer societies. Many recent arguments about other aspects of the role played by females in human social and technological evolution depend on this belief, even though it is rarely argued out fully. At one end of the scale other primates show little evidence for differences in food collecting behaviour between females and males, while at the other all modern foragers apparently divide subsistence tasks on the basis of sex. The question, therefore, is when and why this difference came about, and whether looking after young offspring would have a limiting effect on hunting by females. One view[1] suggests that although males unburdened by young might have caught meat more often

than females, a regular division of labour would probably have come quite late in human evolution, as the physical differences between females and males are insufficient to make one sex or the other more suitable for either task. Recent work has also questioned whether meat actually filled a significant part of the early human diet, suggesting that this would have been far more like that of other primates, based almost entirely on a wide range of plant foods. What meat was eaten in the earliest phases of the Palaeolithic was probably scavenged, rather than hunted. Both these factors are problematic for the traditional view, as they suggest that hunting was neither an important factor in physical evolution, nor in the social and economic balance between female and male activities. Both sexes would have obtained vegetable foods and occasional meat, and brought some of their day's collection back to the homebase for sharing.

If there was little division of labour in the earliest phase of human development, when and why did it become usual? Two chronological points may have provided possible contexts. Initially, hominids would have been content to catch small game or to scavenge meat caught by other animals, or to collect those that had died naturally, but perhaps around 100,000 years ago they developed suitable tools and techniques for hunting large animals. While hunting small game would not have been hazardous, big-game hunting might often have resulted in death or injury to the hunter rather than the hunted. In small societies, such as these early human groups and present-day forager societies, every unexpected death is a serious blow to the viability of the community, particularly the death of women of child-bearing age. Mobility would also have been more important in hunting large game; the hunter would have to move rapidly and quietly, with hands free to throw a spear or shoot an arrow. It would not be possible to do this while carrying a bag or basket of gathered food, nor a young child, who might cause an additional hazard by making a noise at a crucial moment. Thus gathering and hunting become incompatible as simultaneous occupations; pregnant women and those carrying very small infants would have found hunting difficult, though gathering is quite easily combined with looking after young children. It is therefore possible that at this stage women began to hunt less, until a regular pattern of dividing subsistence tasks was established.[5]

Another possible context for the origin of the division of labour[6] is the change in environment which hominids found when they first entered Europe. It is argued that this spread could not have occurred until the perceptual problems of coping with a new environment had been resolved, by splitting food foraging into separate tasks. During the Lower Palaeolithic in East Africa, plants and animals would have been abundant, so vegetable foods and small game would have provided plenty of easily obtainable food with only the occasional large game caught to supplement the diet. As the hominid population increased and went in search of new territory, some hominids moved north into Europe. There they encountered colder conditions in which plant foods were harder to come by, so meat would have formed a more significant part of their diet. If this problem was not serious enough to necessitate a solution when hominids first moved into Europe, it would have become so with the onset of the last glaciation when conditions became very much colder and vegetation more sparse (this period equates archaeologically with the Upper Palaeolithic). The time and danger involved in hunting large animals became more worthwhile, but would not have provided a regular, guaranteed source of food, and would have been more dangerous. A solution might have been for only part of the community to concentrate on hunting, while the rest continued gathering plants and small animals. It is likely that this division would usually have been on a female-male basis for the reasons already suggested.

On the other hand, more detailed studies of chimpanzee behaviour suggest that there may be slight differences in the food collecting behaviour of females and males of non-human primates, which could argue for an early gathering/hunting division.[7] Although chimpanzees eat very little animal flesh, males make nearly all the kills and eat more of the meat; however, termite fishing, involving the use of sticks as fishing rods to poke into the termite mounds, a skilled task requiring patience and simple tool use, is far more commonly carried out by females. Whether the 'changing environment' theory or the latter argument is preferred, both hypotheses suggest that a division of labour on the basis of sex would have been an early development in human history.

Tool-using was once thought to be a distinctly human attribute, but in simple form it is now known to be shared with several of the higher primates, and even other animals and birds. Most early theories suggested that tool-using by humans was intimately linked with hunting, which in turn was assumed to be a male task, and that the earliest tools would have been spears for hunting animals and stone knives or choppers for butchery. This idea was partly encouraged by the archaeological evidence of the early stone tools, most of which are thought to have had such functions. However, this is partly a circular argument, as on the one hand the function of these tools is far from certain, and many would have been just as useful for cracking nuts or digging roots, and on the other, the very earliest tools would almost certainly have been made of wood, skins or other perishable material. Artefacts such as digging sticks, skin bags, nets, clubs and spears can be made entirely of organic materials, and would not have survived, so the extant stone tools are probably quite late in the sequence of hominid tool use. The evidence of tool use by other primates and by modern foragers, combined with a more balanced theoretical view, suggests that other factors and possibilities need to be considered.

One of the most significant human tools must be the container. Whether it be a skin bag, a basket, a wooden bowl or pottery jar, it allows us to carry items around or store them safely in one place. The container may have been one of the earliest tools to be invented, though unfortunately there is little archaeological evidence to demonstrate this. Chimpanzees can carry things in the skinfold in their groin, but when hominids became bipedal this skin was stretched and the fold was lost. The use of a large leaf or an animal skin, carried over one arm or the developing shoulder, or tied to the waist, might have replicated this lost natural carrier.[8] One of the most important things that a female hominid would need to carry would be her young offspring. The complex interaction of bipedalism, food gathering, the loss of hair for the infant to cling to, and changes in the structure of the toes which made them useless for clinging to its mother would have made it necessary for the mother to carry the child. The development of a sling for supporting the infant, found in almost all modern societies, including foraging groups, is likely to have been among the earliest applications of the container.

The first tools to aid in foraging and preparing foodstuffs are perhaps more likely to have been used in connection with plant foods and small animals than in the hunting of large mammals. The tools and actions required for termite fishing, for example, are not unlike those required for digging up roots more easily. Modern foraging groups often choose a particularly suitable stone to use as an anvil for cracking nuts, which they leave under a particular tree and then return to it on subsequent occasions. Higher primates also use stones for cracking nuts, so it is very likely that early hominids would have done this even before tools were used for hunting. The role of women as tool inventors, perhaps contributing many of the major categories of tools which are most essential even today, cannot be dismissed.

The introduction of food gathering, as opposed to each individual eating what food was available where it was found, was another significant advance which would both have necessitated and been made possible by the invention of the container. More food might be gathered than was needed immediately by one individual, either for giving to someone else or for later consumption. With the exception of parents feeding very young offspring, this behaviour is unusual among other animals and presumably would not have been common amongst the very earliest hominids, but gradually developed to become a hallmark of human behaviour. Another change would have involved carrying this food to a base, which would imply both conceptual and physical changes, made possible by the use of containers, and may also have made it necessary to walk on two legs, leaving the hands free to carry the food, either directly or in containers. The development of consistent sharing, not only with offspring but with others in the group, and exchanging food brought from different environments of savanna and forest would have been a stage towards living in regular social groups.

Environmental changes would also have led to social changes within early hominid groups. In savanna grassland, as opposed to forest, it would have been more difficult to find safe places to sleep overnight, and water would have been harder to obtain. Once a suitable location was discovered, there would have been a greater tendency to remain there as long as possible rather than sleeping in a different place each night, thus introducing the idea of a homebase.

Women also played a key role in social development. A major difference between human development and that of other animals is the greater length of time during which infants need to be cared for and fed: this has probably contributed to a number of human characteristics, including food sharing and long-term male-female bonding. The sharing of food between mother and offspring would necessarily have continued for longer in early hominids than in other primates, and it is argued that when a mammal too large to be consumed by the hunters alone was killed, the males would have shared it with those who had shared with them in their youth, that is their mothers and sisters, rather than with their sexual partners. This argument is supported by a primate study[9] which shows that banana sharing almost always takes place within matrifocal groups rather than between sexual partners. This has important implications for the primacy or otherwise of monogamy and marriage. Several scholars have also pointed out that in this situation the female would choose to mate with a male who was particularly sociable and willing to share food with his partner while she was looking after a very young infant. As well as preferring those most willing to share, females would choose those males who appeared to be most friendly. Not surprisingly, female chimpanzees will not mate with males who are aggressive towards them. The more friendly-looking males would probably have been smaller, or nearer in size to the female, and would have had less pronounced teeth, and therefore have been less aggressive-looking. Over thousands of years this female sexual preference would have led to gradual evolutionary changes in favour of smaller, less aggressive, males.

The stronger tie between mother and offspring caused by the longer period of time during which human infants need to be cared for would have resulted in closer social bonds than are found in other species. The primary bond between mother and offspring would be supplemented by sibling ties between sisters and brothers growing up together. Older offspring would be encouraged or socialised to contribute towards the care of younger siblings, including grooming, sharing food, playing and helping to protect them. The natural focus of such a group would clearly be the mother rather than, as is so often supposed, any male figure. Moreover, this group behaviour would lead to increased sociability in the male as well as in the species in general. The role of the female, both in fostering this increased sociability in the species and as the primary teacher of technological innovations during this long period of caring, must be recognised.

An increase in human sociability, and particularly female sociability, would have had a number of other positive side-effects. As a result of a mutual willingness to share food and

food resources, each individual would have had more access to overlapping gathering areas when a particular resource was abundant. This in turn might greatly increase the chances of the offspring being well fed and therefore surviving, and thus of the survival of the species in general. As the ability to communicate precisely increased with the development of language, it would have become possible for humans to have ordered social relationships with more individuals and other groups. This would have evolved into a pattern very similar to that found in modern foraging groups, many of which include distant relations who regularly meet up with other groups in the course of their annual movements. Males who had moved out of the matrifocal group in order to mate would have learnt a pattern of friendly contact with their ancestral females when they met them in the course of their foraging.

It can therefore be argued that the crucial steps in human development were predominantly inspired by females. These include economic and technological innovations, and the role of females as the social centre of groups. This contrasts sharply with the traditional picture of the male as protector and hunter, bringing food back to a pair-bonded female. That model treats masculine aggression as normal, assumes that long-term, one-to-one, male-female bonding was a primary development, with the male as the major food provider, and that male dominance was inherently linked to hunting skills. None of these patterns, however, accords with the behaviour of any but the traditional Western male. Other male primates do not follow this pattern, nor do non-Western human groups, in particular those foraging societies whose lifestyle in many ways accords most closely with putative early human and Palaeolithic cultural patterns.

NOTES

1. Zihlman, 1981.
2. Slocum, 1975.

3. For example, Tanner, 1981; Martin and Voorhies, 1975.
4. Zihlman, 1981; Isaac and Crader, 1981.
5. Zihlman, 1978; the same arguments are used by Friedl, 1975 and 1978, who explains in more detail than here why present-day foragers divide food collecting tasks along gender lines.
6. Dennell, 1983, 55.
7. McGrew, 1981; Goodall, 1976.
8. Tanner and Zihlman, 1976.
9. McGrew, 1981, 47.

REFERENCES

Dennell, R. 1983. *European Economic Prehistory.* London: Academic Press.

Friedl, E. 1975. *Women and Men: An Anthropologist's View.* New York: Holt, Rinehart and Winston.

———. 1978. "Society and sex roles." *Human Nature* 1: 68–75.

Goodall, J. 1986. *The Chimpanzees of Gombe: Patterns of Behavior.* Cambridge, MA: Harvard University Press.

Isaac, G. and Crader, D. 1981. "To what extent were early hominids carnivorous?" In Teleki, G. (ed.), *Omnivorous Primates: Gathering and Hunting in Human Evolution.* New York: Columbia University Press.

Martin, M. K. and Voorhies, B. 1975. *Female of the Species.* New York: Columbia University Press.

McGrew, W. 1981. "The female chimpanzee as a human evolutionary prototype." In Dahlberg, Frances (ed.). *Woman The Gatherer.* New Haven: Yale University Press.

Slocum, S. 1975. "Woman the gatherer: male bias in anthropology." In Reiter, Rayna R. (ed.), *Toward an Anthropology of Women.* New York: Monthly Review Press.

Tanner, N. 1981. *On Becoming Human.* Cambridge: Cambridge University Press.

Tanner, N. and Zihlman, A. 1976. "Woman in evolution. Part 1: Innovation and selection in human origins." *Signs* 1(3): 585–608.

Zihlman, A. 1978. "Women in evolution. Part 2: Subsistence and social organization among early hominids." *Signs* 4: 4–20.

———. 1981. "Woman as shapers of human adaption." In Dahlberg, Frances (ed.). *Woman the Gatherer.* New Haven: Yale University Press.

Conflict and Violence Among the !Kung

Richard B. Lee

The purpose of this chapter is two-fold: (1) to document the extent, frequency, and seriousness of fighting among the !Kung and (2) to attempt to place !Kung hunter-gatherer violence into an ecological and evolutionary perspective. . . .

Excerpted from Richard B. Lee, *The !Kung San* (New York: Cambridge University Press, 1979), pp. 370–400. Reprinted with the permission of Cambridge University Press.

LEVELS OF VIOLENCE

It is useful to distinguish, as the !Kung do, three levels of conflict: talking, fighting, and deadly fighting. A *talk* is an argument that may involve threats and verbal abuse, but no blows. A *fight* is a dispute that includes an exchange of blows but without the use of weapons. A *deadly fight* is one in which the deadly weapons—poisoned arrows, spears, and clubs—are used whether or not someone is killed. The 81 cases of violence I collected are divided among these three levels of violence as follows: verbal disputes, 10; fights without weapons, 34; fights with weapons, 37 (15 non-fatal, 22 fatal). . . .

TALKING: ARGUMENTS AND VERBAL ABUSE

The San do not fight much, but they do talk a great deal. In fact, they may be among the most talkative people in the world. Much of this talk verges on argument, often for its own sake and usually ad hominem, as ably documented by Lorna Marshall (1961, 1976). Accusations of improper meat distribution, improper gift exchange (*hxaro*), laziness, and stinginess are the most common topics of these disputes. Often they are followed by a group split, as one or both of the principals leaves the camp for a cooling-off period. N!eishin!a and his brother-in-law ≠Toma/ /gwe at Dobe, for example, have been coalescing and splitting for years. Every year or so one or the other packs up after an argument and takes off with his group, only to recombine the following season.

The most common kind of argument heard is called *hore hore* or *oba oba*, !Kung words that mean "yakity-yak." It is often punctuated by a joke that breaks the tension and leaves the participants rolling on the ground helpless with laughter. Simply because these arguments happen to be funny does not mean that they lack seriousness. They *are* serious, and they proceed along the knife edge between laughter and anger. Indeed, one of the purposes of this kind of argument is to provoke one's opponent to anger so that one can retort with injured innocence: "What's the matter, we were only kidding" (see Lee 1969).

When disputants get really angry (i.e., when both parties drop the pretense of good humor), a talk ensues. The "talk" (*n ≠ wa*), first described by Marshall (1961:232), is an outpouring of verbal anger with extravagant statements delivered in a stylized staccato form. A good example of the n ≠ wa is John

Marshall's film, *An Argument About a Marriage* (1973). Of this level of verbal conflict, the !Kung say that *si lx" asi dui* ("their hearts rise up"). The point of potential danger has been passed, and the combatants are no longer completely in control of the situation. Fighting may break out directly, or the talk may move on to another level: verbal abuse involving sex.

The third and final phase of conflict on the verbal level is *za* ("sexual insulting"). The za mode occupies the ambiguous position of being both the highest form of affectionate joking between appropriate kin in the "joking relationship" and the deadliest affront leading directly to fighting. The primary za form addressed to males is *!ki nuwa n!u* ("may death pull back your foreskin"), a grave insult among a people who do not practice circumcision and among whom the glans penis is exposed only during sexual arousal. For females the most common za forms are *!ki du a !gum* ("death on your vagina") and *!gum/twisi ≠ dinyazho* ("long black labia"), the latter a reference to the elongated labia minora characteristic of San and Khoi-Khoi female genitalia. According to the !Kung, to be the recipient of za in anger arouses intense feelings of *dokum* ("shame"), leading to suicide or assault. . . .

FIGHTING: HAND TO HAND

Not all fights are resolved at the verbal level. On at least 34 occasions during 1963–9 peace making failed and people came to blows. There were probably other cases I did not hear about. Based on accounts of 17 incidents actually witnessed by the research group, !Kung fights tend to have the following characteristics. They are of short duration; the actual time during which blows are exchanged varies between 30 seconds and 5 minutes. Assaults are sudden and in earnest; once begun, there are no ritualized phrases or slanging matches interspersed with the fighting. An exception to this rule is the play fighting occasionally observed among young males aged

18 to 35. Here there can be lengthy sequences of posturing and sparring interspersed with bouts of wrestling. Of five such cases observed during fieldwork, two turned serious, three did not. Four of the five cases involved only males; one involved a husband and wife. There are no instances of play fights among women.

In the case of serious fights, the atmosphere among the bystanders tends to be hysterical, although the combatants themselves often fight in dead silence, grim-faced and tight-lipped. Wrestling and punching at close quarters rather than fisticuffs seems to be the major technique for both sexes. The object of the fighter is to get a headlock on his opponent and force him to the ground. We saw no evidence of kicking or intent to harm the genitals. After the first exchange of blows, attempts are made by third parties to restrain the combatants. The fighters are forcibly separated and held back facing each other. After the fighting ceases, there is an eruption of talking and shouting by everyone—again except for the combatants, who remain silent. The discussion of the fight may continue for several hours after the event, and punching may flare again. On the other hand, we have seen people burst into laughter only a few minutes after a fight. After the tension is broken, partisans of the opposing sides may be seen joking with one another whereas only minutes before they were grappling. We did not see formal attempts at reconciliation—such as handshaking—following a fight. However, the trance dance that sometimes follows a fight may serve as a peace-making mechanism where trance performers give ritual healing to persons on both sides of the argument. . . .

Women are involved in fights almost as frequently as men (23 vs. 26 times), but men are the *initiators* of the attack almost three times as frequently as women (25 vs. 9 times). In only 1 instance did a woman attack a man, although women attacked other women on 8 occasions. The severity of the attacks were mild. In most cases the only injuries sustained were a few cuts and scratches. In six instances,

however, a riding crop or a stick was used and in two of these the victim suffered concussion and scalp wounds. In the most serious case, a brawl at !Kangwa in January 1969 in which a man received a deep gash on the skull, drunkenness was a precipitating factor. The misuse of alcohol, a substance unknown until the 1960s, appears to be an increasingly serious social problem in the 1970s. . . .

The causes of these fights are not always easy to discern, because the precipitating event may give few clues to the underlying cause. Adultery was the most common single factor: Accusations of adultery cropped up in 2 (of 11) male-male fights and 2 (of 14) male-female fights, but was a factor in 5 (of 8) female-female fights. The incidence of fights within a family was high: In 10 of the 14 male-female fights a husband attacked his wife, and in the 1 female-male encounter a woman attacked her husband. Despite the higher frequency of male-initiated attacks, women fought fiercely and often gave as good or better than they got.

In total, 48 people appeared as principals in these 34 fights, 37 people appeared only once, but 11 others took part in two or more fights. One nasty man with a reputation for unruliness was responsible for 4 of the 34 fights; 3 others (2 men and 1 woman) each cropped up in three different fights. . . .

FIGHTING WITH WEAPONS

Arrow fights have several general features. They occurred most commonly *within* living groups or between neighboring groups. Only a few of the killings occurred as a result of special expeditions for the purpose of fighting. However, two informants said that raiding expeditions had occurred in the very distant past, during the youth of the grandparent generation of the oldest living people. In the 22 cases, the outbreak of fighting was usually spontaneous; only 5 killings were the result of premeditated sneak attacks. The !Kung fight in public, usually in full view of everyone, and many people get involved.

The fight takes place in or near the camp—the site of domestic activities. There are no special fighting grounds or prearranged times for fighting. Nor are there any special weapons. . . .

ANALYSIS OF HOMICIDES

All the killers were males between the ages of 20 and 50. In 17 cases, there was a single killer; in 1 case, two killers; and in 1 case, three killers. In 3 additional cases between one and three men were involved. Two of the men were multiple killers. . . . There were no female killers and only 3 of the 22 victims were female. The low incidence of women in deadly fights contrasts sharply with the picture for less serious fights among the !Kung, in which over two-thirds of the cases involved females. The low incidence of females in deadly fights also contrasts sharply with the proportions of females reported as killers and as victims in other African societies and in Western industrial nations. Table [1] compares !Kung homicide rates, by sex, with rates in three other African societies and in Philadelphia and Britain. Female offenders, absent among the !Kung, make up 2 to 9 percent of the killers in the three African societies, and 18 and 32 percent of the killers in the two Western studies. Similarly, females as victims tend to be much more common in other African societies and in the West. . . .

TABLE 1. Incidence of Females as Killers and Victims Among the !Kung and Other Societies

Society	No. of cases	Percent Female Killers	Percent Female Victims
!Kung	22	0.0	13.6
Tiv (Nigeria)[a]	122	4.0	18.0
Soga (Uganda)[a]	100	2.0	45.0
Luo (Uganda)[a]	47	9.0	25.0
Philadelphia[b]	(1948–52)	18.0	24.0
Britain[b]	(1900–48)	32.0	57.0

[a]Data from Bohannan (1960:240).
[b]Data from Wolfgang (1958:46ff.).

Among the !Kung, the male monopoly of the lethal hunting weapons may partly account for the absence of woman killers, but still leaves unexplained the low incidence of woman victims compared with other societies. The answer may lie in the relatively high status !Kung women have relative to men. . . .

Victimology

Wolfgang (1958) following Hentig (1948) has employed the term *victimology* to refer to the study of who gets killed and the relationship of victim to killer. This perspective is useful for analyzing !Kung homicides. The data show that unlike the situation in Western societies, where up to a quarter of homicides occur within the family, among the !Kung close kin do not kill one another. No case concerns killing a parent, a child, or a sibling, and only one describes a husband killing a wife. This case, concerned with the wife's infidelity, was the only instance of intentional homicide of a woman. . . . In [one case] a young man killed his father's younger brother in an arrow fight. In the other cases the kin tie was more distant. In all cases the victim was personally known to the killer and probably related by some kinship connection. In no case was the victim a stranger. . . .

Hunter-Gatherer Violence: An Evolutionary Perspective

We have examined !Kung conflict in detail, with special attention to homicide. That the !Kung do fight and sometimes kill has been thoroughly documented. It remains to be determined whether the !Kung violence rate is high or low by the standards of other societies. A total of 22 killings over 50 years in a base population of approximately 1500 gives a homicide rate of 29.3 per 100,000 person-years. This rate is high by African standards. Southall (1960:228) has calculated the homicide rates from court records for 23 Ugandan tribes during the late colonial period 1945–54. The figures range from 1.1 to 11.6 homicides per 100,000 population with a mode of 4.0 to 6.0.

The rates for urban industrial societies are also lower than the !Kung figure. In the United States in 1972, there were some 18,880 homicide victims for a rate of 9.2 per 100,000 population, one-third that estimated for the !Kung. Only in a few American cities did the homicide rate exceed that of the !Kung: Washington, D.C., 32.8; Baltimore, 36.8; Detroit, 40.1; and Cleveland, 41.3 (U.S. Bureau of the Census 1974).

At first glance, the !Kung homicide rate seems to rank very high, making the !Kung level of conflict comparable to the level in America's most troubled urban centers. However, these statistics unduly favor the United States. One reason the American homicide rate is as low as it is, is the availability of excellent hospital emergency room care for victims of knife attacks and gunshot wounds. Were it not for these medical facilities many more cases entered on the police books as aggravated assaults would be entered instead as homicides. Another hidden source of homicides is contained in automobile accidents, a significant proportion of which have a homicidal intent but are not reported as such in the crime statistics. But the most important difference between homicide rates among the !Kung and the modern nation-state has still to be mentioned. The figure of 22 dead plus a few other possible cases represents all the killing the !Kung did for 50 years; they do not engage in warfare. The American state, on the other hand, was waging a war in Vietnam characterized by massive bombing of the rural population. While 18,800 Americans were murdered at home, at least 10 times that number of Vietnamese and Americans died violently in 1972 as a result of the war. In calculating the rate, one should add the Vietnamese base population (30 million) to that of the United States (210 million). Adding Vietnamese, as well as American, casualties in Vietnam, and allowing for underreporting of domestic violence in the United States, brings the comparable American homicide rate to over 100 per 100,000 population. Even in times of peace, domestic underreporting alone would probably account for triple the current homicide rate of 9.2.

Other Western nations have recent homicide rates that are much lower than that of the United States. Canada, England, France, and Germany had homicide rates in the 1950s and 1960s that ranged between 1.0 and 2.5 per 100,000 population. Yet the same comments about emergency medical care and underreporting apply to the underestimation of homicide in these countries; and, of course, the tremendous slaughter of the populations of Europe during the two world wars is not represented in the annual reporting of domestic violence. If the millions of English, French, and Germans killed in 1914–18, and 1939–45 were prorated in the homicide statistics for these countries for the interwar and postwar periods, the rates for other industrial nations would equal or surpass the revised American figures of 100 per 100,000 population.

The balance sheet in this perspective clearly favors the hunter-gatherers, who manage to keep their killing rates low even in the absence of our elaborate system of police, courts, and prisons.

This revised view of the level of violence in one of the "simplest" societies on earth compared with the most "advanced" should lead us to reconsider the role so often ascribed to the state in the evolution of social control. It has been argued that the great advantage of the state in societal evolution is that it creates an overriding mechanism for containing and resolving social conflict. Sahlins (1968) has called the state a society especially constituted to maintain law and order. The vast administrative hierarchies of the state are, of course, absent in band and tribal societies. An alternative but complementary view is to regard the process of social evolution leading to the state as one of *externalizing* violence rather than *controlling* or *eliminating* it. Such a view enables us to see the evolution of social control in a different light. As human societies have evolved from bands (like the !Kung) to tribes and chiefdoms, each step up in the level of sociocultural integration has reduced the problems of violence at the previous level of integration, *but has opened up new forms of violence at the new level.* So, for example, in the nineteenth century the Batswana chiefdom imposed its order on the band-level San hunters in Eastern Botswana, only to wage inter-tribal warfare on a much larger scale against neighboring chiefdoms such as the Matebele and the Kalanga-Shona. Then at the end of the nineteenth century, the British industrial state brought the Pax Britannica to the warring chiefdoms of Southern Africa. But a generation later, the British mobilized thousands of Tswana warriors' sons to fight in the Mediterranean theater against the German and Italian national states. At each new level of integration, the scale on which violence is practiced becomes greater in terms of the numbers involved, the degree of organization, the length and intensity of the conflict, and the technological sophistication. Warfare, in Paul Goodman's phrase, has become less passionate precisely as it has become more violent. In this perspective the lowly !Kung, for all the fierceness of their poisoned arrows, may well be the harmless people after all.

The !Kung themselves should have the final word on the subject of violence. One afternoon I was interviewing about hunting success four men who had also been participants in several cases of homicide. As I asked them about how many kudu, gemsbok, and giraffe they had killed, it suddenly occurred to me to pose the question: "And how many men have you killed?"

Without batting an eye, ≠Toma, the first man, held up three fingers; ticking off the names on his fingers, he responded: "I have killed Debe from N≠amchoha, and N//u, and N!eisi from /Gam."

I duly recorded the names and turned to Bo, the next man. "And how many have you killed?"

Bo replied, "I shot //Kushe in the back, but she lived."

Next was Bo's younger brother, Samk"xau: "I shot old Kan//a in the foot, but he lived."

I turned to the fourth man, Old Kashe, a kindly grandfather in his late sixties, and asked: "And how many men have *you* killed?"

"I have never killed anyone," he replied.

Pressing him, I asked: "Well then how many men have you shot?"

"I never shot anyone," he wistfully replied. "I always missed."

REFERENCES

Bohannan, P. 1960. Homicide among the Tiv of Central Nigeria. In Paul Bohannan (ed.). *African Homicide and Suicide*, pp. 30–64. New York: Atheneum.

Hentig, H. 1948. *The Criminal and His Victim: Studies in the Sociobiology of Crime*. New Haven: Yale University Press.

Lee, R. B. 1969. Eating Christmas in the Kalahari. *Natural History* (December): 14–22, 60–63.

Marshall, J. 1973. *An Argument about a Marriage* (film). Somerville, MA: Center for Documentary Anthropology.

———. 1961. Sharing, talking and giving: Relief of social tensions among !Kung Bushmen. *Africa* 31: 231–249.

———. 1976. *The !Kung of Nyae Nyae*. Cambridge, MA: Harvard University Press.

Sahlins, M. 1968. *Tribesmen*. Englewood Cliffs, NJ: Prentice Hall.

Southall, A. 1960. Homicide and suicide among the Alur. In Paul Bohannan (ed.). *African Homicide and Suicide*, pp. 214–229. Princeton: Princeton University Press.

U.S. Bureau of the Census. 1974. *Statistical Abstracts of the United States, 1973*. Washington, DC: Government Printing Office.

Wolfgang, M. E. 1958. *Patterns in Criminal Homicide*. Philadelphia: University of Pennsylvania Press.

The Case for Social Maternity: Adoption of Children by Urban Baule Women

Mona Etienne

In interpreting the adoption of children by urban Baule women of the Ivory Coast,[1] I will focus on such transactions in parenthood as evidence that maternity, like paternity is social as well as natural.[2] In analyzing the data, I will also try to emphasize the ways in which Baule women behave as autonomous social agents, controlling their own destiny—and often determining that of others. I suggest that this autonomy, like the adoption phenomenon itself, is not specific to the contemporary postcolonial urban context, but is rooted in precolonial Baule society.

That history and structure can be summarized as follows:

Colonized in the late nineteenth century and conquered only in the early twentieth, Baule society could hardly be characterized as "egalitarian," in the reductive sense, but there was no centralized political authority and there were no clear-cut principles of stratification, certainly no class structure. Early administrators were impressed by the independent spirit of the Baule in general and by what one described as "the preponderant role of women."[3] The Baule were primarily farmers and land was accessible to all, a woman normally farming in partnership with a man, typically her husband, *and having rights to the surplus production of specific crops.*

Craft production, trade, and gold-prospecting were major sources of wealth. In all of these activities, the woman had her share, both of the labor and of the profits.[4]

Physical warfare was the province of men, but it was supported by a women's ritual that constituted magical warfare. It is said that men who went to war against the will of village women would die in combat.

Political authority was limited, only magicoreligious sanctions were in effect, but such authority as existed was vested in women as well as men; there is ample evidence that the almost total disappearance of women chiefs was due to colonization. The one clear indication of a limit on women's access to positions of authority is the principle of virilocality. A married woman normally resided in her husband's household and this prevented her from being household head or kin group elder. Baule society was not however strongly gerontocratic. There was leeway for the acquisition of wealth by all adults. Differential wealth and status were made possible both by individual enterprise and by the access an individual had to the labor of dependents—mainly children, junior kin and captives.

A head of household or kin group elder had more ready access to the labor of dependents than others. There is however clear evidence that even within her husband's household a woman could have her own dependents and profit by their labor. Besides her daughters, she could also have captives of her own, along with junior female kin living and working with her. Junior members of a woman's kin group were acquired more or less definitively by fosterage or adoption. There was in fact an established custom whereby a married woman who went to reside with her husband was accompanied by a sister, a classificatory sister or a classificatory daughter, who remained with her if she had no daughter of her own at the time of marriage.

Although this usage can be seen to reflect a concern with maintaining a married woman's

From *Dialectical Anthropology* 4:237–242, 1979. Reprinted by permission of Kluwer Academic Publishers.

kin ties, my data also suggest the concern with a woman's having her own personal dependent, a child of her own, *who is not shared with the husband,* and also a concern with maintaining precise interindividual bonds with the mother, aunt or older sister who gives her the child.

Baule marriage is marked by brideservice and symbolic gifts of consumable goods; there is no bridewealth that gives a father and paternal kin undisputed rights in children.

Descent is cognatic with matrilineal emphasis,[5] and, although there are some rules governing the relationship between a child and its maternal and paternal kin, conflicting rights in children tend to make the option of the mother herself decisive. This shows up in adoption transactions although consent of the father is required.

It is perhaps significant that in pre-colonial Baule society, where pawning of persons existed, only maternal kin, including the mother herself, could pawn a child.

Another pertinent aspect of Baule society is that, although natural maternity, like natural paternity, is highly valued, sterility does not carry with it the onus described for some other African societies and sterility does not justify divorce. To be alone, without children, without dependents, is the saddest of conditions. It is also a threat for the future, since children are a guarantee of security in old age. Rights in children, however, are not determined by reproductive capacity alone. As I shall explain, sterility can even be a positive advantage for the urban woman.

Since early colonization, Baule women have been migrating to urban centers. Although some come to town as wives of male migrants, many come as single women, on their own initiative. Their principal motivation is to seek wealth and status. For the most part, urban migrants maintain active ties with the village; and status is a function not only of wealth, but of the network of social relations wealth facilitates and is facilitated by. To return to the village well-dressed and with gifts is essential. To build a house there, even though one may never live in it, is a much sought-after goal. To leave an inheritance that will make for an important funeral and remembrance after death is an ultimate achievement. Without people, however, without dependents who will live in the house, carry out the funeral, take the inheritance, speak your name after death, wealth is futile. To fulfill these needs, children, whether natural or social are indispensable, just as they are indispensable to constitute the wealth itself and to build relationships in the present and the future.

It is necessary here to indicate the ways in which illiterate women acquire wealth in town. To a certain extent they try to appropriate the advantage of men, who have greater access to the cash economy. Baule women are rarely prostitutes in the European sense, but they may try to profit by their sexual relationships or enter into temporary marriages with a man who is at least generous enough to assume all household expenses and make occasional gifts, leaving the woman free to trade and keep her profits. A woman who has established herself in petty trade can eventually maintain both herself and dependents without a man's support. Women who are unsuccessful return to the village, often with the hope of trying again. For reasons that I shall not elaborate on here, fertility is often an obstacle to urbanization. Pregnancy favors a return to the village, that, with further pregnancy, may become definitive. It is therefore not surprising that successful urban women tend to be sterile or of low fertility.

In addition to property in the village, these women acquire their own urban compounds and can maintain dependents who consolidate their ties with the village and eventually serve their interests in many ways. They have the advantage of being able to acquire children either temporarily or permanently when the most burdensome period of motherhood is past, at an age where a child starts to become an asset rather than a liability, and at a moment in their own lives when they are economically capable of taking responsibility for a child. Sterile women are also preferential candidates as adoptive mothers because the adoptee will not be in competition with natural children.

Transfers of parental rights and obligations range from minimal to maximal and can involve children and partners of both sexes and of varying degrees of kinship, as well as non-kin and, sometimes, non-Baule. Rather than review all of these variables and the combinations in which they appear, I will describe the different forms of transfer briefly and then focus on quasi-total transfer, or *adoption*, with women as the principal participants. (Rural to urban is today the preferential direction of adoption. Although urbanization may have intensified transfers of children, it is also possible that the lower incidence of rural to rural transfers may be only a recent phenomenon, a result of the draining toward the city of children who would formerly have been transferred between rural kin.)

Clear-cut cases of temporary transfer always refer to a specific reason. A child may be sent to a guardian or foster parent for schooling or as a temporary household aid. When these transfers take place between distant kin or non-kin, the child is often treated as a servant. As in all rural-urban transfers there is nevertheless the idea that the child, even when taken on as a household aide and treated as a servant, is receiving an education in the ways of the city and thus a chance at success. Children themselves may enter into such relationships on their own initiative. Baule children, in any case, *are not forced into such fosterage situations against their will*, nor are they exploited in the sole interest of their parents. These transfers may however relieve the burden on a fertile and economically disadvantaged family and, at the same time, create ties with the city that can serve in the future.

A child may also be sent on a temporary basis to remain with an older sister or other close kin for a specified period of time or for a given task, for example to help after childbirth. This kind of transfer is, to a certain extent, part of the normal rights and obligations of close kin. If however the arrangement has not been precise enough or the foster parent begs time and again to keep the child a little longer and the child wants to remain, the ensuing relationship may be interpreted after the fact as a case of adoption, the foster mother ultimately assuming all the rights and obligations of an adoptive mother.

Cases in which the child is given simply to go with the woman, to accompany her, are the object of contradictory interpretations by informants, who refer sometimes to the closeness of kinship, sometimes to the age of the child as criteria of whether there is fosterage or adoption. Again the nature of the transfer will often be defined *a posteriori*.

In the clear-cut case of adoption, the child is given with the words "This is your own child," "Take this child for yourself," or even "Here is a child to put in your belly." Ideally the adopted is a baby and may even be promised before birth, although the actual transfer will take place only after weaning, sometimes very much later. In this type of transfer, the emphasis is on the relationship between the natural and the adoptive parent. In the case of close kin such as sisters, beyond the obligations they normally have to each other and to each other's children, the gift of a child is supposed to mark something extra, a special bond of affection. But a child can also be given to a more distant kinswoman, an affine, or even a stranger "to show that you love her." Here any suggestion that the child may be considered a burden, and given for that reason is inadmissible. When a fertile woman gives a child to a sterile woman or an older woman who has no young children, the gift is seen in terms of generosity and sharing. It would be selfish to do otherwise.

The fact remains that adoption here serves to adjust the imbalance of natural maternity. It may also serve to adjust the imbalance between natural maternity and a woman's desire to raise children, either at a given moment in her life or in general. Although all women are supposed to desire their children, the Baule recognize an unequal distribution of both the penchant, and the talent for active motherhood. Some women receive many children in adoption because they are considered to raise children well, while others systematically give their children to sisters or mothers because they simply do not like raising children.

If these cases make it appear that, in spite

of the ideology, adoption serves to get rid of unwanted or excess children, many others appear to confirm the ideology and reveal the importance of the bond between natural and adoptive parents. A much-desired first-born, often promised before birth, may be given to an adoptive mother as proof of the natural mother's special affection for her. This can occur as a form of indirect exchange following a previous adoption. When a young woman has been given a younger sister to accompany her in marriage, she may later give her first-born to this adoptive daughter. Where this is not possible, because the original adoptive mother is old or sterile, one finds reinforcement and perpetuation of the original bond by duplication: An adoptee, as proof of her affection for her adoptive mother, is supposed to replace herself when she leaves to marry, ideally by the gift of her first-born. Not to offer a child to one's adoptive mother is a way of saying that the adoptee does not love her, is not happy with the way she was raised. In one case of a very old woman I found duplication of adoption over several generations.

In true adoption, life-long rights and obligations of the natural parent are transferred. An adoptive mother will assume all expenses for the child in health and in illness, perhaps send her/him to school; and she can authorize marriage without consulting the natural parents. The adult adoptee will maintain ties with the adoptive parent, returning to her in case of divorce of difficulty, caring for her in old age, eventually burying her, and possibly becoming her heir.

Ties with the natural parents are not, however, broken. A child adopted in babyhood must be taught who its natural parents are, and incest prohibitions are defined through them. They receive visits and gifts from the child, and they must be informed, if not consulted, when the child is married.[6]

It is particularly interesting, however, that, juridically at least, the bond between adoptee and adoptive parent is in some ways stronger than the bond between a child and its natural parents. As noted, Baule children have considerable autonomy and often leave home on their own. If a child insists, the natural parent cannot object. The bond between adoptee and adoptive parent, however, has the character of a sacred gift. The child must not leave, especially to return to the natural parents. If she/he does, both natural and adoptive parents must do everything possible to see that the child returns. To act otherwise would suggest that the former want to take the child back and the latter want to return it. A child will, of course, especially in cases of extreme mistreatment, sometimes return to its natural parents; but this is never accomplished easily or without conflict and bad feelings.

While there are such cases of returned children, there are also others in which women who give their first-born in adoption subsequently have no other children and are in dire straits for lack of a child helper. In such cases, the child may be sent temporarily to help the natural mother, but there can be neither a request nor an offer that she/he be given back permanently.

In another sense, the rights of an adoptive parent are stronger than those of natural parents. As suggested previously, in natural parenthood, rights in the child are considered to be shared between mother and father, although mother-right is stronger, especially in the case of girl children and babies of both sexes. The adoptive parent, however, who is most often a woman, receives the child in her name only. Her husband, if she has one, may sometimes create ties with the child by contributing to its welfare, but the transfer itself gives rights only to the woman. The adoptive mother therefore acquires, even within her husband's household, a child that is hers alone, that materializes her personal bond with the child's natural family, and, if she raises the child to successful adulthood, guarantees her future security.

Transactions involving males follow, as might be expected, similar rules.[7] Whereas a girl is traditionally considered the appropriate adoptive child for a woman because of the sexual division of labor, and women still adopt more girls for their labor value and for rights in their future children, a boy who is sent to school may become part of the urban educated elite, even the modern political power structure. If this happens, he will not forget his adoptive mother—or his natural parents. Particularly foresighted women therefore tend to give and receive a certain number of boy children as urban adoptees. Further, in spite of the generally stronger rights of mothers and maternal kin, precisely the most prestigious urban women frequently receive adoptive children both through male kin and on the initiative of fathers themselves.

These cases are important, because they show that networks constituted by urban women through adoption are not strictly female networks. Rather, while they appear to be female-dominated, they include male elements. Here the adoption data correlate with my observations of compounds, where one finds men as well as women among the urban woman's constituency of dependents.[8]

Let me note finally that further exploration of similar material will contribute to undermining the assumption that, whereas paternity is eminently social, maternity is irrevocably natural. The biological fact that only women give birth to children is seen by some as the theoretical key to male dominance—dominance that is perhaps too easily considered to be amply demonstrated by the empirical data. At the same time, the tendency of male-centered anthropology to assume that, when women's reproductive capacity is controlled or manipulated, the agents of this social action are necessarily men, is but another instance of the more general tendency to see only men as social actors. Thus the empirical data feed back into the theoretical orientation that posits the universal subordination of women.

When a contemporary theorist who has also done fieldwork in Africa—I am referring here to Meillassoux—says: "Woman, in spite of her irreplaceable function in reproduction, never intervenes as a vector of social organization. She disappears behind the man; her father, her brother, her husband"[9] we must ask ourselves to what extent the theory accounts for the reality of other societies, and its incarnation in an anthropology that makes women disappear behind fathers, brothers and husbands. I believe that only systematic attempts to make women visible, to determine whether in fact they do or do not appear as vectors of social organization, can begin to answer this question. And if they do, as among the Baule, what are the occasions for their visibility and their autonomy?

NOTES

1. This is a paper presented at the 76th annual meeting of the American Anthropological Association, Houston, Texas, 1977. An extended version of this article will be published in French: *L'Homme*, XIX (3/4, Juin/ Décembre, 1979). Data are based on 1962–63 fieldwork among rural Baule, supported by the Ivory Coast government (Ministère de Plan) in the context of the Bouaké Regional Study (Etude régionale de Bouaké), and on 1974–75 fieldwork among urban Baule of Abidjan, supported by Grant No. 3067 from the Wenner-Gren Foundation. I thank the Ivory Coast Ministère de la Recherche Scientifique and the Institut d'Ethnologie of the University of Abidjan for authorizing 1974–75 research, and the Institut de Linguistique for use of audio equipment.

2. See Nicole-Claude Mathieu, "Paternité biologique, maternité sociale," in Andrée Michel (ed.). *Femmes, sexisme et société.* (Paris: Presses universitaires de France, 1977), pp. 39–48. A critique of male bias in anthropological views of reproduction, this article strongly influenced not only the present analysis, but also my 1974–75 fieldwork. Written in 1974, it explicitly suggests adoption as one insufficiently explored object of research and as a "sign of the social manipulation of biological engendering" ("signe de la manipulation sociale de l'engendrement biologique", pp. 43–44).

3. ". . . le rôle prépondérant des femmes . . . ", p. 139 in J. F. Bouet, "Quelques opérations militaires á la Côte d'Ivoire en 1909," *Revue des troupes coloniales*, IX (1910), 2ème sem., pp. 134–153. Early observers are unanimous in noting the high status of Baule women.

4. Concerning women's control of cloth, an important item in long-distance trade, see Mona Etienne. "Women and Men, Cloth and Colo-

nization: The Transformation of Production—Distribution Relations among the Baule (Ivory Coast)", *Cahiers d'Etude Africaines*, vol. 65, XVII (1), (1977), pp. 41–64.

5. Baule kinship nomenclature is of the "generation" or "Hawaiian" type. The correlation of institutionalized adoption with this type of nomenclature and cognatic descent is frequently noted, usually with reference to non-African societies and especially Polynesia. For excellent case studies, see Vern Carroll (ed.), *Adoption in Eastern Oceania* (Hawaii: University of Hawaii Press, 1970). The only serious exploration of the subject by an Africanist is Esther Goody, "Some Theoretical and Empirical Aspects of Parenthood in West Africa," in C. Oppong, G. Adaba et al. (eds.), *Marriage, Fertility and Parenthood in West Africa* (Papers from the XVth Seminar of the International Sociological Association Committee on Family Research, Lomé, Togoland, January 1976). Changing African Family No. 4, Canberra: Australian National University; n.d., pp. 227–271.

6. An adoptee's relationship to the ancestors is determined by birth and must be maintained. In disagreement with Goody (*op. cit.*) and in accord with the Oceanists (Carroll, *op. cit.*), I use the term "adoption", in spite of its different connotations in our own society, to mark the specificity of a form of transfer significantly distinct from those that can be called "fosterage".

7. Of the three positions involved in a transfer: giver, adoptee and recipient, males appear least frequently as recipients in true adoption, although they often receive older children in fosterage, especially for schooling. The raising of young children is woman's work and creates strong emotional ties. The giver would not want such ties to develop with an unrelated woman (the wife of the recipient) and eventually cause problems in case of divorce.

8. During my 1974–75 fieldwork, the suggestions of Naomi Quinn, "Asking The Right Question: A Re-examination of Akan Residence," Wm. M. O'Barr, David H. Spain and Mark Tessler (eds.), *Survey Research in Africa* (Evanston, IL: Northwestern University Press, 1973), pp. 168–183, proved invaluable in establishing relationships of dependency in general and adoption in particular. The questions, "By whom is she/he here?" and "Who takes care of (is responsible for) her/him?" applied to all inhabitants of each compound studied, revealed relationships that genealogical and "head of household" bias would have obscured. For example, a woman residing in her brother's compound could be the autonomous head of a sub-group, a child residing in the same compound as its mother could be the adoptee of another woman.

9. ". . . la femme, malgré sa fonction irremplaçable dans la reproduction, n'intervient jamais comme vecteur de l'organisation sociale. Elle disparait derrière l'homme: son père, son frère ou son époux." See Claude Meillassoux, *Femmes, Greniers et Capitaux* (Paris: Maspéro, 1975), p. 116. It is interesting that Meillassoux and Marvin Harris give explanations of "male dominance" that are diametrically opposed, but founded on similar assumptions. For Meillassoux (*op. cit.*), women become subordinate with the development of horticulture because their reproductive capacity is *so valuable* to societies that rely on increased population to increase production; for Harris, male dominance emerges in the first moments in human history because women's reproductive capacity is *so dangerous* to a world threatened by overpopulation. (See "Why Men Dominate Women," *The New York Times Magazine*, November 13, 1977, p. 46ss., and W. T. Divale and M. Harris, "Population, Warfare and the Male Supremacist Complex," *American Anthropologist*, vol. 78, no. 3 (1976), pp. 521–538.)

Both theorists assume that men are the social actors, that men manipulate women's reproductive capacity but women do not (even in infanticide!). It must be noted to Meillassoux's credit that he does attempt to explain why men are the actors and women the objects in the earliest struggle to control their child-bearing potential; but his argument begs the question, reifying women to explain their reification. It belongs to the realm of anthropological mythology and, if one accepts the ground rules, could easily be converted into its opposite, an argument for matriarchy.

Lifeboat Ethics: Mother Love and Child Death in Northeast Brazil

Nancy Scheper–Hughes

I have seen death without weeping
The destiny of the Northeast is death
   Cattle they kill
To the people they do something worse
      —Anonymous Brazilian singer (1965)

"Why do the church bells ring so often?" I asked Nailza de Arruda soon after I moved into a corner of her tiny mud-walled hut near the top of the shantytown called the Alto do Cruzeiro (Crucifix Hill). I was then a Peace Corps volunteer and a community development/health worker. It was the dry and blazing hot summer of 1965, the months following the military coup in Brazil, and save for the rusty, clanging bells, of N. S. das Dores Church, an eerie quiet had settled over the market town that I call Bom Jesus da Mata. Beneath the quiet, however, there was chaos and panic. "It's nothing," replied Nailza, "just another little angel gone to heaven."

Nailza had sent more than her share of little angels to heaven, and sometimes at night I could hear her engaged in a muffled but passionate discourse with one of them, two-year-old Joana. Joana's photograph, taken as she lay propped up in her tiny cardboard coffin, her eyes open, hung on a wall next to one of Nailza and Ze Antonio taken on the day they eloped.

Nailza could barely remember the other infants and babies who came and went in close succession. Most had died unnamed and were hastily baptized in their coffins. Few lived more than a month or two. Only Joana, properly baptized in church at the close of her first year and placed under the protection of a powerful saint, Joan of Arc, had been ex-

pected to live. And Nailza had dangerously allowed herself to love the little girl.

In addressing the dead child, Nailza's voice would range from tearful imploring to angry recrimination: "Why did you leave me? Was your patron saint so greedy that she could not allow me one child on this earth?" Ze Antonio advised me to ignore Nailza's odd behavior, which he understood as a kind of madness that, like the birth and death of children, came and went. Indeed, the premature birth of a stillborn son some months later "cured" Nailza of her "inappropriate" grief, and the day came when she removed Joana's photo and carefully packed it away.

More than fifteen years elapsed before I returned to the Alto do Cruzeiro, and it was anthropology that provided the vehicle of my return. Since 1982 I have returned several times in order to pursue a problem that first attracted my attention in the 1960s. My involvement with the people of the Alto do Cruzeiro now spans a quarter of a century and three generations of parenting in a community where mothers and daughters are often simultaneously pregnant.

The Alto do Cruzeiro is one of three shantytowns surrounding the large market town of Bom Jesus in the sugar plantation zone of Pernambuco in Northeast Brazil, one of the many zones of neglect that have emerged in the shadow of the now tarnished economic miracle of Brazil. For the women and children of the Alto do Cruzeiro the only miracle is that some of them have managed to stay alive at all.

The Northeast is a region of vast proportions (approximately twice the size of Texas) and of equally vast social and developmental problems. The nine states that make up the region are the poorest in the country and are representative of the Third World within a dynamic and rapidly industrializing nation. Despite waves of migrations from the interior to the teeming shantytowns of coastal cities, the majority still live in rural areas on farms and ranches, sugar plantations and mills.

Life expectancy in the Northeast is only forty years, largely because of the appallingly high rate of infant and child mortality. Approximately one million children in Brazil under the age of five die each year. The children of the Northeast, especially those born in shantytowns on the periphery of urban life, are at a very high risk of death. In these areas, children are born without the traditional protection of breast-feeding, subsistence gardens, stable marriages, and multiple adult caretakers that exists in the interior. In the hillside shantytowns that spring up around cities or, in this case, interior market towns, marriages are brittle, single parenting is the norm, and women are frequently forced into the shadow economy of domestic work in the homes of the rich or into unprotected and oftentimes "scab" wage labor on the surrounding sugar plantations, where they clear land for planting and weed for a pittance, sometimes less than a dollar a day. The women of the Alto may not bring their babies with them into the homes of the wealthy, where the often-sick infants are considered sources of contamination, and they cannot carry the little ones to the riverbanks where they wash clothes because the river is heavily infested with schistosomes and other deadly parasites. Nor can they carry their young children to the plantations, which are often several miles away. At wages of a dollar a day, the women of the Alto cannot hire baby sitters. Older children who are not in school will sometimes serve as somewhat indifferent caretakers. But any child not in school is also expected to find wage work. In most cases, babies are simply left at home alone, the door securely fastened. And so many also die alone and unattended.

Bom Jesus da Mata, centrally located in the plantation zone of Pernambuco, is within commuting distance of several sugar planta-

tions and mills. Consequently, Bom Jesus has been a magnet for rural workers forced off their small subsistence plots by large landowners wanting to use every available piece of land for sugar cultivation. Initially, the rural migrants to Bom Jesus were squatters who were given tacit approval by the mayor to put up temporary straw huts on each of the three hills overlooking the town. The Alto do Cruzeiro is the oldest, the largest, and the poorest of the shantytowns. Over the past three decades many of the original migrants have become permanent residents, and the primitive and temporary straw huts have been replaced by small homes (usually of two rooms) made of wattle and daub, sometimes covered with plaster. The more affluent residents use bricks and tiles. In most Alto homes, dangerous kerosene lamps have been replaced by light bulbs. The once tattered rural garb, often fashioned from used sugar sacking, has likewise been replaced by store-bought clothes, often castoffs from a wealthy *patrão* (boss). The trappings are modern, but the hunger, sickness, and death that they conceal are traditional, deeply rooted in a history of feudalism, exploitation, and institutionalized dependency.

My research agenda never wavered. The questions I addressed first crystallized during a veritable "die-off" of Alto babies during a severe drought in 1965. The food and water shortages and the political and economic chaos occasioned by the military coup were reflected in the handwritten entries of births and deaths in the dusty, yellowed pages of the ledger books kept at the public registry office in Bom Jesus. More than 350 babies died in the Alto during 1965 alone—this from a shantytown population of little more than 5,000. But that wasn't what surprised me. There were reasons enough for the deaths in the miserable conditions of shantytown life. What puzzled me was the seeming indifference of Alto women to the death of their infants, and their willingness to attribute to their own tiny offspring an aversion to life that made their death seem wholly natural, indeed all but anticipated.

Although I found that it was possible, and

hardly difficult, to rescue infants and toddlers from death by diarrhea and dehydration with a simple sugar, salt, and water solution (even bottled Coca-Cola worked fine), it was more difficult to enlist a mother herself in the rescue of a child she perceived as ill-fated for life or better off dead, or to convince her to take back into her threatened and besieged home a baby she had already come to think of as an angel rather than as a son or daughter.

I learned that the high expectancy of death, and the ability to face child death with stoicism and equanimity, produced patterns of nurturing that differentiated between those infants thought of as thrivers and survivors and those thought of as born already "wanting to die." The survivors were nurtured, while stigmatized, doomed infants were left to die, as mothers say, *a mingua*, "of neglect." Mothers stepped back and allowed nature to take its course. This pattern, which I call mortal selective neglect, is called passive infanticide by anthropologist Marvin Harris. The Alto situation, although culturally specific in the form that it takes, is not unique to Third World shantytown communities and may have its correlates in our own impoverished urban communities in some cases of "failure to thrive" infants.

I use as an example the story of Zezinho, the thirteen-month-old toddler of one of my neighbors, Lourdes. I became involved with Zezinho when I was called in to help Lourdes in the delivery of another child, this one a fair and robust little tyke with a lusty cry. I noted that while Lourdes showed great interest in the newborn, she totally ignored Zezinho who, wasted and severely malnourished, was curled up in a fetal position on a piece of urine- and feces-soaked cardboard placed under his mother's hammock. Eyes open and vacant, mouth slack, the little boy seemed doomed.

When I carried Zezinho up to the community day-care center at the top of the hill, the Alto women who took turns caring for one another's children (in order to free themselves for part-time work in the cane fields or washing clothes) laughed at my efforts to save Ze, agreeing with Lourdes that here was a baby without a ghost of a chance. Leave him alone, they cautioned. It makes no sense to fight with death. But I did do battle with Ze, and after several weeks of force-feeding (malnourished babies lose their interest in food), Ze began to succumb to my ministrations. He acquired some flesh across his taut chest bones, learned to sit up, and even tried to smile. When he seemed well enough, I returned him to Lourdes in her miserable scrap-material lean-to, but not without guilt about what I had done. I wondered whether returning Ze was at all fair to Lourdes and to his little brother. But I was busy and washed my hands of the matter. And Lourdes did seem more interested in Ze now that he was looking more human.

When I returned in 1982, there was Lourdes among the women who formed my sample of Alto mothers—still struggling to put together some semblance of life for a now grown Ze and her five other surviving children. Much was made of my reunion with Ze in 1982, and everyone enjoyed retelling the story of Ze's rescue and of how his mother had given him up for dead. Ze would laugh the loudest when told how I had had to force-feed him like a fiesta turkey. There was no hint of guilt on the part of Lourdes and no resentment on the part of Ze. In fact, when questioned in private as to who was the best friend he ever had in life, Ze took a long drag on his cigarette and answered without a trace of irony, "Why my mother, of course!" "But of course," I replied.

Part of learning how to mother in the Alto do Cruzeiro is learning when to let go of a child who shows that it "wants" to die or that it has no "knack" or no "taste" for life. Another part is learning when it is safe to let oneself love a child. Frequent child death remains a powerful shaper of maternal thinking and practice. In the absence of firm expectation that a child will survive, mother love as we conceptualize it (whether in popular terms or in the psychobiological notion of maternal bonding) is attenuated and delayed with consequences for infant survival. In an environment already precarious to young life, the emotional detachment of mothers toward some of their babies contributes even further to the spiral of high mortality—high fertility in a kind of macabre lock-step dance to death.

The average woman of the Alto experiences 9.5 pregnancies, 3.5 child deaths, and 1.5 stillbirths. Seventy percent of all child deaths in the Alto occur in the first six months of life, and 82 percent by the end of the first year. Of all deaths in the community each year, about 45 percent are of children under the age of five.

Women of the Alto distinguish between child deaths understood as natural (caused by diarrhea and communicable diseases) and those resulting from sorcery, the evil eye, or other magical or supernatural afflictions. They also recognize a large category of infant deaths seen as fated and inevitable. These hopeless cases are classified by mothers under the folk terminology "child sickness" or "child attack." Women say that there are at least fourteen different types of hopeless child sickness, but most can be subsumed under two categories—chronic and acute. The chronic cases refer to infants who are born small and wasted. They are deathly pale, mothers say, as well as weak and passive. They demonstrate no vital force, no liveliness. They do not suck vigorously; they hardly cry. Such babies can be this way at birth or they can be born sound but soon show no resistance, no "fight" against the common crises of infancy: diarrhea, respiratory infections, tropical fevers.

The acute cases are those doomed infants who die suddenly and violently. They are taken by stealth overnight, often following convulsions that bring on head banging, shaking, grimacing, and shrieking. Women say it is horrible to look at such a baby. If the infant begins to foam at the mouth or gnash its teeth or go rigid with its eyes turned back inside its head, there is absolutely no hope. The infant is "put aside"—left alone—often on the floor in a back room, and allowed to die. These symptoms (which accompany high fevers, dehydration, third-stage malnutrition, and encephalitis) are equated by Alto women with madness, epilepsy, and worst of all, ra-

bies, which is greatly feared and highly stigmatized.

Most of the infants presented to me as suffering from chronic child sickness were tiny, wasted famine victims, while those labeled as victims of acute child attack seemed to be infants suffering from the deliriums of high fever or the convulsions that can accompany electrolyte imbalance in dehydrated babies.

Local midwives and traditional healers, praying women, as they are called, advise Alto women on when to allow a baby to die. One midwife explained: "If I can see that a baby was born unfortuitously, I tell the mother that she need not wash the infant or give it a cleansing tea. I tell her just to dust the infant with baby powder and wait for it to die." Allowing nature to take its course is not seen as sinful by these often very devout Catholic women. Rather, it is understood as cooperating with God's plan.

Often I have been asked how consciously women of the Alto behave in this regard. I would have to say that consciousness is always shifting between allowed and disallowed levels of awareness. For example, I was awakened early one morning in 1987 by two neighborhood children who had been sent to fetch me to a hastily organized wake for a two-month-old infant whose mother I had unsuccessfully urged to breast-feed. The infant was being sustained on sugar water, which the mother referred to as *soro* (serum), using a medical term for the infant's starvation regime in light of his chronic diarrhea. I had cautioned the mother that an infant could not live on *soro* forever.

The two girls urged me to console the young mother by telling her that it was "too bad" that her infant was so weak that Jesus had to take him. They were coaching me in proper Alto etiquette. I agreed, of course, but asked, "And what do *you* think?" Xoxa, the eleven-year-old, looked down at her dusty flip-flops and blurted out, "Oh, Dona Nanci, that baby never got enough to eat, but you must never say that!" And so the death of hungry babies remains one of the best kept secrets of life in Bom Jesus da Mata.

Most victims are waked quickly and with a minimum of ceremony. No tears are shed, and the neighborhood children form a tiny procession, carrying the baby to the town graveyard where it will join a multitude of others. Although a few fresh flowers may be scattered over the tiny grave, no stone or wooden cross will mark the place, and the same spot will be reused within a few months' time. The mother will never visit the grave, which soon becomes an anonymous one.

What, then, can be said of these women? What emotions, what sentiments motivate them? How are they able to do what, in fact, must be done? What does mother love mean in this inhospitable context? Are grief, mourning, and melancholia present, although deeply repressed? If so, where shall we look for them? And if not, how are we to understand the moral visions and moral sensibilities that guide their actions?

I have been criticized more than once for presenting an unflattering portrait of poor Brazilian women, women who are, after all, themselves the victims of severe social and institutional neglect. I have described these women as allowing some of their children to die, as if this were an unnatural and inhuman act rather than, as I would assert, the way any one of us might act, reasonably and rationally, under similarly desperate conditions. Perhaps I have not emphasized enough the real pathogens in this environment of high risk: poverty, deprivation, sexism, chronic hunger, and economic exploitation. If mother love is, as many psychologists and some feminists believe, a seemingly natural and universal maternal script, what does it mean to women for whom scarcity, loss, sickness, and deprivation have made that love frantic and robbed them of their grief, seeming to turn their hearts to stone?

Throughout much of human history—as in a great deal of the impoverished Third World today—women have had to give birth and to nurture children under ecological conditions and social arrangements hostile to child survival, as well as to their own well-being. Under circumstances of high childhood mortality, patterns of selective neglect and passive infanticide may be seen as active survival strategies.

They also seem to be fairly common practices historically and across cultures. In societies characterized by high childhood mortality and by a correspondingly high (replacement) fertility, cultural practices of infant and child care tend to be organized primarily around survival goals. But what this means is a pragmatic recognition that not all of one's children can be expected to live. The nervousness about child survival in areas of northeast Brazil, northern India, or Bangladesh, where a 30 percent or 40 percent mortality rate in the first years of life is common, can lead to forms of delayed attachment and a casual or benign neglect that serves to weed out the worst bets so as to enhance the life chances of healthier siblings, including those yet to be born. Practices similar to those that I am describing have been recorded for parts of Africa, India, and Central America.

Life in the Alto do Cruzeiro resembles nothing so much as a battlefield or an emergency room in an overcrowded innercity public hospital. Consequently, morality is guided by a kind of "lifeboat ethics," the morality of triage. The seemingly studied indifference toward the suffering of some of their infants, conveyed in such sayings as "little critters have no feelings," is understandable in light of these women's obligation to carry on with their reproductive and nurturing lives.

In their slowness to anthropomorphize and personalize their infants, everything is mobilized so as to prevent maternal overattachment and, therefore, grief at death. The bereaved mother is told not to cry, that her tears will dampen the wings of her little angel so that she cannot fly up to her heavenly home. Grief at the death of an angel is not only inappropriate, it is a symptom of madness and of a profound lack of faith.

Infant death becomes routine in an environment in which death is anticipated and bets are hedged. While the routinization of death in the context of shantytown life is not hard to understand, and quite possible to empathize with, its routinization in the formal institutions of public life in Bom Jesus is not as easy to accept uncritically. Here the social production of indifference takes on a different, even a malevolent cast.

In a society where triplicates of every form are required for the most banal events (registering a car, for example), the registration of infant and child death is informal, incomplete, and rapid. It requires no documentation, takes less than five minutes, and demands no witnesses other than office clerks. No questions are asked concerning the circumstances of the death, and the cause of death is left blank, unquestioned and unexamined. A neighbor, grandmother, older sibling, or common-law husband may register the death. Since most infants die at home, there is no question of a medical record.

From the registry office, the parent proceeds to the town hall, where the mayor will give him or her a voucher for a free baby coffin. The full-time municipal coffinmaker cannot tell you exactly how many baby coffins are dispatched each week. It varies, he says, with the seasons. There are more needed during the drought months and during the big festivals of Carnaval and Christmas and São Joao's Day because people are too busy, he supposes, to take their babies to the clinic. Record keeping is sloppy.

Similarly, there is a failure on the part of city-employed doctors working at two free clinics to recognize the malnutrition of babies who are weighed, measured, and immunized without comment and as if they were not, in fact, anemic, stunted, fussy, and irritated starvation babies. At best the mothers are told to pick up free vitamins or a health "tonic" at the municipal chambers. At worst, clinic personnel will give tranquilizers and sleeping pills to quiet the hungry cries of "sick-to-death" Alto babies.

The church, too, contributes to the routinization of, and indifference toward, child death. Traditionally, the local Catholic church taught patience and resignation to domestic tragedies that were said to reveal the imponderable workings of God's will. If an infant died suddenly, it was because a par-

ticular saint had claimed the child. The infant would be an angel in the service of his or her heavenly patron. It would be wrong, a sign of a lack of faith, to weep for a child with such good fortune. The infant funeral was, in the past, an event celebrated with joy. Today, however, under the new regime of "liberation theology," the bells of N. S. das Dores parish church no longer peal for the death of Alto babies, and no priest accompanies the procession of angels to the cemetery where their bodies are disposed of casually and without ceremony. Children bury children in Bom Jesus da Mata. In this most Catholic of communities, the coffin is handed to the disabled and irritable municipal gravedigger, who often chides the children for one reason or another. It may be that the coffin is larger than expected and the gravedigger can find no appropriate space. The children do not wait for the gravedigger to complete his task. No prayers are recited and no sign of the cross made as the tiny coffin goes into its shallow grave.

When I asked the local priest, Padre Marcos, about the lack of church ceremony surrounding infant and childhood death today in Bom Jesus, he replied: "In the old days, child death was richly celebrated. But those were the baroque customs of a conservative church that wallowed in death and misery. The new church is a church of hope and joy. We no longer celebrate the death of child angels. We try to tell mothers that Jesus doesn't want all the dead babies they send him." Similarly, the new church has changed its baptismal customs, now often refusing to baptize dying babies brought to the back door of a church or rectory. The mothers are scolded by the church attendants and told to go home and take care of their sick babies. Baptism, they are told, is for the living; it is not to be confused with the sacrament of extreme unction, which is the anointing of the dying. And so it appears to the women of the Alto that even the church has turned away from them, denying the traditional comfort of folk Catholicism.

The contemporary Catholic church is caught in the clutches of a double bind. The new theology of liberation imagines a kingdom of God on earth based on justice and equality, a world without hunger, sickness, or childhood mortality. At the same time, the church has not changed its official position on sexuality and reproduction, including its sanctions against birth control, abortion, and sterilization. The padre of Bom Jesus da Mata recognizes this contradiction intuitively, although he shies away from discussions on the topic, saying that he prefers to leave questions of family planning to the discretion and the "good consciences" of his impoverished parishioners. But this, of course, sidesteps the extent to which those good consciences have been shaped by traditional church teachings in Bom Jesus, especially by his recent predecessors. Hence, we can begin to see that the seeming indifference of Alto mothers toward the death of some of their infants is but a pale reflection of the official indifference of church and state to the plight of poor women and children.

Nonetheless, the women of Bom Jesus are survivors. One woman, Biu, told me her life history, returning again and again to the themes of child death, her first husband's suicide, abandonment by her father and later by her second husband, and all the other losses and disappointments she had suffered in her long forty-five years. She concluded with great force, reflecting on the days of Carnaval '88 that were fast approaching:

> No, Dona Nanci, I won't cry, and I won't waste my life thinking about it from morning to night. . . . Can I argue with God for the state that I'm in? No! And so I'll dance and I'll jump and I'll play Carnaval! And yes, I'll laugh and people will wonder at a *pobre* like me who can have such a good time.

And no one did blame Biu for dancing in the streets during the four days of Carnaval—not even on Ash Wednesday, the day following Carnaval '88 when we all assembled hurriedly to assist in the burial of Mercea, Biu's beloved *casula*, her last-born daughter who had died at home of pneumonia during the festivities. The rest of the family barely had time to change out of their costumes. Severino, the child's uncle and godfather, sprinkled holy water over the little angel while he prayed: "Mercea, I don't know whether you were called, taken, or thrown out of this world. But look down at us from your heavenly home with tenderness, with pity, and with mercy." So be it.

II.
Archaeology and Gender

A popular introductory archaeology text began its career fifteen years ago with the title *Men of the Earth* (Fagan 1974). For the last several editions (Fagan 1977–1991) it has been called *People of the Earth*. This change is deliberate and illustrates a growing sensitivity on the part of some archaeologists to the importance of considering the contribution of women, as well as men, to the history of our species. An archaeological focus on gender provides a lens for reassessing myths about the past that glorify men as the agents of cultural change. As some archaeologists seek to reinstate women as agents and as subjects, widely held assumptions about "mankind" and "man's past" are challenged by a focus on women's involvement in production, politics, and the generation of symbol systems in past societies. In contrast to earlier archaeological orientations (see Conkey and Spector 1984 for a review of archaeological approaches), an "engendered" archaeology assumes that the process of survival throughout human history has of necessity involved a collaborative effort between men and women. Those who advocate a feminist-informed archaeology have explored such issues as women's participation in the creation of wealth (for example, women's production of textiles or ceramics), consequences of women's rule in state societies, images of powerful women in prehistoric art, and women's roles in the development of agriculture.

Questions of fundamental importance regarding the sexual division of labor in past societies may benefit from an archaeological perspective that includes women's interests. Rather than assuming that "earliest human groups were conscious of and elaborated sex differences into differentially valued, gender-exclusive task groups," Spector and Whelan (1989:73) suggest that an archaeology of gender needs to begin by raising questions about the origins of a sexual division of labor and by determining what gender differentiation might have accomplished among early human populations (Spector and Whelan 1989:72–73; see also Ehrenberg, this book).

As Conkey (this book) suggests, in the study of gender in archaeology, we are reminded of the importance of confronting presuppositions and values that guide our work, however "scientific" we presume our methodologies to be. She outlines a number of challenges for future archaeological research. First, archaeologists must recognize and eliminate biased reconstructions of gender roles in the past that derive from our own cultural assumptions. Second, they must pay more attention to theories about gender in analyzing their data. Third, archaeologists need to use their data to make explicit inferences about men and women in prehistory. Finally, Conkey points out biases not only in analysis but also in the very practice of archaeology. Eliminating gender bias from archaeology, as Conkey suggests, will require a major commitment to the same critical reflection that has characterized other branches of anthropology. As Nelson and Kehoe (1990:4) observe, "disentangling our culture-bound assumptions from the actual archaeological record will be a long and wrenching procedure."

Nelson's discussion of Upper Paleolithic "Venus" figurines in archaeology textbooks (in this book) illustrates Conkey's point about the potential for distortion in the archaeological record when cultural values affect archaeological analysis. Nelson demonstrates that most textbooks convey the same ideological message in their treatment of Venus figurines—that adult male humans are fascinated by women's bodies and view them as signs of fertility. The widely held assumption that Upper Paleolithic figurines possibly depicting human females are fertility fetishes is, according to Nelson, poorly founded. Feminist analysis of the figurines suggests alternative explanations regarding their production, functions, and symbolism and serves as a warning that "reinforcing present cultural stereotypes by projecting them into the past allows whole generations of students to believe that our present gender constructs are eternal and unchanging" (Nelson 1990:19).

In an effort to better explain contemporary gender relations archaeological evidence has offered a means to understanding the present by reconstructing our evolutionary past. Scholarly and public imaginations have been drawn to the possibility that archaeological data might document the existence of a matriarchal society in which women occupied a privileged position as rulers. If powerful women could be found in history or prehistory, this would serve as evidence that male dominance is not inevitable.

Images of matriarchy exist in both western and nonwestern societies. Nineteenth-century evolutionists such as J. J. Bachofen (1967) described a history of humankind that passed from a state of primitive communal marriages, through mother right, or a rule of women, to patriarchy. Similar myths of matriarchy have been recorded in several South American societies (Bamberger 1974:266). According to Bamberger these myths share a common theme, that of women's loss of power through moral failure. The myths describe a past society in which women held power; however, through their inability to handle power when they had it, the rule of women was eventually replaced by patriarchal leadership.

Rather than representing historical events, the myths of matriarchy serve as a tool to keep woman bound to her place. They reinforce current social relations by justifying male dominance (Bamberger 1974:280). There is no historical or archaeological evidence of matriarchial societies in which women systematically and exclusively dominated men. In spite of the absence of such evidence the idea remains popular, precisely because it conveys the possibility of a future society characterized by female dominance that is reminiscent of the matriarchal past.

Culturally based assumptions can be avoided by paying more careful attention to a range of sources at our disposal in the archaeological record. The reconstruction of gender roles and relations in past societies may be facilitated by representations of women and men in burials, images, and written texts. Literary texts pertaining to early Sumer, for instance, portray women in supportive, nurturing roles, acting to further the interests of male political rulers or heroes (Pollock 1991). In some texts, women are also described as political officeholders, or queens. Pollock concludes that some women seem to have had significant political and economic power, although few of them were written about, compared to the number of men in such positions whose lives were more fully recorded (Pollock 1991). Women also held offices in the temple hierarchy as priestesses; it is possible that these were the primary positions of power available to women. An informative example is that of the priestess Enheduanna, installed at Ur by her father King Sargon. Literary texts suggest that she acted to further her father's political ambitions as well as her own authority (Pollock 1991). These texts, as well as other representations such as burials and images, suggest that Sumerian women were not pawns to be manipulated by men, but were able to attain positions of high status and power.

Similarly, recent access to Maya history by decipherment of glyphic texts on public monuments has shown that some royal women played politically central roles in their kingdoms. Hypogamy, or the marriage of higher-status women to lower-status men, insured the alliance of these lower-status men to higher-status men of their wives' families. Hypergamy, or the marriage of lower-status women to higher-status men, also occurred. More importantly, the women involved in marriage alliance and royal politics were anything but passive pawns in the games of men. Freidel and Schele (in this book) look at the lives and exploits of powerful Maya women in two classic period kingdoms to show that generalities based on limited data often fail in the face of detailed information. They also show that royal women can emerge as extraordinary heroic figures and great politicians when their stories are known. In the case of Lady Wak-Chanil-Ahaw they explore what happens when a woman revives a failing kingdom. Lady Xok raised the most beautiful temple in her city as a great Queen in payment for the bitter disappointment of having the heir to the throne be the child of another wife to her lineage. The various forms of power exercised by these women suggest that while there were no matriarchies in the past, women could control important resources and influence the course of public events. Little is know about the lives of commoner women, whose exploits are less visible in texts and other representations. The limited information available on commoner Maya women highlights the need for innovative conceptual and methodological approaches to the archaeological record that will help reconstruct gender roles in past societies.

Conkey and Spector discuss the general problem of the "archaeological invisibility" of women (1984:5), which, they contend, is more the result of a false notion of objectivity and of the gender paradigms archaeologists use than of an inherent invisibility of such data (Conkey and Spector 1984:6). Questions that would elicit information about prehistoric gender behavior or organization are too infrequently asked, while researchers "bring to their work preconceived notions about what each sex ought to do, and these notions serve to structure the way artifacts are interpreted" (for example, the presumption of linkages between projectile points with men and pots with women) (Conkey and Spector 1984:10). In contrast, goals for a feminist archaeology would include gender-inclusive reconstructions of past human behavior, the development of a specific paradigm for the study of gender, and an explicit effort to eliminate androcentrism in the content and mode of presentation of archaeological research (Conkey and Spector 1984:15).

REFERENCES

Bachofen, Johann. 1967. *Myth, Religion and Mother Right* [*Die Mutterrecht* 1861 orig.]. London: Routledge and Kegan Paul.

Bamberger, Joan. 1974. The Myth of Matriarchy: Why Men Rule in Primitive Society. In Michelle Z. Rosaldo and Louise Lamphere (eds.). *Woman, Culture, and Society*, pp. 263–281. Stanford: Stanford University Press.

Conkey, Margaret W. and Janet Spector. 1984. Archaeology and the Study of Gender. In Michael B. Schiffer (ed.). *Advances in Archaeological Method and Theory*, Vol. 7, pp. 1–29. New York: Academic Press.

Fagan, Brian. 1974. *Men of the Earth*. Boston: Little, Brown and Co.

Nelson, Sarah M. and Alice B. Kehoe. 1990. Introduction. In Sarah M. Nelson and Alice B. Kehoe (eds.). *Powers of Observation: Alternative Views in Archeology*, pp. 1–10. Archeological Papers of the American Anthropological Association, Number 2.

the challenge of understanding more explicitly what gender is about so we can develop a theory of gender that is useful in archaeological research. Third, there is the challenge of making explicit inferences about gender and about men and women, using archaeological data to help answer questions concerning what might have happened in prehistory.

On one hand, archaeologists have not taken gender as an important research question; they have, in fact, come quite late to the field of gender studies or to any kind of insights from feminist theory. The first major paper that reviewed archaeology and the study of gender (Conkey and Spector 1984) came more than ten years after the first major books in sociocultural anthropology, and most archaeology in North America is housed in departments of anthropology. On the other hand, archaeology has not been silent about gender. Our accounts of prehistoric societies have been "saturated" with gender, but most of these accounts are—as we will see—male centered, or androcentric. At this point in the development of gender studies within archaeology, at least half of the task of thinking about men and women in prehistory is to question the gendered accounts that pervade our reconstructions of past societies and of how cultures have changed with time.

CHALLENGING GENDER BIAS

Although many archaeologists maintain that it is very difficult to know, or to make inferences, about gender relations or even about male and female activities in prehistoric societies, gender assertions are made regularly in interpretations. Often these assertions are so implicit that archaeologists don't really "see" them as specific ideas that need to be confirmed or tested. Most ideas about gender have come from the implicit and stereotypical gender models of our own sociopolitical lives (e.g., women at home) or from the androcentric ethnographies of sociocultural anthropology. In the early 1970s when anthropology "discovered" the widespread androcentric

biases in ethnographic accounts, most of archaeology—which really *depends* on ethnographic analogies—was not paying much attention!

To take apart, or deconstruct, archaeological interpretations can be very useful, but this should not be taken as an end in itself. Rather, this critical scrutiny is part of the way in which we come to see not just *that* research and "results" can be biased, but exactly *how* they are biased and in what ways. This historical analysis of archaeological accounts is a necessary part of the process whereby we transform what we do. In reviews of the treatment of gender in the archaeological literature of the 1960s through the early 1980s, Mary Kennedy, Janet Spector, and I found some significant problems that are worth summarizing to understand how bias works (Conkey and Spector 1984).

First, we found that women—if they are present at all in reconstructions of prehistory—are usually depicted in a narrow range of passive, home-oriented tasks; they are often "exchanged" as wives, the objects of art and image making, and symbols of fertility and sexuality. In contrast prehistoric men are shown as very public, far ranging (adventurous), productive, active, and responsible for most of the significant changes in human evolution, especially technological innovations. These kinds of representations led Ruth Hubbard (1982) to write an article entitled, "Have only men evolved?"

Second, archaeologists often go through interpretive "contortions" to avoid suggesting that some prehistoric women might actually have been strong, active, or determining people in cultural life. For example one archaeological account of burials interpreted the same artifacts quite differently when they were found in a woman's grave than when found in a man's (Winters 1968). A pestle buried with a woman was there because in life she had done foodprocessing and grinding with it; the same kind of pestle in a man's grave was there because he had *made* it. If a spearthrower (*atlatl*) was found in a man's grave, it was because he had *used* it; if found in a woman's grave, it was a gift to her, or, the ar-

Nelson, Sarah M. 1990. Diversity of the Upper Paleolithic "Venus" Figurines and Archeological Mythology. In Sarah M. Nelson and Alice B. Kehoe (eds.).
*Powers of Observation: Alternative Views in Arche-
ology*, pp.11–23. Archeological Papers of the
American Anthropological Association, Number 2.
Pollock, Susan. 1991. Women in a Men's World: Images of Sumerian Women. In Joan Gero and Mar-

garet Conkey (eds.). *Engendering
Women and Prehistory*. Oxford: Ba:
Spector, Janet D. and Mary K. Whelar
porating Gender into Archaeolog
Sandra Morgen (ed.). *Gender and
Critical Reviews for Research and
65–95. Washington, DC: American
cal Association.

Men and Women in Prehistory: An Archaeological Challenge

Margaret W. Conkey

The *entire village* left the next day in about 30
canoes, leaving us alone with the *women and children* in the abandoned houses.

—Levi-Strauss 1936, as cited by Michard-
Marshale and Ribery 1982:7, in Eichler and
Lapointe 1985:11.

When we close our eyes and think about the
human societies and groups that lived thousands of years ago, what kinds of men and
women do we "see"? What are they doing?
What kinds of roles and relationships do we
imagine? When we think about this we realize
that there must have been many different
roles and relationships. There must have
been men of power and women of power,
men with children and women as decision
makers, men making pots and women making stone tools, men and women working together in the fields, men in trance and women
as healers.

Yet, all too often archaeological accounts
and the popular reconstructions of past societies that appear in magazines or coffeetable
books suggest a much simpler picture: men
hunting, women gathering plants, men mak-

ing tools, women with children
wood. Why do we have such si
very familiar kinds of reconstru
tainly part of the explanation is t
ogists have not done much that e
about gender, yet they have dev
els or reconstructions that inv
These reconstructions derive fro
problematic sources: from ethn
counts that are gender biased
previous quote from Levi-Straus:
beliefs that twentieth century (m
white, male) archaeologists hol
der, about men and women, an
prehistoric societies "worked" a
We are all, of course, quite susce
own cultural ideas, ideals, an
Most North American archae
taken somewhat longer to be as
self-critical about this than som
thropological colleagues.

Thus, to think about men ar
prehistoric societies and to thin
gender roles, gender ideologies
relations raises several archaec
lenges. First, there is the challe
nizing and stripping away the
plied gender reconstructions. S

Original material prepared for this text.

chaeologist speculated, there really were (female) "Amazons" in this river valley. If trade goods were buried with a man, it was because he controlled the trading; if in a woman's grave, it was because she simply "had" the items. Thus, bias and differential representations of men and women can emerge in archaeological interpretations. Men, in prehistoric societies, often performed (various) "activities"; women (more passively) engaged in "tasks." Male activities are often described in more detail, and they are portrayed more frequently than female ones.

Ethnographers have noted that in many horticultural societies (those that cultivate plants with a simple technology) women do most of the field labor; they are often associated with plants. Archaeologists have long been fascinated with how and why some prehistoric people developed horticulture, which predominated over hunting-gathering-fishing as a way of life and as a subsistence system. In one study of how archaeologists account for the cultural innovation of "horticulture" (the domestication of plants) in the eastern woodlands of the United States, the analysts—Pat Watson and Mary Kennedy (1991)—show how the two major accounts have suggested some of the most obscure or contorted ways in which horticulture was developed to avoid suggesting that women might have been the innovators. One account accepts the idea that women were extremely familiar with plant resources when these societies were primarily collecting wild foods for their resources and the idea that *after* the "invention" of agriculture, women were the primary crop tenders. However, according to this account invention happened because shamans—men, of course—came to control the production and reproduction of the squashes that they used for gourd rattles in their ceremonies. Indeed, squashes were among some of the early cultivated plants in this region, but it is very difficult to link the speculative notion about shamans in one narrow context to such a major change in subsistence practices.

The other account suggests that because human occupation sites are areas of soil disturbance, this would have been a likely place for stray seeds from wild plants to have been "naturally" encouraged to the point of deliberate further modifications by humans. In other words the plants just about domesticated themselves. As Watson and Kennedy argue these two primary interpretations seem to go to considerable extremes to avoid disrupting the "sacred association" of women-passive-plants.

From this and other critiques it is clear that unexamined and present assumptions about gender have crept into archaeological interpretation. Explicit attention to women as active and as having varied roles and positions is usually absent. There is also a lack of consideration of other kinds of gender relations than those of the idealized mid-twentieth century—white, western, middle-class—with a sexual division of labor and a male-dominated, androcentric society. The reconstructions of our most ancient hominid ancestors, more than 2 million years ago, show a monogamous nuclear family unit: The male strides ahead across the savannah landscape, carrying a pointed stick as tool and/or as weapon. The female is several steps behind, carrying a young child on her hip.

The most widely touted version (Lovejoy 1981) of the social life of early hominids is that of men (mobile, risk taking, and adventurous), who "provision" the females and young with the most desirable resources (especially meat); the waiting women cluster for protection at a "home base," while making limited forays for gathered foods. Clearly, this is a familiar picture to us, not because it has been well demonstrated with archaeological (or other) data, but because it represents a culturally idealized (yet culturally limited) view of gender and socioeconomic relationships.

Such an interpretation is problematic. It invites and reifies the idea that there are deep and specific *continuities* in how men and women relate to each other in gender roles and gender positions. By suggesting that mobile men have been provisioning dependent and relatively constrained women and children for more than 2 million years, this account strongly implies that this is "natural" and therefore legitimate. Specific and narrow gender relations are universalized—"it's always been this way"—and convey the (mistaken) idea that these relationships and gender stereotypes are inevitable and immutable (unchanging and unchangeable).

The kinds of biased archaeological views I have discussed are promoted and reinforced by androcentric ethnographic and ethnoarchaeological accounts.[1] When John Yellen (1977) reported on his ethnoarchaeological studies of the !Kung people of the Kalahari desert of southern Africa, he first noted how research has shown that the female gathering of food accounts for most of the !Kung diet (60 to 80 percent). In writing about his observations based on living with and interviewing various !Kung people, however, he finds that "in practice, it is much easier to talk to the men because each day is in some way unique and stands out in the hunter's mind. Asking women where they went produces much less detailed and reliable information" (Yellen 1977:62–63).

Although this kind of reporting raises another central issue—the relationship between the observer and the people being studied—the *effects* of this kind of statement on the reader are insidious and powerful. This is particularly because ethnoarchaeological studies of contemporary people like the !Kung have been carried out specifically to build models for interpreting prehistoric hunter-gatherers. If women are never named and if they are portrayed as somehow wandering around the Kalahari with no clear recollection of what they did or where they have been, how can we avoid using these impressions in our visions of past social life?

So far we have seen how bias can creep into archaeological accounts when the analysts do not consciously reflect on their assumptions nor explicitly use some theoretical models about gender. The differential use of language to describe men and women has further contributed to problematic accounts of their activities and contributions to human societies. Further archaeology, like all other research, is influenced by and embedded in the social and political worlds within which it

is practiced. At this point in the development of our field the topic with which we are concerned is just as much the gender of archaeology as the archaeology of gender.

There is now a very well established body of literature that shows how the values, cultural assumptions, and social contexts of the researchers can and do strongly affect the kind of science that is practiced.[2] *All* sciences are social; every fact has a factor, a maker, who is a person of a certain nationality, race, class, ethnicity, and gender. In many instances some of these factors do affect their research (e.g., Latour and Woolgar 1986). For example, to draw further on the !Kung case given previously, it is more likely that Yellen did not get precise information from the women because he is a western, foreign man than because they didn't know where they go and what they do. As an ethnographer Yellen was admittedly attracted to male information because !Kung men would and could speak to him and give him information in *his* terms. This needs to be recognized before an ethnographer writes in a way that creates gender differences, in this case in knowledge between !Kung men and women, that perpetuate androcentric accounts to be accepted and applied by other researchers.

In archaeology it is also true that women tend to be relegated to or take up what are considered to be more marginal positions and jobs. Usually this is the lab analysis or "housework" of archaeology (Gero 1985). In Americanist archaeology the statistics confirm that it has been predominantly a white male enterprise; Robert Ascher (citing Kidder 1949) discusses the two types of archaeologists as being either "hairy-chested" or "hairy-chinned" (Ascher 1960). *Who* the practitioners are affects the kinds of questions that are given priority in research and thus the interpretations of the past.

Gero (1991a) has shown, for example, that when archaeologists replicate various prehistoric tools and technologies through experiments, male archaeologists do all the manufacturing (and they especially manufacture the finished tools, the projectile points thought central to the hunting of wild game), and female archaeologists do much of the edge-wear or use-wear analysis. For this they study in the laboratory the polishes left on the edges of tools and used pieces from the various activities, such as hide working and plant or wood processing. Furthermore, Gero (1991b) has also shown how the studies of American Paleoindian cultures have been dominated by male archaeologists and how the primary picture of Paleoindian lifeways is one that focuses almost exclusively on activities presumed to be male, especially the hunting of big game, with all the associated tools and strategies.

The point of studies like Gero's is not merely to "expose" and critique androcentric thinking. It is a serious charge to note that the nature of archaeological knowledge about the past is directly created by the topics that are given research priority and that these are very much influenced by the gender, class, race, ethnicity, and nationality of the practitioners (and of those who fund archaeology). Rather, the point of such studies is to understand how such factors work and to ask critical questions, such as "where *do* archaeologists get the assumptions about gender and social life that underlie their interpretations?"[3]

MAKING GENDER EXPLICIT IN ARCHAEOLOGICAL RESEARCH

I have already noted how ideas about gender drawn from ethnography or ethnoarchaeology must be critically evaluated because of long-standing biases (Moore 1988). Additionally, archaeologists have been drawing primarily on specific theoretical frameworks in the last several decades that have very little to offer in terms of making inferences about social processes and social life, except in a general way. That is, the preferred—and in many ways very productive—theories have been cultural ecology (how humans relate to their environment), cultural evolution (how societies and cultures change), and systems theory (how societies and cultures "work" on a grand scale). There is very little in these theories about social *relations* and much less about

gender. Even most materialist approaches have never looked at how cultural materials are part of gender relations; until recently, most material culture studies in archaeology have not viewed artifacts as active means through which social relations are produced. If archaeologists thought materials could be used to "say" something about past societies, it was usually a direct "reflection" of relatively static social phenomena, such as status (e.g., a burial item reflects the status of the deceased) or "group" (e.g., an artifact style reflects the existence of a specific "ethnic group"). When material culture and artifacts are understood as an active part of the definition and transformation of social relationships, we can then ask how the artifacts have been part of these social processes, including gender relations. For example, one ethnoarchaeological study (Braithwaite 1982) has shown how, among the Azande of the Sudan (Africa), the decorated ceramics (not the plainware) are used by women to serve food to men because this exchange and interface between men and women is considered potentially dangerous and ambiguous. The use of decorated ceramics is integral to, and signifies, the tensions and the enactments of these male/female gender relations.

However, although gender, like many other aspects of social life, was probably present in past societies (at least since the establishment of modern humans), it may not be something we can always "get at."[4] We know there were both men and women (as well as children) in prehistory, and we suspect that gender often may have been a powerful—but highly variable—dimension of social life. Just because gender inquiry is enjoying some popularity now, it should not necessarily become the goal of most archaeological research. Whether gender is considered in analyses will depend on the questions being asked, the particular archaeological contexts being studied, and the kinds of archaeological data involved. As in *all* archaeological research the kinds of questions asked successfully will be closely linked to, if not somewhat constrained by, each case. However, it is clear that by taking gender as an explicit focus, there can be important and rich insights into past human lives.

In all societies it is not just gender *per se* that is of anthropological interest, but gender relations, because gender identity, roles, and ideologies are established in relation to others of similar and different genders, roles, and classes.[5] We have seen what problems arise in archaeological interpretation when certain assumptions about gender and gender roles are not made explicit or questioned. Many archaeologists think that gender studies in archaeology are simply linking certain artifacts and activities to men or women, which is a limited view. Even then, as in the different interpretations of grave goods discussed previously, they often do not question or consider the assumptions they are making about roles and activities.

By *not* taking gender seriously archaeologists often miss powerful evidence and rich interpretations. For example, some anthropologists (e.g., Silverblatt 1987) have shown how the development of complex societies, such as the state, were often partly accomplished by a shift from societies based on kinship to relations based more on economics and politics. This means there were significant changes in gender relations. How then could archaeologists possibly explain the "rise of the state" *without* analysis of the role of gender in the successful transformations and subsequent maintenance of the state itself?

Brumfiel's (1991) recent analysis of the Aztec state in the Valley of Mexico has shown how the tribute system (the collection and redistribution of textiles), the fundamental politicoeconomic basis for state maintenance, was in large part based on female labor: Women either made textiles directly or cooked and prepared food for market "sale" to obtain the textiles for the tribute payments. How did these gender roles emerge and become established? When gender relations are viewed as one of the (many) processes "at work" in cultural change and in how humans cope and live their daily lives, we *do* get a much more human picture and a more detailed picture of the past.

There have been a number of important attempts to take gender and gender relations seriously in archaeological interpretation, and some of these are worth reviewing. For example, the traditional view on hunter-gatherers is that they lived their lives more or less dictated by their environments because they did not produce their own food. This has easily led to interpretations of hunter-gatherers either in ecological terms (focusing on such things as "resource-procurement strategies") or in biological terms (that they had to be involved in "viable mating networks"). There is little room in such characterizations for real people with social and interpersonal lives and relationships.

One archaeologist has taken a different perspective on some California hunter-gatherers (Jackson 1991). Archaeology and ethnography have shown that as a group California hunter-gatherers had much more complex social relations, alliances, and trade networks than the more "stereotypically simple" hunter-gatherer societies. Usually such phenomena as alliances and trade are viewed as ways to move resources and not to be too controlled by the environment. Although many of these people knew about the practices of agriculture (from some of their southwestern neighbors), this was not a part of their ways; however, we know that they did control the production of some resources, such as the deliberate burning of wild grasses, which could increase productivity. Often the location of their sites is described in terms of "maximizing" their access to desired or necessary resources.

But instead of thinking about these people primarily in economic terms (and terms derived from the "maximization" principles of western capitalism), we could think about them through the lens of gender. Jackson, using historic, ethnohistoric, and archaeological data on the Western Sierra Mono people, came up with a model for their food-getting and food-preparation (which are standard archaeological topics) that features women doing most of the processing of the staple crop—acorns. When he asked what the *implications* of this might be for other aspects of Mono life, he arrived at some interesting observations. For one thing much of this acorn processing (and storage) occurred in locations where outcrops of bedrock lay exposed because they created mortars, or places *in* the bedrock, for grinding acorns. Often "granaries" were built over the bedrock mortars to store the acorns. These mortars are thus "fixed" on the landscape, and it was at these locales that other activities—of men, women, and children—were often focused. Thus, these locations of women's work structured settlement patterns and social relations. In this case Jackson suggested that women's production served as an economic and social focus for Mono daily life. As a result we get a glimpse into how gender roles and relations were integral to prehistoric lifeways.

As suggested previously the many instances of large-scale cultural change, which are a favorite topic of archaeological inquiry, can be better understood if we understand how gender roles and relations were involved. Christine Hastorf (1991) studied what happened in an area of highland Peru when the Inka tried to move in and establish sociopolitical control. The study shows how changing gender relations and changes in something as mundane as food preparation and consumption have much to do with large-scale sociopolitical transformations. Hastorf's research is a powerful example, not just because it involves explicit attention to gender, but because several lines of evidence converge to reinforce the interpretation. This kind of archaeological reasoning is particularly important because one line of evidence (such as changes in location of food processing) might not be adequate to make a strong case, in this instance for shifts in gender roles and relations.

First Hastorf analyzed the pollen found in soil samples from dwelling areas or "patios," and she documented changes in the kinds of plant foods processed, including an increase in corn. Her analysis of the spatial distribution of food processing and consumption suggests that food processing, for example, was becoming more focused in certain patios. This more concentrated food production seemed to occur within individual domestic units primarily associated with women. This insight is reinforced by ethnohistoric information about sexual and spatial divisions of labor.

Second Hastorf looked at the bone chemistry of skeletons buried at different phases in the transformation to greater control by the Inka. From bone chemistry we can infer certain aspects of people's dietary intake (because the chemical composition of food leaves some "signatures" during the growth of human bone). Corn is one food product that leaves a quite distinctive signature because of its carbon content. The bone chemistry analysis showed that the diets of men and women were about the same at the beginning of the transformation, but by the time the Inka had taken over the region, there were marked differences in male and female diets. The consumption of corn in some form increased in the men. Drawing on ethnohistoric accounts of the political life of the Inkas, Hastorf suggests that men consumed corn mostly in the form of a corn-based beer, which was central to the feasting offered as tribute and as a political symbol of Inka control. The general picture of the transformation is one whereby household food production increased and men consumed increasingly more corn, probably in the form of beer.

Hastorf's study is an archaeological inquiry into what happens with the "rise of a state:" How did the Inka expand their territory and get other people to give in to them? In daily lives how does this happen? Most archaeological accounts tend to invoke large-scale processes, such as ecological pressure, warfare, and mobilization of labor for public works. Again we might ask, what happens if we inquire into how such a sociopolitical change impacts on, and was affected by, gender roles and relations? As with Brumfiel's work with the Aztecs it appears as if changing gender roles and women's labor are crucial to the establishment and maintenance of the political tributes that sustain some empires. Furthermore, archaeology performed at the level of the household—which has not been as popular as studying the big ceremonial centers and public buildings of complex societies—can be not at all marginal to answering large questions about political power and the "rise of states."

Much of the archaeological research that asks about gender and about the implications of gender for other sociocultural processes has drawn on ethnohistoric records about male and female activities and positions in society. Such data have been used to make archaeological inferences about gender more credible. It may not be possible to have such strong culturally specific starting assumptions about gender in many prehistoric situations, although as we have seen this has not always deterred archaeologists from assuming a lot about gender in prehistory. Regardless of the source or the relative strength of starting assumptions, it is, as with all archaeological interpretations, up to us to make our assumptions explicit and to make our inferences "tight." They must be as well grounded as possible.

Archaeologists may not be able to consider gender in every instance. However, the one thing to be learned from both social and gender theory and from archaeological studies in which gender has been taken seriously is that gender can be one of many powerful relations that embody the dialectics of human life. Also the one thing to be learned from studies of gender in archaeology is that the human past was also full of tensions, conflicts, and cooperation between men and women (and other possible genders). Without attention to this when possible we will have an impoverished and often mechanistic view of human lives.

We have learned in anthropology, history, archaeology, sociology, and other fields of the tremendous range and variability in gender relations, meanings, and gendered lives, even within a single society or culture. We have also learned of variations in archaeological contexts in which we are specifically inquiring into gendered social lives. It is thus increasingly unlikely that we will be able to account for hundreds of societies for long periods of time and in wide geographic areas with just one "account" or story of gender—whether that is a story of androcentric or gynecentric (women centered) social life. We are beginning to appreciate how dynamic and fluid gender relations can be and how diverse the possibilities and practices are that existed for, and were engaged in by, men and women for tens of thousands of years of past human lives.

NOTES

1. I make a distinction here between research and interpretation that is "sexist" and that which is androcentric or gynecentric. Sexism involves statements, attitudes, and theories that presuppose, assert, or imply inferiority (of one sex or the other), that accept as legitimate the subordination of one sex to the other, and that view prescriptions for defining roles on the basis of sex as legitimate and unproblematic. Androcentrism or gynecentrism is less intentional. Human life is perceived from a male (androcentrism) or female (gynecentrism) perspective without considering or describing the activity or position of the other sex or gender.

2. Within archaeology, there is an increasing amount of work being done that not only documents the different status of men and women in the field (Gero 1985; Kramer and Stark 1989; and a range of papers in Walde and Willows 1991), but also shows how the "profile of practitioners" substantively affects the kind of interpretations we develop (see also in Hastorf 1991; Trigger 1986). Also there are accounts about how the preferred topics for discussion and explanation (e.g., technological innovations as crucial to culture change) are also highly gendered (usually male) (see for example, Conkey and Williams 1991; Wylie 1991).

3. There is a rich and important literature on the concept of gender that I cannot discuss here. It is important to recognize the distinction between sex, which is biologically based, and gender. Gender is, at one level, the cultural and social construction of sex, but it is more complex than merely mapping cultural constructs onto one sex or another. There can be, for example, more than two genders, such as in the *berdache* of some native American people. Because there is often some relation between sex and whatever genders develop, some analysts have referred to this area of inquiry as the "sex/gender system" (see Fausto-Sterling 1985; Harding 1983).

Archaeologists who wish to make inferences about gender need to consider the rich theoretical literature and understand that gender is not just another static variable for which we can find a material correlate in the archaeological record (see the critique by Stacey and Thorne 1985; Conkey 1991).

4. Archaeologists continue to debate what our "objects of knowledge" can be, especially in terms of what we call the "level of resolution." With reference to gender research there are those who are not convinced we can make inferences about individual human behavior in the past (e.g., Hayden 1991) and those who argue that "ethnographic variables" (such as gender relations) are outside the scope of a "scientifically credible" archaeology (e.g., Binford 1983, 1986; but see Wylie 1991 for a critique of these views with particular reference to gender).

5. Gender is a complex social process, involving such aspects as gender roles (what people do, what is considered appropriate), gender ideology (what meanings are assigned to male, female, or other genders; these are not universal in the sense that there are some essential, unchanging notions of male and female), and gender identity (feelings about one's own gender). Gender is, above all, highly variable; it is a social and cultural way of marking differences, and it is entangled with other social and cultural phenomena, such as (in our current western societies) ethnicity, class, and religion.

REFERENCES

Ascher, Robert. 1960. Archaeology and the public image. *American Antiquity* 25(3):402–403.

Binford, Lewis R. 1983. *Working at Archaeology.* New York: Academic Press.

———. 1986. Data, relativism, and archaeological science. *Man* (n.s.) 22:391–404.

Braithwaite, Mary. 1982. Decoration as ritual symbol: A theoretical proposal and an ethnographic study in southern Sudan. In Ian Hodder (ed.). *Symbolic and Structural Archaeology*, pp. 80–88. Cambridge, England: Cambridge University Press.

Brumfiel, Elizabeth. 1991. Weaving and cooking: Women's production in Aztec Mexico. In Joan Gero and Margaret Conkey (eds.). *Engendering Archaeology: Women and Prehistory*, pp. 224–254. Oxford: Basil Blackwell.

Conkey, Margaret W. 1991. Does it make a difference? Feminist thinking and archaeologies of gender. In Dale Walde and Noreen Willows (eds.). *The Archaeology of Gender*. Chacmool Archaeological Association. Calgary, Alberta: Department of Archaeology, University of Calgary.

Conkey, Margaret W. and Janet Spector. 1984. Archaeology and the study of gender. In Michael B. Schiffer (ed.). *Advances in Archaeological Method and Theory*, Vol. 7, pp. 1–38. New York: Academic Press.

Conkey, Margaret and Sarah H. Williams. 1991. Original narratives: The political economy of gender in archaeology. In M. DiLeonardo (ed.). *Gender at the Crossroads of Knowledge: Feminist Anthropology in the Post-Modern Era*. Berkeley and Los Angeles: University of California Press.

Eichler, Margrit and Jeanne Lapointe. 1985. *On the Treatment of the Sexes in Research*. Ottawa: Social Sciences and Humanities Research Council of Canada.

Fausto-Sterling, Anne. 1985. *Myths of Gender: Biological Theories about Women and Men*. New York: Basic Books.

Gero, Joan M. 1985. Socio-politics of archaeology and the woman-at-home ideology. *American Antiquity* 50:342–350.

———. 1991a. Genderlithics: Women's roles in stone tool production. In Joan Gero and Margaret Conkey (eds.). *Engendering Archaeology: Women and Prehistory*, pp. 163–193. Oxford: Basil Blackwell.

———. 1991b. The social world of prehistoric facts: Gender and power in knowledge construction. Paper presented at "Women in Archaeology" conference, Albury, New South Wales, Australia, February 1991. (To be published by the Australian National University, Department of Anthropology and Prehistory; Laurajane Smith and Hilary DuCros, editors.)

Harding, Sandra. 1983. Why has the sex/gender system become visible only now? In Sandra Harding and Merrill B. Hintikka (eds.). *Discovering Reality: Feminist Perspectives on Epistemology, Metaphysics, Methodology, and Philosophy*, pp. 311–324. Boston: Reidel.

Hastorf, Christine A. 1991. Gender, space, and food in prehistory. In Joan Gero and Margaret Conkey (eds.). *Engendering Archaeology: Women and Prehistory*, pp. 132–162. Oxford: Basil Blackwell.

Hayden, Brian. 1991. Observing prehistoric women. Paper presented at Anthropology and Archaeology of Women Conference, Appalachian State University, Boone, NC (May 1991).

Hubbard, Ruth. 1982. Have only men evolved? In R. Hubbard, M. S. Henfin, and B. Fried (eds.). *Biological Woman—the Convenient Myth*, pp. 17–46. Cambridge: Schenkman.

Jackson, Thomas L. 1991. Pounding acorn: Women's production as social and economic focus. In Joan Gero and Margaret Conkey (eds.). *Engendering Archaeology: Women and Prehistory*, pp. 301–328. Oxford: Basil Blackwell.

Kidder, A. V. 1949. Introduction. *Prehistoric Southwesterners from Basketmaker to Pueblo*, by Charles Amsden. Los Angeles: Southwest Museum.

Kramer, Carol and Miriam Stark. 1988. The status of women in archaeology. *Anthropology Newsletter* 29(9):11–12. Washington, DC: American Anthropological Association.

Latour, Bruno and Stephen Woolgar. 1986. *Laboratory Life: The Construction of Scientific Facts*, 2nd ed. Princeton: Princeton University Press.

Levi-Strauss, Claude. 1936. Contribution à l'étude de l'organization sociale des Indiens Bororo. *Journal de la Societe des Americanistes de Paris* 28:269–304.

Lovejoy, Owen. 1981. The origin of man. *Science* 211:341–350.

Michard-Marshale, Claire and Claudine Ribery. 1982. *Sexisme et Science Humaine*. Lille: Presses Universitaires de France.

Moore, Henrietta. 1988. *Feminism and Anthropology*. Oxford: Polity Press.

Silverblatt, Irene. 1987. *Moon, Sun, and Witches: Gender Ideologies and Class in Inca and Colonial Peru*. Princeton: Princeton University Press.

Stacey, Judith and Barrie Thorne. 1985. The missing feminist revolution in sociology. *Social Problems* 32(4):301–316.

Trigger, Bruce G. 1984. Alternative archaeologies: Nationalist, colonialist, imperialist. *Man* (n.s.) 19:355–370.

Walde, Dale and Noreen Willows (eds.). 1991. *The Archaeology of Gender*. Proceedings of the Chacmool Conference, 1989. Calgary, Alberta: Chacmool Archaeological Association, Department of Archaeology.

Watson, Patty Jo and Marcy C. Kennedy. 1991. The development of horticulture in the eastern woodlands of North America: Women's role. In Joan Gero and Margaret Conkey (eds.). *Engendering Archaeology: Women and Prehistory*, pp. 255–275. Oxford: Basil Blackwell.

Winters, Howard. 1968. Value-systems and trade cycles of the late archaic in the Midwest. In S. R. Binford and L. R. Binford (eds.). *New Perspectives in Archaeology*, pp. 175–222. Chicago: Aldine.

Wylie, M. Alison. 1991. Gender theory and the archaeological record: Why is there no archaeology of gender? In Joan Gero and Margaret Conkey (eds.). *Engendering Archaeology: Women and Prehistory*, pp. 31–54. Oxford: Basil Blackwell.

Yellen, John. 1977. *Archaeological Approaches to the Present*. New York: Academic Press.

Diversity of the Upper Paleolithic "Venus" Figurines and Archeological Mythology

Sarah M. Nelson

Among the earliest depictions of human beings, dating back to perhaps 30,000 years ago, are small figurines of nude females, which are found across a broad belt in Europe from the Pyrenees in southern France to the Don river in the USSR, with outliers in Siberia. Every anthropologist is familiar with these Upper Paleolithic "Venus" figurines. They are used to titillate freshman classes, and photographs or drawings, especially of the figurines from Willendorf and Dolni Vestoni e, routinely enliven introductory textbooks.

Current trends in literary criticism lean toward deconstruction of "texts," in which both words and situations may serve as the text for analysis. In this [reading], I would like to deconstruct some texts in a narrower sense, using the example of the Venus figurines to demonstrate that introductory textbooks of archeology and physical anthropology produce gender metaphors which, by ignoring much of the scholarship on the figurines, reaffirm the folk model of gender preferred by our culture.

FIGURINE DESCRIPTIONS

The figurines themselves have only gender in common. They are diverse in shape, in pose, in the somatic details depicted, and in ornamentation (Soffer 1988, Fleury 1926, Abramova 1967, Luquet 1926, Delporte 1979).

They seem to represent differences in age as well (Rice 1981). Yet the textbooks tend to represent the figurines as all the same, and then to leap from this purported sameness to a supposed function for all figurines over their 3000 mile and perhaps 10,000 year spread (Soffer [1988], although Gamble [1986, 1987] asserts that most figurines fall within a 2000 year range). We need to explore this phenomenon of perceiving sameness in the diverse figurines, and ask why it occurs.

The texts our students read describe the figurines and frequently ascribe a function to them. There is little indication in the bibliographies that the authors of the texts have read any primary sources about the figurines, or that they are conversant with the rich literature which explores the variation in both the figurines themselves and the possible meanings and functions of the figurines. Rather, it seems that a kind of folklore is repeated, a folklore of the anthropology profession, too well known to require documentation.

The textbooks utilized in this study represent an unsystematic nonrandom sample—all that happen to be on my bookshelves, supplemented with those of my colleagues. Of 20 introduction to archeology or archeology and physical anthropology textbooks thus examined, eight concentrate on methodology and do not mention the figurines, while the other twelve contain cursory remarks on one to three pages. It is these twelve texts which constitute the study sample.

Table 1 shows the distribution of what is written regarding the physical characteristics of the figurines. Six of the textbooks mention

TABLE 1. Description of Figurines

Author	Sexual	Abdomen	Breasts	Buttocks	Hips	Pregnant	Fat
Barnouw (1978)	×	×	×		×	×	
Campbell (1988)		×	×	×			×
Chard (1975)			×	×	×	×	×
Clark (1977)			×	×	(thighs)		×
Eddy (1984)	×		×	×			
Fagan (1986)	×		×				
Hester & Grady (1982)			×		×		
Jurmain et al. (1981)	×						
Pfeiffer (1985)	(stylized)						
Poirier (1987)		×	×	×			
Smith (1976)	×		×	×		×	
Wenke (1984)	×						

exaggerated sexual characteristics as a prominent feature, whether or not they specify which traits are meant. The most common feature to be singled out is the breasts, described as "large," "generous," or "pendulous." All but one of the texts characterize the figurines as having either exaggerated sexual characteristics or large breasts, and four include both. Buttocks are mentioned five times, once described as "protruding," while hips, once with the adjective "broad," are specified three times. Only one author mentions both, showing that he makes a distinction between hips and buttocks. We are left to guess whether these terms are intended to refer to hindquarters in general in the other cases, or whether one set of authors indeed has protruding buttocks in mind (i.e., steatopygia), and the other really means broad hips (i.e., steatomeria) (Boule and Vallois 1957:318). In one confusing case, an illustration of Willendorf, without a trace of steatopygia but with undoubted steatomeria, is pictured side by side with a Khoi-San woman, of whom the reverse is clearly the case—that is, protruding buttocks without broad hips (Campbell 1988:508).

The assertion that pregnancy is depicted in the figurines occurs in the textbook sample three times, and one additional author points out the exaggerated "belly," allowing him the satisfying alliteration of "breasts, belly, and buttocks." Three of the authors describe the

figurines as fat. The only author to refrain from asserting or implying fatness does not describe the figurines at all, but contents himself with an illustration of Willendorf (Pfeiffer 1985:203). Reading these descriptions, one would suppose that the Willendorf statuette, easily the most familiar, was typical or normal or modal. Instead, it is one of the least stylized and the most obese—referred to in another context with admiration as representing "resplendent endomorphy" (Beller 1977:78).

The generalizations in the textbooks do some violence to the facts. Few of the statuettes represent gross obesity, and some are quite slender (Fig. 1). Even the first figurines found in the 1890s were classified by Piette into svelte and obese classes (Delporte 1979:73). Half a century ago Passemard (1938) examined all the then-known figurines to see whether they were steatopygous, a description quite popular at that time, and came to the conclusion that most were not. Saccasyn Della Santa (1947:9–13) reviewed the literature on the figurines again, and also concluded that they were not meant to represent steatopygia.

An unpublished statistical study of the variation in body shapes made 22 measurements on each figurine for which both frontal and profile photographs could be found—24 measurable figurines in all. The statuettes sorted into distinct groups of 10 obese (wide hips and thick body), 3 steatopygous (pro-

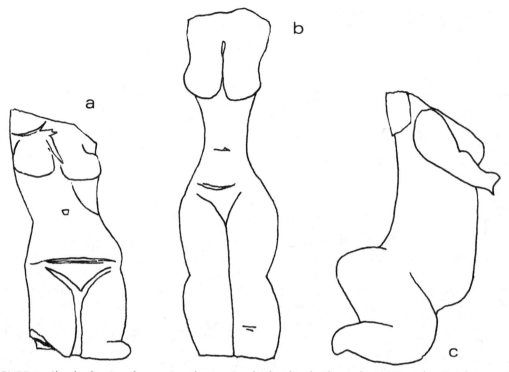

FIGURE 1   Slender figurines from a. Petrokovi e, Czechoslovakia; b. Elisevitchi, USSR; and c. Sireul, France

truding buttocks), and 11 normal (Nelson n.d.). Another study shows that only 39 percent of these figurines could possibly represent pregnancy, slightly over half (55 percent) have pendulous breasts, 45 percent have broad hips, and 13 percent have protruding buttocks. Twenty-two percent have none of these characteristics, (Nelson and Bibb n.d.). Bodyshapes depicted in the figurines have been divided into three or four categories by intuitive studies as well, such as those by Fleury (1926), Abramova (1967), and Luquet (1926).

Rice (1981) has suggested that this variability in body shape reflects different age groups, and has shown that different body characteristics can be so interpreted, with a high correlation between ratings. The distribution of the figurines in these age categories corresponds to the expected age pyramid for foraging societies.

Failure to acknowledge the variability of the figurines makes it easier to produce sweeping generalizations about their probable meaning or function. This is evident in the textbook interpretations. By far the most common function ascribed to the figurines is that of "fertility" (Table 2), specifically so designated in seven of the 12 texts, and called "procreation" and "maternity" by one text each. This ascription is usually not explained at all, or weakly expressed at best. For example, "It seems unlikely that Upper Paleolithic women actually looked like that, but perhaps it was an ideal type or expressed a wish for fertility" (Barnouw 1978:176). Apparently in conjunction with the fertility function is the idea of a "cult" or "Mother Goddess," since the five authors who use one or both of these expressions attach them to the fertility notion. Only one author rejects fertility as an explanation, on the grounds that hunters are not concerned with human fertility. Rather he explicitly suggests that the figurines are erotic: "Pleistocene pinup or centerfold girls" (Chard 1975:182).

TABLE 2. Functions of Figurines

Author	Fertility	Goddess/Cult	Erotic	Artistic/Stylized
Barnouw (1978)	×			
Campbell (1988)	×	×		
Chard (1975)	rejects		×	
Clark (1977)	× (maternity)			ö
Eddy (1984)	×	×	×	
Fagan (1986)	×	×		
Hester & Grady (1982)	×			×
Jurmain et al. (1981)	×	×	×	ö
Pfeiffer (1985)				×
Poirier (1987)	×	×		
Smith (1976)	×		×	×
Wenke (1984)			ö	×

HIDDEN ASSUMPTIONS

The brief descriptions and interpretations of the female figurines contain and to some extent conceal unexamined assumptions about gender. Among them are: that the figurines were made *by* men, that the figurines were made *for* men, that nakedness is necessarily associated with eroticism, and that depiction of breasts is primarily sexual.

Underlying the description of the female figurines as erotic or reproductive is a masculist construction of the world, in which females are assumed to exist primarily for the use of males, sexually or reproductively. The scholarly literature is replete with explicit examples of this worldview, which the textbooks reflect.

A few quotations from the scholarly literature will demonstrate that males are usually assumed to be the sculptors of the figurines. The italics are mine throughout. "How did the artist's vision, which reflected the ideal of *his* time, see her? For as with man, we can never know what she really looked like . . . so we have to make do with the version her comparison, man, had of her" (Berenguer 1973:48). The possibility that it was *her* version appears not to have crossed Berenguer's mind. Although this mindset focuses on males exclusively, it is not confined to males only, as shown from this quote from a woman, "He [the artist] desired only to show the female erotically and as the source of all abundance—in her he portrayed not woman but fertility" (Hawkes 1964:27). Referring to the not uncommon find of broken-off legs, Campbell (1982:410) suggests that "they may have cracked off in the baking, or when the ancient ceramicist tossed aside a work that failed to please *him*." (Most of the figurines of course are carved.) In case there is any doubt about the use of the specific rather than the generic use of the term "man", Leroi-Gourhan (1967:90) makes it crystal clear that "prehistoric man" doesn't include females, speaking of "the first figurines representing prehistoric man—or at least *his wife*."

If the figurines are assumed to have been made by men, then it follows that they were created for male purposes. Even when they were first discovered, the Abbé Breuil (1954, cited in Ucko and Rosenfeld 1973:119) said they were for "pleasure to Paleolithic man during his meals" (do we have a euphemism here?). Berenguer (1973:52) focuses on reproductivity: "we may deduce man's obsessive need for women who would bear *him* lots of children to offset the high mortality rate caused by the harsh living conditions." Von Königswald worried about other possessions, "It certainly is an old problem: how could man protect *his* property, mark a place as 'his home', 'his living site' so that others would recognize and respect it, especially in a period where there were no houses, just *abris* and caves?" He concludes that men made the "grotesque" figurines to guard their property, and scare off intruders! Delporte (1979:308) muses more philosophically, "for [paleolithic men] as for us . . . the mother who gives and transmits life is also the woman who gives and shares pleasure: could the paleolithic have been insensitive to this novel duality?" [my translation]. Could the present be insensitive to the fact that there were paleolithic women as well as men? Are women to be denied their own sensitivity, or indeed their own existence as sentient beings?

The fact that the figurines were unclothed, or scantily clothed, for several wear belts and other decorations (a fact that is noted only by Clark [1977:105] among our textbook sample), surely has been essential to the interpretation of eroticism, in spite of the fact that there are many other possible reasons for the depiction of nudity. For example, people may have been usually unclothed inside the cave or hut, so that nakedness was not a special condition. The figurines could have been teaching devices for girls' puberty rites, as Marshack (1972:283) has suggested.

Nakedness frequently has different connotations when men rather than women are the sculptor's subject. For example, a naked male torso from Harappa is shown under the heading "Figures of Authority," in *The First Cities*, a widely used book from the Time-Life series (Hamblin 1973:133). The text tells us:

> Although male figures rarely appear among sculptures dug up at Mohenjo-Daro and Harappa, the few that do all seem to represent men of importance. In the three works reproduced here, there is a common theme, however varied the pieces themselves may be: regality or godliness.

As Conkey and Spector (1985:11) point out in another context, changing the rules of interpretation according to sex will not reveal anything about prehistoric gender roles. Rather it comforts us in supposing that things have always been the same.

In spite of being naked, however, it would seem that the fat figurines have little sex appeal to modern male scholars. This has called forth various explanations, ranging from assertions that they are stylized, to a suggestion that you cannot tell *what* might have turned on those prehistoric men (you can almost see the shrug and the wink), to a rejection of the erotic argument on the grounds that the figurines are simply too grotesque! In all of this discussion, passivity of women is assumed.

It is deserving of some comment that breasts are equated with eroticism in the textbooks, more by juxtaposition of words than by explicit statements. Sometimes, though, the equation is specified. There is one carving, referred to as the "rod with breasts," which evoked the following paean: "This statuette shows us that the artist has neglected all that did not interest *him*, stressing *his* sexual libido only where the breasts are concerned — a diluvial plastic pornography." (Absolon 1949). Surely anthropologists of all people know that exposed breasts are not at all uncommon in the warmer parts of the world, and cause little comment or excitement except for visiting tourists and perhaps a segment of the readership of *National Geographic*.

The "rod with breasts" is an interesting example of the extension of the underlying attitude toward women that is revealed in some generalizations about the figurines. Enigmatic carvings are declared to represent breasts, buttocks, or vulvae, reducing women to their "essentials" (Fig. 2). Especially the notion of the "vulvae" (some of which look rather like molar teeth), "has become an *idée fixe* and one of the most durable myths of prehistory" (Bahn 1986:99). The "rods" from Dolni Vestonice could be as easily perceived as stylized male genitalia, but if they were so described the eloquence would probably be in a different vein. It is hard to imagine exchanging the genders in the quote by Absolon above.

Alternative explanations, based on variability rather than generalizations, are not lacking in the scholarly literature. The figurines have been argued to represent priests or ancestors or clan-mothers, to show women as actors with a ritual function (Klima 1962:204, Abramova 1967:83, Hancar 1940). These

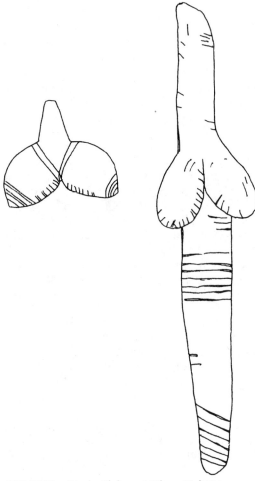

FIGURE 2 "Rod with breasts" from Dolni Vestonice, Czechoslovakia.

possibilities are not even hinted at in the texts, with one sole exception (Campbell 1988:481).

ARCHEOLOGICAL MYTHOLOGY

What are the possible reasons for the selective reporting found in the textbooks? First, to be fair, is the summary nature of the texts. Little space is given to the figurines, and it is necessary to paint a broad picture with a few strokes. But the selection of this particular way of viewing the Upper Paleolithic figures

as fat, as sexual, and as representing fertility, can be linked to our own cultural stereotypes and assumptions about the nature of men, women, sexuality, and reproduction. I suggest that our own culture makes these generalizations seem so natural, so satisfying, that there is no reason to examine them. The "text" read into the figurines is ours.

Several archeologists have commented on the problems of reading our unconscious assumptions about the present into the past. "History and prehistory constitute bodies of knowledge used to legitimize social policies and to validate social trajectories" (Moore and Keene 1983:7). This tendency has been traced to the dominant paradigm in archeology: "Because of the logic of empiricist epistemology, theories rising on empiricist foundations potentially serve only to recreate in the past the dominant cultural ideologies of the present" (Saitta 1983:303). We must recognize "the importance of taking into account the conceptions we hold of our own society which inevitably mediate our understanding of the past" (Miller and Tilley 1984:2).

Recent research on gender roles in cultural anthropology proposes that "male and female, sex and reproduction, are cultural or symbolic constructs" (Ortner and Whitehead 1981:6). These constructs are often reflected in origin stories as "metaphors for sexual identity" (Sanday 1981:56), which Sanday calls "scripts." I am suggesting that culturally constructed gender roles, and our attitudes and beliefs about sex and reproduction, enter into the selectivity of reporting on the Upper Paleolithic figurines. The reading of the metaphors of the figurines derives from a masculist script.

I do not wish to impute either evil intentions or inferior scholarship to the authors of these textbooks. It is important to note the unconscious nature of the acceptance of cultural scripts. But that does not make them less pernicious. Reinforcing present cultural stereotypes by projecting them into the past allows whole generations of students to believe that our present gender constructs are eternal and unchanging. Especially those who deal in prehistory need to be alert to our cultural biases, and not imply that present gender roles are external verities.

Marvin Harris points out that "our ordinary state of mind is always a profoundly mystified consciousness. . . . To emerge from myth and legend to mature consciousness we need to compare the full range of past and present cultures" (Harris 1974:5). The trick is to examine the past without the mystification.

I am not proposing that alternative explanations are necessarily better, only that the diversity of the figurines should be taken into account. Maybe women made some of the figurines. Maybe the figurines were used for women's purposes. Maybe it isn't relevant whether men find them sexy or not. If an explanation feels intuitively right, perhaps that is the best reason to reexamine it.

REFERENCES

Abramova, Z. A. 1967. Paleolothic Art in the USSR. *Arctic Anthropology* 4(2):1–179.

Absolon, K. 1949. The Diluvial Anthropomorphic Statuettes and Drawings, Especially the So-called Venus Statuettes Discovered in Moravia. *Artibus Asiae* 12:201–220.

Bahn, P. G. 1986. No Sex Please, We're Aurignacians. *Rock Art Research* 3(2):99–105.

Barnouw, V. 1978. *Physical Anthropology and Archaeology*. 3rd ed. Homewood, IL: The Dorsey Press.

Beller, A. S. 1977. *Fat and Thin*. New York: Farrar, Strauss and Giroux.

Berenguer, M. 1973. *Prehistoric Man and His Art*. M. Heron, trans. London: Souvenir Press.

Boule, M., and H. Vallois. 1957. *Fossil Man*. New York: Dryden Press.

Campbell, B. G. 1982. *Humankind Emerging*. 3rd ed. Boston: Little, Brown.

———. 1988. *Humankind Emerging*. 5th ed. Glenview, IL: Scott, Foresman and Company.

Chard, C. 1975. *Man in Prehistory*. 2nd ed. New York: McGraw-Hill.

Clark, G. 1977. *World Prehistory in New Perspective*. 3rd ed. Cambridge: Cambridge University Press.

Conkey, M. and J. Spector. 1985. Archaeology and the Study of Gender. In *Advances in Archaeological Method and Theory*. Vol. 7. M. B. Schiffer, ed. Pp. 1–38. New York: Academic Press.

Delporte, H. 1979. *l'Image de la Femme dans l'Art Préhistorique*. Paris: Picard.

Eddy, F. W. 1984. *Archaeology, A Cultural-Evolutionary Approach*. Englewood Cliffs: Prentice Hall.

Fagan, B. 1986. *People of the Earth: An Introduction to World History*. 5th ed. Boston: Little, Brown.

Fleury, C. 1926. Quelques Considerations sur la Pseudo-steatopygie des Venus Aurignaciennes. *Archives Suisses d'Anthropologie Generale* 11(1): 137–141.

Gamble, C. 1986. *The Paleolithic Settlement of Europe*. Cambridge: Cambridge University Press.

———. 1987. Interaction and Alliance in Palaeolithic Society. *Man* (n.s.) 17:92–107.

Hamblin, D. J. 1973. *The First Cities*. New York: Time-Life Books.

Hancar, F. 1940. Problem der Venus Statuetten im Eurasiatischen Jung-Palaolithikum. *Praehistorische Zeitschrift:* 30–31.

Harris, M. 1974. *Cows, Pigs, Wars and Witches: The Riddles of Culture*. New York: Random House.

Hawkes, J. 1964. The Achievements of Paleolithic Man. In *Man Before History*. C. Gabel, ed. Pp. 21–35. Englewood Cliffs: Prentice Hall.

Hester, J. J. and J. Grady. 1982. *Introduction to Archaeology*, 2nd ed. New York: Holt, Rinehart and Winston.

Jurmain, R., H. Nelson, H. Kurashina, and W. Turnbaugh. 1981. *Understanding Physical Anthropology and Archaeology*. St. Paul: West Publishing Co.

Klima, B. 1962. The First Ground-Plan of an Upper Paleolithic Loess Settlement in Middle Europe and its Meaning. In *Courses Toward Urban Life*. R. Braidwood and G. Willey, eds. Pp. 193–210. Chicago: Aldine.

Koenigswald, G. H. R. von. 1972. Early *Homo sapiens* as an Artist: The Meaning of Paleolithic Art. In *The Origin of Homo sapiens, Ecology and Conservation*, Vol. 3. F. Bordes, ed. Pp. 133–139. Proceedings of the Paris Symposium 1969.

Laurent, P. 1965. *Heureuse Prehistoire*. Perigeux: Pierre Fanlac.

Leroi-Gourhan, André. 1967. *Treasures of Prehistoric Art*. Translated by N. Guterman. New York: Henry N. Abrams.

Luquet, G. H. 1926. *L'Art et la Religion des Hommes Fossiles*. Paris: Masson et Cie.

Marshack, A. 1972. *The Roots of Civilization*. New York: McGraw-Hill.

Miller, D. and A. Tilley. 1984. Ideology, Power and Prehistory: An Introduction. In *Ideology, Power and Prehistory*. Daniel Miller and Christopher Tilley, eds. Pp. 1–15. Cambridge: Cambridge University Press.

Moore, J. A. and A. S. Keene. 1983. Archaeology and the Law of the Hammer. In *Archaeological Hammers and Theories*. J. A. Moore and A. S. Keene eds. Pp. 3–13. New York: Academic Press.

Nelson, S. M. n.d. "Venus" Figurines as Evidence of Sedentism in the Upper Paleolithic. (On file, Department of Anthropology, University of Denver.)

Nelson, S. M., and L. Bibb. n.d. Notes and Statistics on Venus Figurines. (On file, Department of Anthropology, University of Denver.)

Ortner, S. B., and H. Whitehead (eds.). 1981. *Sexual Meanings: The Cultural Construction of Gender and Sexuality*. Cambridge: Cambridge University Press.

Passemard, L. 1938. *Les Statuettes Feminines Paléolithiques Dites Venus*. St. Nîmes: Libraire Teissier.

Pfeiffer, J. 1985. *The Emergence of Humankind*. 4th ed. New York: Harper and Row.

Poirier, F. E. 1987. *Understanding Human Evolution*. Englewood Cliffs, NJ: Prentice Hall.

Rice, P. C. 1981. Prehistoric Venuses: Symbols of Motherhood or Womanhood? *Journal of Anthropological Research* 37(4):402–416.

Saccasyn Della Santa, E. 1947. *Les Figures Humaines du Paléolithique Superior Eurasiatique*. Paris: Amberes.

Saitta, D. J. 1983. The Poverty of Philosophy in Archaeology. In *Archaeological Hammers and Theories*. James A. Moore and Arthur S. Keene, eds. Pp. 299–304. New York: Academic Press.

Sanday, P. R. 1981. *Female Power and Male Dominance: On the Origins of Sexual Inequality*. Cambridge: Cambridge University Press.

Smith, J. W. 1976. *Foundations of Archaeology*. Beverly Hills: Glencoe Press.

Soffer, O. 1988. Upper Paleolithic Connubia, Refugia and the Archaeological Record for Eastern Europe. In *Pleistocene Old World: Regional Perspectives*. O. Soffer, ed. Pp. 333–348. New York: Plenum Publishing Co.

Ucko P. J. and A. Rosenfeld. 1973. *Palaeolithic Cave Art*. New York: McGraw-Hill.

Wenke, R. 1984. *Patterns in Prehistory, Humankind's First Three Million Years*. 2nd ed. New York: Oxford University Press.

Maya Royal Women: A Lesson in Precolumbian History

David Freidel and Linda Schele

The lowland Maya civilization flourished on the Yucatan peninsula for 2,000 years before the Spanish arrived on their shores in the early sixteenth century. What particularly distinguishes the Maya civilization from the others of Mesoamerica is its literature. Some other cultures, such as the Zapotec of Oaxaca, Mixe societies of Veracruz, and the early highland Maya of Guatemala, had written scripts that approximated spoken language as did the Maya script. Yet only the lowland Maya have left posterity a sizable collection of texts. Together these texts on carved stone, painted walls, pottery vessels, and other small artifacts are a bare remnant from a civilization that mostly wrote alfresco on screen-fold books of bark paper sized with lime plaster. Nevertheless, they reveal dimensions of ancient society in the New World that are barely hinted at in other regions known primarily or exclusively through their archaeological remains.

One of the lessons from textual history is that women were much more than pawns in Maya power politics. In three cases already documented (and with the prospect of more to come with continued decipherment), the performance of royal women proved decisive to the destiny of particular late Classic period (A.D. 600 to A.D. 900) kingdoms.[1] We will briefly summarize one of these dramatic episodes in Maya history that shows how women propelled themselves to the center stage of an ancient civilization. We think there is a basic lesson to be learned by archaeologists who must deal with the remains of past complex societies without the guide of written texts detailing state politics. Despite some lip service

Original material prepared for this text.

to the contrary, current introductory archaeology texts relate the rise and fall of such ahistorical civilizations as if women did not exist and as if only men ruled and made the critical decisions guiding governments. We think, on the basis of our experience with the ancient Maya, that in some early class-structured societies with hereditary elites, such as the Maya classes of *ahaw* (supreme lord) or *sahal* (noble vassal), women ruled with men in the context of court politics revolving around family alliances and feuds. Governments ruled by royal dynasties did not merely profit by the participation of women, such participation was mandatory and necessary. The political reproduction of power required the physical reproduction of rulers, a process in which women played a clear role. Beyond this biological fact, Maya rulers inherited the social, political, and religious potential for power from their mothers and their fathers. Our cases illustrate these points.

THE GREAT CLASSIC MAYA WARS

The seventh century witnessed bloody and endemic wars of conquest between the great houses of the Maya in the interior forests of the Yucatan peninsula. King Tok-Chan-K'awil (Blade-Sky-Spirit)[2] of the minor realm of Dos Pilas came to the throne as Holy Lord in A.D. 645 but rapidly transformed his small holding into one of the great Maya conquest states. Tok-Chan-K'awil consolidated his hold over the southern forest region called the Petexbatun not only through battle, but also through judicious polygamous marriage to several princesses from smaller kingdoms in the area. His ambition stretched across the vast and rich farmlands of the interior forest now called Peten in Guatemala, and his wars and alliances embroiled the greatest kingdoms of that region. One threat to his plans came from the city of Caracol to the north and east of Dos Pilas. Caracol had defeated another venerable northeastern city, Naranjo, and now held undisputed sway over the strategic eastern trade routes to the Caribbean coast from the interior. Even more importantly Tok-Chan-K'awil had defeated the great and geographically central city of Tikal, capturing and sacrificing King Shield-Skull. Now Shield-Skull's successor at Tikal, King Hasaw-Chan-K'awil (Battle Standard-Sky-Spirit), was rising in vengeance against him. Tok-Chan-K'awil needed allies on Tikal's northeastern flank prepared to attack if Tikal thrust southward toward Dos Pilas.

LADY WAK-CHANIL-AHAW AND THE REVIVAL OF NARANJO

To check Tikal and Caracol at the same time, Tok-Chan-K'awil enlisted his daughter Wak-Chanil-Ahaw (Risen-Sky-Lord) to a dangerous mission. He arranged to send her to Naranjo to marry into the defeated royal house of that city, to revive it, and to marshal its forces against his enemies. Hasaw-Chan-K'awil came to the throne of Tikal on May 6, A.D. 682, readying his war with his enemies. By August 30 of that same year Wak-Chanil-Ahaw had successfully crossed the forest past Tikal without being captured and had arrived at Naranjo. It takes little imagination to know the courage and resolve of this woman, riding in her sedan chair as a living declaration of war more than 100 kilometers over jungle paths through enemy territory. Every moment of that journey she faced capture and death by sacrifice at the hands of Hasaw-Chan-K'awil on the west side of the trail, Caracol's king on the east side, and the allies of Caracol in the middle.

No doubt to the people of Naranjo her arrival was nothing short of miraculous, and her three-day ceremonial was precisely that. Her duty was to rededicate the sacred temple of the city. In the thinking of the Maya she reopened the Naranjo portal to the Otherworld, allowing communication and magical power to pass from the world of the ancestors to the world of the living. The usual way to accomplish this for a royal woman was to pierce her tongue in self-sacrifice with a lancet of black volcanic glass and then to pull a cord through it as she entered an ecstatic trance and brought forth her ancestor to bless the place. From the texts of this city, we know that it was her work and not that of her husband, whose name is never mentioned in the histories of Naranjo. The ignominious defeat of Naranjo by Caracol under his aegis or that of his father stripped him of the privilege of history. Without Wak-Chanil-Ahaw the kingdom of Naranjo would have slipped quietly into obscurity.

THE BIRTH OF THE HEIR AND THE NARANJO WARS

Five years after her dedication of the Naranjo royal temple, Wak-Chanil-Ahaw gave birth to a royal heir, dubbed Smoking-Squirrel by scholars, on January 6, A.D. 688. There is little doubt that although her husband may have been alive, she ruled during this period, because she was the only one with a royal history from Naranjo at this time. Clearly, however, Tok-Chan-K'awil of Dos Pilas was anxious to see his daughter's command of this strategic city consolidated. When the boy was only five years old he ascended to the throne of Naranjo on May 31, A.D. 693. Out of deference to the humiliated royal house of Naranjo, the scribes of the city never explicitly announced the parentage of the new king, but the systematic way that they linked the arrival of Wak-Chanil-Ahaw at Naranjo, the birth of Smoking-Squirrel, and the declaration of Wak-Chanil-Ahaw's parentage in Tok-Chan-K'awil in a single text makes it certain that she is the mother of the king.

Soon after the boy became king, on June 20, A.D. 693, Naranjo went to war against the allies of Caracol. Obviously, a five-year-old child had little to do with this bloody work.

Wak-Chanil-Ahaw successfully prosecuted this war against the kingdom of Ucanal, capturing a lord named Kinichil-Kab. On a retrospective stela celebrating this victory, Wak-Chanil-Ahaw shows herself standing upon the prostrate captive in the time-honored stance of conquest taken by Maya kings. This was only the opening battle in a protracted series of campaigns by the newly refurbished dynasty of Naranjo against the Caracol hegemony. One hundred days later Naranjo attacked Ucanal again, and on February 1, A.D. 695, Naranjo delivered a major defeat against this border kingdom ally of Caracol. This victory involved an unnamed lord from Dos Pilas, probably a relative of Wak-Chanil-Ahaw, and it shows that Dos Pilas played an active military role in the success of Naranjo.

Naranjo continued to attack to the south and east under the aegis of Smoking-Squirrel and his mother for many years. Between them, they successfully broke the power of Caracol in the central forests after that kingdom had wreaked havoc on Tikal and other cities for many generations. Wak-Chanil-Ahaw clearly played the key role in this success in the early and critical years of the fledgling new dynasty at Naranjo. The result of her success was a mixed blessing for her father, Tok-Chan-K'awil of Dos Pilas. The relief of Tikal from the oppression of Caracol no doubt gave Hasaw-Chan-K'awil of Tikal the opportunity to prepare for war against his enemies—including Dos Pilas. At the same time, Hasaw-Chan-K'awil was surely aware of the military success that Wak-Chanil-Ahaw's armies had enjoyed in their wars against Caracol. She was a dangerous player in the great war that he could ill afford to attack without inviting a devastating counterattack by her father from the south. She, in turn, held the Tikal king in check from attacking directly south against Dos Pilas to avenge the sacrifice of his own father.

In the end Hasaw-Chan-K'awil chose to attack north against a different enemy, Jaguar-Paw of Calakmul, a protégé of Tok-Chan-K'awil of Dos Pilas. Tikal succeeded and Hasaw-Chan-K'awil restored the honor of his family and his kingdom in the forests of the

Maya. Still, he never attacked Wak-Chanil-Ahaw or her son Smoking-Squirrel. Indeed, so far as we can tell, he never attacked Dos Pilas directly. Together with her son, a great woman ruled Naranjo and stood sentinel from the northeast; Dos Pilas held Tikal in check. Wak-Chanil-Ahaw's father Tok-Chan-K'awil, and then her brother Pakal-Chan-K'awil, enjoyed the security to expand and consolidate the hegemony of Dos Pilas into one of the largest conquest states of the Classic Maya world.

Far to the west and a few years later in the drainage of the mighty Xokol Ha, now called the Usumacinta river, two queens nearly tore their kingdom asunder in their struggle to determine who would inherit the throne. The kingdom was Yaxchilan, its capitol, a city graced with white temples, carved and terraced on a mountain facing northeast over the forested swamps of the interior. On August 24, A.D. 709, Lady Eveningstar, daughter of the royal house of Calakmul and queen to Shield-Jaguar, Holy Lord of Yaxchilan, gave birth to a son named Bird-Jaguar after his illustrious grandfather, Wak-Tun-Bird-Jaguar of Yaxchilan. The event brought no happiness to Lady Xoc, cowife to Lady Eveningstar and the senior wife of the Yaxchilan king. Her family was local to the kingdom, a vassal lineage to the house of Yaxchilan. Yet it was a noble house that had received a woman, Lady Tahal-Tun, from the same wife-giving family that had provided Lady Pakal as queen to the dynasty and mother to the reigning king, her husband. She was, technically, Shield-Jaguar's mother's father's sister's daughter—first cousin once removed. Lady Xoc had every reason and precedent to support her claim to give birth to the heir to the throne, but now there was a rival claimant. The logic of Lady Eveningstar's claim no doubt derived from the powerful alliance that would result if the heir was from two great royal houses strategically spanning the great forest.

We don't know exactly when Shield-Jaguar declared for his son Bird-Jaguar, but it was certainly before the boy was thirteen. We do know that the consequences were to thrust Yaxchilan to the brink of civil war, some families supporting the precedent that the heir should come from the union of the dynasty with a vassal noble house of Yaxchilan and others supporting the king's alliance to Calakmul. Shield-Jaguar went out among his noble vassals and performed public sacrifices at their provincial capitols to cement their loyalty to him and his heir. The king attempted to settle the struggle by conceding to Lady Xoc an extraordinary privilege: She was to dedicate a new royal temple in the most important location in the city. This beautiful temple contained carved stone lintels over the doorways featuring portraits of Lacy Xoc with Shield-Jaguar and with his ancestor. Shield-Jaguar went to war to bring back sacrificial victims to bless this temple. There was a catch, however. The text of one of the lintels celebrates a hierophany, a conjunction of planets in the sky; this conjunction occurs a magic number of days, 52, after the birth of Bird-Jaguar to Lady Eveningstar. In this indirect and discrete fashion Lady Xoc was required to acknowledge through her dedication of a royal temple that the dynastic heir was to be Bird-Jaguar. In this way Lady Xoc won the privilege of writing sacred history for herself in one of the most beautiful set of Maya carvings, but she had to inscribe against the starfield that her rival's son would rule the kingdom.

On the other hand while Lady Eveningstar won the crown for her son, she forfeited her claim to history all through the lifetime of her husband. Never once in all of his inscriptions does Shield-Jaguar mention Lady Eveningstar's existence. It is only because Bird-Jaguar won his struggle for the throne and inscribed retrospective history about his mother that we know of her. It was not an easy fight. All through his waning years Shield-Jaguar worked to confirm and sanctify his son's claim to succeed him. After his death there were ten long years before Bird-Jaguar actually acceded to the throne. We surmise that Bird-Jaguar was battling against rival claimants derived from Lady Xoc and her patriline. Although he does not mention the civil wars we find him out in the provincial capitols cementing alliances with noble vassals and cele-brating victory in wars by sacrificing captives. It was not until Lady Xoc died on April 3, A.D. 749, and her rival Lady Eveningstar died on March 13, A.D. 751, that Bird-Jaguar could finally take his throne on February 10, A.D. 752.

Despite Lady Eveningstar's success, Lady Xoc had taught the kings of Yaxchilan a bitter lesson in local civics. Bird-Jaguar made certain that his own heir was born to a noble woman from one of his own vassal lineages. His wife, Lady-Great-Skull, and her brother, Great-Skull, figure prominently in his official history in ceremonies carved on lintels, along with his son Chel-Te. In light of the events we can document from Bird-Jaguar's life we think his attribution by modern scholars as "Bird-Jaguar the Great" is well earned. He was clearly a charismatic and very able military and political leader. Without such skill he may have failed to repair the breach caused by his father's decision to choose him for heir. A struggle of great women underscored that the fate of major Maya kingdoms depended on them as much as their husbands and sons.

The role of Maya royal women in the history of this ancient civilization is beginning to come into focus. We have had clues for some time in the form of sumptuous tomb furniture accompanying some elite women. Slowly we have moved in our understanding of the texts from initial hypotheses that the exchange of women between dynasties strengthened alliances between their male rulers to more subtle and complicated scenarios in which Maya women have emerged as powerful personalities and active politicians. As the archaeologists continue to excavate and as the epigraphers continue to decipher texts more completely, we expect the role of royal women to become even more central in our interpretations of this New World civilization.

NOTES

1. We derive this historical narrative from our book, *A Forest of Kings, The Untold Story of the Ancient Maya* (Schele and Freidel, 1990) and specifically from chapters five and eight of

that book. In our book we provide extensive footnotes to show which texts we are using to substantiate our interpretations of Maya history. As in any other historical inquiry, interpretations are subject to change with new information. Ours are vulnerable to evidence from future archaeological research or more effective translation of existing texts. Already in this outline of the complex events surrounding the life of Wak-Chanil-Ahaw, we have changed some interpretations in our book. We are drawing on new evidence supplied by the Vanderbilt University research in the Petexbatun region and at the site of Dos Pilas. This research is directed by Arthur Demarest and Stephen Houston.

2. The name given this Holy Lord, k'ul ahaw, which is what the Maya called kings, is a decipherment of the main elements of his glyphs. He is called Ruler A of Dos Pilas in the scholarly literature, and also Flint-Sky-God K. Flint in Maya is tok; sky is chan; and one of God K's names is k'awil. At the present time the literature on ancient Maya kings and queens is a hodge-podge of the real names they called themselves and a variety of nametags supplied by scholars just to keep track of them.

III.
Domestic Worlds and Public Worlds

In 1974, in an attempt to document a universal subordination of women, Michelle Rosaldo (1974:18) proposed a paradigm relating "recurrent aspects of psychology and cultural and social organization to an opposition between the 'domestic' orientation of women and the extra-domestic or 'public' ties, that, in most societies, are primarily available to men." The domestic-public model led Rosaldo to suggest that women's status is highest in societies in which the public and domestic spheres are only weakly differentiated, as among the Mbuti pygmies. In contrast "women's status will be lowest in those societies where there is a firm differentiation between domestic and public spheres of activity and where women are isolated from one another and placed under a single man's authority, in the home. Their position is raised when they can challenge those claims to authority . . . " (Rosaldo 1974:36). Accordingly, women may enhance their status by creating a public world of their own or by entering the men's world. In

addition, the most egalitarian societies will be those in which men participate in the domestic domain.

Correspondingly, Sanday (1974) suggests that women's involvement in domains of activity such as subsistence or defense may be curtailed because of their time and energy commitment to reproduction and mothering. Men, on the other hand, are free to form broader associations in the political, economic, and military spheres that transcend the mother-child unit. While the linkage of women with the domestic and men with the public domains may imply a biological determinism based on women's reproductive roles, Rosaldo (1974:24) argues that the opposition between domestic and public orientations is an intelligible but not a necessary arrangement.

One aspect of women's domestic responsibilities is that it is women who primarily raise children. Nancy Chodorow (1974) develops a theory linking adult sex role behavior to the fact that children's early involvement is with their female parent. Chodorow argues that girls are integrated through ties with female kin into the world of domestic work. Age, rather than achievement, may define their status, while boys must "learn" to be men. Unlike girls, boys have few responsibilities in childhood and are free to establish peer groups that create "public" ties. To become an adult male a boy is often obliged to dissociate himself from the home and from female kin. According to Rosaldo (1974:26), "the fact that children virtually everywhere grow up with their mothers may well account for characteristic differences in male and female psychologies" as well as setting the stage for adult organization of activities.

As scholarship devoted to an understanding of gender issues has evolved, the influential domestic-public model has been the focus of considerable controversy, revolving around three related issues: whether male domination is universal, whether male domination is explained by the domestic-public dichotomy, and whether the concept of domestic-public has relevance in all cultures.

Lamphere (in this book) reviews the formulation of the domestic-public model, and discusses the subsequent critiques of its applicability. Rosaldo herself, rethinking her original position, said that while male dominance appears widespread, it does not "in actual behavioral terms assume a universal content or a universal shape. On the contrary, women typically have power and influence in political and economic life, display autonomy from men in their pursuits, and rarely find themselves confronted or constrained by what might seem the brute fact of male strength" (1980:394). While the domestic-public opposition has been compelling, Rosaldo suggests that the model assumes too much rather than helping to illuminate and explain (see, for example, Mathews in this book).

As Lamphere observes, it has become increasingly clear that the domestic-public opposition is the heir to nineteenth-century social theory rooted in a dichotomy contrasting home and woman, with a public world of men, and reflecting an understanding of political rights based on sex. It has also been noted that conceptualizing

social life as dichotomized into domestic and public domains does not make sense in societies in which management of production occurs within the household and in which household production itself involves the management of the "public" economy (Leacock 1978:253).

In contrast, in an industrial society, where home and workplace are clearly demarcated, the domestic-public opposition may have explanatory value. For example, Murcott (in this book) analyzes one domestic task, cooking, as part of an exploration of economic relations in the family and of the division of labor between spouses. Interviews with Welsh housewives indicate that ideas about home cooking reflect understandings of the relationship between domestic and paid labor. The informants shared the view that proper eating must occur at home and that a cooked dinner is necessary to family health and well-being. Murcott suggests that the emphasis on having a proper dinner waiting for the husband when he comes in from work underscores the symbolic importance of the return home: "the cooked dinner marks the threshold between the public domains of school or work and the private sphere behind the closed front door" (Murcott, this book).

Alice Yun Chai (in this book) considers the relevance of the domestic-public distinction to Korean immigrant women in Hawaii and examines the adaptive strategies of these women in response to their disadvantageous political and economic position in the larger society. She shows that Korean immigrant women attempt to gain status in the public sphere often in sales or clerical jobs; eventually, because of structural barriers, women create a public world of their own in family businesses engaging male and female relatives. These businesses integrate home and workplace, the public and private spheres, as husband and wife strive together to improve the family economy and educate children.

This research suggests that the public-private distinction has implications for the interplay among gender, status, and power. While traditional conceptions of power emphasized formal political behavior and authority associated with a status conferring the "right" to impose sanctions (Lamphere 1974:99), informal power strategies such as manipulation and maneuvering are also important aspects of political activity. The analysis of Korean immigrant women indicates that a thorough understanding of women's strategies requires an examination of multiple factors: status in the public world, interpersonal influence, and the relationship between them.

Cynthia Nelson (in this book) also examines the concept of power, focusing on images of women and power in the domestic and public domains in the societies of the Middle East. Ethnographies of the Middle East have commonly differentiated two social worlds, a woman's private world and a man's public world. Women's concerns are domestic, men's political. Nelson argues that the assignment of private and public reflects the imposition of western cultural categories on the Middle East; the meaning of power is influenced by these categorizations, as well as by the limitations of data obtained by male ethnographers from male informants. This is a point made forcefully by Annette Weiner (1976) in her reanalysis of Trobriand exchange. She argues that "we unquestioningly accept male statements about women as factual evidence for the way a society is structured. . . . Any study that does not include the role of women—as seen by women—as part of the way the society is structured remains only a partial study of that society. Whether women are publicly valued or privately secluded, whether they control politics, a range of economic commodities, or merely magic spells, they function within that society, not as objects, but as individuals with some measure of control" (1976:228).

Similarly, Nelson argues that by asking such questions as "How do women influence men?" "Who controls whom about what?" "How is control exercised?" it becomes apparent that women exercise a greater degree of power in social life than is often appreciated. In addition, she challenges the idea that the social worlds of men and women are reducible to private and public domains, with power limited to men in the public arena. Nelson's review of ethnographies addressing the role and position of women in Middle Eastern society suggests that women play a crucial role as structural links between kinship groups in societies in which family and kinship are fundamental social institutions. Women are in a position to influence men through ritual means, to channel information to male kin, and to influence decision making about alliances; consequently, women do participate in "public" activities, and women's exclusive solidarity groups exercise considerable social control and political influence. The conceptions of power as defined by the western observer are particularly challenged by literature on women done by women that offer a perspective on the position of Middle Eastern women derived from the actors themselves.

In the course of her critique of the application of the domestic-public opposition to social organization in the Middle East, Nelson challenges long-standing assumptions regarding women's subordination and male dominance. Yun Chai's argument also demonstrates that women engage in strategies that have political implications within the ethnic community. Thus, the association between political power and a public domain that excludes women is called into question. Similarly, in studies of peasant societies Rogers (1975) and others (Friedl 1967; Reigelhaupt 1967) contend that the sector of life over which peasant women have control—the household—is in fact the key sphere of activity, socially, politically, and economically. Men occupy public and prestigious positions of authority within the village sphere, but these activities do not have the impact on daily life that household activities have. In light of these analyses demonstrating women's power and influence, we are reminded that the universality of male dominance appears untenable.

In reflecting on feminist research in anthropology, Rosaldo critiques the very tendency to look for universal truths and origins. Rather, anthropologists need to develop theoretical perspectives that analyze the relationships of men and women in a broader social context (Rosaldo 1980:414), involving inequality and hierarchy. As Henrietta Moore emphasizes, while women in many societies share some experiences and problems, women have had very different encounters with racism, colonialism, the penetration of capitalism, and international development. We need to move from assumptions of the shared experience of "women" to a critical analysis of "concepts of difference" (Moore 1988:9).

REFERENCES

Chodorow, Nancy. 1974. Family Structure and Feminine Personality. In Michelle Z. Rosaldo and Louise Lamphere (eds.). *Woman, Culture, and Society*, pp. 43–67. Stanford: Stanford University Press.

Friedl, Ernestine. 1967. The Position of Women: Appearance and Reality. *Anthropological Quarterly* 40: 97–108.

Lamphere, Louise. 1974. Strategies, Cooperation, and Conflict Among Women in Domestic Groups. In Michelle Z. Rosaldo and Louise Lamphere (eds.). *Woman, Culture, and Society*, pp. 97–113. Stanford: Stanford University Press.

Leacock, Eleanor. 1978. Women's Status in Egalitarian Society. Implications for Social Evolution. *Current Anthropology* 19(2): 247–275.

Moore, Henrietta L. 1988. *Feminism and Anthropology*. Minneapolis: University of Minnesota Press.

Riegelhaupt, Joyce. 1967. Saloio Women: An Analysis of Informal and Formal Political and Economic Roles of Portuguese Peasant Women. *Anthropological Quarterly* 40: 109–126.

Rogers, Susan Carol. 1975. Female Forms of Power and the Myth of Male Dominance: A Model of Female/Male Interaction in Peasant Society. *American Ethnologist* 2: 727–756.

Rosaldo, Michelle Z. 1974. Theoretical Overview. In Michelle Z. Rosaldo and Louise Lamphere (eds.). *Woman, Culture, and Society*, pp. 17–43. Stanford: Stanford University Press.

———. 1980. The Use and Abuse of Anthropology: Reflections on Feminism and Cross-Cultural Understanding. *Signs* 5(3): 389–418.

Rosaldo, Michelle Z. and Louise Lamphere (eds.). 1974. *Woman, Culture, and Society*. Stanford: Stanford University Press.

Sanday, Peggy R. 1974. Female Status in the Public Domain. In Michelle Z. Rosaldo and Louise Lamphere (eds.). *Woman, Culture, and Society*, pp. 189–207. Stanford: Stanford University Press.

Weiner, Annette B. 1976. *Women of Value, Men of Renown: New Perspectives in Trobriand Exchange*. Austin: University of Texas Press.

The Domestic Sphere of Women and the Public World of Men: The Strengths and Limitations of an Anthropological Dichotomy

Louise Lamphere

Since 1974 there has been a burgeoning interest within anthropology in the study of women, sex roles, and gender. Anthropology has long been a discipline that contained important women (Elsie Clews Parsons, Ruth Benedict, and Margaret Mead among the

Original material prepared for this text.

most famous) and a field in which women have been studied as well (e.g., Kaberry 1939, 1952; Landes 1938, 1947; Leith-Ross 1939; Underhill 1936; and Paulme 1963). However, with the publication of *Woman, Culture, and Society* (Rosaldo and Lamphere 1974) and *Toward an Anthropology of Women* (Reiter 1975) women scholars, many of whom were identified as feminists, began to critique the androcentric bias in anthropology, to explore women's status in a wide variety of societies, and to provide explanatory models to understand women's position cross-culturally.

One of the most powerful and influential models was proposed by Michelle Rosaldo in her introductory essay to *Woman, Culture, and Society* (1974). Her argument began by asserting that although there is a great deal of cross-cultural variability in men's and women's roles, there is a pervasive, universal asymmetry between the sexes. "But what is perhaps most striking and surprising," Rosaldo writes, "is the fact that male, as opposed to female, activities are always recognized as predominantly important, and cultural systems give authority and value to the roles and activities of men" (Rosaldo 1974:19).

One of the quotes we chose to appear at the beginning of the book, a passage from Margaret Mead's *Male and Female,* sums up what we saw in 1974 in all the ethnographies and studies we examined. "In every known society, the male's need for achievement can be recognized. Men may cook, or weave, or dress dolls or hunt hummingbirds, but if such activities are appropriate occupations of men, then the whole society, men and women alike, votes them as important. When the same occupations are performed by women, they are regarded as less important" (Mead 1949:125). Not only were there differential evaluations of women's activities, but, Rosaldo argues, "everywhere men have some *authority* over women, that [is] they have culturally legitimated right to her subordination and compliance" (1974:21)

Having argued for a pervasive sexual asymmetry across cultures, not just in terms of cultural values, but also in terms of power and authority, Rosaldo accounted for this difference between men and women in terms of a dichotomy.[1] She argued that women are associated with a "domestic orientation," while men are primarily associated with extra domestic, political, and military spheres of activity. By "domestic" Rosaldo meant "those min-

imal institutions and modes of activity that are organized immediately around one or more mothers and their children." In contrast the "public" referred to "activities, institutions, and forms of association that link, rank, organize, or subsume particular mother-child groups. Put quite simply, men have no single commitment as enduring, time-consuming, and emotionally compelling—as close to seeming necessary and natural—as the relation of a woman to her infant child; and so men are free to form those broader associations that we call 'society,' universalistic systems of order, meaning, and commitment that link particular mother-child groups."

Rosaldo, along with Sherry Ortner and Nancy Chodorow who also wrote essays in *Woman, Culture, and Society,* insisted that the connection between women's role in reproduction (the fact that women everywhere lactate and give birth to children) and their domestic orientation is not a necessary one. In other words biology is not destiny. Women's domestic orientation was structurally and culturally constructed and "insofar as woman is universally defined in terms of a largely maternal and domestic role, we can account for her universal subordination" (Rosaldo 1974:7).

"Although" Rosaldo writes, "I would be the last to call this a necessary arrangement or to deny that it is far too simple as an account of any particular empirical case, I suggest that the opposition between domestic and public orientations (an opposition that must, in part, derive from the nurturant capacities of women) provides the necessary framework for an examination of male and female roles in any society" (Rosaldo 1974:24).

For Rosaldo, then, women were involved in the "messiness" of daily life; they were always available for interruption by children. Men could be more distanced and may actually have separate quarters (such as men's houses) away from women's activities. Men could thus "achieve" authority and create rank, hierarchy, and a political world away from women. The confinement of women to the domestic sphere and men's ability to create and dominate the political sphere thus accounted for men's ability to hold the greater share of power and authority in all known cultures and societies.

At the time Rosaldo wrote her overview and in the introduction we both wrote, we were faced with building a framework where none existed. Despite the number of monographs on women, Margaret Mead's work and that of Simone de Beauvoir (1953) were the most provocative, and perhaps the only, theoretical works we knew.[2] The argument for universal sexual asymmetry followed in a long tradition in anthropology where scholars have sought to look for what is broadly "human" in all cultures. In addition to language, anthropologists have discussed the universality of the incest taboo, marriage, and the family. The notion that women might be universally subordinate to men thus made sense as a first attempt at theory building in this newly revived "subfield" within anthropology.

Although Rosaldo argued for universal subordination, she was careful to make clear that women are not powerless. They exercise informal influence and power, often mitigating male authority or even rendering it trivial (Rosaldo 1974:21). In addition, there are important variations in women's roles in different cultures, and variation was discussed in most of the rest of the articles in the collection. For example, Sanday and Sacks compared women's status in a number of different societies, while Leis examined the structural reasons why women's associations are strong in one Ijaw village in Nigeria, yet absent in another. Finally, in my own article I examined the differences in women's strategies within domestic groups in a number of societies, which related to the relative integration or separation of domestic and political spheres.

Since 1974 the hypothesis of universal subordination of women and the dichotomous relationship between women in the domestic sphere and men in the public sphere have been challenged and critiqued by a number of feminist anthropologists. As appealing as this dichotomy seemed in the abstract it turned out to be difficult to apply when actually looking at examples of women's activities in different cultures. For example, in an important article written about the same time as Rosaldo's introduction, Rayna Reiter (now Rayna Rapp) described women's and men's distinct lives in a small French village in the south of France. "They inhabited different domains, one public, one private. While men fraternized with whomever they found to talk to in public places, women were much more enmeshed in their families and their kinship networks" (Reiter 1975b:253). However, two categories of public space fell into women's domain: the church and three shops, including the local bakery. Men tended to avoid women's places, entering the bakery, for example, only when several men were together and joking, "Let's attack now" (Reiter 1975b:257).

Reiter argues that men and women use public space in different ways and at different times. "The men go early to the fields, and congregate on the square or in the cafes for a social hour after work. Sometimes they also fraternize in the evenings. These are the times when women are home cooking and invisible to public view. But when the men have abandoned the village for the fields, the women come out to do their marketing in a leisurely fashion. The village is then in female hands. In the afternoon, when the men return to work, the women form gossip groups on stoops and benches or inside houses depending on the weather" (Reiter 1975b:258). Despite the powerful imagery—women associated with the private or domestic domain and men with public space—the description also shows that the dichotomy is not neat. After all women are in public a great deal; they have taken over, in some sense, the Church and the shops and even the public square in the middle of the day.

In Margery Wolf's description of women in a Taiwanese village based on data she collected in the late 1950s, she emphasizes that because researchers have focused on the dominance of patrilineal descent in the family, they have failed to see women's presence. "We have missed not only some of the system's subtleties but also its near-fatal weaknesses" (Wolf 1972:37). Women have different interests than men and build uterine families—strong ties to their daughters, but primarily to their sons who give their mothers loyalty and a place in the patrilineal extended family. Outside the family in the community women formed neighborhood groups—around a store, at a platform where women washed their clothes in the canal, or under a huge old tree. In a village strung out between a river and a canal, there was no central plaza dominated by men as in the South of France.

In Peihotien Wolf did not describe a cultural geography where women were in a private sphere and men in the public one; rather there was more of a functional separation—men and women had different activities and interests. They were often located in the same places but had a different relationship to the patrilineal extended family and the male-dominated community. Women's lack of power led them to different strategies, different tactics that often undermined male control of the household and even the community. As Sylvia Yanagisako (1987:111) has pointed out the notion of domestic-public entails both a spatial metaphor (of geographically separated or even nested spaces) and a functional metaphor (of functionally different activities or social roles) in the same conceptual dichotomy. Analysts often "mix" these different metaphors in any particular analysis—sometimes using domestic-public spatially and at other times functionally.

Even in the Middle East, the association of women with a private domain (and a lack of power) and men with a public domain (and the center of politics) was too simple, as Cynthia Nelson pointed out in her article, "Public and Private Politics: Women in the Middle Eastern World" (1974; reprinted in this book). Because they are born into one patrilineal group and marry into another, women are important structural links between social groups and often act as mediators. Because there are segregated social worlds, all-female institutions are important for enforcing social norms: Women fill powerful ritual roles as sorceresses, healers, and mediums; women

are important sources of information for their male kin; and women act as "information brokers," mediating social relations within both the family and the larger society.

From Rosaldo's point of view, these aspects of women's power are primarily "informal" and very different from the public, legitimate roles of men. Nevertheless, even though Nelson affirms the separation of male and female worlds (both spatially and functionally), what is "domestic" has public ramifications (the arrangement of a marriage, the transmission of highly charged political information) and the shadow of the family and kin group (the "domestic") is present in even the most "public" of situations. What at first seemed like a simple straightforward dichotomy, in light of actual case material seems very "slippery" and complex.

Furthermore, in many cultures, particularly those with an indigenous band or tribal structure, a separation of "domestic" and "public" spheres makes no sense because household production was simultaneously public, economic, and political. Leacock pointed out the following after reviewing the literature on the Iroquois during the seventeenth and eighteenth century:

> Iroquois matrons preserved, stored, and dispensed the corn, meat, fish, berries, squashes, and fats that were buried in special pits or kept in the long house. Brown (1970:162) notes that women's control over the dispensation of the foods they produced, and meat as well, gave them de facto power to veto declarations of war and to intervene to bring about peace. . . . Women also guarded the "tribal public treasure" kept in the long house, the wampum quill and feather work, and furs. . . . The point to be stressed is that this was "household management" of an altogether different order from management of the nuclear or extended family in patriarchal societies. In the latter, women may cajole, manipulate, or browbeat men, but always behind the public facade; in the former case, "household management" was itself the management of the "public economy." (Leacock 1978:253)

Sudarkasa has made much the same point about women in West African societies such as the Yoruba. She argues that many of the political and economic activities anthropologists discuss as public are actually embedded in households (Sudarkasa 1976, as quoted in Rapp 1979:509). Furthermore, "in West Africa, the 'public domain' was not conceptualized as 'the world of men.' Rather, the public domain was one in which both sexes were recognized as having important roles to play" (Sudarkasa 1986:99).

A more appropriate conception would be to recognize two domains, "one occupied by men and another by women, both of which were internally ordered in a hierarchical fashion and both of which provided 'personnel' for domestic and extradomestic (or public) activities" (Sudarkasa 1986:94).

Furthermore, a careful examination of "domestic domain" indicates that the categories of "woman" and "mother" overlap in Western society, but the meaning of motherhood may be vastly different in another society. Women may not be exclusively defined as mothers and childrearers in terms of their status and cultural value (see Moore 1988:20–29 for a discussion of this point).

In addition to the issue of whether the domestic-public dichotomy can provide an adequate *description* of men's and women's spatial and functional relationships in our own and other societies, the model has problems as an *explanation* of women's status. One of these problems is the inherent circularity of the model. A central point is to account for the nature of these domains, yet they are already assumed to exist widely and are treated as categories in terms of which women's activities (such as food preparing, cooking, child care, washing) can be classified (as opposed to male hunting, warfare, political councils). Comaroff says that the model "can only affirm what has already been assumed—that is, that the distinction between the domestic and politico-jural is an intrinsic, if variable, fact of social existence" (Comaroff 1987:59). When the model is used to explain women's positions in different societies in relation to these two orientations, the reasoning is equally circular. To put it in the words of Yanagisako and Collier, "The claim that women become ab-

sorbed in domestic activities because of their role as mothers is tautological given the definition of 'domestic' as 'those minimal institutions and modes of activity that are organized immediately around one or more mothers and their children'" (Yanagisako and Collier 1987:19).

Finally, we have come to realize that the concepts of domestic and public were bound up in our own history and our own categories grounded particularly in a Victorian heritage. Rosaldo, in a thoughtful reevaluation of her model, came to argue this position herself.

> The turn-of-the-century social theorists whose writings are the basis of most modern social thinking tended without exception to assume that women's place was in the home. In fact, the Victorian doctrine of separate male and female spheres was, I would suggest, quite central to their sociology. Some of these thinkers recognized that modern women suffered from their association with domestic life, but none questioned the pervasiveness (or necessity) of a split between the family and society. (Rosaldo 1980:401–402)

Rosaldo traced the historical roots of domestic-public from the nineteenth century evolutionists through twentieth century structural functionalists to her own work. Instead of two opposed spheres (different and apart), Rosaldo suggested an analysis of gender relationships, an examination of inequality and hierarchy as they are created particularly through marriage (Rosaldo 1980:412–413).

The dichotomy has been usefully employed in several ways since 1974. First, several authors have shown us how it works in Western societies (e.g., France and the United States where it arose historically and still has an important ideological function) (Reiter 1975; Collier, Rosaldo, and Yanagisako 1982). In a related way analysts have explored the meanings surrounding domestic activities of women, putting together a much more complex picture of women's relation to men in this sphere (Murcott 1983; Chai 1987; both are reprinted in this book). Second, anthropological analysis has helped us to understand the historical development of domestic-public spheres in societies under colonialism. John Comaroff's analysis of the Tshidi chiefdom in South Africa during the early twentieth century is an excellent example of this approach (1987:53–85). Finally, some analysts have used the cultural concepts of other societies to critique our own model of domestic-public orientations. Sylvia Yanagisako's essay on the clear separation of "inside-outside" domains (a spatial metaphor) and "work-family" activities (a functional dichotomy) in Japanese American culture demonstrates how the anthropological model of domestic-public mixes these metaphors, which has made analysis confusing and difficult (Yanagisako 1987).

Despite these useful attempts at examining women's lives through the lens of a domestic-public opposition, many of us would agree with Rayna Rapp's 1979 summary of the problems with this dichotomy.

> We cannot write an accurate history of the West in relation to the Rest until we stop assuming that our experiences subsume everyone else's. Our public/private conflicts are not necessarily the same as those of other times and places. The specific oppression of women cannot be documented if our categories are so broad as to decontextualize what "womaness" means as we struggle to change that definition. A Tanzanian female farmer, a Mapuche woman leader, and an American working-class housewife do not live in the same domestic domain, nor will the social upheavals necessary to give them power over their lives be the same. We must simultaneously understand the differences and the similarities, but not by reducing them to one simple pattern. (Rapp 1979:511)

Thus, many of us have tired of the domestic-public dichotomy. We feel it is constraining, a "trap," while new approaches try to get away from dichotomous thinking. These approaches do one of several things. Often they take history seriously, examining women's situation as it has evolved, often in a colonial context. Furthermore, they treat women as active agents and following Collier (1974), as people who have interests, often divergent from men, and who act on them. Third, they

often focus on gender relationships, rather than only on women. Finally, they do not treat all women as part of a single universal category of "woman." Rather women are usually analyzed in terms of their social location. Age, class, race, ethnicity, and kinship are all likely to divide women, so newer analyses examine women's strategies and identities as they are differently shaped. Several examples will illustrate some of the different approaches taken in recent years.

Collier's examination of Comanche, Cheyenne, and Kiowa gender relationships (1988) illustrates the recent focus on gender and on the multiple positions that men and women hold in societies in which the domestic-public dichotomy seems inappropriate. This is because these "spheres" are integrated, and there is no firm line between domestic and public space (see Lamphere 1974 and Leacock above).

The Comanche are an example of a bride service society in which, like many hunter-gather societies, men and women were relatively autonomous, the concept of femininity was not elaborated, and the greatest status differences were between unmarried and married men. Marriage established men as having something to achieve (e.g., a wife), leaving women without such a cultural goal. Young men, through providing meat for their in-laws (bride service), become equal adults, and older men, through egalitarian relations and generosity, become the repositories of wisdom and knowledge. Politics focused on the issue of sexuality and on male-male relationships, which often erupted in conflict and violence. Women celebrated their health and sexuality, and hence the roles of "woman the gatherer" or even "woman the mother" did not emerge as cultural themes.

Among the Cheyenne, an equal bridewealth society, and among the Kiowa, an unequal bridewealth society, marriage relationships were structured in a much different way in the nineteenth century, so gender relationships had a much different content, politics were more hierarchical, and ideology played a different role. Collier's interest is not in the subordination of women in these three societies, because in all three there are several kinds of inequality: between men and women, between older women and girls, between unmarried men and married men, and between kin and affines. An interest in "spheres" and "domains" has been replaced by an emphasis on relationships and an analysis that focuses on the ways in which inequality gets reproduced through marriage transactions, claims on the labor of others, and giving and receiving of gifts. Dominance and subordination become a much more layered, contextualized phenomenon—more interesting than the simple assertion that women are universally subordinated. The processes through which women's inequality (and that of young men) is constructed are laid bare, rather than flatly asserted.

Mary Moran's study of civilized women (1990) explores the historical beginnings and present day construction of the category "civilized," which does confine educated women among the Glebo of southeastern Liberia to a "domestic sphere." The dichotomy between "civilized" and "native" (or even tribal or country) is a result of missionization and has created a status hierarchy differentially applied to men and to women. Men, once educated and with a history of paid wage work, never lose their status as "civilized," while women, even though married to a "civilized man," may lose their status if they do not dress correctly, keep house in specific ways, and refrain from farming and marketing. Native women, who market or have farms, are more economically independent but occupy positions of lower prestige. Here we see not only the importance of historical data in examining how cultural categories evolve, but also the ways in which both civilized and native women actively manage their status positions. Civilized women, through the practice of fosterage, recruit younger women to their households to carry out the more elaborate household routines in which they must engage and to train these fostered daughters to become civilized themselves.

The civilized-native dichotomy represents the juxtaposition of two systems. One is a parallel-sex system in which native men and women are represented by their own leaders in two linked but relatively autonomous prestige hierarchies (as suggested by Sudarkasa 1986). The other is a single-sex system (based on a Western model) in which men in political positions represent both sexes, and women have little access to prestige except through their husbands. Thus, this is a much more complex system than one based on a domestic-public dichotomy. There are dichotomous categories—civilized-native, male-female— but they do not fit neatly together. Moran speaks of categories as "gender sensitive" and suggests that "The Glebo have inserted gender into the civilized/native dichotomy to the point that women's status is not only more tenuous and vulnerable than men's but also very difficult to maintain without male support." In some respects civilized women trade off dependency for prestige, but Moran provides a sympathetic picture of how both civilized and native women manage their lives.

Lila Abu-Lughod's study (1986) of Bedouin women's ritual poetry gives us further insights into the complexity of women who in 1974 we would have simply thought of as "confined to a domestic sphere." Among the Bedouin women's marriages are arranged; wives wear black veils and red belts (symbolizing their fertility); and women must behave within a code of behavior that emphasizes family honor and female modesty and shame. When confronted with loss, poor treatment, or neglect, the public discourse is one of hostility, bitterness, and anger. In the case of lost love the discourse is of militant indifference and denial of concern. In contrast, Bedouin poetry, a highly prized and formally structured art, expresses sentiments of devastating sadness, self-pity, attachment, and deep feeling (Abu-Lughod 1986:187). Although both men and women recite poetry for women it may express conflicting feelings concerning an arranged marriage, a sense of loss over a divorce, or sentiments of betrayal when a husband marries a new wife. The poems are used to elicit sympathy and get help, but they also constitute a dissident and subversive discourse. Abu-Lughod sees ritual poetry as a corrective to "an obsession with morality and an overzealous adherence to the ideology of honor. . . . Poetry reminds people of another way of being and encourages, as it reflects, another side of experience. . . . And maybe the vision [offered through poetry] is cherished because people see that the costs of this system, in the limits it places on human experiences, are just too high" (Abu-Lughod 1986:259). Bedouin women in this portrait are not simply victims of patriarchy confined to a domestic sphere; they are active individuals who use a highly valued cultural form to express their deepest sentiments, acknowledge an alternative set of values, and leave open the possibility of subverting the system in which they are embedded.

A large number of studies have been conducted in the United States that loosely focus on what used to be termed the domestic sphere and the public world of work. As in the Native American, African, and Middle Eastern cases cited previously, when one begins to examine a topic in detail, global notions like domestic-public seem too simple to deal with the complexities of women's lives. Clearly work and home are distinctly separated spheres in the United States. Women who have been employed in the paid labor force have experienced the disjunction of spending eight or more hours of the day in a place of employment where they are "female workers" and the rest of their time in the home where they are daughters, wives, and/or mothers. With this comes responsibilities for cooking, cleaning, and providing nurturance, care, and intimacy for other family members. Several recent studies have examined the contradictions women face when combining work and family, the impact of paid employment on family roles, and vice versa. I will refer to only three examples of this growing literature.

Patricia Zavella's research on Chicana cannery workers examines women's networks that link the workplace and the family (Zavella 1987). Calling these "work-related networks," Zavella describes groups of friends who saw each other outside work and who were members of a kin network employed in the same cannery. Women used work-related networks as sources of exchange for information, baby sitters, and emotional support. Networks operated in more political ways as workers organized a women's caucus and filed a complaint with the Fair Employment Practices Commission. Women's cannery work was seasonal and had relatively little impact on power relations in the family or the household division of labor. On the other hand work-related networks of friends or kin were an important "bridging mechanism" helping women to deal with the contradictions and demands that came from two different spheres.

Karen Sacks' study of hospital workers at the Duke Medical center examines the ways in which black and white women brought family notions of work, adulthood, and responsibility to work with them and used these values to organize a walk out and subsequent union drive (1988). Sacks focuses on the activities of "center women"—leaders in the union drive. Unlike the men who were often the public speakers at rallies and events, the center women organized support on an interpersonal, one-to-one basis. Rather than emphasizing the bridging aspect of women's networks, Sacks shows how the family is "brought to work" or in the old terminology how the "domestic" influences the "public."

In my own research I have traced the changes in the relationship between women, work, and family historically through the study of immigrant women in a small industrial community, Central Falls, Rhode Island (Lamphere 1987). Using the twin notions of productive and reproductive labor, I examined the rise of the textile industry in Rhode Island and the recruitment of working daughters and later of working mothers to the textile industry and to the other light industries that have replaced it since World War II. Rather than seeing production and reproduction as a rigid dichotomy (like public and domestic), I have used these categories to study relationships and to examine the kinds of strategies that immigrant women and their families forged in confronting an industrial system where wage work was a necessity and where working-class families had no control over the means of production. Such an approach revealed a great deal of variability both between and within ethnic groups—the Irish, English, French-Canadian, and Polish families who came to Central Falls between 1915 and 1984 and the more recent Colombian and Portuguese immigrants. Examination of strikes and walk outs in the 1920s and 1930s and my own experience as a sewer in an apparel plant in 1977 led me to emphasize the strategies of resistance the women workers used on the job, as well as the impact of women's paid labor on the family itself. When daughters were recruited as workers in textile mills, the internal division of labor within the household did not materially change because wives and mothers continued to do much of the reproductive labor necessary to maintain the household. Fathers, teenage sons, and daughters worked for wages. In the current period, in contrast, as more wives have become full-time workers, immigrant men have begun to do some reproductive labor, particularly child care. Immigrant couples often work different shifts and prefer to care for children themselves rather than trust baby sitters from their own ethnic group. In my study I argue that "the productive system as constituted in the workplaces has shaped the family more than issues of reproduction have shaped the workplace" (Lamphere 1987:43).

More recently Patricia Zavella, Felipe Gonzalez, and I have found that young working mothers in sunbelt industries have moved much further than Cannery women or New England industrial immigrant women in changing the nature of the household division of labor (Lamphere, Gonzalez, and Zavella nd). These new committed female workers have been employed since high school and do not drop out of the labor force for long periods of time to have children. Thus, they and their husbands construct a family life around a two-job household. Although some couples have a "traditional" division of housework (women do the cooking and the majority of the cleaning and husbands take out the garbage, do minor repairs, and fix the car), many husbands participate in "female chores" and do substantial amounts

of child care (often caring for children while the wife is at work). Here we see the impact of what we used to call the "public sphere" on the domestic one, but in our analysis we have focused more on the varied ways that Anglos and Hispanics (including single mothers) have negotiated household and child-care arrangements, viewing husbands and wives as mediating contradictions. Subtle similarities and differences among and between working class Anglo and Hispanic women have emerged from this analysis, making it clear that the impact of work in the public work is not a monolithic but a variegated process.

In summary the dichotomy between the public world of men and domestic world of women was, in 1974, an important and useful starting point for thinking about women's roles in a cross-cultural perspective. As anthropologists have written more detailed and fine-grained studies of women's lives in a wide variety of other cultures and in our own society, we have gone beyond the use of dichotomies to produce analyses of the complex and layered structure of women's lives. We now treat women more historically, viewing them as social actors and examining the variability among women's situations within one culture and in their relationship to men.

NOTES

1. Rosaldo says that "the opposition does not *determine* cultural stereotypes or asymmetries in the evaluations of the sexism, but rather underlies them, to support a very general . . . identification of women with domestic life and of men with public life" (Rosaldo 1974:21–22). Thus, I would argue, Rosaldo did not attempt to *explain* women's subordination through the dichotomy, but saw it as an underlying structural framework in any society that supported subordination and that would have to be reorganized to change women's position.

2. It is interesting that we did not know of Elsie Clews Parsons' extensive feminist writing during 1910 to 1916, much of which is reminiscent of the kind of position we took in *Woman, Culture, and Society*. In another article I have

noted the similarities between Shelly's prose and that of Parsons (see Lamphere 1989 and Parsons 1913, 1914, 1915).

REFERENCES

Abu-Lughod, Lila. 1986. *Veiled Sentiments: Honor and Poetry in a Bedouin Society.* Berkeley and Los Angeles: University of California Press.

Brown, Judith. 1970. Economic organization and the position of women among the Iroquois. *Ethnohistory* 17(3/4):131–167.

Chai, Alice Yun. 1987. Freed from the elders but locked into labor: Korean immigrant women in Hawaii. *Women's Studies* 13:223–234.

Collier, Jane. 1974. Women in politics. In Michelle Z. Rosaldo and Louise Lamphere (eds.). *Woman, Culture, and Society.* Stanford: Stanford University Press.

———. 1988. *Marriage and Inequality in Classless Societies.* Stanford: Stanford University Press.

Collier, Jane, Michelle Rosaldo, and Sylvia Yanagisako. 1982. Is there a family? New anthropological views. In Barrie Thorne and Marilyn Yalom (eds.). *Rethinking the Family: Some Feminist Questions.* New York and London: Longman.

Comaroff, John L. 1987. Sui genderis: Feminism, kinship theory, and structural "domains." In Jane Fishburne Collier and Sylvia Junko Yanagisako (eds.). *Gender and Kinship: Essays Toward a Unified Analysis.* Stanford: Stanford University Press.

de Beauvoir, Simone. 1953. *The Second Sex.* New York: Alfred A. Knopf. Originally published in French in 1949.

Kaberry, Phyllis M. 1939. *Aboriginal Women, Sacred and Profane.* London: G. Routledge.

———. 1952. *Women of the Grassfields.* London: H. M. Stationery Office.

Lamphere, Louise. 1974. Strategies, cooperation, and conflict among women in domestic groups. In Michelle Z. Rosaldo and Louise Lamphere (eds.). *Woman, Culture, and Society.* Stanford: Stanford University Press.

———. 1987. *From Working Daughters to Working Mothers: Immigrant Women in a New England Industrial Community.* Ithaca, NY: Cornell University Press.

———. 1989. Feminist anthropology: The legacy of Elsie Clews Parsons. *American Ethnologist* 16(3):518–533.

Lamphere, Louise, Felipe Gonzales, and Patricia Zavella. (eds.). Working Mothers and Sunbelt Industrialization: New Patterns of Work and Family. Submitted to Cornell University Press.

Landes, Ruth. 1938. *The Ojibwa Woman, Part 1: Youth.* New York: Columbia University. Contributions to Anthropology, Vol. 31.

———. 1947. *The City of Women: Negro Women Cult Leaders of Bahia, Brazil.* New York: Macmillan.

Leacock, Eleanor. 1978. Women's status in egalitarian society: Implications for social evolution. *Current Anthropology* 19(2):247–275.

Leith-Ross, Sylvia. 1939. *African Women: Study of the Ibo of Nigeria.* London: Faber and Faber.

Mead, Margaret. 1949. *Male and Female.* New York: William Morrow and Co.

Moran, Mary H. 1990. *Civilized Women: Gender and Prestige in Southeastern Liberia.* Ithaca, NY: Cornell University Press.

Moore, Henrietta L. 1988. *Feminism and Anthropology.* Minneapolis: University of Minnesota Press.

Murcott, Anne. 1983. "It's a pleasure to cook for him": Food, mealtimes and gender in some South Wales households. In Eva Gamarnikow, D. H. J. Morgan, June Purvis, and Daphne Taylorson (eds.). *The Public and the Private.* London: Heinemann Educational Books.

Nelson, Cynthia. 1974. Public and private politics: Women in the Middle East. *American Ethnologist* 1:551–563.

Parsons, Elsie Clews. 1913. *The Old Fashioned Woman.* New York: G. P. Putnam's Sons.

———. 1914. *Fear and Conventionality.* New York: G. P. Putnam's Sons.

———. 1915. *Social Freedom: A Study of the Conflicts Between Social Classifications and Personality.* New York: G. P. Putnam's Sons.

Ong, Aihwa. 1987. *Spirits of Resistance and Capitalist Discipline.* Albany, NY: State University of New York Press.

Paulme, Denise (ed.). 1963. *Women of Tropical Africa.* Berkeley: University of California Press.

Rapp, Rayna. 1979. Anthropology. *Signs* 4(3): 497–513.

Reiter, Rayna (ed.). 1975a. *Toward an Anthropology of Women.* New York: Monthly Review Press.

———. 1975b. Men and women in the South of France: Public and private domains. In Rayna Reiter (ed.). *Toward an Anthropology of Women.* New York: Monthly Review Press.

Rosaldo, Michelle. 1974. Woman, culture and society: A theoretical overview. In Michelle Z. Rosaldo and Louise Lamphere (eds.). *Woman, Culture, and Society.* Stanford: Stanford University Press.

————. 1980. The uses and abuses of anthropology. *Signs* 5(3): 389–417.

Rosaldo, Michelle Z. and Louise Lamphere (eds.). 1974. *Woman, Culture, and Society.* Stanford: Stanford University Press.

Sacks, Karen. 1988. *Caring by the Hour: Women, Work, and Organizing at the Duke Medical Center.* Urbana and Chicago: University of Illinois Press.

Sudarkasa, Niara. 1976. Female employment and family organization in West Africa. In Dorothy McGuigan (ed.). *New Research on Women and Sex Roles.* Ann Arbor: Center for Continuing Education of Women.

————. 1986. The status of women in indigenous African Societies. *Feminist Studies* 12: 91–104.

Underhill, Ruth. 1936. *Autobiography of a Papago Woman.* Supplement to *American Anthropologist* 38(3), Part II. Millwood, NY: American Anthropological Association.

Wolf, Margery. 1972. *Women and the Family in Rural Taiwan.* Stanford: Stanford University Press.

Yanagisako, Sylvia Junko. 1987. Mixed metaphors: Native and anthropological models of gender and kinship domains. In Jane Fishburne Collier and Sylvia Junko Yanagisako (eds.). *Gender and Kinship: Essays Toward a Unified Analysis.* Stanford: Stanford University Press.

Yanagisako, Sylvia Junko and Jane Fishburne Collier. 1987. Toward a unified analysis of gender and kinship. In Jane Fishburne Collier and Sylvia Junko Yanagisako (eds.). *Gender and Kinship: Essays Toward a Unified Analysis.* Stanford: Stanford University Press.

Zavella, Patricia. 1987. *Women's Work and Chicano Families: Cannery Workers of the Santa Clara Valley.* Ithaca, NY: Cornell University Press.

"It's a Pleasure to Cook for Him": Food, Mealtimes and Gender in Some South Wales Households

Anne Murcott

INTRODUCTION

I think it lets him know that I am thinking about him—as if he knows that I am expecting him. But it's not as if 'oh I haven't got anything ready' ... Fair play, he's out all day ... he doesn't ask for that much ... you know it's not as if he's been very demanding or—he doesn't come home and say 'oh, we've got chops again', it's really a pleasure to cook for him, because

Reprinted with permission from Eva Gamarnikow, David H. J. Morgan, June Purvis, and Daphne Taylorson (eds.), *The Public and the Private* (London: Heinemann Educational Books, Ltd., 1983), pp. 78–90. Copyright © 1983 British Sociological Association.

whatever you ... oh I'll give him something and I think well, he'll like this, he'll like that. And he'll always take his plate out ... and he'll wash the dishes without me even asking, if I'm busy with the children. Mind, perhaps his method is not mine.

Every now and then an informant puts precisely into words the results of the researcher's analytic efforts—providing in the process a quotation suitable for the title! The extract reproduced above, explaining the importance of having the meal ready when her husband arrives home, comes from one of a series of interviews on which this paper is based.[1] The discussion starts by remembering that 'everyone knows' that women do the cooking: all the women interviewed—and the few husbands/boyfriends or mothers who came in and out—took it for granted that cooking was women's work. Informants may not enjoy cooking, or claim not to be good at it; they may not like the arrangement that it is women's work, or hanker after modifying it. But all recognise that this is conventional, some volunteer a measure of approval, most appeared automatically to accept it, a few resigned themselves and got on with it.

Studies of the organisation of domestic labour and marital role relationships confirm that cooking continues to be a task done more by women than men; this is also the case cross-culturally (Stephens, 1963; Murdock and Provost, 1973). Emphasis in the literature has shifted from Young and Willmott's (1975) symmetrical view of sharing and marital democracy. Now rather more thoroughgoing empirical study suggests their assessment is little more than unwarranted optimism (Oakley, 1974a and b; Edgell, 1980; Leonard, 1980; Tolson, 1977). This work improves on earlier studies of the domestic division of labour by going beyond behaviourist enquiry about 'who does which tasks' to consider the meanings attached to them by marital partners. The distribution of work turns out not to correlate neatly with assessments of importance or allocation of responsibility. (Oakley, 1974b; Edgell, 1980).

Part of this effort (in particular, Oakley, 1974a and b) has in addition attempted to analyse domestic work as a 'job like any other', considering housewives' work satisfaction, routines, supervision and so on. While this line of enquiry has undoubtedly made visible much of women's lives conventionally rendered invisible, it has perhaps not gone far enough. The study of housework as an occupation needs to attend in addition to features such as quality control, timekeeping, client as well as worker satisfaction, and perhaps further consideration of who, if anyone, is a housewife's boss. As will be seen, each of these is implicated in the discussion that follows.

These occupational aspects of housework provide, moreover, additional means of examining the relationship of the domestic division of labour to the economic structure as a whole. Recent commentary has also proposed that the view of the family as stripped of all but the residual economic function of consumption is ill-conceived and over-simplified. Domestic labourers refresh and sustain the existing labour force and play a key part in reproducing that of the future—as well as providing a reserve of labour themselves. The precise manner in which the political economy is to be accounted continues to be debated (West, 1980; Fox, 1980; Wajcman, 1981). For the moment, however, the general drift of that discussion can be borne in mind by recalling the everyday terminology of eating; food is consumed, meals have to be produced. The language favoured in cookbooks echoes that of industry and the factory (Murcott, 1983a). Homecooking may nicely embody the terms in which the family and household's place in the division of labour has to be seen. It may also provide a convenient arena for the further exploration of the economic and labour relations in the family and the relation of the marital partners to the means of production of domestic labour (Middleton, 1974).

Examination of the household provision of meals in these terms is, however, some way in the future. This paper does no more than offer some empirical foundation on which such study might build. It brings together informants' ideas about the importance of cooking, their notions of propriety of household eating and indicates their relation to gender. It starts with views of the significance of good cooking for home life, and goes on to deal with the place of cooking in the domestic division of labour. The familiar presumption that women are the cooks is extended to show that their responsibility in this sphere is tempered with reference to their husband's, not their own, choice. The paper concludes with brief comment on possible ways these data may illuminate some of the questions already raised.

HOME COOKING

> Aside from love, good food is the cornerstone of a happy household . . . (Opening lines of a 1957 cookbook called *The Well Fed Bridegroom*).

Right through the series of interviews three topics kept cropping up; the idea of a proper meal, reference to what informants call a 'cooked dinner' and the notion that somehow home is where proper eating is ensured. Moreover, mention of one like as not involved mention of another, sometimes all three. The composite picture that emerges from the whole series suggests that these are not merely related to one another in some way, but virtually equated.

It first needs to be said that informants seemed quite comfortable with a conception of a proper meal—indeed the very phrase was used spontaneously—and were able to talk about what it meant to them. Effectively a proper meal is a cooked dinner. This is one which women feel is necessary to their family's health, welfare and, indeed, happiness. It is a meal to come home to, a meal which should figure two, three or four times in the week, and especially on Sundays. A cooked dinner is easily identified—meat, potatoes, vegetables and gravy. It turns out that informants displayed considerable unanimity as to what defines such a dinner, contrasting it to, say, a 'snack' or 'fried'. In so doing they made apparent remarkably clear rules not only for its composition but also its preparation and taking. I have dealt with their detail and discussed their implications in full elsewhere (Murcott, 1982). But in essence these rules can be understood as forming part of the equation between proper eating and home cooking. And, as will be noted in the next section, they also provide for the symbolic expression of the relationship between husband and wife and for each partner's obligation to their home.

The meal for a return home is, in any case, given particular emphasis—a matter which cropped up in various contexts during the interviews. Thus, for some the very importance of cooking itself is to be expressed in terms of homecoming. Or it can provide the rationale for turning to and making a meal, one to be well cooked and substantial—not just 'beans on toast . . . thrown in front of you'.

The actual expression 'home cooking'—as distinct from 'cooking for homecoming'—received less insistent reference. Informants were straightforward, regarding it as self-evident that people preferred the food that they had at home, liked what they were used to and enjoyed what they were brought up on. Perhaps untypically nostalgic, one sums up the point:

> When my husband comes home . . . there's nothing more he likes I think than coming in the door and smelling a nice meal cooking. I think it's awful when someone doesn't make the effort . . . I think well if I was a man I'd think I'd get really fed up if my wife never bothered . . .

What was prepared at home could be trusted—one or two regarded the hygiene of restaurant kitchens with suspicion, most simply knew their chips were better than those from the local Chinese take-away or chippy. Convenience foods had their place, but were firmly outlawed when it came to a cooked dinner. In the ideal, commercially prepared items were ranged alongside snacks, and light, quick meals: lunches and suppers in contrast to proper dinners. Informants talked about home cooking, but used this or some such phrase infrequently; the following is an exception:

> I'd like to be able to make home-made soups and things, it's just finding the time and getting organised, but at the moment I'm just not organised . . . I think it would probably be more good for us than buying . . . I suppose it's only—I'd like to be—the image of the ideal housewife is somebody who cooks her own food and keeps the household clean and tidy.

The sentiments surrounding her valuation of home-made food are not, however, an exception. Time and again informants linked not only a view of a proper meal for homecoming, but a view of the proper parts hus-band and wife are to play on this occasion. So cooking is important when you are married.

> you must think of your husband . . . it's a long day for him at work, usually, . . . even if they have got a canteen at work, their cooking is not the same as coming home to your wife's cooking . . . I think every working man should have a cooked meal when he comes in from work . . .

Cooking is important—though not perhaps for everybody 'like men who don't cook'—for women whose 'place [it is] to see the family are well fed'.

In this section, I have indicated that infor-mants virtually treat notions of proper meals, home-based eating and a cooked dinner, as equivalents. The stress laid on the homecom-ing not only underlines the symbolic signifi-cance attached to both the meal and the re-turn home. It simultaneously serves as a reminder of the world beyond the home being left behind for that day. Put another way, the cooked dinner marks the threshold between the public domains of school or work and the private sphere behind the closed front door. In the process of describing these notions of the importance of cooking in the home, it becomes apparent that the familiar division of labour is assumed.

COOKING IN THE DOMESTIC DIVISION OF LABOUR

As noted in an earlier section, all those inter-viewed took it for granted that it is the women who cook. What they had to say refers both to conventions in general, and themselves and their circumstances in particular.[2] There are two important features of their general pre-sumption that women are the cooks; one indi-cates the terms in which it is modifiable, the other locates it firmly as a matter of marital justice and obligation. The upshot of each of these is to underline the manner in which the domestic preparation of meals is securely an-chored to complementary concepts of con-duct proper to wife and husband.

To say that women cook is not to say that it is only women who ever do so. It is, however, to say that it is always women who daily, rou-tinely, and as a matter of course are to do the cooking. Men neither in the conventional ste-reotype nor in informants' experience ever cook on a regular basis in the way women do.[3] Husband/boyfriends/fathers are 'very good really'; they help informants/their mothers with carrying the heavy shopping, preparing the vegetables, switching the oven on when told, doing the dishes afterwards (cf. Leon-ard, 1980). Such help may be offered on a regular enough basis, notably it is available when the women are pregnant, dealing with a very young infant, unwell or unusually tired. But none of this is regarded as men doing the cooking.

More significantly, it is not the case that men do not cook—in the strict sense of taking charge of the transformation of foodstuffs to some version of a meal. They may make breakfast on a Sunday, cook only 'bacon-y' things, can do chips or 'his' curries: all exam-ples, incidentally, of foods that do *not* figure in the proper cooked dinner (Murcott, 1983c).

For some, however, competence in the kitchen (and at the shops) is suspect: he'll 'turn the potatoes on at such and such a time . . . but leave him he's hopeless' and another just 'bungs everything in'. For others, it is men who make better domestic cooks than women, are more methodical, less moody. Another couple jokingly disagree: she 'not taken in' by Robert Carrier on TV, he claim-ing that 'the best chefs are men'. The point is that either way, of course, informants do re-gard gender as relevant to the question of who is to cook.

It is not even the case that all men cannot cook the proper, homecoming meal. One or two, when out of work for a while, but his wife still earning (this only applied to those having a first baby) might start the meal or even have it ready for her return. But once he is em-ployed again he does not continue to take this degree of responsibility, reverting either to 'helping' or waiting for her to do it. Now and again, wives have learned to cook not at school or from their mothers, but from their husbands. But it was still assumed that it was for the woman to learn. This was even so in one instance where the informant made a 'confession . . . my husband does the cooking'. But now that she was pregnant and had quit paid work she would take over; 'it would be a bit lazy not to'. Like others for whom the cooking may have been shared while both were employed, cooking once again became the home-based wife's task (cf. Bott, 1957, p. 225; Oakley, 1980, p. 132).

The issue is, however, more subtle than an account of who does what, or who takes over doing what. Men and women's place involve mutual obligation. 'I think a woman from the time she can remember is brought up to cook . . . Whereas most men are brought up to be the breadwinner.' The question of who does the cooking is explicitly a matter of justice and marital responsibility. A woman talks of the guilt she feels if she does not, despite the greater tiredness of late pregnancy, get up to make her husband's breakfast and something for lunch—'he's working all day'. Another insists that her husband come shopping with her so he knows the price of things—he's 'hopeless' on his own—but she has a clear idea of the limits of each person's responsibility: each should cook only if the wife *has* to earn rather than chooses to do so.

Here, then, I have sought to show that informants subscribed in one way or another to the convention that it is women who cook. In the process it transpired that it is certain sorts of cooking, i.e. routine, homecoming cooking, which are perennially women's work. The meal that typically represents 'proper' cooking is, of course, the cooked dinner. Its composition and prescribed cooking techniques involve prolonged work and attention; its timing, for homecoming, prescribes when that work shall be done. To do so demands the cook be working at it, doing wifely work, in time that corresponds to time spent by her husband earning for the family (Murcott, 1982). This is mirrored in Eric Batstone's (1983) account of the way a car worker's lunch box prepared by his wife the evening before is symbolic of the domestic relationship which

constitutes the rationale for his presence in the workplace; he endures the tedium of the line in order to provide for his wife and family. It transpired also that men do cook in certain circumstances, but such modification seems to reveal more clearly the basis for accounting cooking as part of a wife's responsibility (to the family) at home corresponding to the husband's obligation (to the family) at work, i.e. their mutual responsibilities to each other as marriage partners.

WHO COOKS FOR WHOM?

At this point I introduce additional data which bear on cooking's relation to the question of marital responsibility. Repeatedly informants indicated that people do not cook for themselves; evidently it is not worth the time and effort.[4] But the data suggest implications beyond such matters of economy. Two interrelated features are involved: one is the distinction already alluded to in the previous section, between cooking in the strict sense of the word and cooking as preparation of a particular sort of meal. The other enlarges on the following nicety. To observe that people do not cook for themselves can mean two things. First it can imply that a solitary person does not prepare something for themselves to eat while on their own. But it can also imply that someone does not do the cooking on their own behalf, but in the service of some other(s). Examination of the transcripts to date suggests that not only could informants mean either or both of these, but also that each becomes elided in a way that underlines the nuances and connotations of the term cooking.

The question of a lone person not cooking themselves a meal unsurprisingly cropped up most frequently with reference to women themselves, but men, or the elderly were also thought not to bother.

Informants are clear, however, that not cooking when alone does not necessarily mean going without. Women 'pick' at something that happens to be in the house, have a bar of chocolate or packet of crisps later in the evening or a 'snack'. Men will fry something, an egg or make chips. No one said that a man would go without altogether (though they may not know), whereas for themselves—and women and girls in general—skipping a meal was thought common enough. Men—and occasionally women—on their own also go back to their mother's or over to their sister's for a meal. One informant was (the day of my interview with her) due to go to her mother's for the evening meal, but fearful of being alone in the house at night, she was also due to stay there for the next few days while her husband was away on business.

The suggestion is, then, that if a person is by themselves, but is to have a proper meal, as distinct from 'fried' or a 'snack' then they join a (close) relation's household. The point that it is women who cook such meals receives further emphasis. Indeed, when women cook this particular meal, it is expressly *for* others. In addition to the temporary lone adults just noted who return to mothers or sisters, women in turn may cook for the older generation, as well as routinely cooking for children or for men home at 'unusual' times if unemployed or temporarily of a different shift.

This conventional requirement that women cook for others is not always straightforward in practice. At certain stages in an infant's life the logistics of producing meals for husband *and* child(ren) there as well meant the woman felt difficulties in adequately meeting the obligations involved. And not all informants enjoyed cooking; most just accepted that it needed doing, though there were also those who took positive, creative pleasure in it (cf. Oakley, 1974b). Part of this is expressed in the very satisfaction of providing for others something they should be getting, and in turn will enjoy.

More generally cooking can become tiresome simply because it has to be done day-in, day-out. The pleasure in having a meal prepared for you becomes all the more pointed if routinely you are cooking for others.[5] In the absence of any data for men, it can only be a guess that going out for a meal is thus specially enjoyable for women. But for those who on occasion did eat out this clearly figures in

their pleasure. Even if it rarely happened, just the idea of having it put in front of you meant a treat: 'it's nice being spoiled'.

The question 'who cooks for whom?' can now begin to be answered. Apparently it is women who cook for others—effectively, husbands and children. If husbands and children are absent, women alone will not 'cook', indeed many may not even eat. It is the others' presence which provides the rationale for women's turning to and making a proper meal—that is what the family should have and to provide it is her obligation. Men—and children—have meals made for them as a matter of routine: but for women it is a treat. That solitary men do not 'cook' for themselves either, and may go to a relative's for meals (cf. Rosser and Harris, 1965; Barker, 1972), or that a woman on her own may also do so does not detract from the main proposal that it is women who cook for others. For it is not only that informants or their husbands will go temporarily back to their mother's, not their father's, home-cooking. It is also that both men and women revert to the status of a child for whom a woman, a mother, cooks. The mother may actually be the adult's parent, but they—and I with them—may stretch the point and see that she may be mother to the adult's nieces or nephews or indeed, as in the case of cooking for the elderly, she may be mother to the adult's grandchildren.

The appreciation that it is women who cook for others elaborates the more familiar convention, discussed above, that in the domestic division of labour cooking is women's work. First of all it indicates that this work is service work. Cooking looks increasingly like a task quite particularly done for others. Second, when cooking for others women are performing a service to those who are specifically related (sic) rather than for a more generalised clientele known only by virtue of their becoming customers. The marital—and parental—relationship defines who is server, who served.

That said, there remains the question of deciding what the server shall serve. As already discussed in an earlier section, the conventional expectation shared, it seems, by both woman and man, is that meals shall be of a certain sort—a cooked dinner for a certain occasion, most commonly the return home from work, or the celebration of Sunday, a work-free day. The 'rules' involved are not entirely hard and fast, or precisely detailed. Cooked dinners are neither daily nor invariable affairs (Murcott, 1982). And the cooked dinner itself can properly comprise a number of alternative meats (and cuts) and range of different vegetables. What then, determines the choice of meat and vegetables served on any particular day? Some of the factors involved, as will be seen in the next section, once again echo ideas of responsibility and mutual obligation.

DECIDING WHAT TO HAVE

A number of factors feature in deciding what to have for a particular day's meal.[6] First, a question of cost was taken for granted. This does not necessarily mean keeping expenditure to a minimum—eating in the customary manner despite hard times was highly and expressly valued by some. Second, the conventional provision of proper dinners itself contributed to the determination of choice. These two factors present themselves as marking the limits within which the finer decisions about what the precise components of the day's dinner are to be. Here reference to their husband's—and, to a lesser extent, children's—preferences was prominent in informants' discussion of such detailed choices.

It was indicated earlier that in an important sense women's cooking is service work. This sort of work has two notable and interrelated aspects affecting decisions and choice: is it the server or served who decides what the recipient is to want? Exploring the mandate for professionals' work, Everett Hughes (1971, p. 424) highlights a key question: 'professionals do not merely serve: they define the very wants they serve'. Servants, and service workers such as waitresses (Whyte, 1948; Spradley and Mann, 1975) compliantly provide for the wants identified by the served. On

the face of it, then, the professional has total and the waitress nil autonomy. Examples reflecting this sort of range occurred among informants varying from one woman apparently always deciding, through to another always making what he wants for tea. But in the same way that the maximum autonomy of the professional is continually, to a certain degree, a matter of negotiation and renegotiation with clients, and that, similarly, the apparent absence of autonomy is modified by a variety of more or less effective devices waitresses use to exert some control over customers, so a simple report of how meal decisions are reached can, I propose, either conceal negotiations already complete, or reveal their workings.

Thus informants interested in trying new recipes still ended up sticking to what they usually made because their husbands were not keen. Others reported that 'he's very good' or 'never complains' while some always asked what he wanted. A non-committal reply however did not necessarily settle the matter, for some discovered that being presented with a meal she had then decided on could provoke adverse and discouraging remarks. But it was clear that even those who claimed not to give their husbands a choice were still concerned to ensure that he agreed to her suggestion. It is almost as if they already knew what he would like, needed to check out a specific possibility every now and then but otherwise continued to prepare meals within known limits. Deciding what to have already implicitly took account of his preferences so that the day-to-day decision *seemed* to be hers.

The material presented in this section provides only a glimpse of this area of domestic decision-making. Other aspects need consideration in future work. For instance, what degree of importance do people attach to the matter (cf. Edgell, 1980, pp. 58–9)? Attention also needs to be paid to wider views of the legitimacy of choice in what one eats. In what sense do restaurant customers choose and mentally subnormal patients not? Does a child that spits out what it is fed succeed in claiming a choice or not? And in apparently acquiescing to their husband's choice, are wives circumscribing their own? But it looks as if deciding what to have is of a piece with a shared view of marital responsibility whereby he works and so deserves, somehow, the right to choose what she is to cook for him.

GENDER AND THE PRODUCTION OF MEALS

> I know a cousin of mine eats nothing but chips, in fact his mother-in-law had to cook him chips for his Christmas dinner and she went berserk . . .

This 'atrocity story' recapitulates various elements of the preceding discussion. Such unreasonableness is, no doubt, unusual but its artless reporting emphasises a number of points already made. Not only do chips break the rules of what should properly figure in a Christmas meal, superior even to the Sunday variant of a cooked dinner, but it remains, however irksome, up to the woman to prepare what a man wants. The burden of this paper, then, may be summarised as revealing allegiance to the propriety of occasion such that a certain sort of meal is to mark home (male) leisure versus (male) work-time, and that such meals are cooked by women for others, notably husbands, in deference, not to the woman's own, but to men's taste.

This examination of cooking, mealtimes and gender within the household has implications for the continuing analysis of domestic work as work. While it does not shed light on why such work is women's, only reasserting that conventionally this is so, it clearly casts the work of meal provision as service work.

The everyday way of describing dishing up a meal as serving food is embedded in a set of practices that prescribe the associated social relationships as of server and served. As already observed this involves two interrelated matters: control over the work, and decisions as to what are the 'wants' the worker shall serve, what the work shall be. Each is considered in turn.

Oakley (1974a and b) reports that one of the features of housewifery that women value is the feeling of autonomy. Care is needed,

though, not to treat such attitudes as tantamount to their analysis. Just because housewives express their experiences in terms of enjoying being their own boss does not mean that their conditions of work can be analysed in terms of a high degree of autonomy. The material presented in this paper suggests that doing the cooking is not directed by the woman herself, but is subject to various sorts of control.

First of these is the prescription for certain kinds of food for certain occasions. The idea of the cooked dinner for a homecoming is just such an example of cultural propriety. Related to this is a second control, namely that the food is to be ready for a specific time. Mealtimes construed in this way may exert just the same sort of pressure on the cook as any other production deadline in industry. Third, control is also exerted via the shared understanding that it is the preferences of the consumer which are to dictate the exact variant of the dinner to be served. What he fancies for tea constrains the cook to provide it. These kinds of control in the domestic provision of meals find their counterpart in the industrial concerns of quality control, timekeeping and market satisfaction. A woman cooking at home may not have a chargehand 'breathing down her neck' which is understandably a source of relief to her. But this does not mean to say that she enjoys autonomy—simply perhaps that other controls make this sort of oversight redundant. Evidence either way is extremely sparse, but Ellis (1983) suggests that failing to cook according to her husband's wishes can contribute to a wife's battering.

Linked to the issue of control of domestic cooking is the question of decision-making. Edgell (1980) has drawn attention to the degree of importance couples attach to different aspects of family living about which decisions have to be made. He distinguishes assessments of importance from, first, whether the decision is mainly the wife's or husband's responsibility and second, from the frequency with which the decision has to be made. So, for instance, moving is the husband's decision, perceived to be very important and infrequent, a contrast to the matter of spending on food. What Edgell does not make clear, however, is quite what either his informants or he mean by 'importance'. As an analytic device, the idea does not distinguish between family matters which partners may identify as both important and somehow major or permanent such as moving, and those identified as mundane, or fleeting but important nonetheless, such as daily eating. Like refuse collection or sewage work which is regarded as vital but low status, the importance attached to meals may not be remarked in the general run of things, though noticed particularly if absent. But that does not necessarily mean that both husband and wife regard it as unimportant. And, harking back to the question of autonomy in decision-making, reports such as Edgell's that food spending, cooking or whatever is regarded as the wife's responsibility, cannot, of itself, be seen as evidence of her power and freedom from control in those areas. For as Jan Pahl (1982, p. 24) has so cogently observed, 'being able to offload certain decisions and certain money-handling chores on to the other spouse can itself be a sign of power'. The delegate may be responsible for execution of tasks, but they are answerable to the person in whom the power to delegate is originally vested.

The preliminary analysis offered in this paper has theoretical and political implications concerning power and authority in marriage and the relation between domestic and paid work. The exploration of ideas about cooking and mealtimes starts to provide additional approach to detailing the means of domestic production. And the sort of work women are to do to ensure the homecoming meal provides a critical instance of the juncture between the control of a worker and the (his) control of his wife. The meal provides one illustration not only of a point where the public world of employment and the private world of the home meet one another; it also shows how features of the public take precedence within the private. For the stress informants lay on this mealtime offers an interesting way of understanding how the industrial rhythms which circumscribe workers are linked to the rhythms which limit women's domestic work (cf. Rotenberg, 1981). And women's continual accommodation to men's taste can also be seen as a literal expression of wives' deference to husbands' authority (Bell and Newby, 1976; Edgell, 1980, p. 70). This acquiescence to his choice provides the cultural gloss to the underlying economic relationship whereby industry produces amongst other things both the wage, and the raw materials it buys, for the domestic to produce what is needed to keep the industrial worker going. Part of the conjugal contract that each in their own way provide for the other, it does indeed become 'a pleasure to cook for him'.

ACKNOWLEDGEMENTS

I am very grateful to all those necessarily anonymous people who made the research possible and who generously gave their time to answer my questions. I should like to record my appreciation of conversations with Tony Coxon, Sara Delamont, Robert Dingwall, Rhian Ellis, Bill Hudson and Phil Strong at various stages during the preparation of this paper and of the computing help and advice Martin Read provided. Only I and not they are to blame for its deficiencies. And I must thank Lindsey Nicholas, Joan Ryan, Sheila Pickard, Myrtle Robins and Margaret Simpson very much, despite flu all round, and an unusually scrawly manuscript, for their help in typing both drafts.

NOTES

1. In order to begin remedying sociology's neglect (Murcott, 1983b) of food beliefs and of the social organisation of eating, I conducted a single-handed exploratory study (supported by a grant from the SSRC) holding unstructured tape-recorded interviews with a group of 37 expectant mothers attending a health centre in a South Wales valley for antenatal care (22 pregnant for the first time), 20 of whom were interviewed again after the baby's birth. No claim is made for their representativeness in any hard and fast sense,

though they represent a cross-section of socio-economic groups. For present purposes the data are treated as providing a composite picture. The prime concern here is to indicate the range and variety of evidence gathered. An instance that occurs once only thus becomes as interesting as one occurring 30 times. This is reflected in the discussion by the deliberate use of phrases such as 'some informants' rather than '6 out of 37'. In any case reference to numbers of instances is no more exact, and risks implying a spurious representativeness.

These qualifications are most important. But for the sake of a tolerably readable account I do not hedge every other sentence with reminder of these limitations. Yet they do actively have to be taken as read.

2. Informants referred not only to themselves but also to mothers, sisters, sisters-in-law and women friends doing cooking.

3. No informant who had children old enough to cook currently shared the household with them.

4. Market researchers know how to trade on such reports. During the period of interviewing a TV commercial was running which sought to persuade busy housewives not to neglect themselves but have a frozen ready-cooked meal at lunchtime.

5. Interestingly, no one talked of hospital meals put in front of them as a treat. (None had a home delivery.) Rather it was the quality of the food provided which informants concentrated on. Institution cooking could not be home cooking.

6. It might have been expected that nutritional criteria would figure in these decisions. Analysis so far suggests that cultural prescriptions for proper eating at home override what is known about healthy eating. (Murcott, 1983d).

REFERENCES

Barker, D. L. 1972. 'Keeping close and spoiling,' *Sociological Review*, 20(4), 569–590.

Batstone, E. 1983. 'The hierarchy of maintenance and the maintenance of hierarchy: Notes on food and industry,' in A. Murcott (ed.), *The Sociology of Food and Eating*, Gower.

Bell, C. and Newby, H. 1976. 'Husbands and wives: The dynamics of deferential dialectic,' in D. L. Barker and S. Allen (eds.), *Dependence and Exploration in Work and Marriage*, Longmans.

Bott, E. 1957. *Family and Social Network*, Tavistock.

Edgell, S. 1980. *Middle Class Couples: A Study of Segregation, Domination and Inequality in Marriage*, Allen and Unwin.

Ellis, R. 1983. 'The way to a man's heart . . . ,' in A. Murcott (ed.), *The Sociology of Food and Eating*, Gower.

Fox, B. (ed.). 1980. *Hidden in the Household*, Toronto: Women's Press.

Hughes, E. C. 1971. 'The humble and the proud,' in *The Sociological Eye: Selected Papers*, Aldine-Atherton.

Leonard, D. 1980. *Sex and Generation*, Tavistock.

Middleton, C. 1974. 'Sexual inequality and stratification theory,' in E. Parkin (ed.), *The Social Analysis of Class Structure*, Tavistock.

Murcott, A. 1982a. 'On the social significance of the "cooked dinner in South Wales," *Social Science Information*, 21(4/5), 677–695.

———. 1983a. 'Women's place: Cookbook's image of technique and technology in the British Kitchen,' *Women's Studies International Forum*, 6(2) (forthcoming).

———. (ed.) 1983b. *The Sociology of Food and Eating*, Gower.

———. 1983c. 'Cooking and the cooked,' in A. Murcott (ed.), *The Sociology of Food and Eating*, Gower.

———. 1983d. 'Menus, meals and platefuls,' *International Journal of Sociology and Social Policy* (forthcoming).

Murdock, G. P. and Provost, C. 1973. 'Factors in the division of labour by sex: A cross-cultural analysis,' *Ethnology*, XII(2), 203–225.

Oakley, A. 1974a. *Housewife*, Penguin.

———. 1974b. *The Sociology of Housework*, Martin Robertson.

———. 1980. *Women Confined: Towards a 'Sociology of Childbirth,'* Martin Robertson.

Pahl, J. 1982. 'The allocation of money and the structuring of inequality within marriage,' *Board of Studies in Social Policy and Administration*, University of Kent, mimeo.

Rosser, C. and Harris, C. 1965. *The Family and Social Change*, Routledge and Kegan Paul.

Rotenberg, R. 1981. 'The impact of industrialisation on meal patterns in Vienna, Austria,' *Ecology of Food and Nutrition*, 11(1), 25–35.

Spradley, J. O. and Mann, B. J. 1975. *The Cocktail Waitress: Women's Work in a Man's World*, John Wiley.

Stephens, W. N. 1963. *The Family in Cross-cultural Perspective*, Holt, Rinehart and Winston.

Tolson, A. 1977. *The Limits of Masculinity*, Tavistock.

Wajcman, J. 1981. 'Work and the family: Who gets "the best of both worlds?"' in Cambridge Women's Studies Group, *Women in Society*, Virago.

West, J. 1980. 'A political economy of the family in capitalism: Women, reproduction and wage labour,' in T. Nichols (ed.), *Capital and Labour: A Marxist Primer*, Fontana.

Whyte, W. F. 1948. *Human Relations in the Restaurant Industry*, McGraw-Hill.

Young, M. and Willmott, P. 1975. *The Symmetrical Family*, Penguin.

Freed from the Elders but Locked into Labor: Korean Immigrant Women in Hawaii

Alice Yun Chai

An immigrant's class in her home country plays a large part in the kinds of adaptive strategies she develops in the new. Men and women do not necessarily have the same experiences, either of class or of immigration. This paper is a study of middle class, professional and educated Korean women immigrants married to professional and student husbands in Hawaii. It focuses on the differential impacts that immigration has on women and men in changing their division of labor, their relative statuses, social identities and their class positions.

BACKGROUND TO IMMIGRATION

Urban Middle Class Ideals in Korea

Marriage in Korea is ideally a complementary relationship in which husband and wife divide

From *Women's Studies* 13(3):223–234, 1987. Reprinted with permission of Gordon and Breach, Science Publishers, Inc. This article is based on a longer essay entitled "Adaptive Strategies of Recent Korean Women in Hawaii," in Janet Sharistanian (ed.), *Beyond the Public/Dichotomy: Contemporary Perspectives on Women's Public Lives* (New York: Greenwood Press, 1987).

the labor into male and female tasks, as well as having separate friendship networks and leisure pursuits. Younger, educated couples are more likely to participate in joint leisure activities such as family outings, films and concerts, or to visit relatives and friends. Wives who live in households separate from their husbands' parents have more contact with their own parents than do those who live with their in-laws.

The wife's domain is home and motherhood, the husband's economic provision. Both are indispensible to the welfare of the family, and husbands and wives respect each other's autonomy and competence within their separate domains. It is not acceptable for married women of relatively high socioeconomic status to enter the labor force, though in poorer urban and rural families it is acceptable because the incomes of both spouses are necessary to the family's economic support.

The Korean "domestic" and "public" domains divide social labor somewhat differently than they do in the United States. Korean women's household responsibilities are much broader than their American counterparts. Many urban middle class wives in

Korea have at least one non-nuclear family member living with them, usually a house-maid or a single female relative. Heavy tasks and repairs that in the United States are the responsibilities of a husband are not part of the cultural domain of Korean middle class husbands. Workers are hired for these tasks, but wives do the hiring and supervision.

As domestic specialists, wives make decisions about family finances from real estate to consumption. Most husbands give all their pay to their wives, who in turn give their husband an allowance to cover his daily expenses. In addition, most middle class urban wives supplement their husband's incomes by participating in mutual financing associations called *Kye*, as well as in other business ventures.

Koreans in Hawaii

The Korean population in Hawaii and in the United States remained relatively small until the liberalized Immigration Act of 1965 which permitted not only spouses and children, but also parents, married children and siblings of American citizens to enter the country (H. Kim 1977: 91). Between 1970 and 1976, the number of Koreans in Hawaii increased almost 300%, making them the second fastest-growing Asian group in the state (Hawaii Commission on Manpower and Full Employment 1978). Hawaii's 9,868 Korean immigrants between 1970 and 1978 made up 15.6% of its immigrant population.

WOMEN'S LIVES

For this study I interviewed 27 women at length, informally, in Korean and in their homes. All are Christians (as are most Korean immigrants), and belong to one of Honolulu's two largest Korean Protestant churches. Most of the women had been urban full-time homemakers, high school or college educated, Protestants or Buddhists prior to emigration to Hawaii no more than seven years prior to being interviewed (the average was

four years). All the women had married in Korea when they were between the ages of 20 and 30—those with less schooling tended to marry younger than college-educated—and were between the ages of 21 and 48, living in Honolulu with husbands and school-aged children when I talked with them.

Most women said they came to Hawaii to join their own or their husband's relatives. Many hoped for economic improvement, and for educational and occupational opportunities for their children (Koo and Yu 1981: 11). About half said they would like to move to the U.S. mainland for their children's higher education, or to return to Korea after their children finished their schooling.

Almost all (23 women) had already become citizens or were applying to do so. Their reasons were pragmatic: to vote for Korean electoral candidates, to get financial aid for their children, to invite relatives to visit or emigrate. Only one woman said she would not obtain American citizenship because she did not want to forsake her allegiance to Korea. The remaining three had not come to any decision about citizenship.

MIDDLE CLASS WOMEN IN WORKING CLASS JOBS

Unlike the immigrants of the early 1900s, who had been largely uneducated, poor and of rural origin (Chai 1981: 328–344), recent Korean immigrants are well-educated. One-third of the household heads surveyed in 1975 had at least one year of post-secondary education, and more than three-fourths of that group had completed college (Hawaii, Commission on Manpower and Full Employment 1977: 27). Of the women who migrated to Hawaii between 1968 and 1975, 68% had at least a high school education (Gardner and Wright 1979: Table 6). Over two-thirds of the immigrants who reported an occupation were in the professional, technical or managerial categories.

However, few of these workers have the opportunity to practice in the fields for which they trained. This is primarily because of discrimination in employment and the refusal of local professional accreditation agencies to issue licenses on the basis of their previous education and training, and only secondarily because of language barriers. Recent immigrants often work at low-status, low-paying unskilled or semi-skilled jobs (Hawaii, Commission on Manpower and Full Employment 1977: 38). More than half of all recent Korean immigrants to Hawaii worked in service jobs. The median income of immigrant men ($7,400) was less than half that for American born Korean men ($16,600). For immigrant and American-born Korean women, the differences were even greater ($2,750 and $8,857), while the contrasts between men's and women's earnings are equally striking (Gardner and Wright 1979: Table 16).

This situation is even sharper for Korean women with college degrees. Here, an estimated 60% of liberal arts graduates work as operatives, sales or clerical workers (Hyungchan Kim 1977: 107). In Los Angeles, where Korean immigrant women also have higher labor force participation rates than native born women with children, most found work in garment and bead factories. An alternative pattern, to be explored below, was for self-employment in small retail shops (Bok-Lim C. Kim 1978: 186).

Many Korean immigrant women who identified as full-time homemakers in Korea moved into the labor force after they came to Hawaii (Hawaii, Commission on Manpower and Full Employment 1977: 33; H. Kim 1974: 23–42). Two-thirds of the women I interviewed did not work outside the home when they first came to Hawaii. Half of these had been teachers, in technical jobs or small businesses before and after marriage, but had stopped working after the arrival of children. The other half had never been employed. These women's husbands' occupations were evenly distributed among clerical, technical, professional and business fields. Their median monthly family income in 1979 was $1,000.

Two-thirds of the women I interviewed said they had to change from being homemakers to being working women for eco-

nomic survival. All 27 women remembered their first jobs in Hawaii. Nine worked as kitchen helpers in Korean or Japanese-owned restaurants; six women worked in dress-making factories; and three women worked as hotel maids in white or Japanese-owned hotels; three were jewelry makers or farm workers; and three were sales or clerical workers for Korean or Japanese employers. Their second jobs were not significantly different, in that there was more horizontal than vertical mobility, from one to another entry-level job.

Available jobs arise from the interplay among English proficiency, skills, age, sex and marital status. English was the most common language used at work, followed by Korean and Japanese together, and then by English and Japanese together. Women faced a variety of obstacles in getting jobs and trying to work continuously. They tend to be confined to jobs with the lowest status and wages, to short-term, fluctuating employment, and they are often the last hired and the first to lose their jobs in the more volatile tourist, garment and jewelry industries.

Immigrant women's need for employment is also related to discrimination faced by their men. The women's husbands, most of whom had been professional, managerial or white collar workers in Korea, found themselves working as janitors, gardeners, painters, and dishwashers. Some men were able to move into more technical and semi-skilled work, or became store-owners.

By the time these women described their third jobs, there was a noticeable shift toward being unpaid workers in family-owned businesses—typically grocery stores, restaurants and gift shops. To start such a business by herself, with her husband or another relative, was preferable to moving from service or factory work to clerical or sales work. Women preferred the freedom, decision-making power and flexibility of working hours (though it sometimes meant longer hours and harder work) that a small business provided. Those women who aspired to such businesses usually had worked as kitchen helpers or seamstresses for several years, frequently working 10–16 hours a day, seven days a week often at more than one job in order to save enough money to start their business.

DOMESTIC STRATEGIES

Economic demands of immigrant life changed women's attitudes in some ways. Because of their experiences in Hawaii, three-fourths of the women came to believe that it was psychologically and socially beneficial (beyond the economic benefits) for married women to work outside the home. However, most women interviewed said that it was very difficult for mothers of small children to work in Hawaii because of the absence of extended family support and suitable babysitters.

Even mothers with older children feel badly about not being able to spend more time with their children. A mother of four children ranging in age from 7–20, who worked at a sewing factory during the day and as a kitchen helper at a club at night, and whose husband worked as a janitor, noted:

> Even though the life here is much harder than Korea and my husband wants to go back to Korea or move to the mainland for the easier life and the better job opportunities, I have to bear it because of the children's education. I think Korean women in Korea who are full-time housewife/mother are much happier and better off than Korean women here. I have developed a bad headache and dizzy spells since I came due to fatigue from overwork.

In Hawaii, the division of labor between husbands and wives is more like the American ideal than the Korean. Men do outdoor and technical chores, women the indoor ones. Wives, assisted by daughters and/or female relatives do most of the cooking, cleaning, dishwashing, laundry and child care. Husbands help with grocery shopping if the wife does not drive, or if the family has only one car. They also assisted with yard work and home repair. In only a few families, husbands and sons helped occasionally with cleaning, laundry and dishwashing.

Older women and those who had been married in Korea before immigrating to the United States complained about their husbands' refusal to help with household tasks, since their husbands still expected to be waited on as they had been in Korea.

> Life is very hard in America. We have to work as hard as men at work place and have to come home and do more work. Many Korean husbands in America still want their wives to serve them as they did in Korea, and marital conflict occurs because of this. In Korea, since we usually had some domestic help we did not work as hard physically as we do now and did not have as much mental tension as we have here because of double work loads and the language barrier.

Finances too are arranged differently. In Hawaii, equal numbers of husbands and wives were responsible for family budgets and took care of paying bills or going to the bank. Because wives had less time, and tended to have fewer language and driving skills, many husbands were forced to share some of these family responsibilities. However, husbands were doing a traditional wife's work reluctantly and temporarily until they gained the needed skills.

In the midst of changing areas of responsibility, most women felt that their husbands retained final authority to approve or reject their wives' decisions about their behavior. Several wives said that they could not take night shift kitchen work because of their husband's objections. One middle-aged wife with a teenage daughter explained:

> I suffer most because of the language barrier. . . . Next hardest thing is too much work, both at work and at home because my husband still wants to be served and he does not even give me freedom to go to English classes at night. But I go to English classes against his will anyway. I can only endure for so long, but if I cannot take it any more, I will have to leave him.

More wives said that their marital relationship improved in Hawaii. (Only two women said that the relationship had been better in Korea.) This was because their husbands came home directly from work, rather than going to stag parties with male friends or colleagues as they did in Korea, and because there were no elderly relatives living with them who might inhibit their spontaneous reactions to each other. Sources of conflict centered around fatigue and irritation from hard physical labor, and around husbands' refusal to help with housework while demanding wives' services. One-third of the women said they had less frequent sexual intercourse in Hawaii because of long working hours, different shifts and fatigue. One woman lost all sexual interest because she was so pessimistic and depressed, but gave in to her husband's sexual demands because it was the only ego booster left to him.

Almost half the women said that their health deteriorated since immigration, and that they experienced insomnia, stomach disorders, headaches, chest pain, dizziness, loss of appetite and weight, eye ailments or frigidity. Eight reported no real changes in health, and five had improved health.

Korean wives feel especially burdened because they are not accustomed to double responsibilities of work and home. Though they only take on wage work from economic necessity, the fact of earning a regular wage has affected both their perceptions of and their actual relations with their spouses. They come to doubt their husbands' right to dominate them, and they insist on their sharing in the housework. They also refuse to meet their husbands' demands for the preparation of Korean food, which is quite time-consuming when added to cooking American food for the children. Women's wage earning may lead to a more flexible division of labor, decision-making and parental responsibility, as well as to less sex segregation in social life and public places.

In Hawaii, couples tend to engage in joint family, social and religious activities to a greater extent than they did in Korea. The greater isolation of the nuclear family and the wives wage-earning status account for this change and explain why female immigrants tend to make greater demands on their husbands for joint activities. Another factor is

changed kinship networks, more specifically, women's separation from their mothers and other close female relatives.

On the one hand, since spouses need each other more, they have learned to share and cooperate in ways they would not have learned in Korea. Men whose work shifts were different from those of their wives often cared for children while their wives worked. Husbands were especially likely to help with household chores when their wives worked and when no older child or adult female was available at home. On the other hand, the absence of kin also makes life more difficult because women have no one to depend on for day-to-day child rearing help.

Relations between parents and children are also stress points. Half the women said they disciplined their children, while half said that both parents did so, husbands dealing with older sons and wives with daughters. Many women were unhappy about lack of control over their children as they got older.

> They themselves control their own lives. Do you think they would listen to their old-fashioned immigrant parents?. . . . The only way to control our children in America is by withdrawing material things and money.

Seventeen of 27 women said they were very much concerned about their children being influenced by negative aspects of American youth culture, such as premarital sex (especially for daughters), smoking, drinking and drug use.

Apart from their problems with language and communication, the children of immigrants themselves felt that Hawaii's schools were academically relatively easy compared to Korean schools. All students felt greater freedom and independence after moving to Hawaii.

Women put great stress on their children's education. Children provide future emotional support and financial security for their mothers. While mothers experience racial and sexual discrimination at work, and are often demeaned by it, they enjoy great prestige in the family in their valued role as mothers. Giving birth to sons is still regarded as the most important function of married urban Korean women. Moreover, women whose lives have been devoted to child-bearing feel psychological security and vicarious status achievement through their sons' academic and occupational success (Chai 1978: 46).

However, economic burdens prevent women from giving children the kind of care for which they have immigrated. At the same time, their roles as homemakers and mothers are reinforced by sexual discrimination to severely restrict their employment opportunities. This is a frustrating double bind for many women.

ADAPTIVE STRATEGIES: NETWORKS AND ORGANIZATIONAL PARTICIPATION

Koreans form a highly organized ethnic community in Hawaii, with many overlapping associations that generate and distribute money, labor, jobs, clients and information (Bonacich, Light and Wong 1976: 443). As a group, middle and upper middle class Korean immigrants participate in a variety of organized activities: professional and social associations, Korean ethnic churches, church-sponsored English classes, and Korean language newspapers.

New immigrants often live temporarily with resident relatives until they can find housing. Patterns in Hawaii departed from Korean patterns of living with the husband's family. More new immigrants lived with the wife's kin than the husband's during resettlement. Likewise, the number of women who said they were sending money to their own parents in Korea was greater than those who said they were sending money to their husband's parents. This may be because they earn their own money and do not need to ask their husbands for it.

Eighteen of the women I interviewed attended Korean Protestant churches regularly: one attended the Catholic church and another was a Buddhist. Church and English classes were women's main organized socializing, though some did participate in auxiliary activities of their husbands' alumni, professional or recreational associations. Most women had been members of high school or college alumni associations in Korea. These met at least monthly for lunch and a *kye* meeting. Those with whom immigrant women had most frequent contact were church friends, relatives, co-workers and English-class mates. Indeed, these classes were important sources of companionship and emotional support for these women.

When the women were asked what advice they would give to relatives or friends planning to come to America, one-third said they would advise against it if the person were more well-to-do than average in Korea. The remainder would encourage immigration, provided the person were well-informed and genuinely prepared to face hardships, or if they were young and had skills that were useful in America. Significantly, no one suggested immigrating for the sake of their children's education and their future.

Over half said that they would not have come had they known of the hardships they were to experience. Over half said that their only hope for the future was their children's success. Nevertheless, they were prepared to live independently from their children in old age unless the children wanted their parents to live with them. One-third wanted to return to Korea in their old age to live with their relatives and friends because they saw around them the loss of status, the isolation and the loneliness of the elderly in America.

SUMMARY AND CONCLUSION

Research for this paper began with the premise that particular domains of behavior and institutional arrangements in specific societies must be observed before cross-cultural generalizations about women can be made. I examined the multiple dimensions of middle class, married Korean immigrant women's roles in both the private and public domains of behavior and in specific institutional contexts in order to show women's economic, domestic, social and psychocultural adaptive strategies from the perspectives of the women themselves.

As a family strategy for survival in the new society, and because of a lack of viable alternatives, Korean middle class immigrant women obtain employment in unskilled or semi-skilled service jobs. The decision that these women should work is explained in terms of family survival, since Korean immigrant men are unable to transfer their professional and vocational training and experience to comparable positions in Hawaii.

Korean immigrant women attempt to enter the American labor market in female sales or clerical jobs. Since this channel is open to few immigrant women because of English language and structural barriers, the women create a public world of their own by developing and engaging in family businesses with the cooperation of male and female relatives. They seek small business opportunities where wives and husbands can become their own bosses and work together with their children nearby. Thus they integrate the public and private spheres and enjoy more flexible working hours than they would otherwise in the poorly paid menial jobs that keep them away from home and that require a separation between the workplace and home.

Success in this family strategy establishes a separate ethnic public sphere with its own ladders of achievement and brings immigrant women a certain economic status and some power in the majority culture. This in turn enables their children (who have acquired language skills and American credentials) to achieve social and political status. This is not so different from the situation in Korea, where these women's status would increase as they reared occupationally successful sons, and where mothers lived vicariously in the public sphere through their children's achievement.

In Hawaii, because of the double burden of home and work and the absence of an extended kin network, immigrant women feel that they cannot be effective mothers. Their inadequate English, limited knowledge of American cultures, and their work at degrading jobs have lessened their maternal authority. These may be the major reasons for their psychosomatic symptoms—which actually reaffirm the centrality of motherhood in their lives. Because traditional cultural values emphasize the importance of motherhood—and this is reinforced by low status, low paying jobs—women consider themselves mothers and wives first. They regard their menial jobs as only temporary means of earning supplementary income for their children's education. The goal is still to raise successful children. Despite the fact that they contribute significantly to the economic well-being of the family, their meager earnings and the structural limitations placed on them by American society force their continued dependence on their husbands. Furthermore, because of the structural barriers in the larger society, both husbands and wives are forced to rely on each other and to look to the Korean community for security and support. This study affirms Heidi I. Hartmann's observation that "The conflicts inherent in class and patriarchal society tear people apart, but the dependencies inherent in them can hold people together" (Hartmann 1981: 394).

REFERENCES

Bonacich, Edna, Ivan Light and Charles Choy Wong. 1976. Small Business Among Koreans in Los Angeles. In Emma Gee, ed. *Counterpoint: Perspectives on Asian America*. Los Angeles: Asian American Studies Center, University of California, pp. 437–449.

Chai, Alice. 1978. Korea: Urban Profile. *Impulse* (Honolulu: East-West Center). Winter: 44–46.

———. 1981. Korean Women in Hawaii: 1903–1945. In Hilah F. Thomas and Rosemary Skinner Keller, eds. *Women in New Worlds*. Nashville: Abingdon, pp. 328–344.

Gardner, Robert W. and Paul A. Wright. 1979. Asian Female Immigrants on Oahu, Hawaii. Paper prepared for the Women in the Cities Working Group, 5–23 March, Honolulu, East-West Population Institute.

Hartmann, Heidi I. 1981. The Family as the Locus of Gender, Class, and Political Struggle: The Example of Housework. *Signs*, 6, 3:366–394.

Hawaii, Commission on Manpower and Full Employment, Immigration Services Center. 1977. *Immigration in Hawaii: 1965–1975*. Prepared by Irene D. Makiya.

———— 1978. *Immigrants in Hawaii Fourth Annual Report*.

Kim, Bok-Lim C. 1978. *Asian Americans: Changing Patterns and Changing Needs*. Association of Korean Christian Scholars Series, No. 4. Urbana: AKCS Publication Services.

Kim, Hyung-chan. 1974. Some Aspects of Social Demography of Korean Americans. *International Migration Review*, Spring: 23–42.

————. 1977. Ethnic Enterprises Among Korean Immigrants in America. In Hyung-chan Kim, ed. *The Korean Diaspora*. Santa Barbara: ABC-Clio, Inc., pp. 85–107.

Koo, Hagen and Eui-Young Yu. 1981. Korean Immigration to the United States: Its Demographic Pattern and Social Implications for Both Societies. *Papers of the East-West Population Institute* No. 74. Honolulu: East-West Center Population Institute.

Public and Private Politics: Women in the Middle Eastern World[1]

Cynthia Nelson

THE ETHNOGRAPHIC IMAGE

One of the most commonly held assumptions found in the ethnographic literature discussing the political significance of women in the society at large is that the decisions that women take do not have repercussions on a very wide range of institutions. The general argument is most clearly stated by Mary Douglas:

> The social division of labour involves women less deeply than their menfolk in the central institutions—political, legal, administrative, etc.—of their society. They are indeed subject to control. But the range of controls they experience is simpler, less varied. Mediated through fewer human contacts, their social responsibilities are more confined to the domestic range . . . their social relations certainly carry less

Reproduced by permission of the American Anthropological Association from *American Ethnologist* 1:3, August, 1974. Not for further reproduction.

> weighty pressure than those which are also institutional in range. This is a social condition they share with serfs and slaves. Their place in the public structure of roles is clearly defined in relation to one or two points of reference, say in relation to husbands and fathers. As for the rest of their social life, it takes place at the relatively unstructured interpersonal level, with other women. . . . Of course I would be wrong to say that the network of relations a woman has with others of her sex is unstructured. A delicate patterning certainly prevails. But its significance for society at large is *less than the significance of men's relations with one another in the public role system* (1970:84).

Nowhere is this assumption more uncritically taken for granted than in the ethnographic descriptions of pastoral and sedentary societies in the Middle East in which the assertion is made that there are dual and separate worlds of men and women in which the former world is public and the latter world is private. Typical of such assertions is the following:

The women's world is not merely more narrowly circumscribed like in most civilizations; it is also provided with a complicated system of devices for cushioning off: i.e., safeguards which provide limited access to each other's worlds. The women's world has two major manifestations: *the home* (tent) and *the private communication patterns between women of several homes.* For men there is limited access to the former and practically no access to the latter and this is paralleled by lack of interest by the men about the women's world. . . . The men's world has two major manifestations: *the sphere of earning a living and the public sphere of communications including public affairs.* Access of women to the former is limited and formally none in the latter — old grandmothers being an exception. But women are keenly interested in male affairs!!! No doubt that the two worlds have their regular meeting point in the home, for this is where a good deal of clearing goes on continuously (van Nieuwenhuijze 1965:71).

Inherent in this statement as well as most other discussions on sex roles found in the ethnographies of the Middle East, and particularly those centering on nomadic societies, is not only the commonplace notion that the human universe is segregated into two social worlds marked out by the nature of the two sexes, but also that these two social worlds are by definition characterized as being *private* (the women's) and *public* (the men's) (Asad 1970; Barth 1961; Cole 1971; Cunnison 1966; Marx 1967; Pehrson 1966; Peters 1966). The former world is invariably described as domestic, narrow, and restricted, whereas the latter is described as political, broad, and expansive. Authority is also segregated in terms of this dichotomy. The home is regarded as the woman's for all *internal purposes.* Her authority in domestic affairs is an established fact. For *external purposes,* the home is the man's, the assumption being that whatever articulates the household to the public sphere is by definition political and thereby a male concern. And the inference drawn from this assumption is that women are far more interested in men's affairs than vice versa.

Also inherent in the ethnographic accounts of these two social worlds is the notion that what is the concern of women is the domestic and not the political. This raises the whole question of the meaning of "power" and "the political" and why this should be linked to such notions as "private (domestic)" and "public (political)." By assigning private and public to the different social worlds of men and women described for certain Middle Eastern societies, I would argue that western social scientists have imposed their own cultural categories onto the experiential world of the Middle East and that the whole discussion of "power" in these societies is influenced by these categorizations.

Most anthropologists working in the Middle East tend to view power in the classic functionalist tradition. Following Radcliffe-Brown, they define the political system as the maintenance or establishment of social order within a territorial framework by the organized exercise of coercive authority through the use or possibility of use of physical force.

Barth, for example, explores the kinds of relationships that are established between persons (only males as it turns out) among the Swat Pathans and the way in which these may be systematically manipulated to build up positions of authority and the variety of political groups. The main sources of authority/power available to persons are ownership of land, the provision of hospitality, and a reputation for honor. Most statuses and rights are usually defined by contractual agreements between persons. In these circumstances, each man's aim may be seen as the adoption of the strategy that will best serve his interest. "Physical force or the threat of it is in Swat a characteristic sanction in a great many relations" (Barth 1959:53). Barth sees Swat Pathans as being driven by self-aggrandizing passion and maximizing rationale and represents the political activity of the dominant land-owning class as the foundation of social order. As Asad has so cogently pointed out, Barth's model is an anarchic, conflict-ridden, violent society which reflects Barth's Hobbesian model of human nature (Asad 1972:74–94).

Criticizing the functionalist position, Asad argues for a distinction between power and authority. For Asad, power refers to the relation between agent and an object as a means, that is, to the opposition of exploiter and exploited, whereas authority refers to the subordination of human consciousness to a legitimate rule (and contingently to those who determine the rule) (Asad 1972:86). Asad sees the problem of political domination in terms of a dialectical relationship and raises an important alternative in terms of the way ethnographers tend to look at political systems. But he, too, tends to view power and authority as the exclusive concern of men. "The overall authority of the household head is based on the fact that he has greater power and moral responsibility than any other member of the household" (Asad 1970:100–101).

Given the fact that most ethnographers of the Middle East have been European or American males who, by virtue of their foreignness and maleness, have had limited if no access to the social world of women, we seem to be confronted with the normative image of the society as reported to male ethnographers by male informants.[2] Lienhardt expresses this dilemma cogently:

> And though the segregation of women from men not closely related to them is one of the things that must at once meet the eye of any visitor to the towns and villages of the Trucial Coast, this segregation makes it difficult for a visitor to gain any precise knowledge of the women's position. Apart from its being difficult for a man to talk to women there, it is not even proper for him to ask very much about them, particularly to ask in any detail about specific cases . . . one can easily be misled, particularly in assessing the extent of male dominance (1972:220).

From the ethnographic literature, we know precious little about how women in these societies view their situation, whether they feel they have "power" and how they wield it. If we had better knowledge of the "lived-in-world" of nomadic women, we might come up with different images of the society and the definitions of power. Also, we might ask what could the contributions to our knowledge and un-

derstanding of the relationship of women and power be, if we were to re-think the notions of "power" and recognize its special feature as a particular kind of social relation rather than as an embodied quality institutionalized in types of social structures. Some social scientists have argued along the following lines:

> The initial problem of defining social power is to recognize its special features as a particular kind of social relation, as reciprocity of influence. *Reciprocity of influence*—the defining criterion of the social itself—is never entirely destroyed in power relations, except physical violence when one treats another as object. We cannot sever power relations from their roots in social interaction. One actor controls the other with respect to particular situations and spheres of conduct—or scopes—while the other actor is regularly dominant in other areas of situated conduct (Wrong n.d.).

Olesen has suggested in an unpublished paper that the concept of "the negotiated order" is a useful idea for understanding reciprocity of influence in interactive situations (Olesen 1973). Persons in an interactive situation, she argues, negotiate the rules that define and circumscribe that relationship.

Assuming that men and women are involved in "negotiating their social order"—i.e., the rules and roles of social interaction—we must not lose sight of the fact that social action is always "situated action" and circumscribed by culturally given constructs of social reality, the social stock of knowledge at hand, as Schutz would say (1962:120–134). What becomes relevant for the purposes of our discussion is to recognize that despite the existence of segregated social worlds and the implication that there exists a differential distribution of social knowledge—the man's and the woman's—this knowledge is structured in terms of relevances, and women's relevance structures intersect with those of men at many points. Applying this to the ethnographic situation, we must ask how women can and do influence men to achieve their own objectives. The notion of power implied in the concept of the negotiated order is the potential for levying sanctions, the potential for influencing further actions of others (as well as one's own). Sanctions are not just threats of physical force but capacities for influencing the behavior (action) of others. They are ways of creating possible lines of action for others as well as for oneself.

Looking at power from this perspective, we are forced to raise a different set of ethnographic questions, questions that have been neglected perhaps due to not recognizing the ongoing dialectical process of social life in which both men and women are involved in a reciprocity of influence *vis-à-vis* each other. What are the normative constructs that facilitate, limit, and govern "negotiation"? What are the sanctions open to women? In what ways can and do women set up alternatives for men by their own action? How do women influence men? Who controls whom about what? How is control exercised? How do women control men? Other women? How conscious are women of their capacity to influence? In other words, what are women doing in this reciprocity?

In the remainder of this essay I would like to challenge the notion that the social worlds of men and women, despite the element of segregation, are reducible to spheres of private and public with power limited to males in a so-called public arena. By using data from ethnographic studies by both men and women concerning women in the Middle East, I shall suggest that women can and do exercise a greater degree of power in spheres of social life than has heretofore been appreciated.

THE ETHNOGRAPHIC EVIDENCE

The detailed and scholarly work of Ilse Lichtenstädter (1935) on *Women in the Aiyam Al-'Arab* offers an interesting analysis of the role that the Arabic women played in the warfare of her tribe and thus presents us with a view of the life and position of women in pre-Islamic Arabia.[3] Although the material deals with nomadic society during the

Jahiliya, it is still informative about the manner in which women were depicted in everyday life and how they exercised political influence in the man's world.

According to the Aiyam narratives, the women's influence was felt beyond the tent. Through marriage she played an important role in Arab policy by being the link and mediator through which powerful alliances between tribes were accomplished. As matron she acted as counsellor to her son who very often submitted to the advice of his mother and, whenever it was possible, she tried to gain influence over her son in order to bring an enmity to an end. Lichtenstädter points out:

> That Fatima bint al-Khurshub tried, though unsuccessfully, to mediate between her son and Qais b. Zuhari shows that she could be sure that her opinion would at least be heard. In this case, however, the son did not accept his mother's advice; the events proved that she was right (1935:65).

In warfare the woman very often was the cause of quarrels and great feuds. She was also employed as a spy and, if captured in war, was the source of great ransoms. As the women were not far from the spot where the battle took place, they were able to watch the bustle of the fight and incite their men by acclamations. When in the greatest distress and danger, the Arabs had recourse to a device which was meant to excite their desire of fighting to the highest degree: they exposed their women, particularly noble women, to danger by forcing them to fall from their camels and litters in order to show the warriors that they must fight or die (Lichtenstädter 1935:43).

In summarizing her analysis, Lichtenstädter suggests that pre-Islamic nomadic society was a society that treated women with esteem and one in which they were allowed to take part in public life. "From the Aiyam tales pre-Islamic Arab women played a part in the life of their tribe and exercised an influence which they lost only later in the development of Islamic society" (1935:81). "But as during the time of Jahiliya women were *not* separated from men but lived in close intercourse with them they could readily get to know their plans and projects" (1935:83). "In addition the conditions of life were such that in times of distress clever advice was eagerly accepted and followed regardless whence it came, even if offered by a woman. In this sense we are justified in speaking of the 'influence' of a woman without exaggerating her importance in the public life of an Arab tribe" (1935:85).

Emrys Peters also describes the manner in which women can and do exercise influence over men in pastoral societies, for example, as mediators between natal and affinal groups in marriage alliances, as controllers of the products or the property, and as wielders of authority in the domestic sphere.

> *The pivotal points in any field of power* in this, a superficially dominant patrilineal, patrilocal and patriarchal society where the male ethos is vulgar in its brash prominence, *are the women.* What holds men together, what knots the cords of alliances are not men themselves, but the women who depart from their natal household to take up residence elsewhere with a man, and who, in this critical position communicate one group to another (Peters 1966:15).

Among the Bedouin of Cyrenaica men may boast of their dominance over women (and certainly this might be expected with male informants channeling information to male ethnographers), but they are constrained in their actions by the control women possess over the preparation of food, the provision of hospitality, the comforts of shelter, and the reputation for honor. Men may control the economic resources—land, water, animals—the durable properties, but women control the products. Utilization of the products, the dividends of their investments, are granted to women, and through these they acquire legal rights in men. Bereft of controlling rights in property, women are nevertheless critical in its manipulation. They possess the legal right to protection and support against husband as daughter or sister of the

man who holds the bridewealth. Women mediate between the two, make demands on the men as a right, and are given public support (Peters 1966; Mohsen 1967).

Marx makes the same point about Bedouin of Negev—that women in multiplex role situations increase their potential for negotiation:

> A marriage link acts as a very effective communicative device between groups because the woman who conveys the communications is so intimately bound up with both her husband and sons and with her father and brothers. She has the interest of both groups at heart and would suffer most from an estrangement between the two groups. At the same time she is on the inside of both groups and *thus able to assert her influence over the sections* through the men to whom she is closely connected, as well as through women (1967:157).

Cunnison, while arguing that women occupy no formal position of power or authority among the Baggara Arabs, does suggest that:

> Women have a profound influence on politics in two respects. Firstly, they are arbiters of men's conduct, and they can make or break a man's political career. They do this by singing songs of praise or alternatively of mockery. The brave man and the cowardly man have their fame spread. The man who is undistinguished in either direction goes unsung. The songs sweep the country, and the reputations are made and broken by them. Secondly, a policy decision that the men of a camp or a *surra* (kin group) make is influenced by the kind of reactions that the women of the group are likely to have (1966:117).

In these respects, at least for the Baggara, women have a significance in the public *role* system of the society. Cunnison also points out that the Baggara ideas about the value of manliness involve the closely related aims of wealth, women, and power.

> Cattle attract women and allow a man to marry more than one wife. The possession of cattle plays an important part in the relations of men and women. It implies that a man is endowed

with those qualities that Baggara men and women alike regard as most admirable. Herd building means easier access to women who play a positive part in spreading a man's virtue or challenging man's honour. Although there is often argument about amount of bridewealth to be paid, debate is not between two families; instead the men of both families agree and unite in argument to try to beat down the price. The bride's mother backed by the women of the family is demanding. Final word is that of the bride's mother. She can try to stop a marriage that she or her daughter don't want by refusing to lower the price. "Let us chase him off with our demands" (1966:116).

The Pehrsons in their study of the Marri Baluch describe the strategies used by women to achieve influence over men: (1) playing men off against each other; (2) seeking alliance and support from other women; and (3) minimizing contact with the husbands (1966:59).

In another monograph on *La Femme Chaouia de L'Aures* (1929), Gaudry draws our attention to the *power* that women can exert over men in their capacity as saints, sorceresses, magicians, and healers. The Auresian woman has, like the man, the cult of *mzara*, places sanctified by the passage of a saint, and the woman, just as the man, affiliates herself to religious organization. Gaudry describes a female Marabout, Turkeyya:

> There existed a Marabout of great virtue named Turkeyya who was most pious and exerted a great influence on her many clients and adepts. There was also a male Marabout, Sidi Moussa, seeing that his authority had diminished with a number of his followers felt peeved. He decided to put an end to this competition with his dangerous rival and he devised a simple plan to get rid of her. He appealed to one of his devouts and entrusted him to kidnap Turkeyya and marry her. As a Marabout can only enter into a family of Marabout she lost, from this mis-marriage, *all the authority she had* (1929:235).

Sorcery is another means by which women can be said to exert their influence over males in Chaouia society, and as a sorceress woman has more power over the man than as a saint because of her ability to divine the future, enhance love, deter evil, and heal illness. According to Gaudry:

> It can be said that the superstitious fear of the women which filled the Berber mind allowed the women to *impose an inferior religion of which they are the priestesses* which is a response to a collective need (1929:246).

All old women are more or less sorcerers, learning their craft from their mothers. They teach women to prepare lotions which can "tame any man." Men fear them, and some forbid their wives to receive them. A sorceress has power over the male through the women. Says a male Chaouia proverb:

> The child of male sex comes to the world with 60 *jnoun* in his body; the child of the female sex is born pure; but every year, the boy gets purified of a jinn, whereas the girl acquires one; and this is the reason that old women, 60 years and with 60 *jnoun* are sorcerers more malignant than the devil himself. Blind she sews more material, lame she jumps over rocks and deaf she knows all the news (Gaudry 1929:267).

Gaudry's work raises a fundamental issue that has *not* been the focus of much recent ethnographic field research among Middle Eastern societies; that is, the degree to which men perceive women exercising power over them through the idiom of the supernatural. Crapanzano's recent work on the Hamadsha in Morocco, however, is suggestive of the powerful significance of the "camel-footed she-demon, A'isha Qandisha" on men in the curing rituals (1972:327–348).

> Should one of A'isha's followers disobey her, he is immediately struck and suffers grave misfortune or bodily harm. The Hamadsha, her special devotees, are said to be favored by A'isha and are very proud of the intimacy of their relations with her (1972:333).

It must be noted that both Gaudry's and Crapanzano's work was conducted among Islamicized Berber cultures of North Africa among whom saint cult worship is predominant (Gellner 1969; Geertz 1968). Nevertheless, both ethnographers underscore the fear and veneration expressed by men toward these female supernatural figures and suggest lines of inquiry for further investigation. The paucity of ethnographic description surrounding the relationship of women to the religious system, in general, and the supernatural, in particular, suggests more a lack of interest on the part of ethnographers than it does a lack of concern on the part of the actors in Middle Eastern Islamic societies. This does not seem to be the case when we look at studies of women in societies of sub-Saharan Africa (Lebeuf 1971; Hofer 1972). Perhaps if we were to turn to the more recent ethnographic studies focusing specifically on women in pastoral and sedentary societies of the Middle East, we might discover evidence that suggests women do exercise control in society in a variety of ways.[4]

Farrag, in her study of social control among the Mzabite women, demonstrates convincingly how moral, social, and religious control is exercised over women by women through a specific all-female religious institution called the Azzabat. Both men and women have a very important stake in the conduct of their women in that there is a firm belief that god's anger befalls the whole community as a result of any sexual misconduct on the part of women.[5] Because of the frequent and prolonged absence of the men in the community for purposes of trade, the women have assumed an increasing importance in the mechanisms of social control over women.

> Although social changes since independence have also affected the power of the Azzabat, they still exercise a far stricter control over the women than the Ozzaba (male religious group) do over the men (Farrag 1971:318).

Yet, at the same time, increasing demands are now being made by the men for the "modernization" of the women, thus creating a situation in which certain inconsistencies and ambivalences are created. The thrust of Farrag's argument is to show how breaches of

certain norms are still effectively and formally sanctioned through all-female religious institutions coupled by informal sanctions of the power of mothers-in-law, public opinion, and gossip, regardless of social status. The implications of Farrag's article to the main thesis of this paper are obvious. Instead of an image of segregated social worlds of men and women, in which women are relegated to the private domestic sphere, we find all-female institutions responsible for the sanctioning of breaches of social norms—certainly a most public concern.

Approaching her study of women from the perspective of social stratification, Vanessa Maher, in a recent study among townswomen in the Middle Atlas of Morocco, makes an exhaustive analysis of the social mechanisms, both political and ideological, by which women are confined to the traditional status-based mode of social relationship "where women are not working for wages because participation in the public sphere of the market is considered immoral" (1972:15). Given this segregation of men's and women's roles, the dependence of women on women becomes all the more necessary, especially in late pregnancy and early childbirth. These feminine links of cooperation that form are independent of those formed by the male's kindred of cooperation and operate to redress the balance of power between men and women. Maher argues that the market principles and prerogatives of kinship and status struggle for hegemony with the result that there is a structural conflict between the social necessities of marriage and the superior rewards of kinship (status-based relations), especially for women. The chief locus of conflict is marriage, and Maher argues that lacking political control over their own lives and lacking religious worth as second-rate Moslems, women are forced to turn to intrigue and witchcraft—weapons used in the power struggle between men and their wives.

Nancy Tapper (1968) explores this theme in more depth in her study of a women's sub-society among the pastoral Shahsavans in Iran. In this women's sub-society she describes how women establish among themselves a range of relationships in which *women may gain achieved status in the community* as midwives, ceremonial cooks, and religious leaders.

> In each *tira* (clan or family group) . . . were one or two women held to be knowledgeable on religious matters. Commonly, they are women who, with a male relative, have made the pilgrimage to the shrine of Imam Reza at Mashhad and are thereafter referred to by the title of *Mashadi*. In fact the position of Mashadis among women is comparable to that of a Hajji among men. The Mashadis are among the few women who pray regularly; their position is a highly conservative one and they firmly support traditional Shahsavan customs and moral attitudes, sometimes by reference to imaginary Koranic injunctions. The opinions of such a woman in matters of family law and custom are sought by both men and women and her advice is given equal weight with that of a man (Tapper 1968:17).

Al-Torki, in her pioneering study of townwomen in Jeddah, Saudi Arabia (1973a), postulates that in societies where the segregation of women prevents their participation in public affairs, elaborate networks of friendship and gift-exchange will be found. These networks are likely to enable the participants to gather vital information, which gives them considerable informal control over decisions that are nominally the exclusive prerogative of males. In Jeddah the women exercise considerable control over marriage alliances.

> This control has far-reaching consequences in a society where kinship dominates as a structural principle in local and national politics. Obviously, their influence must derive from a different source of power than control of resources. I suggest that the women's eminent control of information in matters relating to the arrangement of marriage constitutes this source. The very nature of the women's exchange networks gives them an almost exclusive access to information on which the decisions of their male relatives depend. By manipulating their knowledge to accommodate their own interests in potential marriages, the women actually manage to direct or impede the men's efforts to establish marriage alliances (1973b:5).

Lienhardt (1972) underscores this proposition in his description of marriage and the position of women in Trucial Coast society. Since shaikhs, great and small, are political personages, their marriages have a much clearer political dimension than the marriages of other people. Here some women achieve remarkable influence and power. Lienhardt suggests that the marriage of shaikhs with Bedouin women may be one of the reasons why the women of shaikhly families in general seem to lead a less secluded life than most others. When they are women of strong character, the senior women of ruling families can play an important part in affairs. One remarkable woman of the Trucial Coast, Shaikha Hussah bint al-Murr, the mother of the present ruler of Dubai and wife of his predecessor, came so far out into open public affairs as to hold her own *majlis* ('public meeting'), not for women but for men, sitting receiving visitors, as people said, like a shaikh, and when her husband ruled it is said that more men visited her *majlis* than visited his. This remarkable lady was an outstanding figure in both politics and business. On the one hand, she played a leading part in a political struggle that led to civil war and the subsequent expulsion of the reformist party. On the other, she restored her husband's family fortunes by property development, trade, and, one gathers, that profitable but risky enterprise of Dubai, smuggling with Persia and India (1972:229–230).

This may be an extreme example of the potential importance of leading women in public affairs; however, it suggests that we must re-evaluate the metaphors of private and public in terms of domestic and political. What Lienhardt's and the other ethnographic material suggest is that women do approach public affairs but they do so from private positions. In public, women are separated from men, and men mix widely in the public circle of the market. The women, on the other hand, mix in a large number of smaller groups, more exclusive than the society of men and consisting largely of closer and more distant kin affines, and other women who are friends of the women of the family, e.g., *azzabat*, female sub-societies, and kindred of cooperation as discussed above. In the societies we have been discussing, families are one of the basic groupings in its economic and political, as well as its moral aspects. Here, in some senses, the range of women is greater than that of men, and it is the very segregation of women and the impropriety of discussing them in male company that makes this so. Women, in general, are a necessary part of the network of communications that provides information for their menfolk, and at the head of the social hierarchy are some women who form a focus for the smaller groupings of women and a bridge between their concerns and the public concerns of men.

Once we begin to examine the role and position of women in Middle Eastern society from the standpoint of the woman and to describe the woman's view of the social worlds in which she lives and interacts, it becomes clear that our ethnographic imagery about domestic spheres being private and female and public spheres being political and male is misleading. This is not to argue that only women can understand or do ethnography about women, but only to suggest that by taking the standpoint of the woman, by examining her taken-for-granted assumptions about her social worlds, we discover another image of power and influence operative in society. I take the position that to place oneself imaginatively into the inner self of another (including a set of interacting "others" of which the ethnographer is one) is not only necessary, but it is the very foundation of social life (Berger and Luckman 1967; Schutz 1962; Mills 1967). Also, by re-evaluating the notion of power from the standpoint of reciprocity of influence, we can specify ethnographically those particular situations in which women can and do exercise influence over men. Based on the evidence presented, what are these situations?

One dominant theme repeated throughout the ethnographies is the crucial role women play as structural links between kinship groups in societies where family and kinship are the fundamental institutions of everyday life. Simultaneously the woman as daughter, sister, wife, and mother acts as an "information-broker," mediating social relations within the family and larger society. The implications for power (reciprocity of influence) are obvious in that by these networks of relationships, the woman is in a position to channel or withhold information to the male members of the kindred. And in this position the woman influences decision-making about alliances, actually sets up marriage relations, and informs male members of the household what is going on in other homes. But of course the "home" in question is not that of a tiny nuclear family, but of a wider family group. And this family group is one upon which many of the affairs of the society—social, economic, political—turn.

The ethnographies do support the idea of segregated social worlds but rather than seeing this as a severe limitation on women, the evidence suggests that the segregation of women can alternatively be seen as an exclusion of men from a range of contacts which women have among themselves. This emphasizes a second major theme emerging from our data, particularly from sources on women written by women, and that is that women form their own exclusive solidarity groups and that these groups exercise considerable social control (Farrag 1971; Maher 1972). Also, by seeking alliance and support from other women in the community, certain women achieve high social status in the community and consequently exercise political influence (Aswad 1967; Tapper 1968).

From the ethnographic data summarized above it is evident that women *do* participate in public activities, activities which have their reverberations and intentions in large-scale societal networks.

A third realm in which women emerge as having influence over men is through the religious or supernatural. That is, in those situations where women are publicly acknowledged as having power, it is associated with the supernatural and the fear that men have of women's sexuality or, better expressed, as the felt threat to male esteem of women's sexual misconduct. Through witchcraft, sorcery, divination, and curing, women are instrumental in influencing the lives of men.

A final point to be mentioned is the degree to which the public image of a man is influenced by the particular behavior of his women—through ridiculing, through gossip, through honor and shame (Schneider 1971; Cunnison 1966).

IMPLICATIONS FOR ETHNOGRAPHY

The main thrust of this essay has been to challenge the prevalent ethnographic image of the position of women in selected pastoral and sedentary societies of the Middle East. Specifically, it has addressed itself to the question: In what sense can we speak of women exercising power in those societies which are avowedly patrilineal, patrilocal, and patriarchal? This raised the whole issue of the conception of power as viewed by Western ethnographers in their writings about Middle Eastern society—a view that defines the sphere of masculine activity as the public—in the Greek *polis* sense, and the sphere of feminine activity as the private and domestic. What becomes defined as the public and private spheres, however, are less the categorizations of the world by the actors living in these societies than they are the metaphors of the observers who are recording the actions of men and women in these societies.[6]

The fundamental implication for ethnography emerging from this essay rests on the following question: What are the kinds of data generated in a field situation in which accessibility to the social worlds of men and women is predicated primarily on the sex role of the observer? As sex roles circumscribe the way the actors interact with each other in society, it is of fundamental importance to realize that sex roles also circumscribe the way in which actor and ethnographer interact with each other. The sex-linked aspect of social interaction places the actor and ethnographer in situations of communication in which the so-called "raw data" of ethnography are the very

products of this communication. In other words, it is the interactive situation itself which produces (or generates) the data from which ethnographies are written. An awareness of this phenomenon suggests to me a quite different strategy of fieldwork than has hitherto been expressed in the ethnography of the Middle East, particularly on the important question of the position of women. What I would suggest is that we, as ethnographers, become more imaginative in the creation of our models of the activities, norms, and interpersonal linkages that make up a society's political processes. My descriptions of women as information brokers, as reputation builders and maintainers, as "power" of their own, all concern a better filling in of all the links. We must get away from the simplistic, mechanical models (either those implicit ones of the ethnographers—such as Barth's Hobbesian view of politics—or the official ones of the informants). We must become conscious that our data are not "gathered" but manufactured and grounded in the interactive foundations of the research process itself. Not being conscious of this phenomenon has led to an ethnographic image of women and power in the Middle East that is both incomplete and misleading.[7] We must ask ourselves how do we come to understand the world of the opposite sex? And as ethnographers, what are the criteria by which we have selected data to record the "true image" of society?

For most ethnographers of the Middle East, there exists an implicit assumption that "reality," the data, exist "out there" waiting to be described and that it matters little what the social position of the informant is since "as a bearer of the culture" he (or she) is as informed as anyone else. Unfortunately, this view overlooks one of the most critical problems in fieldwork—the importance of the social distribution of knowledge (Berger and Luckman 1967; Mannheim 1936; Schutz 1962). It also denies the relevance of the interactive situation as the source of our knowledge about the society and the implications of these shortcomings have been the focus of this paper.

On the one hand, I have pointed out that when we examine the literature of the Middle East on women done by women, our ethnographic image of women and power is considerably different from that of the male ethnographers. On the other hand, when I examined the literature of the male ethnographers, I discovered hints that the women in these societies are not as powerless as the ethnographer themselves had concluded. In other words, there exists internal evidence that our images are incomplete, that the dynamics of power and authority are much more subtle than we have been led to believe, and that our theoretical perspectives about the position of women in Middle Eastern society must be the common-sense world of the actors themselves.

NOTES

1. This is a much revised version of an earlier paper delivered at a symposium on nomadic-sedentary interaction in Middle Eastern societies held at the American University in Cairo, March 17–21, 1972 (Nelson 1973). The emergence of the present paper, however, is in large part due to the many stimulating and provocative discussions while on sabbatical at the Institute of International Studies, 1973–1974, with colleagues at the University of California, May N. Diaz, Lucile Newman, Elvi Whittaker, and, particularly, Virginia L. Olesen, whose incisive and critical comments forced me to sharpen my own ideas considerably. To Hildred Geertz, a note of appreciation for suggesting a closer link between the central argument of the paper and its title.

2. The argument might be made that women share the man's construction of the social world, but this seems to me more of an implicit taken-for-granted assumption than an ethnographic fact. Until we know that this is the case, based on ethnographic evidence emerging from studies of women's views about their social world, we are making generalizations from information channeled from male informants to ethnographers.

3. Although Lichtenstädter's analysis is drawn from written materials rather than from personal observations, her insights are suggestive of themes emerging from more recent ethnographic studies (Lienhardt 1972). Dr. Abdou (personal communication) of the University of Riyadh drew my attention to the fact that the Prophet Mohammed worked for a female merchant whom he later married—Khadidja. He commented that "generally speaking the Bedouin women of Saudi Arabia participate more as men in society than do their urban counterparts." Abdou attributes this to the greater Turkish influence on the seclusion of women in the urban centers. He also noted that in the Saudi Arabian town of Tadmur there are special women's markets where only women are sellers. This phenomenon is also recorded among the Berbers of the High Atlas and Rif Mountains of Morocco (Benet 1970:182, 193; Hart 1970:38).

4. Evidence that my generalizations about women and power in Arab society also held true for Arabicized Berbers in North Africa is found in several recent published and unpublished manuscripts (Alport 1970; Benet 1970; Hart 1970; Murphy 1970; Mason 1973; Joseph 1973). Subsequent to the submission of this essay, a useful exploration of this topic among pastoral nomads in the Sudan came to my attention. I wish to thank Elinor Kelly of the University of Manchester for generously sharing with me her unpublished thesis from the University of London.

5. Supporting this image of women from yet another part of Moslem Africa is the following excerpt from an *Agence France-Presse* news item quoted in the June 23, 1973 issue of the *San Francisco Chronicle:*

   Kano, Nigeria—Single women are being ordered to get married immediately or leave Northern Nigeria because religious authorities here say that the current drought in West Africa is caused by prostitution and immorality. . . . Many unmarried women are reported to have fled their homes following the get-married-or-leave order by the Emirs in the Moslem area. Landlords have been ordered not to let out rooms to single women since, according to one Emir, "because of prostitution there has been no rain."

6. One historian of the Middle East has suggested that among nomads there is no equivalent Arabic term for the concept "public"

arena. The tent and the camp are not synonyms for public and private (Dols, personal communication).

7. The recent exchange between Abou Zahra (1970) and Antoun (1968) on the meaning of the modesty code in the Middle East is an excellent example of conflicting ethnographic images.

REFERENCES CITED

Abou-Zahra, Nadia. 1979. On Modesty of Women in Arab Muslim Villages: A Reply. American Anthropologist 72(5):1079–1088.

Alport, E. A. 1970. The Mzab. *In* Peoples and Cultures of the Middle East, Vol. II. L. Sweet, Ed. New York: The Natural History Press, pp. 225–241.

Al-Torki, Soraya. 1973a. Religion and Social Organization of Elite Families in Urban Saudi Arabia. Unpublished Ph.D. dissertation. University of California, Berkeley.

———. 1973b. Men-Women Relationship in Arab Societies: A Study of the Economic and Political Conditions of the Status of Women. Unpublished research proposal.

Antoun, Richard. 1968. On the Modesty of Women in Arab Muslim Villages: A Study in the Accommodation of Traditions. American Anthropologist 70(1):671–697.

Asad, Talal. 1970. The Kababish Arabs: Power, Authority and Consent in a Nomadic Tribe. London: C. Hurst.

———. 1972. Market Model, Class Structure and Consent. Man 7(1):74–94.

Aswad, Barbara. 1967. Key and Peripheral Roles of Noble Women in a Middle East Plains Village. Anthropological Quarterly 40(3):139–153.

Barth, Fredrik. 1959. Political Leadership among Swat Pathans. London School of Economics Monographs on Social Anthropology, 19. London.

———. 1961. Nomads of South Persia: Basseri Tribe of the Khameseh Confederacy. Boston: Little, Brown.

Benet, Francisco. 1970. Explosive Markets: The Berber Highlands. *In* Peoples and Cultures of the Middle East, Vol. I. Louise Sweet, Ed. New York: The Natural History Press, pp. 173–203.

Berger, Peter, and T. Luckman. 1967. The Social Construction of Reality. New York: Doubleday (Center Book).

Bujra, Abdullah. 1966. The Relationship between the Sexes amongst the Bedouin in a Town. Unpublished paper delivered at the Mediterranean Social Science Conference, Athens.

Cole, Donald. 1971. Social and Economic Structure of the Al Murrah: A Saudi Arabian Bedouin Tribe. Unpublished Ph.D. dissertation. University of California, Berkeley.

Crapanzano, Vincent. 1972. The Hamadsha. *In* Scholars, Saints and Sufis: Muslims Religious Institutions Since 1500. Nikki R. Keddie, Ed. Berkeley: University of California Press, pp. 327–348.

Cunnison, Ian. 1966. The Baggara Arabs: Power and Lineage in a Sudanese Nomad Tribe. Oxford: Clarendon Press.

Douglas, Mary. 1970. Natural Symbols: Explorations in Cosmology. New York: Random House (Pantheon).

Evans-Pritchard, E. E. 1971. The Senusi of Cyrenaica. Oxford: Clarendon Press.

Farrag, Amina. 1971. Social Control amongst the Mzabite Women of Beni-Isguen. Middle Eastern Studies, Winter (3):317–327.

Gaudry, Mathea. 1929. La Femme Chaouia de L'Aures. Paris: Geuthner.

Geertz, Clifford. 1968. Islam Observed. New Haven, CT: Yale University Press.

Gellner, Ernest. 1969. Saints of the Atlas. Chicago: University of Chicago Press.

Hart, David M. 1970. Clan, Lineage, Local Community and the Feud in a Rifian Tribe. *In* Peoples and Cultures of Middle East, Vol. II. Louise Sweet, Ed. New York: The Natural History Press, pp. 3–75.

Hofer, Carol. 1972. Mende and Sherbro Women in High Office. Canadian Journal of African Studies 6(2):151–164.

Joseph, Roger. 1973. Choix ou Force: Une Etude sur la Manipulation Sociale. Unpublished manuscript.

Lebeuf, Annie. 1971. The Role of Women in the Political Organization of African Societies. In Women of Tropical Africa. Denise Paulme, Ed. Berkeley: University of California Press, pp. 93–119.

Lichtenstädter, Ilse. 1935. Women in Aiyam al-Arab. London: The Royal Asiatic Society.

Lienhardt, Peter A. 1972. Some Social Aspects of the Trucial States. *In* The Arabian Peninsula: Society and Politics. D. Hopwood, Ed. London: Allen and Unwin, pp. 219–229.

Maher, Vanessa. 1972. Social Stratification and the Role of Women in the Middle Atlas of Morocco.

Unpublished Ph.D. dissertation. Cambridge University.

Mannheim, Karl. 1936. Ideology and Utopia. New York: Harcourt, Brace (Harvest Books.)

Marx, Emmanuel. 1967. Bedouin of the Negev. New York: Praeger.

Mason, John. n.d. Sex and Symbol in a Libyan Oasis. Unpublished manuscript.

Mohsen, Safia. 1967. Legal Status of Women among the Awlad Ali. Anthropological Quarterly 40(3):153–166.

Mills, C. W. 1967. Situated Actions and the Vocabulary of Motives. *In* Power Politics and People. Oxford: Oxford University Press, pp. 439–452.

Murphy, Robert F. 1970. Social Distance and the Veil. *In* Peoples and Cultures of the Middle East, Vol. I. Louise Sweet, Ed. New York: The Natural History Press, pp. 290–314.

Nelson, Cynthia. 1973. Women and Power in Nomadic Societies of the Middle East. *In* The Desert and the Town Nomads in the Greater Society. Cynthia Nelson, Ed. Berkeley: Institute of International Studies, University of California, pp. 43–59.

Nieuwenhuijze, C. A. O. van. 1965. Social Stratification in the Middle East. The Hague: E. J. Brill.

Olesen, Virginia L. 1973. Notes on the Negotiation of Rules and Roles in Fieldwork Studies. Unpublished manuscript. San Francisco: Department of Social and Behavioral Sciences, University of California.

Pehrson, Robert. 1966. The Social Organization of the Marri Baluch. Viking Fund Publications in Anthropology, 53. New York.

Peters, Emrys. 1966. Consequences of the Segregation of the Sexes among the Arabs. Unpublished paper delivered at the Mediterranean Social Science Council Conference, Athens.

Rosenfeld, Henry. 1968. The Contradictions between Property, Kinship, and Power as Reflected in the Marriage System of an Arab Village. *In* Contributions to Mediterranean Sociology. J. Peristiany, Ed. The Hague: Mouton, pp. 247–260.

San Francisco Chronicle. June 23, 1973.

Schneider, Jane. 1971. Honor, Shame and Access to Resources in Mediterranean Societies. Ethnology 10(1):1–24.

Schutz, Alfred. 1962. Collected Papers, Vol. II: The Problem of Social Reality. The Hague: Martinus Nijhof.

Sweet, Louise. 1970. Peoples and Cultures of the Middle East, Vols. 1 & 2. New York: The Natural History Press.

Tapper, Nancy. 1968. The Role of Women in Selected Pastoral Islamic Society. Unpublished M. A. thesis. S.O.A.S. London.

Wrong, Dennis H. n.d. Some Problems in Defining Social Power. Unpublished manuscript.

IV.

The Cultural Construction of Gender and Personhood

We all live in a world of symbols that assign meaning and value to the categories of male and female. Despite several decades of consciousness raising in the United States, advertising on television and in the print media perpetuates sexual stereotypes. Although "house beautiful" ads are less prominent as women are increasingly shown in workplace contexts, body beautiful messages continue to be transmitted. In children's cartoons women are still the helpless victims who the fearless male hero must rescue. Toys are targeted either for little boys or little girls and are packaged appropriately in colors and materials culturally defined as either masculine or feminine.

To what extent are these stereotypes of men and women and the symbols with which they are associated universal? If they are universal, to what extent are they rooted in observed differences about the biological nature of men and women that are made culturally significant? These questions have interested scholars as they have attempted to account for both similarity and difference among the people of the world.

Making the assumption that the subordination of women exists in all societies—a "true universal"—Ortner (1974:67) sought to explain the pervasiveness of this idea not in the assignation of women to a domestic sphere of activity, but in the symbolic constructions by which women's roles are evaluated. Ortner argues that women, because of their reproductive roles, are universally viewed as being closer to nature, while men are linked with culture. She defines culture as "the notion of human consciousness, or . . . the products of human consciousness (i.e., systems of thought and technology), by means of which humanity attempts to assert control over nature" (1974:72). That which is cultural and subject to human manipulation is assigned more worth than that which is natural; hence, women and women's roles are denigrated or devalued, whether explicitly or implicitly.

The nature-culture dichotomy is a useful explanatory model in the United States where, according to Martin (1987:17), "women are intrinsically closely involved with the family where so many 'natural,' 'bodily' (and therefore lower) functions occur, whereas men are intrinsically closely involved with the world of work where (at least for some) 'cultural,' 'mental,' and therefore higher functions occur. It is no accident that 'natural' facts about women, in the form of claims about biology, are often used to justify social stratification based on gender."

While this model may be applicable in some cultures, its universality has been challenged not only by those who point out that nature-culture is a dichotomy of western thought in particular (Bloch and Bloch 1980; Jordanova 1980; Moore 1988), but also by those who provide ethnographic data to indicate its lack of salience in other cultures around the world (Strathern 1980). Similarly, the assumption that women are universally subordinated while men are dominant (Ortner 1974:70) appears questionable through the lens of recent ethnographic reanalyses. The critique of the concepts of universal subordination and of the nature-culture dichotomy has stimulated significant research on how gender identity and gender roles are constructed in particular cultural contexts (Errington and Gewertz 1987; Ortner and Whitehead 1981; Weiner 1976). Whether and under what conditions social asymmetry between men and women emerges in the process of this construction is open to empirical investigation.

The cultural construction of gender in a particular society involves definitions of what it means to be male or masculine, female or feminine, and these definitions vary cross-culturally. While masculinity is thought to have a powerful biological component in the United States, among the Sambia of New Guinea, it is constructed in the context of ritual. The Sambia, like many other societies in New Guinea (Brown and Buchbinder 1976; Herdt 1982; Meigs 1984), are characterized by a high degree of segregation and sexual antagonism between men and women, both of which are reinforced by powerful taboos. These taboos, and other facets of Sambian male identity including that of the warrior, are inculcated during a series of initiation rituals whereby boys are "grown" into men. As Herdt (in this book) observes, the Sambia "perceive no imminent, naturally driven fit between one's birthright sex and one's gender identity or role" (1982:54). Indeed, Sambian boys and men engage in what some societies would label homosexual activity, yet they do it to create masculinity. It is precisely for this reason that an analytical distinction is often made between "sex" as a biological classification and "gender" as a set of learned social roles.

Through the rituals of manhood Sambian boys are progressively detached from the world of women, a world they occupied for the first six or seven years of their lives and which they must now learn to both fear and devalue. This process of detachment has been identified by Chodorow (1974) as a major phase of human male development. If it is unmarked and therefore ambiguous in most western cultures, it is marked in many nonwestern cultures and often associated with male circumcision. Among the Mende of Sierra Leone (Little 1951), for example, boy initiates are seized from their homes by the force of spirits—men wearing masks and long raffia skirts. In this act they are dramatically and suddenly separated from their childhood, carried into the bush where they will spend several weeks in seclusion and transition, before they reemerge as men.

Initiation rituals that prepare girls for their roles as women and instruct them in what it means to be a woman in a particular cultural context can also be found in various societies around the world (Brown 1963; Richards 1956). However, the transition to womanhood is often part of a more subtle and continuous process of enculturation and socialization. In a description of Hausa socialization Callaway (in this book) demonstrates how girls in this society learn how to behave in culturally appropriate ways. The Hausa are an Islamic people who live in northern Nigeria. Historically, ruling class Hausa women had significant authority and social standing, but with the expansion of Islam this position was eroded and a sexually segregated society characterized by female subordination emerged. Hausa girls marry young, generally upon reaching puberty. At that time they enter *kulle* or seclusion. In seclusion, the social roles of women are specifically defined and their sexual activities are limited. Though a Hausa woman becomes part of her husband's family, her place is secured only by bearing sons, and all her children belong to her husband. Hausa women are taught the expected life course from early childhood.

In Hausa society, Callaway (1987:22) claims, "the reproduction of 'masculine' and 'feminine' personalities generation after generation has produced psychological and value commitments to sex differences that are tenaciously maintained and so deeply ingrained as to become central to a consistent sense of self." This self is defined by reproductive roles and by deference to men; thus a good daughter-in-law gives her first born child to her husband's mother, an act that strengthens family ties.

Conceptions of the self or personhood are, as Henrietta Moore (1988:39) has observed, "cross-culturally as variable as the concepts of 'woman' and 'man.'" Personhood is constituted by a variety of attributes. In addition to gender, it may comprise age, status in the family and in the community, and physical appearance or impairment. In many cultures naming is also an important mechanism for constructing personhood. In the United States, for instance, the use of Ms. to replace Mrs. and Miss is an acceptable option. It is increasingly common for married women to retain the name that they were born with rather than replace it with one that only gives them an identity in relation to someone else—their husband.

Among the Chambri of New Guinea initial identity or personhood is gained through a totemic name given by a child's patrilineal and matrilateral relatives. According to Errington and Gewertz (1987:32, 47), "these names both reflect and affect the transactions which constitute a person's fundamental social relationships and identity.... Totemic names allow both men and women to pursue respectively their culturally defined preoccupations of political competition and the bearing of children. The totemic names available to men, however, convey different sorts of power and resources than do those available to women.... Men seek to augment their own power through gaining control of the names of others.... The power conveyed by [women's] names cannot shape social relationships as does the power of names men hold, but, instead, ensures reproduction."

Women's names among the Chambri work in different ways from those of men, but they nonetheless enable women to claim personhood in Chambri society. The married Chinese women described by Watson (in this book) have an entirely different experience. They are denied individuating names, and through this denial their personhood is in question. They remain, says Watson, "suspended between the anonymous world of anybodies and the more sharply defined world of somebodies." In contrast with the namelessness of Chinese women, men in Chinese culture acquire numerous names as they pass through the life cycle. Nowhere is the difference more apparent than at marriage—a time when a man acquires a name that symbolizes his new status and public roles and a woman loses her girlhood name and becomes the "inner person." Like the Hausa women who assume an identity with respect to their husbands, Chinese women begin newly married life by learning the names and kinship terms for all their husbands' ancestors and relatives. Namelessness follows them to the grave—anybodies in life, they become nobodies at death.

In many societies personhood for women is also associated with conceptions of the body and often centers on reproductive functions. One reproductive process that has particular salience is menstruation. Understandings of the symbolic meanings of menstruation influence men's and women's ideologies of gender. Buckley and Gottlieb (1988:3) suggest that "while menstruation itself has at least a degree of biological regularity, its symbolic voicings and valences are strikingly variable, both cross-culturally and within single cultures."

Among numerous groups in New Guinea, men engage in a range of symbolic behaviors to cleanse themselves of what they believe are the harmful effects of contact with women—for example, tongue scraping and smokehouse purification. Menstrual blood, a natural female substance, is culturally defined as one of the most powerful pollutants. The Mae Enga, for example, believe that "contact with [menstrual blood] or a menstruating woman will, in the absence of appropriate counter-magic, sicken a man and cause persistent vomiting, turn his blood black, corrupt his vital juices so that his skin darkens and wrinkles as his flesh wastes, permanently dull his wits, and eventually lead to a slow decline and death" (Meggitt 1964:207).

Male beliefs about the dangers of menstrual blood can be found in a number of other cultures around the world (Buckley and Gottlieb 1988). In some contexts men appear to devalue female reproductive roles by defining menstruation as the unfortunate lot of women. For example, a creation story of a group of pastoral nomads in northern Iran goes as follows: "In the beginning men had menstruation and not women. But blood would go down their pants and it was very uncomfortable. So they went to God and complained about their situation, asking Him to give menstruation to women who had skirts. At the time of childbirth, it used to be men who had pains. Again they complained to God, and He gave the pain to women, as He had done with menstruation" (Shahshahani 1986:87).

This creation story, like many beliefs about menstrual pollution, represents a male view that not only associates women with nature and men with culture, but also helps to explain and support sexual asymmetry in that culture. Buckley (in this book) addresses a different form of male bias in his discussion of menstrual beliefs and practices among the Yurok Indians of North America—that of the western male ethnographer who is working with his own construction of "the curse." In his reanalysis of Yurok data Buckley found that while precontact Yurok men considered women, through their menstrual blood, to be dangerous, Yurok women viewed it as a positive source of power. Rather than looking on the forced monthly seclusion as isolating and oppressive, women viewed it as a source of strength and sanctuary. This female voice, expressing the power and position that is sometimes associated with menstrual taboos, has begun to emerge in other cultural descriptions (Gottlieb 1982; Keesing 1985; Lawrence 1988). As Rosaldo (1974:38) has put it pollution beliefs can form the basis for solidarity among women.

What Buckley is suggesting is not that the male point of view is wrong or unimportant, but that it is only a partial representation. Gender roles and gender identities are constructed by both men and women in any society.

REFERENCES

Ardener, Edwin. 1975. Belief and the Problem of Women. In Shirley Ardener (ed.). *Perceiving Women*, pp. 1–18. New York: John Wiley and Sons.

Bloch, Maurice and Jean Bloch. 1980. Women and the Dialectics of Nature in Eighteenth-Century French Thought. In Carol MacCormack and Marilyn Strathern (eds.). *Nature, Culture and Gender*, pp. 25–41. Cambridge: Cambridge University Press.

Brown, Judith K. 1963. A Cross-Cultural Study of Female Initiation Rites Among Pre-Literate Peoples. *American Anthropologist* 65(4): 837–853.

Brown, Paula and Georgeda Buchbinder. 1976. *Man and Woman in the New Guinea Highlands*. Washington, DC: American Anthropological Association, Special Publication, number 8.

Buckley, Thomas and Alma Gottlieb (eds.). 1988. *Blood Magic: The Anthropology of Menstruation*. Berkeley: University of California Press.

Buckley, Thomas and Alma Gottlieb. 1988. A Critical Appraisal of Theories of Menstrual Symbolism. In Thomas Buckley and Alma Gottlieb (eds.). *Blood Magic: The Anthropology of Menstruation*, pp. 3–50. Berkeley: University of California Press.

Callaway, Barbara J. 1987. *Muslim Hausa Women in Nigeria. Tradition and Change*. Syracuse: Syracuse University Press.

Chodorow, Nancy. 1974. Family Structure and Feminine Personality. In Michele Z. Rosaldo and Louise Lamphere (eds.). *Woman, Culture, and Society*, pp. 43–67. Stanford: Stanford University Press.

Errington, Frederick and Deborah Gewertz. 1987. *Cultural Alternatives and a Feminist Anthropology: An Analysis of Culturally Constructed Gender Interests in Papua New Guinea*. Cambridge: Cambridge University Press.

Gottlieb, Alma. 1982. Sex, Fertility and Menstruation Among the Beng of the Ivory Coast: A Symbolic Analysis. *Africa* 52(4): 34–47.

Herdt, Gilbert. 1982. *Rituals of Manhood. Male Initiation in Papua New Guinea*. Berkeley and Los Angeles: University of California Press.

Hogbin, Ian. 1970. *The Island of Menstruating Men*. Scranton, PA: Chandler.

Jordanova, L.J. 1980. Natural Facts: A Historical Perspective on Science and Sexuality. In Carol MacCormack and Marilyn Strathern (eds.). *Nature, Culture and Gender,* pp. 42–69. Cambridge: Cambridge University Press.

Keesing, Roger. 1985. Kwaio Women Speak: The Micropolitics of Autobiography in a Solomon Island Society. *American Anthropologist* 87: 27–39.

Lawrence, Denise. 1988. Menstrual Politics: Women and Pigs in Rural Portugal. In Thomas Buckley and Alma Gottlieb (eds.). *The Anthropology of Menstruation,* pp. 117–136. Berkeley: University of California Press.

Little, Kenneth L. 1951. *The Mende of Sierra Leone: A West African People in Transition.* London: Routledge and Kegan Paul.

Martin, Emily. 1987. *The Woman in the Body: A Cultural Analysis of Reproduction.* Boston: Beacon Press.

Meggitt, M.J. 1964. Male-Female Relationships in the Highlands of Australian New Guinea. *American Anthropologist* 66(4, part 2): 204–224.

Meigs, Anna S. 1984. *Food, Sex, and Pollution: A New Guinea Religion.* New Brunswick, NJ: Rutgers University Press.

Moore, Henrietta. 1988. *Feminism and Anthropology.* Minneapolis: University of Minnesota Press.

Ortner, Sherry. 1974. Is Female to Male as Nature to Culture? In Michelle Z. Rosaldo and Louise Lamphere (eds.). *Woman, Culture, and Society, pp.66–87.* Stanford: Stanford University Press.

Ortner, Sherry and Harriet Whitehead. 1981. *Sexual Meanings: The Cultural Construction of Gender and Sexuality.* Cambridge: Cambridge University Press.

Richards, Audrey I. 1956. *Chisungu: A Girls' Initiation Ceremony Among the Bemba of Northern Rhodesia.* London: Faber and Faber.

Rosaldo, Michelle. 1974. Woman, Culture, and Society: A Theoretical Overview. In Michelle Z. Rosaldo and Louise Lamphere (eds.). *Woman, Culture, and Society,* pp. 17–42. Stanford: Stanford University Press.

Shahshahani, Soheila. 1986. Women Whisper, Men Kill: A Case Study of the Mamasani Pastoral Nomads of Iran. In Leela Dube, Eleanor Leacock, and Shirley Ardener (eds.). *Visibility and Power: Essays on Women in Society and Development,* pp. 85–97. Delhi: Oxford University Press.

Strathern, Marilyn. 1980. No Nature, No culture: The Hagen Case. In Carol MacCormack and Marilyn Strathern (eds.). *Nature, Culture and Gender,* pp. 174–222. Cambridge: Cambridge University Press.

Weiner, Annette. 1976. *Women of Value, Men of Renown.* Austin: University of Texas Press.

Rituals of Manhood: Male Initiation in Papua New Guinea

Gilbert H. Herdt

Sambia are a mountain-dwelling hunting and horticultural people who number some 2,000 persons and inhabit one of New Guinea's

Reprinted with permission from Gilbert H. Herdt, *Rituals of Manhood: Male Initiation in Papua New Guinea* (Berkeley, University of California Press, 1982), pp. 50–57. Copyright © 1982 The Regents of the University of California.

most rugged terrains. The population is dispersed through narrow river valleys over a widespread, thinly populated rain forest; rainfall is heavy; and even today the surrounding mountain ranges keep the area isolated. Sambia live on the fringes of the Highlands, but they trace their origins to the Papua hinterlands; their culture and economy thus reflect a mixture of influences from both of those areas. Hunting still predominates as a masculine activity through which most meat protein is acquired. As in the Highlands, though, sweet potatoes and taro are the staple crops, and their cultivation is for the most part women's work. Pigs are few, and they have no ceremonial or exchange significance; indigenous marsupials, such as possum and tree kangaroo, provide necessary meat prestations for all initiations and ceremonial feasts (cf. Meigs 1976).

Sambia settlements are small, well-defended, mountain clan hamlets. These communities comprise locally based descent groups organized through a strong agnatic idiom. Residence is patrivirilocal, and most men actually reside in their father's hamlets. Clans are exogamous, and one or more of them together constitute a hamlet's landowning corporate agnatic body. These men also form a localized warriorhood that is sometimes allied with other hamlets in matters of fighting, marriage, and ritual. Each hamlet contains one or two men's clubhouses, in addition to women's houses, and the men's ritual life centers on their clubhouse. Marriage is usually by sister exchange or infant betrothal, although the latter form of prearranged marriage is culturally preferred. Intrahamlet marriage is occasionally more frequent (up to 50 percent of all marriages in my own hamlet field site) than one would expect in such small segmentary groupings, an involutional pattern weakened since pacification.

Sambia male and female residential patterns differ somewhat from those of other Highlands peoples. The nuclear family is an important subunit of the hamlet-based extended family of interrelated clans. A man, his wife, and their children usually cohabit within a single, small, round hut. Children are thus reared together by their parents during the early years of life, so the nuclear family is a residential unit, an institution virtually unknown to the Highlands (Meggitt 1964; Read 1954). Sometimes this unit is expanded through polygyny, in which case a man, his cowives, and their children may occupy the single dwelling. Girls continue to reside with their parents until marriage (usually near the menarche, around fifteen to seventeen years of age). Boys, however, are removed to the men's clubhouse at seven to ten years of age, following their first-stage initiation. There they reside exclusively until marriage and cohabitation years later. Despite familial cohabitation in early childhood, strict taboos based on beliefs about menstrual pollution still separate men and women in their sleeping and eating arrangements.

Warfare used to be constant and nagging among Sambia, and it conditioned the values and masculine stereotypes surrounding the male initiatory cult. Ritualized bow fights occured among neighboring hamlets, whose members still intermarried and usually initiated their sons together. At the same time, though, hamlets also united against enemy tribes and in staging war parties against them. Hence, warfare, marriage, and initiation were interlocking institutions; the effect of this political instability was to reinforce tough, strident masculine performance in most arenas of social life. "Strength" (*jerundu*) was—and is—a pivotal idea in this male ethos. Indeed, strength, which has both ethnobiological and behavioral aspects, could be aptly translated as "maleness" and "manliness." Strength has come to be virtually synonymous with idealized conformity to male ritual routine. Before conquest and pacification by the Australians, though, strength had its chief performative significance in one's conduct on the battlefield. Even today bitter reminders of war linger on among the Sambia; and we should not forget that it is against the harsh background of the warrior's existence that Sambia initiate their boys, whose only perceived protection against the inconstant world is their own unbending masculinity.

Initiation rests solely in the hands of the men's secret society. It is this organization that brings the collective initiatory cycle into being as jointly performed by neighboring hamlets (and as constrained by their own chronic bow fighting). The necessary feast-crop gardens, ritual leadership and knowledge, dictate that a handful of elders, war leaders, and ritual experts be in full command of the actual staging of the event. Everyone and all else are secondary.

There are six intermittent initiations from the ages of seven to ten and onward. They are, however, constituted and conceptualized as two distinct cultural systems within the male life cycle. First-stage (*moku,* at seven to ten years of age), second-stage (*imbutu,* at ten to thirteen years), and third-stage (*ipmangwi,* at thirteen to sixteen years) initiations—bachelorhood rites—are collectively performed for regional groups of boys as age-mates. The initiations are held in sequence, as age-graded advancements; the entire sequel takes months to perform. The focus of all these initiations is the construction and habitation of a great cult house (*moo-angu*) on a traditional dance ground; its ceremonialized building inaugurates the whole cycle. Fourth-stage (*nuposha:* sixteen years and onward), fifth-stage (*taiketnyi*), and sixth-stage (*moondangu*) initiations are, conversely, individually centered events not associated with the confederacy of interrelated hamlets, cult house, or dance ground. Each of these initiations, like the preceding ones, does have its own ritual status, social role, and title, as noted. The triggering event for the latter three initiations, unlike that for the bachelorhood rites, is not the building of a cult house or a political agreement of hamlets to act collectively but is rather the maturing femininity and life-crisis events of the women assigned in marriage to youths (who become the initiated novices). Therefore, fourth-stage initiation is only a semipublic activity organized by the youths' clansmen (and some male affines). Its secret purificatory and other rites are followed by the formal marriage ceremony in the hamlet. Fifth-stage initiation comes at a woman's menarche, when her husband is secretly introduced to additional purification and sexual techniques. Sixth-stage initiation issues from the birth of a man's wife's first child. This event is, de jure, the attainment of manhood. (The first birth is elaborately ritualized and celebrated; the next three births are also celebrated, but in more truncated fashion.) Two children bring full adulthood (*aatmwunu*) for husband and wife alike. Birth cer-

emonies are suspended after the f[...] since there is no reason to belabo[...] now obvious: a man has proved hi[...] petent in reproduction. This sequence of male initiations forms the basis for male development, and it underlies the antagonistic tenor of relationships between the sexes.

It needs stating only once that men's secular rhetoric and ritual practices depict women as dangerous and polluting inferiors whom men are to distrust throughout their lives. In this regard, Sambia values and relationships pit men against women even more markedly, I think, than occurs in other Highlands communities (cf. Brown and Buchbinder 1976; Meggitt 1964; Read 1954). Men hold themselves as the superiors of women in physique, personality, and social position. And this dogma of male supremacy permeates all social relationships and institutions, likewise coloring domestic behavior among the sexes (cf. Tuzin 1980 for an important contrast). Men fear not only pollution from contact with women's vaginal fluids and menstrual blood but also the depletion of their semen, the vital spark of maleness, which women (and boys, too) inevitably extract, sapping a man's substance. These are among the main themes of male belief underlying initiation.

The ritualized simulation of maleness is the result of initiation, and men believe the process to be vital for the nature and nurture of manly growth and well-being. First-stage initiation begins the process in small boys. Over the ensuing ten to fifteen years, until marriage, cumulative initiations and residence in the men's house are said to promote biological changes that firmly cement the growth from childhood to manhood. Nature provides male genitals, it is true; but nature alone does not bestow the vital spark biologically necessary for stimulating masculine growth or demonstrating cold-blooded self-preservation.

New Guinea specialists will recognize in the Sambia belief system a theme that links it to the comparative ethnography of male initiation and masculine development: the use of ritual procedures for sparking, fostering, and maintaining manliness in males (see Berndt

1962; Meigs 1976; Newman 1964, 1965; Poole 1981; Read 1965; Salisbury 1965; Strathern 1969, 1970). Sambia themselves refer to the results of first-stage collective initiation—our main interest—as a means of "growing a boy"; and this trend of ritual belief is particularly emphatic.

Unlike ourselves, Sambia perceive no imminent, naturally driven fit between one's birthright sex and one's gender identity or role.[1] Indeed, the problem (and it is approached as a situation wanting a solution) is implicitly and explicitly understood in quite different terms. The solution is also different for the two sexes: men believe that a girl is born with all of the vital organs and fluids necessary for her to attain reproductive competence through "natural" maturation. This conviction is embodied in cultural perceptions of the girl's development beginning with the sex assignment at birth. What distinguishes a girl (*tai*) from a boy (*kwulai'u*) is obvious: "A boy has a penis, and a girl does not," men say. Underlying men's communications is a conviction that maleness, unlike femaleness, is not a biological given. It must be artificially induced through secret ritual; and that is a personal achievement.

The visible manifestations of girls' fast-growing reproductive competence, noticed first in early motor coordination and speech and then later in the rapid attainment of height and secondary sex traits (e.g., breast development), are attributed to inner biological properties. Girls possess a menstrual-blood organ, or *tingu,* said to precipitate all those events and the menarche. Boys, on the other hand, are thought to possess an inactive tingu. They do possess, however, another organ—the *kere-ku-kereku,* or semen organ—that is thought to be the repository of semen, the very essence of maleness and masculinity; but this organ is not functional at birth, since it contains no semen naturally and can only store, never produce, any. Only oral insemination, men believe, can activate the boy's semen organ, thereby precipitating his push into adult reproductive competence. In short, femininity unfolds naturally, whereas masculinity must be achieved; and here is where the male ritual cult steps in.

Men also perceive the early socialization risks of boys and girls in quite different terms. All infants are closely bonded to their mothers. Out of a woman's contaminating, life-giving womb pours the baby, who thereafter remains tied to the woman's body, breast milk, and many ministrations. This latter contact only reinforces the femininity and female contamination in which birth involves the infant. Then, too, the father, both because of postpartum taboos and by personal choice, tends to avoid being present at the breast-feedings. Mother thus becomes the unalterable primary influence; father is a weak second. Sambia say this does not place girls at a "risk"—they simply succumb to the drives of their "natural" biology. This maternal attachment and paternal distance clearly jeopardize the boys' growth, however, since nothing innate within male maturation seems to resist the inhibiting effects of mothers' femininity. Hence boys must be traumatically separated—wiped clean of their female contaminants—so that their masculinity may develop.

Homosexual fellatio inseminations can follow this separation but cannot precede it, for otherwise they would go for naught. The accumulating semen, injected time and again for years, is believed crucial for the formation of biological maleness and masculine comportment. This native perspective is sufficiently novel to justify our using a special concept for aiding description and analysis of the data: masculinization (Herdt 1981:205 ff). Hence I shall refer to the overall process that involves separating a boy from his mother, initiating him, ritually treating his body, administering homosexual inseminations, his biological attainment of puberty, and his eventual reproductive competence as *masculinization.* (Precisely what role personal and cultural fantasy plays in the negotiation of this ritual process I have considered elsewhere: see Herdt 1981: chaps. 6, 7, and 8.)

A boy has female contaminants inside of him which not only retard physical development but, if not removed, debilitate him and eventually bring death. His body is male: his tingu contains no blood and will not activate. The achievement of puberty for boys requires semen. Breast milk "nurtures the boy," and sweet potatoes or other "female" foods provide "stomach nourishment," but these substances become only feces, not semen. Women's own bodies internally produce the menarche, the hallmark of reproductive maturity. There is no comparable mechanism active in a boy, nothing that can stimulate his secondary sex traits. Only semen can do that; only men have semen; boys have none. What is left to do, then, except initiate and masculinize boys into adulthood?

NOTE

1. I follow Stroller (1968) in adhering to the following distinctions: the term *sex traits* refers to purely biological phenomena (anatomy, hormones, genetic structure, etc.), whereas *gender* refers to those psychological and cultural attributes that compel a person (consciously or unconsciously) to sense him- or herself, and other persons, as belonging to either the male or female sex. It follows that the term *gender role* (Sears 1965), rather than the imprecise term *sex role,* refers to the normative set of expectations associated with masculine and feminine social positions.

REFERENCES

Berndt, R. M. 1962. *Excess and Restraint: Social Control among a New Guinea Mountain People.* Chicago: University of Chicago Press.

Brown, P., and G. Buchbinder (eds.). 1976. *Man and Woman in the New Guinea Highlands.* Washington, D.C.: American Anthropological Association.

Herdt, G. H. 1981. *Guardians of the Flutes: Idioms of Masculinity.* New York: McGraw-Hill.

Meggitt, M. J. 1964. Male-female relationships in the Highlands of Australian New Guinea. In *New Guinea: The Central Highlands,* ed. J. B. Watson, *American Anthropologist,* 66, pt. 2 (4):204–224.

Meigs, A. S. 1976. Male pregnancy and the reduction of sexual opposition in a New Guinea Highlands society. *Ethnology* 15 (4):393–407.

Newman, P. L. 1964. Religious belief and ritual in a New Guinea society. In *New Guinea: The Central Highlands,* ed. J. B. Watson, *American Anthropologist* 66, pt. 2 (4):257–272.

———. 1965. *Knowing the Gururumba.* New York: Holt, Rinehart and Winston.

Poole, F. J. P. 1981. Transforming "natural" woman: female ritual leaders and gender ideology among Bimin-Kuskumin. In *Sexual Meanings,* ed. S. B. Ortner and H. Whitehead. New York: Cambridge University Press.

Read, K. E. 1954. Cultures of the Central Highlands, New Guinea. *Southwestern Journal of Anthropology* 10 (1):1–43.

———. 1965. *The High Valley.* London: George Allen and Unwin.

Salisbury, R. F. 1965. The Siane of the Eastern Highlands. In *Gods, Ghosts, and Men in Melanesia,* P. Lawrence and M. J. Meggitt, pp. 50–77. Melbourne: Melbourne University Press.

Sears, R. R. 1965. Development of gender role. In *Sex and Behavior,* ed. F. A. Beach, pp. 133–163. New York: John Wiley and Sons.

Stoller, R. J. 1968. *Sex and Gender.* New York: Science House.

Strathern, A. J. 1969. Descent and alliance in the New Guinea Highlands: some problems of comparison. Royal Anthropological Institute, *Proceedings,* pp. 37–52.

———. 1970. Male initiation in the New Guinea Highlands societies. *Ethnology* 9(4):373–379.

Tuzin, D. F. 1980. *The Voice of the Tambaran: Truth and Illusion in Ilahita Arapesh Religion.* Berkeley, Los Angeles, and London: University of California Press.

Hausa Socialization

Barbara J. Callaway

The Hausa ethos of male domination and the Islamic emphasis on male supremacy combine to structure distinct conceptions of life for men and women. Perceptions of a woman's life cycle stress her current status in relation to men and her reproductive status as well as her approximate age—*jinjiniya* (female infant), *yarinya* (girl), *budurwa* (maiden or virgin), *mata* (woman or wife), *bazarawa* (divorced or widowed), or *tsohuwa* (old woman). The corresponding terms for males stress biological age—*jinjiri,* (infant), *yaro* (young boy), *miji* (young man), and *tsoho* (old man) (Schildkrout 1981, 96).

Married Muslim women in Hausaland live in seclusion (*kulle*). In Kano State—in contrast to other Islamic areas in West Africa— the practice appears to be increasing as the city and the countryside become more involved in the national cash economy (Abell 1962; Hill 1977; M. G. Smith 1955).

Hausa culture emphasizes siring large numbers of children, and in Kano the average number of living children per woman is seven.[1] Countries with Islamic majorities generally have the highest population growth rates in the world today. Nigeria has one of the highest (3.5 percent annually). While pronatal tendencies are strong in all Nigerian societies, they are most evident in the Islamic north, where family planning is not considered a legitimate focus of public policy. In Kano, a metropolitan area of over five million people, no family planning office or publicly available information on either planning or birth control was available as late as 1983.[2]

The number of children born to a given

Reprinted with permission from Barbara J. Callaway, *Muslim Hausa Women in Nigeria* (Syracuse, NY: Syracuse University Press, 1987), pp. 28–35 (text only).

woman is not necessarily indicative of the number for whom she is responsible. Widespread fostering and the practice of a woman's avoiding contact with her firstborn child (*kunya*) creates a great deal of fluidity in children's lives. Eighty percent of 500 Hausa children surveyed in Kano State for one study were not raised by their biological parents (Hake 1972, 23–24). Of these, 41.5 percent were raised by paternal grandmothers, 16.7 percent by stepmothers, 19.8 percent by other relatives, and 5.5 percent by "friends of the family." The giving of children for fostering indicates the strength of the bonds linking spatially dispersed kin. The firstborn child generally is given to an older woman who has no child currently living with her. A good daughter-in-law demonstrates that she is "polite" by giving her first child to her husband's mother, and in so doing strengthens ties between the two families (Interview #16, Kano, October, 1982).

Childhood is generally a mixture of good-natured freedom and harsh corporal punishment and deprivation. When 175 students at the Advanced Teachers College (male) and Women's Teachers College in Kano were asked if their childhoods had been happy or sad or both, 57.4 percent of the 102 men and 56.8 percent of the 73 women replied "both." One-third of these translated "sad" as referring to harsh punishment by parents or other adults. One-fifth complained of lack of sufficient food or clothing as children. "My brother was kind—but his wife was not good; she often gave me too little to eat." "I was not fed properly in my uncle's house where I went to live." "I lived with a stepmother, who had many children, and so I was neglected most of the time." Sixty percent of these students claimed never to have had a conversation with an adult while growing up. Eighty percent of the girls claimed to have been "often afraid" (questionnaire administered by Aisha Indo Yuguda, 1983).

While the birth of a new baby is cause for celebration in nearly all families, no matter what the economic status, the birth of a son is usually celebrated on a more lavish scale than that of a daughter. Among wealthier families, when a boy is born it is customary to slaughter *sa* or *sanuja* (a cow or an ox) for the *radin suna* (naming ceremony). When a girl is born, it is customary to slaughter a lesser animal, such as *tunkiya* (sheep) or *akuya* (goat) (Kabir 1981). In the home little girls are assigned domestic duties from about age five. By age six they are dressed in imitation of adult women and begin to be viewed as future wives. They go outside only for specific reasons, such as running errands for their mothers who cannot go out, selling food and handicrafts from bowls or baskets on top of their heads, and carrying messages; they do not go out to play. Little boys, at about age six, are sent out to play and sleep with other boys in the *zaures* or *soro* (entranceways) to their homes. They are ousted from their mother's rooms at night and virtually become visitors in her space during the day. By age ten, boys cross the line into female space less often. They eat with other boys, seldom with sisters or mothers. Boys whose fathers are artisans or traders may be apprenticed to their fathers or other adult men by age eleven or twelve. Even those going to school beyond the primary years spend little time "at home" and avoid contact with women as they approach adulthood. Adulthood means separation, even avoidance, between male and female. "The transition to manhood means moving out of the domain of female authority, into the world of men, and ultimately into marriage, where male dominance is as yet unchallenged" (Schildkrout 1978, 131).

As she grows up, a girl is made aware of her second-class status. In addition to housework, she is assigned child-care responsibilities, and she is made aware that her sex is a potential source of shame and dishonor. A girl's inferior status vis-à-vis her brothers, father, or male kin is early and constantly emphasized. She is told *ki dinga yin abu kamar mace,* "to behave like a woman." A girl should sit quietly, talk softly, cover her head, and never disagree with a male. *Ba ki ganin ke mace ce, she namiji ne,* meaning "Can't you see you are a woman while he is a man?" (and thus superior) is a refrain repeated to her from her earliest years. She will also hear *ke mace ce, gidan wani zaki,* ("after all, you are a woman and you are going to someone else's house"), or *"komai abinki, gidan wani zaki"* ("No matter what you do you are going to someone else's house") (Kabir 1981).

When a girl shows signs of independence of character, she will be snubbed by her peers and told that *tunda ke mace ce, a karkashin wani kike,* "You are a woman and you are under someone's (male) authority." The girl seeking to join boys at play may be greeted with a popular children's song:

> *Mai wasa da maza karya*
> *Tunda na gan ta na rena ta.*
>
> ("She who plays with boys is a bitch
> When I see her, I detest her.")

Finally, girls are repeatedly admonished that *Duk mace a bayan namiji take*—"Every woman is inferior to a man" (Interviews #6, Kano, January 20, 1982; and #21, Kano, February 24, 1983).

For the overwhelming majority of girls, it is almost inconceivable to aspire to anything other than the role of wife or mother. Normally, girls are expected to be married by the time they reach puberty. The widespread introduction of Western education (*boko*) is beginning to postpone the age of marriage for girls who go to school, but even in this event, there is great pressure to marry young, before age sixteen. Girls who are not married while in secondary school (all such noncommercial schools in Kano are single sex) are viewed with suspicion and it is said that *an gama da ita,* meaning, "They have finished with her," implying that she is no longer a virgin and therefore not a good candidate for a first wife (Interviews #11 and 12, Kano, March 8 and March 12, 1982).

Although they may have heavy household responsibilities, girls are sent out to hawk wares for their mothers and are relatively free until they are abruptly married and secluded. After that, even though they are still very young, like adult women they can leave their houses only for naming ceremonies, marriages, funerals, and medical care. If they go out, it is usually at night and an older woman generally accompanies them as escorts. They must cover their heads and be accountable for their visits (Schildkrout 1979).

Since most girls are married by age twelve to fourteen, they are virtually confined to the female quarters of their compounds all their lives. If a girl is married as young as ten, she will not be expected to cook or have sexual relations with her husband until puberty begins, but she enters *kulle* and loses the freedom associated with childhood. For all practical purposes, the house or compound is a woman's world. From the time she marries and enters *kulle* until after her childbearing years, a woman has virtually no freedom of movement or association. This socialization process is pervasive and thorough. Opportunities for broadening one's experiences or raising one's expectations are few.

Unlike girls, boys do not reach adult status until they become economically productive, usually in their late twenties or early thirties, because it is one of the requirements of Islam that men do not marry until they can provide shelter, clothing, and food for their wife or wives. While in 1982, ninety percent of the 92 Muslim women students at Bayero University were married, only fifteen percent of the 2000 men students were married (Bayero University 1982).

Even in matters of religion, a woman's inferiority is underscored. While all Muslims are equal before Allah, menstruating or pregnant women are considered "religiously impure." In addition, women cannot lead the community in prayer, do not officiate at religious festivals, and rarely attend mosque. Even at the mosque on the campus at Bayero University in Kano, women may attend only by standing in a separate room out of sight of the male worshipers and may not be in public areas of the mosque during Friday prayers. Hence, the thrust of socialization through religion is to emphasize a properly subordinate place for women.

Unlike other urban settings, Kano provides no specifically female organizations for Hausa women. The one exclusively women's club in Kano, the Corona Society, a British-based international service organization for women, had no Hausa Muslim Kano women as members. The National Association of Women's Societies of Nigeria (the federally recognized umbrella organization for women's associations) had no Kano chapter, although it asked the Corona Society to help organize one; no interest in affiliation with such an organization was expressed in Kano. Although interested in the idea of women's organizations, elite Kano women preferred to avoid the visibility entailed in membership. They seemed to perceive some advantage in their current status and not many advantages in radically changing it.

At Bayero University no northern Nigerian woman holds a position of regular faculty rank (there was one female teaching assistant in sociology), nor do women generally participate in University-sponsored conferences or symposia. As of 1983, the University had never sponsored a program dealing with women's issues or concerns; no course in the curriculum deals specifically with women's history or issues.

If women are absent from the public realm, within their own restricted but private world they enjoy considerable autonomy. Houses are a woman's domain. Women can enter virtually any house, but men can enter few and then they rarely go beyond the entranceway, or, in the case of wealthier homes, the man's sitting room. Women are secluded, but men are excluded from women's space. Even kinship does not open the door, for a man would not normally enter the house of a younger married sister or the female section of his younger brother's house. He might, with the husband's permission, enter the house of an older married sister (Schildkrout, 1978a, p. 115). "It shall be no crime in them as to their fathers, or their sons, or their brothers, or their brother's sons, or their sister's sons, or their women, or the slaves which their right hands possess, if they speak with them unveiled" (*Qur'an* 3:33 and 33:55). Thus, young men and women are not thrown together in situations where they could form relationships that could lead to marriage; the system of arranged marriages, in which girls are married early and boys much later, means that relationships between unrelated young people of equal status but opposite sex are almost nonexistent. The fact that men and women live in separate and distinct worlds has profound psychological implications for women. While men's authority over women in the public domain is nearly complete, in the private domain, where interaction is highly limited and age differences between men and women are great, the differences in their interests are also great and thus the authority of men is quite precarious.

Hausa households are large and multigenerational abodes. Women are constantly surrounded by female consanguineal and affinal relatives and the children of all. The average number of persons in the households visited during the course of this study was twenty, but it was not unusual for fifty persons to be eating at a particular house or compound. Often, while fifteen to twenty people might actually be resident in a particular house, many others might be eating and sleeping there. In Kano it is exceedingly rare to visit a Hausa woman in her home and find her alone—women appear to be never alone. Thus, the large city does not provide the alleged anonymity and lower visibility attributed to urban life. Within seclusion, women maintain wide networks, through which news of the world and changing events moves in an unending flow. Marriages, naming ceremonies, and other rituals are constant. Goods, services, and money flow rapidly, and visiting of extended kin is incessant; large families ensure movement and wide-ranging networks of exchange. Nothing is as simple as it looks. Kano City, although rapidly industrializing, is nonetheless reminiscent of nonindustrial towns, where the sense of a small, face-to-face community is maintained in the midst of an urban area. When a woman leaves her compound or receives visitors to it, all her neighbors know; the many men standing outside their compounds speculate as to the identity of a stranger and the nature of his or her business.

To the casual observer, life behind the mud wall of the compound appears secure and peaceful, but time spent there brings hundreds of sad stories. Women complain of heavy labor, of marriages of young daughters against their wills, of child brides brought into the household, of forced sexual cohabitation at puberty regardless of mental or emotional development, of early motherhood and infant death. There is no sewage system, running water is unreliable, and animals roam freely. Illness, needless death, and especially female and infant mortality are commonplace. Said a mother of a twelve-year-old on her wedding day, "may the day be cursed when she was born a woman."

NOTES

1. Reproductive histories of 82 women with children in two Kano wards (Kurawa and Kofar Mazugal) were taken by Schildkrout in 1977. Of these, seventy-nine had children and three were "caregivers" (i.e., they had been given children to foster). The 79 women had given birth to a total of 164 children, or an average of 8.2 each. Women without children are assumed to be unable to conceive.

2. As of 1983, the president of the Planned Parenthood Society of Nigeria, a member of a distinguished Kano family, saw nothing disconcerting in the fact that no office of the organization existed in the city. He asserted that Kano women knew he was president of the society and were free to come to his house and request a note from him to the appropriate doctor in the city hospital if they wanted information on birth control assistance (Interview #23, 1983).

REFERENCES

Abell, H. C. 1962. "Report to the Government of Nigeria (Northern Region) on the Home Economics Aspects of the F.A.O. Socio-Economic Survey of Peasant Agriculture in Northern Nigeria: The Role of Rural Women in Farm and Home Life." Rome: F.A.O. (mimeograph).

Bayerto University, Kano. 1980–1982. *Annual Report*. Kano: Bayerto University, Office of the Registrar.

Hake, James M. 1972. *Child-Rearing Practices in Northern Nigeria*. Ibadan: Ibadan University Press.

Hill, Polly. 1977. *Population, Prosperity and Poverty: Rural Kano 1900–1970*. Cambridge: Cambridge University Press.

Kabir, Zainab sa'ad. 1981. "The Silent Oppression: Male-Female Relations in Kano." Kano: Bayerto University Faculty Seminar, Department of Sociology (May) (mimeography).

Schildkrout, Enid. 1978. "Age and Gender in Hausa Society: Socio-Economic Roles of Children in Urban Kano." In *Sex and Age as Principles of Social Differentiation*. A.S.A. Monograph 17, ed. J. S. Fontaine, 109–37. London: Academic Press.

———. 1979. "Women's Work and Children's Work: Variations among Moslems in Kano." In *Social Anthropology of Work*, A.S.A. Monograph 19, ed. S. Wallman, 69–85. London: Academic Press.

———. 1981. "The Employment of Children in Kano." In *Child Work, Poverty and Underdevelopment*, ed. Gerry Rodgers and Guy Standing, 81–112. Geneva: International Labor Office.

Smith, M. G. 1955. *The Economy of the Hausa Communities of Zaire*. Colonial Research Studies, 16. London: Her Majesty's Stationary Office.

The Named and the Nameless:
Gender and Person in Chinese Society

Rubie S. Watson

In Chinese society names classify and individuate, they have transformative powers, and they are an important form of self expression. Some names are private, some are chosen for their public effect. Many people have a confusing array of names while others are nameless. The theory and practice of personal naming in Chinese society is extremely complex and unfortunately little studied.

For the male villagers of rural Hong Kong, naming marks important social transitions: the more names a man has the more "socialized" and also, in a sense, the more "individuated" he becomes. To attain social adulthood

a man must have at least two names, but most have more. By the time a male reaches middle age, he may be known by four or five names. Village women, by contrast, are essentially nameless. Like boys, infant girls are named when they are one month old, but unlike boys they lose this name when they marry. Adult women are known (in reference and address) by kinship terms, teknonyms, or category terms such as "old woman."

In Chinese society personal names constitute an integral part of the language of joking, of boasting, and of exhibiting one's education and erudition. The Chinese themselves are fascinated by personal names: village men enjoy recounting stories about humorous or clumsy names, educated men appreciate the elegance of an auspicious name, and all males worry about the quality of their own names and those of their sons. To a large extent women are excluded from this discourse. They cannot participate because in adulthood they are not named, nor do they name others. Until very recently the majority of village women were illiterate and so could not engage in the intellectual games that men play with written names. Women were not even the subjects of these conversations.

The namelessness of adult women and their inability to participate in the naming of others highlights in a dramatic way the vast gender distinctions that characterize traditional Chinese culture. The study of names gives us considerable insight into the ways in which gender and person are constructed in Chinese society. Judged against the standard of men, the evidence presented here suggests that village women do not, indeed cannot, attain full personhood. The lives of men are punctuated by the acquisition of new names, new roles, new responsibilities and new privileges; women's lives, in comparison, remain indistinct and indeterminate.

In his essay "Person, Time, and Conduct in Bali," Clifford Geertz argues that our social world "is populated not by anybodies . . . but by somebodies, concrete classes of determinate persons positively characterized and appropriately labeled" (1973:363). It is this process by which anybodies are converted into somebodies that concerns me here. Do men and women become "somebodies" in the same way? Are they made equally determinate, positively characterized and labeled?

Although this discussion is based primarily on field research carried out in the Hong Kong New Territories, examples of naming practices have been drawn from other areas of Chinese culture as well. It is difficult to determine the extent to which the patterns described in this paper are indicative of rural china in general.[1] Available evidence suggests that there is considerable overlap between Hong Kong patterns of male naming and those of preliberation Chinese society and present-day rural Taiwan (see for example Eberhard 1970; Kehl 1971; Sung 1981; Wu 1927). Unfortunately, there have been no studies that specifically examine the differences between men's and women's naming, although brief references in Martin Yang's study of a Shantung village (1945:124) and in Judith Stacey's account of women in the People's Republic (1983:43, 131) suggest that the gender differences discussed here are not unique to Hong Kong. In making these statements I do not wish to suggest that there are no substantial differences in personal naming between rural Hong Kong and other parts of China. A general survey of personal naming in China, especially one that takes the postrevolution era into account, has yet to be done.

This paper draws heavily on ethnographic evidence gathered in the village of Ha Tsuen, a single-lineage village located in the northwest corner of the New Territories. All males in Ha Tsuen share the surname Teng and trace descent to a common ancestor who settled in this region during the 12th century (see R. Watson 1985). For most villagers postmarital residence is virilocal/patrilocal. The Ha Tsuen Teng practice surname exogamy, which in the case of a single-lineage village means that all wives come from outside the community. These women arrive in Ha Tsuen as strangers and their early years of marriage are spent accommodating to a new family and new community. The Teng find this completely natural; "daughters," they say, "are born looking out; they belong to others."

Patrilineal values dominate social life in Ha Tsuen. Women are suspect because they are outsiders. As Margery Wolf points out, Chinese women are both marginal and essential to the families into which they marry (1972:35). They are necessary because they produce the next generation, yet as outsiders their integration is never complete. Women are economically dependent on the family estate, but they do not have shareholding rights in that estate. Half the village land in Ha Tsuen is owned by the lineage (see R. Watson 1985:61–72), and the other half is owned by private (male) landlords. Women have no share in this land; they do not own immovable property nor do they have rights to inherit it.

Few married women are employed in wage labor, and since the villagers gave up serious agriculture in the 1960s, most women are dependent on their husbands' paychecks for family income. At the time I conducted my research (1977–78) Ha Tsuen had a population of approximately 2500—all of whom are Cantonese speakers.

NAMING AN INFANT

Among the Cantonese a child's soul is not thought to be firmly attached until at least 30 days after its birth. During the first month of life the child and mother are secluded from all but the immediate family. After a month has passed, the child is considered less susceptible to soul loss and is introduced into village life. The infant is given a name by his or her father or grandfather at a ceremony called "full month" (*man yueh*). If the child is a son, the "full month" festivities will be as elaborate as the family can afford; if, on the other hand, a girl is born, there may be little or no celebration (except, perhaps, a special meal for family members). The naming ceremony for a boy normally involves a banquet for neighbors and village elders, along with the distribution of red eggs to members of the community. The first name a child is given is referred to as his or her *ming*.[2]

This name (*ming*) may be based on literary or classical allusions. It may express a wish for the child's or family's future, or it may enshrine some simple event that took place at or near the time of the child's birth. Examples of this kind of naming are found not only in Ha Tsuen but in other areas of China as well. Arlington, in an early paper on Chinese naming, describes how the name "sleeve" was given to a girl of his acquaintance who at the time of her birth had been wrapped in a sleeve (1923:319). In the People's Republic of China, people born during the Korean War might be called "Resist the United States" (Fan-mei) or "Aid Korea" (Pang-ch'ao). Alternatively, children may be given the name of their birthplace, for example, "Born in An-

hwei" (Hui-sheng) or "Thinking of Yunnan" (Hsiang-yun). In the past girl babies might be named Nai ("To Endure"). This name was given to infant girls who survived an attempted infanticide. One way of killing an infant was to expose it to the elements. If a girl survived this ordeal, she might be allowed to live. In these cases the name Nai commemorated the child's feat of survival.[3]

A child's name may express the parents' desire for no more children. For instance, in Taiwan a fifth or sixth child may be named Beui, a Hokkien term meaning "Last Child." Alternatively, a father may try to assure that his next child will be a son by naming a newborn daughter "Joined to Brother" (Lien-ti). There are several girls with this name in Ha Tsuen. A father or grandfather might express his disappointment or disgust by naming a second or third daughter "Too Many" (A-to)[4] or "Little Mistake" (Hsiao-t'so) or "Reluctant to Feed" (Wang-shih). A sickly child might be given the name of a healthy child. My informants told me that a long-awaited son may be given a girl's name to trick the wandering ghosts into thinking the child had no value and therefore could be ignored (see also Sung 1981:81–82). For example, a Ha Tsuen villager, who was the only son of a wealthy family (born to his father's third concubine), was known by everyone as "Little Slave Girl" (in Cantonese, Mui-jai).

In most cases the infant receives a *ming* during the full month ceremony but this name is little used. For the first year or two most children are called by a family nickname ("milk name" or *nai ming*). Babies are sometimes given milk names like "Precious" (A-pao), or A-buh (mimicking the sounds infants make) or "Eldest Luck," or "Second Luck," indicating sibling order.

Some care and consideration is given to a child's *ming*, especially if it is a boy. By referring to the Confucian classics or by alluding to a famous poem, the name may express the learning and sophistication of the infant's father or grandfather. The name, as we will see, may also save the child from an inauspicious fate. Commonly girls' names (*ming*) are less distinctive and less considered than are boys' names. And, as we have seen, girls' names may also be less flattering: "Too Many" or "Little Mistake." Often a general, classificatory name is given to an infant girl; Martin Yang reports from rural Shantung that Hsiao-mei ("Little Maiden") was a "generic" girls' name in his village (1945:124).

Most Chinese personal names are composed of two characters, which follow the one character surname (for example, Mao Tse-tung or Teng Hsiao-ping). One of the characters of the *ming* may be repeated for all the children of the same sex in the family or perhaps all sons born into the lineage during one generation (for example, a generation or sibling set might have personal names like Hung-hui, Hung-chi, Hung-sheng, and so on.). Birth order may also be indicated in the child's name. In these cases part of the name indicates group affiliation and sibling order. However, one of the characters is unique to the individual and so the child is distinguished from his siblings. A variation on this theme occurs when a parent or grandparent selects a name for all sons or grandsons from a group of characters that share a single element (known as the radical—a structured component found in every Chinese character). For example, Margaret Sung (1981:80) in her survey of Chinese naming practices on Taiwan notes that in some families all son's names may be selected from characters that contain the "man" radical (for example, names like "Kind" [Jen], "Handsome" [Chun], or "Protect" [Pao]).

Individuation of the name, Sung points out, is very strong in Chinese society (1981:88). There is no category of words reserved specifically for personal names and care is taken to make names (particularly boys' names) distinct. The Chinese find the idea of sharing one's given name with millions of other people extraordinary.[5] In Taiwan, Sung notes that individuation of one's name is so important that the government has established a set of rules for name changes (1981:88). According to these regulations a name can be changed when two people with exactly the same name live in the same city or county or have the same place of work. "Inelegant" names or names shared with wanted criminals can also be changed.

In Ha Tsuen a boy might be named, in Cantonese, Teng Tim-sing, which translates Teng "To Increase Victories"; another person could be called Teng Hou-sing, "Reliably Accomplish" (Teng being the shared surname). Parents, neighbors, and older siblings will address the child or young unmarried adult (male or female) by his or her *ming* or by a nickname. Younger siblings are expected to use kin terms in addressing older siblings. It should be noted that, in contrast to personal names, Chinese surnames do not convey individual meaning. When used in a sentence or poem, the character *mao* (the same character used in Mao Tse-tung) means hair, fur, feathers, but when it is used as a surname it does not carry any of these connotations.

THE POWER OF NAMES: NAMES THAT CHANGE ONE'S LUCK

Names classify people into families, generational sets, and kin groups. Ideally, Chinese personal names also have a unique quality. Personal names carry meanings; they express wishes (for more sons or no more daughters), mark past events ("Sleeve" or "Endure"), and convey a family's learning and status. Beyond this rather restricted sense there is, however, another level of meaning. According to Chinese folk concepts each person has a unique constitution—a different balance of the five elements (fire, water, metal, earth, and wood). When the child is about one month old a family will usually have a diviner cast the child's horoscope. The horoscope consists of eight characters (*pa tzu*)—two each for the hour, day, month, and year of birth. The combination of these characters determines in part what kind of person one is (what kind of characteristics one has) and what will happen in future years. However, the *pa tzu* do not represent destiny; one is not bound to act out this fate.

By means of esoteric knowledge a person's fate can be changed. Perhaps the most common method of accomplishing such a change is through naming. For example, if one of the five elements is missing from a person's constitution or is not properly balanced with other elements, the name (*ming*) may then include a character with the radical for that element. In the event of illness the diviner may suggest that the patient suffers from an imbalance of wood and that the radical for this element be added to the child's name. In such a case the character *mei* (plum), for example, may replace one of the original characters of the *ming* and thus save the child from a bad fate, illness, or perhaps death. *Mei* achieves this astounding feat not because there is anything intrinsically wood-like about *mei* but because the written character *mei* has two major components: *mu*, the radical for wood and another symbol that is largely phonetic. It is the written form of the character that is important here; in spoken Chinese there is nothing that suggests that *mei* has within it the element wood. I will return to this point later.

Significantly, it is not only one's own horoscope that matters; one must also be in balance with the horoscopes of parents, spouses, and offspring. It is particularly important that the five elements of mother and child be properly matched to ensure mutual health.[6] If conditions of conflict arise and nothing is done to resolve this conflict, the child may become ill and even die. A name change, however, can rectify the situation. It is obvious that Chinese personal names *do* things: they not only classify and distinguish but also have an efficacy in their own right.

GENDER DIFFERENCES AND THE WRITTEN NAME

As noted above, even in childhood there are important gender distinctions in naming. Girls nearly always have less elaborate full month rituals than their brothers, and less care is taken in choosing girls' names. The greatest difference between the sexes, however, pertains not to the aesthetics of naming but to the written form of the name.

Until the 1960s in Ha Tsuen and in rural Hong Kong generally births were seldom registered with government agencies. Except in cases of a bad fate, there was no compelling reason for girls' names ever to appear in written form. There was rarely any need to attach their names to legal documents. Girls did not inherit land, they had no rights in property, and their given names were not entered in genealogies (on this point see also Hazelton 1986) or on ancestral tablets (see below). Until the 1960s girls rarely attended primary schools. Consequently, nearly all village women born prior to 1945 cannot write or recognize their own names.

Commenting on the role of nicknames, Wolfram Eberhard makes the point that in spoken Chinese with its many homonyms, a two-word combination may fail to express clearly what the speaker wants to convey. The intended meaning of a name (that is, the two-character *ming*) is only apparent when it is written. Nicknames, Eberhard notes, are not normally meant to be written and, hence, are usually longer (often three or four characters) than a person's *ming* (1970:219). Given the ambiguities, a great deal of play is possible with the spoken form of names. For example, Hsin-mei can mean "New Plum" or "Faithful Beauty" depending on the tones that one uses in pronouncing the characters. In the written form the meaning of this name is perfectly clear, but in the spoken form it can be misunderstood or misconstrued, sometimes with disastrous consequences. The Manchu (Ch'ing) authorities played the naming game when they changed the written form of one of Sun Yat-sen's many names. During Sun's long political career, he used a variety of names and aliases (see Sharman 1934), one being Sun Wen (*wen* translates as "elegant," "civil," "culture"). In Manchu attacks on Sun the character *wen* pronounced with a rising tone (elegant, culture) was replaced by another character *wen* pronounced with a falling tone (which translates as "defile"). The change was effected simply by adding the water radical to the term for elegant. *Wen* (defile), it should be noted, was also the name of a famous criminal in southern China during the last years of Manchu rule.

Upon seeing a person's written name, the beholder may comment on the beauty, the refinement, the auspicious connotations of the characters. As long as it is simply spoken, however, it is in a sense "just a name." Although women have names, these do not convey as much information as do men's names, for the obvious reason that the former were rarely written. Until recently New Territories women were not given names with a view to their written effect. The written form of "Too Many" may be offensive or unpleasant in a way that the spoken form is not.

Given that it is the written form of names that has force, that informs, that can be used to change a bad fate, there is justification for thinking that those whose names are rarely or never written are at some disadvantage. Girls, it would appear, did not have names in the same way that boys did.[7] It is also clear that girls' names are less expressive, less individuating than their brothers' names are. Fathers strove to make son's names distinctive, unique—whereas girls' names tended to classify (for example, Endure, Little Maiden) or to be used as a vehicle for changing circumstances external to the girl herself (for example, Joined to Brother). Many girls of course had names like Splendid Orchid, Morning Flower, Resembling Jade, but in general they were more likely than were their brothers to be given negative names, stereotypic names, or goal-oriented names. These gender distinctions are significant, but the contrast between men and women becomes even more dramatic when we consider adult naming practices.

MEN'S NAMING

When a Ha Tsuen man marries, he is given or takes (often he chooses the name himself) a marriage name, or *tzu*. Considering the importance of the written name it is significant that *tzu* is the same character that is commonly used for "word" or "ideograph." The marriage name is given in a ceremony called *sung tzu*, which literally means "to deliver written characters." This ceremony is an integral part of the marriage rites and is held after the main banquet on the first day of wedding festivities.

In Ha Tsuen, the marriage name (always two characters) is written on a small rectangular piece of red paper and is displayed in the main reception hall of the groom's house (alternatively, it may be hung in the groom's branch ancestral hall). This name is chosen with regard to its effect in the written form. Great care is taken in choosing the characters; they often have origins in the Confucian classics. In Ha Tsuen one of the two characters of this marriage name is usually shared by a lineage generational set. In some kin groups a respected scholar may be asked to choose a poem or aphorism to be used in generational naming. Each generation will then take in turn one character of the poem as part of their (*tzu*) name. Of course, this makes the selection of an auspicious, learned name more difficult and also more intellectually challenging. Naming at this level can become a highly complicated game.

In choosing a marriage name (*tzu*) the groom demonstrates his sophistication, learning, and goals. Among the people I studied, the possession of a marriage name is essential for the attainment of male adulthood, which gives a man the right to participate in important lineage and community rituals. In Ha Tsuen the correct way to ask whether a man has full ritual rights in the lineage is to inquire, "Does X have a *tzu*?", not "Is X married?" Marriage names are not used as terms of address; they may, however, appear in lineage genealogies and in formal documents.

By the time a man is married he will have acquired a public nickname (*wai hao*, literally an "outside name"). This is usually different from the family nickname he had in infancy or the "school name" given to him by a teacher.[8] Nicknames are widely used as terms of address and reference for males in the village; in fact, a man's birth and marriage names may be largely unknown.

In a discussion of naming among the Ilongot, Renato Rosaldo emphasizes the process by which names come into being (1984:13). Rosaldo argues that names are negotiated, and that naming, like other aspects of Ilongot social life, is a matter of give and take, challenge and response (1984:22). Rosaldo's approach is particularly useful for understanding Chinese nicknaming. *Ming* (birth names) are formally bestowed by one's seniors, one chooses the *tzu* (marriage name) and, as we will see, the *hao* (courtesy name) oneself. Nicknames (*wai hao*), however, are negotiated; both the namer and the named play the game. By setting up this dichotomy between nicknames and other given names, I do not mean to suggest that these two categories have no common features nor that *ming*, marriage names, and courtesy names are simply the consequence of a set of rigidly applied rules and structures. It is clear, however, that nicknames fit into the transactional world of local politics, friendship, and informal groups more comfortably than do formal names.

In Chinese society, one can gain a reputation for cleverness by giving nicknames that are particularly apt or make witty literary allusions. Chinese nicknames are highly personalized and often refer to idiosyncratic characteristics. They may also be derogatory or critical, whereas one's formal names would never be intentionally unflattering (especially for a man). Nicknames may refer to a physical quality (for example, "Fatty") or a personal quality ("Stares at the Sky" for someone who is a snob). Nicknames may also protect ("Little Slave Girl") or they may equalize, at least temporarily, unequal relationships. The richest and most powerful man in one New Territories village was nicknamed "Little Dog." In one respect this was a useful nickname for an extremely wealthy man whose political career depended on being accepted by everyone in the community. Rather than rejecting his derogatory nickname he embraced it.

In Ha Tsuen when a man reaches middle age or when he starts a business career, he usually takes a *hao*—"style" or "courtesy" name. A man chooses this name himself. Sung notes that such names are "usually dissyllabic or polysyllabic, and [are] selected by oneself bas[ed] upon whatever one would like to be" (1981:86). Some people have more than one courtesy name. The *hao* is a public name par excellence. Such names, Eberhard points out, are often used on occasions when a man wants "to make his personal identity clear without revealing his personal name (*ming*)" (1970:219). In the past, and to some extent today,[9] the *ming* was considered to be too intimate, too personal to be used outside a circle of close friends and kin (Eberhard 1970:218). "The Chinese I know hide their names," writes Maxine Hong Kingston in *Woman Warrior;* "sojourners take new names when their lives change and guard their real names with silence" (1977:6).

Sung notes that *hao* names are no longer popular in present-day Taiwan except among high government officials (1981:86). However, in Hong Kong *hao* are still widely used; they are commonly found, for example, on business cards, and of course many painters or writers sign their work with a *hao*.

In one sense courtesy names are different from birth and marriage names. One achieves a courtesy name. They are a mark of social and economic status, and a poor man who gives himself such a name may be accused of putting on airs. Any man may take a *hao* but if he is not a "man of substance," the *hao* is likely to remain unknown and unused. With poor men or politically insignificant men these names, if they have them at all, may appear only in genealogies or on tombstones.

Some Ha Tsuen men have posthumous names (*shih-hao*) that they take themselves or have conferred upon them by others. Among the imperial elite posthumous names or titles were given to honor special deeds. In the village, however, taking or giving a *shih-hao* is left to individual taste. The practice has declined in recent years.

The preceding discussion suggests that names mark stages in a man's social life. The possession of a birth name, school name, nickname, marriage name, courtesy name, and posthumous name attest to the fact that a man has passed through the major stages of social adulthood. By the time a man reaches middle age he has considerable control over his names and naming. He names others (his children or grandchildren, for example) and he chooses his own marriage, courtesy, and posthumous names. He also has some control over the use of these names. This is especially true of a successful businessman or politician whose business associates may only know his courtesy name, his drinking friends one of his nicknames, his lineage-mates his birth name, and so on. The use of names is situational and involves some calculation both on the part of the named and those with whom he interacts.

Beidelman, in an article on naming among the Kaguru of Tanzania, emphasizes the point that the choice of name reflects the relation between the speaker and the person to whom he speaks (1974:282; see also Willis 1982). The choice of one name or another, or the use of a kin term rather than a personal name, is a tactical decision. In Ha Tsuen the use of nicknames, pet names, birth names, courtesy names is, like the use of kin terms, highly contextual. Intimates may address each other by a nickname when they are among friends but not when strangers are present, family nicknames may be used in the household but not outside of it, birth names and surnames with titles may be used in formal introductions but not in other settings. A man might be addressed by a kin term or a nickname depending on the speaker's goals. One can give respect by using a courtesy name or claim intimacy by using a nickname. In a single lineage village like Ha Tsuen, where all males are agnatic kinsmen, the strategic use of kin terms and personal names provides a fascinating glimpse into social relationships.

Surprisingly, however, this flexibility does not continue into old age. When a man reaches elderhood at age 61, his ability to control his names diminishes just as his control over his family and corporate resources weakens. In Ha Tsuen and in China generally men often hand over headship of the family when they become elders. The village code of

respect requires that male elders be addressed by a kin term (for example, in Cantonese *ah baak*, FeB, or a combination of the given name and kin term, for example, *ah Tso baak*). Only an exceptional man, a scholar or wealthy businessman, will continue to be called by one of his personal names after his 60th birthday. For example, no villager would dare refer to or address the 93-year-old patriarch of the wealthiest family in Ha Tsuen as *ah baak*. In general, however, with advancing age the playful aspects of names and naming are taken away as is a man's power to transact his name. In old age a man has little control over what he is called, and in this respect his situation is similar to that of a married woman. As with wives, old men have left (or are leaving) the world of public and financial affairs to become immersed in the world of family and kinship where they are defined not by a set of distinctive names but by their relationship to others.

"NO NAME" WOMEN

At one month a Ha Tsuen girl is given a name (*ming*); when she marries this name ceases to be used. Marriage is a critical rite of passage for both men and women, but the effect of this rite on the two sexes is very different. Just as a man's distinctiveness and public role are enhanced by his marriage and his acquisition of a marriage name, the marriage rites relegate the woman to the inner world of household, neighborhood, and family. On the one hand, the marriage rites seek to enhance the young bride's fertility, but on the other hand, and in a more negative vein, they also dramatize the bride's separation from her previous life and emphasize the prohibitions and restrictions that now confine her. When the young bride crosses her husband's threshold, what distinctiveness she had as a girl is thrust aside. It is at this point that she loses her name and becomes the "inner person" (*nei jen*), a term Chinese husbands use to refer to their wives.

While the groom is receiving his marriage name on the first day of marriage rites, his bride is being given an intensive course in kinship terminology by the elderly women of Ha Tsuen. Marriage ritual provides a number of occasions for the formal, ritualized exchange of kin terms (for a description of marriage rites in Ha Tsuen see R. Watson 1981). These exchanges, which always feature the bride, instruct the new wife and daughter-in-law in the vast array of kin terms she must use for her husband's relatives. The prevalence of virilocal/patrilocal residence means that the groom remains among the kin with whom he has always lived. It is the bride who must grasp a whole new set of kin terms and learn to attach these terms to what must seem a bewildering array of people. Two women resident in the groom's village (called in Cantonese *choi gaa*, "bride callers") act as the bride's guides and supporters during the three days of marriage rites, and it is their responsibility to instruct the bride in the kin terminology she will need in order to survive in her new environment.

These ritualized exchanges of kin terms do more, however, than serve as a pedagogic exercise; they also locate and anchor the bride in a new relational system. As the groom acquires his new marriage name—a name, it should be noted, that denotes both group or category membership *and* individual distinctiveness—the bride enters a world in which she exists only in relation to others. She is no longer "grounded" by her own special name (*ming*), however prosaic that name might have been; after marriage she exists only as someone's eBW or yBW or as Sing's mother, and so on. Eventually even these terms will be used with decreasing frequency; as she approaches old age, she will be addressed simply as "old woman" (*ah po*) by all but her close kin.

When I first moved into Ha Tsuen, I quickly learned the names of the male residents (mostly nicknames). But for the women I, like other villagers, relied on kin terms or category terms. Significantly, the rules that govern the use of these terms are not dependent on the age of the women themselves, but rather are a function of the lineage generation of their husbands. Women married to

men of an ascending generation to the speaker (or the speaker's husband) may be addressed as *ah suk po* (a local expression meaning FyBW) or by the more formal *ah sam* (also meaning FyBW). For women married to men of one's own generation (male ego) the terms *ah sou* (eBW) or, if one wanted to give added respect, *ah sam* (FyBW) may be used.

A woman may also be referred to by the nickname of her husband plus "leung" (for example, ah Keung leung), or by a teknonym. For their part married women ordinarily use kin terms for their husbands' agnates and for other women in the village. I was told that a woman must use kin terms for men older in age or generation than her husband. Between husband and wife teknonyms are often used so that the father of Tim-sing might address his wife as *ah Sing nai* (ah is a prefix denoting familiarity, *Sing* is part of the son's *ming*, nai is "mother" or, literally, "milk"). In addressing their husbands, women might use nicknames; my neighbor always called her husband "Little Servant."[10]

Although there is some flexibility in deciding what to call a woman, the reference and address terms used for women in Ha Tsuen are very rigid compared to those employed for men. Furthermore, among women there is no possibility of self-naming. Men name themselves, women are named by others. Similarly, Ha Tsuen women are more restricted than their husbands in the tactical use they can make of names and kin terms. Whereas a man may refer to or address his neighbor by his nickname ("Fatty"), his *ming* (*ah Tim*), or by a kin term, decorum dictates that his wife use either a kin term appropriate to her husband's generation or one appropriate to her children. In Cantonese society, and presumably in China generally, adults often address and refer to each other by a version of the kin term their children would use for that person. I suspect, but at this point cannot document, that women are far more likely to do this than are men.

While it is true that a man has little choice in the reference or address terms he uses for women, he does have considerable freedom in distinguishing among his male acquaintances, friends, and kin. Women, as outlined above, have a restricted repertoire for both sexes. In this sense adult women may be said to carry a particularly heavy burden for guarding the kinship and sexual order. No adult woman is free to act alone or to be treated as if she were independent. The terms by which she is addressed and the terms she uses to address others serve as constant reminders of the hierarchical relations of gender, age, and generation.

As men grow older, as they become students, marry, start careers, take jobs, and eventually prepare for ancestorhood, their new names anchor them to new roles and privileges. These names are not, however, only role markers or classifiers. Ideally, they assign people to categories and at the same time declare their uniqueness. The pattern of naming in Chinese society presents an ever changing image of men. Viewed from this perspective Chinese males are always growing, becoming, accumulating new responsibilities and new rights.

Peasant women, on the other hand, experience few publicly validated life changes, and those that they do undergo link them ever more securely to stereotyped roles. Women's naming leaves little room for individuation or self-expression. Unlike males, whose changes are marked by both ascribed (for example, elderhood) *and* achieved criteria (such as student, scholar, businessman, writer, politician), a woman's changes (from unmarried virgin to married woman, from nonmother to mother, from reproducer to nonreproducer) are not related to achievement outside the home. Instead of acquiring a new name at marriage or the birth of a first child, women's changes are marked by kin terminology or category shifts. At marriage the bride loses her *ming* and becomes known by a series of kin terms. At the birth of a child she may add a teknonym ("Sing's mother"), and as she approaches and enters old age more and more people will address her simply as "old woman" (*ah po*).

The most dramatic changes that women make are the shift from named to unnamed at marriage and the gradual shift from kin term

to category term as their children mature and marry.[11] It would appear that as a woman's reproductive capacity declines, she becomes less grounded in the relational system. She becomes, quite simply, an "old woman" much like any other old woman. Of course, family members continue to use kin terms for these elderly women, especially in reference and address, but gradually their anonymity increases. Unlike men, women do not become elders. There is no ceremony marking their entry into respected old age. They move from reproductively active mother to sexually inactive grandmother with no fanfare and with little public recognition of their changed status.

Even in death a woman has no personal name. On the red flag that leads the spirit of the deceased from the village to the grave is written the woman's father's surname (for example, *Lin shih*, translated "Family of Lin"); no personal name is added. For men, the deceased's surname plus his courtesy and/or posthumous name is written on the soul flag. Neither do women's personal names appear on the tombstone where, here again, only the surname of the woman's father is given ("Family of Lin"). In Ha Tsuen women do not have separate ancestral tablets; if they are commemorated at all, they appear as minor appendages on their husbands' tablets. And, once more, they are listed only under the surnames of their fathers. In subsequent generations whatever individuating characteristics a woman might have had are lost—not even a name survives as testimony of her existence as a person.

CONCLUSIONS

If one were to categorize Ha Tsuen villagers on a social continuum according to the number and quality of their names, married peasant women would stand at the extreme negative pole.[12] To my knowledge they share this dubious distinction with no other group. In the past even male slaves (*hsi min*) and household servants had nicknames (see J. Watson 1976:365). They may not have had *ming* or surnames as such but they did possess names that distinguished them from others. It is important to note that it is not only the possession of multiple names that matters but also the fact that, at one end of the continuum, people have no control over their own names while, at the other end, they name themselves and others.

At marriage women find themselves enmeshed in the world of family and kinship. It is a world, as noted in the introduction, that they belong to but do not control. In Ha Tsuen brides arrive as outsiders but quickly, one might even say brutally, they become firmly entrenched in their new environment. Village women can only be identified within the constellation of male names or within the limits of kinship terminology. Unlike their husbands and brothers, women—having no public identity outside the relational system—are defined by and through others.

In Ha Tsuen women are excluded from participation in most of the formal aspects of lineage or community life and they are not involved in decision making outside the home. Ha Tsuen women do not inherit productive resources; they are also restricted in the uses to which they can put their dowries (R. Watson 1984). Furthermore, women in Ha Tsuen cannot become household heads and, even today, they do not vote in local elections. They do not worship in ancestral halls nor do they join the cult of lineage ancestors after death. Although individual peasant women may attain considerable power within their households, they are said to have gained this power by manipulation and stealth. Women by definition cannot hold positions of authority.

In a discussion of male and female naming among the Omaha Sioux, Robert Barnes writes: "The names of Omaha males provide men with distinctive individuality, while also linking each unmistakably to a recognized collectivity. The possibility of acquiring multiple names in adulthood enhances individual prominence for men" (1982:220). Barnes goes on to say that women's names "barely rescue them from a general anonymity, neither conferring uniqueness nor indicating

group membership" (1982:22). As among the Sioux, personal naming among Chinese men is a sign of both individual distinctiveness and group membership, while naming practices among village women simply confirm their marginality.

In Ha Tsuen the practice of personal naming reflects and facilitates the passage from one social level to another. Names establish people in social groups and give them certain rights within those groups. With each additional name, a man acquires new attributes. Maybury-Lewis has argued that among many Central Brazilian societies names give humans their "social persona and link [them] to other people" (1984:5; see also Bamberger 1974). Names, Maybury-Lewis writes, "transform individuals into persons" (1984:7). Naming may not be as central to Chinese social organization and ideology as it is among the societies of Central Brazil, yet there is no doubt that, for Chinese men, names have a transformative power that binds them as individuals to society.

In Ha Tsuen the ultimate goal of all males is to produce an heir, to have a grandson at one's funeral, to leave property that guarantees the performance of one's ancestral rites. The possession of many names testifies to the fact that a man has completed the cycle of life. Full personhood is not acquired at birth, at marriage, or even at the death of one's father. It is a process that continues throughout life and is punctuated by the taking and bestowing of names. One might argue that it is a process that extends even beyond death as the named ancestor interacts with the living. If, as Grace Harris suggests, personhood involves a process of social growth "in the course of which changes [are] wrought by ceremony and ritual" (1978:49), then Chinese women never approximate the full cycle of development that their menfolk experience.[13] In stark contrast to men, women become less distinct as they age. The changes they undergo remain largely unrecognized and unnoticed.

In Chinese society, as in other societies, there is a tension between the notion of the unique individual (the individual as value) and the notion of the person tied to society.[14] In some sense the great philosophical systems of Taoism and Confucianism represent these two poles. Among men, naming involves a dual process through which they achieve personhood by being bound to society, while at the same time they acquire an enhanced sense of individuality and distinctiveness. The peasant women described in this paper seem to have been largely excluded from the individuating, individualizing world of personal naming. The situation with regard to personhood is, however, another matter. It would be wrong to say that peasant wives are nonpersons; rather, they are not persons in the same sense or to the same degree as are husbands and sons. Viewed from the perspective of names, peasant women are neither fully individuated nor "personed." In life as in death they remain suspended between the anonymous world of anybodies and the more sharply defined world of somebodies.

NOTES

Acknowledgments. The research for this study was conducted in 1977–78 and was made possible by a grant from the Social Science Research Council (Great Britain) and by the University of London Central Research Fund. An earlier version of this paper was presented at the 1984 American Anthropological Association Annual Meetings. Versions of this paper were also presented at the University of London Intercollegiate Anthropology Seminar and at the University of Rochester's Anthropology Colloquium. I thank the members of those seminars for their suggestions and criticisms. I owe a special debt to Jack Dull, Hsu Cho-yun, Sun Man-li, Roderick MacFarquhar, and James Watson, all of whom have helped in this project. Deborah Kwolek, Judy Tredway, and Martha Terry of the Asian Studies Program at the University of Pittsburgh helped in the preparation of the manuscript and I thank them for their assistance.

Cantonese terms are in Yale romanization and Mandarin terms follow the Wade-Giles system.

This paper is dedicated to the memory of my friend and fellow anthropologist Judith Strauch (1942–85).

1. There are bound to be regional, temporal, urban-rural, and class differences in Chinese naming practices. A general discussion of Chinese naming awaits further research.

2. In Taiwan the *ming* is the legal name (it appears in the official household register) and is sometimes called the *cheng ming* (correct name) (Sung 1981:70). In Hong Kong this name may or may not be the name used on legal documents.

3. I am grateful to Professor Jack Dull for pointing out to me the significance and frequency of the personal name Nai among Chinese women.

4. In a similar vein a fifth or sixth child might be named "To End" or "To Finish." One can find such names in the Hong Kong and Taipei telephone directories (see also Sung 1981:81).

5. In China there are no given names like John that are shared by millions of people; on this point see Sung 1981:85.

6. In a discussion of the cosmic relationship between mother and child Marjorie Topley writes of her Cantonese informants:

   The constitutional imbalance of a child with a queer fate may also involve other parties. First, the child may be polarized in the same direction as someone with whom it has a continuous relationship. Then both parties may suffer from continual illness. This may be corrected by adding an element to the child's name so it is compatible with that of the other party [1974:240].

7. This is changing now that girls go to school and their births are registered.

8. In the past when village boys started school at age five or six (girls did not attend school until the 1960s), the schoolmaster gave each student a school or "study name" (*hsueh-ming*). School names are no longer very important in the New Territories.

9. In the past officials' *ming* could not be used except by intimates (see Eberhard 1970 and Sung 1981).

10. After having gained some insight into the micropolitics of my neighbor's household, the name seemed well chosen.

11. Once a son marries reproduction becomes a matter for the younger generation, and in Ha Tsuen it was considered shameful for the mother of a married son to become pregnant.

12. It should be noted here that men do not constitute a uniform category in this regard. Highly literate men make up one extreme but

many poorly educated or uneducated men fall somewhere between the two extremes. Like the names of their sisters, their names may be inelegant and rarely seen in written form, but unlike adult women, they do retain their names after marriage.

13. On this point see also LaFontaine 1985:131.
14. For discussions of the concept of the individual as value and the self in Chinese society see for example de Bary 1970; Shiga 1978:122; and more recently Elvin 1985; Munro 1985 (especially essays by Hansen, Yu, Munro, and de Bary).

REFERENCES CITED

Arlington, L. C. 1923. The Chinese Female Names. China Journal of Science and Arts 1(4):316–325.

Bamberger, Joan. 1974. Naming and the Transmission of Status in a Central Brazilian Society. Ethnology 13:363–378.

Barnes, Robert B. 1982. Personal Names and Social Classification. *In* Semantic Anthropology. David Parkin, ed. pp. 211–226. London: Academic Press.

Beidelman, T. O. 1974. Kaguru Names and Naming. Journal of Anthropological Research 30:281–293.

de Bary, William Theodore. 1970. Individualism and Humanitarianism in Late Ming Thought. *In* Self and Society in Ming Thought. Wm. Theodore de Bary, ed. pp. 145–247. New York: Columbia University Press.

Eberhard, Wolfram. 1970. A Note on Modern Chinese Nicknames. *In* Studies in Chinese Folklore and Related Essays. Wolfram Eberhard, ed. pp. 217–222. Indiana University Folklore Institute Monograph Series, Vol. 23. The Hague: Mouton.

Elvin, Mark. 1985. Between the Earth and Heaven: Conceptions of the Self in China. *In* The Category of the Person. Michael Carrithers, Steven Collins, Steven Lukes, eds. pp. 156–189. Cambridge: Cambridge University Press.

Geertz, Clifford. 1973. Person, Time, and Conduct in Bali. *In* The Interpretation of Cultures. pp. 360–411. New York: Basic Books.

Harris, Grace. 1978. Casting Out Anger: Religion among the Taita of Kenya. Cambridge: Cambridge University Press.

Hazelton, Keith. 1986. Patrilines and the Development of Localized Lineages: The Wu of Hsiu-ming City, Hui-chou, to 1528. *In* Kinship Organization in Late Imperial China. Patricia B. Ebrey and James L. Watson, eds. pp. 137–169. Berkeley: University of California Press.

Kehl, Frank. 1971. Chinese Nicknaming Behavior: A Sociolinguistic Pilot Study. Journal of Oriental Studies 9:149–172.

Kingston, Maxine Hong. 1977. The Woman Warrior: Memories of a Girlhood among Ghosts. New York: Vintage Books. (Originally published in hardcover by Alfred Knopf, 1976.)

La Fontaine, Jean. 1985. Person and Individual: Some Anthropological Reflections. *In* The Category of the Person. Michael Carrithers, Steven Collins, and Steven Lukes, eds. pp. 123–140. Cambridge: Cambridge University Press.

Maybury-Lewis, David. 1984. Name, Person, and Ideology in Central Brazil. *In* Naming Systems. Elisabeth Tooker, ed. pp. 1–10. 1980 Proceedings of the American Ethnological Society. Washington, DC: American Ethnological Society.

Munro, Donald (ed.). 1985. Individualism and Holism: Studies in Confucian and Taoist Values. Ann Arbor: University of Michigan Press.

Rosaldo, Renato. 1984. Ilongot Naming: The Play of Associations. *In* Naming Systems. Elisabeth Tooker, ed. pp. 11–24. 1980 Proceedings of the American Ethnological Society. Washington, DC: American Ethnological Society.

Sharman, Lyon. 1934. Sun Yat-sen: His Life and its Meaning. Stanford, CA: Stanford University Press.

Shiga, Shuzo. 1978. Family Property and the Law of Inheritance in Traditional China. *In* Chinese Family Law and Social Change. David Buxbaum, ed. pp. 109–150. Seattle: University of Washington Press.

Stacey, Judith. 1983. Patriarchy and Socialist Revolution in China. Berkeley: University of California Press.

Sung, Margaret M. Y. 1981. Chinese Personal Naming. Journal of the Chinese Language Teachers Association 16(2):67–90.

Topley, Marjorie. 1974. Cosmic Antagonisms: A Mother-Child Syndrome. *In* Religion and Ritual in Chinese Society. Arthur Wolf, ed. pp. 233–249. Stanford, CA: Stanford University Press.

Watson, James L. 1976. Chattel Slavery in Chinese Peasant Society: A Comparative Analysis. Ethnology 15:361–375.

Watson, Rubie S. 1981. Class Differences and Affinal Relations in South China. Man 16:593–615.

———. 1984. Women's Property in Republican

China: Rights and Practice. Republican China 10(12):1–12.

———. 1985. Inequality Among Brothers: Class and Kinship in South China. Cambridge: Cambridge University Press.

Willis, Roy. 1982. On a Mental Sausage Machine and other Nominal Problems. *In* Semantic Anthropology. David Parkin, ed. pp. 227–240. London: Academic Press.

Wolf, Margery. 1972. Women and the Family in Rural Taiwan. Stanford, CA: Stanford University Press.

Wu, Ching-chao. 1927. The Chinese Family: Organization, Names, and Kinship Terms. American Anthropologist 29:316–325.

Yang, Martin C. 1945. A Chinese Village: Taitou, Shantung Province. New York: Columbia University Press.

Menstruation and the Power of Yurok Women

Thomas Buckley

In 1976 Lowell Bean and Thomas Blackburn encouraged the ongoing renewal of anthropological interest in native California through publication of a collection of relatively recent theoretical essays. In their introduction to the volume the editors stress the possibilities inherent in the truly vast accumulation of data on aboriginal Californian peoples to be found in the descriptive ethnographies of earlier investigators, and especially in the "undigested" original field notes of these ethnographers. Bean and Blackburn (1976:5–10) emphasize the necessity for approaching such materials from new theoretical perspectives so as to realize their potentials. Several recent papers on Californian cultures stress such possibilities as well, suggesting that the real value in exploring these cultures lies in opportunities for developing hypotheses of significance to general theory

Reprinted with permission from Thomas Buckley and Alma Gottlieb (eds.), *Blood Magic: Explorations in the Anthropology of Menstruation* (Berkeley: University of California Press, 1988), pp. 187–209. Copyright © 1988 The Regents of the University of California.

regarding hunter-gatherers far beyond the confines of native California. Data on the area are increasingly recognized as being uniquely fruitful in just this regard (e.g., Gould 1975; Blackburn 1976).

That significant new work on native California continues to appear belies the Kroeberian notion that the ethnographic records of California's aboriginal peoples have been completed as far as possible and, moreover, that they have been exhausted analytically. Clearly more skeptical scholars have been mistaken in the conservatism of their questioning "whether late-coming ethnologists, working with . . . apparently imperfect old data and such new data as can be elicited from younger informants . . . can actually develop a viable new analytic system . . . at this late date" (Elsasser 1976:96). Specifically, I question the dim view taken in some quarters of the value of contemporary Indian consultants' testimony regarding their traditional cultures. Surviving Californian cultures have proved unexpectedly resilient. It is indeed, as Bean and Blackburn (1976:8–9) point out, the possibility of doing sound new fieldwork in native California that in part accounts for the extreme usefulness today of older unpublished field materials.

Following these anthropologists, I suggest that contemporary research in and analyses of California cultures may best be undertaken in a threefold manner. New fieldwork among knowledgeable consultants should be seen in relation to earlier accounts, especially those available in various archives. Each sheds light on the other. Contemporary testimony often reveals the importance of data that were neglected in published work, and these earlier data may provide unplumbed information that could be highly useful in interpreting the nature of both cultural change and persistence in a given surviving culture. A theoretical component is needed, however, to take full advantage of the existence of these two strata of field materials, and this third component must overcome the limitations in vision implicit in prior neglect of significant portions of the earlier data. Particularly in the Californian case, such limitations seem to indicate a certain blindness to broadly suggestive, complex orders of systematic organization, variation, and interrelation in native cultures, and it is with these that I am most concerned here.

"MOONTIME"

The Yurok Indians today live largely within or near their aboriginal homelands in coastal and riverine northwestern California, close by the Klamath River and the present California-Oregon border. Their culture, though greatly changed since the time of first massive contact with European-Americans during the gold rush, retains a certain, albeit transformed, uniqueness.

One evening in 1978 I went with an Indian friend to his house to eat. He would be doing the cooking, he explained on the way, because his Yurok wife was "on her moontime" (menstruating)[1] and they were keeping the old ways as best they could. This meant that his wife went into seclusion for ten days dur-

ing and after her flow, cooking and eating her own food by herself.

According to traditional "Indian law" (here, rules for conduct), a menstruating woman is highly polluting and will contaminate the family house and food supply if she comes into contact with either. Thus in the old days, a special shelter for menstrual seclusion was built near the main house, and special food for a family's menstruating women was separately collected, stored, and prepared for consumption in this shelter. In my friend's modern house a back room had been set aside for his wife's monthly use. Separate food storage as well as cooking and eating utensils were furnished in the kitchen.

I hadn't expected to find the old, seemingly anachronistic menstrual practices being approximated in this environment. Aside from the exclusion of women from ceremonial activities during their menses, and the fact that some men refrain from deer hunting while their wives and daughters are menstruating, I had not found adherence to the old menstrual rules to be widespread among contemporary Yurok—certainly not to the extent that they were being followed in this house. Even here, however, these rules were not kept to the letter. The young woman appeared when we arrived and joined the conversation, explaining to me that she often got restless in her back room and so wandered around the house talking with her husband when he was home, although they neither ate nor slept together during her "moontime." She then went on to talk about what she was doing and why and how she felt about it.

She said that she had been instructed in the menstrual laws by her maternal aunts and grandmother, who in their times were well-known, conservative Yurok women. Her understanding of menstruation came largely from these sources. She began her account of this understanding by telling me that as a foster child in non-Indian homes she had been taught that menstruation is "bad and shameful" and that through it "women are being punished." On her return to Yurok society, however, "my aunts and my grandmother taught me different."[2] The difference was that these women stressed the positive aspects of menstruation and of Yurok menstrual rules. Briefly, here is what the young woman said.

A menstruating woman should isolate herself because this is the time when she is at the height of her powers. Thus the time should not be wasted in mundane tasks and social distractions, nor should one's concentration be broken by concerns with the opposite sex. Rather, all of one's energies should be applied in concentrated meditation "to find out the purpose of your life," and toward the "accumulation" of spiritual energy. The menstrual shelter, or room, is "like the men's sweathouse," a place where you "go into yourself and make yourself stronger." As in traditional male sweathouse practice, or "training" (*hohkep-*), there are physical as well as mental aspects of "accumulation." The blood that flows serves to "purify" the woman, preparing her for spiritual accomplishment. Again, a woman must use a scratching implement, instead of scratching absentmindedly with her fingers, as an aid in focusing her full attention on her body by making even the most natural and spontaneous of actions fully conscious and intentional: "You should feel all of your body exactly as it is, and pay attention."

The woman continued: There is, in the mountains above the old Yurok village of Meri·p, a "sacred moontime pond" where in the old days menstruating women went to bathe and to perform rituals that brought spiritual benefits. Practitioners brought special firewood back from this place for use in the menstrual shelter. Many girls performed these rites only at the time of their first menstruation, but aristocratic women went to the pond every month until menopause. Through such practice women came to "see that the earth has her own moontime," a recognition that made one both "stronger" and "proud" of one's menstrual cycle.

Finally, the young woman said that in oldtime village life all of a household's fertile women who were not pregnant menstruated at the same time, a time dictated by the moon; that these women practiced the bathing rituals together at this time; and that men associated with the household used this time to "train hard" in the household's sweathouse. If a woman got out of synchronization with the moon and with the other women of the household, she could "get back in by sitting in the moonlight and talking to the moon, asking it to balance [her]."

THE CLASSIC APPROACH

My immediate reaction to all of this was somewhat as follows. The woman and her husband, who were both deeply involved in the contemporary renascence of Indian culture and identity and were committed to living in an "Indian way," as they understood it, had revived aspects of traditional menstrual practice as a means of expressing their commitment to "Indianness." Because the old Yurok menstrual rules had reflected the male-dominant gender asymmetry that ordered the underlying symbolic code—an asymmetry specifically challenged by modern notions of women's rights—these old rules had been rationalized and reinterpreted. Through this process they had come to be newly understood from a perspective that allowed resolution of conflicting desires for both a strong link to the Indian past and for political modernity.

I reacted this way because having studied the received ethnographies of traditional Yurok and neighboring cultures carefully, I found the young woman's testimony incredible. According to a composite picture drawn from published data bearing on the topic of menstruation in Yurok, Karok, Hupa, and Tolowa ethnographies, menstruation and everything associated with it was simply negative—in Yurok, *kimoleni* (dirty, polluting). Menstrual blood itself was thought by Yurok to be a dire poison, and menstruating women were believed to contaminate whatever they came into contact with—houses, food, hunting gear, weapons, canoes, water, trails, and, above all, the men's wealth objects central to these acquisitive societies and emblematic of spiritual ascendancy (Bushnell and Bushnell 1977). Menstruating women, beyond contaminating concrete objects, were perhaps most dangerous through their negative effect on men's psychic or spiritual life. These women spoiled men's "luck" (*heyomoks-*)— their ability to exercise power in, among other things, the accumulation of wealth. A menstruating woman who seduced an unwary man was therefore cišah ([worse than] a dog), the lowest form of mammalian life. Strong antipathy between menstruous women and the world of spirits seems suggested by the use of menstruating virgins to drive off the spirits (*wo·gey*) that attempted to steal the "souls" (*hewec-*) of infants.

Thus menstruating women were isolated in special shelters, ate carefully segregated foods, and used scratching bones, being so highly charged with negative energy that they could not touch even themselves for fear of poisoning. In Yurok society, far from being permitted to travel into the very "pure" (*mɨw.ɨks.y.h̓*) mountains to bathe, these women bathed daily and seemingly compulsively in the Klamath River, waters already thought to be polluted by corpses, dogs, aborted fetuses, and menstrual blood—"things" (*so·k*). Finally, regarding discrepancies between the modern Yurok woman's testimony on the positive nature of menstruation and the received ethnographies, the latter nowhere explicitly suggest that either the moon or synchrony was a consideration in aboriginal menstrual practices.[3]

Reports of entirely negative coding of menstruation itself (as distinct from female puberty) are, of course, staples of the ethnographic accounts of a great many cultures, to the extent that they seem collectively to suggest an ethnological truism: Menstruation is, for a great many peoples, virtually the definitive form of pollution. Currently this apparent truism is being widely used as the basis for a strong element in more general, politically motivated critiques of male-dominant gender asymmetry in certain cultures (e.g., Delaney, Lupton, and Toth 1976). Supported by further neglected Yurok data to which I now turn, however, I suggest that we be circum-

spect in evaluating received ethnographies, realizing the double male biases that are implicit in a great many of them (i.e., in the descriptions of male anthropologists based on the testimony of primarily male consultants). Moreover I suggest that we be open to far more complex kinds of symbolic, or conceptual, structuring than are accommodated in what may be simplistic and overly universalistic views of menstruation qua pollution. We should bear in mind the ambivalent nature of pollution itself in many cultural systems, where, far from being a *simply* negative concept, pollution is understood to comprise an ambiguous manifestation of a neutral (hence potentially positive) energy (Douglas 1966; compare Bean 1977). Finally, we should continue to consider seriously Edwin Ardener's (1972:1–3) proposition that the world of women in culture is not characteristically defined by the same "neat, bounded categories given by the male informant" (King 1983:109).

KROEBER'S FIELD NOTES

A few weeks after the conversation sketched earlier I went to Berkeley, where I spent several days going through the A. L. Kroeber Papers, now in the Manuscript Division of the Bancroft Library, University of California, Berkeley (call number 71/83c). I was particularly interested in Kroeber's Yurok field notes (cartons 6 and 7). I discovered, in the course of my readings, a set of notes and textual transcriptions detailing interviews with a Yurok woman at the village of Wecpus in 1902 (carton 7). Kroeber never utilized either the texts or most of the descriptions collected from this woman, identified only as "Weitchpec Susie," in his various publications (but see Kroeber 1925:45).

These notes and transcriptions concern menstruation and childbirth and, along with some expository comments by Susie on these topics, include a long formula used by women in ritual bathing during menstruation, a myth relating the origins of both menstruation and these rituals, and other esoterica—fragments of prayers and myths concerning various aspects of childbirth. To my surprise, these materials to an extent confirmed the traditional authenticity of the young woman's modern understanding of menstruation as a powerful, positive phenomenon with esoteric significance. Additionally, Kroeber's notes provide a good deal of fresh insight into the structure of menstrual symbolism when viewed from a feminine perspective.

According to the myth recited in English by Susie, menstruation originated in a capricious joke, initiated by Coyote (*segep*).[4] Coyote said, "I think be best way if woman have flowers. When she have flowers she will see blood." The hero Pulekuk^werek aided and abetted Coyote, cutting his ankle and putting the blood on a girl's thigh. Coyote said, "You got flowers now." Girl: "No!" Coyote: "Yes, I see blood on your legs." Coyote and Pulekuk^werek then instituted both the girls' puberty ritual and the regimen to be followed during subsequent menses. The duration of monthly continence and ritual observance (ten days), proper costume (a bark skirt, grass arm and leg bands), specially treated foods of a limited kind (acorns gathered and stored for the purpose, similarly secured dried fish, no red meats or fresh fish), isolation in a special shelter, a program of bathing and of firewood gathering, and use of the long prayer to bring wealth are all specified (notes for 8 June 1902, pp. 1–8).

After Coyote has outlined the basic menstrual procedures he falters, not knowing how to continue. A spirit-woman speaks to him from the sky:

Need not be afraid of that [menstruation]. We [spirits] are around here in sky, all we women thus, flowers, and we never afraid on it, because we have medicine for it. Now you look way over other side (upriver). Now I always wash way over there myself. . . . Now you can look, look at that lake right in the middle of the sky, you can see how many trails come on that lake. . . . Those trails are dentalia's trails some of them, some woodpecker head's, some white deerskin's, everything, that's where I always wash myself, because that money that's his water, his lake. Now you can look where I stand. You can see blood all around where I stand now, be-

cause I'm that way now. I'm flowers. I can go out on that lake, and wash, and they'll make me good luck just the same. . . . You tell that girl to do that. . . . Whenever goes to wash in water anyplace, tell her just that way. . . . Tell her I wash in sky, using that water. So he'll be good luck; if talk that way, will be just same as if wash that lake on sky. (Notes 8 June 1902, pp. 4–5)

The menstrual formula (described later) comprises these instructions given by the menstruating spirit woman to Coyote and Pulekuk^werek.[5]

Pulekuk^werek, it should be noted, was the most ascetic and spiritual of the "Beforetime People." His total abstinence from sexual intercourse suggests asexuality, rather than the pronounced maleness of the two Yurok tricksters Coyote and Wohpekumew (a trickster-hero). It was Pulekuk^werek, however, who epitomized human virtues for Yurok men, for it was he who, along with being a formidable warrior, instituted the men's sweathouse and the wealth quest austerities to be followed by men. A comparison between his and Coyote's instructions for menstruating women and Pulekuk^werek's for male wealth questing is illuminating.

Ten days was the standard period for men's "training" related to all important undertakings—most significantly, here, to wealth questing and to "luck" seeking in alpine lakes. During this period men secluded themselves in the sweathouse, maintained strict continence, avoided all contacts with fecund women, and ate only specially gathered, stored, and prepared foods (the same staples as utilized in menstrual provender). These men bathed twice daily. A primary feature of such sweathouse training was the gathering of firewood for use in the sweathouse. Grass anklets were worn by these men for protection against snakebite and as an esoteric aid in traveling into the mountains to gather wood and to practice various rituals. Men in training for wealth acquisition gashed their legs with flakes of white quartz, the flowing blood being thought to carry off psychic impurity, preparing one for spiritual attainment: The common ten-day men's training periods alternated with periods of greater relaxation and less austerity, in which the "balance" of a "complete" life was restored—the aim of well-trained Yurok men being to keep "in the middle" (*wogi*). (It is relevant to note that in the sweathouse-focal training of both male and female "doctors" [*kegey*]—held to bring wealth as well as curing powers—a skirt of shredded maple bark was worn.)

The recitation of formulas was a central feature of all Yurok training, and such recitations, correctly executed, were believed to bring wealth. It has long been thought that the wealth quest and hence use of such formulas were, with the exception of female *kegey*, strictly male prerogatives. However, the menstrual formula collected from Susie not only substantiates the comparisons between male and female training suggested by the Coyote myth but calls this ethnographic assumption into question.

The formula speaks of a small lake, "up in the middle of the sky" (*wonoye²ik*), where menstruating women may see a great many *Dentalia Indianorum* (dentalium shells were prized Yurok wealth objects). Women are instructed in the formula to dive to the lake's bottom to pick up a small stone and then to return with it to their homes. As a result of these actions (and of properly reciting the formula itself), women may expect to grow wealthy in later life, their menstrual practices attracting dentalium to their houses. Translating from the Yurok text recited for Kroeber by Susie:

> You will be rich if you wash. You go in, you will be rich. Human being, money will come into your house. You go in—you'll be rich. You better go. Go up in the sky. Look! Look! Wash in the lake—just once. Sink down completely. Don't submerge yourself twice. A pile of dentalium is here.
>
> You will go in, go in the water. Only one time. You will lie with your head downstream. Take a stone. You will take it into your house so you will be rich. (Notes 8 June 1902, items 4065–4066; my translation)

The middle of the sky in Yurok cosmography is the most pure, least polluted place in the universe, the source of the most valuable and powerful of things, including many wealth objects. It may be reached, in trance, only by those who are themselves completely pure. It seems to have been a consciously metaphorical location for, as trained people well knew, they physically ascended only into the hills and mountains rising above the coastal and riverine villages.[6] In the most powerful kinds of training, the terrain of the Blue Creek drainage, above Meri·p, was utilized. Such ascents were, however, closely restricted to those who, through ritual austerities, were free of polluting influence.

Men making such ascents while seeking the power of wealth acquisition visualized dentalia and the trails of slime left by them, reciting formulas to attract the shells into their later possession. Diving in alpine lakes is a recurrent motif in accounts of male esoteric practice, as is the retrieval of wealth-attracting stone talismans from various watery places.

There are, then, direct parallels in conception, ritualization, and goal orientation between male training and female menstrual practice. However, and most important, whereas Yurok men feared menstrual pollution as, above all, driving away wealth (that is, spiritual attainment), Yurok women who used the formula understood that it was precisely during their menses that they could most easily attract wealth (i.e., attain spiritual ascendancy).

Finally, we find that whereas men considered menstruating women who seduced men to be *cišah* ([worse than] dogs), the same term was applied by women to men who forced their attentions on them during their own ten-day menstrual training periods (according to the Kroeber papers). Clearly, then, there are two gender-specific views, of which only one—that of the male—has become known through published ethnographies.[7]

The contemporary Yurok woman's notion of "accumulation" now rings true in retrospect. The primary activity of men engaged in wealth questing (that is, in a quest for spiritual advancement), while they were actually in and around the sweathouse, was "meditating" (*kocpoks*) directed toward personal centering and empowerment. It was in such meditation, according to the most knowledgeable of elderly male consultants, that one actually "made medicine" and grew "stronger," rather than in the rituals for which such "thinking" prepared one and which accompanied the meditative "accumulation" of identity, insight, and control. Wealth was believed to accrue only to those who had "done their thinking" precisely and openly (see Buckley 1979).

We find further inferential support of the traditional nature of the young woman's positive view of the power of menstruation in "Weitchpec Susie's" 1902 accounts of childbirth. Susie's English gloss of the Yurok formula for easing labor contains the passage, "*wes?onah* . . . said, 'You call my name whenever hard to come baby, then you call me to help you,' he said to Indians. 'Is my *?e?gur?* [medicine basket].' Whenever you call that to open you will hear baby crying coming." Kroeber notes that "the woman's vagina is Sky's [*wes?onah's*] *?e?gur*" (notes for 8 June 1902, p. 16). Two pieces of information are necessary to put the childbirth formula into perspective. First, the Yurok (?)*wes?onah* is polysemous, meaning "sky"; "that which exists" (the phenomenal world); and "cosmos," the universe as noumenon, a metaphysical first principle—today, in English, "creation" and/or "the Creator." Second, both traditional elkhorn dentalium purses and the medicine baskets (*?e?gur?*) used by men in the Jump Dance, which contain various power tokens, have labialike openings.

We may interpret this material in light of both the menstrual myth and formula and general tendencies in the Yurok worldview. The medicines of (?)*wes?onah*, from the "feminine" perspective, are babies, the by-products of birth, and menstrual blood—all of which are highly polluting from the "masculine" perspective. From an (aristocratic "feminine" point of view, however, these things, while polluting in certain contexts, are *also* pure: pure enough, that is, to be to the "cosmos" what wealth and other tokens of spiritual ascendancy are to human beings. Like wealth objects, from this perspective they are themselves *m.auuks.cy.h* (pure).[8] Such multiple

coding is common in Yurok philosophy, which repeatedly stresses complementary perspectives in which things held to be *kimoleni* (dirty) from one perspective are revealed to be *m.auuks.cy.h* from another (Buckley 1980). We find, then, that the young contemporary woman's account is quite reliable as an expression of a far older traditional Yurok women's perspective. Its reliability is founded, no doubt, in her memory of the instruction she received through her female relatives, who, it would seem, emphasized what I have characterized as an aristocratic feminine perspective over the more negative male one recorded in received ethnographies. This being so in the general case, we are obliged to pay close attention to her testimony regarding synchrony and lunar influence. Although to this point investigation has rested on solid data and clearly relevant comparison, here we can only speculate, for there are few earlier ethnographic data on these topics. There are, however, recent biological research results that appear to be pertinent.

The work of Martha McClintock (1971, 1981) has established the phenomena of human intragroup menstrual synchrony and suppression. The menstrual cycles of frequently interacting women—in college dormitories, for instance—tend to become synchronized over time, the greatest increase in synchrony among individuals occurring within four months. Such synchronization of groups within all-female populations is related to the extent and frequency of contacts between individual women, groups of close friends comprising the most evident synchronous groups (McClintock 1971). In more recent experiments (Quadagno, Shubeita, Deck, and Francouer 1979; Graham and McGrew 1980), McClintock's results have been replicated and extended to populations including both males and females.

The aboriginal Yurok residential group was an extremely flexible unit. An ideal type may be suggested through the term "household." I use this term to refer to the narrowly extended unit of population defined through consanguinity, affinity, adoption, and—above all—common residence. Such a household comprised three or four generations of patrilineally related males and their wives and unmarried daughters, those married daughters with in-marrying husbands and their children, and, in many cases, adoptive kin, both male and female. This unit was centered at a named, patrilineally inherited "family house" (*ʔoʔlel*). The family house was usually the property of the senior male but was strictly the domain of the women who lived and slept there with the children. The lives of most males after puberty were centered in the household's sweathouse (*ʔɪʔgɪc*), where the men spent much of their time, both waking and sleeping.

When a descent group outgrew its family house, a second one was built close by, sharing the name of the first, and its men used the sweathouse belonging to the owner of the original family house. There was approximately one sweathouse for every two family houses in a Yurok village. The people closely associated with these three structures, then, constituted the household. The normative village comprised approximately three such households, the members of each being (putatively) related to those of the others (hence exogamy was generally practiced, intravillage marriage usually being considered incestuous). By my estimate, based on 1852 census figures, each family house sheltered an average of five women and children, of whom, we may hypothesize, at least two were fertile women. Thus a *household's* potentially menstruating women would have numbered four or more (see Kroeber 1925:16–17).

We can only presume that, aboriginally, the related women of Yurok households interacted both frequently and regularly. The findings of McClintock and others are pertinent here, and a myth from the neighboring Karok encourages such comparison. The myth, relating the origins of the Pleiades, tells of several sisters who shared a house and who menstruated at the same time. The *idea* of household menstrual synchrony was indeed present in the area (Harrington 1931:142–145). Indeed, we have a historical account of women menstruating simultaneously at the coastal Yurok village of *ʔespew* in the later

nineteenth century. According to Robert Spott, when his "aunt," the doctor Fanny Flounder, was dancing for her power in that village's sweathouse, she was secretly cursed by a menstruating woman. Trying to discover the culprit, "they summoned the menstruating women . . . only one of them would not come" (Spott and Kroeber 1942:62). At the approximate time, there were four family houses at *ʔespew* (Waterman 1920:261).

What of the claim that synchronously menstruating women practiced the requisite rituals together? If this was indeed the case, why, we must ask, were small, individual menstrual shelters built? Why not communal shelters, like the men's sweathouses that the menstrual shelters seem functionally to parallel? It is possible that communal shelters were used. There is very little information on the subject in either ethnographic descriptions or in native texts and none on the actual size of the shelters. Although several early ethnographers mention menstrual "huts" in northwestern California, none of them ever actually saw one, for these shelters had fallen from use before the earliest trained observers arrived. Goddard (1903:17–18), working among the Hupa in 1900, noted that not even traces of the Hupa "huts" remained at the time of his fieldwork. The detailed Yurok village maps drawn by Waterman (1920) in the early part of this century, which show all structures and structural remains in each village, show neither these "menstrual huts" (*mekʷʔr*) nor their remains. All accounts of these shelters found in ethnographic notes and publications are thus both vague and incomplete, as the minimal accounts themselves suggest.

Kroeber (1925:80), for example, tells us only that "a hut was used by Yurok women in their periodic illnesses. This was a small and rude lean-to of a few planks, near the house or against its side." Yet in northwestern California surely such flimsy shelter for valuable, necessary, and beloved women (Gould 1966; Spott and Kroeber 1942) would have been perceptibly maladaptive, even among the apparently male-dominant Yurok and especially so during the months between October and May when a great deal of cold rain customarily falls. I suggest the the paucity of ethnographic detail regarding menstrual shelters and much else reflects an understandable and pervasive bias (note Kroeber's use of the word "illnesses") and reticence in delving into and publishing material on the entire topic of menstruation, as further suggested by Kroeber's neglect of most of the Susie material in his published work.

In fact, it is quite possible that the aboriginal Yurok used large, dome-shaped communal brush menstrual shelters. Brush menstrual shelters have been reported for the Hupa of 1890 (A. R. Pilling, personal communication, 1981). In 1984 an elderly Yurok woman reported that she knew, at second hand, of three Yurok women who had undergone their first menstrual seclusion simultaneously in a single brush shelter (see later discussion). Finally, an 1850 sketch of the Yurok village of Curey by J. Goldsborough Bruff shows at least one, and possibly two, dome-shaped structures in association with plank houses (Kroeber, Elsasser, and Heizer 1977:257). If the Bruff drawing does depict one or more menstrual shelters, it indeed supports the synchrony hypothesis, for the structures shown are large ones—the clearer of the two being approximately the size of the sweathouse by which it stands. Comparative material from the Northwest Coast and the Plateau supports both the elderly woman's testimony and the drawing as evidence.

The Yurok have long been recognized as being importantly influenced by more "climactic" Northwest Coast cultures (e.g., Drucker 1963[1955]). We may legitimately turn to the farther Northwest Coast seeking comparative suggestions. We find among the Tlingit, for example, substantial brush and plank "birth houses," used for monthly menstrual seclusion as well as for labor and childbirth. These houses were heated by fires, used for sweating, and were large enough to hold four adult women (de Laguna 1972:501–502, 519, 527). The influence of Plateau cultures on those of northwestern California, though not yet systematically established, seems probable. It is of interest, then, that communal birth and menstrual seclusion houses were

once common among the Chilcotin, Okanogen, Tenino, and others in the Plateau culture area (Ray 1939).

Regarding the posited use of the moon in restoring menstrual synchrony on the occasions when it had been disrupted, we note recent biological research and findings. The timing of ovulation in certain nonhuman mammalian females and in female humans can be manipulated by exposure to light relatively stronger than that to which subjects are accustomed at a given time of day or night (Hoffman, Hester, and Towns 1965; Reinberg, Halberg, Ghata, and Siffre 1966; Matsumoto, Igarashi, and Nagaoka 1968; Dewan 1967, 1969; Presser 1974). There is evidence that light of the intensity of the full moon can affect the timing of ovulation and hence of menstruation in human females (Menaker and Menaker 1959; Hauenschild 1960; Cloudsley 1961:85–93).

More recently Dewan, Menkin, and Rock (1978) have demonstrated that the onset of menstruation itself may be directly affected by the exposure of ovulating women to light during sleep. The menstruation of ovulating women exposed to the light of a 100-watt bulb during the fourteenth through sixteenth or seventeenth nights of their cycles (counting the onset of menstruation as day 1) became regularized, with a significant number of the forty-one experimental subjects' cycles being regularized at twenty-nine days, the normative menstrual cycle (Dewan et al. 1978:582–583). The three to four nights of exposure was predicated on the natural duration of full moonlight during the lunar month (the mean synodic lunar month is 29.53 days). However, the researchers held it "probable" that one night's exposure would suffice to regularize the onset of menstruation (1978:582).

Light thus affects the onset of menstruation directly and, through affecting the onset of ovulation, indirectly as well. My young Yurok consultant did not specify in what phase of the moon women "talked" to it, "asking it to balance them." It is probable, however, that only the full moon provides enough photic stimulation (probably to the pineal gland) to affect either ovulation or, directly, the onset of menstruation twelve to fourteen days later. Such onset is at the time of the new moon, which, according to the biological model (Cloudsley 1961:85–93; Dewan et al. 1978:581), comprises the naturally occurring lunar phase for the onset of menstruation. Elderly Yurok men have told me that intensive male training was always undertaken "during the dark of the moon." It seems probable, then, that women indeed "talked" to the full moon and that both synchronized menstruation and male training occurred during the period bracketed by the new moon. Yurok men's training for positive medicines ("luck") emphasizes light in its symbolism. Thus the intensification of training, much of it undertaken at night, during the new moon seems inconsistent—but, indeed, it makes good sense in the full biological context of village life.[9]

The Yurok word for "moon" is *wonesleg*, from *wonews* (overhead) and *leg(ay-)* (to pass regularly). There is evidence for precontact use of sweathouses as calendrical observatories in northwestern California (Goldschmidt 1940). In 1907 Kroeber gathered data on the construction and use of Yurok sweathouses for observation of both solar and lunar yearly cycles (in Elmendorf 1960:26). Such material evidence substantiates contemporary Yurok testimony on the accuracy of traditional timekeeping and the closeness of lunar prediction, and adds support to the young woman's assertion that Yurok women once utilized the moon's light in temporal regulation of biological cycles. I am suggesting, that is, a parallelism between male (sweathouse) and female uses of the moon consistent with cross-gender conceptual and ritual parallelisms discussed earlier.[10]

One important object of male lunar observation was that of correctly scheduling the great interareal ritual and ceremonial events that were once held in accordance with one-, two-, and three-year cycles in more than a dozen northwestern Californian centers. These events, customarily—if erroneously—lumped together as "world renewal dances," included esoteric components enacted by

priests and their helpers, as well as public dances attended by very large audiences (Kroeber and Gifford 1949). Each had to be completed, in all aspects, within a single lunation and it had to end in the dark of the moon (p. 130; Kroeber, in Elmendorf 1960:28). The public dances themselves usually lasted approximately ten days, following the esoteric preparations. Menstruating women were prohibited from attending these dances. Whatever other symbolism was involved, the timing of these events makes particular sense in light of the biological model for menstruation at the new moon. According to this model, the two weeks before the new moon would have been the optimum time for the public dances: the time when the most women were free of menstrual restrictions and could attend.

The possible significance of menstrual synchrony in precontact Yurok culture, however, is far broader than this emphasis on ceremonialism suggests. *If* Yurok women once shared menstrual periods in synchrony and were able to control this synchrony to some degree, it would have meant that for ten days out of every twenty-nine all of the fertile women who were not pregnant were removed, as a group, from their households' mundane activities and plunged into collective contemplative and ritual exercises aimed at the acquisition of wealth objects and other spiritual boons. Logically, this would have been the ideal time for all of the younger men in the sweathouse to undertake their own ten-day periods of intense training, which, as did women's menstrual practices, emphasized continence and avoidance of contact with fecund members of the opposite sex.

Because they would have contaminated any food that they touched during their menses, all fecund women were removed from the subsistence quest for ten days out of every twenty-nine (pregnant women followed their own extended restrictions). Because the subsistence quest was *dominated* by women, who either provided foods themselves (e.g., acorns, shellfish) or were required actresses in male-focal subsistence activities—necessary for cleaning, butchering, and drying the fish and game that men caught—it is clear that during the ten-day menstrual period a woman's household's subsistence quest would have been somewhat hampered. This is even more clear in light of the fact that men could not hunt (or fight) while their wives were menstruating. If all of the women of a household menstruated in synchrony, these activities would have been very severely curtailed. If this was the case, it would be logical to think that the household's subsistence quest (and feuding) would have been brought virtually to a halt, men as well as women refraining from all but the most casual collecting of food. (Note that demand for fresh fish and game was reduced through the food avoidance rules for both menstruating women and men in training.) Such interruptions would not necessarily have been risky in northwestern California, where food supplies were abundant and dependable (cyclic occurrence of staple fish and acorns being of long duration) and where food (especially acorns and smoked-dried fish) was successfully stored in large quantities (Gould 1966, 1975).

A possibility, then, is that the monthly round transformed the Yurok household, for one-third of every month, into an esoteric training camp in which most (aristocratic) men and women between puberty and middle age devoted themselves to their respective practices aimed at the acquisition of wealth and self-knowledge, supported by both younger and older males and females (with the exception of pregnant women and new mothers, who followed their own equally restrictive regimes for the entire gestation period and for ninety days after giving birth).

This speculation accords well with both the oft-noted spirituality and asceticism of aboriginal Yurok culture and the expression of these tendencies in Yurok social organization. Male Yurok began to undertake wealth-bringing austerities at puberty, as did the women; and like the women, they had largely ceased such activities by late middle age, when, in the native theory, they began to enjoy the fruits of their labors. There was, then, a well-defined group in every household capable of managing ongoing affairs

and supporting the monthly practices of the men and women between puberty and middle age. For example, the special foods of men in training were prepared by postmenopausal women and prepubescent girls, who also attended women secluded during their menses.

If we are anywhere near the mark in these speculations, it is clear that the menstrual power of Yurok women did not manifest itself only on a gender-specific, esoteric level of knowledge and practice—one that paralleled identical features of opposite-gender life—but that it had profound, pragmatic implications as well in dictating the temporal structuring of activities for entire households on a monthly basis.

CONCLUSION

I have shown that for some precontact Yurok women at least, menstruation was not viewed solely as a virulent form of contamination but was understood as spiritual potency potentially, if ambiguously, providing a route to knowledge and wealth. It is quite likely that in agreement with many contemporary native northwestern Californians other than my principal informant, and with a traditional male-dominated understanding, some aboriginal Yurok women did view their periods as times, simply, of negative pollution. It is also likely that still others were deeply ambivalent. However, some—most likely aristocratic—women held a seemingly gender-specific, at least partially positive view of menstruation, encoding it within a gender-specific mythic and ritual context.

I suggest, moreover, that the women of aboriginal Yurok households menstruated in synchrony, utilizing the light of the moon to regularize their menstrual cycles, and that the menstruating women of (aristocratic) households used their shared periods of menstrual seclusion for the practice of spiritual disciplines. Moreover I propose that both the subsistence quests and fighting patterns of all of the active men of these households, as well as their own programs of esoteric training, were keyed to the synchronous menstrual cycles of the household's women. To an extent these propositions have been justified by recent Yurok testimony, unavailable to me when I first published on these topics (Buckley 1982).

During 1984 Arnold R. Pilling, my senior colleague in Yurok studies, spent part of the summer working with the late Lowana Brantner, a Yurok woman of Meta, then in her mid-seventies. Pilling recorded on tape over twenty-two hours of data concerning Mrs. Brantner's life and Yurok traditional patterns. In the process of that interviewing he collected such data as Mrs. Brantner knew of other females' first menstruation rites and many comments on her own lengthy first menstrual seclusion. In regard to the latter, Mrs. Brantner reported that among the women who came to supervise and instruct her during this period was the renowned *kegey* Fanny Flounder (e.g., Spott and Kroeber 1942:158–164).

Mrs. Brantner also noted that she was the only girl from Meta undergoing menstrual seclusion during the year of her training and, in fact, for over a generation before, while Fanny had been the only female of her village secluded the year that Fanny had been trained at the undercut of a waterfall in a canyon along Gold Bluffs. Mrs. Brantner noted, however, that in the case of one woman with whom she had discussed first menstrual seclusion there had been three girls from a single village being secluded in one brush shelter at once. When Pilling expressed surprise that three girls from one village would have their first menstruation at the same time, Mrs. Brantner said that they *should:* since the whole village had their "mating season" at the same time (i.e., late summer–early fall), the "birthing season" fell at the same time for all as well (in May–June [compare Erikson 1943]). Therefore all the girls of a village had their first menstruation at once, according to Mrs. Brantner (Arnold R. Pilling, personal communications 1985, 1986).

Lowana Brantner's recollections add considerable weight to my own consultant's assertions regarding Yurok menstrual synchrony and menstrual practice as a context for spiritual training, which initiated the present inquiry. Still, empirical proof of the hypotheses that have grown out of that original testimony remains lacking. Unfortunately it is too late to test these hypotheses in the Yurok case. Yet as I have suggested, there are certain possibilities that can and should be explored in contemporary face-to-face societies in which strong menstrual restrictions and gender-specific knowledge and practices still exist.

Such research can be combined with a close examination of early information concerning cultures that are today much changed from their aboriginal precursors. Contemporary native testimony and far earlier ethnographic materials may stand in an intricate relationship. By exploring this relationship we may, in some cases, clarify both our received understandings of the past and our (possibly mistaken) interpretations of the present. In such analyses, particularly but not exclusively in the cases of native Californian cultures, it is especially important that we attend to the often entirely neglected raw field data of earlier investigators.

NOTES

Acknowledgments. I especially thank Tela Lake, Yurok, without whose testimony this work could not have been done, and Martha McClintock, Committee on Human Development, University of Chicago, who also contributed in important ways. I am grateful, too, to the late Dewey George, Yurok, and the late Harry K. Roberts for information on male esoteric training used in this chapter, and to Arnold R. Pilling and Richard Keeling for a variety of ethnographic details. Of course I take full responsibility for the uses I have made of everyone's respective contribution. Research undertaken in California and incorporated here was supported by the Jacobs Research Fund of the Whatcom Museum Foundation in 1976 and 1978 and by the Danforth Foundation in 1978. I also thank the Bancroft Library, University of California at Berkeley, and Professor Karl Kroeber for their kind permission to quote from the A. L. Kroeber Papers at the Bancroft.

An earlier version of this chapter appeared in *American Ethnologist*, vol. 9, no. 1 (1982):47–60. The present version, in which I have corrected certain errors and have made several additions, should be regarded as the more definitive of the two.

1. The English language euphemism "moon-time," used by some Yurok today in reference to menstrual periods, reflects a central symbolic relationship between the moon and menses in contemporary Yurok culture. It is not clear, however, just when "moontime" came into use among English-speaking Yurok, nor are there sufficient data to establish a likely time. In 1902 one of Kroeber's consultants used the English "flowers" in reference to menstruation, and "moontime" does not appear in any of the other early published or archival material on the Yurok. We cannot, then, use the term "moontime" as evidence of a moon/menses relationship in aboriginal Yurok culture. (Both flowers and moon-related menstrual imagery are very widespread, far beyond the confines of both native California and the modern era [Delaney, Lupton, ant Toth 1976; Gottlieb, this volume].)

   The explicit Yurok verb meaning "to menstruate" is *kıkıcp-*, the prefix *kıkı-* indicating both cyclic and erratic oscillation. This verb is not used, however, in any of the Yurok texts collected by Kroeber. Here the common Yurok term for a menstruating woman, *wespurawok*, is euphemistic, alluding to a woman who bathes in the (Klamath) river. Such euphemisms are frequently used in Yurok in avoidance of more explicit terms, use of which under many circumstances is considered to be offensive and even polluting.

2. The woman was perhaps dramatizing her relationship to her far older female relatives. It is quite possible that she did not herself receive the information from them but at second hand, from her mother, for the youngest of the women of whom she spoke died while she herself was a young girl in a foster home. (Such dramatization is frequently encountered among Yurok today, many of whom stress their links with the past by telescoping time and people in accounts of their own nurture.)

   Later I argue that the value of the young woman's testimony is established by its resonance with a far older account, that given in 1902 by Weitchpec Susie, and with the contemporary testimony of another, elderly Yurok woman. Again, the evaluation of con-

temporary testimony in dialectic with other evidence is a central methodological concern in the present chapter.

3. The classic ethnographic accounts in which the earliest published data on menstrual practices in northwestern California are to be found are S. Powers ([1877] 1976); Goddard (1903); Kroeber (1925); Harrington (1932); and Drucker (1937). Information on male training for wealth acquisition among these peoples, referred to later, is found in the same sources. Additional material on Yurok training appears in Spott and Kroeber (1942); Elmendorf (1960); Kroeber (1976); and Pilling (1978).

4. No reason is given in the Kroeber notes for Coyote's action. A parallel Chilula Indian account, however, states that a girl had rejected the trickster's sexual advances and that he acted out of spite. The Chilula once neighbored the Yurok.

5. Note that in this text the perpetual purity of the spirits—the *wo·gey*—is cast in quite a different light than in the received ethnography (e.g., Erikson 1943): the female *wo·gey* themselves menstruate, even in the "spirit world." The fact is but one of many that needs attention in a careful reconsideration of traditional Yurok world view, male and female.

6. A Yurok woman fully trained as a *kegey* (doctor) told Kroeber about using the angelica roots she gathered in the mountains. The full account was recorded in English in 1907 and is among the Kroeber Papers, carton 7. I include a partial version here.

   I ... always throw *woˀlp'eˀy* [angelica] in the fire. I talk this way:
   "Now this *woˀlp'eˀy*, I got it *wesˀonah hiwoˀnik*, right up in the middle of the sky...."
   It didn't come from there in fact, but one just talked that way and threw it in the fire, so that all kinds of money would just come right to this house.

   Clearly the "lake in the middle of the sky" comprises such metaphorical usage, this lake being symbolized by any water used to bathe in during menstruation, most commonly the Klamath River and, far less certainly, the "moontime pond' above Meri·*p*.

7. In all likelihood the actual situation was far more complex. Some women undoubtedly shared what I have characterized here as a

"male" perspective, viewing menstruation as a dire pollutant. Again, one old Yurok-trained "aristocratic" male voiced the kind of perspective I here characterize as female in conversations with me in 1970, long before I had begun the present inquiry. Finally, it is probable that some—perhaps many—women were highly ambivalent and shared *both* "male" and "female" perspectives on menstruation. Susie herself, for instance, told Kroeber that menstruous women polluted trails.

Such diversity was probably resolved to an extent by Yurok quasi-class structure. Esoteric knowledge among Yurok tended to be concentrated in the upper echelons of aboriginal society among what, for lack of a better term, may be called "aristocratic" descent groups (see Buckley 1980). Weitchpec Susie was a member of such a group, as was the old man mentioned earlier, and as is—although less significantly today—the young woman whose testimony initiated the present study.

It is likely, and in keeping with what may be known of the sociology of aboriginal Yurok knowledge, that the positive view of menstruation developed here was class- as well as gender-specific, but also that its occurrence to some extent crossed both class and gender lines. In any case the present analysis must be viewed as pertaining particularly to aboriginal Yurok women of aristocratic descent groups. As Pilling (1978) points out, these groups overwhelmingly have provided ethnographers, informants, and we know far more about them than about the lower strata of traditional Yurok society.

8. Erikson (1943:295) writes that the Yurok "believe [that] babies come from the sky." The Kroeber notes discussed here, however, suggest that the meaning of this "belief" was far more complex, at least for "educated" (teno·wok) aristocratic women. Babies come from (ʔ)wesʔonah (the cosmos) by way of its "medicine basket" (the uterus).

9. Menstruation at the new moon is in accord both with Cloudsley's and Dewan's biological model and with the folk-physiological models of many nonindustrial peoples. However, these models contrast with Cutler's (1980) findings that statistically correlate menstruation among a sample of contemporary women in Philadelphia and the "light" lunar period (between the first and third lunar quarters). If Cutler's findings are significant (and the variables here are extraordinarily complex), more

comprehensive cross-cultural models should perhaps be pursued. Lamp's hypothesis (this volume) that menstruation occurs among Temne women in two groups—a "light" lunar phase group and a "dark" one, in Cutler's terms—may be relevant to this still unresolved matter.

10. Harry K. Roberts, who spent much of his youth in the Spott household at Requa, told me that "old-time" women kept careful track of their monthly cycles using stick calendars in order to plan for travel and ritual. Pregnancy, according to Roberts, was also carefully charted, a stick being set aside each month rather than each day (as is the case with menstrual stick calendars).

REFERENCES

Ardener, Edwin. 1972. Belief and the problem of women. In *The interpretation of ritual: Essays in honour of A. I. Richards,* ed. Jean la Fontaine, London, Tavistock, pp. 135–158.

Bean, John Lowell. 1977. Power and its applications in native California. In *The anthropology of power,* ed. Raymond D. Fogelson and Richard N. Adams. New York: Academic Press, pp. 117–131.

Bean, John Lowell and Thomas C. Blackburn. 1976. Introduction. In *Native Californians: A theoretical retrospective,* ed. J. L. Bean and T. C. Blackburn. Socorro, N. M.: Ballena Press, pp. 5–10.

Blackburn, Thomas C. 1976. Ceremonial integration and social interaction in aboriginal California. In *Native Californians: A theoretical retrospective,* ed. J. L. Bean and T. C. Blackburn. Socorro, N.M.: Ballena Press, pp. 225–244.

Buckley, Thomas. 1979. Doing your thinking: Aspects of traditional Yurok education. *Parabola* 4, no. 4:29–37.

———. 1980. Monsters and the quest for balance in native northwest California. In *Manlike monsters on trial: Early records and modern evidence,* ed. Marjorie Halpin and Michael Ames. Vancouver: University of British Columbia Press, pp. 152–171.

———. 1982. Menstruation and the power of Yurok women: Methods in cultural reconstruction. *American Ethnologist* 9:47–60.

Bushnell, John and Donna Bushnell. 1977. Wealth, work, and world view in native Northwest California. In *Flowers in the Wind,* ed.

Thomas C. Blackburn, Socorro, N.M.: Ballena Press, pp. 120–182.

Cloudsley, T. J. L. 1961. *Rhythmic activity in animal physiology and behavior.* New York: Academic Press, pp. 85–93.

de Laguna, Frederica. 1972. *Under Mount Saint Elias: The history and culture of the Yakutat Tlingit,* 3 vols. Smithsonian Contributions to Anthropology, vol. 7. Washington, DC.: Smithsonian Institution Press, pp. 72, 501–527.

Delaney, Janice, Mary Jane Lupton, and Emily Toth. 1976. *The curse: A cultural history of menstruation.* New York: Dutton.

Dewan, E. M. 1967. On the possibility of a perfect rhythm method of birth control by periodic light stimulation. *American Journal of Obstetrics and Gynecology* 99:1016–1019.

———. 1969. Rhythms. *Science and Technology* 20:20–28.

Dewan, E. M., M. F. Menkin, and J. Rock. 1978. Effect of photic stimulation on the human menstrual cycle. *Photochemistry and Photobiology* 27:581–585.

Douglas, Mary. 1966. *Purity and danger: An analysis of concepts of pollution and taboo.* London: Routledge and Kegan Paul.

Drucker, Philip. 1963. *Indians of the Northwest coast.* Garden City, N.Y.: Natural History Press. (Original edition: New York: McGraw-Hill, for the American Museum of Natural History, Anthropological Handbook No. 10, 1955.)

Elmendorf, William W. 1960. The structure of Twana culture with comparative notes on the structure of Yurok culture by A. L. Kroeber. *Washington State University Research Studies* 28, no. 3, Monographic supplement 2. Pullman, Washington.

Elsasser, Albert B. 1976. Review of Native Californians. *Journal of California Anthropology* 3, no. 2:95–96.

Erikson, Erik H. 1943. Observations on the Yurok: Childhood and World Image. *University of California Publications in American Archaeology and Ethnology* 35, no. 10:257–302.

Goddard, P. E. 1903. Life and culture of the Hupa. *University of California Publications in American Archaeology and Ethnology* 1, no. 1:1–88.

Goldschmidt, Walter R. 1940. A Hupa calendar. *American Anthropologist* 42:176–177.

Gould, Richard A. 1966. The wealth quest among the Tolowa Indians of northwestern California. *Proceedings of the American Philosophical Society* 110:67–87.

———. 1975. Ecology and adaptive response among the Tolowa Indians of northwestern California. *Journal of California Anthropology* 2, no. 2:148–170.

Graham, C. A. and W. C. McGrew. 1980. Menstrual synchrony in female undergraduates living on a coeducational campus. *Psychoneuroendocrinology* 3:245–252.

Harrington, J. P. 1931. Karuk texts. *International Journal of American Linguistics* 6:121–161, 194–226.

Hauenschild, C. 1960. Lunar periodicity. *Cold Spring Harbor Symposium on Quantitative Biology* 25:491–497.

Hoffman, R. A., J. A. Hester, and C. Towns. 1965. Effect of light and temperature on the endocrine system of the golden hamster. *Comparative Biochemistry and Physiology* 15:525–533.

King, Helen. 1983. Born to bleed: Artemis and Greek women. In *Images of women in antiquity,* eds. Averil Cameron and Amelie Kuhrt. Detroit: Wayne State University Press, pp. 109–127.

Kroeber, A. L. 1925. *Handbook of the Indians of California.* Bureau of American Ethnology, Bulletin 78. Washington, D.C.: Government Printing Office, pp. 16–17, 45.

Kroeber, A. L. and E. W. Gifford. 1949. World renewal: A cult system of native Northwest California. *Anthropological Records* 13.

Kroeber, Theodora, A. B. Elsasser, and R. F. Heizer. 1977. *Drawn from life: California Indians in pen and brush.* Socorro, N.M.: Ballena Press, pp. 257.

Matsumoto, S., M. Igarashi, and Y. Nagaoka. 1968. Environmental anovulatory cycles. *International Journal of Fertility* 13:15–23.

McClintock, Martha K. 1971. Menstrual synchrony and suppression. *Nature* 229, no. 5285:244–245.

———. 1981. Social control of the ovarian cycle and the function of estrous synchrony. *American Zoologist* 21:243–256.

Menaker, W. and A. Menaker. 1959. Lunar periodicity in human reproduction: A likely unit of biological time. *American Journal of Obstetrics and Gynecology* 77:905–914.

Pilling, Arnold R. 1978. Yurok. In *Handbook of North American Indians,* vol. 8, ed. R. F. Heizer. Washington, D.C.: Smithsonian Institution Press, pp. 137–154.

Presser, H. B. 1974. Temporal data relating to the human menstrual cycle. In *Biorhythms and human reproduction,* ed. M. Ferin, F. Halberg, R. M. Richart, and R. L. Van de Wiele. New York: Wiley, pp. 145–160.

Quadagno, D. M., H. M. Shubeita, J. Deck, and D.

Francouer. 1979. A study of the effects of males, exercise, and all-female living conditions on the menstrual cycle. (Abstract.) *Conference on Reproductive Behavior,* Tulane University, New Orleans.

Ray, Verne F. 1939. *Cultural relations in the plateau of northwestern America.* Los Angeles: F. W. Hodge Anniversary Fund, Southwest Museum, Vol. 2.

Reinberg, A., F. Halberg, J. Ghata, and M. Siffre. 1966. Spectre thermique (rhythmes de la température rectale) d'une femme adulte avant, pendant, et apres son isolement souterrain de trois mois. *Comptes Rendus de l'Academie Scientifique D.* 262:782–785.

Spott, Robert and A. L. Kroeber. 1942. Yurok narratives. *University of California Publications in American Archaeology and Ethnology* 35:143–256.

Waterman, T. T. 1920. Yurok geography. *University of California Publications in American Archaeology and Ethnology* 16, no. 5:177–314.

V.
Culture and Sexuality

The study of sexuality in anthropology is a relatively recent research emphasis. Classic anthropological monographs have reported exotic sexual practices in the course of ethnographic description (for example, we learn in Malinowski's *The Sexual Life of Savages* [1929] that the Trobriand islanders may bite each others' eyelashes in the heat of passion), but other than occasional esoterica, a naturalistic, biological bias has dominated the study of sexuality. However, as Vance observes (1984:8), "although sexuality, like all human cultural activity, is grounded in the body, the body's structure, physiology, and functioning do not directly or simply determine the configuration or meaning of sexuality." Rather, sexuality is in large part culturally constructed. Just as we may inquire into the culturally variable meanings of male and female and masculinity and femininity, we may examine the ways in which sexuality is invested with meaning in particular societies (Ortner and Whitehead 1981:2).

Sexuality, as a topic of analysis, links the personal and the social, the individual and society. To Americans sex may imply medical facts, Freud, and erotic techniques, but all of these aspects of sexuality are socially shaped and inevitably curbed. Within every culture there are measures for the management of sexuality and gender expression (Ortner and Whitehead 1981:24–25) and sanctions for those who break the rules.

These sanctions may be imposed at the level of the family, the lineage, the community, or the state. Indeed, Foucault (1981) has suggested that a feature of the recent past is the increasing intervention of the state in the domain of sexuality. In this regard Ross and Rapp (1981:71) conclude that it is not accidental that contemporary western culture conceptualizes sex as a thing in itself, isolated from social, political, and economic context: "The separation with industrial capitalism of family life from work, of consumption from production, of leisure from labour, of personal life from political life, has completely reorganized the context in which we experience sexuality. . . . Modern consciousness permits, as earlier systems of thought did not, the positing of 'sex' for perhaps the first time as having an 'independent' existence." However, Caplan (1987:24) warns that while western culture may have a concept of sexuality divorced from reproduction, marriage, or other social domains, it is not possible to analyze sexuality without reference to the economic, political, and cultural matrix in which it is embedded.

A comparative perspective informs us that the attributes of the person seen as sexual and erotic vary cross-culturally. For example, scarification, the corsetted waist, bound feet, and the subincised penis are admired and provocative in particular cultures. Such attributes as these are not only physical symbols of sexuality, but indicators of status. Similarly, Sudanese women enforce infibulation, or pharonic circumcision causing serious pain and health risks to young women, for the honor of the lineage. In the name of power young men applied as recruits to the palace eunuch staff in Imperial China carrying their genitals in jars (Ortner and Whitehead 1981:24). These examples are reminders of the power of social concerns and cultural meanings in the domain of sexuality.

It has been argued that sexual intercourse, while personal, can also be a truly political act. For example, in hunting and gathering societies claims to women are central in men's efforts to achieve equal status with others (Collier and Rosaldo 1981:291). Through sexual relations with women, men forge relationships with one another and symbolically express claims to particular women. Shostak (in this book) presents the perspective of a !Kung woman, Nisa, on sex, marriage, and fertility in the broader context of a hunting and gathering society in which women have high status.

In !Kung society children learn about sex through observation. Boys and girls play at parenthood and marriage. If they are caught playing at sex, they are scolded but are not severely punished. No value is placed on virginity, and the female body need not be covered or hidden. A girl is not expected to have sex until the onset of menstruation, usually age 16. During adolescence, both heterosexual and homosexual sex play is permitted, and sexual liaisons outside of marriage are also permissible.

The !Kung believe that without sex, people can die, just as without food, one would starve. Shostak observes that "talk about sex seems to be of almost equal importance [to eating]. When women are in the village or out gathering,

or when men and women are together, they spend hours recounting details of sexual exploits. Joking about all aspects of sexual experience is commonplace" (1983:265). According to Nisa, "If a woman doesn't have sex . . . her thoughts get ruined and she is always angry" (Shostak 1983:31).

From Nisa Shostak elicits the history of her relationships with men, in particular her former husband and constant admirer, Besa, who abandons her while she is pregnant but later tries to persuade her to return and live with him as his wife. Although he seeks the intervention of the headman, Nisa refuses to return to him, and the headman supports her decision. Nisa's characterization of sexuality among the !Kung suggests that for both men and women engaging in sex is necessary to maintaining good health and is an important aspect of being human.

In contrast, for the past 150 years Anglo-American culture has defined women as less sexual than men. This represents a major shift from the widespread view prior to the seventeenth century that women were especially sexual creatures (Caplan 1987:3). By the end of the nineteenth century the increasingly authoritative voice of male medical specialists argued that women were characterized by sexual anesthesia (Caplan 1987:3). Victorian ideas about male sexuality emphasized the highly sexed and baser nature of men. In contrast, Muslim concepts of female sexuality (Mernissi 1987:33) cast the woman as aggressor and the man as victim. Imam Ghazali, writing in the eleventh century, describes an active female sexuality in which the sexual demands of women appear overwhelming and the need for men to satisfy them is a social duty (Mernissi 1987:39). Women symbolize disorder and are representative of the dangers of sexuality and its disruptive potential.

The example of the Kaulong of New Guinea further illustrates the extent to which understandings of male and female sexual natures are cultural products (Goodale 1980). Both sexes aspire to immortality through the reproduction of identity achieved through parenting. Sexual intercourse, which is considered animal-like, is sanctioned for married people. Animals are part of the forest and nature, so the gardens of married couples are in the forest. The only sanctioned purpose of sex and marriage is reproduction; sex without childbearing is viewed as shameful. Suicide was formerly considered an acceptable recourse for a childless couple. Sexual activity is thought to be dangerous to men and women in different ways: polluting for men and leading to the dangers of birth for women. Goodale notes that girls are encouraged to behave aggressively toward men, to initiate sex, and to select the husband of their choice. In contrast, men are reluctant to engage in sex, are literally "scared to death of marriage," and rarely take the dominant role in courtship (Goodale 1980:135). Thus, the Kaulong view seems to reverse the western idea of the passive woman and the active man (Moore 1988:17).

Attempting to explain such variations in cultural constructions of sexuality, Caplan (1987) suggests that when desire for children is high, fertility and sexuality are hardly distinguished; biological sex is important and impediments to procreation (e.g., contraception, homosexuality) are viewed as wicked. Caplan shows that Hindu tradition values celibacy, although there may be a life stage in which an individual is sexually active. The spirit is valued over the flesh, and celibacy represents a purer and higher state than sexual activity. In contrast, a spirit-flesh dichotomy is less common in Africa and the Caribbean, where sexual activity is thought to be a part of healthy living (Nelson 1987:235–236). When fertility is less valued, sexual activity is more open and less regulated, and sexuality becomes an aspect of self, not of parenthood. Thus, control of female fertility is linked to control of sexual behavior; when sexual activity is thought to be a prerequisite for good health, there tends to be greater sexual autonomy for women.

Gender, referring to sociocultural designations of behavioral and psychosocial qualities of sexes (Jacobs and Roberts 1989), is commonly contrasted with sex, or the observable biophysiological, morphological characteristics of the individual. Gilmore (in this book) examines the relationship between sex and gender in his analysis of the often dramatic ways in which cultures construct appropriate manhood. He finds a recurring notion that "real manhood is different from simple anatomical maleness, that it is

not a natural condition that comes about spontaneously through biological maturation but rather is a precarious or artificial state that boys must win against powerful odds" (1990:11).

To Gilmore the answer to the manhood puzzle lies in culture. He examines a post-Freudian understanding of masculinity as a category of self-identity, showing how boys face special problems in separating from their mother. A boy's separation and individuation is more perilous and difficult than a girl's, whose femininity is reinforced by the original unity with her mother. Thus, to become separate the boy must pass a test, breaking the chain to his mother. Ultimately, Gilmore concludes that manhood ideologies force men to shape up "on penalty of being robbed of their identity." Men are not innately different from women, but they need motivation to be assertive.

Gilmore notes that some cultures also provide for alternative gender constructs. Popular thinking in the United States dichotomizes two sexes, male and female, and corresponding gender identities, masculinity and femininity, leaving little room for culturally defined variance. Some research suggests at least three phenotypic sexes in human cultures: female, male, and androgynous or hermaphroditic people. This classification refers to characteristics observable to the naked eye rather than to medical classifications of sex types based on chromosomal evidence (Jacobs and Roberts 1989:440). Linguistic markers for gender reveal culturally specific epistemological categories (Jacobs and Roberts 1989:439). Accordingly, in English one may distinguish woman, lesbian, man, or gay male. The Chuckchee counted seven genders—three female and four male—while the Mohave reportedly recognize four genders—a woman, a woman who assumes the roles of men (berdache), a man, or a male berdache who assumes the roles of women (Jacobs and Roberts 1989:439–440). Thus, cross-cultural research suggests that we need to use categories of sex and gender that reflect the evidence of diversity rather than rigid classification systems.

In any culture genders are recognized, named, and given meaning in accordance with that culture's rules or customs (Jacobs and Roberts 1989:446). When a baby is born people generally rely on the appearance of the infant's external genitalia to determine whether that child will be treated as female or male. As a child grows more criteria come into play, such as the phenotypic expression of sex—facial hair, voice, and breast development. In some societies spiritual development and interests may be used as criteria for gender attribution. One such example is the hijras of Indian society. The hijra role attracts people who in the West might be called eunuchs, homosexuals, transsexuals, transvestites, or hermaphrodites.

The hijra role is deeply rooted in Indian culture, and it accommodates a variety of sexual needs, gender behaviors and identities, and personalities. Nanda (in this book) shows that Hinduism encompasses ambiguities and contradictions in gender categories without trying to resolve them. In Hindu myths, rituals, and art, the theme of the powerful man-woman is significant; mythical figures who are androgynes figure in popular Indian culture. Thus the hijra represents an institutionalized third gender role.

Hinduism holds that all people contain both male and female principles, and in some sects male transvestism is used as a way of achieving salvation. There are many references in Hinduism to alternative sexes and sexual ambiguity. However, hijras are viewed ambivalently and can inspire both fear and mockery. Ancient writings indicate criticism of homosexuality, but in actuality homosexuals were tolerated, following the counsel of the classic Hindu text, the Kamasutra, that in sex one should act according to the custom of one's country and one's own inclination. Hijras see themselves as humans, neither man nor woman, calling into question basic social categories of gender. The accommodation of the hijras reflects the extent to which contradictions are embraced and tolerated in Indian culture.

Additional examples of cultures that tolerate gender ambiguity are found in Native American societies, in which a male who felt an affinity for female occupation, dress, and attributes could choose to become classified as a berdache. Williams (in this book) discusses alternative gender identities for Native American women whom he calls amazons; others refer to them as "cross gender females" or female berdache. According to Williams' use of the term, an amazon is a woman who has manifested an unfeminine character from infancy, has shown no interest in heterosexual relations, and might have expressed a wish to become a man. Such women were known for their bravery and skill as warriors. For example, Kaska Indians would select a daughter to be a son if they had none; after a transformation ritual the daughter would dress like a man and be trained for male tasks. Ingalik Indians also recognize such a status; in this society the amazons even participated in male-only sweat baths. The woman was accepted as a man on the basis of her gender behavior (Williams, in this book).

The assignment of this changed gender "operates independently of a person's morphological sex and can determine both gender status and erotic behavior" (Williams 1986:235). In some societies a woman could choose to be a man, as among the Kutenai Indians. The "man-like woman" was greatly respected, although the Kutenai did not recognize a berdache status for men. A tribe with an alternative gender role for one sex did not necessarily have one for the other, and the roles were not seen as equivalent. The Mohave also recognized the status of amazons, subjecting these women to a ritual that authorized them to assume the clothing, sexual activity, and occupation of the opposite, self-chosen sex. It is sometimes believed that such women do not menstruate because menstruation is a crucial part of the definition of a woman. However, the category of amazon is distinct from that of men or women. It is another gender status. Thus, some Native American cultures have a flexible recognition of gender variance, and they incorporate fluidity in their world view.

Sexuality, as differentiated from sex and gender, refers to sexual behaviors, feelings, thoughts, practices, and sexually based bonding behaviors (bisexuality, heterosexuality, homosexuality) (Jacobs and Roberts 1989:440). Sexual identity, involving an individual's self-attribution of sex preferences and practices, is both a response to and an influence on sexuality. In western culture today sexuality is thought to comprise an important part of one's identity, the core of self (Caplan 1987:2). In the United

States, where heterosexual relations are the norm, the dominant ideology suggests that heterosexuality is innate and natural. Lesbianism may be threatening to male dominance, while male homosexuality threatens male solidarity and the sense of masculine identity. In other cultures, however, gender and sexuality are conceptually separate. For example, Shepherd (1987) shows that for Swahili Muslims of Mombasa, Kenya, being in a homosexual relationship does not change one's gender, which is essentially assigned by biological sex.

In American society sexuality is an integral part of identity on a personal and a social level. Sexuality not only classifies one as male or female, but is an aspect of adult identity. In contrast, in Jamaica or parts of Africa childbirth, rather than sexuality, confers adulthood. The linkage of sexual identity and gender leads to an identification of gay men and lesbians in terms of their homosexuality, although they do not necessarily change their gender. In this culture a lack of fit between sex, gender, and sexuality causes suspicion. In addition, the conflating of sexuality and gender makes it hard to conceptualize homosexual parents. Bozett (in this book) points out that there is almost no scientific literature on this subject, although there is somewhat more discussion of lesbian mothers than of gay fathers. Custodial gay fathers are less common and have been less accessible for research, although there may be as many as 3 million gay men who are natural fathers, not including those who adopt children, are stepfathers, or are foster parents.

Recent interest in gay families and gay parenting reflects the awareness that the "traditional" nuclear family now describes fewer than one-third of families with children (Bozett 1987:40). Bozett's research on children of gay fathers suggests that the father-child relationship does not significantly change when the child becomes aware of the father's homosexuality. While the children may not approve, the bond to their father remains. Because of embarrassment or concern that others will think they are gay, the children may seek to use social control strategies that will protect their public image of themselves. Gay fathers attempt to prevent homophobic harassment of their children and to prevent them from being socially marginalized. Fathers' homosexuality does not seem to influence children's sexual orientation.

The articles in this part reveal that there are a number of possible combinations of sex, gender, and sexuality, leading to different and culturally acceptable identities (Caplan 1987:22). Although western categorizations impose a particular rigidity on gender concepts, cross-cultural data demonstrate that these identities are not fixed and unchangeable. This realization necessitates a critique of these western classifications and provokes a number of stimulating questions: Are heterosexuality and homosexuality equally socially constructed? Is there cross-cultural variation in the extent to which sexuality represents a primary aspect of human identity? Is desire itself culturally constituted?

REFERENCES

Caplan, Pat. 1987. Introduction. In Pat Caplan (ed.). *The Cultural Construction of Sexuality*, pp. 1–31. London: Tavistock.

Collier, Jane F. and Michelle Z. Rosaldo. 1981. Politics and Gender in Simple Societies. In Sherry Ortner and Harriet Whitehead (eds.). *Sexual Meanings: The Cultural Construction of Gender and Sexuality*, pp. 275–330. Cambridge: Cambridge University Press.

Foucault, Michel. 1981. *The History of Sexuality*. Harmondsworth: Penguin.

Goodale, Jane C. 1980. Gender, Sexuality and Marriage: a Kaulong Model of Nature and Culture. In Carol P. MacCormack (ed.). *Nature, Culture and Gender*, pp. 119–143. Cambridge: Cambridge University Press.

Jacobs, Sue-Ellen and Christine Roberts. 1989. Sex, Sexuality, Gender, and Gender Variance. In Sandra Morgen (ed.). *Gender and Anthropology: Critical Reviews for Research and Teaching*, pp. 438–462. Washington, DC: American Anthropological Association.

Malinowski, Bronislaw. 1929. *The Sexual Life of Savages in Northwestern Melanesia*. New York: Harvest Books.

Mernissi, Fatima. 1987. *Beyond the Veil: Male-Female Dynamics in Modern Muslim Society*. Bloomington and Indianapolis: Indiana University Press.

Moore, Henrietta L. 1988. *Feminism and Anthropology*. Minneapolis: University of Minnesota Press.

Nelson, Nici. 1987. 'Selling her kiosk': Kikuyu Notions of Sexuality and Sex for Sale in Mathare Valley, Kenya. In Pat Caplan (ed.). *The Cultural Construction of Sexuality*, pp. 217–240. London: Tavistock.

Ortner, Sherry B. and Harriet Whitehead. 1981. Introduction: Accounting for Sexual Meanings. In Sherry Ortner and Harriet Whitehead (eds.). *Sexual Meanings: The Cultural Construction of Gender and Sexuality*, pp. 1–29. Cambridge: Cambridge University Press.

Ross, E. and R. Rapp. 1981. Sex and Society: A Research Note from Social History and Anthropol-

ogy. *Comparative Studies in Society and History* 20:51–72.

Shepherd, Gill. 1987. Rank, Gender, and Homosexuality: Mobasa as a Key to Understanding Sexual Options. In Pat Caplan (ed.). *The Cultural Construction of Sexuality*, pp. 240–271. London: Tavistock.

Shostak, Marjorie. *Nisa: The Life and Words of a !Kung Woman*. Cambridge, MA: Harvard University Press.

Vance, Carole S. 1984. Pleasure and Danger: Toward a Politics of Sexuality. In Carole S. Vance (ed.). *Pleasure and Danger: Exploring Female Sexuality*, pp. 1–29. Boston: Routledge and Kegan Paul.

Women and Men in !Kung Society

Marjorie Shostak

After Besa and I had lived together for a long time, he went to visit some people in the East. While there, he found work with a Tswana cattle herder. When he came back, he told me to pack; he wanted me to go and live with him there. So we left and took the long trip to Old Debe's village, a Zhun/twa village near a Tswana and European settlement. We lived there together for a long time.[1]

While we were there, my father died. My older brother, my younger brother, and my mother were with him when he died, but I wasn't; I was living where Besa had taken me. Others carried the news to me. They said that Dau had tried to cure my father, laying on hands and working hard to make him better. But God refused and Dau wasn't able to see what was causing the illness so he could heal

him. Dau said, "God is refusing to give up my father."

I heard and said, "Eh, then today I'm going to see where he died." Besa and I and my children, along with a few others, left to take the long journey west. We walked the first day and slept that night. The next morning we started out and slept again that night; we slept another night on the road, as well. As we walked, I cried and thought, "Why couldn't I have been with him when he died?" I cried as we walked, one day and the next and the next.

The sun was so hot, it was burning; it was killing us. One day we rested such a long time, I thought, "Is the sun going to stop me from seeing where my father died?" When it was cooler, we started walking again and slept on the road again that night.

We arrived at the village late in the afternoon. My younger brother, Kumsa, was the first to see us. When he saw me, he came and hugged me. We started to cry and cried to-

Reprinted by permission of the publishers from *Nisa: The Life and Words of a !Kung Woman* by Marjorie Shostak, Cambridge, MA: Harvard University Press, Copyright © 1981 by Marjorie Shostak.

gether for a long time. Finally, our older brother stopped us, "That's enough for now. Your tears won't make our father alive again."

We stopped crying and we all sat down. My mother was also with us. Although my father never took her back again after the time she ran away with her lover, she returned and lived near him until he died. And even though she slept alone, she still loved him.

Later, my mother and I sat together and cried together.

We stayed there for a while, then Besa and I went back again to live in the East where he had been working for the Europeans. A very long time passed. Then, my brother sent word that my mother was dying. Once again we made the journey to my family and when we arrived I saw her: she was still alive.

We stayed there and lived there. One day, a group of people were going to the bush to live. I said, "Mother, come with us. I'll take care of you and you can help me with my children." We traveled that day and slept that night; we traveled another day and slept another night. But the next night, the sickness that had been inside her grabbed her again and this time, held on. It was just as it had been with my father. The next day, she coughed up blood. I thought, "Oh, why is blood coming out like that? Is this what is going to kill her? Is this the way she's going to die? What is this sickness going to do? She's coughing blood . . . she's already dead!" Then I thought, "If only Dau were here, he would be able to cure her. He would trance for her every day." But he and my younger brother had stayed behind. Besa was with us, but he didn't have the power to cure people. There were others with us as well, but they didn't help.

We slept again that night. The next morning, the others left, as is our custom, and then it was only me, my children, my husband, and my mother; we were the only ones who remained. But her life was really over by then, even though she was still alive.

I went to get her some water and when I came back, she said, "Nisa . . . Nisa . . . I am an old person and today, my heart . . . today

you and I will stay together for a while longer; we will continue to sit beside each other. But later, when the sun stands over there in the afternoon sky and when the new slim moon first strikes, I will leave you. We will separate then and I will go away."

I asked, "Mother, what are you saying?" She said, "Yes, that's what I'm saying. I am an old person. Don't deceive yourself; I am dying. When the sun moves to that spot in the sky, that will be our final separation. We will no longer be together after that. So, take good care of your children."

I said, "Why are you talking like this? If you die as you say, because that's what you're telling me, who are you going to leave in your place?" She said, "Yes, I am leaving you. Your husband will take care of you now. Besa will be with you and your children."

We remained together the rest of the day as the sun crawled slowly across the sky. When it reached the spot she had spoken of, she said—just like a person in good health— "Mm, now . . . be well, all of you," and then she died.

That night I slept alone and cried and cried and cried. None of my family was with me[2] and I just cried the entire night. When morning came, Besa dug a grave and buried her. I said, "Let's pull our things together and go back to the village. I want to tell Dau and Kumsa that our mother has died."

We walked that day and slept that night. We walked the next day and stopped again that night. The next morning, we met my brother Kumsa. Someone had told him that his mother was sick. When he heard, he took his bow and quiver and came looking for us. He left when the sun just rose and started walking toward us, even as we were walking toward him. We met when the sun was overhead. He stood and looked at me. Then he said, "Here you are, Nisa, with your son and your daughter and your husband. But Mother isn't with you . . ."

I sat down and started to cry. He said, "Mother must have died because you're crying like this," and he started to cry, too. Besa said, "Yes, your sister left your mother behind. Two days ago was when your mother and sister separated. That is where we are coming from now. Your sister is here and will tell you about it. You will be together to share your mourning for your mother. That will be good."

We stayed there and cried and cried. Later, Kumsa took my little son and carried him on his shoulders. I carried my daughter and we walked until we arrived back at the village. My older brother came with his wife, and when he saw us he, too, started to cry.

After that, we lived together for a while. I lived and cried, lived and cried. My mother had been so beautiful . . . her face, so lovely. When she died, she caused me great pain. Only after a long time was I quiet again.

Before we returned to the East, I went with Besa to visit his family. While I was there, I became very sick. It came from having carried my mother. Because when she was sick, I carried her around on my back. After she died, my back started to hurt in the very place I had carried her. One of God's spiritual arrows must have struck me there and found its way into my chest.

I was sick for a long time and then blood started to come out of my mouth. My younger brother (he really loves me!) was visiting me at the time. When he saw how I was, he left to tell his older brother, "Nisa's dying the same way our mother died. I've come to tell you to come back with me and heal her." My older brother listened and the two of them traveled to where I was. They came when the sun was high in the afternoon sky. Dau started to trance for me. He laid on hands, healing me with his touch. He worked on me for a long time. Soon, I was able to sleep; then, the blood stopped coming from my chest and later, even if I coughed, there wasn't any more blood.

We stayed there for a few more days. Then, Dau said, "Now I'm going to take Nisa with me to my village." Besa agreed and we all left together. We stayed at my brother's village until I was completely better.

Besa and I eventually moved back East again. But after we had lived together for a long time, we no longer were getting along.

One day I asked, "Besa, won't you take me back to my family's village so I can live there?" He said, "I'm no longer interested in you." I said, "What's wrong? Why do you feel that way?" But then I said, "Eh, if that's how it is, it doesn't matter."

I was working for a European woman at the time, and when I told her what Besa was saying to me, she told him, "Listen to me. You're going to chase your wife away. If you continue to speak to her like this, she'll be gone. Today, I'm pregnant. Why don't you just let her be and have her sit beside you. When I give birth, she will work for me and help me with the baby."

That's what we did. We continued to live together until she gave birth. After, I helped wash the baby's clothes and helped with other chores. I worked for her for a long time.

One day, Besa broke into a little box I had and stole the money she had paid me with. He took it and went to drink beer. I went to the European woman and told her Besa had taken five Rand[3] from me and had left with it. I asked her to help me get it back. We went to the Tswana hut where everyone was drinking and went to the door. The European woman walked in, kicked over a bucket and the beer spilled out. She kicked over another and another and the beer was spilling everywhere. The Tswanas left. She turned to Besa and said, "Why are you treating this young Zhun/twa woman like this? Stop treating her this way." She told him to give her the money and when he gave it to her, she gave it to me. I went and put the money in the box, then took it and left it in her kitchen where it stayed.

Later Besa said, "Why did you tell on me? I'm going to beat you." I said, "Go ahead. Hit me. I don't care. I won't stop you."

Soon after that, I became pregnant with Besa's child. But when it was still very tiny, when I was still carrying it way inside, he left me. I don't know what it was that made him want to leave. Did he have a lover? I don't know. He said he was afraid of a sore I had on my face where a bug had bitten me. It had become swollen, and eventually the Europeans helped to heal it. Whatever it was, his heart had changed toward me and although my heart still liked him, he only liked me a very little then. That's why he left.

It happened the day he finished working for the Europeans. He came back when the sun was low in the sky and said, "Tomorrow, I'm going to visit my younger brother. I have finished my work and have been paid. I'm going, but you'll stay here. Later, Old Debe and his wife can take you back to your brothers' village." I said, "If you are leaving, won't I go with you?" He said, "No, you won't go with me." I said, "Why are you saying you'll go without me? If I go with you and give birth there, it will be good. Don't leave me here. Let me go with you and give birth in your brother's village." But he said, "No, Old Debe will bring you back to your family."

When I saw Old Debe, he asked me what was wrong. I said, "What is Besa doing to me? If he doesn't want me, why doesn't he just end it completely? I've seen for a long time that he doesn't want me." I thought, "Besa . . . he took me to this faraway village, got me pregnant, and now, is he just going to drop me in this foreign place where none of my people live?"

Later, I said to Besa, "Why did you take me from my people? My brothers are still alive, yet you won't take me to them. You say someone else will. But, why should someone else, a near stranger, take me to my family after you've given me this stomach. I say you should take me to them, take me there and say, 'Here is your sister. Today I am separating from her.' Instead, you're saying you'll just leave me here, with these strangers? I followed you here, to where you were working, because you wanted me to. Now you're just going to leave me? Why are you doing this? Can there be any good in it?"

I continued, "You're the one who came here to work. Yet, you have no money and have no blankets. But when you had no more work and no more money, I worked. I alone, a woman. I entered the work of the European and I alone bought us blankets and a trunk. I alone bought all those things and you covered yourself with my blankets. When you weren't working, you asked people to give you things.

How can you leave me here in this foreign place after all that?" He answered, "What work could I have done when there wasn't any to be had?"

I said, "It doesn't matter, because I can see that you will only be here for a few more nights, then you will go. I know that now. But, if you leave me like this today, then tomorrow, after you have gone and have lived with your brother, if you ever decide to come to where I am living, I will refuse you and will no longer be your wife. Because you are leaving me when I am pregnant."

The next morning, early, he tied up his things and left. He packed everything from inside the hut, including all our blankets, and went to his brother's village to live. I thought, "Eh, it doesn't matter, after all. I'll just sit here and let him go." He left me with nothing; the people in the village had to give me blankets to sleep with.

Besa, that man is very bad. He left me hanging like that.

Once he left, I saw that I would be staying there for a while. I thought, "Today I'm no longer going to refuse other men, but will just be with them. Then, maybe I will miscarry. Because this is Besa's child and didn't he leave it and go? I won't refuse other men and will just have them. I will drop this pregnancy; then I will go home."

That's when Numshe entered the hut with me. He spoke to me and I agreed. People said, "Yes, she will enter the hut with him. But when he tastes her,[4] the pregnancy will be ruined." Old Debe's wife said, "That won't be so bad. If her pregnancy is ruined, it won't be a bad thing. Because Besa dropped her. Therefore, I will sit here and take care of her. Later, I will bring her to her family."

I lived there for a long time. I lived alone and worked for the Europeans. Then one day, just as my heart had said, my body felt like fire and my stomach was in great pain. I told Old Debe's wife, "Eh-hey, today I'm sick." She asked, "Where does it hurt? Do you want some water? Where is the sickness hurting you." I said, "My whole body hurts, it isn't just my stomach." I lay there and felt the pains, rising again and again and again. I thought, "That man certainly has made me feel bad; even today, I'm lying here in great pain."

She looked at my stomach and saw how it was standing out. She said, "Oh, my child. Are you going to drop your pregnancy? What is going to happen? Will you be able to give birth to this child or will it be a miscarriage? Here, there are just the two of us; I don't see anyone who will bring more help to you. If you miscarry, it will be only us two." I said, "Yes, that's fine. If I drop this pregnancy, it will be good. I want to drop it, then I can leave. Because my husband certainly doesn't want it."

We stayed together all day. When the sun was late in the sky, I told her it was time and we went together to the bush. I sat down and soon the baby was born. It was already big, with a head and arms and a little penis; but it was born dead. Perhaps my heart had ruined my pregnancy. I cried, "This man almost ruined me, did he not?" Debe's wife said, "Yes, he destroyed this baby, this baby which came from God. But if God hadn't been here helping you, you also would have died. Because when a child dies in a woman's stomach, it can kill the woman. But God . . . God gave you something beautiful in giving you this baby and although it had death in it, you yourself are alive." We left and walked back to the village. Then I lay down.

After that, I just continued to live there. One day I saw people visiting from Besa's village. I told them to tell him that our marriage had ended. I said, "Tell him that he shouldn't think, even with a part of his heart, that he still has a wife here or that when we meet another time in my village that he might still want me." That's what I said and that's what I thought.

Because he left me there to die.

Soon after, a man named Twi saw me and said, "Did your husband leave you?" I said, "Yes, he left me long ago." He asked, "Then won't you stay with me?" I refused the first time he asked as well as the second and the third. But when he asked the next time, I

agreed and we started to live together. I continued to work for the European woman until my work was finished and she told me I could go home. She gave us food for our trip and then all of us—Old Debe, his wife, Twi, and me—traveled the long distance back to where my family was living.

Twi and I lived together in my brothers' village for a long time. Then, one day, Besa came from wherever he had been and said, "Nisa, I've come to take you back with me." I said, "What? What am I like today? Did I suddenly become beautiful? The way I used to be is the way I am now; the way I used to be is what you left behind when you dropped me. So what are you saying? First you drop me in the heart of where the white people live, then you come back and say I should once again be with you?" He said, "Yes, we will pick up our marriage again."

I was stunned! I said, "What are you talking about? This man, Twi, helped bring me back. He's the man who will marry me. You're the one who left me." We talked until he could say nothing more; he was humbled. Finally he said, "You're shit! That's what you are." I said, "I'm shit you say? That's what you thought about me long ago, and I knew it. That's why I told you while we were still living in the East that I wanted you to take me back to my family so we could end our marriage here. But today, I came here myself and you only came afterward. Now I refuse to have anything more to do with you."

That's when Besa brought us to the Tswana headman to ask for a tribal hearing. Once it started, the headman looked at everything. He asked me, "Among all the women who live here, among all those you see sitting around, do you see one who lives with two men?" I said, "No, the women who sit here . . . not one lives with two men; not one among them would I be able to find. I, alone, have two. But it was because this man, Besa, mistreated and hurt me. That's why I took this other man, Twi, who treats me well, who does things for me and gives me things to eat." Then I said, "He is also the man I want to marry; I want to drop the other one. Because Besa has no sense. He left me while I was pregnant and the pregnancy almost killed me. This other one is the one I want to marry."

We talked a long time. Finally, the headman told Besa, "I have questioned Nisa about what happened and she has tied you up with her talk; her talk has defeated you, without doubt. Because what she has said about her pregnancy is serious. Therefore, today she and Twi will continue to stay together. After more time passes, I will ask all of you to come back again." Later, Twi and I left and went back to my brothers' village to sleep.

The next day, my older brother saw a honey cache while walking in the bush. He came to tell us and take us back there with him; we planned to stay the night in the bush. We arrived and spent the rest of the day collecting honey. When we finished, we walked toward where we were planning to camp. That's when I saw Besa's tracks in the sand. I said, "Everyone! Come here! Besa's tracks are here! Has anyone seen them elsewhere?" One of the men said, "Nonsense! Would you know his tracks . . . " I interrupted, "My husband . . . the man who married me . . . I *know* his tracks." The man's wife came to look, "Yes, those are Besa's tracks; his wife really did see them."

The next morning, Besa walked into the camp. Besa and Twi started to fight. My older brother yelled, "Do you two want to kill Nisa? Today she is not taking another husband. Today she's just going to lie by herself." I agreed, "Eh, I don't want to marry again now."

Twi and I continued to live together after that. But later we separated. My older brother caused it, because he wanted Besa to be with me again. He liked him and didn't like Twi. That's why he forced Twi to leave. When Twi saw how much anger both Dau and Besa felt toward him, he became afraid, and finally he left.

I saw what my brother had done and was miserable; I had really liked Twi. I said, "So, this is what you wanted? Fine, but now that you have chased Twi away, I'll have nothing at all to do with Besa." That's when I began to refuse Besa completely. Besa went to the headman and said, "Nisa refuses to be with

me." The headman said, "Nisa's been refusing you for a long time. What legal grounds could I possibly find for you now?"

After more time passed, a man who had been my lover years before, started with me again. Soon we were very much in love. He was so handsome! His nose . . . his eyes . . . everything was so beautiful! His skin was light and his nose was lovely. I really loved that man, even when I first saw him.

We lived together for a while, but then he died. I was miserable, "My lover has died. Where am I going to find another like him—another as beautiful, another as good, another with a European nose and with such lovely light skin? Now he's dead. Where will I ever find another like him?"

My heart was miserable and I mourned for him. I exhausted myself with mourning and only when it was finished did I feel better again.

After years of living and having everything that happened to me happen, that's when I started with Bo, the next important man in my life and the one I am married to today.

Besa and I lived separately, but he still wanted me and stayed near me. That man, he didn't hear; he didn't understand. He was without ears, because he still said, "This woman here, Nisa, I won't be finished with her."

People told Bo, "You're going to die. This man, Besa, he's going to kill you. Now, leave Nisa." But Bo refused, "Me . . . I won't go to another hut. I'll just stay with Nisa and even if Besa tries to kill me, I'll still be here and won't leave."

At first, Bo and I sneaked off together, but Besa suspected us; he was very jealous. He accused me all the time. Even when I just went to urinate, he'd say that I had been with Bo. Or when I went for water, he'd say, "Did you just meet your lover?" But I'd say, "What makes you think you can talk to me like that?" He'd say, "Nisa, you are not still my wife? Why aren't we living together? What are you doing?" I'd say, "Don't you have other women or are they refusing you, too? You have others so why are you asking me about what I'm doing?"

One night, Bo and I were lying down inside my hut and as I looked out through the latched-branch door, I saw someone moving about. It was Besa; I was able to see his face. He wanted to catch us, hoping I would feel some remorse and perhaps return to him.

I said, "What? Besa's here! Bo . . . Bo . . . Besa's standing out there." Bo got up; Besa came and stood by the door. I got up and that's when Besa came in and grabbed me. He held onto me and threatened to throw me into the fire. I cursed him as he held me, "Besa-Big-Testicles! Long-Penis! First you left me and drank of women's genitals elsewhere. Now you come back, see me, and say I am your wife?" He pushed me toward the fire, but I twisted my body so I didn't land in it. Then he went after Bo. Bo is weaker and older than Besa, so Besa was able to grab him, pull him outside the hut, and throw him down. He bit him on the shoulder. Bo yelled out in pain.

My younger brother woke and ran to us, yelling, "Curses to your genitals!" He grabbed them and separated them. Bo cursed Besa. Besa cursed Bo, "Curses on your penis!" He yelled, "I'm going to kill you Bo, then Nisa will suffer! If I don't kill you, then maybe I'll kill her so that you will feel pain! Because what you have that is so full of pleasure, I also have. So why does her heart want you and refuse me?"

I yelled at him, "That's not it! It's you! It's who you are and the way you think! This one, Bo, his ways are good and his thoughts are good. But you, your ways are foul. Look, you just bit Bo; that, too, is part of your ways. You also left me to die. And death, that's something I'm afraid of. That's why you no longer have a hold over me. Today I have another who will take care of me well. I'm no longer married to you, Besa. I want my husband to be Bo."

Besa kept bothering me and hanging around me. He'd ask, "Why won't you come to me? Come to me, I'm a man. Why are you afraid of me?" I wouldn't answer. Once Bo answered, "I don't understand why, if you *are* a man, you keep pestering this woman? Is what you're doing going to do any good? Because I won't leave her. And even though you bit me and your marks are on me, you're the one who is going to move out of the way, not me. I intend to marry her."

Another time I told Bo, "Don't be afraid of Besa. You and I will marry; I'm not going to stay married to him. Don't let him frighten you. Because even if he comes here with arrows, he won't do anything with them." Bo said, "Even if he did, what good would that do? I am also a man and am a master of arrows. The two of us would just strike each other. That's why I keep telling him to let you go; I am the man you are with now."

The next time, Besa came with his quiver full of arrows, saying, "I'm going to get Nisa and bring her back with me." He left with another man and came to me at my village. When he arrived, the sun was high in the sky. I was resting. He said, "Nisa, come, let's go." I said, "What? Is your penis not well? Is it horny?"

People heard us fighting and soon everyone was there, my younger and older brothers as well. Besa and I kept arguing and fighting until, in a rage, I screamed, "All right! Today I'm no longer afraid!" and I pulled off all the skins that were covering me—first one, then another, and finally the leather apron that covered my genitals. I pulled them all off and laid them down on the ground. I cried, "There! There's my vagina! Look, Besa, look at me! This is what you want!"

The man he had come with said, "This woman, her heart is truly far from you. Besa, look. Nisa refuses you totally, with all her heart. She refuses to have sex with you. Your relationship with her is finished. See. She took off her clothes, put them down, and with her genitals is showing everyone how she feels about you. She doesn't want you, Besa. If I were you, I'd finish with her today." Besa finally said, "Eh, you're right. Now I am finished with her."

The two of them left. I took my leather apron, put it on, took the rest of my things and put them on.

Mother! That was just what I did.

Besa tried one last time. He went to the headman again, and when he came back he told me, "The headman wants to see you." I thought, "If he wants to see me, I won't refuse."

When I arrived, the headman said, "Besa says he still wants to continue your marriage." I said, "Continue our marriage? Why? Am I so stupid that I don't know my name? Would I stay in a marriage with a man who left me hanging in a foreign place? If Old Debe and his wife hadn't been there, I would have truly lost my way. Me, stay married to Besa? I can't make myself think of it."

I turned to Besa, "Isn't that what I told you when we were still in the East?" Besa said, "Mm, that's what you said." I said, "And, when you left, didn't I tell you that you were leaving me pregnant with your baby. Didn't I also tell you that?" He said, "Yes, that's what you said." I said, "And didn't I say that I wanted to go with you, that I wanted you to help make our pregnancy grow strong? Didn't I say that and didn't you refuse?" He said, "Yes, you said that." Then I said, "Mm. Therefore, that marriage you say today, in the lap of the headman, should be continued, that marriage no longer exists. Because I am Nisa and today, when I look at you, all I want to do is to throw up. Vomit is the only thing left in my heart for you now. As we sit together here and I see your face, that is all that rises within and grabs me."

The headman laughed, shook his head and said, "Nisa is impossible!" Then he said, "Besa, you had better listen to her. Do you hear what she is saying? She says that you left her while she was pregnant, that she miscarried and was miserable. Today she will no longer take you for her husband." Besa said, "That's because she's with Bo now and doesn't want to leave him. But I still want her and want to continue our marriage."

I said, "What? Besa, can't you see me? Can't you see that I have really found another man? Did you think, perhaps, that I was too old and wouldn't find someone else?" The headman laughed again. "Yes, I am a woman. And that which you have, a penis, I also have something of equal worth. Like the penis of a

chief . . . yes, something of a chief is what I have. And its worth is like money. Therefore, the person who drinks from it . . . it's like he's getting money from me. But not you, because when you had it, you just left it to ruin."

The headman said, "Nisa is crazy; her talk is truly crazy now." Then he said, "The two of you sleep tonight and give your thoughts over to this. Nisa, think about all of it again. Tomorrow, I want both of you to come back."

Besa went and lay down. I went and lay down and thought about everything. In the morning, I went to the headman. I felt ashamed by my talk of the night before. I sat there quietly. The headman said, "Nisa, Besa says you should stay married to him." I answered, "Why should he stay married to me when yesterday I held his baby in my stomach and he dropped me. Even God doesn't want me to marry a man who leaves me, a man who takes my blankets when I have small children beside me, a man who forces other people to give me blankets to cover my children with. Tell him to find another woman to marry."

The headman turned to Besa, "Nisa has explained herself. There's nothing more I can see to say. Even you, you can hear that she has defeated you. So, leave Nisa and as I am headman, today your marriage to her is ended. She can now marry Bo."[5]

Besa went to the headman one more time. When he tried to discuss it again, saying, "Please, help me. Give Nisa back to me," the headman said, "Haven't you already talked to me about this? You talked and talked, and the words entered my ears. Are you saying that I have not already decided on this? That I am not an important person? That I am a worthless thing that you do not have to listen to? There is no reason to give Nisa back to you."

I was so thankful when I heard his words. My heart filled with happiness.

Bo and I married soon after that.[6] We lived together, sat together, and did things together. Our hearts loved each other very much and our marriage was very very strong.

Besa also married again not long after—this time to a woman much younger than me. One day he came to me and said, "Look how wrong you were to have refused me! Perhaps you thought you were the only woman. But you, Nisa, today you are old and you yourself can see that I have married a young woman, one who is beautiful!"

I said, "Good! I told you that if we separated, you'd find a young woman to marry and to sleep with. That is fine with me because there is nothing I want from you. But you know, of course, that just like me, another day she too will be old."

We lived on, but not long after, Besa came back. He said that his young wife was troubled and that he wanted me again. I refused and even told Bo about it. Bo asked me why I refused. I said, "Because I don't want him." But what he says about his wife is true. She has a terrible sickness, a type of madness. God gave it to her. She was such a beautiful woman, too. But no longer. I wonder why such a young woman has to have something like that . . .

Even today, whenever Besa sees me, he argues with me and says he still wants me. I say, "Look, we've separated. Now leave me alone." I even sometimes refuse him food. Bo tells me I shouldn't refuse, but I'm afraid he will bother me more if I give anything to him. Because his heart still cries for me.

Sometimes I do give him things to eat and he also gives things to me. Once I saw him in my village. He came over to me and said, "Nisa, give me some water to drink." I washed out a cup and poured him some water. He drank it and said, "Now, give me some tobacco." I took out some tobacco and gave it to him. Then he said, "Nisa, you really are adult; you know how to work. Today, I am married to a woman but my heart doesn't agree to her much. But you . . . you are one who makes me feel pain. Because you left me and married another man. I also married, but have made myself weary by having married something bad. You, you have hands that work and do things. With you, I could eat. You would get water for me to wash with. Today, I'm really in pain."

I said, "Why are you thinking about our dead marriage? Of course, we were married once, but we have gone our different ways. Now, I no longer want you. After all that happened when you took me East—living there, working there, my father dying, my mother dying, and all the misery you caused me—you say we should live together once again?"

He said that I wasn't telling it as it happened.

One day, he told me he wanted to take me from Bo. I said, "What? Tell me, Besa, what has been talking to you that you are saying this again?" He said, "All right, then have me as your lover. Won't you help my heart out?" I said, "Aren't there many men who could be my lover? Why should I agree to you?" He said, "Look here, Nisa . . . I'm a person who helped bring up your children, the children you and your husband gave birth to. You became pregnant again with my child and that was good. You held it inside you and lived with it until God came and killed it. That's why your heart is talking this way and refusing me."

I told him he was wrong. But he was right, too. Because, after Besa, I never had any more children. He took that away from me. With Tashay, I had children, but Besa, he ruined me. Even the one time I did conceive, I miscarried. That's because of what he did to me; that's what everyone says.

NOTES

1. This chapter covers about five years, beginning when Nisa was in her early thirties (c. the mid 1950s).
2. In fact, her husband and children were with her.
3. The Rand is a South African currency that was then legal tender in Bechuanaland (pre-independence Botswana). It was worth between $1.20 and $1.50. Five Rand was a very large sum of money to the !Kung at that time—perhaps as much as two months wages at a typical menial task.
4. Tastes her: A euphemism for sexual intercourse.
5. The procedure for divorce in traditional !Kung culture would have been less complicated and would have proceeded more quickly.
6. Nisa and Bo married around 1957, when Nisa was about thirty-six years old.

The Manhood Puzzle

David D. Gilmore

> There are continuities of masculinity that transcend cultural differences.
> —Thomas Gregor, *Anxious Pleasures*

Are there continuities of masculinity across cultural boundaries, as the anthropologist Thomas Gregor says (1985:209)? Are men everywhere alike in their concern for being "manly?" If so, why? Why is the demand made upon males to "be a man" or "act like a man" voiced in so many places? And why are boys and youths so often tested or indoctrinated before being awarded their manhood? These are questions not often asked in the growing literature on sex and gender roles. Yet given the recent interest in sexual stereotyping, they are ones that need to be considered if we are to understand both sexes and their relations.

Regardless of other normative distinctions made, all societies distinguish between male and female; all societies also provide institutionalized sex-appropriate roles for adult men and women. A very few societies recognize a third, sexually intermediary category, such as the Cheyenne *berdache*, the Omani *xanith,* and the Tahitian *mahu* . . . but even in these rare cases of androgynous genders, the individual must make a life choice of identity and abide by prescribed rules of sexual comportment. In addition, most societies hold consensual ideas—guiding or admonitory images—for conventional masculinity and femininity by which individuals are judged worthy members of one or the other sex and are evaluated more generally as moral actors. Such ideal statuses and their attendant images, or

models, often become psychic anchors, or psychological identities, for most individuals, serving as a basis for self-perception and self-esteem (D'Andrade 1974:36).

These gender ideals, or guiding images, differ from culture to culture. But, as Gregor and others (e.g., Brandes 1980; Lonner 1980; Raphael 1988) have argued, underlying the surface differences are some intriguing similarities among cultures that otherwise display little in common. Impressed by the statistical frequency of such regularities in sexual patterning, a number of observers have recently argued that cultures are more alike than different in this regard. For example, Gregor (1985:200) studied a primitive Amazonian tribe and compared its sex ideals to those of contemporary America. Finding many subsurface similarities in the qualities expected of men and women, he concludes that our different cultures represent only a symbolic veneer masking a bedrock of sexual thinking. In another study, the psychologist Lonner (1980:147) echoes this conclusion. He argues that culture is "only a thin veneer covering an essential universality" of gender dimorphism. In their comprehensive survey of sex images in thirty different cultures, Williams and Best (1982:30) conclude that there is "substantial similarity" to be found "panculturally in the traits ascribed to men and women."

Whether or not culture is only a thin veneer over a deep structure is a complicated question: as the rare third sexes show, we must not see in every culture "a Westerner struggling to get out" (Munroe and Munroe 1980:25). But most social scientists would agree that there do exist striking regularities in standard male and female roles across cultural boundaries regardless of other social arrangements (Archer and Lloyd 1985:283–

84). The one regularity that concerns me here is the often dramatic ways in which cultures construct an appropriate manhood—the presentation or "imaging" of the male role. In particular, there is a constantly recurring notion that real manhood is different from simple anatomical maleness, that it is not a natural condition that comes about spontaneously through biological maturation but rather is a precarious or artificial state that boys must win against powerful odds. This recurrent notion that manhood is problematic, a critical threshold that boys must pass through testing, is found at all levels of sociocultural development regardless of what other alternative roles are recognized. It is found among the simplest hunters and fishermen, among peasants and sophisticated urbanized peoples; it is found in all continents and environments. It is found among both warrior peoples and those who have never killed in anger.

Moreover, this recurrent belief represents a primary and recurrent difference from parallel notions of femaleness. Although women, too, in any society are judged by sometimes stringent sexual standards, it is rare that their very status as woman forms part of the evaluation. Women who are found deficient or deviant according to these standards may be criticized as immoral, or they may be called unladylike or its equivalent and subjected to appropriate sanctions, but rarely is their right to a gender identity questioned in the same public, dramatic way that it is for men. The very paucity of linguistic labels for females echoing the epithets "effete," "unmanly," "effeminate," "emasculated," and so on, attest to this archetypical difference between sex judgments worldwide. And it is far more assaultive (and frequent) for men to be challenged in this way than for women.

Perhaps the difference between male and female should not be overstated, for "femininity" is also something achieved by women who seek social approval. But as a social icon, femininity seems to be judged differently. It usually involves questions of body ornament or sexual allure, or other essentially cosmetic behaviors that enhance, rather than create,

an inherent quality of character. An authentic femininity rarely involves tests or proofs of action, or confrontations with dangerous foes: win-or-lose contests dramatically played out on the public stage. Rather than a critical threshold passed by traumatic testing, an either/or condition, femininity is more often construed as a biological given that is culturally refined or augmented.

TESTS OF MANHOOD: A SURVEY

Before going any further, let us look at a few examples of this problematic manhood. Our first stop is Truk Island, a little atoll in the South Pacific. Avid fishermen, the people of Truk have lived for ages from the sea, casting and diving in deep waters. According to the anthropologists who have lived among them, the Trukese men are obsessed with their masculinity, which they regard as chancy. To maintain a manly image, the men are encouraged to take risks with life and limb and to think "strong" or "manly" thoughts, as the natives put it (M. Marshall 1979). Accordingly, they challenge fate by going on deep-sea fishing expeditions in tiny dugouts and spearfishing with foolhardy abandon in shark-infested waters. If any men shrink from such challenges, their fellows, male and female, laugh at them, calling them effeminate and childlike. When on land, Trukese youths fight in weekend brawls, drink to excess, and seek sexual conquests to attain a manly image. Should a man fail in any of these efforts, another will taunt him: "Are you a man? Come, I will take your life now" (ibid.:92).

Far away on the Greek Aegean island of Kalymnos, the people are also stalwart seafarers, living by commercial sponge fishing (Bernard 1967). The men of Kalymnos dive into deep water without the aid of diving equipment, which they scorn. Diving is therefore a gamble because many men are stricken and crippled by the bends for life. But no matter: they have proven their precious manhood by showing their contempt for death (ibid.:119). Young divers who take precautions are effeminate, scorned and ridiculed by their fellows.

These are two seafaring peoples. Let us move elsewhere, to inland Black Africa, for example, where fishing is replaced by pastoral pursuits. In East Africa young boys from a host of cattle-herding tribes, including the Masai, Rendille, Jie, and Samburu, are taken away from their mothers and subjected at the outset of adolescence to bloody circumcision rites by which they become true men. They must submit without so much as flinching under the agony of the knife. If a boy cries out while his flesh is being cut, if he so much as blinks an eye or turns his head, he is shamed for life as unworthy of manhood, and his entire lineage is shamed as a nursery of weaklings. After this very public ordeal, the young initiates are isolated in special dormitories in the wilderness. There, thrust on their own devices, they learn the tasks of a responsible manhood: cattle rustling, raiding, killing, survival in the bush. If their long apprenticeship is successful, they return to society as men and are only then permitted to take a wife.

Another dramatic African case comes from nearby Ethiopia: the Amhara, a Semitic-speaking tribe of rural cultivators. They have a passionate belief in masculinity called *wand-nat*. This idea involves aggressiveness, stamina, and bold "courageous action" in the face of danger; it means never backing down when threatened (Levine 1966:18). To show their wand-nat, the Amhara youths are forced to engage in whipping contests called *buhe* (Reminick 1982:32). During the whipping ceremonies, in which all able-bodied male adolescents must participate for their reputations' sake, the air is filled with the cracking of whips. Faces are lacerated, ears torn open, and red and bleeding welts appear (ibid.:33). Any sign of weakness is greeted with taunts and mockery. As if this were not enough, adolescent Amhara boys are wont to prove their virility by scarring their arms with red-hot embers (Levine 1966:19). In these rough ways the boys actualize the exacting Amhara "ideals of masculinity" (Reminick 1976:760).

Significantly, this violent testing is not enough for these virile Ethiopians. Aside from showing physical hardihood and courage in the buhe matches, a young man must demonstrate his potency on his wedding night by waving a bloody sheet of marital consummation before the assembled kinsmen (ibid.:760–61). As well as demonstrating the bride's virginity, this ceremonial defloration is a talisman of masculinity for the Amhara groom. The Amhara's proof of manhood, like that of the Trukese, is both sexual and violent, and his performances both on the battlefield and in the marriage bed must be visibly displayed, recorded, and confirmed by the group; otherwise he is no man.

Halfway around the world, in the high mountains of Melanesia, young boys undergo similar trials before being admitted into the select of club of manhood. In the New Guinea Highlands, boys are torn from their mothers and forced to undergo a series of brutal masculinizing rituals (Herdt 1982). These include whipping, flailing, beating, and other forms of terrorization by older men, which the boys must endure stoically and silently. As in Ethiopia, the flesh is scored and blood flows freely. These Highlanders believe that without such hazing, boys will never mature into men but will remain weak and childlike. Real men are made, they insist, not born.

PARALLELS

To be sure, there are some contextual similarities in these last few examples. The Amhara, Masai, and New Guinea Highlanders share one feature in common beyond the stress on manhood: they are fierce warrior peoples, or were in the recent past. One may argue that their bloody rites prepare young boys for the idealized life of the warrior that awaits them. So much is perhaps obvious: some Western civilizations also subject soft youths to rough hazing and initiations in order to toughen them up for a career of soldiering, as in the U.S. Marines (Raphael 1988). But these trials are by no means confined to militaristic cultures or castes. Let us take another African example.

Among the relatively peaceful !Kung Bushmen of southwest Africa (Thomas 1959; Lee 1979), manhood is also a prize to be grasped through a test. Accurately calling themselves "The Harmless People" (Thomas 1959), these nonviolent Bushmen have never fought a war in their lives. They have no military weapons, and they frown upon physical violence (which, however, sometimes does occur). Yet even here, in a culture that treasures gentleness and cooperation above all things, the boys must earn the right to be called men by a test of skill and endurance. They must single-handedly track and kill a sizable adult antelope, an act that requires courage and hardiness. Only after their first kill of such a buck are they considered fully men and permitted to marry.

Other examples of stressed manhood among gentle people can be found in the New World, in aboriginal North America. Among the nonviolent Fox tribe of Iowa, for example, "being a man" does not come easily (Gearing 1970:51). Based on stringent standards of accomplishment in tribal affairs and economic pursuits, real manhood is said to be "the Big Impossible," an exclusive status that only the nimble few can achieve (ibid.:51–52). Another American Indian example is the Tewa people of New Mexico, also known as the Pueblo Indians. These placid farmers, who are known today for their serene culture, gave up all warfare in the last century. Yet they subject their boys to a severe hazing before they can be accounted men. Between the ages of twelve and fifteen, the Tewa boys are taken away from their homes, purified by ritual means, and then whipped mercilessly by the Kachina spirits (their fathers in disguise). Each boy is stripped naked and lashed on the back four times with a crude yucca whip that draws blood and leaves permanent scars. The adolescents are expected to bear up impassively under the beating to show their fortitude. The Tewa say that this rite makes their boys into men, that otherwise manhood is doubtful. After the boys' ordeal, the Kachina spirits tell them, "You are now a man. . . . You are made a man" (Hill 1982:220). Although Tewa girls have their own (nonviolent) initiations, there is no parallel belief that girls have to be *made* women, no "big impossible" for them; for the Tewa and the Fox, as for the other people above, womanhood develops naturally, needing no cultural intervention, its predestined arrival at menarche commemorated rather than forced by ritual (ibid.:209–10).

Nor are such demanding efforts at proving oneself a man confined to primitive peoples or those on the margins of civilization. In urban Latin America, for example, as described by Oscar Lewis (1961:38), a man must prove his manhood every day by standing up to challenges and insults, even though he goes to his death "smiling." As well as being tough and brave, ready to defend his family's honor at the drop of a hat, the urban Mexican, like the Amhara man, must also perform adequately in sex and father many children. Such macho exploits are also common among many of the peasant and pastoral peoples who reside in the cradle of the ancient Mediterranean civilizations. In the Balkans, for instance, the category of "real men" is clearly defined. A real man is one who drinks heavily, spends money freely, fights bravely, and raises a large family (Simic 1969, 1983). In this way he shows an "indomitable virility" that distinguishes him from effeminate counterfeits (Denich 1974:250). In eastern Morocco, true men are distinguished from effete men on the basis of physical prowess and heroic acts of both feuding and sexual potency; their manly deeds are memorialized in verses sung before admiring crowds at festivals, making manhood a kind of communal celebration (Marcus 1987:50). Likewise, for the Bedouin of Egypt's Western Desert, "real men" are contrasted with despicable weaklings who are "no men." Real Bedouin men are bold and courageous, afraid of nothing. Such men assert their will at any cost and stand up to any challenge; their main attributes are "assertiveness and the quality of potency" (Abu-Lughod 1986:88–89). Across the sea, in Christian Crete, men in village coffee shops proudly sing paeans to their own virility, their self-promotion having been characterized as the "poetics of manhood" by Michael Herzfeld (1985a:15). These Cretans must demonstrate their "manly selfhood" by stealing sheep, procreating large families, and besting other men in games of chance and skill (ibid.).

Examples of this pressured manhood with its almost talismanic qualities could be given almost indefinitely and in all kinds of contexts. Among most of the peoples that anthropologists are familiar with, true manhood is a precious and elusive status beyond mere maleness, a hortatory image that men and boys aspire to and that their culture demands of them as a measure of belonging. Although this stressed or embattled quality varies in intensity, becoming highly marked in southern Spain, Morocco, Egypt, and some other Mediterranean-area traditions, true manhood in other cultures frequently shows an inner insecurity that needs dramatic proof. Its vindication is doubtful, resting on rigid codes of decisive action in many spheres of life: as husband, father, lover, provider, warrior. A restricted status, there are always men who fail the test. These are the negative examples, the effete men, the men-who-are-no-men, held up scornfully to inspire conformity to the glorious ideal.

Perhaps these stagy routes to manhood seem bizarre to us at first glance. But none of them should surprise most Anglophone readers, for we too have our manly traditions, both in our popular culture and in literary genres. Although we may choose less flamboyant modes of expression than the Amhara or Trukese, we too have regarded manhood as an artificial state, a challenge to be overcome, a prize to be won by fierce struggle: if not "the big impossible," then certainly doubtful.

For example, let us take a people and a social stratum far removed from those above: the gentry of modern England. There, young boys were traditionally subjected to similar trials on the road to their majority. They were torn at a tender age from mother and home, as in East Africa or in New Guinea, and sent away in age sets to distant testing grounds that sorely took their measure. These were the public boarding schools, where a cruel "trial by ordeal," including physical violence and terrorization by elder males, provided a passage to a "social state of manhood" that their parents thought could be achieved in no

other way (Chandos 1984:172). Supposedly, this harsh training prepared young Oxbridge aristocrats for the self-reliance and fortitude needed to run the British Empire and thereby manufactured "a serviceable elite as stylized as Samurai" (ibid.:346). Even here, in Victorian England, a culture not given over to showy excess, manhood was an artificial product coaxed by austere training and testing.

Similar ideas motivated educators on both sides of the Atlantic, for example, the founders of the Boy Scouts. Their chartered purpose, as they put it in their pamphlets and manuals, was to "make big men of little boys" by fostering "an independent manhood," as though this were not to be expected from nature alone (cited by Hantover 1978:189). This obsessive moral masculinization in the English-speaking countries went beyond mere mortals of the day to Christ himself, who was portrayed in turn-of-the-century tracts as "the supremely manly man," athletic and aggressive when necessary, no "Prince of Peace-at-any-price" (Conant 1915:117). The English publicist Thomas Hughes dilated rhapsodically about the manliness of Christ (1879), while his colleagues strove to depict Christianity as the "muscular" or "manly" faith. Pious and articulate English Protestants loudly proclaimed their muscular religion as an antidote to what Charles Kingsley derided as the "fastidious maundering, die-away effeminacy" of the High Anglican Church (cited in Gay 1982:532). Boys, faiths, and gods had to be made masculine; otherwise there was doubt. The same theme runs through much British literature of the time, most notably in Kipling, as for example in the following lines from the poem "If":

If you can fill the unforgiving minute
With sixty seconds worth of distance run,
Yours is the Earth, and everything that's in it,
And—which is more—you'll be a Man, my son!

Consequent only to great deeds, being a Kiplingesque man is more than owning the Earth, a truly imperial masculinity consonant with empire building. The same theme of "iffy" heroism runs through many aspects of popular middle-class American culture today. Take, for example, the consistent strain in U.S. literature of masculine *Bildungsroman*—the ascension to the exalted status of manhood under the tutelage of knowledgeable elders, with the fear of failure always lurking menancingly in the background. This theme is most strongly exemplified by Ernest Hemingway, of course, notably in the Nick Adams stories, but it is also found in the work of such contemporaries as William Faulkner and John Dos Passos, and in such Hemingway epigones as Studs Terkel, Norman Mailer, James Dickey, Frederick Exley, and—the new generation—Robert Stone, Jim Harrison, and Tom McGuane. This "virility school" in American letters (Schwenger 1984:13), was sired by Papa Hemingway (if one discounts Jack London) and nurtured thereafter by his acolytes, but it is now in its third or fourth generation and going strong (for a feminist view see Fetterly 1978).

In contemporary literary America, too, manhood is often a mythic confabulation, a Holy Grail, to be seized by long and arduous testing. Take, for example, this paradigmatic statement by Norman Mailer (1968:25): "Nobody was born a man; you earned manhood provided you were good enough, bold enough." As well as echoing his spiritual forebears, both British and American, Mailer articulates here the unwritten sentiments of the Trukese, the Amhara, the Bushmen, and countless other peoples who have little else in common except this same obsessive "quest for male validation" (Raphael 1988:67). Although some of us may smile at Mailer for being so histrionic and sophomoric about it, he nevertheless touches a raw nerve that pulsates through many cultures as well as our own. Nor is Mailer's challenge representative of only a certain age or stratum of American society. As the poet Leonard Kriegel (1979:14) says in his reflective book about American manhood, "In every age, not just our own, manhood was something that had to be won."

Looking back, for instance, one is reminded of the cultural values of the antebellum American South. Southerners, whatever their class, placed great stress on a volatile manly honor as a defining feature of the southern character, a fighting principle. Indeed, Bertram Wyatt-Brown, in his book *Southern Honor* (1982), has argued convincingly that this touchy notion was a major element behind southern secessionism and thus an important and underrated political factor in U.S. history. A defense of southern "manliness" was in fact offered by Confederate writers of the time, including the South Carolina firebrand Charles C. Jones, as one justification for regional defiance, political separation, and, finally, war (cited in McPherson 1988:41). And of course similar ideals are enshrined in the frontier folklore of the American West, past and present, as exemplified in endless cowboy epics.

This heroic image of an achieved manhood is being questioned in America by feminists and by so-called liberated men themselves (Pleck 1981; Brod 1987). But for decades, it has been widely legitimized in U.S. cultural settings ranging from Italian-American gangster culture to Hollywood Westerns, private-eye tales, the current Rambo imagoes, and children's He-Man dolls and games; it is therefore deeply ingrained in the American male psyche. As the anthropologist Robert LeVine (1979:312) says, it is an organization of cultural principles that function together as a "guiding myth within the confines of our culture." But given the similarities between contemporary American notions of manliness and those of the many cultures discussed above, can we drop LeVine's qualifying phrase about "the confines of our culture"? Can we speak instead of an archetype or "deep structure" of masculinity, as Andrew Tolson (1977:56) puts it? And if so, what explains all these similarities? Why the trials and the testing and the seemingly gratuitous agonies of man-playing? Why is so much indoctrination and motivation needed in all these cultures to make real men? What is there about "official" manliness that requires such effort, such challenge, and such investment? And why should manhood be so desirable a state and at the same time be conferred so grudgingly in so many societies? These are some of the questions I want to consider here. Only a broadly comparative approach can begin to answer them.

MANHOOD AND GENDER ROLE

Let us pause at this point to take stock. What do we know so far about the origins of such gender imagery? Until very recently, studies of male and female were wedded to a persistent paradigm derived from mechanistic nineteenth-century antecedents. Most pervasive was the idea of generic types, a Universal Man counterpoised to a Universal Woman—a sexual symmetry supposedly derived from self-evident dualisms in biology and psychology (Katchadourian 1979:20). Freud, for example, held that anatomy was destiny, and Jung (1926) went so far as to develop universal principles of masculinity and femininity which he conveyed as "animus" and "anima," irreducible cores of sexual identity. Western literature and philosophy are full of such fundamental and supposedly immutable dualisms (Bakan 1966); they are also found in some Asian cosmologies, for example, the Chinese Yin and Yang, and in countless sets of binary oppositions both philosophical and scientific (e.g., Ortner 1974). What could be a neater polarity than sex? Our view of manhood in the past was often a simple reflection of these polar views of male and female "natures" or "principles." This view had some scientific support among biologists and psychologists, many of whom held that the aggressiveness of masculinity, including the testing and proving, was merely a consequence of male anatomy and hormones: men seek challenges because they are naturally aggressive. That is simply the way they are; women are the opposite. Period.

The way we look at sex roles, however, has changed drastically in the past two decades. Although appealing to many, sex dualisms and oppositions are definitely out of fashion, and so are sexual universals and biological determinisms. Part of the reason, aside from the recent movement away from static structural dualisms in the social sciences generally,

lies in the feminist revolution of the past twenty years. Starting in the 1960s, the feminist attack on the bipolar mode of sexual thinking has shaken this dualistic edifice to its roots; but to be fair, it was never very sturdy to begin with. For example, both Freud and Jung accepted an inherent mixture of masculinity and femininity within each human psyche. Although he distinguished male and female principles, Jung to his credit admitted the existence of animus and anima to degrees in all people; bisexuality was in fact one of the bedrocks of Freud's psychological reasoning. In every human being, Freud (1905:220) remarks, "pure masculinity or femininity is not to be found either in a psychological or a biological sense. Every individual on the contrary displays a mixture."

Moreover, feminists of various backgrounds and persuasions (see, for example, Baker 1980; Sanday 1981; Otten 1985) have convincingly demonstrated that the conventional bipolar model based on biology is invalid and that sex (biological inheritance) and gender (cultural norms) are distinct categories that may have a relationship but not an isomorphic identity. Most observers would agree that hormones and anatomy do have an effect on our behavior. The biological anthropologist Melvin Konner has convincingly shown this in his book, *The Tangled Wing* (1982). Assessing the latest scientific and clinical literature in this highly acclaimed survey, Konner concludes that testosterone (the main male sex hormone) predisposes males to a slightly higher level of aggressivity than females (see also Archer and Lloyd 1985;138–39). But, as Konner freely admits, biology does not determine all of our behavior, or even very much of it, and cultures do indeed vary to some degree in assigning sex roles, measured in jobs and tasks. Discrete concepts of masculinity and femininity, based on secondary sex characteristics, exist in virtually all societies, but they are not always constructed and interfaced in the same way. Gender is a symbolic category. As such, it has strong moral overtones, and therefore is ascriptive and culturally relative—potentially changeful. On the other hand, sex is rooted in anatomy and is therefore fairly constant (Stoller 1968). It is now generally accepted, even among the most traditional male researchers, that masculine and feminine principles are not inherent polarities but an "overlapping continuum" (Biller and Borstelmann 1967: 255), or, as Spence and Helmreich put it (1979:4), "orthogonal dimensions."

Still, as we have seen from the examples above, there exists a recurrent cultural tendency to distinguish and to polarize gender roles. Instead of allowing free play in sex roles and gender ideals, most societies tend to exaggerate biological potentials by clearly differentiating sex roles and by defining the proper behavior of men and women as opposite or complementary. Even where so-called "third sexes" exist, as for example the Plains Indian berdache and the Omani xanith, conventional male and female types are still strongly differentiated. So the question of continuities in gender imaging must go beyond genetic endowment to encompass cultural norms and moral scripts. If there are archetypes in the male image (as there are in femininity), they must be largely culturally constructed as symbolic systems, not simply as products of anatomy, because anatomy determines very little in those contexts where the moral imagination comes into play. The answer to the manhood puzzle must lie in culture; we must try to understand why culture uses or exaggerates biological potentials in specific ways.

PREVIOUS INTERPRETATIONS

Some feminists and other relativists have perceived the apparent contradiction between the theoretical arbitrariness of gender concepts and the empirical convergence of sex roles. Explanations have therefore been offered to account for it. The existing explanations are interesting and useful, and I do not argue against them on the grounds of logical consistency. Rather, I think that the wrong questions have been asked in this inquiry. Most explanations have been phrased in one of two ways, both ideologically satisfying de-

pending upon one's point of view, but neither getting us very far analytically.

First, the question has been phrased by the more doctrinaire Marxists and some radical feminists in an idiom of pure conflict theory. They see gender ideology as having a purely exploitative function. Thus they ask, inevitably, cui bono? Since many male ideologies include an element of gender oppressiveness, or at least hierarchy (in the view of liberated Western intellectuals), some of these radicals regard masculine ideologies as masks or justifications for the oppression of women. They see male ideologies as mystifications of power relationships, as examples of false consciousness (see, for example, Ortner 1981; Godelier 1986). This explanation is probably true for some cases, at least as a partial explanation, especially in some extreme patriarchies where male dominance is very pronounced. But it cannot be true as a universal explanation, because it cannot account for instances in which males are tested for manhood but where there is relative sexual equality. We have seen one example of this in the African Bushmen (Thomas 1959; Lee 1979; Shostak 1981). Although these nonsexist foragers are often held up by feminists as a model of sexual egalitarianism (Shostak 1981), Bushmen boys must prove their manhood by hunting prowess. They must also undergo tests of hardiness and skill from which girls are excluded. . . . Their manhood is subject to proof and, conceptually, to diminishment or loss. The same is true of the Fox and the Tewa of North America. So if a conception of manhood has no oppressive function in these societies, what is it doing there? It seems that the conflict theorists are missing something.

The second idiom of explanation is equally reductionistic. Here, biological or psychological processes are given analytical priority. There are two forms of biopsychological reductionist argument. The first is biological/evolutionary à la Lionel Tiger in *Men in Groups* (1971). Tiger holds that men worry about manhood because evolutionary pressures have predisposed them to do so. Once we were all hunters, and our success and therefore the survival and expansion of the group depended upon our developing genetically determined "masculine tendencies," aggression and male bonding being principal among them. This sociobiological argument is useful in certain cases, again, most notably in the violent patriarchies. But it is demonstrably false as a universal explanation because there are many societies where "aggressive" hunting never played an important role, where men do not bond for economic purposes, where violence and war are devalued or unknown, and yet where men are today concerned about demonstrating manhood. Further, this argument commits the historical fallacy of proposing a historical explanation for a cultural trait that persists under changed circumstances.

The second genetic reductionism is the standard psychoanalytic one about male psychic development. It is based squarely on an orthodox reading of Freud's Oedipus complex and its derivative, castration anxiety. This orthodoxy has been challenged recently with a neo-Freudian viewpoint stressing other aspects of male development, which I find much more powerful. . . . The standard psychoanalytic view holds that men everywhere are defending against castration fears as a result of identical oedipal traumas in psychosexual development. Masculinity cults and ideals are compensations erected universally against such fears (Stephens 1967; Kline 1972).

In this view, the norms of masculinity are projected outward from the individual psyche onto the screen of culture; public culture is individual fantasy life writ large. I think this explanation is useful in some cases but supererogatory. More damaging, it fails to give proper weight to social constraints that enforce male conformity to manhood ideals; as we shall see, boys have to be encouraged—sometimes actually forced—by social sanctions to undertake efforts toward a culturally defined manhood, which by themselves they might not do. So the explanation cannot be one based solely on psychic projections. Moreover, the orthodox psychoanalytic view can also be demonstrated to be false at a universal level, for there are empirical exceptions to the culture of manhood. There are a few societies that do not place the usual stress on achieving a masculine image; in these exceptional "neuter" societies, males are freed from the need to prove themselves and are allowed a basically androgynous script, which, significantly, they find congenial. As these exceptions do exist, . . . the answer to the masculinity puzzle must have a social side to it, because formal variation cannot be explained on the basis of a psychological constant such as castration anxiety.

SOME HELP FROM THE POST-FREUDIANS

At this point we have to call upon some alternative models of male psychosexual development that accommodate social and relational factors. A psychological theory of masculinity that I find useful . . . derives in part from recent work by the post-Freudian ego psychologists. The list of relevant theorists and their works is long but may be reduced here to Erik Erikson, Ralph Greenson, Edith Jacobson, Margaret Mahler, Gregory Rochlin, Robert Stoller, and D. W. Winnicott.

The basic idea here concerns the special problems attached to the origin of masculinity as a category of self-identity distinct from femininity. The theory begins with the assumption that all infants, male and female, establish a primary identity, as well as a social bond, with the nurturing parent, the mother. This theory already departs from the classic Freudian assumption that the boy child has from the first a male identity and a natural heterosexual relationship with his mother that culminates in the oedipal conflict, that the boy's identity as male is axiomatic and unconflicted. This new theory goes on to posit an early and prolonged unity or psychic merging with the mother that Freud (1914) discussed under "primary narcissism," a period when the infant fails to distinguish between self and mother. The argument is that the physical separation of child and mother at birth does not bring with it a psychological separation of equivalent severity or finality.

As the child grows, it reaches the critical threshold that Mahler (1975) has called separation-individuation. At this juncture its growing awareness of psychic separateness from the mother combines with increased physical mobility and a motoric exercise of independent action, for example, walking, speaking, manipulating toys. These independent actions are rewarded socially both by parents and by other members of the group who want to see the child grow up (Erikson 1950). Boys and girls alike go through these same trial stages of separation, self-motivation, encouragement and reward, and proto-personhood; and both become receptive to social demands for gender-appropriate behavior. However, according to this theory, the boy child encounters special problems in the crucible of the separation-individuation stage that impede further progression toward independent selfhood.

The special liability for boys is the different fate of the primal psychic unity with the mother. The self-awareness of being a separate individual carries with it a parallel sense of a gender identity—being either a man or a woman, boy or girl. In most societies, each individual must choose one or the other unequivocally in order, also, to be a separate and autonomous person recognizable as such by peers and thus to earn acceptance. The special problem the boy faces at this point is in overcoming the previous sense of unity with the mother in order to achieve an independent identity defined by his culture as masculine—an effort functionally equivalent not only to psychic separation but also to creating an autonomous public persona. The girl does not experience this problem as acutely, according to this theory, because her femininity is reinforced by her original symbiotic unity with her mother, by the identification with her that precedes self-identity and that culminates with her own motherhood (Chodorow 1978). In most societies, the little boy's sense of self as independent must include a sense of the self as different from his mother, as separate from her both in ego-identity and in social role. Thus for the boy the task of separation and individuation carries an added burden and peril. Robert Stoller (1974:358) has stated this problem succinctly:

> While it is true the boy's first love object is heterosexual [the mother], he must perform a great deed to make this so: he must first separate his identity from hers. Thus the whole process of becoming masculine is at risk in the little boy from the day of birth on; his still-to-be-created masculinity is endangered by the primary, profound, primeval oneness with mother, a blissful experience that serves, buried but active in the core of one's identity, as a focus which, throughout life, can attract one to regress back to that primitive oneness. That is the threat latent in masculinity.

To become a separate person the boy must perform a great deed. He must pass a test; he must break the chain to his mother. He must renounce his bond to her and seek his own way in the world. His masculinity thus represents his separation from his mother and his entry into a new and independent social status recognized as distinct and opposite from hers. In this view the main threat to the boy's growth is not only, or even primarily, castration anxiety. The principal danger to the boy is not a unidimensional fear of the punishing father but a more ambivalent fantasy-fear about the mother. The ineradicable fantasy is to return to the primal maternal symbiosis. The inseparable fear is that restoring the oneness with the mother will overwhelm one's independent selfhood.

Recently, armed with these new ideas, some neo-Freudians have begun to focus more specifically on the puzzle of masculine role modeling cults. They have been less concerned with the questions of gender identity and castration anxiety than with the related questions of regression and its relation to social role. In a recent symposium on the subject, the psychoanalyst Gerald Fogel (1986:10) argues that the boy's dilemma goes "beyond castration anxiety" to a conflicted effort to give up the anaclitic unity with the mother, which robs him of his independence. In the same symposium, another psychoanalyst (Cooper 1986:128) refers to the comforting sense of omnipotence that this symbiotic unity with the mother affords. This sense of omnipotence, of narcissistic completeness, sensed and retained in fantasy as a blissful experience of oneness with the mother, he argues, is what draws the boy back so powerfully toward childhood and away from the challenge of an autonomous manhood. In this view, the struggle for masculinity is a battle against these regressive wishes and fantasies, a hard-fought renunciation of the longings for the prelapsarian idyll of childhood.

From this perspective, then, the manhood equation is a "revolt against boyishness" (Schafer 1986:100). The struggle is specifically "against regression" (ibid.). This revisionist theory provides us with a psychological key to the puzzle of manhood norms and ideals. Obviously, castration fear is also important from an individual point of view. But manhood ideologies are not only intrapsychic; they are also collective representations that are institutionalized as guiding images in most societies. To understand the meaning of manhood from a sociological point of view, to appreciate its social rather than individual functions and causes, regression is the more important variable to consider. The reason for this is that, in aggregate, regression poses a more serious threat to society as a whole. As we shall see, regression is unacceptable not only to the individual but also to his society as a functioning mechanism, because most societies demand renunciation of escapist wishes in favor of a participating, contributing adulthood. Castration anxiety, though something that all men may also need to resolve, poses no such aggregate threat to social continuity. In sum, manhood imagery can be interpreted from this post-Freudian perspective as a defense against the eternal child within, against puerility, against what is sometimes called the Peter Pan complex (Hallman 1969).

REFERENCES

Abu-Lughod, Lila. 1986. *Veiled Sentiments: Honor and Poetry in a Bedouin Society.* Berkeley: University of California Press.

Archer, John, and Barbara Lloyd. 1985. *Sex and Gender.* Cambridge: Cambridge University Press.

Bakan, David. 1966. *The Duality of Human Existence.* Chicago: University of Chicago Press.

Baker, Susan W. 1980. Biological influences on human sex and gender. *Signs* 6:80–96.

Bernard, H. Russell. 1967. Kalymnian sponge diving. *Human Biology* 39:103–30.

Biller, Henry B., and Lloyd Borstelmann. 1967. Masculine development: An integrative view. *Merrill-Palmer Quarterly* 13:253–94.

Brandes, Stanley H. 1980. *Metaphors of Masculinity: Sex and Status in Andalusian Folklore.* Philadelphia: University of Pennsylvania Press.

Brod, Harry (ed.). 1987. *The Making of Masculinities: The New Men's Studies.* Boston: Allen and Unwin.

Chandos, John. 1984. *Boys Together: English Public Schools, 1800–1864.* New Haven: Yale University Press.

Chodorow, Nancy. 1978. *The Reproduction of Mothering.* Berkeley: University of California Press.

Conant, Robert W. 1915. *The Virility of Christ.* Chicago: no publisher.

Cooper, Arnold M. 1986. What men fear: The facade of castration anxiety. In *The Psychology of Men: New Psychoanalytic Perspective*, ed. Gerald Fogel, F. M. Lane, and R. S. Liebert, pp. 113–30. New York: Basic Books.

D'Andrade, Roy G. 1974. Sex differences and cultural institutions. In *Culture and Personality: Contemporary Readings*, ed. Robert A. LeVine, pp. 16–39. Chicago: Aldine.

Denich, Bette. 1974. Sex and power in the Balkans. In *Women, Culture, and Society*, ed. Michelle Rosaldo and Louise Lamphere, pp. 243–62. Stanford: Stanford University Press.

Erikson, Erik. 1950. *Childhood and Society.* New York: Norton.

Fetterly, Judith. 1978. *The Resisting Reader: A Feminist Approach to American Fiction.* Bloomington, Ind.: Indiana University Press.

Fogel, Gerald I. 1986. Introduction: Being a man. In *The Psychology of Men: New Psychoanalytic Perspectives*, ed. Gerald Fogel, F. M. Lane, and R. S. Liebert, pp. 3–22. New York: Basic Books.

Freud, Sigmund. 1905. Three Essays on the Theory of Sexuality, III: The Transformations of Puberty. *Standard Edition*, ed. James Strachey 7:207–30. London: Hogarth Press (1975).

———. 1914. On narcissism. *Standard Edition*, ed. James Strachey, 14:67–102. London: Hogarth Press (1975).

Gay, Peter, 1982. Liberalism and regression. *Psy-*

choanalytic *Study of the Child* 37:523–45. New Haven: Yale University Press.

Gearing, Frederick O. 1970. *The Face of the Fox.* Chicago: Aldine.

Godelier, Maurice. 1986. *The Making of Great Men.* Cambridge: Cambridge University Press.

Gregor, Thomas. 1985. *Anxious Pleasures: The Sexual Life of an Amazonian People.* Chicago: University of Chicago Press.

Hallman, Ralph, 1969. The archetypes in Peter Pan. *Journal of Analytic Psychology* 14:65–73.

Hantover, Jeffrey P. 1978. The Boy Scouts and the validation of masculinity. *Journal of Social Issues* 34:184–95.

Herdt, Gilbert H. 1982. Fetish and fantasy in Sambia initiation. In *Rituals of Manhood,* ed. Gilbert H. Herdt, pp. 44–98. Berkeley: University of California Press.

Hertzfeld, Michael. 1985. *Gender pragmatics: agency, speech and bride-theft in a Cretan mountain village.* Anthropology 9:25–44.

Hill, W. W. 1982. *An Ethnography of Santa Clara Pueblo, New Mexico,* ed. and annotated by Charles H. Lange, Albuquerque, N. Mex. : University of New Mexico Press.

Hughes, Thomas. 1879. *The Manliness of Christ.* London: Macmillan.

Jung, Carl. 1926. *Psychological Types.* New York: Harcourt, Brace and Co.

Katchadourian, Herant A. 1979. The terminology of sex and gender. In *Human Sexuality: Comparative and Developmental Perspectives,* ed. Herant A. Katchadourian, pp. 8–34. Berkeley: University of California Press.

Kline, Paul. 1972. *Fact and Fantasy in Freudian Theory.* London: Methuen.

Konner, Melvin. 1982. *The Tangled Wing: Biological Constraints on the Human Spirit.* New York: Harper Colophon Books.

Kriegel, Leonard, 1979. *On Men and Manhood.* New York: Hawthorn Books.

Lee, Richard B. 1979. *The !Kung San: Men, Women, and Work in a Foraging Society.* Cambridge: Cambridge University Press.

Levine, Donald N. 1966. The concept of masculinity in Ethiopian culture. *International Journal of Social Psychiatry* 12:17–23.

Levine, Robert A. 1979. Anthropology and sex: Developmental aspects. In *Human Sexuality: Comparative and Developmental Perspectives,* ed. Herant A. Katchadourian, pp. 309–31. Berkeley: University of California Press.

Lewis, Oscar. 1961. *The Children of Sanchez.* New York: Random House.

Lonner, Walter J. 1980. The search for psycholog-ical universals. In *Handbook of Cross-Cultural Psychology,* ed. Harry C. Triandis and William W. Lambert, 1:143–204. Boston: Allyn & Bacon.

McPherson, James M. 1988. *Battle Cry of Freedom: The Civil War Era.* New York: Oxford University Press.

Mahler, Margaret, et al. 1975. *The Psychological Birth of the Human Infant.* New York: Basic Books.

Mailer, Norman. 1968. *Armies of the Night.* New York: New American Library.

Marcus, Michael. 1987. "Horsemen are the fence of the land": Honor and history among the Ghiyata of eastern Morocco. In *Honor and Shame and the Unity of the Mediterranean,* ed. David D. Gilmore, pp. 49–60. Washington, D.C.: American Anthropological Association, Special Pub. no. 22.

Marshall, Mac. 1979. *Weekend Warriors.* Palo Alto, CA: Mayfield.

Munroe, Robert L. and Ruth H. Munroe. 1980. Perspectives suggested by anthropological data. In *Handbook of Cross-Cultural Psychology,* ed. Harry C. Triandis and William W. Lambert 1:253–317. Boston: Allyn and Bacon.

Ortner, Sherry B. 1974. Is female to male as nature is to culture? In *Woman, Culture, and Society,* ed. Michelle Z. Rosaldo and Louise Lamphere, pp. 67–88. Stanford: Stanford University Press.

———. 1981. Gender and sexuality in hierarchical societies: The case of Polynesia and some comparative implications. In *Sexual Meanings,* ed. Sherry B. Ortner and Harriet Whitehead, pp. 359–409. Cambridge: Cambridge University Press.

Otten, Charlotte M. 1985. Genetic effects on male and female development and on the sex ratio. In *Male-Female Differences: A Bio-Cultural Perspective,* ed, Roberta L. Hall, pp. 155–217. New York: Praeger.

Pleck, Joseph. 1981. *The Myth of Masculinity.* Cambridge, Mass.: MIT Press.

Raphael, Ray. 1988. *The Men from the Boys: Rites of Passage in Male America.* Lincoln, Nebr.: University of Nebraska Press.

Reminick, Ronald A. 1976. The symbolic significance of ceremonial defloration among the Amhara of Ethiopia. *American Ethnologist* 3:751–63.

———. 1982. The sport of warriors on the wane: a case of cultural endurance in the face of social change. In *Sport and the Humanities,* ed. William H. Morgan, pp. 31–36. Knoxville, Tenn.: Bureau of Educational Research and Service, University of Tennessee Press.

Sanday, Peggy R. 1981. *Female Power and Male Dominance: On the Origins of Sexual Inequality.* Cambridge: Cambridge University Press.

Schafer, Roy. 1986. Men who struggle against sentimentality. In *The Psychology of Men: New Psychoanalytic Perspectives*, ed. Gerald I. Fogel, L. M. Lane, and R. S. Liebert, pp. 95–110. New York: Basic Books.

Schwenger, Peter. 1984. *Phallic Critiques: Masculinity and Twentieth-Century Literature.* London: Routledge and Kegan Paul.

Shostak, Marjorie. 1981. *Nisa: The Life and Words of a !Kung Woman.* Cambridge, Mass.: Harvard University Press.

Simic, Andrei. 1989. *Management of the male image in Yugoslavia.* Anthropological Quarterly 42: 89–101.

Spence, Janet, and Robert L. Helmreich. 1979. *Masculinity and Femininity: Their Psychological Dimensions, Correlates and Antecedents.* Austin, Tex.: University of Texas Press.

Stephens, William N. 1967. A cross-cultural study of menstrual taboos. In *Cross-Cultural Approaches*, ed. Clellan S. Ford, pp. 67–94. New Haven: HRAF Press.

Stoller, Robert. 1968. *Sex and Gender.* New York: Science House.

————. 1974. Facts and fancies: An examination of Freud's concept of bisexuality. In *Women and Analysis*, ed. Jean Strousse, pp. 343–64. New York: Dell.

Thomas, Elizabeth Marshall. 1959. *The Harmless People.* New York: Vintage Books.

Tiger, Lionel. 1971. *Men in Groups.* New York; Random House.

Tolson, Andrew. 1977. *The Limits of Masculinity: Male Identity and the Liberated Woman.* New York: Harper and Row.

Williams, John E., and Deborah L. Best. 1982. *Measuring Sex Stereotypes: A Thirty-Nation Study.* Beverly Hills: Sage Publs.

Wyatt-Brown, Bertram. 1982. *Southern Honor: Ethics and Behavior in the Old South.* New York: Oxford University Press.

Neither Man nor Woman: The Hijras of India

Serena Nanda

The hijra role is a magnet that attracts people with many different kinds of cross-gender identities, attributes, and behaviors—people whom we in the West would differentiate as eunuchs, homosexuals, transsexuals, hermaphrodites, and transvestites. Such individuals, of course, exist in our own and perhaps all societies. What is noteworthy about the hijras is that the role is so deeply rooted in Indian culture that it can accommodate a wide variety of temperaments, personalities, sexual needs, gender identities, cross-gender behaviors, and levels of commitment without losing its cultural meaning. The ability of the hijra role to succeed as a symbolic reference point giving significant meaning to the lives of the many different kinds of people who make up the hijra community, is undoubtedly related to the variety and significance of alternative gender roles and gender transformations in Indian mythology and traditional culture.

Whereas Westerners feel uncomfortable with the ambiguities and contradictions inherent in such in-between categories as transvestism, homosexuality, hermaphroditism, and transgenderism, and make strenuous attempts to resolve them, Hinduism not only accommodates such ambiguities, but also views them as meaningful and even powerful.

In Hindu mythology, ritual, and art—important vehicles for transmitting the Hindu world view—the power of the combined man/woman is a frequent and significant theme. Indian mythology contains numerous examples of androgynes, impersonators of the opposite sex, and individuals who undergo sex changes, both among deities and humans. These mythical figures are well known as part of Indian popular culture, which helps explain the ability of the hijras to maintain a meaningful place for themselves within Indian society in an institutionalized third gender role.

One of the most important sexually ambivalent figures in Hinduism with whom hijras identify is Shiva, a deity who incorporates both male and female characteristics.[1] Shiva is an ascetic—one who renounces sex—and yet he appears in many erotic and procreative roles. His most powerful symbol and object of worship is the phallus—but the phallus is almost always set in the *yoni*, the symbol of the female genitals. One of the most popular forms of Shiva is that of *Ardhanarisvara*, or half-man/half-woman, which represents Shiva united with his shakti (female creative power). Hijras say that worshipers of Shiva give them special respect because of this close identification, and hijras often worship at Shiva temples. In the next chapter, I look more closely at the identification of the hijras with Shiva, particularly in connection with the ritual of emasculation.

Other deities also take on sexually ambiguous or dual gender manifestations. Vishnu and Krishna (an *avatar*, or incarnation, of Vishnu) are sometimes pictured in androgynous ways. In one myth, Vishnu transforms himself into Mohini, the most beautiful woman in the world, in order to take back the sacred nectar from the demons who have stolen it. In another well-known myth, Krishna takes on the form of a female to destroy a demon called Araka. Araka's strength came from his chasteness. He had never set eyes on a woman, so Krishna took on the form of a beautiful woman and married him. After 3 days of the marriage, there was a battle and Krishna killed the demon. He then revealed himself to the other gods in his true form. Hijras, when they tell this story, say that when Krishna revealed himself he told the other gods that "there will be more like me, neither man nor woman, and whatever words come from the mouths of these people, whether good [blessings] or bad [curses], will come true."

In Tamil Nadu, in South India, an important festival takes place in which hijras, identifying with Krishna, become wives, and then widows, of the male deity Koothandavar. The story behind this festival is that there were once two warring kingdoms. To avert defeat, one of the kings agreed to sacrifice his eldest son to the gods, asking only that he first be allowed to arrange his son's marriage. Because no woman could be found who would marry a man about to be sacrificed, Krishna came to earth as a woman to marry the king's son, and the king won the battle as the gods promised.

For this festival, men who have made vows to Koothandavar dress as women and go through a marriage ceremony with him. The priest performs the marriage, tying on the traditional wedding necklace. After 1 day, the deity is carried to a burial ground. There, all of those who have "married" him remove their wedding necklaces, cry and beat their breasts, and remove the flowers from their hair, as a widow does in mourning for her husband. Hijras participate by the thousands in this festival, coming from all over India. They dress in their best clothes and jewelry and ritually reaffirm their identification with Krishna, who changes his form from male to female.

Several esoteric Hindu ritual practices involve male transvestism as a form of devotion. Among the Sakhibhava (a sect that worships Vishnu) Krishna may not be worshiped directly. The devotees in this sect worship Radha, Krishna's beloved, with the aim of becoming her attendant: It is through her, as Krishna's consort, that Krishna is indirectly worshiped. The male devotees imitate feminine behavior, including simulated menstruation; they also may engage in sexual acts with men as acts of devotion, and some devotees even castrate themselves in order to more nearly approximate a female identification with Radha (Bullough, 1976:267–268; Kakar, 1981; Spratt, 1966:315).

Hinduism in general holds that all persons contain within themselves both male and female principles. In the Tantric school of Hinduism, the Supreme Being is conceptualized as one complete sex containing male and female sexual organs. Hermaphroditism is the ideal. In some of these sects, male (never female) transvestism is used as a way of transcending one's own sex, a prerequisite to achieving salvation. In other Tantric sects, religious exercises involve the male devotee imitating a woman in order to realize the woman in himself: Only in this way do they believe that true love can be realized (Bullough, 1976:260).

Traditional Hinduism makes many specific references to alternative sexes and sexual ambiguity among humans as well as among gods. Ancient Hinduism, for example, taught that there was a third sex, which itself was divided into four categories: the male eunuch, called the "waterless" because he had desiccated testes; the "testicle voided," so called because he had been castrated; the hermaphrodite; and the "not woman," or female eunuch (which usually refers to a woman who does not menstruate). Those who were more feminine (whether males or females) wore false breasts and imitated the voice, gestures, dress, delicacy, and timidity of women (Bullough, 1976:268). All of these categories of persons had the function of providing alternative techniques of sexual gratification, some of which are mentioned in the classical Hindu sex manual, the Kamasutra.

Another ancient reference to a third sex, one that sounds similar to the hijras, is a prostitute named Sukumarika ("good little girl"), who appears in a Sanskrit play. Sukumarika is accused of being sexually insatiable. As a third sex, she has some characteristics advantageous in her profession: "She has no breasts to get in the way of a tight embrace, no monthly period to interrupt the enjoyment of passion, and no pregnancy to mar her beauty" (O'Flaherty, 1980:299).

As just suggested, ancient Hindus, like contemporary ones, appeared to be ambivalent about such third gender roles and the associated alternative sexual practices. The figure of Sukumarika, for example, was considered inauspicious to look upon and, not coincidentally, similar to the hijras today, inspired both fear and mockery. Historically, both eunuchism and castration were looked down on in ancient India, and armed women and old men were preferred to eunuchs for guarding court ladies (Basham, 1954:172). Whereas homosexuality was generally not highly regarded in ancient India, such classic texts as the Kamasutra, however, did describe, even prescribe, sexual practices for eunuchs, for example, "mouth congress."[2]

Homosexuality was condemned in the ancient lawbooks. The Laws of Manu, the first formulation of the Hindu moral code, held that men who engaged in anal sex lost their caste. Other medieval writers held that men who engaged in oral sex with other men were reborn impotent. But homosexuals were apparently tolerated in reality. Consistent with the generally "sex positive" attitude of Hinduism, Vatsyayana, author of the Kamasutra, responded to critics of oral and anal sex by saying that "in all things connected with love, everybody should act according to the custom of his country, and his own inclination," asking a man to consider only whether the act "is agreeable to his nature and himself" (Burton, 1964:127).

Even the gods were implicated in such activities: Krishna's son Samba was notorious for his homosexuality and dressed as female, often a pregnant woman. As Sambali, Samba's name became a synonym for eunuch (Bullough, 1976:267). An important ritual at the Jagannatha temple in Orissa involves a sequence in which Balabhadra, the ascetic elder brother of the deity Jagannatha, who is identified with Shiva, is homosexually seduced by a transvestite (a young man dressed as a female temple dancer) (Marglin, 1985:53). In some Hindu myths a male deity takes on a female form specifically to experience sexual relations with another male deity.

Islam also provides a model of an in-between gender—not a mythological one, but a true historical figure—in the traditional role of the eunuch who guarded the ladies of the harem, under Moghul rule. Hijras often mention this role as the source of their prestige in Indian society. In spite of the clear connection of hijras with Hinduism, Islam not only provides a powerful positive model of an alternative gender, but also contributes many elements to the social organization of the hijra community. Hijras today make many references to the glorious, preindependence Indian past when the Muslin rulers of princely states were exceedingly generous and reknowned for their patronage of the hijras (see Lynton & Rajan, 1974).

Today the religious role of the hijras, derived from Hinduism, and the historical role of the eunuchs in the Muslim courts have become inextricably entwined in spite of the differences between them. Hijras are distinguished from the eunuchs in Muslim courts by their transvestism and their association with men. Muslim eunuchs dressed as males and associated with women and, unlike the hijras, were sexually inactive. More importantly, the role of hijras as ritual performers is linked to their sexual ambiguity as this incorporates the elements of the erotic and the ascetic; Muslim eunuchs had no such powers or roles. Today, the collapsing of the role of the hijra and that of the Muslim eunuchs leads to certain contradictions, but these seem easily incorporated into the hijra culture by hijras themselves; only the Western observer seems to feel the need to separate them conceptually.

The hijras, as human beings who are neither man nor woman, call into question the basic social categories of gender on which Indian society is built. This makes the hijras objects of fear, abuse, ridicule, and sometimes pity. But hijras are not merely ordinary human beings; . . . they are also conceptualized as special, sacred beings, through a ritual transformation. The many examples that I have cited above indicate that both Indian society and Hindu mythology provide some positive, or at least accommodating, roles for such sexually ambiguous figures. Within the context of Indian social roles, sexually ambiguous figures are associated with sexual specializations; in myth and through ritual, such figures become powerful symbols of the divine and of generativity.

Thus, where Western culture strenuously attempts to resolve sexual contradictions and ambiguities, by denial or segregation, Hinduism appears content to allow opposites to confront each other without resolution, "celebrating the idea that the universe is boundlessly various, and . . . that all possibilities may exist without excluding each other" (O'Flaherty, 1973:318). It is this characteristically Indian ability to tolerate, even embrace, contradictions and variation at the social, cultural, and personality levels that provides the context in which the hijras cannot only be accommodated, but even granted a measure of power.

NOTES

1. The Hindu Triad, or Trinity, is made up of Brahma, the creator; Vishnu, the preserver (protector and sustainer of the world); and Shiva, the destroyer. Brahma is the Supreme Being and the creator of all creatures. Vishnu is believed to descend into the world in many different forms (*avataras*, or incarnations) and is worshiped throughout India. One of Vishnu's incarnations is Ram. Krishna is sometimes considered an aspect or incarnation of Vishnu but more commonly is worshiped as a god in his own right. Shiva is the god of destruction or absorption, but he also creates and sustains life. In addition to the Triad Hinduism includes a large number of deities, both male and female, all of whom are aspects of the Absolute. This concept of the Absolute Reality also includes matter and finite spirits as its integral parts; the divine spirit is embodied in the self and the world, as well as in more specifically religious figures. The religious concepts of Hinduism are expressed in the two great Hindu epics, the Mahabharata and the Ramayana, both of

which are familiar to every Hindu and many non-Hindus as well. These epics, along with other chronicles of the gods and goddesses, are frequently enacted in all forms of popular and elite culture. Thus, for the hijras, particularly the Hindu hijras, the incorporation of these divine models of behavior into their own world view and community image is in no way unusual.

2. In an editor's note Burton (1962:124) suggests that this practice is no longer common in India and has been replaced by sodomy, which was introduced after the Muslim period began in the tenth century. In a later chapter (Nanda 1990) we will see that Meera, a hijra elder, specifically says that oral sex is "not a good thing and goes against the wishes of the hijra goddess" and that it brings all kinds of problems for those who practice it.

REFERENCES

Basham, A. I. 1954. *The Wonder That Was India*. New York: Grove Press, p. 172.

Bullough, V. 1976. *Sexual Variance in Society and History*. Chicago: University of Chicago Press, pp. 260, 267–268.

Burton, R. F. (Trans.) 1962. *The Kama Sutra of Vatsyayana*. New York: E. P. Dutton, p. 127.

Kakar, Sudhir. 1981. *The Inner World: A Psychoanalytic Study of Childhood and Society in India*. Delhi: Oxford University Press.

Lynton, H. and Rajan, M. 1974. *Days of the Beloved*. Berkeley: University of California Press.

Marglin, Frederique Apffel. 1985. Female Sexuality in the Hindu World. In Clarissa Atkinson, Constance H. Buchanan, and Margaret R. Miles (Eds.), *The Immaculate and the Powerful*. Boston: Beacon Press, pp. 39–59.

Nanda, Serena. 1990. Neither Man Nor Woman: The Hijras of India. Belmont, California: Wadsworth Publishing Co.

O'Flaherty, Wendy Doniger. 1973. *Siva: The Erotic Ascetic*. New York: Oxford University Press, p. 318.

———. 1980. *Women, Androgynes, and Other Mythical Beasts*. Chicago: University of Chicago Press, p. 299.

Spratt, Philip. 1966. *Hindu Culture and Personality: A Psychoanalytic Study*. Bombay: Manaktalas.

Amazons of America: Female Gender Variance

Walter L. Williams

When Pedro de Magalhães de Gandavo explored northeastern Brazil in 1576, he visited the Tupinamba Indians and reported on a remarkable group of female warriors.

There are some Indian women who determine to remain chaste: these have no commerce with men in any manner, nor would they consent to

it even if refusal meant death. They give up all the duties of women and imitate men, and follow men's pursuits as if they were not women. They wear the hair cut in the same way as the men, and go to war with bows and arrows and pursue game, always in company with men; each has a woman to serve her, to whom she says she is married, and they treat each other and speak with each other as man and wife.[1]

Gandavo and other explorers like Orellana were evidently so impressed with this group of women that they named the river which flowed through that area the River of the Amazons, after the ancient Greek legend of women warriors.

To what extent did this recognized status for women exist among Native Americans? The sources are few, since European male explorers dealt almost entirely with aboriginal men. Most documents are unclear about anything to do with women, and as a result it is difficult to make conclusions about those females who took up a role similar to that of the Tupinamba Amazons. But we can begin by making it clear that this institution was not the same as berdache. As specified earlier, the term *berdache* clearly originated as a word applying to males. Anthropologist Evelyn Blackwood has done a thorough search of the ethnographic literature and found mention of a recognized female status in thirty-three North American groups. Because she sees it as distinct from berdachism, she does not use the term "female berdache" but instead calls this role "cross-gender female." She notes that it was most common in California, the Southwest, the Northwest, and the Great Basin, but she also notes a few instances among peoples of the Subarctic and the northern Plains.[2]

Because I have some disagreement with the concept of gender crossing, and also because "cross-gender female" is linguistically awkward, I prefer the word *amazon*. This term is parallel to berdache, but it is a status specific to women that is not subservient to male definitions. American Indian worldviews almost always recognize major differences between amazons and berdaches. With the single exception of the Navajo, those cultures that recognize alternative roles for both females and males, have distinct terminologies in their languages that are different for each sex. The Papago word translates as "Light Woman," and such women even up to the 1940s were considered simply socially tolerated variations from the norm.[3] Among the Yumas of the Southwest, berdaches are called *elxa'*, while amazons are called *kwe'rhame*. They are defined as "women who passed for men, dressed like men and married women." There is no ceremony marking their assumption of the role, as there is for the *elxa'*.[4]

The parents of a *kwe'rhame* might try to push her into feminine pursuits, but such a child manifested an unfeminine character from infancy. She was seen as having gone through a change of spirit as a result of dreams. In growing up she was observed to hunt and play with boys, but she had no interest in heterosexual relations with them. According to Yuman informants in the 1920s, a *kwe'rhame* "wished only to become a man." Typical of amazons in several cultures, she was said to have a muscular build and to desire to dress like a man, and it was also claimed that she did not menstruate. A Yuman *kwe'rhame* married a woman and established a household with herself as husband. She was known for bravery and for skillful fighting in battle.[5]

RAISING A FEMALE HUNTER

While there are parallels between berdaches and amazons, female amazons are also very different from male berdaches. Among the Kaska Indians of the Subarctic, having a son was extremely important because the family depended heavily on big-game hunting for food. If a couple had too many female children and desired a son to hunt for them in their old age, they would simply select a daughter to "be like a man." When the youngest daughter was about five years old, and it was obvious that the mother was not going to produce a son, the parents performed a transformation ceremony. They tied the dried ovaries of a bear to a belt which she always wore. That was believed to prevent menstruation, to protect her from pregnancy, and to give her luck on the hunt. According to Kaska informants, she was dressed like a male and trained to do male tasks, "often developing great strength and usually becoming an outstanding hunter."[6]

The Ingalik Indians of Alaska, closely related to the Kaska as part of the Dene culture, also recognized a similar status for females. Such a female even participated in the male-only activities of the *kashim*, which involved sweat baths. The men ignored her morphological sex in this nude bathing, and accepted her as a man on the basis of her gender behavior.[7] Other notable Subarctic amazons from the eighteenth century included the leader of the eastern Kutchin band from Arctic Red River, and a Yellowknife Chipewayan who worked for peace between the various peoples of the central Subarctic.[8]

Among the Kaskas, if a boy made sexual advances to such a female, she reacted violently. Kaska people explained her reaction thus: "She knows that if he gets her then her luck with game will be broken." She would have relationships only with women, achieving sexual pleasure through clitoral friction, "by getting on top of each other."[9] This changed-gender demonstrates the extreme malleability of people with respect to gender roles. Such assignment operates independently of a person's morphological sex and can determine both gender status and erotic behavior.

TRANSFORMATION INTO A MAN

In other areas, becoming an amazon was seen to be a choice of the female herself. Among the Kutenai Indians of the Plateau, for example, in what is now southern British Columbia, such a female became famous as a prophet and shaman. She is remembered in Kutenai oral tradition as being quite large and heavy boned. About 1808 she left Kutenai to go with a group of white fur traders, and married one of them. A year later, however, she returned to her people and claimed that her husband had operated on her and transformed her into a man. Kutenai informants from the 1930s told ethnographer Claude Schaeffer that when she returned she said: "I'm a man now. We Indians did not believe the white people possessed such power from the supernaturals. I can tell you that they do, greater power than we have. They changed my sex while I was with them. No Indian is able to do that." She changed her name to Gone-To-The-Spirits, and claimed great spiritual power. Whenever she met people she performed a dance as a symbol of her transformation.[10]

Following her return, she began to dress in men's clothes, and to carry a gun. She also began to court young women. After several rebuffs she met a divorced woman who agreed to marry her. "The two were now to be seen constantly together. The curious attempted to learn things from the consort, but the latter only laughed at their efforts." A rumor began that Gone-To-The-Spirits, for the pleasure of her wife, had fashioned an artificial phallus made of leather. But whatever their sexual technique, the wife later moved out because of Gone-To-The-Spirits's losses in gambling. Thereafter, Gone-To-The-Spirits changed wives frequently.

Meanwhile, she began to have an interest in warfare and was accepted as a warrior on a raid. Upon coming to a stream, Kutenai oral tradition recalled, the raiders would undress and wade across together but she delayed so as to cross alone. On one of these crossings, her brother doubled back to observe her. He saw her nude and realized that her sex had not been changed at all. Seeing him, she sat down in the water and pretended that her foot was injured. Later, trying to protect her reputation, she told the others that she was injured in the stream and had to sit. She declared that she hereafter wished to be called *Qa'nqon ka'mek klau'la* (Sitting-In-The-Water-Grizzly).

Her brother did not tell what he saw, but refused to call her by her new name. Later, she took still another wife, and as she had done with previous wives eventually began accusing her of infidelity. Qa'nqon was of a violent temper, and when she began to beat this wife, the brother intervened. He yelled out angrily, in the hearing of the entire camp: "You are hurting your woman friend. You have hurt other friends in the same way. You know that I saw you standing naked in the stream, where you tried to conceal your sex. That's why I never call you by your new name."[11]

After this, according to Kutenai informants, all the people knew that Qa'nqon had not really changed sex. It is conceivable that the community already knew about her sex before this pronouncement since Qa'nqon's ex-wives must have spread the truth. The oral tradition does not explain why women continued to marry the temperamental Qa'nqon. Soon after this incident, evidently, she and a wife (whether the same woman or another is unknown) left to serve as guides for white traders. The couple seemed to get along fine once they arrived at Fort Astoria on the Columbia River in 1811.

One trader named Alexander Ross characterized them as "two strange Indians, in the character of man and wife." "The husband," he said, "was a very shrewd and intelligent Indian" who gave them much information about the interior. Later, this trader learned that "instead of being man and wife, as they at first gave us to understand, they were in fact both women—and bold adventurous amazons they were." Qa'nqon served as guide for Ross's party on a trip up the Columbia to the Rocky Mountains. Ross recounted that "the man woman" spread a prophesy among the tribes they passed, saying that the Indians were soon going to be supplied with all the trading goods they desired.

> These stories, so agreeable to the Indian ear, were circulated far and wide; and not only received as truths, but procured so much celebrity for the two cheats, that they were the objects of attraction at every village and camp on the way; nor could we, for a long time, account for the cordial reception they met with from the natives, who loaded them for their good tidings with the most valuable articles they possessed— horses, robes, leather, and higuas [?]; so that, on our arrival at Oakinacken [Okanagon, near the present-day border of British Columbia and Washington State], they had no less than twenty-six horses, many of them loaded with the fruits of their false reports.[12]

Another white traveler in the area nearly a decade later heard the Indians still talking about Qa'nqon, whom they referred to as "Manlike Woman." She had acquired a widespread reputation as having supernatural powers and a gift of prophesy. Her most important prediction was that there would soon be a complete change in the land, with "fertility and plenty" for all tribes. According to this traveler, writing in 1823, she had predicted that the whites would be removed and a different race of traders would arrive "who

would supply their wants in every possible manner. The poor deluded wretches, imagining that they would hasten this happy change by destroying their present traders, of whose submission there was no prospect, threatened to extirpate them."[13] What we can see from these stories is that Qa'nqon sparked a cultural movement similar to "cargo-cults" that twentieth-century anthropologists have observed among Melanesians and other tribal peoples coming in close contact with Western trade cargo goods. This movement also reflected the dissatisfaction the Indians felt with the white traders.

After establishing her fame, Qa'nqon returned to settle with the Kutenai and became noted as a shamanistic healer among her people. A twentieth-century elderly headman named Chief Paul remembered his father telling stories of her curing him of illnesses when he was a child. In 1825 she accompanied a Kutenai chief to the Hudson's Bay Company post among the Flathead Indians, taking the role of interpreter. The company trader described her as "a woman who goes in men's clothes and is a leading character among them. . . . [She] assumes a masculine character and is of some note among them."[14]

In 1837 she was traveling with some Flatheads when a Blackfoot raiding party surrounded them. Through her resourcefulness the Flatheads made an escape while she deceived the attackers. The Blackfeet were so angry that they tried to kill her, but after several shots she was still not seriously wounded. They then slashed her with their knives. But according to Kutenai oral tradition, "Immediately afterwards the cuts thus made were said to have healed themselves. . . . One of the warriors then opened up her chest to get at her heart and cut off the lower portion. This last wound she was unable to heal. It was thus *Qa'nqon* died." Afterward, the story goes, no wild animals disturbed her body.[15]

This story, which was passed down among the Kutenai for over a century, signifies the respect the Indians had for the shamanistic power of the "Manlike Woman." Even the animals recognized this power and respected it. It should be noted that the Kutenai did not recognize a berdache status for males. A tribe that had an alternative gender role for one sex did not necessarily have another role for the other sex. Native Americans did not see the two roles as synonymous so equating amazons with berdaches does not clarify the matter.

MANLIKE WOMAN

The Mohaves, like other cultures, have different words for berdaches and amazons. *Hwame* girls are known to throw away their dolls and refuse to perform feminine tasks. It is said that they dreamed about their role while still in the womb. Adults recognize this pattern and, according to ethnographer George Devereux, make "occasional half-hearted and not very hopeful attempts to discourage them from becoming inverts. When these efforts fail, they are subjected to a ritual, which is half 'test' of their true proclivities and half 'transition rite' and which authorizes them to assume the clothing and to engage in the occupations and sexual activities of their self-chosen sex." Adults then help the *hwame* to learn the same skills that boys are taught.[16]

Mohaves believe that such females do not menstruate. In the worldview of many American Indians, menstruation is a crucial part of defining a person as a woman. Some amazons may have in fact been nonmenstruating, or, since they wished to be seen as men, if they did menstruate they would hide any evidence of menses. The other Indians simply ignored any menstrual indicators out of deference to their desire to be treated like men.[17]

Mohaves also accept the fact that a *hwame* would marry a woman. There is even a way to incorporate children into these female relationships. If a woman becomes impregnated by a man, but later takes another lover, it is believed that the paternity of the child changes. This idea helps to prevent family friction in a society where relationships often change. So, if a pregnant woman later takes a *hwame* as a spouse, the *hwame* is considered the real father of the child.[18]

George Devereux, who lived among the Mohaves in the 1930s, was told about a famous late nineteenth-century *hwame* named Sahaykwisa. Her name was a masculine one, indicating that she had gone through the initiation rite for *hwames*. Nevertheless, she dressed more like a woman than a man, proving that cross-dressing is not a requirement for assuming amazon status. While she was feminine in appearance and had large breasts, Mohaves said that she (typical of others like her) did not menstruate. As evidence of this, they pointed out that she never got pregnant, despite the fact that she hired herself out as a prostitute for white men.

Sahaykwisa used the money that she received from this heterosexual activity to bestow gifts on women to whom she was attracted. With her industriousness as a farmer (a woman's occupation) and as a hunter (a man's occupation), she became relatively prosperous. She was also noted for her shamanistic ability to cure venereal diseases. Shamans who treated venereal diseases were regarded as lucky in love. This fame, plus her reputation as a good provider, led women to be attracted to her.

Sahaykwisa's first wife was a very pretty young woman, whom many men tried to lure away from her. Motivated by jealousy, they began teasing her, "Why do you want a *hwame* for a husband? A *hwame* has no penis; she only pokes you with her finger." The wife brushed off the remark saying "That is alright for me." But then later the wife eloped with a man. Such a breakup was not unusual, given the fact that heterosexual marriages among Mohaves were equally subject to change. After a time the wife returned to Sahaykwisa, having found the man less satisfying. People referred to Sahaykwisa by the name Hithpan Kudhape, which means split vulvae, denoting how the *hwame* would spread the genitals during sex. This part of the oral tradition indicates that the Mohaves were well aware that an amazon role involved sexual behavior with women.

While accepting these relationships, Mohaves nevertheless teased Sahaykwisa's wife unmercifully. While teasing is quite common in American Indian cultures generally, in this case it was done so much that the woman left a second time. Sahaykwisa then began to flirt with other women at social dances, soon easily attracting another wife, and then a third one later on. Mohaves explained this by the fact that Sahaykwisa was, after all, lucky in love. Her reputation as a good provider was also an obvious factor. But after the third woman left her, and returned to the man from whom Sahaykwisa stole her, the man attacked the *hwame* and raped her. Rape was extremely uncommon among the Mohaves, so this incident had a major impact on her life.

Sahaykwisa became demoralized and an alcoholic, and ironically began having wanton sex with men. She claimed to have bewitched one man who rejected her advances, and when he died in the late 1890s she boasted about having killed him. The man's son was so enraged by this that he threw her into the Colorado River, where she drowned. In telling this story Devereux's Mohave informants were convinced that Sahaykwisa claimed witchcraft intentionally so that someone would kill her. They explained that she wanted to die and join the spirits of those she had earlier loved.[19]

While this story does not have a happy ending, it does nevertheless point out that female-female relationships were recognized. Sahaykwisa was killed because it was believed that she had killed another person by witchcraft, not because of her gender status or her sexual relations with women.

While the social role of the *hwame* was in some ways like that of men, the story of Sahaykwisa does not support Blackwood's view of gender *crossing*. The Mohaves did not in fact accept Sahaykwisa as a full-fledged man, and the wife was teased on that regard. She was regarded as a *hwame*, having a distinct gender status that was different than men, women, or *alyha*. Mohaves thus had four genders in their society.

To what extent an amazon was accepted as a man is unclear. The variation that existed among Indians of the Far West typifies this matter. The Cocopa *warrhameh* cut her hair and had her nose pierced as men did, and did not get tattooed as women did.[20] Among the late nineteenth-century Klamath a woman named Co'pak "lived like a man. . . . She tried to talk like a man and invariably referred to herself as one." Co'pak had a wife, with whom

she lived for many years, and when the wife died Co'pak "observed the usual mourning, wearing a bark belt as a man does at this time." Nevertheless, this mourning may have been the standard for a "husband" rather than for a "man," and we do not know if Klamath custom made a distinction between the two categories. Co'pak also retained woman's dress, which certainly implies a less than total crossover. Other Klamaths continued to see her as a manlike woman rather than as a man.[21]

A survey of California Indian groups that recognized amazon status revealed that in half of the groups amazons performed both men's and women's work, while in the other half they did only men's work.[22] No doubt this variation of roles is typical of cultural diversity in aboriginal America generally.

Unlike Western culture, which tries to place all humans into strict conformist definitions of masculinity and femininity, some Native American cultures have a more flexible recognition of gender variance. They are able to incorporate such fluidity into their worldview by recognizing a special place for berdaches and another one for amazons. "Manlike Woman" is how Indians described the Kutenai female, and that phrase recurs in anthropological literature when direct translations are given. By paying more attention to words used by Indians themselves, we can make more precise definitions. Gender theory is now beginning to make such distinctions. Terms like gender crossing imply that there are only two genders, and one must "cross" from one to the other. As with the male berdache, most recent theorists argue, the amazon is either a distinct gender role, or is a gender-mixing status, rather than a complete changeover to an opposite sex role.[23]

WARRIOR WOMEN IN THE GREAT PLAINS

When we turn to the nomadic Plains cultures, the picture becomes even more complex. Here, an accepted amazon status was generally lacking. Female divergence into male activity was not recognized as a distinct gender comparable to the institutionalized berdache role. Women could participate in male occupations on the hunt or in warfare, but this did not imply an alternative gender role. Precisely because they had various activities open to them on a casual and sporadic basis, there was not as much need to recognize a specific role for females behaving in a masculine way. For example, they could become "Warrior Women." Such a woman might join a war party for a specific occasion, like a retribution raid for the death of a relative. She might even accumulate war honors, called *coup*. But since it did not affect her status as a woman, she should not be confused with an amazon. Male warriors simply accepted female fighters as acting within the parameters of womanhood, without considering them a threat to their masculinity.[24]

Warrior women were not the same as amazons partly because their menstruation continued to define them as women. Among Plains peoples, as among many other American Indians, blood was seen as an important and powerful spiritual essence. An individual who bled would not be able to control the power of this bleeding, so if a person bled it might disrupt any important activity that depended on spiritual help, like a hunt or a raid. Consequently, if a woman began her period, the raid would have to be delayed while the spirits were placated. As a result of this belief, the "manly hearted women" who sometimes participated in warfare were almost always postmenopausal.[25]

This belief was not just a restriction on women; a male who bled from an accident or a wound had to go through the same efforts to placate the spirits. The matter was more a question of power than of restriction. Menstruation "was not something unclean or to be ashamed of," according to the Lakota shaman Lame Deer, but was sacred. A girl's first period was cause for great celebration. Still, Lame Deer concluded, "menstruation had a strange power that could bring harm under some circumstances."[26] Paula Gunn Allen explains: "Women are perceived to be possessed of a singular power, most vital during menstruation. . . . Indians do not perceive signs of womanness as contamination;

rather they view them as so powerful that other 'medicines' may be cancelled by the very presence of that power." American Indians thought of power not so much in terms of political or economic power, but as supernatural power. Being a matter of spirituality, woman's power comes partly by her close association with the magical properties of blood.[27]

Another possible factor inhibiting the development of amazon status among Plains women had to do with the economic need for their labor and procreation. Women were responsible for the preparation of buffalo meat. Since a successful hunter could kill more bison than one woman could dress and preserve for food or trade, every available woman was needed to do this work. This economic system limited women's choice of occupation and put more pressure on them to marry than in other North American cultures. Furthermore, with the loss of men from warfare, there was the expectation that every woman would marry and have children.[28]

There was such a strong need for female labor that Plains men began taking multiple wives. A typical pattern was for an overworked wife to encourage her husband to take a second wife. The first wife now had higher status, as a senior wife who directed younger women, and the family as a whole benefited from the extra output of the additional wife. Quite often it would be the younger sisters of the first wife who were later brought in as cowives. This pattern gave advantages to women. It kept female siblings together, giving them support and strength throughout their lives. In contrast to Western culture, which keeps women separated by promoting competition among them for men, Plains polygyny meant that wives were added to the family rather than replaced by divorce and serial monogamy.[29]

Despite these pressures on women to marry and procreate, even in the Plains culture there were exceptions. An amazon role was followed by a few females, with the most famous example being Woman Chief of the Crows. She was originally a Gros Ventre Indian who had been captured by Crow raiders when she was ten years old. She was adopted by a Crow warrior, who observed her inclination for masculine pursuits. He allowed her to follow her proclivities, and in time she became a fearless horseback rider and skilled rifle shooter. Edward Denig, a white frontiersman who lived with the Crows in the early nineteenth century, knew Woman Chief for twelve years. He wrote that when she was still a young woman she "was equal if not superior to any of the men in hunting both on horseback and foot. . . . [She] would spend most of her time in killing deer and bighorn, which she butchered and carried home on her back when hunting on foot. At other times she joined in the surround on horse, could kill four or five buffalo at a race, cut up the animals without assistance, and bring the meat and hides home."[30]

After the death of the widowed man who adopted her, she assumed control of his lodge, "performing the double duty of father and mother to his children." She continued to dress like other women, but Denig, writing in 1855, remembered her as "taller and stronger than most women—her pursuits no doubt tending to develop strength of nerve and muscle." She became famous for standing off an attack from Blackfoot Indians, in which she killed three warriors while remaining unharmed herself: "This daring act stamped her character as a brave. It was sung by the rest of the camp, and in time was made known to the whole nation."[31]

A year later she organized her first raid and easily attracted a group of warriors to follow her. She stole seventy horses from a Blackfoot camp, and in the ensuing skirmish killed and scalped two enemies. For these acts of bravery she was awarded *coups,* and by her subsequent successful raids she built up a large herd of horses. As a successful hunter, she shared her meat freely with others. But it was as a warrior, Denig concluded, that her fame was most notable. In every engagement with enemy tribes, including raids on enemy camps, she distinguished herself by her bravery. Crows began to believe she had "a charmed life which, with her daring feats, elevated her to a point of honor and respect not often reached by male warriors." The Crows

were proud of her, composing special songs to commemorate her gallantry. When the tribal council was held and all the chiefs assembled, she took her place among them, as the third-highest-ranked person in the tribe.[32]

Woman Chief's position shows the Crows' ability to judge individuals by their accomplishments rather than by their sex. Their accepting attitude also included Woman Chief's taking a wife. She went through the usual procedure of giving horses to the parents of her intended spouse. A few years later, she took three more wives. This plurality of women added also to her prestige as a chief. Denig concluded, "Strange country this, where [berdache] males assume the dress and perform the duties of females, while women turn men and mate with their own sex!"[33]

Denig's amazement did not denote any condemnation on his part, for individual traders on the frontier often accepted Indian ways of doing things. Rather, he respected his friend as a "singular and resolute woman. . . . She had fame, standing, honor, riches, and as much influence over the band as anyone except two or three leading chiefs. . . . For 20 years she conducted herself well in all things." In 1854 Woman Chief led a Crow peacekeeping mission to her native Gros Ventre tribe. Resentful because of her previous raids against them, some Gros Ventres trapped her and killed her. Denig concluded sadly, "This closed the earthly career of this singular woman." Her death so enraged the Crows that they refused to make peace with the Gros Ventres for many years.[34] Woman Chief's exceptionally high status was rather unique on the Plains; stories that were passed down made her a hero in the classic Plains mode. Even her death, at enemy hands, was typical of the pattern for the honored male warrior.

WIVES OF AMAZONS

What about the wives of the amazon? Woman Chief, like the other amazons, evidently had no difficulty finding women to marry. Yet, these women did not identify as lesbian in the

Western sense of the word. American Indian women were not divided into separate categories of persons as is the case with Anglo-American homosexual and heterosexual women. The white lesbian often sees herself as a member of a minority group, distinct from and alienated from general society. She is seen as "abnormal," the opposite of "normal" women, and often suffers great anguish about these supposed differences. Paula Gunn Allen writes, "We are not in the position of our American Indian fore-sister who could find safety and security in her bond with another woman because it was perceived to be destined and nurtured by non-human entities, and was therefore acceptable and respectable."[35]

With the exception of the amazon, women involved in a relationship with another female did not see themselves as a separate minority or a special category of person, or indeed as different in any important way from other women. Yet, they were involved in loving and sexual relationships with their female mates. If their marriage to an amazon ended, then they could easily marry heterosexually without carrying with them any stigma as having been "homosexual." The important consideration in the Indian view is that they were still fulfilling the standard role of "mother and wife" within their culture. The traditional gender role for women did not restrict their choice of sexual partners. Gender identity (woman or amazon) was important, but sexual identity (heterosexual or homosexual) was not.[36]

WOMEN-IDENTIFIED WOMEN

Socially recognized marriages between an amazon and her wife only tell part of the story. Relationships between two women-identified women were probably more common. American Indians, while not looking down on sex as evil or dirty, generally see it as something private. Consequently, it is not something that is talked about to outsiders, and there is not much information on sexual practices. It is most important for a woman to

have children, but in many tribes a woman's sexual exclusiveness to the child's father is not crucial. Thus, a woman might be sexually active with others without worrying that she or her children would be looked down on. In many Native American societies, a woman has the right to control her own body, rather than it being the exclusive property of her husband. As long as she produces children at some point in her life, what she does in terms of sexual behavior is her own private business.[37]

Individual inclinations, after all, are usually seen as due to a direction from the spirits. This spiritual justification means that another person's interference might be seen as a dangerous intrusion into the supernatural. "In this context," writes Paula Gunn Allen, "it is quite possible that Lesbianism was practiced rather commonly, as long as the individuals cooperated with the larger social customs." Allen wrote a poem to native "Beloved Women" which expresses this attitude of non-interference:

> It is not known if those
> who warred and hunted on the plains . . .
> were Lesbians
> It is never known
> if any woman was a lesbian
> so who can say. . . .
> And perhaps the portents are better
> left written only in the stars. . . .
> Perhaps
> all they signify is best left
> unsaid.[38]

It is precisely this attitude, that sexual relations were not anyone else's business, that has made Indian women's casual homosexuality so invisible to outsiders. Except for some female anthropologists, most white observers of native societies have been males. These observers knew few women, other than exceptional females who acted as guides or go-betweens for whites and Indians. Most writers expressed little interest in the usual female lifestyle. Yet even if they did, their access to accurate information would be limited to bits that they could learn from Indian males.

Given the segregation of the sexes in native society, women would not open up to a male outsider about their personal lives. Even Indian men would not be told much about what went on among the women.[39]

Given these circumstances, it is all the more necessary for women researchers to pursue this topic. Openly lesbian ethnographers would have a distinct advantage. In contrast to institutionalized male homosexuality, female sexual variance seems more likely to express itself informally. Again, enough cross-cultural fieldwork has not been done to come to definite conclusions. However, Blackwood suggests that female-female erotic relationships may be most commonly expressed as informal pairings within the kin group or between close friends.[40]

GENDER AND SEXUAL VARIANCE AMONG CONTEMPORARY INDIAN WOMEN

In what ways do these patterns continue today? An idea of the type of data that might be gathered by contemporary fieldworkers is contained in a report by Beverely Chiñas, who has been conducting research among the Isthmus Zapotecs of southern Mexico since 1966. While she details an accepted berdache status for males, among females the picture is somewhat different. In two decades of fieldwork she has observed several instances of women with children leaving their husbands to live with female lovers. She sees these relationships as lesbian: "People talk about this for a few weeks but get used to it. There is no ostracism. In the case of the lesbians, they continued to appear at fiestas, now as a couple rather than as wives in heterosexual marriages." At religious festivals, she points out, such female couples do not stand out, since every woman pairs up with another woman to dance together as a couple. There is virtually no male-female couple activity in religious contexts. The sexes are always separated in ceremonies, with different roles and duties.[41]

The only negative reaction that Chiñas reports concerned an unmarried daughter of a close friend and informant who "left her mother's home and went to another barrio to live with her lesbian lover. The daughter was only 25 years old, not beyond the expected age of heterosexual marriage. The mother was very upset and relations between mother-daughter broke off for a time but were patched up a year later although the daughter continued to live with her lesbian partner."[42]

The Zapotec mother's anger at her daughter was due to the latter's evident decision not to have children. By refusing to take a husband at least temporarily, the daughter violated the cultural dictate that females should be mothers. It was thus not lesbianism per se that caused the mother-daughter conflict. It would be interesting to know if the mother was reconciled by the daughter's promise that she would get pregnant later. If so, it would fit into the traditional pattern for American Indian women. The importance of offspring in small-scale societies cannot be ignored; female homosexual behavior has to accommodate to society's need to reproduce the population.

Chiñas explains that in such *marimacha* couples, "one will be the *macho* or masculine partner in the eyes of the community, i.e., the 'dominant' one, but they still dress as women and do women's work. Most of the lesbian couples I have known have been married heterosexually and raised families. In 1982 there were rumors of a suspected lesbian relationship developing between neighbor women, one of whom was married with husband and small child present, the other having been abandoned by her husband and left with children several years previously."[43]

These data offer an example of the kind of valuable findings that direct fieldwork experience can uncover. The fact that one of the women was looked on as the macho one, even though she did not cross-dress, points up the relative *un*importance of cross-dressing in a same-sex relationship. An uninformed outsider might have no idea that these roles and relationships exist, and might assume that the practice had died out among the modern Zapotecs.

Since the field research that could answer these questions has not yet been done with enough Native American societies, I am reluctant to agree with Evelyn Blackwood's statement that by the end of the nineteenth century "the last cross-gender females seem to have disappeared."[44] Such a statement does not take into account the less formalized expressions of gender and sexual variance. If I had trusted such statements about the supposed disappearance of the male berdache tradition, I never would have carried out the fieldwork to disprove such a claim.

As also occurs with the berdaches, contemporary Indians perceive similarities with a Western gay identity. A Micmac berdache, whose niece recently came out publicly as gay, reports that the whole community accepts her: "The family members felt that if she is that way, then that's her own business. A lot of married Indian women approach her for sex. A male friend of mine knows that she has sex with his wife, and he jokes about it. There is no animosity. There might be some talking about her, a little joking, but it is no big deal as far as people on the reserve are concerned. There is never any condemnation or threats about it. When she brought a French woman to the community as her lover, everyone welcomed her. They accept her as she is."[45]

Despite the value of such reports, it is clear that a male cannot get very complete information on women's sexuality. I hope that the data presented here will inspire women ethnographers to pursue this topic in the future.

Paula Gunn Allen, who is familiar with Native American women from many reservations, states that there is cultural continuity. She wrote me that "There are amazon women, recognized as such, *today* in a number of tribes—young, alive, and kicking!"[46] They may now identify as gay or lesbian, but past amazon identities, claims Beth Brant (Mohawk), "have everything to do with who we are now. As gay Indians, we feel that connection with our ancestors." Erna Pahe (Navajo), cochair of Gay American Indians, adds that this connection gives advantages: "In our culture [and] in our gay world, anybody can do anything. We can sympathize, we can really

feel how the other sex feels. [We are] the one group of people that can really understand both cultures. We are special." Paula Gunn Allen also emphasizes this specialness, which she sees as applying to non-Indian gay people as well. "It all has to do with spirit, with restoring an awareness of our spirituality as gay people."[47] As with the berdache tradition for males, modern Indian women's roles retain a connection with past traditions of gender and sexual variance. There is strong evidence of cultural revitalization and persistence among contemporary American Indians.

NOTES

1. Pedro de Magalhães de Gandavo, "History of the Province of Santa Cruz," ed. John Stetson, *Documents and Narratives Concerning the Discovery and Conquest of Latin America: The Histories of Brazil* 2 (1922): 89.
2. Evelyn Blackwood, "Sexuality and Gender in Certain Native American Tribes: The Case of Cross-Gender Females," *Signs: Journal of Women in Culture and Society* 10 (1984): 27–42. These tribes are listed on p. 29: California (Achomawi, Atsugewi, Klamath, Shasta, Wintu, Wiyot, Yokuts, Yuki), Southwest (Apache, Cocopa, Maricopa, Mohave, Navajo, Papago, Pima, Yuma), Northwest (Bella Coola, Haisla, Kutenai, Lillooet, Nootka, Okanagon, Queets, Quinault), Great Basin (Shoshoni, Ute, Southern Ute, Southern and Nothern Paiute), Subarctic (Ingalik, Kaska), and northern Plains (Blackfoot, Crow).
3. Alice Joseph, et al., *The Desert People* (Chicago: University of Chicago Press, 1949), p. 227.
4. C. Caryll Forde, "Ethnography of the Yuma Indians," *University of California Publications in American Archeology and Ethnology* 28 (1931): 157; Leslie Spier, *Yuman Tribes of the Gila River* (Chicago: University of Chicago Press, 1933), p. 243.
5. Forde, "Ethnography of the Yuma," p. 157. E. W. Gifford, "The Cocopa," *University of California Publications in American Archeology and Ethnology* 31 (1933): 294.
6. John J. Honigmann, *The Kaska Indians: An Ethnographic Reconstruction* (New Haven: Yale University Press, 1964), pp. 129–30.
7. Cornelius Osgood, *Ingalik Social Culture* (New Haven: Yale University Press, 1958); com-

mented on in Blackwood, "Sexuality and Gender," p. 32.

8. K. J. Crowe, *A History of the Original Peoples of Northern Canada* (Montreal: McGill-Queen's University Press, 1974), pp. 77–78, 90.

9. Honigmann, *Kaska*, pp. 129–30.

10. Claude Schaeffer, "The Kutenai Female Berdache: Courier, Guide, Prophetess, and Warrior," *Ethnohistory* 12 (1965): 195–216.

11. Quoted in ibid.

12. Alexander Ross, *Adventures of the First Settlers on the Oregon or Columbia River* (London: Smith and Elder, 1849), pp. 85, 144–49; quoted in Schaeffer, "Kutenai Female."

13. John Franklin, *Narrative of a Journey to the Shores of the Polar Seas* (London: J. Murray, 1823), p. 152; quoted in Schaeffer, "Kutenai Female."

14. T. C Elliott, ed. "John Work's Journal," *Washington Historical Quarterly* 5 (1914): 190; quoted in Schaeffer, "Kutenai Female."

15. Quoted in Schaeffer, "Kutenai Female," pp. 215–16.

16. George Devereux, "Institutionalized Homosexuality of the Mohave Indians," *Human Biology* 9 (1937): 503. George Devereux, *Mohave Ethnopsychiatry* (Washington, D.C.: Smithsonian Institution, 1969), p. 262.

17. Devereux, *Mohave Ethnopsychiatry*, pp. 416–17.

18. Ibid., p. 262.

19. Ibid., pp. 416–420.

20. E. W. Gifford, "The Cocopa," *University of California Publications in American Archeology and Ethnology* 31 (1933): 257–94.

21. Leslie Spier, *Klamath Ethnography* (Berkeley: University of California Press, 1930), p. 53.

22. Erminie Voegelin, *Culture Element Distribution: Northeast California* (Berkeley: University of California Press, 1942), vol. 20, pp. 134–35.

23. Charles Callender and Lee Kochems, "Men and Not-Men: Male Gender-Mixing Statuses and Homosexuality," *Journal of Homosexuality* II (1985); and by the same authors, "The North American Berdache," *Current Anthropology* 24 (1983): 443–56. See also Harriet Whitehead, "The Bow and the Burden Strap: A New Look at Institutionalized Homosexuality in Native North America" in *Sexual Meanings*, ed. Sherry Ortner and Harriet Whitehead (Cambridge: Cambridge University Press, 1981), pp. 80–115. The beginnings of a sophisticated approach, recognizing cultural variation in the number and statuses of genders, are suggested in M. Kay Martin and Barbara Voorhies, *Female of the Species* (New York: Columbia University Press, 1975), chap. 4.

24. Beatrice Medicine, "'Warrior Women'—Sex Role Alternatives for Plains Indian Women," in *The Hidden Half: Studies of Plains Indian Women*, ed. Patricia Albers and Beatrice Medicine (Washington, D.C.: University Press of America, 1983), p. 269. Though Medicine criticizes Sue-Ellen Jacobs for suggesting that Plains Warrior Women were parallel to berdachism, Jacobs has clarified that "they should not be confused with transsexuals, third gender people, homosexuals or others." Sue-Ellen Jacobs, personal communication, 17 May 1983. See also Whitehead, "Bow and Burden Strap," pp. 86, 90–93; Donald Forgey, "The Institution of Berdache among the North American Plains Indians," *Journal of Sex Research* II (1975): I; and Ruth Landes, *The Mystic Lake Sioux* (Madison: University of Wisconsin Press, 1968).

25. Ibid., pp. 92–93; Oscar Lewis, "The Manly-Hearted Women among the Northern Piegan," *American Anthropologist* 43 (1941): 173–87.

26. John Fire and Richard Erdoes, *Lame Deer, Seeker of Visions* (New York: Simon and Schuster, 1972), pp. 148–49.

27. Paula Gunn Allen, "Lesbians in American Indian Cultures," *Conditions* 7 (1981): 76.

28. Blackwood, "Sexuality and Gender," p. 39; Jeannette Mirsky, "The Dakota," in *Cooperation and Competition among Primitive Peoples*, ed. Margaret Mead (Boston: Beacon Press, 1961), p. 417.

29. The best recent works on the position of Plains women are the essays in Albers and Medicine, *Hidden Half*.

30. Edwin Thompson Denig, *Five Indian Tribes of the Upper Missouri*, ed. John Ewers (Norman: University of Oklahoma Press, 1961), pp. 195–200.

31. Ibid.

32. Ibid.

33. Ibid.

34. Ibid.

35. Allen, "Lesbians," pp. 68, 78–79.

36. Blackwood, "Sexuality and Gender," pp. 35–36.

37. Allen, "Lesbians," pp. 65–66, 73.

38. Ibid.

39. Blackwood, "Sexuality and Gender," p. 38; Allen, "Lesbians," pp. 79–80; Albers and Medicine, *Hidden Half*, pp. 53–73.

40. Evelyn Blackwood, "Some Comments on the Study of Homosexuality Cross-Culturally," *Anthropological Research Group on Homosexuality Newsletter* (3 (Fall 1981): 8–9. Important

source material on female homosexual behavior is in the classic study by Ferdinand Karsch-Haack, *Das Gleichgeschlechtliche Leben der Naturvölker* (The same-sex life of nature peoples) (Munich: Verlag von Ernst Reinhardt, 1911). It and July Grahn, *Another Mother Tongue: Gay Words, Gay Worlds* (Boston: Beacon Press, 1984), are the starting points for future cross-cultural research on lesbianism. Just two examples of female-female relationships which bear further investigation include groups of women silk weavers, "spinsters," in China—see Agnes Smedley, *Portraits of Chinese Women in Revolution* (Old Westbury, N.Y.: Feminist Press, 1976)—and female marriages in Africa—see Denise O'Brian, "Female Husbands in Southern Bantu Societies," in *Sexual Stratification*, ed. Alice Schlegel (New York: Columbia University Press, 1977).

41. Beverly Chiñas, "Isthmus Zapotec 'Berdaches,'" *Newsletter of the Anthropological Research Group on Homosexuality* 7 (May 1985): 3–4.
42. Ibid.
43. Ibid.
44. Blackwood, "Sexuality and Gender," p. 38.
45. Joseph Sandpiper, Micmac informant I, September 1985.
46. Paula Gunn Allen, personal communication, 6 September 1985.
47. Quoted in Will Roscoe, "Gay American Indians: Creating an Identity from Past Traditions," *The Advocate*, 29 October 1985, pp. 45–48.

Children of Gay Fathers

Federick W. Bozett

The scientific literature devoted solely to the topic of children of gay fathers is limited to one report, whereas research on the children of lesbian mothers is more extensive. . . . The reason for this discrepancy is most probably due to the fact that lesbian mothers, like nonlesbian single mothers, are much more likely than fathers, gay or nongay, to have child custody. Lesbian mother custody cases have received considerable publicity (see Julian, 1985), sparking researchers' interest in studying the potential effect of the mothers' sexual orientation and lifestyle on their children. Custodial gay fathers are less common. Because of their relative invisibility, gay fathers and their children have been less accessible for study. Although it has been thought that the numbers of gay fathers (and hence the

numbers of their children) were not sufficiently substantial to warrant study, it is now known that this assumption is erroneous. There are at least 1 to 3 million gay men who are natural fathers. . . . Also, this figure is conservative since it does not take into consideration gay men who adopt children, who are foster or stepfathers, or who achieve fatherhood by other less traditional means (for example, sperm donation). Likewise, it is difficult to estimate the number of children of gay fathers. However, Schulenburg (1985) estimates the combined number of children of lesbian mothers and gay fathers to approximate 6 million, whereas, according to Peterson (1984), there are 14 million. Hence, the number of both gay fathers and their children is sufficient to warrant serious study.

In addition, the American family has been undergoing radical change within the past twenty years. No longer can the term "family" be used to refer to a characteristic or typical family form. The so-called "traditional" nuclear family, which consisted of two biological parents of opposite sex with the father as breadwinner, the mother as homemaker, and one or more children is now less than one-third of all families with children (Hayes, 1980, in Bloom-Feshbach, 1981). Moreover, gay father (and lesbian mother) families appear to be increasing in number. Whether or not the number is real or is an artifact of more homosexually-oriented parents letting their sexual orientation be known is unknown. Nevertheless, as Hunt and Hunt (1977) point out, hundreds of thousands of formerly married individuals, many of whom are parents, are leaving their "heterosexual" marriages and are entering the gay world. Thus, it behooves professionals in many disciplines to have an understanding of this particular family form.

The purpose of this chapter is to present what is known about the children of gay fathers. It is based upon the author's research (Bozett, 1986), the research of Miller (1979), panel presentations by such children at professional meetings attended by the author, and upon informal personal discussions with several of these children. The chapter begins with a discussion of the children's reactions to their fathers' disclosure of his homosexuality. How gay fathers manage their homosexuality and their gay lifestyle vis-à-vis their children is addressed next, and is followed by a discussion of the children's development of their sexual identity. Following this, the advantages and disadvantages of having a gay father are identified. Recommendations for educators and counselors are presented, and the chapter concludes with suggestions for further research.

CHILDREN'S REACTIONS TO HAVING A GAY FATHER

Research by the author in which 19 children of gay fathers were interviewed (6 male and 13 female, ages 14 to 35) found that the overriding concern of these children was their fear that others would think that they, too, were gay if their fathers' homosexuality became known. This fear can be explained on the basis of several theoretical premises. Lindesmith, Strauss, and Denzin (1977) comment that one's "self" cannot be separated from one's social environment, that "self implies others." In addition, Goffman (1963) remarks about the informing nature of the "with" relationship. For example, it is assumed that if an individual is seen with others who have a particular trait, that person, too, has that trait. The presumption is that one is what the others are. In addition, homophobia in the United States is especially acute (Altman, 1982). Thus, fear of identity contamination by the children of gay fathers is understandable.

To manage their public image it was found that children use social control strategies, which are specific behaviors children of gay fathers employ vis-à-vis their father so that they are perceived by others as they want to be perceived—gay or nongay. Acting as agents of control can be thought of as the "identity work" of the children of gay fathers. Heterosexual children use these strategies primarily to assure that others will not think that they are gay. Gay children may or may not use the strategies, depending upon their acceptance of their own homosexuality. It is logical to assume that gay or lesbian children who are unaccepting of their own homosexuality, and thus do not want it known, would behave similarly to nongay children in the use of the strategies. Thus, the father's expression of his homosexuality would be kept in check to prevent others from possibly correctly identifying them as gay (the "with" relationship). However, this is not borne out in the research reported here since all of the gay respondents were accepting of their homosexuality.

Social Control Strategies

The first social control strategy is referred to as *boundary control*, which has three facets. The first of these is control by the child of the *father's* behavior (behavioral or verbal) in order to control expression of his homosexuality. For example, one subject refused to allow her father to bring his lover to her Christmas party although she hoped her father would come alone. Another respondent asked her father to keep his hands off his boyfriend's thigh during a party at her home. The second boundary control strategy is control by the child of their *own* behavior in relation to the father. For example, one child would not invite his father and his father's lover to visit his place of employment because the son was afraid that his fellow workers would correctly identify them as being gay. Another subject did not invite her father to a celebration at her home because "I didn't want people talking about me behind my back or pointing at me going 'Oh, her dad's a fag.' I don't want the shame of it." Another subject refuses to be seen in public with her father since she is certain that his homosexuality is readily evident.

The third boundary control strategy is controlling *others* vis-à-vis the father. An example of this is the child who will not bring certain friends home to keep them from encountering both the father and his lover. The function of boundary control strategies is to keep the boundary of the father's expression of his homosexuality within the limits set by the child. By controlling the father, the self, and others in relation to the father, the child controls others' perceptions of him or herself as being nongay. Moreover, the use of these strategies helps children avoid the embarrassment they feel because of their father's "shameful differentness" (Goffman, 1963, p. 140). In addition, the first two strategies help to inform the gay father of where the boundary of acceptable behavior is drawn (Higgins & Butler, 1982) by their children.

A second major social control strategy is *nondisclosure*. Unless children are certain it is safe to do so, children avoid telling others that their father is gay in order to avoid soiling their own identity. One young respondent stated: "I don't tell anyone else because I'm afraid they won't like me . . . [I'm] afraid they'll think I'm gay." An adult son who lives with his father rarely tells anyone since he thinks others might think he is also gay. He

said, "I [do] not want to be perceived as a person who's gay because I certainly am not!" Nondisclosure may take other forms, such as referring to the father's lover as an "uncle" or a "housemate," or hiding artifacts such as gay newspapers when friends visit (Bozett, 1980). The children believe that not telling others prevents identity contamination, that it helps to maintain relationships, and that it keeps them from becoming social pariahs.

The last social control mechanism is the opposite of the one just discussed, *disclosure*. It was found that the most common reason for disclosing was that others are potential discreditors, that they are homophobic, that they will be derogatory about *them* (the child), if they discover the father is homosexual, and thus others need to be "prepared" before meeting the father. It seems that many of these children attribute exceptional decoding capacity to others; they assume that upon first meeting the father others are able to discern that he is gay. In addition, telling others is highly selective because closure of information channels is usually impossible. For example, one male respondent explained that it was very important to choose who to tell very carefully because "you have to be sure they won't tell somebody else. I was worried [about] people knowing [because] I was afraid of what they'd think of me; maybe it would be embarrassing." A gay informant *does* disclose his father's homosexuality to friends because he talks a lot about his family, and his father's homosexuality is "just one part of my family. It's significant." This may appear to be a contradictory finding but it is not. Gay children who are accepting of their own and their fathers' homosexuality may use the strategy of disclosing their father' homosexuality, thus, through the "with" relationship, allowing their own gay identity to be known, or at least assumed without necessarily disclosing it directly.

Influencing Factors

From the foregoing it is possible for the reader to have the impression that children of gay fathers are concerned in the extreme about their fathers' homosexuality, and that they are excessively embarrassed by it. This is *not* necessarily the case. Although social control strategies are used in order to negotiate a public persona, in the research being reported here it was also discovered that there are *influencing factors* that determine the extent to which the children utilize the strategies just described. *The influencing factors are as important to understanding the reactions of these children as are the social control strategies.*

The first influencing factor is *mutuality*. Mutuality refers to identification by the child with the father. When the child identifies or links him or herself in some way with also being different, or the child feels that he or she varies in some way from societal norms in terms of behavior, lifestyle, values, or beliefs or believes there are other mutual links with the father such as sharing similar tastes in music or movies, then the more accepting the child is of the father as gay, and the less the child uses social control strategies. In addition, for children who consider themselves to be nontraditional, the father's homosexuality seems to help legitimate their own feelings of variance. An example of mutuality is the overweight respondent who remarked, "There's a lot of hostility toward heavy people, too. I don't like being labeled, and I understand what labeling is like. I think it's easier for me to accept a difference in someone else." Another subject explained that both she and her father had a drinking problem that linked them together. An adolescent son stated:

> In some ways I'm kind of jealous of my dad being different because I don't want to be like everyone else; I want to be different. My dad is hip. He likes all the music I do, he likes the movies and TV shows I see, and we just like to do the same things. I think I'm much more like my dad (than my mother) and I think that helps me.[1]

The second influencing factor is *obtrusiveness*, which refers to how discernable the child believes the father's homosexuality to be. What constitutes discernability is determined by each child, but generally it refers to the culturally determined stereotypical symbols and manifestations of gay behavior such as the presence of gay artifacts in the household, the father's use of effeminate gestures, or his wearing excessive jewelry. It also includes the father asking his children to participate with him in gay social settings such as dining in gay restaurants. Any external manifestation that "increases the difficulty of maintaining easeful inattention regarding the stigma" (Goffman, 1963, p. 103) may be considered by the child to be obtrusive. One young son explained that he walks twenty feet behind his dad when his father walks arm and arm with another man, whereas another adolescent subject stated: "I feel at ease when I'm in public with my dad. My dad does not act homosexual. He does not! And Joe [the father's lover] does not act like that."

The third influencing factor is *age* of the children. If they are young they have less control over their own, their fathers', and others' actions, whereas the older the children are the more control they can exercise. For example, younger children may use the strategy of nondisclosure by referring to the father's lover as an uncle, whereas an adult child could avoid that situation entirely if the child so chose. Another facet of age as an influencing factor is the age of the child when he is told his father is gay. The older the child is, the more time the child has to take in society's homonegative attitudes and beliefs (Moses & Hawkins, 1982). However, if the child is told when he is young and grows up in association with gays, then it is more likely that the child will be comfortable with them and be relatively immune to the prejudice of others. This reasoning is supported by Turner, Scadden, & Harris (1985) who found that the fathers in their study related that children who were told at an earlier age were reported to have had fewer difficulties than those who found out when they were older.

The fourth and last influencing factor is *living arrangements*, which is often directly related to age. Living arrangements frequently dictate which controlling strategies are used and the extent of their use. For example, if children live with their father and the father's lover, they may have little control over interactions between themselves and their father, but they do exert control over their friends' contacts with their father. Thus, they may be highly selective regarding which friends they bring home. On the other hand, if children live with their mother or live independent of their parents they will probably have less need to use controlling strategies. These four influencing factors are the ones that were extracted from the interview data. However, the odds are that this is not an exhaustive list. For example, another probable influencing factor is the degree of acceptance by the father of his own homosexuality. It is likely that the more accepting and matter-of-fact fathers are regarding their homosexuality, the easier it is for children to accept.

FATHERS' REACTIONS

Protective Strategies

It should be noted that characteristically gay fathers seem to be highly sensitive to their children's needs. They often attempt to avoid undue overt expression of their sexual orientation and gay lifestyle. It is also common for fathers to advise their children to refer to the father's lover as "uncle" or as "housemate." Also, if the children's friends are present the father and his lover often avoid even simple displays of affection, and the father may also put away gay artifacts such as newspapers or magazines. Another strategy is for custodial gay fathers to place their children in a school outside of their own school district. This provides the children with both school friends and neighborhood friends. If the father's gay identity is discovered by one group who then harasses the children, they still have another set of friends (Bozett, 1980). These are only several of the many means that gay fathers use to keep their homosexuality from public notice in order to protect their children from the torment of others.

However, a father's behavior may inadvertently be indiscrete. An example of the nega-

tive consequences of such behavior was related to the author by a fourteen-year-old son of a friend who explained that his father had visited the boy's school several times with "all his jewelry on. The teachers knew he was gay, and all the kids saw him and figured it out. It was obvious. They started calling me names like 'homoson.' It was awful. I couldn't stand it. I hate him for it. I really do" (Bozett, 1980, p. 178).

Role Modeling

Although gay fathers attempt to protect their children from the hostility of others, many gay fathers also want their children to understand that although the wider society disapproves of homosexuality and homosexual parenting, homosexuality is not a negative attribute, and the father is as moral and virtuous as other men. A Jewish gay father explained it this way:

> Any parent wants to show their kids good role models. As a gay parent you'd want to show your kids good gay role models to reinforce to your child that what you're doing is okay. And not only is it okay for you, but that there are also other gay family units out there that it's okay with. Because as a gay parent, I do have to think in my mind that my child is seeing something that is not the ordinary. And I want to have the obligation for her to at least see that this not ordinary thing is okay. And not only okay with me, but with enough people so she knows that although it may not be ordinary, it's out there, it's happening. And to see that, to make it easier, for whatever the future holds in store for her (Bozett, 1980, p. 176).

This father ended his comments by saying:

> I guess all you can do is give your kids the strongest feeling that what's going on is okay, so at least they'll be able to fight back. It's like being Jewish or being black. That kind of discrimination.
>
> And the kid is going to have to fight back as best as he can and get the best support from home that he can get. This is just one of the realities (Bozett, 1980, p. 178).

There is yet another important facet of role modeling. If the gay father has a child who is gay or lesbian, then he has the responsibility to be a positive gay role model just as nongay fathers serve as role models for their heterosexual children. It is regrettable that most gay or lesbian children have no homosexual adult role models during their formative years. As a consequence, self-acceptance and adaptation to the gay world is often much more difficult than it would be otherwise. It is assumed that gay children who have an adult gay role model would experience a much smoother transition into adulthood than gays without such models. Research is needed, however, to bear this out.

CHILDREN'S DEVELOPMENT OF SEXUAL IDENTITY

Studies of the children of lesbian mothers (Golombok, Spencer, & Rutter, 1983; Green, 1978; Hoeffer, 1978, 1981; Hotvedt & Mandel, 1982; Kirkpatrick, Smith, & Roy, 1981; Weeks, Derdeyn, & Langman, 1975) have found no areas directly related to parental homosexuality. The findings of this research can be summed by the statement of Green (1978): "Children being raised by transsexual or homosexual parents do not differ appreciably from children raised in more conventional family settings on macroscopic measures of sexual identity" (pp. 696–697). . . . Although there are no reported studies on the development of sexual identity of children of gay fathers, there is no reason to assume that the findings would differ appreciably from those reported for the children of lesbian mothers. Even so, this is a much needed area of research.

In the study by Miller (1979), among the 27 daughters and 21 sons whose sexual orientation could be assessed, the fathers reported that one son and three daughters were gay. Among the 25 children in the author's study of gay fathers (Bozett, 1981a,b), no father reported having a gay or lesbian child, although not all of the children were old enough for their sexual orientation to be determined. In the author's study of 19 children of gay fathers (Bozett, 1986), two sons reported being gay, and one daughter considered herself bisexual. The remaining 17 claimed to be heterosexual. Thus, as Miller (1979) points out, the link between parental and children's sexual orientation appears weak. Thus, the myth that gay parents will raise gay children and that gay parents attempt to convince their children to be gay has no support from research data. Likewise, another issue brought up regarding gay fathers is that they may seduce or molest their children. There is no evidence that gay fathers are more likely than nongay fathers to seduce their children or to allow them to be seduced. Child molesters are primarily heterosexual, and the victims are usually female.

In addition, there is some evidence that gay fathers attempt to develop traditional gender identity and sex-role behaviors in their children. Harris and Turner (1986) found that the fathers in their study tended to encourage their children to play with sex-typed toys, whereas half of the gay fathers in the Turner, Scadden, and Harris study (1985) did so. Also, it was not uncommon for fathers of both sons and daughters in the author's gay father research (Bozett, 1981a,b) to express concern regarding the absence of a feminine influence in the household. Most of the fathers in the study by Turner, Scadden, and Harris (1985) are reported to have made an effort to provide an opposite sex-role model for their children. These researchers also state that most of their subjects reported that their children appeared to be developing traditional sex-role identification, and that they considered their childrens' behaviors to be no different from other children of the same age and sex.

Children may, however, worry about their own sexual orientation; they may believe that because their father is gay they will be too (Moses & Hawkins, 1982). This concern may be especially acute for the adolescent who has had a homosexual experience. These children need assurance that homosexual experimentation is not unusual among young people (Woodman & Lenna, 1980). Moreover, children need to understand that they have options. Riddle (1978) points out that children's exposure to cultural and individual diversity can be positive, and that "an increased comfort with diversity could result in a greater ability to make personal choices independent of societal pressures to conform" (p. 53). She continues by stating that

> children do not model specific sexual behaviors unquestioningly; rather, they experiement. After early childhood, peers and significant adults (not necessarily parents) serve as primary role models. Persons are selected as models because of perceived valued traits, and then those particular traits are adopted. What gays have to offer children is a non-traditional, multi-option adult lifestyle model, independent of sexual preference choices (p. 53).

HOMONEGATIVE REACTIONS OF CHILDREN

On the basis of current research, it appears that most children are accepting of their fathers as gay. According to Harris and Turner (1986), and Turner, Scadden, and Harris (1985), *initial* responses of children to learning that their fathers are homosexual as reported by their fathers were closeness, confusion, not understanding, worrying, knowing all along, shame, disbelief, anger, shock, and guilt. Wyers (1984), reporting on the initial impact on children, states that 40 percent of the fathers reported a positive impact, 35 percent were uncertain of the initial impact, and 25 percent indicated the impact was negative. The children's *current* feelings as perceived by the fathers in the first two studies mentioned above were indifferent, supportive, proud, confused, angry, hostile, and ashamed. Wyers writes that 50 percent of the fathers reported the current impact was positive, 45 percent were uncertain of the current impact, and 5 percent indicated that the current impact was negative. In all of these studies the number of children who remained negative toward their fathers as gay was small.

Hence, although most children are accepting of their fathers as gay, some are not. It also seems that almost all children who reject their father as gay continue to accept him in

the role of father. Although rare, it is likely that there are children who react by severing ties altogether. In the author's research (Bozett, 1986) two grown daughters were found to be intensely homophobic. They both exhibited some characteristics of the authoritarian personality type: rigid conformity to middle-class values, little tolerance for ambiguity, generalized hostility, and punitive attitudes regarding sexual "goings on" (Babad, Birnbaum, & Benne, 1983). According to Herek (1984), "Heterosexuals who express hostile attitudes toward homosexual persons tend to endorse traditional ideologies of family, sexuality and sex roles, and often are prejudiced against other minorities as well" (p. 12). The quotations that follow are characteristic of the individual described by Herek. They exemplify the attitudes and feelings of these children toward gay persons and homosexuality in general, and toward their fathers in particular.

> I don't hate gays, I just hate the way they act. I don't like people acting weird which is not to say that I don't want people to be different to be proper. I want them to be polite. I mean my dad's fine as long as he's not acting like a fag. Sure I'd prefer for my dad to still be in the closet. There's no conflict [that way] (Bozett, 1983, p. 10–11).

Another example is the following:

> I'm embarrassed that my father's gay. A lot of times I would just like him to go away. I almost wish he would die because then I can lie about what he was like to the future hypothetical children I'm going to have. It's not normal. Normal people don't go around doing things like that (Bozett, 1984, p. 64).

Note that these statements provide support for the contention of Altman (1982) that "What affronts others is the blatant *sexuality* of homosexuals, not merely their transgression of sex roles" (p. 68).

Although these two children are undoubtedly the exception to the rule, these examples are provided in order to demonstrate some of the range of children's reactions to homosexuality and to having a gay father. This is not to say, however, that these children do not have a *cognitive* understanding of their father. For example, one of the children quoted above explained that on one occasion her father took her to a gay restaurant:

> Fortunately we got a table back in the corner. I remember him sort of making eyes at the waiter. That really pissed me off! It's not intentional. What I think he's trying to do is say, "Look. Accept me. This is the world I've chosen." I know he loves me. He wants to be accepted. And it's really hard for me to do that. It's all right for him to live his life whatever way he's going to, but I'm separate from it and I don't want him to try to pull me into it (Bozett, 1983, p. 11).

Although this daughter understands that her father's attempt to integrate her into his gay world is because he values both her and his gay identity and lifestyle and wants her to share in his pleasure, she rejects his efforts because such participation is in conflict with her value system. In addition, since research has demonstrated significant correlations between the attitudes of parents and those of their children (Ehrlich, 1973), these examples point to the value of gay fathers inculcating in their children as they develop an acceptance and appreciation for an extensive diversity of human behavior.

ADVANTAGES AND DISADVANTAGES OF HAVING A GAY FATHER

Based upon the research literature, it appears that the advantages of having a gay father outweigh the disadvantages. One common advantage is that it seems that many fathers who have disclosed their homosexuality to their children are more open in their communication with them, which seems to evoke a reciprocal response in their children, creating a closer father-child relationship. One daughter explained that before her father came out to her she had only a father, but now she has both a father and a friend. One son remarked that since his father had come out to him

communication "has been much better. Since then I've felt much more comfortable talking about anything. When I first moved in with him, on weekends we would sit and just talk from the time we got up in the morning around 8 o'clock until almost 9 or 10 o'clock at night."

In his recent autobiographical account Robert Bauman (1986), the ultraconservative congressman from Maryland whose highly successful career was destroyed when his homosexuality was made public, writes about his four children and former wife knowing that he is gay. "At least we are able to talk without shame, seeking the truth and debating our differences. 'We would have never known who you are,' my daughter, Vicky, said in her youthful wisdom. And I would have never known my children fully, or myself" (p. 272). That disclosure generally fosters a close relationship is supported by the research on disclosure (Chelune 1979) and by Woodman and Lenna (1980, p. 102) who write that one of the effects of delaying disclosure is to postpone opportunities for a closer relationship with one's children. Another advantage children identify is that they learn to be more tolerant of persons different from themselves.

There appear to be few disadvantages. Two daughters commented that their fathers attempted to become too close, that they were *too* open and revealing about themselves. In this regard, Colman and Colman (1981) remark that children measure their parents against the simple images of parents in the culture and the media, and thus, even though fathers may want to be closer to their children, their children may allow them only more traditional limit-setting roles. The most common disadvantage in the author's research (Bozett, 1986) was that the children may have considered the father's homosexuality to be responsible for the breakup of the family. This topic was discussed by several subjects with considerable emotion. For example, one 33-year-old daughter poignantly stated:

> There's been so much that got taken away by my parents' divorce. I enjoyed the times I spent with my parents. It took that away. We don't

have the house any more that we grew up in, and it was really a special house. It took away a lot of innocence, I guess. The world just looked different. You couldn't trust it so much any more. Things weren't as they seemed. It took away a family. It broke up a unit of people, and over the years I'm learning that that's a really valuable thing to have (Bozett, in press).

It is worth noting, however, that children who feel close to their father and express feelings of love and admiration for him do not necessarily approve of his homosexuality. These children seem to be able to separate their fathers' *gay* identity from his *father* identity. For example, one son who spontaneously discussed his love for his father also said, "I perceive his lifestyle as wrong. I don't want to perceive what he's doing as wrong, really, but I just never have been able to change that perception." Likewise, a daughter who said that her father might "burn in hell" because of his homosexuality also explained that "If he wasn't gay I'd say he was sent from heaven. That's how impressed I am with him. He's smart, he's successful, and he's also a very caring man." Even though these children may not approve of their fathers' homosexuality, their homonegative attitudes and beliefs do not appear to interfere with the father-child relationship. Turner, Scadden, and Harris (1985) generalized from the reports of the fathers in their study that a parent's homosexuality seems to create few long-term problems for children who seem to accept it better than parents anticipate. Note, however, the significance of the word "few"; it is reasonable to assume that some long-term problems may occasionally occur under certain circumstances as a result of parental homosexuality. Turner et al. also write that most of their subjects reported a positive relationship with their children, and that the parents' sexual orientation was of little importance in the overall parent-child relationship. These findings are corroborated in the present study. Furthermore, Turner, Scadden, and Harris (1985) remark that gay parents try harder than traditional heterosexual parents to create stable home lives and positive relationships with their children. Although the original research reported here involved data from children only, it does seem from the children's reports that, in general, they felt their fathers had put forth considerable effort to parent well. Lastly, Harris and Turner (1986) sum their study of gay parents by stating that being gay is compatible with effective parenting, and that the parents' sexual orientation is not the major issue in these parents' relationships with their children. Most certainly, the study reported here supports both of these findings. Yet again a caveat must be introduced in that surely it is possible that for some children the father's homosexuality could be a major issue. For the two homophobic daughters reported on earlier, their fathers' homosexuality was often a major issue in their relationship with him. Whether the fathers perceived it to be an issue in their relationship with their daughters is unknown. In short, it seems that the findings of the research on the children of gay fathers are in general agreement with the research reported on gay fathers.

NOTE

1. Unless otherwise noted quotations in this chapter are derived from unpublished in-depth interviews conducted by the author. The interviews are housed at the Henry A. Murray Research Center at Radcliffe College.

REFERENCES

Altman, D. (1982). The homosexualization of America, the Americanization of the homosexual. New York: St. Martin's.

Babad, E. Y., Birnbaum, M., and Benne, K. D. (1983). *The social self: Group influences on personal identity*. Beverly Hills: Sage.

Bauman, R. (1986). *The gentleman from Maryland: The conscience of a gay conservative*. New York: Arbor House.

Bloom-Feshbach, J. (1981). Historical perspectives on the father's role. In M. E. Lamb (Ed.), *The role of the father in child development*. New York: Wiley.

Bozett, F. W. (1980). How and why gay fathers disclose their homosexuality to their children. *Family Relations, 29*, 173–179.

———. (1981a). Gay fathers: Evolution of the gay-father identity. *American Journal of Orthopsychiatry, 51,* 552–559.

———. (1981b). Gay fathers: Identity conflict resolution through integrative sanctioning. *Alternative Lifestyles, 4,* 90–107.

———. (1983, October). *Gay father-child relationships.* Paper presented at the National Council on Family Relations, St. Paul, MN.

———. (1984). Parenting concerns of gay fathers. *Topics in Clinical Nursing, 6,* 60–71.

———. (1985). Gay men as fathers. In S. M. H. Hanson and F. W. Bozett (Eds.), *Dimensions of fatherhood.* Beverly Hills, CA: Sage.

———. (1986, April). *Identity management: Social control of identity by children of gay fathers when they know their father is a homosexual.* Paper presented at the Seventh Biennial Eastern Nursing Research Conference, New Haven, CT.

———. (in press). Gay fatherhood. In P. Bronstein & C. P. Cowan (Eds.), *Fatherhood today: Men's changing role in the family.* New York: Wiley.

Chelune, G. J. (1979). *Self-disclosure.* San Francisco: Jossey-Bass.

Colman, A., and Colman, L. (1981). *Earth father/sky father.* Englewood Cliffs, NJ: Prentice Hall.

Davidson, G., & Griedman, S. (1981). Sexual orientation stereotypy in the distortion of clinical judgment. *Journal of Homosexuality, 6,* 37–44.

Ehrlich, H. J. (1973). *The social psychology of prejudice.* New York: Wiley.

Goffman, I. (1963). *Stigma.* Englewood Cliffs NJ: Prentice Hall.

Golombok, S., Spencer, A., and Rutter, M. (1983). Children in lesbian and single-parent households: Psychosexual and psychiatric appraisal. *Journal of Child Psychology, 24,* 551–572.

Green, R. (1978). Sexual identity of 37 children raised by homosexual and transexual parents. *American Journal of Psychiatry, 135,* 692–697.

Harris, M. D., and Turner, P. H. (1986). Gay and lesbian parents. *Journal of Homosexuality, 12,* 101–113.

Hayes, C. D. (Ed.), *Work, family, and community: Summary proceedings of an ad hoc meeting.* Washington, D.C.: National Academy of Sciences.

Herek, G. M. (1984). Beyond "homophobia." A social psychological perspective on attitudes toward lesbians and gay men. *Journal of Homosexuality, 10,* 1–21.

Higgins, P. C., and Butler, R. R. (1982). *Understanding deviance.* New York: McGraw-Hill.

Hoeffer, B. (1981). Children's acquisition of sex role behavior in lesbian mother families. *American Journal of Orthopsychiatry, 51,* 536–544.

———. (1978). Single mothers and their children: Challenging traditional concepts of the American family. In P. Brandt, P. Chinn, V. Hunt, & M. Smith (Eds.), *Current Practice in Pediatric Nursing.* Vol. II. St. Louis: C. V. Mosby.

Hotvedt, M. E., and Mandel, J. B. (1982). Children of lesbian mothers. In W. Paul, J. D. Weinrich, J. C. Gonsiorek, & M. E. Hotvedt (Eds.), *Homosexuality: Social, psychological, and biological issues.* Beverly Hills, CA: Sage.

Hunt, M., & Hunt, B. (1977). *The divorce experience.* New York: McGraw-Hill.

Julian, J. (1985). *Long way home: The odessy of a lesbian mother and her children.* Pittsburg, PA: Cleis.

Kirkpatrick, M., Smith, C., and Roy, R. (1981). Lesbian mothers and their children: A comparative survey. *American Journal of Orthopsychiatry, 51,* 545–551.

Lewis, K. S. (1980). Children of lesbians: Their point of view. *Social Work, 25,* 198–203.

Lindesmith, A. R., Strauss, A. L., and Denzin, N. K. (1977). *Social psychology.* New York: Holt, Rinehart, and Winston.

Miller, B. (1979). Gay fathers and their children. *Family Coordinator, 28,* 544–552.

Morin, S. F., and Schultz, S. J. (1978). The gay movement and the rights of children. *Journal of Social Issues, 34,* 137–148.

Moses, A. E., and Hawkins, R. O. (1982). *Counseling lesbian women and gay men: A life-issues approach.* St. Louis: C. V. Mosby.

Peterson, N. (1984, April 30). Coming to terms with gay parents. *USA Today,* p. 30.

Riddle, D. I. (1978), Relating to children: Gays as role models. Journal of Social Issues, *34,* 38–58.

Schulenburg, J. (1985). *Gay parenting.* New York: Anchor Press/Doubleday.

Turner, P. H., Scadden, L., and Harris, M. B. (1985, March). *Parenting in gay and lesbian families.* Paper presented at the first meeting of the Future of Parenting symposium, Chicago, Il.

Weeks, R. B., Derdeyn, A. P., and Langman, M. (1975). Two cases of children of homosexuals. *Child Psychiatry and Human Development, 6,* 26–32.

Woodman, N. J., and Lenna, H. R. (1980). *Counseling with gay men and women.* San Francisco: Jossey-Bass.

Wyers, N. L. (1984). *Lesbian and gay spouses and parents: Homosexuality in the family.* Portland: School of Social Work, Portland State University.

VI.

Equality and Inequality: The Sexual Division of Labor and Gender Stratification

In most societies certain tasks are predominantly assigned to men while others are assigned to women. In European and American cultures it used to be considered "natural" for men to be the family breadwinners; women were expected to take care of the home and raise the children. An underlying assumption of this division of labor was that men were dominant because their contribution to the material well-being of the family was more significant than that of women. Women were dependent on men and therefore automatically subordinate to them.

The "naturalness" of this division of labor has been called into question as women increasingly enter the labor force. However, has this significantly altered the status of women within their families and in the wider society? Or has it simply meant that women are now working a double day, performing domestic tasks that are negatively valued and not considered work once they get home from their "real" day's work? If employment enhances the social position of

women, why is it that women still earn only 65% of what men earn for the same work? Why is there still a high degree of occupational segregation by gender?

What precisely is the relationship between the economic roles of women and gender stratification? Cross-cultural research on the sexual division of labor attempts not only to describe the range of women's productive activities in societies with different modes of subsistence, but also to assess the implications of these activities for the status of women.

In many parts of the world women contribute significantly, if not predominantly, to subsistence. This is perhaps most apparent among hunting and gathering or foraging populations, and for this reason such groups have been labeled the most egalitarian of human societies. Hunters and gatherers used to form the bulk of the human population, but today only a small number remain. They are found in relatively isolated regions; they possess simple technology and therefore make little effort to alter the environment in which they live. They tend to be characterized by a division of labor whereby men hunt and women gather. Friedl (1975:18) outlines four reasons for this division: the variability in the supply of game, the different skills required for hunting and gathering, the incompatibility between carrying burdens and hunting, and the small size of seminomadic foraging populations.

Friedl (1975) further argues that in foraging societies in which gathering contributes more to the daily diet than hunting, women and men share equal status (see also Lee 1979; Martin and Voorhies 1975). Conversely, in societies in which hunting and fishing predominate (such as among the Eskimos), the status of women is lower. It seems that female productive activities enhance the social position of women in society, but Sanday (1974) cautions that participation in production is a necessary but not sufficient precondition. Control over the fruits of their labor and a positive valuation of this labor are other factors to consider, as is the extent to which women are involved in at least some political activities. In addition, the absence of a sharp differentiation between public and private domains (Draper 1975) and the fact that there is no economic class structure and no well-defined male-held political offices (Leacock 1975) have been cited as explanations for the relative egalitarianism in foraging societies compared to more complex societies.

Despite the common assumption that men hunt and women gather, in some foraging societies the division of labor is not sharply defined. This often provides the basis for the highest degree of egalitarianism. Among the Tiwi, Australian aborigines who live on Melville Island off the coast of northern Australia, both men and women hunt and gather. Goodale (1971) demonstrates that resources and technology, rather than activities, are divided into male domains and female domains. Although the big game that Tiwi men hunt provides most of the meat to the group and therefore gives them a dominant position in the society, Tiwi women, who hunt and gather, provide more than half of the food consumed; they share in both the comradery and the spoils of their endeavors. As major provisioners, women are economic assets and a

source of wealth and prestige for men in this polygynous society. Despite the fact that their opportunities for self-expression may be more limited than those of men, with age women acquire social status and can be politically influential. In general Goodale suggests that Tiwi culture emphasizes the equality of men and women in society.

Among the Agta women enjoy even greater social equality with their men than among the Tiwi. This is a society in which the division of labor and the battle of the sexes appear to be virtually absent. Agta women hunt game animals and fish just as men do. Not only do they make significant contributions to the daily food supply, but they also control the distribution of the foods they acquire, sharing them with their family and trading them in the broader community. The Griffins (in this book) argue that these roles are clearly the basis for female authority in decision-making within their families and residential groups.

The Agta case challenges the widely held notion that in foraging societies pregnancy and child care are incompatible with hunting (Friedl 1978:72). Agta women have developed methods of contraception and abortion to aid them in childspacing. When they become pregnant they continue hunting until late in their pregnancy and resume hunting for several months after the birth of the child. At any given time there are always some women available to hunt, during which time children may be cared for by older siblings, grandparents, or other relatives. Reproduction is clearly not a constraint on women's economic roles in this society.

In horticultural societies in which cultivation is carried out with simple hand-tool technology and slash and burn methods of farming, women also have important roles in production (Boserup 1970). One theory argues that the economic importance of female production in horticultural society emerged from women's gathering activities in foraging groups. Horticultural societies vary in the degree to which men participate in crop cultivation as well as whether this cultivation is supplemented by hunting, fishing, and raising livestock. In addition, many horticultural societies are matrilineal (reckoning descent through the female line), and in these societies women tend to have higher status than in those that are patrilineal.

Despite descent systems and economic roles that enhance the status of women among horticulturalists, Friedl (1975) cautions that male control of valued property and male involvement in warfare (an endemic feature in many of these societies) can be mitigating factors that provide the basis for male dominance over women. For example, among horticulturalists in highland New Guinea, women raise staple crops but men raise prestige crops that are the focus of social exchange. This cultural valuation is the foundation for gender stratification.

Murphy and Murphy (in this book) take us through the active day of a woman among the Mundurucú Indians who live in the Amazon region of Brazil. The Mundurucú are a sexually segregated society. Men sleep in a men's house, and women and children share other dwellings. Men hunt, fish, and fell the forest area for gardens. Women plant, harvest, and process manioc. In their daily tasks women form cooperative work groups, have authority, and are the equals of men. To the extent that their work "draws women together and isolates them from the immediate supervision and control of the men, it is also a badge of their independence" (Murphy and Murphy 1985:237).

However, according to a male-dominated ideology, women are subservient to men. Despite the contributions that Mundurucú women make to subsistence, what men do is assigned more value. As Murphy and Murphy state, "Male ascendancy does not wholly derive from masculine activities but is to a considerable degree prior to them" (1985:234). Male domination among the traditional Mundurucú is symbolic. As the Mundurucú become increasingly drawn into a commercial economy based on the rubber trade, men, with their rights to rubber trees and to trading, may gain a more complete upper hand. "The women may well discover that they have traded the symbolic domination of the men, as a group, over the women, as a group, for the very real domination of husbands over wives" (1985:238).

While women's labor is clearly important in horticultural societies, it has been argued that it becomes increasingly insignificant relative to that of men with the development of intensive agriculture. Intensive agriculture is based on the use of the plow, draft animals, fertilizers, and irrigation systems. In a survey of ninety-three agricultural societies, Martin and Voorhies (1975: 283) demonstrate that 81% delegate farming to men who then achieve primacy in productive activities. One explanation for the decline in female participation in agriculture is that the female domestic workload tends to increase when root crops are replaced by cereal crops and when animal labor replaces manual labor (Martin and Voorhies 1975). Cereal crops require more extensive processing, and field animals must be cared for. Both these activities fall to women. In addition, the kin-based units of production and consumption become smaller, and this too adds to the burdens on individual women.

Concomitant with the presumably declining importance of women in agricultural activities is a supposed decline in social status (Boserup 1970). Women's value is defined by their reproductive abilities rather than by their productive activities. It has been suggested that the lesser status of women in some agricultural societies, particularly those of Eurasia, compared to some horticultural societies, as in sub-Saharan Africa, is reflected in the contrast between systems of bridewealth and systems of dowry (Goody 1976). Bridewealth is a compensation to the bride's parents or her kin for the productive and reproductive rights of the bride; dowry, as a form of inheritance, provides a bride with land and other wealth and helps her to attract a husband.

Despite arguments describing a decline in women's status and their relegation to the domestic sphere in association with the emergence of intensive agriculture, cross-cultural data indicate that women in agricultural societies lead much more diverse and complex lives than some theories suggest. In northwestern Portugal women do most of the agricultural activity, inherit property equally, and are often the recipients of a major inheritance that generally includes the parental household (Brettell 1986). This division of labor has emerged because men have been assigned the role of emigrants. Another exception is rural Taiwan, where, despite the patriarchal and patrilineal character of Chinese society, women construct a familial network that gives them a good deal of power and influence in later life (Wolf 1972).

Japanese women have traditionally played an important role in farming, but today these activities are often combined with wage employment. Haruko, a farm woman who lives just outside the town of Unomachi in Ehime Prefecture in western Japan (Bernstein, this book), is the busiest member of her family. Like many urban western women, she juggles wage-paying work with household chores and community responsibilities. She does not define what she does at home, or the assistance that she gives her husband in the rice fields, as real work. Her real work is her job in construction—"man's work" for which she gets paid. Haruko regrets that all these responsibilities have to be carried out at the expense of her children who, she says, "raised themselves" (Bernstein 1983:47).

Haruko perceives of her work not only as a necessary supplement to the family income, but also as a means to the end of a middle-class lifestyle. In Haruko's eyes the money she earns does not have meaning as a symbol of independence. Her status, she claims, comes from feeling that she is needed. Her desire to become just a housewife with time to spare is one expressed by other women in agricultural societies around the world, especially those who have entered the cash economy on a part-time or temporary basis (Brettell 1982).

A final economic adaptation is that of pastoralism or herding. Some pastoralists are fully nomadic, moving their entire communities in accordance with the demands of the herd. Others are involved in cultivation and are therefore transhumant. They engage in seasonal migration. Among pastoralists the ownership, care, and management of herds are generally in the hands of men. Though there are exceptions, male domination of herding tends to be reflected in other aspects of social organization— the near universality of patrilineal descent and widespread patrilocal residence. Pastoral societies are also generally characterized by patriarchy and a dichotomization of the sexes, both symbolically and socially. Segregation of the sexes and gender stratification, in other words, are fundamental attributes of many pastoral people.

The symbolic opposition between men and women is apparent among the Sarakatsani, a group of transhumant shepherds who live in the mountainous regions of the province of Epirus in Greece. According to Campbell (1964) the life of the pastoral Sarakatsani revolves around three things: sheep, children (particularly sons), and honor. "The sheep support the life and prestige of the family, the sons serve the flocks and protect the honour of their parents and sisters, and the notion of honour presupposes physical and moral capacities that fit the shepherds for the hard and sometimes dangerous work of following and protecting their animals" (1964:18). Gender ideology is embedded in these three valued items, especially in the parallel oppositions between sheep and goats on the one hand and men and women on the other. The practical division of labor parallels this symbolic opposition. Women give assistance in the care of animals and make major contributions to their families. The economic roles of husband and wife are complementary. Nevertheless, Sarakatsani husbands have ultimate authority over their wives; obedience to a husband is a moral imperative for a wife. As among the Mundurucú, ideology assigns women to a lesser status, in spite of their economic complementarity.

Men and women are also symbolically and economically complementary among the seminomadic and polygynous WoDaaBe Bororo (Fulani) of Niger, West Africa, described by Dupire (in this book). The WoDaaBe Bororo are characterized by a dramatic spatial and conceptual segregation of the sexes. Each camp is divided into an eastern women's domain and a western men's domain. Herding activities provide about 85% of the Bororo subsistence and are dominated by men. Women, however, are involved in the care and milking of cattle, as well as the care of other animals such as sheep and goats. These economic responsibilities, certain rights of ownership, and the fact that they head matricentric units when their husbands are absent give Bororo women a good deal of autonomy.

Generalizations are often made about the status of women according to different modes of adaptation. However, these readings demonstrate that there is a great deal of diversity within each subsistence strategy. For example, in foraging societies women may hunt as well as gather; in intensive agricultural societies not all women are powerless, dependent, and relegated to the domestic sphere.

While women's contributions to subsistence are important to gender stratification, a number of other factors need to be considered. These include leadership roles in family and kinship units and in the wider community; inheritance of property, control of the distribution and exchange of valued goods, authority in childrearing, and participation in ritual activities. In addition, the ideological definitions of women's roles and valuations of their economic activities are often powerful determinants of status.

To fully understand gender stratification both ideology and participation in production must be taken into account. As Atkinson (1982:248) states, "It is too facile to deny the significance of sexual stereotypes or to presume that women's influence in one context cancels out their degradation in another. Just as we know that women's status is not a unitary phenomenon across cultures, we need to be reminded that the intracultural picture is equally complex."

REFERENCES

Atkinson, Jane. 1982. Review: Anthropology. *Signs* 8: 236–258.

Bernstein, Gail. 1983. *Haruko's World: A Japanese Farm Woman and Her Community*. Stanford: Stanford University Press.

Boserup, Esther. 1970. *Women's Role in Economic Development*. London: G. Allen and Unwin.

Brettell, Caroline B. 1982. *We Have Already Cried Many Tears: The Stories of Three Portuguese Migrant Women*. Cambridge, MA: Schenkman.

———. 1986. *Men Who Migrate, Women Who Wait: Population and History in a Portuguese Parish*. Princeton: Princeton University Press.

Campbell, John K. 1964. *Honour, Family and Patronage*. Oxford: Oxford University Press.

Draper, Patricia. 1975. !Kung Women: Contrasts in Sexual Egalitarianism in Foraging and Sedentary Contexts. In Rayna Reiter (ed.). *Toward an Anthropology of Women*, pp. 77–109. New York: Monthly Review Press.

Friedl, Ernestine. 1975. *Women and Men: An Anthropologist's View*. New York: Holt, Rinehart and Winston.

———. 1978. Society and Sex Roles. *Human Nature*, April: 68–75.

Goodale, Jane C. 1971. *Tiwi Wives: A Study of the Women of Melville Island, North Australia*. Seattle: University of Washington Press.

Goody, Jack. 1976. *Production and Reproduction*. Cambridge: Cambridge University Press.

Leacock, Eleanor. 1975. Class, Commodity, and the Status of Women. In Ruby Rohrlich-Leavitt (ed.). *Women Cross-culturally: Change and Challenge*, pp. 601–616. The Hague: Mouton.

———. 1978. Women's Status in Egalitarian Society: Implications for Social Evolution. *Current Anthropology* 19(2): 247–275.

Lee, Richard. 1979. *The !Kung San*. Cambridge: Cambridge University Press.

Martin, M. Kay and Barbara Voorhies. 1975. *Female of the Species*. New York: Columbia University Press.

Murphy, Yolanda and Robert F. Murphy. 1985. *Women of the Forest*. Columbia: Columbia University Press.

Sanday, Peggy Reeves. 1974. Female Status in the Public Domain. In Michelle Z. Rosaldo and Louise Lamphere (eds.). *Woman, Culture, and Society*, pp. 189–206. Stanford: Stanford University Press.

Wolf, Margery. 1972. *Women and the Family in Rural Taiwan*. Stanford: Stanford University Press.

Woman the Hunter: The Agta

Agnes Estioko-Griffin and P. Bion Griffin

Among Agta Negritos of northeastern Luzon, the Philippines, women are of special interest to anthropology because of their position in the organization of subsistence. They are substantial contributors to the daily subsistence of their families and have considerable authority in decision making in the family and in residential groups. In addition, and in contradiction to one of the sacred canons of anthropology, women in one area frequently hunt game animals. They also fish in the rivers with men and barter with lowland Filipinos for goods and services.[1]

In this chapter, we describe women's roles in Agta subsistence economy and discuss the relationship of subsistence activities, authority allocation, and egalitarianism. With this may come an indication of the importance of the Agta research to the anthropology of women and of hunter-gatherers in general. . . .

Women, especially women in hunting-gathering societies, have been a neglected domain of anthropological research. The recent volume edited by Richard Lee and Irven DeVore (1976) and the *!Kung of Nyae Nyae* (Marshall 1976) begin to remedy the lack but focus solely on the !Kung San of southern Africa. Other works are either general or synthetic (Friedl 1975; Martin and Voorhies 1975), or report narrowly bounded topics (Rosaldo and Lamphere 1974). Sally Slocum, writing in *Toward an Anthropology of Women* (Reiter 1975), has provided impetus for the Agta study. Slocum points out a male bias in studying hunter-gatherers, showing how approaching subsistence from a female view

Abridged with permission from Frances Dahlberg (ed.), *Woman the Gatherer* (New Haven: Yale University Press, 1981), pp. 121–140. Copyright © 1981 Yale University Press.

gives a new picture. From the insights of Slocum we have sought to focus on Agta women, to compare the several dialect groups, and to begin investigating the nature and implications of women as not "merely" gatherers but also hunters.

THE AGTA

The Agta are Negrito peoples found throughout eastern Luzon, generally along the Pacific coast and up rivers into the Sierra Madre interior. . . . Although perhaps fewer in numbers, they are also located on the western side of the mountains, especially on the tributary rivers feeding the Cagayan. In general terms, the Agta of Isabela and Cagayan provinces are not dissimilar to other present and past Philippine Negritos. (See Vanoverbergh 1925, 1929–30, 1937–38; Fox 1952; Garvan 1964; and Maceda 1964 for information on Negritos outside the present study area.) In the more remote locales, hunting forest game, especially wild pig, deer, and monkey, is still important. Everywhere, collection of forest plant foods has been eclipsed by exchange of meat for corn, rice, and cultivated root crops. Fishing is usually important throughout the dry season, while collection of the starch of the caryota palm (*Caryota cumingii*) is common in the rainy season. An earlier paper (Estioko and Griffin 1975) gives some detail concerning the less settled Agta; both Bennagen (1976) and Peterson (1974, 1978*a,b*, n.d.) closely examine aspects of subsistence among Agta in the municipality of Palanan.

A brief review of Agta economic organization will be sufficient for later discussion of women's activities. Centuries ago all Agta may have been strictly hunter-gatherers. Since at least A.D. 1900 the groups near the towns of Casiguran (Headland and Headland 1974) and Palanan have been sporadic, part-time horticulturalists, supplementing wild plant foods with sweet potatoes, corn, cassava, and rice. The more remote, interior Agta, sometimes referred to as *ebuked* (Estioko and Griffin 1975), plant small plots of roots, a few square meters of corn, and a banana stalk or two. They usually plant only in the wet season, harvesting an almost immature crop when staples are difficult to obtain by trade. *Ebuked* neglect crop production, preferring to trade meat for grains and roots.

Lee and DeVore (1968:7) argue that women produce much of the typical hunter-gatherers' diet and that in the tropics vegetable foods far outweigh meat in reliability and frequency of consumption. The Dipags-anghang and Dianggu-Malibu Agta strikingly contradict this idea. They are superb hunters, eat animal protein almost daily, and, as noted above, may have both men and women hunting. (The Tasaday, to the south in Mindanao, may represent an extreme nonhunting adaptation, one in which plant food collection is very dominant [Yen 1976].) Hunting varies seasonally and by techniques used among various groups, but is basically a bow and arrow technology for killing wild pig and deer, the only large game in the Luzon dipterocarp forests. Monkey, although not large, is a reliable rainy season prey. Among Agta close to Palanan and Casiguran, hunting is a male domain. Many hunters pride themselves on skill with bow and arrow; less able hunters may use traps. Dogs to drive game are very desirable in the dry season when the forest is too noisy for daylight stalking of animals.

The collecting of wild plant food is not a daily task. Most Agta prefer to eat corn, cassava, and sweet potatoes, and neglect the several varieties of roots, palm hearts, and greens procurable in the forest. . . . Forest foods are difficult to collect, necessitate residence moves over long distances, and do not taste as good as cultivated foods. Emphasis of trade networks with lowland farmers favors

deemphasis of forest exploitation of plants. Only in the rainy season do Agta actively process a traditional resource, the sago-like caryota palm. Fruits are often picked on the spur of the moment; seldom do parties leave camp solely for their collection.

Trade with farmers is practiced by all Agta known to us. Rumors of Agta "farther into the mountains" who never trade (or cultivate) seem to be without substance. In the report of the Philippine Commission (1908:334), evidence of lowland-Agta trade around 1900 indicates the *ibay* trade partner relationship to have some antiquity. As the lowlander population has increased since World War II, trade has also increased. Agta are more and more dependent on goods and foodstuffs gained from farmers; adjustments of Agta economic behavior continue to be made, with labor on farms being one aspect of change. Agta formerly simply traded meat for carbohydrates. Around Palanan they may now work for cash or kind when residing close to farmers' settlements. Hunting decreases as the demands of cultivation are met. A cycle is created, and further withdrawal from forest subsistence occurs. Farmers live in areas once solely owned by Agta. Debts to farmers increase with economic dependence; freedom of mobility and choice of activity decrease; and Agta in farming areas become landless laborers.

At the same time, Agta seek to get out of the cycle by emulating the farmers. Many Agta within ten kilometers of Palanan Centro are attempting to become farmers themselves. While the success rate is slow, the attempt is real. Again, when questioned by an early American anthropologist, Agta close to Palanan Centro claimed to be planting small rainy season plots with corn, roots, and upland rice (Worcester 1912:841). Living informants confirm the long practice of cultivation, but suggest a recent expansion of Agta fields and commitment to abandoning forest nomadism (especially over the last fifteen years). Around the areas of Disuked-Dilaknadinum and Kahanayan-Diabut in Palanan, Agta are well known for their interest in swidden cultivation. Even the most unsettled Agta farther upriver claim small fields and sporadically plant along the rivers well upstream of lowland farmsteads.

The horticultural efforts of the Agta appear less than is the case, since the social organization and settlement patterns are very different from those of the farmers. Agta throughout Isabela and Cagayan are loosely organized into extended family residential groups. A group, called a *pisan*, is seldom less than two nuclear families and very rarely more than five (in the dry season—perhaps slightly higher average during the wet season). The nuclear family is the basic unit of Agta society, being potentially self-sufficient under usual circumstances. The residential group is organized as a cluster of nuclear families united either through a common parent or by sibling ties. Non-kin friends may be visitors for several weeks, and any nuclear family is able to leave and join another group of relatives at will.

As is typical of hunting-gathering societies, no formal, institutionalized authority base exists. The nuclear family is the decision maker concerning residence, work, and relations with other people. Older, respected individuals, often parents and grandparents of group members, may be consulted, but their opinions are not binding. Often group consensus is desired; people who disagree are free to grumble or to leave.

The settlement pattern is determined, in part, by the seasonal cycle of rains and sunny weather, and by these influences on the flora and fauna exploited for food. Rainy season flooding restricts forest travel, brings hardships in exchange, but is compensated by good condition of the game animals. The dry season permits travel over greater distances and into the remote mountains. Predictable fish resources enhance the advantages of human dispersal; only the need to carry trade meats to farmers inhibits distant residence placement.

WOMEN'S ACTIVITIES

Women participate in all the subsistence activities that men do. Women trade with farmers, fish in the rivers, collect forest plant foods, and may even hunt game animals. Tasks are not identical, however; a modest sexual division of labor does exist. Furthermore, considerable variation is found among the groups of Agta of Isabella and Cagayan provinces. These differences may possibly be ascribed to degree of adjustment of Agta to lowland Filipino culture. Some differences may be due to unique culture histories and to little contact.

Although in Isabela most Agta women do not hunt with bow and arrows, with machetes, or by use of traps, most are willing to assist men in the hunt. Not uncommonly, women help carry game out of the forest. Since mature pig and deer are heavy and the terrain is difficult, this is no small accomplishment. Even in areas around Palanan and Casiguran, women are known to accompany men and dogs into the forest and to guide the dogs in the game drive. Some women are famous for their abilities to handle dogs; one informant, a girl about fifteen years of age, was especially skilled. In Palanan and Casiguran, women and men laugh at the idea of women hunting. Such a practice would be a custom of wild, uncivilized Agta (*ebuked*) far in the mountains, they say. Many of the attributes of *ebuked* seem to be old-fashioned customs still practiced by interior groups.

Two groups studied as part of the present research do have women who hunt. Among the Dipagsanghang Agta, several mature women claim to have hunting skills; they learned these in their unmarried teen years. They only hunt under extreme circumstances, such as low food supplies or great distances from farmers and a supply of corn. All these Agta are found in southern Isabela between Dipagsanghang and Dinapiqui.

In the northernmost section of Isabela and well into Cagayan province, women are active and proficient hunters. While we have termed the Agta here as the Dianggu-Malibu group, we are actually referring to speakers of the southeast Cagayan dialect who live on the river drainage areas of the Dianggu and Malibu rivers.[2] Both the dialect and women who hunt are found over a considerably greater territory, according to informants, reaching north to Baggao, Cagayan, and at least to the Taboan River.

Among the Dianggu-Malibu women some variation, perhaps localized, perhaps personal, is found. On the Dianggu, some of the women questioned, and observed hunting, carried machetes and were accompanied by dogs. They claim to prefer the machete to the bow and arrow, allowing dogs to corner and hold pigs for sticking with the knife. Our sample of actual observations is too small to argue that only immature pigs are killed, but we do know that in the dry season adult male pigs are dangerous in the extreme. Dogs may be killed during hunts. Since Agta dogs are seldom strong animals, we wonder if mature pigs are acquired only occasionally. On the other hand, so many dogs are owned by these Agta that sheer numbers may favor large kills. We have observed two Agta women with as many as fifteen dogs. Other Dianggu women prefer the bow.

On the Malibu River, Agta women are expert bow and arrow hunters. On both of our brief visits to this group, women were observed hunting. They claim to use bows always, and they seek the full range of prey animals. Wild pig is most desired, while deer are often killed. Future work must quantify the hunting details, but women seem to vary slightly from men in their hunting strategies. Informants say they hunt only with dogs. On closer questioning they admit to knowing techniques that do not involve dogs—for example, they may climb trees and lie in wait for an animal to approach to feed on fallen fruit. Among all Agta, hunting practices vary considerably between the rainy and dry seasons. Our fieldwork in Malibu has been confined to the dry season, when dogs are important. In the rainy season solitary stalking is practiced. Field observations should eventually provide quantitative data on women hunting in this season; we must stress that our data are primarily from interview and brief observation. We have not resided among Cagayan Agta long enough to advance quantitatively based generalizations.

Women not only hunt but appear to hunt frequently. Like men, some enjoy hunting more than others. The more remotely located Agta seem most to favor hunting. Even among Agta certain males and females are considered lacking in initiative, a fault that may not be confined to hunting.

Informant data indicate that while women may make their own arrows, the actual blacksmithing of the metal projectile points is a male activity. More field research is necessary to confirm the universality of this detail. Other items of interest pertain to the composition of hunting parties. Most people in any one residence group are consanguineally or affinely related. We have observed several combinations of hunting parties. Men and women hunt together or among themselves. Often sisters, or mother and daughter, or aunt and niece hunt together. At Malibu, two sisters, co-wives of one male, hunt together, and either or both sisters join the husband to hunt. When young children exist, one of the two wives may stay at the residence while the husband and the other wife hunt and fish. Also, sisters and brothers cooperate on the hunt. A woman would not hunt with, for example, a cousin's husband unless the cousin were along.

The only real argument, in our opinion, that has been advanced to support the contention that women must gather and men hunt relates to childbearing and nurture. Among the Agta, during late pregnancy and for the first few months of nursing, a woman will not hunt. In spite of the small size of each residential group, however, some females seem always to be around to hunt, although one or more may be temporarily withdrawn from the activity. Women with young children hunt less than teenagers and older women. On the occasion of brief hunts—part of one day—children are cared for by older siblings, by grandparents, and by other relatives. Occasionally a father will tend a child. Only infants are closely tied to mothers.

Girls start hunting shortly after puberty. Before then they are gaining forest knowledge but are not strong. Boys are no different. We have no menopause data, but at least one woman known to us as a hunter must have passed childbearing age. She is considered an older woman, but since she is strong, she hunts. The pattern is typical of men also. As long as strength to travel and to carry game is retained, people hunt. Our best informant, a young grandmother, hunts several times a week.

Both Agta men and women fish. In fact, from early childhood until the infirmity of old age all Agta fish. If most adults are gone on a hunting trip for several days, the remaining adults and children must obtain animal protein by themselves. Only women in late pregnancy, with young infants, or into old age, withdraw from fishing, which makes considerable demands of endurance as well as skill. Some men excel at working in rough, deep, and cold waters. The everyday techniques for fishing are limited to underwater spear fishing. Glass-lensed wooden goggles, a heavy wire spear or rod varying according to size of fish sought, and an inner-tube rubber band complete the equipment. To fish, people simply swim underwater, seeking fish in the various aquatic environments known for each species. Girls in their teens are very capable at fishing. When fishing individually, women may be major contributors to the daily catch.

When group fishing is undertaken, a drive is conducted. In this operation, a long vine is prepared by attaching stones and banners of wild banana stalks. Two people drag the vine, one on each end and on opposite sides of the river, while the people in the water spear fish startled by the stones and stalks. Women join men in the drives, with older men and women dragging the vine while all able-bodied youths and adults work in the water.

Difficulty of fishing may be characterized as a gradient upon which men and women become less and less able as age and debilities increase. The elderly, when mobile, may still be productive, but instead of true fishing, their activities may be termed collecting. Both the coastal reef areas and freshwater rivers and streams have abundant shellfish, shrimp, and amphibians that may be caught by hand. Elderly women and grandchildren are especially eager to harvest these resources. Older men are not ashamed to follow suit, although the enthusiasm of others for the task seldom

gives old men incentive. Men are much less eager to give up riverine fishing after middle age than are women. Clearly some emphasis on males securing protein is found among Agta. Women, however, seem to have traditionally been active in fishing. Interestingly, as a few Agta adopt lowland fishing technology, especially nets, women seldom participate. Like their female counterparts in lowland society, women are deemed not appropriate in net fishing.

One might expect that, on the basis of worldwide comparison, tropic hunters would really be gatherers, and that women would be the steady and substantial providers. Agta do not fit the generalizations now accepted. Few Agta women regularly dig roots, gather palm hearts, seek fruit, or pick greens. Most Agta daily consume domesticated staples grown by the farmers. Women are, however, very knowledgeable concerning flora and its use, and among the less settled Agta, young girls are still taught all traditional forest lore. Brides-to-be among these Agta are partially evaluated on the basis of their knowledge, skill, and endurance in collecting jungle plant foods.

Roots are collected by women whenever more desirable food is unobtainable, when several wild pigs have been killed and the men want to eat "forest food" with pig fat, or when a visit to relatives or friends calls for a special treat. The interior groups may actually combine meat and wild roots for weeks when camped so far from farmers that exchange for corn is impossible. Downriver Agta consider such a practice a real hardship, not to be willingly endured. Men are known to dig roots, even though they say it is women's work. On long-distance hunts men do not as a rule carry food, and they may occasionally dig roots to alleviate the all meat-fish diet.

As hunting is thought of as a "sort of" male activity among many Agta (in Isabela), processing the starch of the caryota palm is a female activity. Women cruise the forest searching for trees containing masses of the starch; they also chop down the trees, split the trunks, adze out the pith, and extract the flour. Often parties of women and girls work together, speeding up the laborious task. On occasion, men will assist. Extracting the flour starch is moderately heavy work, and tiring. Husbands may help when wives have a pressing need to complete a task quickly. Since much of the final product is given in gift form, the need for haste occurs frequently. Perhaps most important to note is the male participation. Sexual division of labor is tenuously bounded among all Agta. Emphases may exist, but a man can even build a house (i.e., tie the fronds to the frame—a female task).

As noted at the beginning, trade, exchange, and horticulture are not new to Agta. Informants, early photographs, and writings indicate that all but the most remote Agta were not "pure" hunter-gatherers after about A.D. 1900. Since the mountains have been a final retreat—from the earliest Spanish attempts to conquer the Cagayan Valley until the present—Agta must have been in contact with former farmers/revolutionaries in hiding. Keesing (1962), summarizing the peoples of northern Luzon, documents several societies of pagan swiddeners adjacent to or in Negrito territory. The Palanan River drainage area was inhabited by farmers before Spanish contact in the sixteenth century. Doubtless, Agta have participated in economic exchange and social intercourse for centuries. Agta now have institutionalized trade partnerships, at least in Palanan and Casiguran municipalities. Trade partners are called *ibay* (Peterson [1978a,b] discussed the *ibay* relationship in detail), and partnerships may last between two families over two or more generations. *Ibay* exchange meat for grains and roots, or meat for cloth, metal, tobacco, beads, and other goods. Services may be exchanged, especially in downriver areas. Fields may be worked by Agta, who then borrow a carabao, receive corn or rice, and satisfy any of a number of needs. What is important in relation to this chapter is that Agta women may engage in *ibay* partnerships. Among the lowland farmers almost all *ibay* are males. An Agta woman may be an *ibay* with a lowland man. According to our data, an Agta husband often is not also *ibay* with his wife's *ibay*, but he must treat the farmer as he would his own *ibay*. Of course Agta men and women trade with any farmer they choose, but such exchange is without the consideration given to an *ibay*. (Considerations include credit, acts of friendship, and first choice/best deal on goods.) Not only do women have *ibay*, but they very frequently are the most active agents of exchange. In areas where the trade rests mostly on meat and where men do most of the hunting, women are likely to carry out the dried meat and bring back the staple. They therefore gain experience in dealing with the farmers. We should note that many farmers attempt to cheat the Agta by shortchanging them on counts or weights, but they do so on the basis of gullibility or naiveté of the Agta, not on the basis of sex. Agta women are actually more aggressive traders than are men, who do not like confrontation.

Among the Dipagsanghang Agta, women seldom hunt today, and infrequently dig roots. They do carry out meat to trade. They seem to have an easier life, with emphasis on corn, rice, and roots instead of gathering wild foods. However, downriver, close to farmers, Agta women have reversed this trend, and are working harder and longer hours.[3] Intensification of the *ibay* relationship and need to own and cultivate land has forced women to become horticulturalists and wage laborers for farmers. On their own family plots (family-owned, not male- or female-owned) they, together with adult males and youths, clear land, break soil, plant, weed, and harvest. When clearing virgin forest of large trees, women do not participate. They do clear secondary growth in fallowed fields.

In the families that reside close to Palanan . . . men and women work almost daily in the fields of farmers. Women go to the forest to collect the lighter raw materials for house construction, mats, betel chews, medicines, and so on. Men follow a similar pattern, giving up hunting for field labor and a corn and sweet potato diet supplemented by small fish. Again we see a remarkable parallel in the activities of males and females.

Looking more closely at specialized women's activities, one may suggest increasing importance in downriver areas. Women have several domains that they use to gain cash or kind income. As just stated, income from labor in fields adds to the economic power of women. A small-scale traditional pursuit, shared by men and women, is the gathering of copal, a tree resin common to trees (*Agathis philippinensis*) found scattered in the Sierra Madre. Women often collect and carry the resin out to lowland "middlemen," who sell it to the depot in town. While corn and cash may be sought in exchange, cloth is desired in order to make skirts. Medicine and medical treatments for ailing children may be paid for by copal collection. Another example of entrepreneurship by females is a small-scale mobile variety store effort. After working in fields for cash and building a surplus, families may cross the Sierra Madre to the towns of San Mariano, Cauayan, and Ilagan. There Agta, often women, purchase in markets and stores goods for use and resale in Palanan. Palanan Centro itself has no real market, only several small general stores selling goods at highly marked up prices. Since no road reaches Palanan, all manufactured supplies must enter town by airplane from Cauayan or boat from Baler. Freight costs are high. Some Agta women are very eager to hike outside to get tobacco, which always commands a high price and a ready market.

DISCUSSION

The role of women in Agta economic activities has been reviewed. Assessment of an hypothesized egalitarian position of women may be more difficult, and rests on assertions and interpretations drawn from the economic roles. First, drawing in part from Friedl (1975), an argument can be made that women in Agta society have equality with men because they have similar authority in decision making. The authority could be based on the equal contribution to the subsistence resources. Working back, we see that among many Agta, women do contribute heavily to the daily food supply, do perform maintenance tasks with men, and may initiate food

acquisition efforts through their own skills. They do control the distribution of their acquired food, sharing first with their own nuclear family and extended family, then trading as they see fit. They may procure nonfood goods as they desire. Men may do the same; generally spouses discuss what work to do, what needs should be satisfied, and who will do what. Whole residential groups frequently together decide courses of action. Women are as vocal and as critical in reaching decisions as are men. Further examples could strongly validate the hypothesis that women do supply a substantial portion of foods, and the assertion that women have authority in major decision making. Two questions arise. May we accept a causal relationship between percentage of food production and equality? Certainly there are cases to the contrary. According to Richard A. Gould (personal communication), Australian Aboriginal women in various areas collected the bulk of the food, yet remained less than equal (as we will define equality). Second, we may ask if Agta males and females are actually "equal."

Two avenues may suffice in answering this question. First, one might explore a definition of equality, surely a culturally loaded concept. Since Agta women have authority or control of the economic gain of their own labor, they may be equal in this critical domain. Equality must surely be equated with decision-making power and control of one's own production. The second avenue of equality validation by the scientist may be to examine the female's control over herself in noneconomic matters. These could include selection of marriage partner, lack of premarital sexual intercourse proscription, spacing of children, ease of divorce, and polygyny rules.

In marriage, two forms are typical of Agta. One, the less common, is elopement by young lovers. While such marriages admittedly are fragile, elopement is not uncommon. In this case both partners must be willing. Rape and abduction are rare. Rape by Agta men is not known to the authors. Abduction must involve a slightly willing female, and is not done by young people. A mature man might abduct a married woman, crossing the mountains to a safe locale. To abduct a young girl would be difficult. Parents of eloping couples may be enraged, but usually reconcile themselves to the marriage. If the newlyweds stay together, no more is made of it.

The proper form of marriage is one arranged by customary meetings and discussions, as well as exchange of goods between two families. Often neither the bride nor the groom has had much say in the matter, although serious dislike by either would probably kill the negotiations before the marriage. Mothers are the most important in choosing who will marry whom. Even when their children are young, they are looking about for good partners. Word filters around when a young girl is marriageable, and efforts are made to get the appropriate young man and his family into negotiations before an undesirable family appears. Once any family with a prospective groom formally asks, a rejection is given only for strong and good reasons, since the denied family loses considerable face and may be angry enough to seek revenge.[1]

Criteria for choice of a marriage partner are varied. Often a young man in his early twenties marries a girl about fifteen. Girls entering marriage before puberty are not uncommon. In such cases the husband may help raise the girl until the time the marriage is consummated and full wifehood is recognized. Other combinations are seen. One much discussed case was the marriage of a woman in her forties to a man in his mid-twenties. The couple seemed very happy, with the wife paying rather special attention to her husband. The man's mother, a friend of the wife's, decided that the marriage was peculiar but acceptable.

Premarital female chastity is not an idea of much currency. Agta close to farmers will pay lip service to the idea, but should a girl become pregnant she will take a husband. There are no illegitimate Agta children, although an occasional rape of an Agta by a lowland male may produce a child. Since by the time a girl is fertile she likely will be married, illegitimacy is not the issue. Although some data are difficult to collect concerning sex, almost certainly girls are able to engage in sexual activity with relative ease; promiscuity is not favored in any circumstance. Males may have as little or great difficulty in engaging in sex as females. The Agta are widely dispersed in extended family groups; hence appropriate sexual partners are seldom seen. No homosexuality is known to exist.

Agta gossip suggests that many Agta, male and female, married and unmarried, constantly carry on extramarital sexual relations. This may be a function of gossip, and a gross exaggeration. Whatever reality, neither males nor females seem to be especially singled out for criticism.

Women say they space their children. The practice certainly varies hugely from person to person, as does fecundity and luck in keeping children alive. The Agta use various herbal concoctions that supposedly prevent conception, cause abortions shortly after conception, and have several functions related to menstruation. These medicines are known to all Agta and are frequently used. Our census data indicate that some women seem to be successful in spacing births. Other cases note high infant mortality yet no infanticide, female or male. All Agta abhor the idea.

Divorce is infrequent among Agta, with elopement being more prone to failure than are arranged marriages. Divorce does happen often enough, however, for us to look at the causes and relate them to an inquiry into female equality. First, either sex may divorce the other with equal ease. Agta have no possessions. Some gift giving between the two families establishes the marriage, but most of the gifts are food. Cloth, kettles, and minor items make up the rest. Return of marriage gifts is unlikely. Spouses simply take their personal possessions and return to the residential group of close relatives.

Causes for divorce are mainly laziness or improvidence, excessive adultery, or personality clashes and incompatibility, usually caused by a combination of the first two conditions. Skill and success in subsistence activities is of primary importance to marriage. While some Agta are less industrious and less skilled than others, all Agta expect a mate to work hard at all appropriate tasks. Should a male fail, divorce is likely. Occasionally, very young couples experience extra difficulties. These may be accentuated by displeased parents of either party.

Polygamy is not found in most of Isabela. Census data collected to date reveal only monogamy or serial monogamy. That is, spouses may be divorced or widow(er)ed several times in a lifetime. In Cagayan the data are incomplete but startling. Probably some of the strongest support for the equality of women hypothesis, when added to the facts of women as hunters, comes from a study of Agta polygamy. We noted earlier that two co-wives, sisters, hunted together in Malibu. South of Malibu at Blos, another husband and two sisters/co-wives arrangement was found. In the same residential unit we recorded a woman residing with her two co-husbands. They were not brothers; one was older than the wife, one younger. The other women considered this arrangement as humorous, but acceptable. An insight into the male sexual jealousy found in many societies worldwide is the comment of a Palanan Agta man. This old man, when told of the polyandrous marriage to the north, thought for a moment and commented, "Well, perhaps one man with two wives is OK, but a woman with two husbands? I find that totally bad." The women laughed at him.

NOTES

1. Although the authors have worked among the Agta about fourteen months, visits to the northerly group in the Dianggu-Malibu area have been brief. The practice of women hunting was first observed during a survey trip in 1972. We again visited the Dianggu group in 1975. In August 1978 we returned for one week to Dianggu and Malibu, where we verified in greater detail the subsistence activities of women. Data were collected using the Palanan Agta dialect and Ilokano.
2. Dianggu and Malibu are river names used by Agta and nearby Malay Filipinos. On the

Board of Technical Surveys and Maps (Lobod Point, Philippines), the Dianggu is named the Lobod and the Malibu is named the Ilang.
3. Peterson (n.d.) argues that "downriver" Agta women are highly variable in their devotion to labor, older women being hardworking and young mothers not at all industrious.
4. Thomas Headland tells us that rejection of a prospective spouse may be a less serious matter among Casiguran Agta than among those we know.

REFERENCES

Bennagen, Ponciano. 1976. Kultura at Kapaligiran: Pangkulturang Pagbabago at Kapanatagan ng mga Agta sa Palanan, Isabela. M. A. thesis, Department of Anthropology, University of the Philippines, Diliman, Quezon City.

Briggs, Jean L. 1974. Eskimo women: makers of men. In *Many sisters: women in cross-cultural perspective*, ed. Carolyn J. Matthiasson, pp. 261–304. New York: Free Press.

Estioko, Agnes A., and P. Bion Griffin. 1975. The *Ebuked* Agta of northeastern Luzon. *Philippines Quarterly of Culture and Society* 3(4):237–44.

Flannery, Regina. 1932. The position of women among the Mescalero-Apache. *Primitive Man* 10:26–32.

———. 1935. The position of women among the eastern Cree. *Primitive Man* 12:81–86.

Fox, Robert B. 1952. The Pinatubo Negritos, their useful plants and material culture. *Philippine Journal of Science* 81:113–414.

Friedl, Ernestine. 1975. *Women and men: an anthropologist's view*. New York: Holt, Rinehart and Winston.

Garvan, John M. 1964. *The Negritos of the Philippines*, ed. Hermann Hochegger, Weiner beitrage zur kulturgeschichte und linguistik, vol. 14. Horn: F. Berger.

Goodale, Jane C. 1971. *Tiwi wives: a study of the women of Melville Island, north Australia*. Seattle, Wash.: University of Washington Press.

Gough, Kathleen. 1975. The origin of the family. In *Toward an anthropology of women*, ed. Rayna R. Reiter, pp. 51–76. New York: Monthly Review Press.

Hammond, Dorothy, and Alta Jablow. 1976. *Women in cultures of the world*. Menlo Park, Calif.: Benjamin/Cummings.

Harako, Reizo. 1976. The Mbuti as hunters—a

study of ecological anthropology of the Mbuti pygmies. *Kyoto University African Studies* 10:37–99.

Headland, Thomas, and Janet D. Headland. 1974. *A Dumagat (Casiguran)–English dictionary*. Pacific Linguistics Series C. No. 28. Australian National University, Canberra: Linguistics Circle of Canberra.

Howell, F. Clark. 1973. *Early man*, rev. ed. New York: Time-Life Books.

Isaac, Glynn L. 1969. Studies of early culture in East Africa. *World Archaeology* 1:1–27.

———. 1971. The diet of early man: aspects of archaeological evidence from lower and middle Pleistocene sites in Africa. *World Archaeology* 2:278–98.

———. 1978. The food-sharing behavior of proto-human hominids. *Scientific American* 238(4): 90–109.

Jenness, Diamond. 1922. *The Life of the Copper Eskimos. Report of the Canadian Arctic Expedition 1913–1918*, vol. XII, pt. 9. Ottawa: Acland.

Keesing, Felix. 1962. *The ethnohistory of northern Luzon*. Stanford, Calif.: Stanford University Press.

Lancaster, Jane B. 1978. Carrying and sharing in human evolution. *Human Nature* 1(2):82–89.

Landes, Ruth. 1938. *The Ojibwa Woman*. New York: Columbia University Press.

Lee, Richard B. and Irven DeVore. 1968. Problems in the study of hunters and gatherers. In *Man the hunter*, ed. Lee and DeVore. Chicago: Aldine.

———. 1976. *Kalahari hunter-gatherers: studies of the !Kung San and their neighbors*. Cambridge, Mass.: Harvard University Press.

Maceda, Marcelino M. 1964. *The culture of the mamanuas (northeast Mindanao) as compared with that of the other Negritos of Southeast Asia*. Manila: Catholic Trade School.

Marshall, Lorna. 1976. *The !Kung of Nyae Nyae*. Cambridge, Mass.: Harvard University Press.

Martin, M. Kay, and Barbara Voorhies. 1975. *Female of the species*. New York: Columbia University Press.

Peterson, Jean Treloggen. 1974. An ecological perspective on the economic and social behavior of Agta hunter-gatherers, northeastern Luzon, Philippines. Ph.D. dissertation, University of Hawaii at Manoa.

———. 1978*a*. Hunter-gatherer farmer exchange. *American Anthropologist* 80:335–51.

———. 1978*b*. The ecology of social boundaries: Agta foragers of the Philippines. *Illinois Studies in Anthropology No. 11*. University of Illinois, Urbana-Champaign, Ill.

———. n.d. Hunter mobility, family organization and change. In *Circulation in the Third World*, ed. Murray Chapman and Ralph Mansell Prothero. London: Routledge & Kegan Paul.

Philippine Commission. 1908. *8th Annual Report of the Philippine Commission: 1907*. Bureau of Insular Affairs, War Department. Washington, D.C.: Government Printing Office.

Quinn, Naomi. 1977. Anthropological studies on women's status. In *Annual review of anthropology*, ed. Bernard J. Siegel, pp. 181–225. Palo Alto, Calif.: Annual Reviews.

Reiter, Rayna R., ed. 1975. *Toward an anthropology of women*. New York:Monthly Review Press.

Rosaldo, Michelle Zimbalist, and Louise Lamphere, eds. 1974. *Woman, culture and society*. Stanford, Calif.: Stanford University Press.

Slocum, Sally. 1975. Woman the gatherer: male bias in anthropology. In *Toward an anthropology of women*, ed. Rayna R. Reiter, pp. 36–50. New York: Monthly Review Press.

Tanner, Nancy, and Adrienne Zihlman. 1976. Women in evolution. Part I: Innovations and selection in human origins. *Signs: Journal of Women in Culture and Society* 1:585–608.

Tanno, Tadashi. 1976. The Mbuti net-hunters in the Ituri Forest, Eastern Zaire—their hunting activities and band composition. *Kyoto University African Studies* 10:101–35.

Turnbull, Colin M. 1965. *Wayward servants: the two worlds of the African pygmies*. Garden City, NY: Natural History Press.

Vanoverberg, Maurice. 1925. Negritos of northern Luzon. *Anthropos* 20:148–99.

———. 1929–30. Negritos of northern Luzon again. *Anthropos* 24:1–75, 897–911; 25:25–71, 527–656.

———. 1937–38. Negritos of eastern Luzon. *Anthropos* 32:905–28; 33:119–64.

Washburn, Sherwood L., and C. S. Lancaster. 1968. The evolution of hunting. In *Man the hunter*, ed. Richard B. Lee and Irven DeVore, pp. 293–303. Chicago: Aldine.

Worcester, Dean C. 1912. Head-hunters of northern Luzon. *National Geographic* 23(9):833–930.

Yen, D. E. 1976. The ethnobotany of the Tasaday: III. Note on the subsistence system. In *Further studies on the Tasaday*, ed. D. E. Yen and John Nance. Makati, Rizal: PANAMIN Foundation Research Series No. 2.

Woman's Day Among the Mundurucú

Robert Murphy and Yolanda Murphy

Dawn came first as a shift of light and shadow in the eastern sky, etching out of the blackness of the night the outline of the hills on the watershed of the rivers. With it, the forest fell silent, the raucous noises of the night creatures faded, and the great quietude separating the life of the night from that of the day reached its brief ascendancy. As the eastern sky turned a dark, then a lighter, gray, the houses of the Mundurucú village of Cabruá began to emerge from shadows into pale images, and the first stirring of the people was heard.

Borai tossed in her hammock, wrapped it tightly around and snuggled her baby closely against the chill dawn. The child began to whimper, and she took a breast from under her worn dress and placed it by his mouth. While he suckled, Borai lay half-asleep, gazing out through the space between the walls and roof of the house, watching the light strengthen in the east. The eight-month-old baby finished feeding, fell back to sleep, and Borai gently disengaged herself from it and eased out of her warm cocoon into the cold of the wakening house. She yawned and stretched, scratched herself luxuriantly, and then kicked at the dogs nestled around the smoldering household fire.

The earth around the hearth was still warm, and she stood close to it, warming the bottoms of her feet. Borai then took some kindling and placing it next to the fire, took a still glowing end of a piece of wood from last night's fire and blew it into flame. She placed the kindling carefully around the small flame, like spokes about a hub, and when the fire

crackled into life, brought over larger pieces of firewood to prepare for the day's cooking. She swung rather halfheartedly with a piece of firewood at the lingering dogs, chasing them out of the house, and then went to stand at the back door, pensively watching the breaking day.

The sky in the east had by then turned to delicate and striated bands of mauve and pink, and the land in the valley below was beginning to appear from the gloom. The hills beyond the headwaters of the river could now be seen in sharp relief, and the islands of forest in the rolling savannah appeared as dark blotches, their trees gaining distinction as the light grew stronger. The valleys were still covered with the mist of the dawn, and small pockets of fog moved slowly across the faces of the hills. It was a calm and serene period, and the other women of the house only spoke to each other in whispers, lest the stillness of the natural world be torn by human beings.

The life of the village gained momentum as the natural order of the day asserted itself. Before the sun had edged over the horizon, a rooster crowed from somewhere in the underbrush bordering the village, another in the brush near the *farinha*-making shed answered, and the morning litany of cock-crowing was joined by the first snarling fight of dogs competing for a shred of tapir intestine outside the village. In the men's house many of the men were stirring, though a few were still lying in their hammocks, their feet dangling over the small fires they had built beneath. Most of them planned to hunt that day, and they were already testing bow strings and sighting down arrow shafts for straightness. Others squatted by a fire to discuss where to hunt, passing from one to another the single cigarette one of them had rolled.

Reprinted with permission from Robert Murphy and Yolanda Murphy, *Women of the Forest* (New York: Columbia University Press, 1985), pp. 1–20.

Borai's husband, Kaba, broke away from the group of men and came to the house. He sat on a log that served as a seat, and Borai brought him a half gourd of farinha, flour made from bitter manioc, mixed with water. He tilted the container back, pushing the farinha toward his mouth with a hunting knife, and passed it back to her when he had finished. Borai had warmed up, over the fire, two monkey legs left from the previous night's dinner, and she passed one of the legs over to him with a small gourd of salt. He dipped the scrawny and heat-shriveled meat in the salt between each bite, washed it down with water, and went back to join the gathering hunting party. Few words had been exchanged. The baby had a slight cold; Kaba asked how he had spent the night, and he played with the child for a short time before leaving.

Borai's older son by a previous marriage, a boy of twelve, arrived from the men's house for food and water, but left quickly to join the other boys, who were planning a day of stalking fish with bow and arrow in a nearby stream. The boys would roast the small fish near the stream and eat palm fruits, so she did not expect to see him again until the men began to return from the hunt, bringing the boys out of the forest to examine the day's kill. The baby having begun to cry, she picked him out of the hammock and gave him the breast again, then passed the child to her sister's ten-year-old daughter, who put the now squalling baby in a carrying sling passed around her shoulder, forming a seat for the baby on her narrow hip. Freed of her burden, Borai gnawed on monkey bones, took some farinha and water, and then went off some 200 feet from the village to relieve herself. Three thin and mangy dogs, not suited for hunting and thus reduced to scavenging garbage and human waste, followed her, sat patiently on their haunches, and waited.

The sun had cleared the hills and the house was in full motion when Borai returned. Children were laughing, crying, and shouting, emerging from their houses to wander through the village and explore the other four dwellings. Wherever the little ones went,

they were offered a bit of food and fondled, for in this village of ninety people, every child was well known to each adult, and most of them were related in ways that people could not quite specify, however much they categorized their kinship ties. The men by this time had left the village, winding single file down the path that led from the grass-covered hill into the still mist-shrouded forests bordering the stream below. The column of hunters passed out of sight, but the women and children could still hear the barks of the hunting dogs and the deep sounds of the horns of the hunters signaling to each other, ever more faintly until only the low murmur of village life broke the calm that had settled on the community.

As the sun rose, it evaporated the mists, driving away the cool of the dawn and touching the village with a promise of the oppressive heat of midday. It was May, and though the worst of the rains had passed from the uplifted drainage south of the Amazon River, the air remained humid, and afternoon thunderstorms were still frequent. But the streams had receded to the confines of their banks, their waters had cleared, and the small rivulets of the high savannahs flowed cool through the tunnels of forest they watered. The women of Borai's house—her mother, two sisters, the wife of one of her brothers, and a maternal cousin of her mother—gathered up their gourd water containers and, bidding the children to follow, went down to the stream below. As the procession wound through the village and past the back doors of other houses, more women joined them, calling out to each other, while the little children ran down the grassy hill, playing as they went; the boys were empty-handed, but their small sisters carried their own little gourds. As they neared the stream, the older boys finished their morning swim and began to work their way downstream to one of the better fishing holes.

The smallest children, who were naked, ran into the water with shrieks of glee, while their older sisters shucked off their thin dresses and followed them. The older women eased into the stream, taking off their clothes as the water rose higher on their bodies. The water was stinging cold at first, but they soon became accustomed to it, ducking under the surface and splashing each other happily. The women rubbed their bodies with the water and scrubbed the backsides of the smallest children to clean them. They splashed about for another half hour and then slipped on their cotton Mother Hubbard dresses and sat in the sun to warm and dry.

Their ablutions done, the women filled the water gourds, and most started back up the hill to the village. A few stayed behind to wash clothes, dipping them in the water, rubbing their folds against each other, and smacking the wet clothing against flat rocks. Last week, the village had run out of the soap they had gotten from the trader, but most of the dirt was washed out without it. Borai had only two dresses, the one she was wearing and the one being washed; Kaba had promised her another after he had sold some rubber to the trader during the coming months of the dry season.

The washing done, the remainder of the women returned to the village together. Both propriety and fear of lone and wandering males kept any from remaining behind, forcing them to stay in small groups on almost any venture beyond the immediate vicinity of the village. Back at the house, Borai hung her tattered wash on a small cotton bush near the back door and began to clean up garbage, which she simply threw in the underbrush, from the cleared area around the house. She started to sweep out the house with a broom improvised from a few branches, but the baby began to cry in earnest, and she took him from her niece. This time, however, instead of offering the breast to the child, she mashed up a piece of banana with a chunk of boiled sweet manioc and spooned it into his mouth. She then put the baby in its carrying sling and swept the floor in a rather desultory way with one hand, while stroking the baby with the other. One of her sisters joined in the housecleaning, and they swept the remains out the door, where a tame parrot and two hens immediately began to pick through the trash for pieces of grain and fruit. The women watched

in amusement as the hens tried unsuccessfully to drive off the parrot, who reared back in outrage and squawked at the menacing fowl. The sisters then sat in their hammocks and talked to their mother about the day's work ahead; housekeeping in the large, uncompartmented, and dirt-floored dwellings was the least of their chores.

The sun had risen full into the morning sky, but the peak of the day's heat was still four hours away, making most of the women anxious to get their garden work done. The supply of manioc flour in the house had already been eaten, and for the last two days the women of Borai's house had been drawing on the larders of their neighbors. Borai's mother went to the open-walled shed in the middle of the village where manioc flour was made, and began to build a fire in the large earth-walled oven on which the farinha was toasted. She directed her three daughters to fetch tubers from the stream, where they had been soaking in water for the past three days, and sent her daughter-in-law for more firewood. The daughter-in-law put an axe in her carrying basket, which she carried on her back with a bark-cloth tump-line hung across her forehead, and went through the village to ask her cousin to come help her. Borai and her sister stopped at another house to tell the women where they were going and enlisted the support of two of the occupants. The four then set out for the stream on a path which took them well below the area where they bathed and drew water, and they began to load their baskets with the softened, almost crumbling, manioc tubers. The children had been left with their grandmother, allowing the women to take another, more leisurely, bath and to discuss some of the shortcomings of their sister-in-law.

The carrying baskets were heavy with the water-laden manioc, and they squatted in a genuflecting position with their backs to the baskets, passed the tumplines across their foreheads, and slowly stood up, using the full strength of their torsos and necks to lift the burdens. The sun was beating down on the path as they made their way laboriously back up the hill to the village, walking in silence to conserve their strength. Arriving at the farinha shed, they gratefully dropped their loads into a long hollowed-out log used as a tub and sat down in the shade to rest. Borai's baby began crying as soon as he saw her, quickly escaping from his older cousin to crawl through the dirt to his mother. She nursed him, more for comfort than food, and then let him crawl back and forth across her lap. The sister-in-law and her helper returned from the garden, where they had gathered felled, but unburned, wood and chopped it into stove lengths, and dumped the contents of their baskets next to the farinha oven. They too sat in the shade against one of the shed uprights and joined the conversation. Three other women drifted across the weed-choked village plaza to help, and to tell of their own plans to make farinha in two days' time.

The work party having increased to eight, the women decided that the dull and laborious chore could be put off no longer. Borai and her mother stepped into the trough filled with soft manioc and began to walk back and forth, working their feet up and down, to break up the tubers and separate the pulp from the skins. As they worked, the water oozed out of the broken tubers, mixed with the pulp into a thick mass, and squished rather pleasurably between their toes. Another woman began picking out the skins and throwing them to one side. The sister-in-law and her cousin went off to the old garden for more firewood, and three of the other women went down to the stream to get more manioc. One woman remained seated in the shade, helping Borai's niece in keeping the children from underfoot.

Despite the tedium of the work, the conversation in the farinha shed never slowed. Borai's mother brought up the possibility that the trader might pay a visit to the village in the near future, a story she had heard from the wife of a young man who had been visiting on the Tapajós River. One woman added that is seemed to make little difference whether he arrived or not, as he rarely brought very much desirable merchandise. Another commented that on his last visit the trader had brought nothing but *cachaça,* the regional cane rum,

and that the men had exhausted all their credit in becoming thoroughly drunk. Borai's mother reminded the critic that she, too, had drunk her fair share of the trader's rum on that occasion, and the onlookers dissolved in laughter. Given the fact that many of the women had drunk as much as the men would let them have, the subject was quickly turned to the men. One of the chief topics of conversation at the time was the visit in the village of a young man, who was in a late stage of courtship of one of the village's girls. The progress of the romance was carefully examined by the group in the farinha shed, and the young man's merits mercilessly evaluated. One of the women noted that the suitor had a small penis, bringing forth the sour remark that he was not much different from the other men. At least, said another, his penis showed more life than those of most of the other men. The women laughed and all looked over with amusement toward the men's house, where two or three occupants still lingered. The men, aware of the derision, became furiously intent on whatever they were doing, their eyes turned carefully away from the farinha shed.

In the meantime, the work was progressing at a slow and steady pace. Large wads of wet pulp were taken from the trough and placed in the open end of a *tipití*. The tipití was a long tube made of loosely woven palm leaves, with an open mouth at the top and closed at the bottom. The top end was suspended from a rafter, and a long pole was placed through a loop at the bottom. Two of the women sat on the end of the pole, the other end of which was secured near the ground, and the resultant lever pulled powerfully downward on the tipití. This caused it to elongate and constrict, squeezing out the water from the pulp and leaving the contents still moist, ready to be sieved. When only a dribble of water came from the tipití, the women emptied the pulp into a large sieve placed over a shallow basin and gently worked it through the mesh with their fingers. It dropped into the receptacle as a coarse, damp cereal, and the pieces that did not go through were taken by another of the women and pounded with a wooden mortar and pestle.

The day's production of farinha would not last the household much more than a week, and the women agreed that they should put more tubers in the water to soak. Borai and three of the other women took their carrying baskets and machetes and headed out of the village to the gardens. They followed a path from the village plaza that passed in back of one of the houses. The path narrowed through the dense underbrush surrounding the village and emerged suddenly into the open savannah. The land ahead rolled gently. The sandy soil was covered with clumps of short grass and small flowering shrubs, and here and there were small islands of trees, some of which marked the sites of old and abandoned villages. These were easily identified by the scattered fruit palms in their midsts, the end products of palm pits thrown away decades ago. As the women walked single file along the narrow path worn through the grasses, they commented on almost everything they saw—a pair of doves cooing in a distant grove, a parrot flying from one tree clump to another, the activity around a termite hill, a curious cloud formation.

The trail entered suddenly into the forest and dropped to a small stream that bubbled among rocks. A log served as a bridge across the water, but the women stopped to bathe before going on to the garden. The path wound for a while among very tall trees, whose leafy branches almost 100 feet above kept out the sunlight and left the forest floor clear of underbrush. As the trail rose, it became lighter and the underbrush became thicker, for they were entering a tract that had been farmed many years ago and was still under the cover of lower, secondary forest. Shadow gave way to brightness, dark greens to light hues, and coolness to heat as the women broke out of the forest and into the garden.

The garden was no more than two acres in extent, and along with two other producing gardens provided the main source of vegetable food for the household. This garden had been cleared two years earlier and was yielding only manioc on its second planting. One of the women, however, spotted a pineapple growing among the weeds and picked it for her children to eat. The garden was rank with weeds and, since no further planting would be done in it, nobody bothered any longer to keep it cleared. To the women, it looked like any other garden, though an outsider would see nothing more than stumps, felled and charred tree trunks lying at various angles, and a clutter of undergrowth. Most of the higher vegetation, however, was bitter manioc, the tall stalks of which had grown to six feet and over.

The women set to their harvest work, taking the machetes from their baskets and cutting the manioc stalks near their bases. They put the stalks aside, and then proceeded to dig out the tubers clustered at the base of each stalk, like fingers from a hand, with the machetes. Each plant yielded two to five tubers, ranging in size from six inches to over a foot in length; if the manioc had been left in the ground to grow for a few months longer, some would reach a length of two feet or so. After knocking the dirt from the manioc, the tubers were put in the baskets. Before going back, the women made a brief reconnoiter of the garden in search of more pineapples or an unharvested squash. Unsuccessful, they took up their burdens and, with another stopover for a drink of water, went directly to the stream near the village where they put the manioc in a quiet pool to soak.

By the time this chore was done, the sun was almost directly overhead, and the morning breezes had died completely. The village lay beaten down by the sun, quiet and somnolent under the noonday heat. The roosters and chickens were not to be seen, and the few dogs remaining in the village were lying in the shade. One of the men in the men's house was still working on a basket, but the other two had retired to their hammocks in its shady recesses. Borai and her companions went to the farinha shed, where she found her baby crying lustily from hunger. She sat in the shade to nurse him, while watching her mother and another woman slowly turning and stirring the manioc flour, which was being toasted on a copper griddle above the furnace. The women each had a canoe paddle which they used as a spatula to prevent the manioc from burning on the pan and to turn under the flour on top to expose it again to the heat. It would take well over an hour for each panful to become dry and toasted brown, and other women took up the task at intervals of about fifteen minutes to relieve the heat-parched workers.

As the work dragged on, most of its preliminary phases, such as bringing in the manioc, mashing it, running the pulp through the tipití, and sieving the resulting mash, were already largely completed, and many of the helpers from the other houses had drifted away to escape the heat of the oven. Borai was hungry after her morning's work and she went to the dwelling, where she put the baby in her hammock. One of her sisters had cooked some plantains in the coals of the fire and offered her some, and Borai rounded out the meal with manioc mixed with a drink made of palm fruit. She then lay down in the hammock to rest with her child and almost immediately fell into a light sleep.

Borai drowsed in the heavy heat of the afternoon and finally awakened after the baby's fitfulness had turned into crying. She fed him and then went out to the farinha shed, where she gave the baby to one of the young girls and took a turn at toasting the manioc flour. The rest of the farinha-making process was now completed, but two five-gallon cans filled with damp sieved pulp remained to be put on the griddle, and it would be almost dark before they were finally done. Though only one or two women at a time were required for the work, others drifted out from the houses to join in the conversation. The sun was already halfway between its zenith and the horizon, and dark cumulus clouds were beginning to build up in the west. The breezes freshened as the storm approached, dispelling the heat and lifting everybody from their afternoon torpor. One of the women suggested that it was time to get water for the evening meal, and the group scattered to their houses to gather up gourds and children. Some twenty of them trooped down to the stream to bathe off the day's sweat and to immerse themselves in the cold stream, lolling in it until their

teeth chattered and they had to seek the warmth of a sun-bathed rock.

From the distance, still deep back in the forest, the faint sound of a horn was heard, followed a short time later by another, somewhat closer. The women quickly filled the water containers and shooed the children ahead of them as they hurried to get back to the village before the hunting party. The storm, too, was approaching, and the silence of the forest and savannahs was broken by still remote rumbles of thunder. Borai went to her house and placed more wood on the fire, put the baby in the hammock, and waited for the return of her husband.

The hunters split up just outside the village and took the separate paths that led to the back entrances of their houses. Borai was waiting there when Kaba walked through the door carrying a wild pig, weighing about 100 pounds, across his shoulders. He dropped the pig to the floor, put his bow and arrow on a platform under the rafters, and sat to wait for Borai to bring him a half gourd of water and manioc. She commented on the fatness of the wild pig, asking her husband where he had taken it. "We cornered the herd at a crossing of the River of the Wild Turkey, not far from the Cabruá River and at a place where there are still ripe *buriti* palm fruit," he replied. "The arrow of my brother Warú hit this one in the flank, and I brought him down with another over the heart." He went on to tell Borai that four pigs had been killed before the herd broke and ran, and individual hunters had also taken two monkeys, an agouti, and a paca. One of the dogs had been gashed by a boar, but the wound would probably heal. It had been a good hunt.

Kaba saw two men leave the men's house for the stream and hurried after them to take a bath before the storm hit. The other women of Borai's house joined with her in butchering the wild pig. They took long knives, finely honed on smooth rocks, and drew incisions down the stomach and along the legs. Two of them then carefully pulled back the hide, cutting the gristle at points where it stuck the flesh. The skin was stretched out with sticks and hung up outside to dry and cure for later sale to the trader. The pig was then sliced through the ventral section to the viscera, the intestines removed and thrown outside to the ravenously hungry dogs. They fell on it ferociously, snarling and fighting while they gulped down whole chunks of the offal. The rest of the pig was quartered, the head and neck put aside as a fifth portion. Pieces of meat were then taken by the women to all the houses in the village, and by the time the usual reciprocity had been observed, almost a whole wild pig was ready for cooking in each dwelling.

The fire was now burning strongly, and Borai half filled a bell-bottomed ceramic pot with water and placed it in the center of the hearth, the flames licking up its sides. As the water heated, she cut a hind quarter of pig into chunks, which she placed in the pot for the evening meal. When the water came toward a boil, she threw in several pinches of salt. Her mother and one of the young girls, in the meanwhile, were cracking Brazil nuts and grating their meats, throwing the fragrant and milky pulp into the pot. The women then sat by the fire, stirring the pot, savoring the smells, and talking happily about the excellence of the meat. The men had by this time returned from their baths and were resting in their hammocks in the men's house, recalling events in the day's hunt, and laughing at some of their misadventures.

The sky had now turned completely dark, though there was still an hour and a half before the sun would set, and a cool breeze blew in advance of the storm. Suddenly the storm struck, with brilliant flashes of lightning and sharp claps of thunder which reverberated off the hills across the valley. The rain fell in sheets, the wind driving it into the open sides of the men's house, forcing some of the occupants to move further into the back and others to run for the walled dwelling houses. The roofs all leaked in places, but the residents had already arranged their hammocks and belongings in dry locations, and nobody paid much attention to the puddles forming on the floor. Borai's mother, nonetheless, took the occasion to ask her sons-in-law when they

were going to build a new village. "The roofs are old and leak, the house poles creak in the wind, and one of the children was almost bitten by a scorpion in the underbrush," she said. "Do we have to wait until our gardens are a half-day's walk away before you men decide to move?" Kaba stared intently at his toes and muttered that they were talking about building another village during the next rainy season. There was no time now, for soon after the next full moon most of the people would be leaving to collect rubber on the larger rivers. Enjoying his discomfiture, the old woman reminded him that this is what the men had said last year and then went back to stirring the pot.

The front of the storm had passed, the wind died down, and the rain became lighter. Several of the men wandered back from the dwellings of the women to the men's house and climbed into their hammocks under the shelter of the overhanging roof. Many of the little boys trailed after them to play among the hammocks, and one three-year-old girl toddled along, too; her father took her into his hammock and played with her while talking to the other men. Everybody was in good spirits. There was enough food in the village for at least two days, the rain had made the day's end cool, and the smells of cooking wild pig occasionally wafted over from the houses. The men chatted with each other from their hammocks, and, in one, three teenage boys were rolling about in obvious sex play, unnoted by the adults.

In the houses, the boiled meat was now cooked, and Borai took a large gourd, filled it with meat and broth, while one of her sisters filled another with freshly made farinha. They brought them across the plaza to the cleared area in front of the men's house, where Kaba took them and called to the other men. Other women were bringing food to their husbands, too, and the men, with most of the boys squatting around them, sat on their haunches in a ring about the bowls. The men took spoons and scooped up meat and broth from the common bowls, occasionally dipping their hands into the farinha bowls and throwing the manioc flour into their mouths with quick tosses. The hunters were hungry after a long day with little more than farinha and water and ate steadily, but quietly and soberly; boisterous and noisy behavior while eating would offend the spirit protectors of the game animals. Other spirits had to be appeased, too, and one of the men took a gourd of meat into the closed chamber adjoining the men's house, where he offered the meat to the ancestral spirits, saying, "Eat grandfathers, and make me lucky in the hunt." The offering made, he brought the bowl of meat back out and placed it with the others.

After the meal had been cooked, the women of Borai's house placed a babricot over the fire. This consisted of a tripod with a horizontal rack of green wood strips running across it a foot from the base. The remaining meat was placed on the babricot, where it would slowly roast and smoke until bedtime. The meat would then be removed, but it would be placed over a low fire again in the morning to complete the cooking process and prevent rotting. One of the women stayed by the fire to turn the meat occasionally and to hit any dogs that approached it. The other women, and the girls and little boys, sat around the pot of boiled meat, filling little half gourds with the stew and eating. The meat was tender, and the sauce of broth and Brazil nut milk delicious. There had been little meat in the village for the past few days, and they all gorged themselves. They also knew that by the third day, the remaining meat would be tough and barely chewable.

Dusk is very brief in the tropics, and the sunset glowed brilliantly against the broken clouds in the clearing western sky. The colors shifted, modulated, changed, and were suddenly gone. Night rapidly enfolded the village, and the people who were watching the setting sun remained a moment in silence and reentered their dwellings. In each house, the women lit small kerosene lamps which cast a flickering glow over the interiors, supplementing the flames of the fires. Borai sat in her hammock, talking with her mother about plans for the next day's work, while her baby sat in the sling on her hip and nursed, more for solace than for food. A few of the children of the house were playing with a puppy, pulling its tail, twisting its legs, and preventing it from running away from them.

Borai and her mother went back to the farinha shed in the middle of the village to finish toasting the manioc flour. They stoked the fire back to life and after letting the oven warm up, poured in the remaining pulp. The glow from the open front of the oven cast a dim and flickering light over their work as they slowly turned and stirred the flour. Other women wandered from their houses to join the group, though the women of the chief's house, who were miffed because they felt they were being gossiped against, stayed home. Finally, unable to bear the thought that the farinha-shed group really was talking about them, two of the chief's daughters joined them. Everybody took a turn at stirring the farinha, but interest centered on a plan to gather *assaí* palm fruits the next morning at a grove a few miles away. The fruit drink, and the abundance of roast meat, would make the day a festive one, and they would hold a dance in the evening.

Across the village plaza, a small fire was burning in front of the men's house. A poorly played guitar was trying to pick out the strain of a Brazilian song heard at a trader's post, and another man was softly playing one of their own songs on a traditional flute. The conversation of the men drifted across as a low murmur, broken occasionally by a raucous cry from one of the boys. After a while, the music stopped, but the silence was soon broken by a deep vibrant note from one of the karökö, the long tubular musical instruments which contained the ancestral spirits and which the women were forbidden even to see. The first notes were joined by the second and then the third karökö, playing in counterpoint to each other, slowly, repetitively, and in measured cadence. The men fell silent for a moment, then the conversation picked up again, the guitarist tried futilely to catch the elusive melody, and one of the boys dumped another from his hammock. But the mournful notes of the karökö dominated the village, shut out the night noises, accentuated the calm.

"There they go again," said Borai, as the first sounds of the karökö reached the farinha shed. The women listened for a moment, trying to identify the players by style and skill, laughing at an off-note played by one of the younger men. They then turned back to their conversation and the work of farinha toasting. Many of the little ones were becoming cranky from tiredness, and their mothers caressed them, or nursed the infants. One five-year-old climbed onto his mother's lap to nurse, but giggles from the older girls made him give up after a few minutes. The farinha was finally finished, scooped out of the pan with the paddles into loosely woven baskets lined with palm leaves, and placed on a storage rack in the house. A large bowl of the freshly made flour was kept in the shed, and the women occasionally dipped their fingers into it, enjoying the tanginess of the still hot grains. Some of the women brought their children back to their hammocks and remained in the houses; the rest of the group lingered a while and then went home, two by two, leaving the farinha shed to a few dogs huddled near the warmth of the oven.

The men's house had grown quiet as people drifted off to sleep, and finally the last sounds of the karökö faded. The players emerged from the enclosed sacred chamber, climbed into their hammocks, talked a while, and then fell asleep. One of the men drowsily told the boys to be quiet, and they, too, rolled up inside their hammocks, still whispering to each other. The dying fire cast in flickering outline the arching, open-ended roof of the men's house and the two rows of hammocks.

Borai took the meat off the babricot, placing it in a covered basket, which she put on a storage rack. She threw a bit of dirt on the fire to bank it for the night, removed the babricot, and then slid gently into her hammock so as not to waken the already sleeping baby. Two of the other women went outside to urinate, but they stayed near the house, as the underbrush in the night was a hiding place of the *Yurupari* and other evil spirits. They reentered, blew out the kerosene lamp, and the house fell into silence.

The hills in the east began to emerge from the total blackness as a three-quarter moon rose, bathing the countryside and the village in pale light. The circle of houses around the village plaza could now be clearly seen; yet nothing moved, and the only sounds were an occasional cough or a baby's whimper. Traces of smoke from the smoldering fires were picked up by the moonlight, and the inside of the farinha shed was tinged with orange by the glowing embers of the dying fire. The village was silent, but the forests were not. From far off in the distance, a band of howler monkeys made an ululating uproar, and the noise of tree frogs near the stream was a steady backdrop of tone, broken by the cries of night birds and the chirping of crickets in the brush around the village. Borai listened for a very short while before tiredness overtook her; her last thought before drifting into full sleep was a hope that her husband would not decide to pay a night visit. A woman's day had ended.

Haruko's Work

Gail Lee Bernstein

"I lead a relatively relaxed life," Haruko told me, kneeling on the floor, folding the laundry, a few days after my arrival in Bessho. "I have a circle of four or five close friends who are, like myself, only housewives. Most other women in this area work outside in factories or stores. I prefer not to work, because I don't need the money that much and would rather have free time. Working women are so busy they don't have time to help their husbands." I gradually discovered that in reality she had very little free time; in fact she had stayed home from work only to help me get settled.

During the first weeks of my stay, the pace of Haruko's daily routine quickened noticeably. It soon became evident that she was more than just "a housewife." Although machinery had freed both women and men from most of the arduous work of rice cultivation, many other farming chores remained, and they usually fell to the women. In addition, once the harvest season was over, Haruko, like most other women in Bessho, sought part-time wage-paying work nearby. Watching her daily activities over several months, I concluded that Haruko was the busiest member of her family.

Yet it was not always easy to ascertain exactly what work Haruko and other farm women performed. For one thing, farm women did not consider their round of household chores to be work, and they viewed vegetable farming as merely an extension of their domestic sphere of activity—a part of cooking. Nor did they define rice cultivation as work. Even though they had labored side by

Reprinted from *Haruko's World: A Japanese Farm Woman and Her Community* by Gail Lee Bernstein with the permission of the publishers, Stanford University Press. © 1983 by the Board of Trustees of the Leland Stanford Junior University.

side with men in the paddies, transplanting rice seedlings in late spring or early summer, weeding together with other women during the remainder of the summer, and again working with their menfolk during the harvest in early fall, farm women referred to such labor as "helping my husband." Only wage labor constituted work. Thus to rely on simple questions like, "What work do you do?" was to invite deceptive answers, because even women who farmed almost entirely on their own but were not employed "outside" for pay, might reply, "I do not work; I stay at home."

In addition, women's work included numerous separate, discrete tasks that varied according to the season of the year and the time of day, and that were performed in countless different places inside and outside the house, the shed, and other farm buildings and on various plots of land scattered throughout the hamlet. Every day I had to ask Haruko where she would be working, and even after she told me, "I'll be hoeing in the vegetable field," I often could not find her, because the family farmed several vegetable fields in different places. By the time I did locate her, she might be finished with the hoeing and on to another task, such as separating out the weeds from the edible grasses she had picked the day before.

Equally difficult to study was the diversity of part-time, wage-paying jobs women performed. Their jobs in factories, shops, and offices or as orderlies in hospitals and as day laborers on other farmers' land took them out of the hamlet during the day. To observe such work required trailing after each hamlet woman and gaining entry into half a dozen different work sites. Also, the work was often temporary: small factories hiring only a few women might close down for several months during an economic slump, and women working as agricultural hired hands might be laid off after the harvest was over.

By tagging after Haruko for several months, I was eventually able to compile a list—by no means complete—of her work responsibilities. They fell broadly into three categories: homemaking, farming, and wage earning.

As a homemaker, Haruko had more extensive responsibilities than ever before: not only was she in charge of such traditional domestic work as cooking, cleaning, sewing, and participating in communal functions, but in recent years she had assumed the newer tasks of shopping, paying the bills, and guiding her children's education. Except in matters relating to the children, Shō-ichi, like most Japanese men, removed himself altogether from these domestic concerns.

Haruko's daily round of household chores began at six o'clock, when recorded Westminster chimes, broadcast from the loudspeaker installed on the roof of the hamlet social hall, awakened the farmers of Bessho and set her scurrying around the house. Every morning she prepared a breakfast of *misoshiru* (bean-paste soup enriched with white cubes of bean curd, an egg, and a few garden greens), boiled rice, and green tea. The children, who needed to be coaxed awake, ate toasted white bread. Before sitting down to breakfast at seven o'clock, Haruko placed six cups of green tea as offerings on the Buddhist altar in the bedroom. Whenever she made special food, such as rice balls, she also offered some to *hotoke-sama*, the spirits of the ancestors of Shō-ichi's family.

After sending the children off to school at eight o'clock in a flurry of last-minute searches for clothing and books and hastily delivered instructions, Haruko ran a load of wash in the washing machine and hung it out to dry. She also aired the heavy mattresses and quilts to prevent mildew, a perennial problem in Japan's humid climate. These two tasks were part of her morning routine on every clear day, but regardless of the weather, at five o'clock every single evening, just before starting dinner, she filled the deep bath tub with hot water for the family's bath. Going without the daily bath was unthinkable; and if Haruko was detained, Obāsan or Yōko did this chore in her place. Her routine did not include housecleaning, however. There were neither windows to wash nor furniture to dust, and since shoes were removed at the door, the tatami-covered floor remained clean and required only sweeping. Such cleaning as was necessary was relegated to rainy days, when farmers do not work in the fields.

Lunch was a simply prepared meal of rice, processed or raw fish, and leftovers. For dinner, taken punctually at six o'clock, Haruko again made boiled rice, this time served with numerous side dishes, each on its own little plate, such as raw tuna or mackerel, boiled octopus, sliced vinegared cucumbers, noodles, seaweed, or spinach sprinkled with sesame seeds, and green tea. Thanks to Shō-ichi's pig business the family enjoyed more meat than other farm families, and occasionally they also ate small cubes of fried chicken bought at the Agricultural Cooperative supermarket in Unomachi.

As the woman of the house, Haruko also had several traditional community obligations that were impossible to shirk. Custom demands that all the women in a *kumi* (a grouping of several neighboring households) help prepare food for receptions following the funerals or weddings of member families. Furthermore, each household sends one woman to attend regular meetings of the Women's Guild of the Agricultural Cooperative Association. Haruko and other Bessho farm wives took turns serving in administrative capacities within the guild. They also participated in the cooking classes sponsored by the guild, as well as in meetings of the Parent-Teacher Association.

In addition to being a homemaker, Haruko was the family's chief farm worker. She grew the fruits and vegetables consumed by the household almost entirely on her own: carrots, peppers, Chinese cabbage, spinach, strawberries, broccoli, corn, onions, and a small scallion called *nira*. In the summertime, after the rice crop was planted, she prepared year-long supplies of staple food items such as pickled vegetables and bean paste for *misoshiru,* and she further supplemented the family diet with wild grasses picked in the hills surrounding the rice plain or along the road. Once, when Haruko was not feeling well, Shō-ichi offered to plant the onions, but she had to tell him what to do.

Since the money for modernizing agriculture had been diverted primarily to the rice paddies, vegetables were still grown in tiny, scattered fields. Haruko's garden was actually four different plots of land: a vegetable patch in front of the house, another one across the road from the house, a cabbage patch down the road toward town, and a potato field about a half mile away in the opposite direction. While the men were learning to use the new rice-transplanting machines and the combines, Haruko worked with an old iron grubbing fork and a scythe. To enrich the soil, she relied on organic materials: chicken manure for fertilizer, and chicken feathers and rice husks for mulch. To irrigate a nearby vegetable field, she drew water from a spigot in front of the goldfish pond and carried it in a watering can.

Haruko did not always farm alone. For one week in autumn, for example, she worked with Obāsan and Shō-ichi harvesting potatoes, which were grown on a quarter-acre plot and fed to the pigs. (Farmers who ate mainly potatoes during the war do not care for them now, though their children have developed a taste for them.) The three worked silently in the fields from ten o'clock in the morning until five at night, stopping only for one hour at noon, when a siren announced the lunch break, and again at three o'clock, when they took a snack of green tea, tangerines, and a sweet cake. The women's work consisted of cutting the potato vines with a scythe, arranging them in piles, and tying them together. Then they put the potatoes in sacks for Shō-ichi to load onto his truck. Shō-ichi also operated a small, motor-driven plow that turned over the soil after the potatoes were harvested. Neighbors carted away the vines and fed them to their cows.

Haruko also worked with her mother-in-

law and husband on a neighborhood team husking rice. The group, which included Obā-san's sister and the sister's husband, son, and daughter-in-law, together with two neighbors, had collectively purchased a wooden husking machine in the early 1960's. It was run by a generator. Before purchasing the husker, they had paid a husking company to do the job for them, and before that, when Obāsan came to Bessho as a bride, a hand-operated device had been used to turn the rice around for hours at a time. The fall of 1974 was the last time the husking group would work together; beginning with the next harvest, all the rice would be husked mechanically in a large machine operated by the Agricultural Cooperative.

Members of the husking group took turns husking rice at each other's houses, and the host family was expected to provide refreshments. On the morning when it was their turn to use the machine, Obāsan and Haruko were up early getting the house in order and preparing the food. While Obāsan raked a gravel area in front of the house, where the gangling wooden contraption would be set up, Haruko turned on the rice steamer, made a swipe at the cobweb strung from the overhead lampshade in the living room to the side wall, climbed the persimmon tree for some fruit, leaped on her scooter for a quick errand to town, and, upon returning, set out the straw baskets used to carry the family's rice kernels from the storage shed to the husker. Shō-ichi telephoned to town for an order of beer.

Once the work team assembled (all but one worker arrived at exactly eight o'clock), the women and the men worked separately on each side of the husker. There was no need to delineate chores or to explain how the work would be done: everyone knew exactly what to do. The women filled the straw baskets with rice, hauled them to the machine, and poured in the rice, while the men weighed the husked rice as it flowed out of the machine, recorded the amount, and sacked and hauled the rice back to the storage shed.

Two hours later, the work was done and a mid-morning feast was served. Mats were spread out between the machine and the side of the road. The workers gathered in a circle, the women on one side, kneeling, and the men on the other, sitting cross-legged. An abundance of food was pressed on the guests, who ritually refused once or twice before accepting rice cakes, raw fish, assorted vegetables, hardboiled eggs, fruit, tea, beer, and *sake*. Haruko peeled persimmons, cut them into four slices each, and handed them around. Sitting on dust and gravel by the side of the road, after two hours of labor, it was nevertheless possible at that moment to feel like royalty being wined and dined, filling one's belly, laughing and joking, indulged by the host and hostess, whose turn to be served would come the following day, when the wooden husker would be wheeled down the road to work at another house.

One of Haruko's principal farm chores was feeding the pigs, which were housed in a wooden structure several hundred yards behind the house. More than half of the Utsunomiyas' annual income came from the pig business. Twice a day, once in the morning and once at night, the couple fed the ninety pigs and cleaned the pigsty. There were about twelve pens, with seven or eight pigs in each. Haruko poured feed into the trough and mixed water in with it, while her husband cleaned the pens one by one, shoveling out the dung. They worked quickly and in silence. The stench and the flies seemed not to trouble either of them.

"Which of your tasks do you least like?" I asked Haruko one day, emerging from the pigsty to take a deep breath of fresh air. The air inside the sty was suffocating, and the pink, flesh-colored pigs, crowded into their stalls, were loudly squealing for food. Haruko was pouring feed from a tank into a wheelbarrow. Without looking up, she answered, "If you farm, you can't say you hate any work."

Shō-ichi operated a larger pig business in the mountains about twenty minutes' drive from the house. He and five other men raised one thousand pigs and took turns staying overnight to feed the animals, clean the pens, and tend to any emergencies.

Occasionally Haruko went along to help Shō-ichi and the other men at the pig farm.

Neither she nor her husband showed any sentimentality toward the animals. A mother pig, too exhausted after giving birth to move into the warmer quarters prepared for her and her piglets, and uncomfortable with a stillborn infant inside her, was first punched and then prodded with a hog catcher that was attached to her snout. Dead piglets from other litters lay in the aisle between the pens. Frightened pigs being weighed for market were kicked in the face, pulled by the ears or tails, or punched on their backs to make them heed. Haruko seemed unperturbed by the din of grunts and squeals, and while some of the men loaded pigs in a basket onto a truck, she calmly swept one of the sties. When the truck drove off, she put down her broom and stood on the pig scale to weigh herself.

An important part of pig farming was mating the pigs. As soon as the male was led into the female's pen, he became aroused, but he could not perform without assistance. Shō-ichi helped guide the penis, and if the pig failed to penetrate, he punched him as a reminder to try again. It took about ten to fifteen minutes to align a pair; copulation itself took only a few seconds. Meanwhile, Haruko stood ready to help, opening the gates to the pen or simply standing on the sidelines cheering and offering advice, like a third-base coach at the world series. "A little higher," she would yell, or "Oh, oh, too bad. OK now, off to the right a bit," alternately laughing at and sympathizing with the efforts of both pig and husband. She shared fully in her husband's work—it was equally her work—and the two performed their tasks like partners.

By early November, Haruko usually looked for part-time, wage-paying jobs. In previous years, she had worked in a small textile factory in Bessho. She had also commuted by bus to Akehama township to pick tangerines as a day laborer, earning four dollars a day (at a time when a tube of lipstick cost five dollars), but since she had returned home from that job too late to prepare the bath and fix dinner, she decided to look for work closer to home. Her options were limited, however.

The local economy offered various small jobs that called for manual dexterity, such as scraping barnacles off oyster shells, wrapping pastry in leaves, or planting tobacco seedlings with chopsticks. This work was often unappealing, however: it usually required either sitting or hunkering for hours at a time, and in such jobs as tobacco planting one was not paid until the crop was harvested and sold.

A few women from Bessho had found office or sales positions in Unomachi, but these positions required special training. When I asked Haruko whether she could get an office job in town, perhaps at the telephone company, where a younger hamlet woman worked, she replied tersely, "I don't have the qualifications." Besides, some of these jobs required a full-time commitment. The best-paying jobs for women, she added, were jobs as schoolteachers, clerks in government offices, shopkeepers, and factory workers. Her own opportunities were confined largely to manual labor.

When day laborers were needed during the reorganization of the rice paddies, Haruko was taken on as a *dokata,* or construction worker (literally, a "mud person"), and she worked on a team with two other women and three men. In most other wage-paying jobs women and men worked apart, at distinct kinds of work, but on the construction teams they worked side by side. The women were paid about $6.65 a day for eight hours' work, and the men were paid about $11.65.[1] They took one hour for lunch and two additional breaks of one-half hour each.

The female *dokata*'s work was physically demanding: women hauled heavy boulders, climbed down into trenches to lay irrigation pipes, constructed bridges over irrigation ditches, and shoveled snow from steep mountain slopes. Though they feminized their work outfits with aprons and bonnets, some were embarrassed when I asked them what work they did, and one female *dokata* replied indirectly, "I do the same work as Haruko."

The *dokata*'s work could be hazardous, too, especially for women unaccustomed to it. In early January, after two months on the construction crew, Haruko was hit on the side of the head by a falling rock. Although her employer had distributed helmets to all workers,

Haruko did not like to wear hers. By a freak coincidence, her head was hit by another falling rock the very next day; she was wearing only her bonnet. This time she began to suffer fainting spells, dizziness, and headaches that prevented her from riding her motor scooter. X-rays did not reveal any bone damage, but the doctor decided that her "nerves" had been affected and prescribed one month's bed rest and a daily dose of eighteen tablets. She was also instructed not to take baths or wash her hair until she recovered. By the end of the month she was feeling better, though a brain scan now showed some abnormality and she had recurrent attacks of asthma. Daily injections at the hospital helped control the asthma; but whenever she tried to work in the fields, the headaches returned. National health insurance and her employee's insurance covered both the bulk of her medical expenses and her loss of income.

Haruko much preferred farming to construction work, she said. She was not thinking of hazards, however, or of physical demands; it was simply that she favored farming over any kind of wage labor. As a farmer, she could see the results of her endeavors. "The greatest pleasure of farming is the autumn harvest," she commented, and on more than one occasion she spoke of the "joy of producing one's own food," and of her "pride" in being the wife of a farmer. She also liked being able to work alongside her husband. Another advantage of farming was that "the farmer is master of himself; he can do whatever he chooses to do." In contrast, outside labor meant "you are used by others." When Haruko had worked in the Bessho knitting mill, she had always been watching the clock, "driven by time," because wages were determined by the worker's productivity—the number of finished goods she produced. Women stood hour after tedious hour in front of the machines, pushing a bobbin from right to left.

Not all farm women shared Haruko's views. Five women working in the Bessho mill, a one-room operation owned by a man in Yawatahama, said they enjoyed the piecework he sent them to do. "Paddy work is hard labor," said one woman. "This is easy." Another said, "We all live in Bessho. We are like relatives. It's pleasant here. Sometimes we sing songs." They worked their own hours, after the farm season was over. From late November they spent most of their time in the factory; in December, however, the factory abruptly closed down, a victim of market fluctuations caused by the oil scarcity in late 1974.

Women working in larger, more impersonal factories echoed some of Haruko's sentiments about factory work. In *Minori* (Harvest) magazine, published by the Women's guild of Uwa township, one woman voiced her complaints: "When I first started working, I felt uneasy about leaving the housework and the children, but there was no other way to pick up ready cash. Under today's completely changed work conditions, nerve fatigue, more than physical labor, is what quickly gets to you. You have to learn your work. You have to think about dealing with people you are working with in the organization. You have a lot of different feelings when you go out work-

ing. And you think: Aren't you taking money but making plainer meals? Can you really manage the household? Are you really taking care of your children's and your husband's health if you come home tired? By working [outside the home] won't you make your family unhappy?"

Factory work in Higashiuwa county consisted primarily of making blue jeans (called g-pants) and canning and packing *mikan* (Japanese tangerines). Women working in blue-jeans factories could earn between $5.60 and $6.60 a day, depending on their experience and the number of jeans they completed. In one factory in Nomura township, women worked from eight in the morning until five at night, with one hour for lunch. Each woman received a flat wage for working on one part of the pants and a bonus depending on the group's productivity as a whole. In a *mikan*-packing plant operated by the Agricultural Cooperative in Unomachi, the women earned $5.10 for eight hours of work; in Yawatahama, about thirty minutes away by

TABLE 1. Sample Daily Wages Paid to Female Workers in Higashiuwa County in 1975 (U.S. dollar equivalent)[a]

Job	Women's Wages	Men's Wages
Dokata in Bessho	6.80 + disability insurance	11.90
Jeans factory in Nomura	5.60–6.60 + bonus	
Mikan-packing plant in Unomachi	5.10 + disability insurance + bonus	
Mikan-packing plant in Yawatahama	7.14–8.50	
Piecework at home	1.20	
Silkworm cultivation in Nomura	7.82	
Textile factory in Nomura	5.10–5.80	11.90
Tobacco planting in nursery beds in Bessho[b]	7.82	9.52
Construction work in cities		16.00–20.00 after room and board
Pruning trees in commonly held forest in Bessho	70% of men's wages	
Rice transplanting in Bessho	equal wages with men	
Public works projects in Bessho	equal wages with men if woman is single head of household	

Note: A blank entry indicates that the information in question was either unavailable or inapplicable.

[a]Computed from the 1975 rate of 294 yen = U.S. $1.00. Some wages had recently been raised by 300–500 yen.

[b]The women placed tobacco seedlings into containers; the men did the planning, organizing, and record keeping. The women were paid their wages only after the crop was sold.

train, similar work paid between $7.14 and $8.50. Daily wages in the cooperative's plant were supplemented by a bonus, however, and by disability insurance like the *dokata*'s wages, which meant that the workers' real income in effect compared respectably with that of other non-salaried workers in the county (see the accompanying table), and was actually greater than that of a *dokata*, who did not work on rainy days.

Whereas the canning plant's equipment for folding and stapling cartons and sending fruit speeding along the conveyor belts was both modern and efficient, conditions of work were neither: some women knelt on cushions in a dimly lit, unheated building placing fruit into cartons, and others stood under a bare electric lightbulb separating out damaged fruit. Factory work was sought after because it paid a wage, but as a contributor to *Minori* wrote, the poor air, the indoor environment, the long work day, and the clatter of the machines could not compare with "farming under the endless blue sky, in clean air, doing the work as you want to do it."

It was difficult to determine what portion of the women's income went toward household expenditures. For one thing, farm women, especially farm women of Haruko's generation, who were unaccustomed to having large sums of money at their disposal, tended not to keep a budget or records of their daily household expenses. As more and more farmers took wage-paying jobs, however, some kind of record keeping was becoming necessary. Since the practice in the countryside, following urban customs, was for men to turn over all of their money to their wives to manage, the Women's Guild of the Cooperative had recently begun to distribute record ledgers to teach farm women how to maintain household budgets separate from the family's farm records. At a meeting of the Uwa branch of the Women's Guild, a guild leader lectured on the virtues of frugality and disciplined spending. "If you follow a budget," she said, "you will not buy merely what your neighbor buys. Also, if you don't go shopping every day, but only every three or five days, you won't buy so much." Similarly,

during the cooking class sponsored by the guild, the instructor slipped in words of advice on budgeting. Women were told first to estimate their income for the coming year and then to apportion their spending as follows: thirty percent for farm equipment, fertilizer, and other farming needs; fifty percent for food, clothing, electricity, telephone, and other household expenses; ten percent for taxes; and the remaining ten percent for savings. If the women followed this advice, said the teacher, they would not overspend. "Budget yourselves," she urged. "Write it down." Haruko asked the instructor to repeat the numbers and hastily scribbled them down, but then forgot what each referred to. "I'm no good at budgeting," she muttered.

The Utsunomiyas were an exception in the sense that Shō-ichi handled money matters: when the family needed money, Shō-ichi withdrew cash from his savings account at the Agricultural Cooperative. He kept most of the vital figures in his head. Writing on the back of a napkin, he estimated that the family's annual income was a little over $10,000—about the average for farmers in Japan. The income from rice was $4,500 and the income from the pig business, in a good year, was $5,600. Government statistics for 1971 showed that, like Shō-ichi, other farmers in the prefecture typically derived sixty to eighty percent of their incomes from nonfarm sources or supplementary farm occupations, such as animal husbandry.[2]

Shō-ichi's estimate did not include Haruko's earnings, which varied from year to year with the availability of part-time and seasonal work. I calculated that in a good year Haruko might earn as much as $700 to $800, which was in keeping with the average earnings of other farm women. A government survey conducted in 1973 showed that forty percent of all farm women took on outside work, and they earned between $330 and $660 annually.[3] My own survey in Higashiuwa county, distributed in the spring of 1975, set the average at about $700, and the head of the local Agricultural Cooperative estimated it to be close to $800.

Why were farm women taking outside jobs?

Or, to put it another way, how were their additional earnings used? In the 1973 government survey, sixty percent of the farm women who reported taking on outside work said that they did so in order to pay for the "basic necessities" of life. In my survey of women in the country, fifty percent said they spent most of their earnings on such essentials as food, and another twenty percent said they spent them on clothing for family members and on their children's education. Haruko believed that Bessho women worked not so much to eat as to make extra cash: "Even the wife of the head of Uwa township works."

When I asked Haruko how she spent her own earnings, however, and whether it was really necessary for her to work, I received conflicting responses. "If I had my choice," Haruko said, "I would rather spend every day knitting sweaters for the children and straightening up the house." Yet although Shō-ichi said she did not have to take part-time jobs, she would not stay at home. She admitted that she liked having the extra spending money, even if earning it meant exhausting herself and, as she once remarked, not being able to complain, because Shō-ichi had not asked her to do it. It is also true that she worried about having to draw on their savings to pay for the machinery. On several occasions, she even implied that her wage-paying jobs were necessary to cover the cost of the new farm equipment, and Obāsan, sharing this view, commented privately about how sad it was that Haruko had to work.

When I pressed the matter further, I hit a sensitive nerve. Shō-ichi claimed that even without Haruko's earnings their income could cover the monthly payments of about eighty dollars for the machines. "Haruko is a worrier," he said. Haruko retorted that I could not be expected to understand the problem, and Shō-ichi countered, "There is no problem!" Later, however, he modified his position, saying that unless the price of rice increased, women's work would still be necessary to supplement farm income.

It is likely that Haruko worked for a variety of reasons. Her earnings, like those of other farm women, helped the family keep pace with inflation, contributed to mechanization efforts, and also satisfied new consumer desires. It was difficult for anyone to determine in exactly which of these areas expenditure was or was not "necessary." Shō-ichi and Haruko incurred many expenses that reflected the steady erosion of the Japanese farmer's traditional sense of self-sufficiency. Fertilizers, chemical sprays, and electricity and the telephone had become virtual necessities. Gasoline and animal feed, both imported, were among the family's greatest expenses, and these costs were tied to fluctuations in world politics and international trade, so that from one year to the next their incomes rose and fell with little predictability. Shō-ichi had a bad year in 1974, when the American corn crop was damaged and the Middle East oil embargo was imposed. The family's expenses thus varied from year to year, making outside sources of cash imperative.

In addition, the desire for ready-made western-style clothing and for packaged food also drove the Utsunomiyas and other farm families in the area to supplement their farm incomes, making them dependent on the wider economy. Farm women everywhere in Japan, exposed to urban goods and life-styles on television screens, expected more out of their life than their parents' generation did. Haruko was no exception, and her greatest pleasure was shopping for western-style clothing. Yōko wanted the fashionable blue jeans, whose popularity was sweeping the countryside and created jobs for women in blue-jeans factories. Hisashi asked for a record player. Both children preferred packaged white bread to boiled rice for breakfast, and they toasted the bread in a new red electric toaster. The children also expected to go beyond the free junior high school level of education to the high school level, for which tuition fees were charged. Haruko's wages, in other words, went toward attaining a middle-class life-style for her farm family.

Even Obāsan entered the paid labor market, working for a pittance in order to accumulate ready cash of her own. The piecework she did at home for a local factory paid her only one dollar a day for seven or eight hours of knitting pocketbooks. Still, the money enabled her to give cash as birthday gifts to her grandchildren.

In their search for wage-paying jobs, residents of Bessho commuted to Unomachi, if they were lucky enough to find employment there, or they traveled by train to Uwajima, Yawatahama, or even Matsuyama. Almost every women in Bessho, except those above the age of sixty and mothers of pre-school children, held some kind of part-time job. As a result of this daily exodus, Bessho by day was a ghost town, a bedroom community whose population of children, men, and women emptied into Unomachi early in the morning and headed for schools, jobs, or the railroad station, leaving behind only children under six years of age tended by their grandparents or even great-grandparents, and dogs, caged or tied up outside.

Unlike younger farm women in their late twenties and early thirties, Haruko did not view her income as a passport to independence. It is true she squirreled away her earnings, saving some for old age, spending the rest as she pleased. But for younger women still living in the shadow of their mothers-in-law, possession of one's own money implied something more. One of Haruko's neighbors, who worked part time as a store clerk and lived with her husband's parents, described how she had deliberately lied to her mother-in-law about the sum she had spent on groceries for the household. She told the older woman she had spent less than she actually had, because she did not want to be fully reimbursed from her mother-in-law's purse. That extra amount represented her small measure of economic independence. Other women hearing the story laughed in agreement.

Haruko viewed her position in the family as depending more on her labor than on her wage earnings. Indeed, work itself, rather than her separate though modest pin money, was Haruko's way of ensuring that her voice would be heard. "Do you want to know why I have a say in this family?" she asked one day, angrily interrupting a conversation I was having with one of her friends about the position of Japanese women. "I'll tell you why. Because I work harder than anybody else. It's for that reason that we've been able to increase our landholdings. You saw how my husband was dressed today to attend Yōko's graduation: in a white shirt, a silk tie, and a brown suit. That's the way it's always been. I've done all the work."

Any discussion of Haruko's household work provoked a similar emotional response. Although she felt angry about the way she had been worked in her husband's household, her belief that her status depended on her labor value made her reluctant to allow her mother-in-law to undertake too many household tasks; she seemed to fear that if she were no longer indispensable, her worth might be diminished. Was it perhaps this fear that also made her less than enthusiastic about her husband's mechanization project, even though it promised to free her from some of the most tiring aspects of rice farming? Haruko needed to be needed.

Haruko's anxiety about further investment in machinery, and her resistance to it, also reflected the more general confusion felt in the farming community over the future role of farm women. Would machinery eliminate altogether the need for female labor in the fields or would it simply tie women to other crops, while removing their husbands from the farm? Over one-third of farm women already farmed on their own. Again, would farm households become dependent on the wage labor of women as well as men, and would enough nonagricultural jobs be available?

In the face of these uncertainties, numerous suggestions from various sources floated around the countryside. A speaker addressing the Agricultural Cooperative in Uwa advised women to make more of their own food, as they did in the self-sufficient economy of the past, but then to sell it. And Shō-ichi, who thought it might be profitable for women to stick with farming, suggested that after the harvest they plant rice paddies with cash crops such as tobacco and wheat.

What such proposals had in common was

the idea of added reliance on women's work of one sort or another; for during the transitional period at least—while the machines were still new and their efficacy uncertain—women were actually being called upon to perform more functions, rather than fewer. It is not surprising that the almost universal complaint of farm women was lack of sufficient time for rest, for domestic work, and for child care. Moreover, mechanization did not necessarily promise the economic security that would ease the demands on women in the near future. "We have put in machines to do our work," wrote one contributor to *Minori,* "and now we must work to pay for the machines. No sooner do we repay our loans than we have to buy machines. We want binders and automobiles. Our ideals are high, our income is low."

It was understandable that most farm wives envied the comparative leisure enjoyed by their middle-class counterparts in the towns, in their more secure roles as the wives of white-collar salaried men. Even Haruko, though she was perhaps too restless and ambitious to enjoy being anything but busy, nevertheless aspired to the kind of life-style such women represented. Many of her friends were affluent town women whose sole responsibility was homemaking, and perhaps she hoped that by her labor, in farming and in part-time work, she too might one day become, literally, just a housewife.

Haruko's town friends, cheerful and girlish, with graceful, refined manners, seemed to belong to a social class that set them apart from Haruko, who was accustomed to strenuous manual labor and blunt, direct communication. Their fashionable dress (skirts with dainty blouses and cardigan sweaters), their curler-set hairstyles, and their hobbies (raising parakeets and growing prize-winning chrysanthemums) gave evidence of their leisure and affluence. Their lives were so comfortable, in fact, that at least one of the women, in her late thirties, had begun jogging to keep her weight down. All of them wore face cream and powder and had beautiful teeth. (They all used dental floss, whereas Haruko was often too tired at night to give her teeth even a perfunctory brushing.) Because they had no need to take jobs, they had withdrawn into their homes, where they concentrated on being attentive mothers and attractive wives.

One day, one of Haruko's town friends bicycled out to the farm, her skirt gently billowing in the breeze, to get cabbage for her son's pet rabbits. Haruko, dressed in her ankle-high boots, baggy pantaloons, and apron, looked more than ever like a gnome, standing next to her elegant friend and loading the homegrown cabbage heads onto the back of the bicycle. The two women, who lived less than one mile apart, were a study in contrasts, and watching them, it was easier to understand why most farm women, inspired by the middle-class feminine ideal of the housewife, wished they were the wives of salaried men and wanted their own daughters to marry one.

NOTES

1. Money values have been calculated from the fall 1974 exchange rate of 300 yen = U.S. $1.00.
2. I am grateful to Ms. Miho Nagata of the Uwa branch of the Farmers Extension Bureau (Nōkyō Kairyō Fukyūshō) for providing this figure.
3. Fujin ni kansuru shomondai chōsa kaigi (Conference for investigating various problems concerning women), ed., *Gendai Nihon josei no ishiki to kōdō* (Contemporary Japanese women's attitudes and behavior) (Okurashō [Ministry of Finance]: Tokyo, 1974), p. 267.

The Position of Women in Pastoral Society (The Fulani WoDaaBe, Nomads of the Niger)

Marguerite Dupire

In Bororo beliefs, the sexes are opposite and complementary, but belong to one and the same human category which is totally different from, and excludes, all other categories. Here it should be briefly mentioned that in the Fulani language masculine and feminine genders do not exist, but nouns are arranged in a number of classes which indisputably indicate a manner of conceiving the universe which is both qualitative (classes of plants, trees, insects, birds, antelopes and the like, liquids, bounded objects) and geometrical or quantitative (plurals, length and duration, small quantities, parts of a whole, diminutives, augmentatives). Among these classes, the ones which appear to us Europeans as the strangest are probably the most important, or at least were so for a pastoralist society.

The first of these is the human class, to which belong both sexes of human beings and a certain number of abstract nouns. With domestic animals, however, males and females belong to different categories (class *ndi* comprising most male domestic animals, castrated and uncastrated; class *nge*, cows). The term used as the generic term for the species is sometimes the one that designates the female of the species (as in the case of the goat, the ass, the cow, the sheep) and sometimes the male (the dog, the horse), the reason for this probably being the importance ascribed,

in the cases where the female term is employed, to the producer of milk, an important feature in the pastoral economy.

The second important class presents a most fascinating riddle to which so far no answer has been found. This is the class *nge*, which includes, as well as the cow (female and generic), also fire and sun. Although no discoverable common element exists between these three things, one must suppose that whatever people it was (the Fulani?) that originally invented this class must have done so in virtue of some essential value shared by all the things assigned to it, and this might also mean that a ritual meaning was attached to them.

Thus, linguistically speaking, while the class of things human is asexual, with domestic animals the males belong to a different class from the females. But there are constant similarities and interrelations between the three orders of animate objects, human, animal and vegetable, all of which depend, for the maintenance of the species, on the same basic principle—prolificacy. Procreative power is thought of as being transferable from one order to the other, evidence for this belief being provided by numerous magic recipes, particularly those concerning the increase of the herd. However, although stress on this common factor is carried to great lengths in the universe of magic, where like is called upon to produce like in a different but parallel order (without any conscious appeal to a superior power), that does not mean that the human order is regarded as sharing anything except this one common factor with the other

Reprinted with permission from Denise Paulme (ed.), *Women of Tropical Africa* (Berkeley and Los Angeles: University of California Press, 1963), pp. 43–53, 75–85. Originally published as *Femmes d'Afrique Noir* by Mouton & Co. in 1960. © Ecole des Hautes Etudes en Sciences Sociales, Paris.

two orders. Thus the human species, male and female, is on a different level from the animal and vegetable kingdoms.

If we leave linguistics and the philosophical concepts they imply and turn to every day life, we find that it is characterized by a cleavage between the sexes, whose contrasted roles are expressed either directly, by the activities each engage in and by the behaviour manifested, or symbolically, by the difference between the male and the female manner of arranging material objects, or by the ritual distribution of meat at ceremonies, to mention only the more obvious instances.

Man and woman complete each other like the prow and poop of a ship, the west and east of a line on the horizon, the head and hindquarters of an animal, the blood and the milk of a living creature. The man precedes and the woman follows, as is indicated by the word for woman, *debbo*, from the root *rew*, to follow. In contrast to what has often been observed in societies of hunters or farmers, it is the man, the herdsman, who, when camp is struck, goes on ahead, with his herd following him, to spy out the grazing lands in advance, while the women, in Indian file behind the pack oxen which are in their charge, follow at the tail-end of the procession, carrying on their heads the household calabashes filled with goods. If the pack ox is primarily a pack animal for the women which a man would scorn to ride, a woman for her part never uses a camel saddle, for when she rides with her husband she sits behind him, astride against the hump.

Within the camp, the arrangement of the women's huts, of the cattle enclosures, and of all material objects always follows the principle of sex differentiation. When the members of an extended family live together, the eldest of the heads of the component individual families—the father or the eldest brother—takes up the position furthest to the south, with his juniors following in order of seniority. But within each separate polygynous group, each man's wives will arrange their huts in hierarchical order in the opposite direction, that is, from north to south. The eastern part of the camp is the women's domain, and the western the men's. Behind each hut (to the east of it), the woman washes her cooking utensils, and also herself. Here she can be metaphorically protected from view, if not actually so, since the hut is no more than a simple screen of thorn, unroofed. This is also the place where she will be buried. The man, on the other hand, does his work on the other side of the hut, for the cattle corral is to the west, near the entrance to the hut, and it is in this corral, or a little beyond it, that his grave will be dug. Because they come under the sphere of masculine activities, the calves are tethered in a row running in the masculine direction, from south to north, arranged according to age, from the oldest to the youngest; while the calabashes belonging to the women are arranged on a raised table in order of decreasing size running in the feminine direction from north to south. In the foreground, then, are the men and the goods that belong specifically to them, while behind are the women with their property arranged in a hierarchy like the men's and according to the same principle, the essential difference between them being expressed by an inversion of orientation: to the women belong the east, and the direction north-south; to the men, the west, and the direction south-north.

In all ceremonies in which the women take part along with the men, they have a customary right to certain portions of the meat. Normally the portions are distributed to groups, according to age-grade, and there are only two occasions when an individual receives a portion: at a betrothal ceremony, when the wife of the paternal uncle of the fiancé (this uncle having directed the distribution of the animal offered up by his brother) and a cross-cousin of the fiancée each receives an individual portion; and at a ceremony for naming a child, when the mother receives a portion of the sacrificial animal. When specially reserved parts such as these, as well as portions assigned to men who have played certain designated roles in the ceremony, have been set aside, the following groups receive collective portions: adults (*ndotti'en:* old men and adult

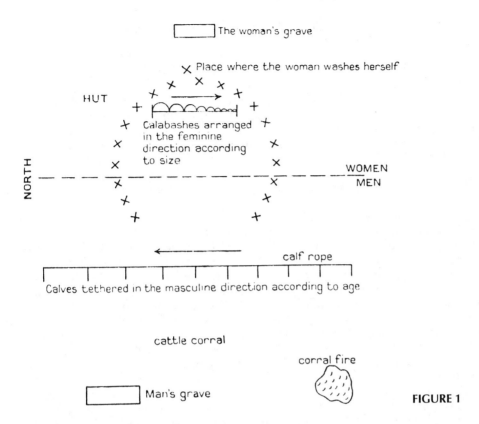

The woman's grave

× Place where the woman washes herself

HUT

Calabashes arranged in the feminine direction according to size

NORTH

WOMEN
MEN

← calf rope

Calves tethered in the masculine direction according to age

cattle corral

corral fire

Man's grave

FIGURE 1

men who have reached the age when they can direct public affairs), young men, young girls, married women and their children, old women. This distribution underlines differences in sex, age, and role, and does so not only quantatively, but also qualitatively, because a particular portion of the animal is assigned to each of these groups in accordance with the idea that certain qualities are shared in magical participation by the human and the bovine species. According to this principle, women have a prior claim not only to the intestines (*reedu*, the belly, comprising the first stomach, the uterus, and the large intestines), which are regarded as the seat of procreation, but also to the hind quarters, including the hinder end of the vertebral column: "Is it not natural that the women should have the hindquarters? Is it not they who follow the men?" So, whether it be the assignment of hindquarters "because they follow" or of the intestines because of their procreative capacities, the distribution of meat to women differentiates not only between age-grades, but also between social roles. Just as the portion assigned to married women is in contrast to that assigned to adult men, so that assigned to young girls is in contrast to that assigned to young men: they receive the heart, the centre of the feelings, while the young men receive the *biol*, a piece of the breast regarded as the organ of potency. The group of senior members on either side (maternal and paternal) of the family each receives one of the two sides of free ribs. As for the cross cousins of the fiancée, young or old they all fight tooth and nail, along with the full cousins who have cut up the animal, for the half of the skin which is their due and from which each individual attempts to cut off a piece to make sandals from. Neither age nor sex counts, and a brutal free-for-all momentarily abolishes all the usual rules of the code of politeness. A young man will jostle his mother-in-law, who may be a cross-cousin with the same rights as he has, and will only say with a laugh: "Too bad! It is my mother-in-law", knowing that she will make a scene when she gets home because he has prevented her from bringing back anything from the slaughter. Everything will calm down later, but on this unique occasion, and in public, the differences of role and of sex are abolished.

At these ceremonies which bring together the kin on both sides as well as the neighbours, the distribution of meat seems to express symbolically a recognition of the various social roles. The women figure as companions of the men, whom they have to follow; as mothers, whose warm flow of affection makes them the paramount representatives of that "kinship through the milk" that characterizes uterine descent; as old women, who have the right to certain special marks of respect; and as cross cousins—and in this capacity they have to compete on the same level as their masculine counterparts, beyond all the rules of kinship, sex, age and status which ordinarily regulate social relations.

DIVISION OF LABOUR

The characteristic association: man-cattle, as against woman-household, is a feature that has already been stressed. The basis of the differences in rights between the sexes must be sought in a division of labour which has the characteristic features common to most cattle-keeping peoples, in Africa at least.[1] To look after the humped cattle, which are only semi-domesticated, demands activities of which a woman is physically incapable. It would be beyond a woman's strength to draw water for the herd in the dry season, to go on long marches to reconnoitre for grazing-lands, to protect the herd against wild animals and thieves, to hold her own with a buyer at the market, to castrate bulls, or to train the pack oxen. This hard, dangerous life, full of uncertainty and of prolonged absences from

the camp, would be incompatible with the duties of motherhood, which require a more sedentary and more regular life.

Thus among the activities required for the care of the herd, only those that are compatible with staying at home are assigned to her: those of milking and of making butter. She also looks after the minor ailments of the animals under her care, and has a direct interest in doing so; but for anything requiring more forceful treatment (blood-letting, yoking . . .) she passes all responsibility over to the head cattlekeeper. Among the Bororo it is inconceivable that a woman should be *jom-na'i*, master of the herd.

It should be noted that this division of labour is not in any way a hard and fast affair. Apart from the period of married life preceding the birth of the first child and the month or two following upon each time she gives birth, there is no period in a woman's life when she may not do the milking. However, although the reason why Bororo men do not undertake this task is because they have never learnt to do so, should the necessity arise, they would not hesitate to assume this feminine role. Thus it is the very conditions of existence that have determined cultural choice. This is proved by the fact that among the semi-nomad Fulani of the Niger it is the men who practise the technique of milking, while the women are unversed in it. The reason why, in this society, it is the herdsmen who have learnt how to milk, is because they spend half the year, parted from the women, looking after the cattle in the bush at some distance from the village. The few milch cows left behind in the village are milked by the older men, while the butter is churned by the women.[2] It is obvious therefore how much these habits, which sometimes persist long after there has been a change in the mode of life, are functional in origin, and not based on any magico-philosophical concepts of irreducible differences between the sexes. In any case, a man sometimes has to intervene when things go wrong with the milking, for if the cow is restive, or if her milk does not flow after the first calving, she has, in the first case, to be controlled by tying her up, or, in the second, to be treated by blowing air into the vagina or, in the last resort, by appealing to a specialist in incantations.

Women also do the milking of the smaller livestock, and here their responsibilities have a wider range (including looking after the animals and negotiating sales), due to the fact that these smaller animals are more amenable to treatment which requires less physical strength. Normally, small flocks of sheep and goats belong to women rather than to men. Being a form of capital that is easily convertible, they provide women with the same kind of "savings bank" as castrated cattle do for men.

Women also undertake all the tasks concerned with the house. As soon as the head of a camp has decided upon the place where they will stay for several days or several weeks, it is the women who build the huts from the thorn branches they have gathered, while their husbands busy themselves with tethering their calves and taking the herd to graze. It is also they who decorate the calabashes, fabricate the mats made out of bark, weave the winnowing fans. They look after the fires belonging to the hut, while the men look after those for the cattle—a task which requires knowledge of the magic talismans associated with it. The women plait the light ropes that are all that is required for their own use, while the men plait the heavy ones needed for drawing water or for tethering the calves; but it is the men who collect the bark used in making them. Helped by her children, the mistress of the house fetches water from the well for domestic purposes, while it is the man's job to draw water for watering the livestock. At the market which both attend, the wife sells her milk and her butter, while the husband buys salt, millet when necessary, and tobacco, sugar and tea for himself, as well as haggling over prices for the sale of cattle.

Both men and women know how to ply a needle for sewing or repairing their own clothes. Nor do men despise doing some cooking, although they usually leave this task to the women. When a man is on his own, or when he is taking part in a ceremony, he cooks meat by grilling it on a skewer, while women boil it in one of the pots they have made.[3]

In this allocation of work between the sexes there is no idea whatsoever of inferiority of status being associated with those tasks normally assigned to women. But it is obvious that in a pastoralist society, in which it is the man who undertakes the heavy work and the responsibilities involved in looking after the cattle, that he, as master of the herd, will achieve social and economic superiority over the woman, whose tasks are confined to managing household affairs and looking after her sheep and goats.

The few fields cultivated by some families at the beginning of the winter season do not employ more than one or two men; and as soon as the crops are sown, these men hasten to rejoin the other members of the camp who are on the move with their herds. Here again it is considerations of a practical order which determine the arrangement, and this is particularly the case with the WoDaaBe, among whom the men are responsible for providing the supply of millet for the family, while the women supply the milk. The Bororo, however, are not unaware of the magical associations which link woman with the fertility of the soil, for one of their recipes for the fertility of the herd includes some seeds from a field belonging to a female sedentary farmer, which are called *umma* (meaning "arise"! in their language).

In the Niger region, WoDaaBe women do not either spin cotton or know how to make cheese, in contrast to their Fulani sisters belonging to tribes that practice sedentary farming.

From this picture it can be seen that upon women fall the less strenuous tasks, but also those which are the most monotonous and which take up the most time. In the dry seasons, they often walk a distance of 20 to 30 kilometers to sell one or two litres of milk in the village. It is the woman who is the first to get up in the morning, at dawn, to pound the grain, when the air is still chilly. But her night will have been undisturbed, unless her baby has wakened her; whereas her husband may have had to stay up half the night getting his herd watered; or he may have had to get up in the middle of the night because a jackal was prowling round the camp.

PROPERTY BELONGING TO WOMEN

From their earliest years, children enjoy undisputed rights of possession over their personal belongings. No mother will give away or exchange her little girl's doll without first asking her permission. With stock, however, the situation is different, for, although both boys and girls are indeed the owners of the cattle given to them by their father, mother, or other relatives, and refer to them in the possessive, yet they have no active control over this property so long as they remain members of the paternal household. The father looks after the cattle, while the mother does the milking and uses the dairy products to supply the needs of the household. If the father's herd is failing to produce enough to support the family, the children cannot raise any objection if the cattle-keeper finds himself forced to sell one of their animals which had been given to them in front of witnesses. It will be accepted philosophically as "God's will", in the same way as nobody will be held responsible for the good or ill luck that may attend the first heifers given to them by their parents. At birth and as the children grow up, portions of the herd are allotted to them which cannot then be re-allotted or compensated for (in principle, at least). These allotted portions remain under the exclusive control of the father until his children marry, or more precisely, until they leave the paternal camp. This economic dependence acts as a stimulus to married sons to set up on their own as soon as possible. When a daughter gets married, the care of her cattle passes from her father to her husband, who is then responsible for their well-being in the interests of his wife and her children. That women consider this question of control to be a delicate one is proved by the fact that young wives

are in the habit of leaving their stock with their father until they can feel sure of the integrity of their husbands, preferring to be temporarily deprived of the dairy products of their herd. Some of them even leave them there for good. When the husband becomes cattle-keeper, he keeps his wife's animals along with his own, but is aware that they do not belong to him.

If a woman wants to sell one of her animals, she must first ask the consent of her husband, and he in turn, should he find himself in difficulties, may not sell one of his wife's animals without her consent. Any sharp practice concerning the cattle will immediately bring complaints on the part of the wife and departure to her family. But if husband and wife get on well together and the husband has shown himself to be trustworthy, his wife is not likely to refuse him one of her animals in order to pay tax or, as is more often the case, to make up the *sadaaki* to be given by one of their sons to his fiancée. In such an event, the combined wealth of husband and wife provides for the maintenance or for the future of their children, thus playing the normal role for which the double contribution of cattle was intended.

Astonishing though it may seem, a wife maintains a much stricter supervision over the *sadaaki*, of which she is only co-owner with her husband, than she does over her own stock given to her by her family. To a woman, keeping the *sadaaki* intact is equivalent to preserving a tangible symbol of her matrimonial rights while also safeguarding the future of her children. For this reason, it is the most socially sacrosanct part of the herd, and the one which must remain the last to be depleted. A wife will as little pardon her husband for having misappropriated their *sadaaki*, especially if he has done so for the children of another wife, as she will be willing to distribute it during her lifetime among her children when they get married. This prevents further quarrels with her husband on the subject without entirely depriving her of her rights to the dairy products, for a mother can easily go to live with one of her sons. Thus a married woman as often as not prefers to hand over her stock to her family or to her children rather than to her husband.

A second way in which women play an important role in the transmission of cattle derives from the manner in which the herd belonging to the father of the family is divided out.

To his chief wife a husband entrusts, in addition to the *sadaaki,* a certain number of milch cows (*darnaaji*), the milk of which will belong to her personally, and which immediately become part of the stock which her children alone will inherit together with the dairy rights. His other wives, with whom he is united by the *teegal* form of marriage, do not receive any *sadaaki,* but he assigns to them a certain number of animals (*senndereeji*) on a scale comparable, in so far as is possible, with the combined *sadaaki* and *darnaaji* of the chief wife. In addition to those cows which have been divided out, the head of the family may possess others which he can entrust to anyone he pleases for varying lengths of time. He is free to dispose of these animals and their progeny as he wishes. Along with the steers and bulls which do not come from the *sadaaki* or *darnaaji* they will form part of the common inheritance of all his children.

This manner of dividing out the herd accentuates the economic basis of the group of full brothers, who share common interests with their mother. Their calves are tethered in front of their hut, and the children get to know them and are aware that they can be certain of inheriting some of them, to the exclusion of their half-brothers and sisters. They understand, too, that the well-being of the animals depends on the care their mother bestows on them and on her firmness in preventing any depredations. In this way, the mother, without herself being its source, is the channel through which a large part of the father's stock is transferred to his children.

A woman enjoys much greater economic independence with regard to the small livestock which she acquires out of her personal savings. She can in fact do what she likes with it. She is free to a considerable degree to put to use the results of her labours. The milk from her cows belongs to her, but out of the income derived from this she must contribute towards the household needs. In principle, the husband is responsible for expenditure required for the cattle (natron, taxes . . .), and for clothing and the supply of millet, while the woman's share of the budget covers expenditure on daily requirements such as cereals, cooking salt, and condiments (which are however a luxury). But actually, in the dry season it is customary to barter milk for millet, and during the winter season the Wo-DaaBe do not eat cereals. There remains the difficult period before the harvest, at the end of the dry season, when the milk yield is low and there is no surplus for exchange. The husband is then often obliged to sell one of his sheep, or even a bullock, although this is an extreme measure to which he is loath to resort. It is in fact also in the wife's interests to safeguard the family capital, and in the dry season it is much more sensible to exchange milk, which is scarce, for millet, than to sell a skinny animal at a low price. Milk and butter are the basis of the household economy. Particularly during the winter season, the women manage to accumulate large quantities of butter stored in calabashes, which, already rancid, is sold in the villages on return from winter quarters. This provides pocket money for buying, for themselves and their children, extra gowns, trinkets, and even sheep. It is astonishing what a Bororo woman manages to do with the small savings from the "butter money", which gradually mount up. During the worst time of the year, four cows give a daily yield of a pat of butter weighing about 250 grammes (costing 15 C.F.A. francs in 1951). This butter is exchanged in the villages or sold on the market, and the women spend quite a lot of their time on these petty commercial transactions.

They may also mend calabashes for village women, or, when food is very scarce, offer to pound grain for a slight payment in cereals or bran. But a young and active Bororo woman will avoid such menial tasks. Similarly, it is only young men who have no cattle of their own who will offer themselves as herdsmen in a locality where they are not known, where they will be less likely to feel ashamed. None of the other articles which women make, such

Rights of Ownership Held by the Nominal Master
of the Herd over His Cattle

Category of cattle	Description and source	Looked after by . . .	Alienation rights held by . . .	Rights to use the milk held by . . .	Inheritance rights held by . . .
birnaaji	Stock held by the head of the family. Acquired through inheritance, gifts, purchases, or *nannga na'i* loans . . .	Father of the family.	Father of the family.	*All the wives alike* as required.	The children of all the wives.
darnaaji	Portion of the stock of the head of the family entrusted to the chief wife, *koowaaDo* (same sources as *birnaaji*).	Father of the family.	Father of the family.	*Only* the wife to whom they have been entrusted.	Only the children of the wife who has rights to the milk.
sadaaki (Western Niger region).	Stock given to the *koowaaDo* wife.	Father of the family even after divorce or repudiation.	*Husband or wife* with the consent of spouse.	*Only* the wife who is co-owner.	Only the children of the wife who is co-owner.
sadaaki (Islamized Eastern Niger region).	Stock given to the *koowaaDo* wife.	Father of the family except in cases of repudiation.	*Husband or wife* with the consent of spouse.	*Only* the wife who is co-owner.	Only the children of the wife who is co-owner.
senndereeji	Portion of the stock of the head of the family entrusted to secondary wives (in place of *sadaaki* and *darnaaji*).	Father of the family.	Father of the family.	*Only* the wife to whom they have been entrusted.	Only the children of the wife who has rights to the milk.
sukaaji of the children.	Gifts received by the children.	Father during their minority, sons after setting up households, husband of married daughters.	Father of the family during their minority, sons on coming of age.	Usually *the wife who is the mother of the children who own the stock.*	This is an inheritance in advance of each child in question.
sukaaji of the wives.	Gifts received by each wife from her family.	Father of the family.	*The wife with the consent of her husband.*	*Only* the wife who is the owner	Only the children of the wife who is the owner.

as mats, winnowing fans or ropes, are sale-able.

Occupied as she is with her house and her children, a woman is nevertheless just as much sentimentally attached to the cattle as the men are. In her earliest years she was accustomed to stroke gently the ears or the vagina of the cow her mother was milking. She has to keep constant watch over the calves entrusted to her, and like her husband and her children, she knows the history of every single animal. When she has to part with a cow that is ill or too old and that has to be killed, it is like parting from a human being, and her sorrow speaks volumes for the attachment she feels for these companions in good times and bad.

It goes without saying that for men as for women the expression *miin-jei*, "I possess", covers various methods of appropriation entailing varying rights: of alienation, of administration, of usufruct. A woman will say of the pack ox that forms part of her *sadaaki* "my pack ox", and it is true that she has exclusive use of it so long as she remains with her husband; but she can neither sell it without her husband's consent, nor take it with her should her marriage be dissolved (this at least is the case among the WoDaaBe groups of the western Niger region).

If a woman's rights over the large livestock are restricted owing to the fact that she is considered incapable of looking after it, those of a married man over the herd of which he is nominally "master" are no less so, (1) by his wife's co-ownership of the *sadaaki*, (2) by each wife's ownership of the cattle given to her by her family, (3) by the wives' exclusive rights over the milk of certain animals, (4) by his children's rights of ownership and of inheritance over the stock divided out during his lifetime.

A glance at the above table in which the various types of ownership are listed will show that a wife not only has exclusive rights to the use of the milk from the animals in one category or another (*darnaaji* and *sadaaki* for the chief wife, *senndereeji* for the others, as well as the *sukaaji* of their children and their own

sukaaji), but also enjoys co-ownership of her *sadaaki* with her husband and exclusive rights of ownership over the animals given to her by her family, although the care of them is entrusted to her husband, the master of the herd. The restrictions on the rights of the father of the family over his cattle are connected with his children's future. As for the wives, their rights to the use of the milk and the co-ownership of the *sadaaki* act as a guarantee for the services they render their husband.

These rights of ownership, co-ownership or merely of use of the milk which a wife enjoys over certain animals are connected with the fact that the capital which these animals represent is inalterably destined to be transmitted to her own children (table col. 6). A mother not only transmits to her children life and "milk", but also channels to them the cattle belonging to their father, simply in virtue of being married to him.

The ownership of all other goods belonging to husband and wife (clothes, furniture and other articles) remains completely separate throughout their married life. When a wife leaves her husband or is repudiated by him, she leaves the hut, people say, with "nothing but the dust" in it, and perhaps also the old blackened cooking pot which would be too cumbersome to take away. She removes all her possessions, including her own livestock and the dowry given to her by her parents. But the presents given to her by her husband's family are left behind: the *sadaaki* and the furniture lent to her by her mother-in-law. Clothes, furniture, and other articles down to sewing needles, are individually acquired either by the husband or by the wife. Marriage does not entail any sharing of such belongings by the couple.

Thus the only rights of ownership that marriage brings to a woman are her rights of co-ownership or of usufruct in cattle belonging to her husband, while her husband only has the use of his wife's possessions (dowry and stock) for as long as she remains with him. Whatever the reasons for the dissolution of a marriage (separation, repudiation, death), the sharing of goods in common ceases with the physical separation of the couple.

The belongings over which a woman possesses permanent rights of alienation or usufruct are, in fact, not those which come from her husband, but those which come from her own family or which have been acquired as a result of her own work under her husband's roof: the gifts of cattle and the dowry given to her by her parents, and the livestock bought with her "butter money".

She is, however, complete mistress of those belongings which do not fall within the large number of restricted categories. But a Bo-DaaDo woman possesses little enough stock: a few cattle calved by the heifer given to her by her parents, supposing it has survived, and a small flock of goats and sheep. It is usually childless women that have the flocks of sheep, because otherwise a married woman finds that most of her slender income goes on necessary household expenses. Among the WoD-aaBe there are no much-sought-after widows whose personally owned cattle and *sadaaki* make them wealthy, such as can be found among the sedentary Fulani, because when a husband dies it is the children and not the wife who inherit the stock. I only came across one widow possessing a small herd of cattle, who was married to an old man without any property at all, and lazy into the bargain. This man who allowed himself to be kept by his wife soon became the laughing-stock of his neighbours. The widow lived with her son, the future inheritor, who threatened to go away, taking the herd with him, if she did not get rid of her good-for-nothing spouse. Even if a widow has no son, her property is controlled by the consanguineous kin who will inherit it, directly if she has made a leviratic marriage with her husband's brother, indirectly if she has opted for some other arrangement.

The Bororo maintain that women are thus incapacitated both because of their lack of physical strength and because of their marital instability. But it is clear that the situation arises from the very nature of the structure of inheritance in this thoroughly patrilineal society.

Since among pastoralists women are usually not owners of capital, that is to say, of cattle, which belong to the men, their economic position would appear to be less favourable than it is in some agriculturalist societies in Africa. There it is land, inalienable in the traditional context, that represents capital, but capital that is less valuable because it is neither mobile nor easily convertible. Hence the position of the women, who are the direct producers, should be, by comparison, higher in relation to the men of the lineage, who own the land that they cultivate. But this would appear to be too summary a generalization, because in some pastoralist societies women do have the right to manage the herd. J. H. Driberg reports that among the Lango a man may not dispose of his property without the permission of his wife, who is co-owner of the property which the children will inherit. She even has sole rights of administration over the property of her husband during the minority of the inheritors. In this society a woman also enjoys far greater political rights than is the case with a BoDaaDo woman, for the widow of a village head may even govern a village during the minority of her son. Thus there is considerable variation in the economic and legal rights of women in African pastoralist societies, whether of Nilotics, Nilo-Hamitics, or Fulani, in spite of the fact that in all of them it is the men who deal with the cattle.

The prestige which her wealth confers upon a woman is similar to that which a man derives from his cattle. At the ceremonies that take place when the lineage segment gathers together in the winter season, the heads of families who are celebrating the marriage of a son parade the herds of the extended family to display in public how many of them there are, and how strong and beautiful they are. The women have their own display, exhibiting their possessions in their huts: calabashes and polished-up spoons from their dowry stores, gourds and countless straw hats from the *kaakol* bags. . . . The whole display bears witness for all to see of feminine wealth, which gives personal prestige to the woman who owns it.

NOTES

1. J. H. Driberg, "The status of women among the Nilotics and Nilo-Hamitics," *Africa*, V, 5, 1932.

2. J. H. Driberg, *op. cit.;* among the Nilotics, the milking is done by the men, but by the women among the Nilo-Hamitics.

3. Driberg (*op. cit.*) has already recorded this difference.

VII.
Gender, Property, and the State

The relationship between sexual inequality, the emergence of class structures, and the rise of the state have been enduring interests in anthropological studies of gender. The subordination of women appears to emerge as an aspect of state formation. According to Gailey (1987:6), "Institutionalized gender hierarchy . . . is created historically with class relations and state formative processes, whether these emerge independently, through colonization, or indirectly through capital penetration." We are led to ask what relationship class and state formation have with the oppression of women and, when gender hierarchy occurs, why women are the dominated gender. How does the state have power to penetrate and reorganize the lives of its members, whether in Sumerian legal codes declaring monogamy for women or in welfare laws in the United States that influence household composition? Eventually, studying state formation may help us understand the origins and interrelationships of class and patriarchy and the social reproduction of inequality.

Much discussion of this subject has centered on Engels' book *The Origin of the Family, Private Property, and the State,* a nineteenth-century text in which Engels argues that the emergence of the concept of private property and its ownership by men, as well as the development of a monogamous family, led to the subordination of women. In Engels' scheme, prior to this gender relations were characterized as egalitarian and complementary. All production was for use, and people worked together for the communal household. Thus, changes in gender relations were linked to changes in material conditions because the ownership of productive property (initially domestic animals) was concentrated in the hands of men. This thesis has been influential in many Marxist and feminist analyses of women's subordination. For example, Leacock notes that "there is sufficient evidence at hand to support in its broad outlines Engels' argument that the position of women relative to men deteriorated with the advent of class society" (Leacock 1973:30).

Following Engels Leacock observes that in early communal society the division of labor between the sexes was reciprocal, and a wife and her children were not dependent on the husband. Further, "the distinction did not exist between a public world of men's work and a private world of women's household service. The large collective household *was* the community, and within it both sexes worked to produce the goods necessary for livelihood" (Leacock 1973:33). In this view the oppression of women was built on the transformation of goods for use into commodities for exchange; the exploitation of workers and of women was generated by this process, which involved the emergence of the individual family as an isolated unit, economically responsible for its members, and of women's labor as a private service in the context of the family. This led to the "world historical defeat of the female sex" (Engels 1973:120; Silverblatt 1988:430).

In a reanalysis of Engels Sacks agrees that women's position declined with the elaboration of social classes but disputes Engels' emphasis on the role of private property in this process (Silverblatt 1988:435). Rather, Sacks links state formation and the decline in the centrality of kinship groups to the deterioration in women's status. She delineates two relationships defining women in noncapitalist societies: sisterhood and wifehood. "Sister" refers to women's access to resources based on membership in a kin group. This relation implies autonomy, adulthood, and possible gender symmetry. "Wife," on the other hand, refers to a relationship of dependency on the husband and his kin. Sacks suggests that the development of states undermined women's status by dismantling the kin group corporations that formed the basis for sister relations (Sacks 1982).

However, critics of Sacks' position have argued that the process of state formation may involve uneven and contradictory developments. For example, elite women in the Kingdom of Dahomey, West Africa, challenged state imperatives by means of control of marketing associations. Thus, Silverblatt rebuts Sacks' evolutionary paradigm, suggesting the inevitability of the decline in women's status with state formation; instead, she suggests that we acknowledge the complex history of the emergence of elite privilege in the rise of the state. In addition, elite women such as the royalty of Dahomey may or may not share the goals of peasant women. They may instead join with male elite in suppressing the authority and power of peasant market women. This illustrates the potential contradictions of gender affiliation on one hand, and class position on the other.

Several anthropologists have observed that Engels lacked reliable ethnographic information and oversimplified the complexities of gender relations in kinship societies and in precapitalist states (Gailey 1987:15). In a critique of Engels Moore argues against his essentialist assumptions that there is a "natural" division of labor in which men are concerned with productive tasks and women with domestic ones. She also disagrees that an inevitable relationship will transpire between property, paternity, and legitimacy in which men "naturally" want to transmit property to genetic offspring (Moore 1988: 47–48).

While Rapp (in this book) agrees with these criticisms, she points out that Engels addresses many current concerns, such as the relationship between women's participation in production and female status and the implications of the separation of the domestic-public domains for women's roles in society (see also Silverblatt 1988:432).

She warns against overgeneralizing when trying to understand the origins of the state and ignoring the history and context in which political formations change. In her view we must examine kinship structures that were supplanted with the rise of the state and replaced by territorial and class specific politics. Kinship domains, formerly autonomous, were subjugated to the demands of emergent elites with repercussions for gender roles and relations.

Among the processes that we need to examine are the politics of kinship, the intensification of military complexes, the impact of trade on social stratification, and the changing content and role of cosmology. For example, in stratified societies the establishment of long-distance trade and tribute systems may affect elite marriage patterns, leading to the emergence of dowry and the exchange of women to cement male political alliances. Similar alliances are forged in societies that have experienced a rise in militarism. When economies change and demand increases for a traded commodity, exploitation of labor to produce it may also increase, and marriage systems that expand trading relations may be solidified through the exchange of women. Women themselves may be important figures in trading networks, as in West Africa and in Mesoamerica, where women are active in the marketplace. Alternatively, the extension of the state into localized communities can significantly influence gender roles and relations. This occurs, for example, by undermining women's ritual responsibilities (see Mathews, this book) or by generating conflict between government policy and the respective interests of men and women (see Browner, this book). Finally, changes in political hierarchies were legitimated by cosmological explanations in early states such as the Inca and the Maya. For example, as Maya society became increasingly stratified, a category of elite rulers known as *ahaw* emerged. These rulers were legitimized by myths that established them as mediators between the natural and supernatural worlds and as protectors of the people. State ideology involved the celebration of both male and female forces and the elite contained both men and women. Mothers of kings were always members of the high elite, and this class affiliation was also validated in myth (Schele and Freidel 1990; Freidel and Schele, this book).

In this book, Ortner also examines the process of state formation, with particular regard to its effect on gender ideology. She analyzes the widespread ideology that associates the purity of women with the honor and status of their families. This pattern is evident in Latin America and the Mediterranean and in societies of the Middle East, India, and China. Broad similarities exist in these varied societies. Ortner questions why the control of female sexual purity is such a ubiquitous and important phenomenon. She notes that all modern cases of societies concerned with female purity occur in states or systems with highly developed stratification, and they bear the cultural ideologies and religions that were part of the emergence of these states.

She argues that no prestate societies manifest the pattern linking female virginity and chastity to the social honor of the group. Thus, concern with the purity of women was, in Ortner's view, structurally, functionally, and symbolically linked to the historical emergence of state structures.

The rise of the state heralds a radical shift in ideology and practice, with the emergence of the patriarchal extended family in which the senior man has absolute authority over everyone in the household. Women are brought under direct control of men in their natal families and later by their husbands and affinal kin. Ideologically women are thought to be in danger, requiring male protection; they are idealized as mothers and for their purity.

One of the central questions in Ortner's discussion is the role of hypergamy (up-status marriage, usually between higher-status men and lower-status women) in state systems. Ortner suggests that one of the significant developments in stratified society involves the transformation through marriage from an essentially equal transaction to a potentially vertical one, where one's sister or daughter could presumably marry into a higher strata (wife of a nobleman, consort of a king). Hypergamy may help to explain the ideal of female purity because concepts of purity and virginity may serve to symbolize the value of a girl for a higher-status spouse. Thus "a virgin is an elite female among females, withheld, untouched, exclusive" (Ortner 1981:32).

Hypergamous marriages often involve the exchange of significant amounts of property, particularly in the form of dowry. The relationship between dowry, inheritance, and female status has been explored in a number of societies with varying marriage patterns. Dowry has been described as a form of premortem inheritance, parallel to men's rights in property accrued through inheritance after death of parents or other legators. However, McCreery (in this book) argues that considering dowry as a form of inheritance prior to death and as part of a woman's property complex obscures an important difference between the clear legal inheritance rights that men possess and the dowry that women may or may not receive. Women obtain dowry at the discretion of their parents or brothers, and dowry is not based on the same rights as other forms of inheritance to which men have access. McCreery uses the cases of China, India, and Ceylon (Sri Lanka) to examine women's property rights and how they relate to dowry. Chinese law more heavily emphasized the family as a corporate group of men related through patrilineal descent and consequently severely restricted the rights of women. Indian law gave greater weight to individual rights, including those of women. Finally, in Ceylon both men and women could own and dispose of private property.

In general, it seems that dowry is not best understood as a form of premortem inheritance to the bride; in Ceylon and China especially the legal bases of dowry and inheritance are distinct. Dowries appear to serve as a means of social mobility in stratified societies in which rights over women are used in competition for higher status.

While dowry has been viewed as a form of inheritance for women, the dowry system in northern India has taken a pernicious turn as brides are burned to death, poisoned, or otherwise "accidentally" killed by husbands and in-laws who believe that the women have brought inadequate dowries. Registered cases of dowry deaths in India in 1987 numbered 1,786, although women's groups contend that the real number is higher. Legislation banning dowries has been ineffective in preventing these murders, and the dowry system continues to be deeply embedded in local culture. Some feminist critics argue that dowry deaths represent a response to a growing materialist consumerism sweeping India that has stimulated demands for larger and ever-increasing dowries.

While the status of Indian women as reflected in the exchange of property at marriage appears to be deteriorating, in other parts of the world women's legal status and property rights have improved through state-sponsored changes in the judicial system. For example, Starr (in this book) examines how in Turkey the impact of capitalistic agriculture and settled village life profoundly affected gender relations

and women's access to property. These changes occurred in the cultural context of Islamic notions of male dominance and female submission and legislation giving equal rights to women.

Ottoman family law gave women rights to divorce and some protection against polygamous marriage, but inheritance practices remained constrained by Islamic law, in which women were under the authority of their husbands, had the status of a minor, received half the share of the patrimony obtained by their brothers, and had no rights to children of a marriage. According to Ataturk's secular reforms in the 1920s, women's rights were expanded to full adult status, equal rights to paternal inheritance, protection for widows, and other legislation promoting equality for women. At first these state-initiated rights were incongruent with cultural practices, but by the late 1960s women had begun to use the courts to protect their rights to property and their reputation. Starr points out that while Engels emphasized the negative impact of private ownership on women's status, in this case law and culture played a positive counterbalancing role resulting in women's emancipation.

In all the works included in this chapter of the book we see the enduring influence of the issues raised by Engels with regard to the relationship between gender, property rights, and state structures. However, cross-cultural data demonstrate that this relationship is much more complex and varied than Engels' original formulation. Equally, universal evolutionary paradigms that posit a uniform impact of the rise of the state on gender roles cannot do justice to the myriad ways in which specific cultural histories, diverse social hierarchies, and systems of stratification affect gender relations and ideology. Thus, Silverblatt (1988:448) asks, "What of the challenges that women and men, caught in their society's contradictions, bring to the dominant order of chiefs and castes, an order they contour and subvert, even as they are contained by it? And what of the other voices, the voices that chiefs and rulers do not (or cannot or will not) express?" The complex histories of the relationship between any particular state and gender relations in it show that while state formation has contributed to the definition of womanhood, women have also contributed to the definition of states (Silverblatt 1988:452).

REFERENCES

Engels, Frederick. 1973. *The Origin of the Family, Private Property and the State.* New York: International Publishers.

Gailey, Christine Ward. 1987. *Kinship to Kingship: Gender Hierarchy and State Formation in the Tongan Islands.* Austin: University of Texas Press.

Leacock, Eleanor Burke. 1973. Introduction. In Frederick Engels (ed.). *The Origin of the Family, Private Property and the State,* pp. 7–57. New York: International Publishers.

Moore, Henrietta L. 1988. *Feminism and Anthropology.* Minneapolis: University of Minnesota Press.

Ortner, Sherry. 1981. Gender and Sexuality in Hierarchical Societies: The Case of Polynesia and Some Comparative Implications. In Sherry B. Ortner and Harriet Whitehead (eds.). *Sexual Meanings: The Cultural Construction of Gender and Sexuality,* pp. 359–410. Cambridge: Cambridge University Press.

Sacks, Karen. 1982. *Sisters and Wives: The Past and Future of Sexual Equality.* Urbana: University of Illinois Press.

Schele, Linda and David Freidel. 1990. *A Forest of Kings.* New York: William Morrow.

Silverblatt, Irene. 1988. Women in States. *Annual Review of Anthropology* 17: 427–461.

Gender and Class: An Archaeology of Knowledge Concerning the Origin of the State

Rayna Rapp

The recent wave of feminism has prompted many anthropologists concerned with the status of women to return to Engels' work, *The Origin of the Family, Private Property, and the State.* While anthropologists vary widely in their assessment of the autonomy of women in prestate societies, there seems to be a general consensus that with the rise of civilization, women as a social category were increasingly subjugated to the male heads of their households. That is, civilizations are properly described as patriarchal. This consensus is based, implicitly or explicitly, on the tradition in which Engels was writing. His schema links the growth of private productive property to the dismantling of a communal kinship base in a prestate society. In this process, marriage

grows more restrictive, legitimacy of heirs more important, and wives generally become means of reproduction to their husbands. At the same time, reciprocal relations amongst kinsfolk are curtailed, unequal access to strategic productive resources gradually develops, and estates or classes arise out of formerly kin-based social organizations. In this analysis, the creation of a class hierarchy is intimately linked to the creation of the patriarchal family. Restrictions on women's autonomy emerge with class society.

Engels' analysis informs many of the themes concerning women that are currently being investigated, such as the relation between productive contribution, control over distribution of products, and female status in society; the relation of the mode of reproduction to the mode of production; and the effects of the relative separation or merger of

From *Dialectical Anthropology* 2:309–316, 1977. Reprinted by permission of Kluwer Academic Publishers.

the domestic and public spheres of activity on the roles available to women.[1] Consciously or not, our questions are often framed within the general territory mapped in *Origins*. Yet the major problematic of the book—the postulated intertwined origins of class oppression and gender oppression—has barely been examined. Engels was working with a paucity of ethnological, archaeological and historical cases; he lacked data on primary or pristine state formation, and knew only minimally of highly stratified prestate societies. We, however, have access to a great deal more information concerning societies in transition between primitivity and civilization with which to examine his theory.[2]

Twentieth-century archaeologists and social theorists have amassed a substantive and growing body of theory and data concerning state origins to which we can, in principle, turn. Yet when we do, we discover that our question is certainly not theirs. We face a double theoretical problem in using their models. First: their search for "prime mover" explanations severely limits the questions that are being asked. There exists within evolutionary anthropology a strongly entrenched tradition which seeks to universalize its explanations. Such theories tend to be extremely reductive, and often condense a multiplicity of processes into unilinear variables. These theories range from a concentration on the extraction of social surplus via increasing division of labor and more productive technology (Childe, 1950, 1952); to a focus on the social-contract necessities of hydraulic societies (Wittfogel, 1955, 1957); to status-limitation, perhaps linked to population pressure (Fried, 1960, 1967); to the effects of population pressure and warfare within circumscribed environments (Carneiro, 1970, Harner, 1970). In the search for universal prime movers, the concern of these theorists has been extremely retrospective. They tend to see the state as an inevitable and efficient solution to a particular set of problems. But when the evolution of the state is viewed as a unilineal success story, we lose the specificity of history. A plethora of ranked chiefdoms, proto-states, city-states, feudal domains, empires and even national states have perished over a span of millenia during which the political apparatus we now identify as "the state" evolved. In overgeneralizing, we ignore history, and the context in which political formations change.[3] This leads to a second theoretical problem. For political structures in the primitive world both arise from, and encounter resistance within the kinship base that organizes prestate societies.[4] *Not* uncoincidentally, it is within the kinship domain that women's subordination appears to occur. Yet kinship barely exists in prime mover theories, except as a backdrop to the progress of the growing state. Kinship structures were the great losers in the civilizational process, and they must be examined if we are to understand both incipient class formation, and the changing domains of women. It seems to me that with the rise of state structures, kinbased forms of organization were curtailed, sapped of their legitimacy and autonomy in favor of the evolving sphere of territorial and class-specific politics. Emergent elites needed access to the primary resources of kin-based groups, especially, their labor power. Formerly autonomous kinship domains were domesticated to increased, institutional demands of production and distribution. What was once the realm of total social reproduction got stripped and transformed to underwrite the existence of more powerful, politicized domains. In the process, not only kinship, but women lost out. This is the process we need to examine.

In recent years, many archaeologists have been inclined to reject prime mover explanations for social stratification in favor of more processual, systemic ones. The refutation of the hydraulic imperative and population pressure models on both theoretical and empirical grounds should make us wary of overly-simple explanations which pump causes out of correlations.[5] The "new archaeology" often uses ethnographic models for hypothesis building.[6] In the process, there are some fascinating hints about the role of kinship structure, and possibly women, in stratification. Some of the processes examined in state formation, such as the politics of kinship, the changing content and role of cosmo-logical systems, the intensification of military complexes, and the role of trade in stimulating or increasing social stratification concern our question directly. I will discuss each of these in schematic form, suggesting some of the lines of inquiry they direct us to pursue.

(1) The politics of kinship: The conical clan floats through the literature, bringing with it an increasing tension in alliance, descent, and the transmission of status positions. Adams awards it an ambiguous and critical role in both Mesoamerica and Mesopotamia, and many anthropologists have examined the internal tensions of ranked kinship systems (Kirchoff, 1959; Sahlins, 1958, 1963; Fried, 1967). In highly ranked kinship systems, the role of women is of crucial importance. They not only transmit status, but may be contenders for leadership positions either directly, or through their children. This seems to be the case in Polynesia and in parts of Africa. As Gailey shows for Tonga (1978), the existence of elite, ranked women became more problematic as stratification increased. We need to know more about marriage patterns in such systems. In archaeology, ethnology, and Western history, we find that elite marriages may be implicated in the politics of establishing and maintaining long-distance trade and tribute systems.[7] Dowry is associated with highly stratified systems and dowered, elite women may appear as pawns in a classic case of male alliances formed via their exchange.[8] Ortner (1976) suggests that in state-organized systems, marriage may shift from a horizontal to a potentially vertical transaction, with a tendency toward hypergamy through which elite women accumulate at the top of the system. These structural properties of the marriage system she links with ideologies requiring sexual purity and protection of women (but not of men). Silverblatt, in a study of Inca elite marriages, suggests that as the Incas extended their rule, they used an indigenous, pre-existing system of male/female ritual domains. These were ranked as male-conqueror/female-conquered. Conquered ayllus, identified as female and potential wives of the

Incas, had to send women to Cuzco to serve in the temples, courts, and as noblemen's wives. For the conquered community, this practice represented a loss of autonomy in marriage patterns, and a burden; at the same time, it made possible upward mobility to the specific males who sent sisters and daughters to Cuzco, separating them out in prestige from the collectivity. The women themselves demonstrated the same sort of ambivalence: they gained a great deal of prestige, but lost any autonomy they might have had in arranging their own marriages and living within their natal communities (1976).

(2) Changing Cosmologies: Both Silverblatt and Ortner aid us to focus on the relation of women to cosmological systems in early states. Along with Wiley (1962, 1971), Eliade (1960), and Adams (1966), they remind us that religious systems were the glue that cemented social relations in archaic societies. Such systems were used, as in the Incaic case, to underwrite and justify changes in political hierarchies. They exhibit signs of ideological warfare on the battleground between local and elite pantheons. Tension about female status is often found within them as well. Eliade claims that the ritual expression of sexual antagonism and the existence of bisexual and/or androgynous gods accompanies the social organizational changes associated with the neolithic. Female and androgynous gods are often subsumed, or covered up, by ascendant male figures. This cover-up is sometimes performed indigenously, and often the work of later missionaries. This sort of layering over female and/or androgynous figures has been uncovered in Mesoamerica (Nash, 1976), Peru (Silverblatt, 1976) and is, of course, a favorite theme of classicists for early Greek society (Arthur, 1976; Pomeroy, 1974). Pagels (1976), working with 2nd century A.D. Gnostic texts, analyzes the symbol system of sects in which the early Christian god was bisexual, and the Holy Family consisted of mother, father, and son. Such sects were organized into non-hierarchical religious communities, in which offices were rotated, and women participated in both teaching and preaching—a far cry from the

ascendant Christian cosmology and practice which became the mainstream tradition. Cosmologies have histories; by peeling away their layers we may learn about how the ascendant estate legitimated itself. Cosmological changes are ideological precipitates of structural tensions; it is clear that their form and content have a great deal to tell us about class and gender.

(3) Intensification of Warfare: As early states became increasingly militaristic, social organization was transformed.[9] We need to know what happened to kinship structure, inheritance and succession in the process. Several case histories lead us to believe that under conditions of intense warfare, men were not only burdened by conscription, but were blessed with increasing power as household heads—a kind of trade-off. Muller (1975) finds this to be the case in feudal Wales. Elite males may gain land, political domains, and alliance-forming wives in the process. Yet the recent sweeping statements about male supremacy and warfare (Harris and Divale, 1976) are overgeneralized, even for state-making groups. Some evidence seems to contradict the association of warfare and an elevation of male status at the expense of female autonomy. I lack data on pristine states, but in the ancient West, the correlation often works the other way: Spartan women held offices, controlled their own property and had a great deal of sexual freedom, allegedly because they kept society functioning while the men were at war. Moreover, producing soldiers was considered as important as training them. In Athens, women's access to public places and roles seems to have increased a great deal during times of warfare, especially the Peloponnesian Wars, during which they left their virtual purdah conditions. In Rome, during the Second Punic War, women gained in inheritance settlements and held public offices formerly closed to them (Pomeroy, 1974). In the medieval Franco-Germanic world, noble women attained approximate parity in politics and property-management during the eras of the most brutal military crisis. McNamara and Wemple argue that their relative autonomy is inversely

linked to the existence of any form of public power structure; to the extent that none exists, women are freer to control their inheritance and their marital destinies (1973). All these examples concern elite women only; we know very little about the effects of warfare on laboring women, who probably suffered then, as they do now. Nonetheless, it is not clear that warfare degrades women's status; the specific context within which military organization and practice occurs must be taken into account. Blood and gore clearly are not universalizable variables in theorizing about women's subordination.

(4) Trade: the role of trade in increasing and/or spreading stratification is an intriguing one.[10] Foreign trade goods may be spread in many ways, by middlemen, via migrations, through central trading centers, and in marriage exchanges, to name but a few. Recent literature tells us that the social relations of a production and distribution which undergird trade may be relations of incipient stratification between classes and genders (Kohl, 1975; Wiley, 1974; Adams, 1974). We need to know who produces goods, who appropriates them, and who distributes them. As demand for a traded commodity increases, exploitation of labor to produce it may arise. Marriage systems may also get intensified to expand the reproduction of trading alliances. The ethnographic literature runs rampant with examples of polygyny to increase access to goods that wives make. There are also many instances of increasing class division linked to increasing bridewealth. Sisters and daughters are sometimes portrayed as pawns in alliances that marry into expanding trade networks.[11] It may be women who are used to "prime the pump" of kinship reciprocity in such circumstances. But appropriation and distribution are not exclusively male functions. In Mesoamerica and the Andes to this day, women are active in the marketplace. Silverblatt (1976) suggests that they were important traders in early Incaic times; Adams records their existence in Mesopotamia as well (1966). And of course, their presence is felt in stratified groups throughout Africa and the Caribbean as well, in contemporary ac-

counts (Mintz, 1971). Under what conditions does long-distance trade pass into the hands of men, and when is it possible for women to continue to perform it? When women are traders, do they constitute an elite, class-stratified group? To the extent that trade is implicated in the intensification of production for exchange, women as producers, reproducers, and traders must be implicated, too.

What I am suggesting in these examples is that structural tensions arise within kinship–based societies and that these need careful examination if we are to understand state-formation. I am making a plea for careful historical reconstructions, informed by a feminist perspective, rather than an overly mechanical and generalizing view which erases certain questions before they can be written.

As we come to identify the factors in state formation as they affect women, we must be careful to think in probablistic rather than deterministic terms. We need to contextualize the relative power of kinship and class, the interplay of domestic and extra-domestic economy, the flexibility within cosmological systems, and the relative autonomy or subordination of women, in light of the possibilities open to each society. We should expect to find variations within state-making (and unmaking) societies over time, and between such societies, rather than one simple pattern.

There is another arena to which we can turn in examining how the processes of state formation and penetration affect gender relations. The area we now rather euphemistically call the Third World has served as a bloody laboratory in which stratification by culture, class and gender occurred. While obviously differing from pristine state formation, this process of rapid penetration by patriarchal national states allows us to see how the conditions of primitivity are shattered. In examining the colonization of the indigenous societies of the Americas, Asia, Africa, we need to be very cautious. Each area is heir to its own particular history, as is each colonizing power. Specific histories condition the patterns of resistance, acceptance, or modification of the social organization produced by colonization. We cannot subsume such complexity into one simple model of precapitalist penetration.

Nonetheless, certain patterns affecting the ways of life of women can be traced at a general level. Wherever women have been active horticulturalists of collective lands, the imposition of private property, taxation, labor migration and cash cropping has had devastating effects. Their realm of productivity and expertise has been deformed and often destroyed (Boserup, 1970; Blumberg, 1976; Tinker, 1976). Depending upon context, they may become either super-exploited, or underemployed, but always more dependent upon men. The evidence also suggests a general pattern concerning political organization: prior to colonial penetration, indigenous cultures appear to have been organized into gender domains on essentially parallel lines. Men and women both had organizational forms and rituals which were conditioned by gender-linked relations of production and distribution.[12] Case histories from Africa, Asia and the Americas suggest that patriarchal, colonizing powers rather effectively dismantled native work organizations, political structures, and ritual contexts. The process of demobilizing women occurs when essentially parallel forms are subsumed into one, and that one is male. Leadership and authority are assigned to activities which are male, while female tasks and roles are devaluated, or obliterated. Van Allen's work (1972) describes the political associations of Igbo women which survived the British freeze, and were effectively used to organize the 1929 tax riots. We have case histories recording the effects of assigning credit, technology and education to men such that traditionally female activities are drastically curtailed, or cease to exist. Female marketing is increasingly circumscribed by the influence of internationalization; its agents prefer to deal with men.[13] Several authors have gone so far as to argue that women thus divested of their social organization and collective roles have become rather like underdeveloped, monocrop regions. Once they lived in a diversified world; now they have been reduced to the role of reproducing and exporting labor power for the needs of the international world economy

(Bossen, 1973; Deere, 1976; Boulding, 1975). Please note: in these processes, class stratification as well as gender stratification is operating. Vast categories of men, too, lose autonomy in the broadest sense. My point is that men and women lose it differently, and their lives are transformed differently.

State formation and penetration is processual; its form and force are highly variable, both within and between societies. Yet it is important to remember that the processes which began millenia ago are ongoing. Cumulatively, they continue to transform the lives of the masses of people who exist under their structures. It is a long way from the Sumerian law codes declaring monogamy for women to the welfare laws of the United States which affect parental dyads and household structure. But in both cases, the power of the state to penetrate and reorganize the lives of its members is clear. As we seek to understand the complex, stratified societies in which we now operate, we are led to reflect on archaic societies in which the dual and intertwined processes of hierarchy we now retrospectively label "class" and "patriarchy" took their origins.

NOTES

1. For analyses implicitly or explicitly influenced by *Origins*, see Brown, 1975; Sacks, 1974; Reiter, 1975; Sanday, 1974; Rubin, 1975; Meillassoux, 1975.
2. Summaries of the state formation literature may be found in Service, 1975; Flannery, 1972; Webb, 1975; Krader, 1968.
3. A less determinant and more processual perspective on stratification and state formation is set forth in Flannery, 1972; Tilly, 1975, and Sabloff & Lamberg-Karlovsky, 1975. Such thinking also informs the corpus of Marxist historiography.
4. This has been a major thrust in S. Diamond's work (1951, 1974).
5. Adams, 1966, presents the most cogent critique of the hydraulic hypothesis. Population pressure models are rejected for Iran in Wright & Johnson, 1975, and for the Valley of Mexico by Brumfiel, 1976 and Parsons, 1974. See Cowgill, 1975 for a theoretical and methodological critique.

6. For instances of the "new archaeology's" use of ethnographic evidences for hypothesis building, see Flannery, 1967; Renfrew, 1975, both volumes edited by Sabloff & Lamberg-Karlovsky, 1974 and 1975, and Adams, 1966 and 1974.
7. Such links are suggested in Flannery, 1967; Wiley & Shimkin, 1971, and by much of the literature on stratified chiefdoms, for example, Sahlins, 1958; Kirchoff, 1959; and Fried, 1967. In European history, we find instances in the international royal marriage patterns. See McNamara & Wemple, 1973, for some of the implications of feudal marriage patterns.
8. See Arthur, 1976; Ortner, 1976; Goody & Tambiah, 1973.
9. The temple and military-complexes figure in the state formation schemes of Steward, 1955; Adams, 1966, and Wiley, 1971, to name but a few.
10. The archaeology of trade is discussed in Sabloff and Lamberg-Karlovsky, 1975, and is critically summarized in both Adams, 1974, and Kohl, 1975. See also Wiley, 1974.
11. Ethnographic examples used to speculate about ancient trade are provided by Adams (1974) who cites materials on the Cheyenne and Blackfoot, and Flannery (1967) who uses Tlingit materials. In these cases, marriage alliances were intensified along with trade.
12. Parallel and interarticulating forms of gender social organization are analyzed in Siskind, 1976; Brown, 1970; Silverblatt, 1976; Van Allen, 1972, and Sacks, 1976.
13. See Mintz, 1971, Boserup, 1970, Tinker, 1976, and Blumberg, 1976 for specific examples. Agricultural schools throughout Africa often closed their doors to women, the traditional horticulturalists. Agricultural machinery for "women's work" often falls into the laps of men as the sole possessors of access to credit.

REFERENCES

Adams, R.M. (1966). *The Evolution of Urban Society.* Chicago: Aldine.

Adams, R.M. (1974). "Anthropological Perspectives on Ancient Trade," *Current Anthropology,* Vol. 15.

Arthur, M. (1976). "Liberated Women: The Classical Era," in Bridenthal and Koontz (eds.), *Becoming Visible: Women in European History.* New York: Houghton and Mifflin.

Blumberg, R. (1976). "Fairy Tales and Facts: Economy, Fertility, Family and the Female.

Boserup, E. (1970). *Women's Role in Economic Development.* London: George Allen and Unwin.

Bossen, L. (1973). "Women in Modernizing Societies." *American Ethnologist,* Vol. 2.

Boulding, E. (1975). "Women, Bread and Babies". University of Colorado, Institute of Behavioral Sciences, Program on Research of General Social and Economic Development.

Brown, J. (1970). "A Note on the Economic Division of Labor by Sex," *American Anthropologist,* Vol. 72.

Brown, J. (1975). "Iroquois Women," in R. Reiter (ed.). *Toward an Anthropology of Women.* New York: Monthly Review Press.

Brumfiel, E. (1976). "Regional Growth in the Valley of Mexico," in Flannery (ed.). *The Early Mesoamerican Village,* New York: Academic Press.

Carneiro, R. (1970). "A Theory of the Origin of the State," *Science,* Vol. 169.

Childe, G. (1950). "The Urban Revolution," *Town Planning Review,* Vol. 21, No. 3.

Childe, G. (1952). "The Birth of Civilization," *Past and Present,* Vol. 2, No. 1.

Cowgill, G. (1975). "Causes and Consequences of Ancient and Modern Population Changes," *American Anthropologist* Vol. 77.

Deere, C. (1976). "Rural Women's Subsistence Production in the Capitalist Periphery," *Review of Radical Political Economics,* Vol. 8.

Diamond, S. (1951). *Dahomey: A Protostate in West Africa.* Ann Arbor: University Microfilms.

Diamond, S. (1974). *In Search of the Primitive: A Critique of Civilization,* New Brunswick, N.J.: Transaction Books.

Eliade, M. (1960). "Structures and Changes in the History of Religions," in Kraeling and Adams (eds.), *City Invincible,* Chicago: University of Chicago Press.

Flannery, K. (1972). "The Cultural Evolution of Civilizations," *Annual Review of Ecology and Systematics,* Vol. 3.

Flannery, K. (1974). "The Olmec and the Valley of Oaxaca," reprinted in Sabloff and Lamberg-Karlovsky (eds.). *The Rise and Fall of Civilizations.* Menlo Park, Ca.: Cummings.

Fried, M. (1960). "On the Evolution of Social Stratification and the State," in S. Diamond (ed.), *Culture and History.* New York: Columbia University Press.

Fried, M. (1967). *The Evolution of Political Society.* New York: Random House.

Gailey, C. (1978). "Origins of the State in Tonga: Gender Hierarchy and Class Formation," *Dialectical Anthropology,* Vol. 3.

Goody, J. and Tambiah, S. (1973). *Bridewealth and Dowry.* Cambridge: Cambridge University Press.

Harner, M. (1970). "Population Pressure and the Social Evolution of Agriculturalists," *Southwestern Journal of Anthropology,* Vol. 26.

Harris, M. and Divale, W. (1976). "Population, Warfare and the Male Supremacist Complex," *American Anthropologist,* Vol. 78.

Kirchoff, P. (1959). "The Principles of Clanship in Human Society," in Fried (ed.), *Readings in Anthropology,* Vol. 2. New York: Crowell.

Kohl, P. (1975). "The Archaeology of Trade," *Dialectical Anthropology,* 1:43–50.

Krader, L. (1968). *Formation of the State.* Englewood Cliffs: Prentice-Hall.

McNamara, J. and Wemple, S. (1973). "The Power of Women through the Family in Medieval Europe: 500–1100," *Feminist Studies,* Vol. 1.

Meillassoux, C. (1975). *Femmes, greniers et capitaux.* Paris: Maspero.

Mintz, S. (1971). "Men, Women, and Trade," *Comparative Studies in Society and History,* Vol. 12.

Muller, V. (1975). "The Formation of the State and the Oppression of Women: England and Wales," manuscript.

Nash, J. (1976). "Aztec Women," manuscript.

Ortner, S. (1976). "The Virgin and the State," *Michigan Papers in Anthropology,* Vol. 2.

Pagels, E. (1976). "When did God Make Man in His Image?" *Signs,* Vol. 2:

Parsons, J. (1974). "The Development of a Prehistoric Complex Society," *Journal of Field Archaeology,* Vol. 1.

Pomeroy, S. (1974). *Goddesses, Whores, Wives and Slaves.* New York: Schocken.

Reiter, R. (1975). "Men and Women in the South of France," in R. Reiter (ed.), *Toward an Anthropology of Women.* New York: Monthly Review Press.

Renfrew, C. (1975). "Trade as Action at a Distance," in Sabloff and Lamberg-Karlovsky (eds.), *Ancient Civilizations and Trade.* Albuquerque, N.M.: University of New Mexico Press.

Rubin, G. (1975). "The Traffic in Women," in R. Reiter (ed.), *Toward an Anthropology of Women.* New York: Monthly Review Press.

Sabloff and Lamberg-Karlovsky (eds.). (1975). *Ancient Civilizations and Trade.* Albuquerque, N.M.: University of New Mexico Press.

Sacks, K. (1974). "Engels Revisited," in Rosaldo and Lamphere (eds.), *Woman, Culture and Society.* Stanford: Stanford University Press.

Sacks, K. (1976). "State Bias and Women's Status," *American Anthropologist*, Vol. 78.

Sanday, P. (1974). "Toward a Theory of the Status of Women," in Rosaldo and Lamphere (eds.), *Woman, Culture and Society*. Stanford: Stanford University Press.

Sahlins, M. (1958). *Social Stratification in Polynesia*. Seattle: University of Washington Press.

Sahlins, M. (1963). "Poor Man, Rich Man, Big-Man, Chief," *Comparative Studies in Society and History*, Vol. 5.

Service, E. (1975). *Origins of the State and Civilization*. New York: Norton.

Silverblatt, I. (1976). "Inca Women: Conquered Moon, Conquering Sun," manuscript, Department of Anthropology, University of Michigan.

Siskind, J. (1976). "Kinship: Relations of Production," manuscript.

Steward, J. (1955). *The Theory of Culture Change*. Urbana: University of Illinois Press.

Tilly, C. (1975). Reflections on the History of European State Making," in Tilly (ed.), *The Formation of National States in Western Europe*. Princeton: Princeton University Press.

Tinker, I. (1976). "The Adverse Impact of Development on Women," in Tinker and Bramsen (eds.), *Women and World Development*. Overseas Development Council.

Van Allen, J. (1972). "Sitting on a Man," *Canadian Journal of African Studies*, Vol. 6.

Webb, M. (1975). "The Flag Follows Trade," in Sabloff and Lamberg-Karlovsky (eds.), *Ancient Civilizations and Trade*. Albuquerque, N.M.: University of New Mexico Press.

Wiley, G. (1962). "The Early Great Styles and the Rise of Pre-Columbian Civilizations," *American Anthropologist*, Vol. 64.

Wiley, G. (1974). "Precolumbian Urbanism," in Sabloff and Lamberg-Karlovsky (eds.), *The Rise and Fall of Civilizations*. Menlo Park, Ca.: Cummings.

Wiley, G. (1974). "Commentary on the Emergence of Civilization in the Maya Lowlands," in Sabloff and Lamberg-Karlovsky (eds.), *The Rise and Fall of Civilizations*. Menlo Park, Ca.: Cummings.

Wiley, G. and Shimkin, D. (1971). "The Collapse of the Classic Maya Civilization in the Southern Lowlands," *Southwestern Journal of Anthropology*, Vol. 27.

Wittfogel, K. (1955). "Oriental Society in Transition," *Far Eastern Quarterly*, Vol. 14, p. 469–478.

Wittfogel, K. (1957). *Oriental Despotism*. New Haven: Yale University Press.

Wright, H. and Johnson, G. (1975). "Population, Exchange and Early State Formation in Southwestern Iran," *American Anthropologist*, Vol. 77.

The Virgin and The State

Sherry B. Ortner

In an extraordinarily wide range of societies in the world one finds a peculiar "complex": ideologically it is held that the purity of the women reflects on the honor and status of their families; and the ideology is enforced by systematic and often quite severe control of women's social and especially sexual behavior. One sees this pattern manifested among peasant societies in Latin America and around the entire Mediterranean area, among pastoral nomadic tribes of the Middle East and southwest Asia, among the castes of India, and among the elites of China. In extreme cases, such as classical Athens or among Brahmins of India, women were confined to the house for life. In imperial Turkey, the sultan had vast numbers of wives and

This article is reprinted from *Feminist Studies*, volume 4, number 3 (October 1978): 19–35, by permission of the publisher, *Feminist Studies*, Inc., c/o Women's Studies Program, University of Maryland, College Park, MD 20742.

daughters "in an elaborately organized harem, or seraglio, with disciplinary and administrative officers, ruled over by [his] mother." Among poorer peasants and nomads, a variety of other devices—veils; rules of body-disguising dress and of modest demeanor; restrictions on expression, communication, and movement; all overseen by the family in particular and the gossip of the community in general—serve to restrict women's social and sexual behavior as effectively as if they were locked up.[1]

Reviewing the variety of cases, one tends to get involved in particular cultural symbolizations and practices, and to lose sight of the broad similarities of pattern. Further, the pattern does not seem to be confined to any particular type of society, or to any consistent stratum: peasants and elites, agriculturalists and pastoral nomads, all seem to embrace some version of the female purity ethic with equal intensity and commitment. It seems difficult to imagine that there might be a single interpretation that would cover, or at least interrelate, all the cases.

In fact, in the anthropological analyses of particular cases, a variety of interpretive frameworks have been used: psychoanalytic, structural, functional, ecological, political, or some mixture of several of these. Let me begin to situate the question of why the control of female sexual purity is such a widespread and virulent phenomenon, by reviewing briefly some of the major attempts at interpretation in the anthropological literature.[2]

In an early essay from a psychoanalytic perspective, Kathleen Gough analyzed the female initiation rites among the Nayar and other groups of the Malabar region of India. Gough interpreted the rituals as signifying the formal renunciation by the girl's consanguineal kinsmen of rights to her sexuality, in a social context in which there is evidently strong incest temptation. Further, during these rites the young girl was actually or symbolically deflowered by a person other than her prospective husband; and Gough interpreted this point as representing male fear of the defloration of virgins in the course of normal sexuality. Although Nayar women do not seem to fit our model in that, following their initiation they had great sexual freedom, we must not forget that their freedom was gained at the expense of Nambudiri Brahmin women, who were subject to virtually total seclusion and control. Untold numbers of Nambudiri women died virgins, while Nambudiri men mated with the conveniently available Nayar.[3]

In a subsequent counteressay, Nur Yalman challenged (and ridiculed) Gough's interpretation and recast the whole argument in terms of the control of female purity. He stressed that the rites establish the purity of the women in their own castes and serve to define and regulate the women's subsequent choices of mates, who must always be of equal or higher caste status. The issue, he argued, is control of caste purity and status as a whole, which must be maintained by regulation of female sexuality, because regardless of the descent principles operating within intracaste kinship groupings, caste as opposed to kin affiliation is always inherited bilaterally. Further, if caste membership is defined as coming only through one parent, that parent is always the mother. Thus for purposes of sustaining caste purity, the woman's purity in particular must be controlled, protected against pollution by lower-caste mates. Men, on the other hand, are free to have sexual relations with anyone, "high or low" as Yalman says, and he then explains this in both cultural and natural terms. Culturally, the Indians distinguish between internal and external pollution. Women are subject to internal pollution in sexual intercourse, which is very hard if not impossible to cleanse, but men are subject only to external pollution in intercourse and can be cleansed by a simple ritual bath. Yet Yalman goes further than this cultural point, and relates the ideology to natural factors: "the bond between the genitor and the child is tenuous; it can always be denied or minimized; the children can always be repudiated by the father."[4]

More recent studies have tended to get away from elusive unconscious factors and symbolic cultural notions of pure and impure, and to stress the brass tacks of economics and politics. Lawrence Watson describes the practices of the Guajiro of Venezuela, among whom the virginity of a girl upon marriage is absolutely demanded, the result being assured by a combination of psychological terrorism and physical punishment, mostly enacted by mothers on their daughters. For a serious offense, "the mother may place the tip of a hot branding iron on the girl's vagina to make the punishment a convincing object lesson." Watson casts his interpretation of this system in terms of the political structure of the society, in which every group is concerned about maintaining its status in a rigid class system; the group's status depends in part upon the quality of the women it can deliver in the marriage alliance process. Especially among the upper classes, influential chiefs overtly use marriage alliances of daughters and sisters as a way of building up followings for political and military backing. "If . . . a woman causes her father or uncle to lose valuable political allies because of deficiencies in her sexual behavior, she becomes a liability and she can seriously impede her lineage's chances of building up a secure base of political support." In this interpretation, the sadistic control of female purity is simply a form of *realpolitik*.[5]

And finally, Jane Schneider presents an argument in terms of ecological and economic factors, and the politics thereof. In her important paper, "Of Vigilance and Virgins . . . ", she begins with the general point that "honor can be thought of as the ideology of a property holding group which struggles to define, enlarge, and protect its patrimony in a competitive arena." She then goes on to argue that both pastoral and peasant societies tend to be highly socially fragmented and "unsolidary," although the reasons for this social fragmentation are different in the two cases. And according to Schneider, honor is the code that keeps this "centrifugal" situation together: it "helps shore up the identity of a group (a family or a lineage) and commit to it the loyalties of otherwise doubtful members. [It] defines the group's social boundaries, contributing to its defense against the claims

of equivalent competing groups. [It] is also important as a substitute for physical violence in the defense of economic interests. . . . Honor regulates affairs among men." But why the honor of the *women?* Why should the women's honor represent the honor of the group as a whole? Because, says Schneider, resolutely practical to the end, among the pastoralists concerned with lineage continuity, female reproductive capacity is valuable, and women are "contested resources much like pastures and water." As for the agrarian peasants, the problem seems primarily to be the potential fragmentation of the family of procreation, with fathers, sons, and brothers set off against one another because of inheritance rules; here the daughters/sisters provide the one shared focus of concern that can hold the group together.[6]

I will restrain my temptation to dissect the circularities and self-contradictions of many of these arguments and will simply say that, with the exception of the psychoanalytic argument, all of them share common functionalist orientations: the purity of women is seen as adaptive for the social coherence, economic viability, or cultural reputation of the group, regardless of whether the group is a caste, lineage, or family. When the theorists try to explain why women in particular should represent the coherence and integrity of the group, rather than, say, a totemic bird or a sacred flute, the answers are more variable—in terms of women's natural childbearing abilities, women's physical structure (internal pollution), women's function as tokens of alliance, or women's symbolic roles in the family. None of these answers is very satisfactory; all use as explanations the very things that need explaining. We are still left with the paradox that male-defined structures represent themselves and conceptualize their unity and status through the purity of their women.

I would argue then that all of these explanations can be lumped together and that they share a set of common failings. First, all are static functional accounts, and lack time depth. Second, all share the common functionalist fallacy of reifying the unit under study and treating it as closed, exclusive, and isolated from a larger social context—the family, lineage, or caste is treated almost as a society in itself. And finally, all explanations, with the exception of the psychoanalytic discussion, take the point of view that the problem is one of male/male relations, in which the women are intermediaries, rather than the problem being, as it at least equally is, a problem of male/female relations. Although each of the arguments contains some useful kernel of truth, none provides a framework for encompassing and accounting for the phenomenon as a whole in cross-cultural, cross-class, and cross-sex perspective.

What I should like to do in this paper, then, is to offer some observations, thoughts, suggestions, and hypotheses for exploring this problem more systematically, and in a way that will illuminate problems of social and cultural process in general, as well as male/female relations in particular.

I would begin by noting that all of the modern cases of societies concerned with female purity are in fact of a certain type, namely, that all are part of, or have historically been part of, states, or at least systems with fairly highly developed stratification.[7] Thus hyperpure Brahmins and hyperpoor Mediterranean peasants share the status of being part-structures, elements in larger stratified political structures. Even when the larger state structures in which they originally developed are no longer organically intact, all of the modern groups in question bear the cultural ideologies, and particularly the religions, which were part of the organic emergence of their ancestral states in the first place. Most of the societies concerned with female purity are involved in so-called great traditions, especially Christianity, Islam, and Hinduism. And these religions evolved in conjunction with the emergence of states (or "civilizations," or empires) which, although most are no longer intact, nonetheless shaped the societies and cultures of the groups that bear their cultural heritages. And most of the peasants whose ancient states have decayed are now involved with modern states in ways that are structurally similar to their places in the original ones.

It is true that there are pre-state societies which, for example, require the virginity of women at marriage, and probably the majority of human societies expect relative sexual faithfulness of women after marriage. But no pre-state societies, as far as I have been able to ascertain, evince the sort of pattern I am concerned with here—the ideological linkage of female virginity and chastity to the social honor of the group, such chastity being secured by the exertion of direct control over women's mobility to the point of lifetime seclusion, and/or through severe socialization of fear and shame concerning sex.[8] What I am suggesting, then, is that this sort of concern with the purity of women was part of, and somehow structurally, functionally, and symbolically bound up with, the historical emergence of systematically stratified state-type structures, in the evolution of human society.[9]

Before examining what the purity of women might have to do with the emergence of states, however, let me sketch very briefly what I see as the patterns and tendencies of female/male relations in pre-state societies, or rather in contemporary societies that have historically been outside of known state systems, and that have not themselves evolved the social, political, and economic characteristics of states. I would begin with the point that there is always, even in the most primitive of known societies, some sort of asymmetry between the sexes. Even the most manifestly egalitarian of band societies accords some edge of authority or charisma or status to men, if only on the view that the big game that the men bring home is superior as food to the women's gathered produce. In slightly more complex band societies, it seems that there is always some sacred center or ritual from which women are excluded. And although women may have their sacred ceremonies, from which men are excluded, the male ceremonies are considered to be for the welfare of the group as a whole, while the women's ceremonies are specific to the welfare of women. Finally, in the most complex of the known band societies, primarily in Australia, male authority is asserted through, and reinforced by systematic control of the marriage system, the exchange of women and goods. Control of the marriage system, always in the hands of men, transforms diffuse authority or charisma into the beginnings of real power and control. Nonetheless, being bartered about in a system of marriage exchange is not the same thing as having one's day-to-day behavior and freedom of movement directly controlled, and in fact women in band societies evidently have a great deal of autonomy of action, as long as they comply with the legal rules of the game. There is also no ideology in these societies about protecting female purity.

If anything, the ideology is just the reverse, and women are often seen as, to some degree, dangerous and polluting. According to Mary Douglas, pollution beliefs are systematically related to cultural category ambiguities and anomalies;[10] the danger and pollution of women would seem to derive in large part from the fact that women systematically appear as ambiguous vis-à-vis two very important, and partly related, category distinctions that may be common to all human societies. The first distinction is the nature/culture dichotomy, and I have discussed at length elsewhere woman's ambiguity vis-à-vis this opposition.[11] The second is the structure/antistructure, or order/disorder dichotomy, in which men and male groups are identified with structure, order, social organization itself. Insofar as women are moved around in marriage, in a social exchange system controlled by, and culturally seen as composed of, structured groups of men, women appear interstitial within the fundamental kinship architecture of society.[12] Further, the ambiguity of women would derive not only from a marriage perspective; insofar as there is descent ideology, whether patrilineal or matrilineal, women are seen as "in between" in these sorts of systems as well, for descent groups (such as clans) see themselves as groups of males, with women as their reproductive agents. With respect to either or both of these oppositions—nature/culture, structure/antistructure—women may appear ambiguous, and hence potentially polluting and dangerous. And although none of the simplest hunting/gathering socie-

ties manifest the phobia about female pollution and danger that appears among, for example, New Guinea horticulturalists, most have a variety of taboos and avoidance rules that seem concerned with keeping at least some of the boundaries drawn.

Now between hunting/gathering band societies on the one hand, and states on the other, there is obviously a vast range of types of societies, of widely varying structure and complexity. I have yet to find or devise a classification scheme that organizes all of them in some satisfactory evolutionary sequence. I will plow right through all this complexity, however, and simply say that through all the types of pre-state societies, female/male relations stay broadly within the pattern established over the range of band societies—from relatively mutualistic and balanced, to the extreme cases of sex antagonism, with male self-segregation, and strong expressions of fear of women as dangerous. But again the expression of and reaction to fear of women in those extreme cases, and here I am thinking largely of New Guinea and South America, involves *exclusion* of women, or attempts thereof, rather than systematic domination and control. My image here is the New Guinea or South American village, with the men huddled in men's houses in the center off-limits to the women, and the women strung out around the periphery in their individual huts with their uterine families. Even in North America, a much less extreme area on this score, we find the male sweat lodges, the kivas into which women are not allowed, and so forth. But as long as the women do not trespass on the off-limits areas, they have considerable autonomy of action, and indeed a certain edge of power insofar as they can appropriate and judiciously imply control of some of the powers with which the male culture endows them. As in band societies, the one area in which men do exercise systematic control over women is the marriage system. Again, however, there is no ideology that the women exchanged in marriage must be virginal, sexually naive, and mystically pure; nor is seclusion of women practiced as a means of controlling their sexuality.

Finally, however, we get to the great divide: the rise of the state. Here there is a radical shift of both ideology and practice. On the ground, we have the emergence of the patriarchal extended family. Indeed here for the first time the term patriarchy becomes applicable, because the structure involves the absolute authority of the father or other senior male over everyone in the household—all junior males and all females. And now women are for the first time brought under direct and systematic control, first by their natal families, and then by their husbands and their affinal kin. Among elites, one has the image of women being rounded up in great numbers and confined in harems and analogous arrangements elsewhere. Among the Brahmins of India, they are locked in great purdah palaces and never emerge into the world. The notion develops that men are directly responsible for the behavior of their women, rendering it part of every man's definition of self and manliness that "his" women never escape his control; his honor, and the honor of his group, are at stake.

At the same time, there is a great shift in the ideology concerning women. Before they were dangerous, but now they are said to be *in danger,* justifying male protection and guardianship. Before they were polluting, and this had to be defended against, but now they are said to be pure, and to need defending. At the same time, one finds for the first time symbolic idealization of woman in the mother-aspect, rather than in the sexual-reproductive aspect. Eventually, as the symbol system gets itself together in one part of the world with which we are all familiar, the ideal woman emerges as all the best things at once, mother and virgin.

Now the way in which I've described the pattern, and the way in which it might, at first glance, be viewed, is in terms of the domestication of women, a sort of Neolithic of the sexes wherein women, like plants and animals, were brought under control in the service of the race. Actually, however, my thinking is to envision the process in terms of the beginnings of the domestication of *men,* as part of a larger pattern of systematization of

hierarchy and control in the evolution of state structures. I will return to this point later.

In any case, the whole business is terribly complex. What I shall do here is simply offer a brief checklist of points that I think would be important to consider in trying systematically to account for the changes in sex-role relations and ideology that seem to be associated with the emergence of the state. The checklist consists of the following items, in no particular order: the question of diffusion, the question of changes in the division of labor, changes in religious thought, changes in family structure, and changes in marriage patterns. I shall only be able to say a few words about each, merely pointing in the direction I think investigation should go.

Diffusion, first, is something that cannot be entirely ruled out. It is possible that the pattern I have described—idealization of female chastity; ideology of protection, control, and seclusion of women—developed in one area of the ancient old world, and reached other early states through trade and other diffusionary mechanisms. Most of the known contemporary societies with this pattern are geographically contiguous, in a broad band from the circum-Mediterranean area, across the Middle East and southwest Asia, across India, and up into China.[13] The new world indigenous states would thus have to be investigated for independent evolution of the pattern.[14] Even if indicated, however, we know that diffusion in itself never explains very much, for peoples hear of many peculiar customs practiced by their neighbors, yet those practices will only be adopted if the social structural and ideological conditions are ripe for their reception. That is, the diffusion would only have taken hold as independently developing societies evolved the sorts of structures within which such a pattern of sex role relations would be functional and meaningful.

The second point, very briefly, is the question of whether changes in the division of labor may have motivated changes in sex-role relations and ideologies. One standard view has it that, with the rise of plow agriculture and/or systematic irrigation systems associated with the rise of states, women were excluded from major roles in the sphere of production, while their reproductive value in the family was more strongly emphasized. My own reading of the data is quite different. It is probably true that men became associated with plowing as a specific activity, and with the engineering and control of irrigation systems, and both of these points are quite important in the symbolics of male prestige. Nonetheless it seems that women continued to be fully productive, and if anything worked even harder than they did before, in both grain production in the western old world and rice production in the east. The gradual withdrawal of women from production (where it happened) was, I think, a very late development. It will thus not account for the emergence of the female purity pattern, although it will have repercussions in that pattern later.

In the domain of religion, next, I would stress the point that an elaborated notion of purity *in general* only comes in systematically with the emergence of state structures. In pre-state societies, including the simplest that we know, one of course finds the notion that exceptional purity, often including temporary celibacy, is required for specific important purposes. Generally, it is associated with some major male undertaking—a hunt, a raid, or a ritual—and is conceived in terms of purifying or at least not polluting male energies, so that they will be strong and focused for the big event. Nonetheless, there is no notion that it would be good for some people, female or male, to strive for permanent exceptional purity, including permanent celibacy. Such notions probably come in with permanent standing priesthoods of some kind, and these of course are standard, virtually diagnostic, features of early states.

If the chastity of priests was the first application of the notion of chastity to a social group, its rationale was probably similar to that for the episodic demands for purity in pre-state societies: the priest is charged with protection of sacred objects and activities, and he (or sometimes she) must be in a permanent state of non-pollution for the job. But it would seem that there is more to it than

this. In particular I would suggest that in state religions and cosmologies, what seems to happen is that the whole purity ceiling is raised, so to speak. That is, one finds systematic elaboration of higher realms of purity and sacredness than existed before, with more exacting demands upon the laity for conforming to religious ideals. Thus it may be a matter of the religion postulating higher, more sacred, and more demanding gods (e.g., the Aztec gods who required human sacrifice), and/or a more articulated after-death state (as, for example, in *The Egyptian Book of the Dead*). Transcendental power, divinity, sacredness, and purity are all more articulated than previously.

It is not at all difficult to account for the emergence of such ideologies in state structures, in relation to the overall increased complexity of society—for example, more complex divine hierarchies may reflect more complex social hierarchies; or more demanding gods may reflect the greater demands of the state and the dominant classes; or more elaborated notions of afterlife may be interpreted as promising the newly emergent masses their rewards later rather than now, and so forth. The situation is of course infinitely more complex than this, but cannot be explored here. My point is simply that one would begin to investigate the elaboration of the notion of female purity by contextualizing it in the emergence of systematic views of transcendental purity in state cosmologies in general. Purity as something that whole categories of people might intrinsically possess, or might systematically be required to sustain, as itself, I think, a product of state-related religious thought. Mind/body dualisms (reflecting, among other things, new divisions of labor between intellectual/artistic/political elites and producing masses), and the control of sexuality, sensuality, and materialism (part of, among other things, a delayed-gratification, reduced-material-expectations, ideology for the masses) would be aspects of this general pattern.

Coming down from the cosmological heights to ground-level social structure, the fourth item covers changes in the structure of the family. Again I will be very brief, although the problem requires detailed scrutiny. The key point is undoubtedly the emergence of the patriarchal family structure, and probably ideally the patriarchal extended family. But the way in which I would look at this phenomenon, as I noted earlier, is in terms of the domestication of men, both as husbands/fathers, and as sons. Probably the catalyst around which the whole thing crystallized was the property holding in one form or another, although it was certainly not yet "private" property. Be that as it may, what I think was at issue was the gradual deepening of involvement of individual males in responsibility, as husbands/fathers, for their specific family units—not just economic responsibility, for that was always accepted, but also what might be called political accountability. The family became in a sense an administrative unit, the base unit in the political-economic structure of the state. The husband/father was no longer simply responsible *to* his family, but also *for* his family vis-à-vis the larger system. It became the base, and often the only base, of his jural status.

Now, judging from contemporary cases, I imagine that such deepening involvement of men in families was accepted only reluctantly, and as part of a tradeoff for patterns of deference and respect from wives and children. The reluctance of males to be involved with their families except on terms of distance, respect, and submission on the part of the other members is still I think to be seen in most of the world today, and the domestication of men is still largely incomplete. Nonetheless, the notion that males are not only economically but also legally and politically responsible for the proper functioning of the family unit seems to be part of the systematic extension of principles of hierarchy, domination, and order in the evolution of states as a whole. Responsible husbands/fathers are more systematically incorporated into the system.

Responsible husbands/fathers, which is to say in this context patriarchal husbands/fathers, in turn keep everyone else in line—the women, of course, but also the sons. Indeed, perhaps the most striking characteristic of the

patriarchal family is the prolongation of dependence and subjugation of sons. This is such an overdetermined phenomenon that one can hardly begin to sort out its sources and components. However, let it suffice to say that sons are held back from the acquisition of property, wives, and emotional maturity by such a powerful combination of forces, emanating from both father and mother, that it is certainly one of the key changes that we see in family structure, regardless of household composition (that is, regardless of whether the family is "extended" or not). Male initiation rites virtually disappear in state societies; and far from fathers and other senior males facilitating, however frighteningly, a young male's passage to adulthood, the young adult male in the patriarchal family remains in a jurally dependent status at least until he is married, and often beyond. In many cases marriage itself becomes the only rite of passage, and thus manhood becomes equated with responsibility for wife and children, part of the pattern described above.

This pattern is likely to have certain psychodynamic implications. One may wish to go the Freudian route, in terms of deep unconscious factors, and I am not immune to the persuasions of a well-done Freudian analysis. Kathleen Gough's paper on female initiation rites, mentioned earlier, is an excellent and very convincing Freudian discussion of the sorts of fears and ideals of women produced in such family situations in the Indian case. However, one can probably account for a lot without recourse to unconscious factors, through careful symbolic analysis of cultural notions of mothers and wives in such systems. The pivotal point of such analysis would be that men were not only "domesticated" as part of the crystallization of authority structures of the state; they were also juvenilized— vis-à-vis women, senior men, and the rulers and overclasses of the system.

Note that I have not tried to postulate motives for either women or men in this process. I have suggested that men were "reluctant" about being domesticated, but I would imagine that women had equally mixed feelings about the greater presence of male authority in the family unit. I do not think it is useful to view this process in terms of (in Engels' famous phrase) "the world historical defeat of women" by men, or other such motivated formulations. The crystallization of patriarchal family corporations was doubtless a precipitate of larger political and economic processes. Nonetheless, once it got going, it became a social force in its own right, affecting not only the further evolution of gender relations, but also the economic and political evolution of the larger system itself.

The final item on the present checklist is the question of changes in marriage systems. I noted earlier that concern for the purity of women is found, in contemporary societies, among both elites and lower strata. In southern Europe, the peasants seem much more concerned about the issue than the upper classes; for elites the relative freedom of their women is a symbol of their modernity, or else simply a symbol of their being above the codes. In India or China, on the other hand, the Brahmins and upper classes were far stricter about the purity of their women than the lower castes and the peasants. In trying to account for the emergence of a code of female purity as part of the emergence of the state, one would perhaps want to begin with the question of which stratum started the whole thing. Thus some might argue that it was probably originally an elite conceit, in that elite women (if not other women) did not need to engage in productive labor, and could be secluded and protected from the pollutions of work and people as a mark of upper-class status. One could argue with equal logic, however, that there are aspects of peasant social life and social structure that would generate a concern for the purity of women, as in Jane Schneider's discussion previously noted.

The way out of the puzzle, I would suggest, lies in stressing the stratified nature of the state as a totality, and seeking the dynamics of the process in the *interaction* between elites and lower strata. In particular, my analytic instinct is to look at patterns of hypergamy (up-status marriage, virtually always between upper men and lower women) in state sys-

tems, and to consider very centrally the possibility that one of the significant developments in stratified societies was the shifting of marriage from an essentially lateral transaction, between essentially equal groups, to at least a potentially vertical transaction, where in one's sister or daughter is potentially a wife or consort of a king or nobleman, or could be dedicated to the temple and the services of the priesthood.

I think it is fairly safe to expect to find patterns and ideals of hypergamy, or what might be called vertical alliance, in stratified societies. Vertical alliance would constitute one of several sorts of paternalistic ties between the strata. But what analytic consequences flow from putting this point at the center of the analysis?

In the first place, as has been noted by others for India, the assumption of systematic hypergamy as an ideal and to some extent as a practice will account for the phenomenon of women accumulating at the top of the system.[15] Because lower-status families are eager to marry their women upwards for political reasons, the elites would accumulate wives. At the same time, the elites would often be unable to get rid of their own sisters and daughters, for there is nowhere further up for those women to go. Thus the emergence harems, purdah palaces, and so forth, would partly be a structural precipitate of the hypergamy system, rather than an indication of (among other possibilities) the extraordinary lust of sultans. At the same time, the accumulation of wives by polygynous royalty and nobility would certainly have value in the symbolics of power, for it would suggest their potency in everything from sex to politics to the fertility of the land. Thus the image of herds of penned-up women that is projected in these sorts of systems flows partly from the dynamics of the marriage system, and not from men rounding up and controlling women as such.

Second, hypergamy may provide the strongest explanation for the purity of women ideal and for certain peculiarities of this ideal. The context of hypergamy is a context of orientation toward upward mobility, through manipulation of marriages. We know that the *economic* value of women becomes a focus in these contexts, for it is here that we find the emergence of dowry, enhancing the girl's value for a higher-status spouse.[16] In addition, however, there is the question of her mystical or spiritual value, her inner worthiness for such an alliance. The notions of virginity and chastity may be particularly apt for symbolizing such value, rather than, for example, external beauty, because virginity is a symbol of exclusiveness and inaccessibility, nonavailability to the general masses, something, in short, that is elite. A virgin is an elite female among females, withheld, untouched, exclusive.

The assumption of hypergamy would also account for one of the major puzzles of the female purity phenomenon, namely, that the women of a given group are expected to be purer than the men, that upon their higher purity hinges the honor of the group. I would argue that the women are *not*, contrary to native ideology, representing and maintaining the group's *actual* status, but are oriented upwards and represent the ideal higher status of the group. One of the problems with the purity literature, I think, has been a failure to get beneath native ideology; the natives justify female purity in terms of maintaining the group's actual status, as a holding action for that status in the system, when in fact it is oriented toward an ideal and generally unattainable status. The unattainability may in turn account for some of the sadism and anger toward women expressed in these purity patterns, for the women are representing the over-classes themselves.

And finally, the hypergamy assumption gives us at least one clue about a girl's (or woman's) motivation for cooperation in her own subordination and control. For if she is a good girl, she has the potential for personal status mobility which in fact exceeds that of most of the men of her group. Here it becomes intelligible that it is often women themselves who actively reproduce the patterns of female purity, socializing their daughters in fear and shame of sex, telling them that it is for their own good (which in a way it is), and spying on and gossiping about

one another's daughters as part of an overall deep internalization of and loyalty to the system. Again the point is the future orientation of the ideology, toward some often quite illusory but nonetheless remotely imaginable status mobility, which the girl herself internalizes as the "someday my prince will come" theme. It is no wonder too that women later may resent their husbands as deeply as husbands resent their wives—not only or even necessarily because of the husbands' direct domination, but for what their husbands represent in status terms. For if the husband is of one's own status level, then one has saved all that purity for nothing, while if he is of the ideal higher status level, he is likely to be an undesirable mate who is willing to take a lowerclass wife because of some personal or social defect—some lecherous old Molièrian widower, or someone of noble credentials but no money.

A final point about hypergamy leads me to my brief conclusions. Note that, once again, women are crossing boundaries, in this case boundaries separating classes or castes or status groups in vertical stratification systems. Thus the ambiguity of femaleness vis-à-vis social categories remains at the core of the problem, and views of women remain bound in the purity/pollution idiom. Perhaps partly because the boundary crossing is in an upward direction, however, the symbolization of ambiguity shifts from danger to purity, although the deep structure, if one may use that phrase, remains the same.

At the ideological level, then, one may say that there has been a fairly simple structural transformation, and nothing much has changed in male attitudes toward and mistrust of women. It is clear in contemporary cultures with female purity ideologies, that women are still feared as ambiguous and dangerous creatures. Nonetheless I wish to close on an optimistic note. Lévi-Strauss has suggested that there is no reason to assume that women and men would, if left to their own devices, form durable bonds of mutual interdependence.[17] The phase of social evolution that I have been discussing may perhaps least depressingly be viewed as a long, painful, and unfinished moment in the dialectic of the evolution of such bonds.[18]

NOTES

This paper was written as an informal talk. It was my first stab in thinking about the problem and is highly speculative. It is really designed to generate and orient further thought and research—my own and others. The version printed here is a very slightly (mostly stylistically) revised version of one printed in *Michigan Discussions in Anthropology* 2 (1976): 1–16. I am grateful to the editors of *Feminist Studies* for encouraging me to reprint it and to *Michigan Discussions in Anthropology* for permission to do so.

1. Quote on the seraglio from *The Encyclopaedia Britannica*, 15th ed., s.v., "Harem." For a Latin American example, see Lawrence Watson, "Sexual Socialization in Guajiro Society," *Ethnology* 11 (1972): 150–56. For the Mediterranean, see Joseph K. Campbell, *Honour, Family, and Patronage* (Oxford, England: Oxford University Press, 1974); J. G. Peristiany, ed., *Honour and Shame: The Values of Mediterranean Society* (Chicago: University of Chicago Press, 1966); Jane Schneider, "Of Vigilance and Virgins: Honor, Shame, and Access to Resources in Mediterranean Society," *Ethnology* 10, no. 1 (1971): 1–24. For the Middle East and South Asia, see Rose Oldfield Hayes, "Female Genital Mutilation, Fertility Control, Women's Roles, and the Patrilineage in Modern Sudan," *American Ethnologist* 2 (1975): 617–33; Hannah Papanek, "Purdah: Separate Worlds and Symbolic Shelter," *Comparative Studies in Society and History* 15 (1973): 298–325; Kathleen Gough, "Female Initiation Rites on the Malabar Coast," *Journal of the Royal Anthropological Institute* 85 (1955): 45–80; Nur Yalman, "On the Purity of Women in the Castes of Ceylon and Malaber," *Journal of the Royal Anthropological Institute* 93 (1963): 25–58. For classical Athens, see Philip Slater, *The Glory of Hera* (Boston: Beacon Press, 1968). For China, see Judith Stacey, "When Patriarchy Kowtows: The Significance of the Chinese Family Revolution for Feminist Theory," *Feminist Studies* 2, no. 2/3 (1975): 64–112. The ethnographic references for this paper are in no way definitive or comprehensive. They are taken from the sources that were at hand during writing. For most areas mentioned in the paper, there is a large body of literature concerning sexual ideology and female sociosexual control.

2. For some general considerations, see also Sigmund Freud, "The Taboo of Virginity," *Standard Edition* 11 (London: Hogarth, 1957): 193–208; Ottokar Nemecek, *Virginity: Prenuptial Rites and Rituals* (New York: Philosophical Library, 1958). For more recent overviews, see Louise Lamphere, "Power, Purity, and the Position of Women: The Implication of Sex-role Ideologies for Social Subordination," (unpublished ms., 1975), and Harriet Whitehead, "The Dynamics of Chastity and the Politics of Mutilation," (unpublished ms., n.d.)

3. Gough, "Female Initiation Rites."

4. Yalman, "On the Purity of Women," p. 41.

5. Watson, "Sexual Socialization," pp. 151, 154. For an even more gruesome case, see Hayes, "Female Genital Mutilation," on infibulation, or Pharaonic circumcision, in the Sudan.

6. Schneider, "Of Vigilance and Virgins," pp. 2, 17, 18, 21.

7. I am referring primarily to what anthropologists call "primary" (or "archaic") states, manifesting the novel social-evolutionary development of specialized centralized decision making and bureaucratized administration. See Henry Wright, "Recent research on the Origin of the State," *Annual Review of Anthropology* 6 (1977): 379–97. See also Rayna Rapp, "Gender and Class: An Archaeology of Knowledge Concerning the Origin of the State," *Dialectical Anthropology* 2 (1977): 309–16.

8. Bradd Shore ("Sexuality and Gender in Samoa: Conceptions and Missed Conceptions," forthcoming in *Sexual Meanings*, eds. Sherry B. Ortner and Harriet Whitehead) describes a similar pattern for Samoa, which would perhaps be characterized as a "prestate" society, but not by much: it has a highly developed system of hierarchical social differentiation.

9. Engels of course related the "defeat" of women to the rise of the state (F. Engels, *The Origin of the Family, Private Property and the State* [New York: International Publishers, 1972]), but my interpretation of this relationship is quite different from his. See also Wilhelm Reich, *The Invasion of Compulsory Sex Morality* (New York: Farrar, Strauss, and Giroux, 1971) for a rather bizarre, if provocative, discussion of these issues.

10. Mary Douglas, *Purity and Danger* (New York and Washington: Praeger, 1966).
11. Sherry B. Ortner, "Is Female to Male as Nature is to Culture?" *Feminist Studies* 1, no. 2 (Fall 1972): 5–32; reprinted in *Woman, Culture, and Society*, eds., M. Rosaldo and L. Lamphere (Stanford: Stanford University Press, 1974).
12. Michelle Z. Rosaldo, "Woman, Culture and Society: A Theoretical Overview," in Rosaldo and Lamphere, *Woman, Culture and Society.*
13. The pattern is also found throughout most of Latin America, presumably imported by the Iberian empires.
14. It seems that the Incas had celibate male and female priesthoods (see Victor von Hagen, *The Realm of the Incas* [New York: New American Library, 1957)], but we do not know whether an ideal of chastity for women was general. As for the Aztecs, Vaillant states that women were supposed to be chaste at marriage, but he does not elaborate on this point (George Vaillant, *The Aztecs of Mexico* [Baltimore: Penguin, 1950]).
15. See, for example, S. J. Tambiah, "Dowry and Bridewealth and the Property Rights of Women in South Asia," in *Bridewealth and Dowry*, eds., J. Goody and S. J. Tambiah (Cambridge, England: Cambridge University Press, 1973).
16. See Jack Goody, "Bridewealth and Dowry in Africa and Eurasia," in Goody and Tambiah, *Bridewealth and Dowry.*
17. Claude Lévi-Strauss, "The Family," in *Man, Culture and Society*, ed., H. Shapiro (New York: Oxford University Press, 1960).
18. I must tack on here one of the more interesting points raised in discussion after I presented this paper as a talk. In many "primitive" societies, sexual activity begins at a very early age (for example, Tiwi men of Australia stretch the vaginas of their child wives with their fingers until the wives are grown enough to engage in full-scale-sexual intercourse). (See Jane Goodale, *Tiwi Wives* [Seattle and London: University of Washington Press, 1971].) It is conceivable then that females in such societies never really develop hymens at all. As premarital chastity is enforced for women to a later age, however, the hymen would have a chance to grow and harden, and would have to be broken more dramatically at first intercourse. The suggestion is, then, that the hymen itself emerges physiologically with the development of sexual purity codes, and thus presumably with the rise of the state.

Women's Property Rights and Dowry in China and South Asia

John L. McCreery

Goody and Tambiah (1973) have provided a major contribution to our understanding of marriage as a social institution. Of particular importance is the way in which these authors draw our attention to the economic aspects of marriage and the ways in which they affect the

From *Ethnology* 15:163–174, 1976. Reprinted with permission of the University of Pittsburgh, Department of Anthropology.

status of women. They have pointed out that bridewealth is associated with lack of social stratification, important economic roles for women, and relatively weak controls over women's sexuality. In contrast dowry is associated with social stratification, restriction of women to the roles of housewife and mother, and emphasis on chastity as a female virtue.

However, in drawing their contrasts between bridewealth and dowry, Goody and

Tambiah—and more especially Goody—have obscured rather than clarified the relationship between women's property rights and dowries: Goody suggests that dowry be treated as a form of inheritance. In fact, I argue, dowry and inheritance are fundamentally different. Where women inherit they exercise rights like those enjoyed by men, but where women receive dowries their rights to inherit are either restricted or non-existent, and their status is markedly lower than that of men (Yalman 1967: 172–179).

Goody (1973: 1, 17) has stated that "dowry can be seen as a form of premortem inheritance to the bride" and as part of a woman's property complex. It is, he says, women's ability in many parts of Asia to acquire the same kinds of property as men (and often from men) which he and Tambiah (1973) want to contrast with the situation associated with bridewealth in Africa in which male and female property are sharply segregated.

What Goody seems to be saying is that dowries can only occur where women have rights to the same kinds of property as men. Because of their rights women either inherit shares of their parents' property or receive them as dowries. Inheritance and dowry are only different ways of implementing the same basic rights.

It has been argued, however, that in China, where dowry was customarily a part of marriage, "Chinese women had practically no property rights" (Lang 1946:44). They might legally own property but usually had no right to inherit property. Whatever they owned was received by them as gifts or as wages. Men had rights to inherit, but women did not.

To consider dowry as a form of pre-mortem inheritance and as part of a woman's property complex would, in the case of China, blur an important distinction between the definite legal rights to inherit enjoyed by men and the privilege of receiving a dowry which might or might not be enjoyed by women at their parents' or brothers' discretion. In this case it makes no sense to consider dowry a form of pre-mortem inheritance based on the same set of rights as other forms of inheritance.

The case of China demonstrates that dowries may not be related to rights to inherit, and thus suggests the need for a closer look at women's property rights and how they relate to whether or not women receive dowries in any society where dowries are given. The scope of this paper is, however, more modest. I first describe women's property rights and how they relate to dowry according to the Ch'ing Code, the statute law of China's last imperial dynasty. I then compare the relevant provisions of the Ch'ing Code to the Indian legal systems described by Tambiah (1973) and the Sinhalese law described by Tambiah (1973) and Yalman (1967). My discussion will be confined to these bodies of law.

In each case we are dealing with legal statutes formulated by members of ruling elites which may differ in some respects from the customs of particular communities. We are also dealing with only a few of the bodies of statute law which might have been considered. These cases suffice, however, to document and to elaborate the critique of Goody's interpretation of dowry which is sketched above.

WOMEN'S PROPERTY RIGHTS AND THE CH'ING CODE

It has been argued that according to the Ch'ing Code a family's[1] property belonged to its head and that no other member of the family could use or dispose of its property without his consent. Only a male could occupy the position of family head, and thus women, excluded from becoming family heads, were also excluded from ownership of family property (Ch'u 1961: 29–31, 103–104).

Only in exceptional circumstances were women allowed to inherit. The law decreed that after the death of a family head his property should be divided equally among his sons. If he had no sons, one of his brother's sons should be appointed his heir. Only if neither sons nor brothers' sons were alive to assert their rights might his daughters inherit. Widows who did not remarry and unmarried daughters were customarily entitled to maintenance from their husband's or father's estate, but ordinarily they had no right to inherit (Chiu 1966: 1–2).

These arguments are based, however, on a highly schematic conception of Chinese law and the social structure defined by it. Their underlying assumption is that the family was the basic property holding unit, and its property was owned by the family head who was free to dispose of it as he pleased.

In fact, legally as well as customarily, individuals, including individual women, might own personal property distinct from family property. Moreover, only a family head who was also the direct ascendant of all of the other family members was free to dispose of its property as he pleased. If, as was often the case, the family head was either junior to some of the family's members or, if senior, only a collateral relative, his power to dispose of the family property was limited by law as well as by custom.

More sophisticated analyses can be found in the papers by McAleavy (1955) and Tai (1963) on which the following discussion is based. According to these authors, a woman might become a family head, but only if there were no competent male to occupy the position. Moreover, a female family head's authority was limited. In particular she was not free to dispose of the family's property in the same way as a male family head who was also the direct ascendant of the family's other members.

A family head's authority varied depending upon his relationships with other family members. His authority included three possible components, rights which belonged to any senior member of a clan in relation to his juniors, rights reserved for direct ascendants, and rights attached to the status of family head per se (McAleavy 1955: 540–541).

A clan was a group of agnates among whom seniority was based, first, on generation and, second, within a generation on relative age. Its membership was defined by patrilineal descent from a common ancestor, and in principle the rights attached to seniority were not dependent on residence or property. The relationship of seniors and juniors

was one of "authority and obedience" (Tai 1963: 5). Seniors had the right to issue commands and demand their juniors' obedience. Their authority was supported by laws which, with a few exceptions, prohibited juniors' taking their seniors to court and punished juniors more severely for offenses against seniors than vice-versa. Except for the specific exceptions discussed below a senior's authority was limited primarily by his own junior position relative to still more senior persons. The law provided no specific regulations, but in principle if two seniors' commands conflicted, the more senior's wishes would have to be obeyed (Tai 1963: 7).

A direct ascendant's authority was virtually absolute. He could not be taken to court by a junior under any circumstances, and offenses against him were the most severely punished. If a family head, a direct ascendant was free to dispose of family property as he saw fit. In contrast a family head who was not a direct ascendant could be taken to court to demand the family property's division or to accuse him of malfeasance in his management or disposal of it. To divide, sell, or pawn the family's property he needed his junior's consent. Thus, while a father's or grandfather's wishes could not be challenged, an uncle's authority was limited (McAleavy 1955: 540; Tai 1963: 9).

A person's direct ascendants included his father and mother, his paternal grandparents, his paternal grandfather's parents and, potentially, any ancestor related to him through a direct patrilineal line for descent. Consequently a number of different individuals might possess a direct ascendant's authority over him. In contrast, the rights specific to a family head were concentrated in a single individual (McAleavy 1955: 542).

The family head's principal right and duty was to manage the family's property (McAleavy 1955: 541). He controlled income and expenditures, decided the division of labor and settled disputes among the family's members (Tai 1963: 6). If the family head were also the most senior direct ascendant of all of the family's other members, his authority was limited only by laws prohibiting willful murder. If, however, the family included persons senior to him or juniors who were not his direct descendants, the family head's authority was limited. He would still have to obey the commands of his seniors and, as we have seen, could not dispose of the family's property without the consent of his juniors to whom he was not a direct ascendant.

Concerning the family head's qualifications the law was specific: "Males first, females later; among the males the most senior is appointed" (Tai 1963: 4). A woman could not be family head if any competent male were available (McAleavy 1955: 9). A widow with a son too young to be family head might act in his stead, but only until he came of age.

As a daughter or wife a woman could not be family head and thus could not freely dispose of family property. A daughter was doubly excluded from the family head's position by being both junior and female. A wife's relationship to her husband and his parents was likened to that of a child to her parents and grandparents (Tai 1963: 6).

If a male family head had died and neither his son nor his grandson were old enough to succeed him, his wife would manage the family property. To pawn or sell it, however, she would have to secure her son or grandson's agreement. She was not free to dispose of the property as her husband had been (Tai 1963: 10).

In any case, if the family head were the owner of the family's property, then women, who ordinarily could not be family heads, would usually not be the owners of family property. Whether or not the family head was the owner of the family property is, however, a debatable question. It has been argued that family property was collectively owned by the family as a corporate group and was not the personal property of the family head. If that were the case then women might have had some property rights as family members, even if they could not become family heads.

The theory that the property belonged to the family head was embodied in *Taiwan Shihō*, the Japanese government's official compilation of the Chinese law and custom in effect in Taiwan when Japan assumed control of the island after the Sino-Japanese War in 1895. Published in 1905, *Taiwan Shihō*, has been

one of the basic sources of Japanese scholarship dealing with Chinese law (McAleavy, 1955: 536). More recently the theory that the family property was the personal property of the family head has been defended by Shiga Shūzō (1967), whose work is cited by Meijer (1971).

To my mind, however, the family head's personal ownership of the family's property has been decisively refuted by Tai (1963: 9–10). Tai points out that the same terminology is applied to division of the family's property both before and after the family head's death. More importantly the theory of the family head's personal ownership fails to explain three points.

First, if a family head's son or grandson entered another family by adoption or by uxori-local marriage he lost the right to share in the division of his natal family's property. If the kinship relation between the son or grandson and his father or grandfather were decisive, then his right to share in the property's division would not have been affected by his leaving one group to enter another. What was decisive was his relationship to the group as a whole, not his relationship to the family head as an individual.

Second, if a family head died and a son or grandson who had entered another family left that family and returned to his natal family before its property was divided, his right to share in the division of its property was restored to him.

Third, even if a family head already had sons and grandsons, if after his death his wife or concubine adopted another son, that adopted son, too, would share in the division of the family's property.

In these two cases, as well, the relationship of the individual to the group as a whole is decisive in determining rights to family property, while his relationship to the family head as an individual is not. If, however, family membership rather than personal relationship to the family head was decisive, then the family property could not have been the family head's personal property in the first place.

Tai also observes that the theory of the family head's personal ownership is based on the ideal case in which the family head is also the direct ascendant of all of the other family members. In that case his authority to command, admonish and punish his juniors and his own immunity of prosecution would allow him to act arbitrarily in disposing of the family's property. These rights, however, were attached to his status as a clan senior and direct ascendant and not to his status as family head per se. As noted above, his authority was limited if the family members included persons who were either his seniors or not his direct descendants. Then the legal rights of other persons, based on their membership in the family as a corporate group, emerged clearly.

We may now turn to the questions whether or not women had rights to the same kinds of property as men and whether or not they had the same kinds of rights. There was no legal classification of property which restricted the kinds of property to which women might have rights. There were, however, laws which implied that the rights of most women were radically different from the rights of most men.

Family members were divided into two categories, "basic shareholders" whose rights to family property were legally defined and "optional shareholders"[2] who might or might not receive property at the basic shareholders' discretion. As a general rule the basic shareholders were men, the direct descendants of a common male ancestor, entitled to shares of their family's property because they, and only they, were qualified to continue the ancestral sacrifices. All of a man's legitimate sons, regardless of whether their mothers were his principal wife or his concubine, were entitled to equal portions of their father's share of the family property. Their rights were divided *per stirpes*, not *per capita*. Women were not permitted to continue the ancestral sacrifices and thus were excluded from being basic shareholders (Tai, 1963: 12).

These general rules were qualified in certain cases. An illegitimate son, i.e., a son whose mother was neither his father's principal wife nor his concubine, was entitled only to half a basic shareholder's portion. Adopted sons were divided into two distinct categories. Those adopted to continue their father's line

of descent were basic shareholders. Others, whose adoptions were acts of charity, were only optional shareholders (Tai, 1963: 13).

Men who married uxorilocally were, like women, not entitled to continue the ancestral sacrifices of the families into which they married and thus could not be basic shareholders with definite rights to family property. Such rights as they had were established by contracts at the time of their marriages. None were attached to their status per se (Tai 1963: 15).

Women were customarily entitled to maintenance and to a trousseau when they married but they had no definite legal rights to them, except for the implicit right implied by the criminal law prohibiting deliberate murder. The law prohibited even parents from willfully starving their daughters to death. When a family's property was divided, the basic shareholders might decide to set aside some part of the property to provide their unmarried sisters with dowries but they were not legally obliged to do so.

Widows of men who had no sons were legally required to adopt sons for them, and only if no possible heirs were available would a widow receive her husband's share of the family property in her own right. A widow who remarried lost her right both to her first husband's share of his family's property and also to the dowry, if any, which she had brought to her first marriage (Tai 1963: 14).

Women, as such, were expected to marry out. If a woman's father had no sons he might, instead of adopting a son, arrange for an in-marrying son-in-law with the hope that his daughter would produce a grandson to continue his line. As we have seen, the uxorilocally marrying man was only an optional shareholder. If her father died before her son was old enough to become family head and assume control of the family property, the woman herself might act as trustee. She was, however, expected to transmit the property intact to her son and was not free to dispose of it however she pleased.

We should also note that when a man died leaving no sons but several daughters, only one of the daughters would marry an in-marrying son-in-law to continue the father's line. The others would marry out in the usual way (Tai 1963: 14).

We can now summarize the legal position of women in relation to family property. As unmarried daughters or as widows they were only optional shareholders who legally might be given nothing at all over and above bare subsistence when the men who were basic shareholders divided the family property. In this respect their rights were subordinate even to those of illegitimate sons. As wives or as mothers they had no legal claims on family property in their own rights, unless as widows they had no sons and none might be adopted.

So far, however, we have only considered family property. There is still the question whether or not women, as individuals, could own personal property distinct from family property.

The *Li Chi*, the classical Book of Rites, had stated the principle that children could not own private property while their parents were alive. In particular, sons and their wives were forbidden to possess their own goods, livestock or implements. As part of the Confucian canon the *Li Chi* had moral authority throughout much of China's history. Nonetheless, personal property is mentioned in historical records as early as the Han dynasty (206 b.c.–220 a.d.) (Tai 1963: 10). A T'ang dynasty (618–906 a.d.) statute implied that rewards for distinguished service to the government, even if given to a family's junior members, were not to be included in the property collectively owned by the family as a corporate group (McAleavy 1955: 545–546).

Another T'ang statute specifically excluded from family property not only the personal items included in a bride's trousseau but also any goods, including land, brought with her as dowry, and the statutes of later dynasties followed this precedent (McAleavy 1955: 546). Ethically speaking, the management and disposal of a wife's property were supposed to be entrusted to her husband, but the husband's control was not legally necessary (Tai 1963: 10).

A distinction was usually made, however, between the personal items (e.g., clothing and jewelry) which constituted a bride's trousseau and the land or other property provided as a dowry. The trousseau was always considered the bride's personal property, but generally the dowry was given not to the bride herself, but instead to the branch of her husband's family composed of herself, her husband and their descendants. Only rarely was the bride's personal ownership stipulated in the marriage agreement (McAleavy 1955: 546).

Usually land or other goods given as dowry were kept apart from a family's common property until the family was divided. Then the dowry was merged with the husband's share of his family property and became the collectively owned property of the new family headed by the husband and wife (McAleavy, 1955: 546). It is clear, however, that women could possess private property.

WOMEN'S PROPERTY RIGHTS IN CHINESE AND INDIAN LAW

Tambiah reminds us that there was no single body of traditional Hindu law. Indian law included two main traditions, the Mitakshara law and the Dayabhaga law. The more widespread Mitakshara law was itself divided into four distinct schools. Tambiah (1973: 74) concentrates primarily on the Mitakshara law at the level of general principles which seem to be shared by all four schools and only comments on the Dayabhaga law where it differs significantly from the Mitakshara. In what follows, Indian law refers to the body of general principles described by Tambiah, and no attempt is made to challenge his description.

The Hindu joint family, as legally defined, is a corporate group including both male and female members, some of whom are co-parceners (i.e., persons entitled to a share of the family's property) while others are only entitled to maintenance. Tambiah quotes Maine (1883: 230) as follows:

> When we speak of a Hindu joint family as constituting a coparcenary, we refer not to the entire number of persons who can trace from a

common ancestor and among whom no partition has ever taken place; we include only those persons who, by virtue of relationship, have the right to enjoy and hold the joint property, to restrain in the acts of each other in respect of it, to burden it with their debts, and at their pleasure to enforce its partition. Outside this body there is a fringe of persons who possess inferior rights such as that of maintenance, or who may, under certain circumstances, hope to enter the coparcenary.

On the face of it this description would seem to apply to traditional Chinese as well as Hindu families. More closely examined, however, it reveals several subtle but basic differences between them. The phrase "to restrain the acts of each other in respect of it" would apply only to senior or collateral relatives of a Chinese family head whose direct descendants had no right to restrain his use or disposal of family property. The phrase "to burden it with their debts" would only apply to the Chinese family head himself, since other family members were prohibited from giving, selling or pawning family property without his consent. Finally, the phrase "to enforce its partition" would once again only apply to family members who were not the family head's direct descendants.

Tambiah states four rules which govern the rights of co-parceners according to Indian law. First, each co-parcener in an undivided family transmits his share to his sons who receive equal portions of it. This rule is identical to Chinese law. Second, the co-parceners include "the three generations next to the owner in unbroken male descent, i.e., a man, his living sons, grandsons and greatgrandsons constitute a single co-parcenary with himself" (Tambiah 1973: 77). According to this rule a four generation group is theoretically the maximum group, which must be divided when the fifth generation is born, lest the fifth generations members lack any property rights at all. In this respect the Indian law differs from the Chinese law which does not restrict the generational depth of family members' relationships. Third, property acquired by a co-parcener without obligation to his father's estate, i.e., by his own learning or

valor or by gifts from friends, is his personal property and not included in the family's estate. In this respect Chinese and Indian law are similar. There is, however, potentially room for difference in the qualification "without obligation to his father's estate," since the scope of that obligation might be conceived quite differently. Fourth, "any co-parcener may sue for partition, and every co-parcener is entitled to a share upon partition," and, moreover, "the Mitakshara explicitly asserts the son's right to partition even against the father's wish" (Tambiah 1973: 77). Like the Chinese law, the Dayabhaga law prohibits a son's demanding partition before his father's death. The Chinese law, moreover, prohibited any direct descendant's demanding partition while any direct ascendant was still alive.

Chinese law gave greater stress to the family as a corporate group than the Indian law. The accent of the Indian law was "on the separate existence of each brother, although brothers form the core of the lineage" (Tambiah 1973: 80). Unlike the Indian law, the Chinese law placed no limit on the generational depth of the family and did prohibit sons or grandsons from demanding the family's division while their fathers or mothers, grandfathers or grandmothers were still alive.

Conversely the Indian law seems to have given greater stress to genealogical relations between individuals than the Chinese law. We have observed that in China a son who left his natal family through adoption but returned to it before its property was divided recovered his right to a share of the property. In contrast, at least according to the Mitakshara system, an adopted son's property rights in relation to his natal family "ceased as if he had then died" (Tambiah 1973: 82). It was stated that "the adopted son shall never take the . . . estate of his natural father" (Derrett 1963: 117). This principle was variously interpreted to allow or not to allow the adopted son's right to property already vested in him at the time of adoption, but there is no suggestion that an adopted son could ever recover his right to a share of his natal family's estate.

It is, I suggest, in this context of greater emphasis on the rights of individuals that we should understand the Indian law that "to unmarried daughters a nuptial portion must be given out of the estate of the father; and his own daughter, lawfully begotten, shall take, like a son, the estate of him who leaves no male issue" (Maine, 1883: 501). In contrast the Chinese law, with its greater stress on the family as a corporate group, makes an unmarried daughter's "nuptial portion" dependent on the wishes of her brothers or uncles who are basic shareholders of the family's property.

In Indian law women's property rights belong to different categories depending, first, on the property's origin and, second, on its devolution after a woman's death. According to Tambiah (1973: 86), dowry includes "clothes and jewelry received by the bride from her parents before marriage, betrothal presents from the bridegroom, presents received by her at marriage from her parents and kin, and gifts received after marriage from her husband."

In contrast, there is property received by inheritance or partition as a member of her husband's family, i.e., as wife, widow or mother and property earned by the woman's labor. Gifts of immovable property, e.g., land or houses, received from the husband after marriage seem to belong to the latter category and not to dowry. The dowry itself is subdivided into two components, property received directly from parents or kin from whom it originates and property originally given to the parents as brideprice and then transmitted by them to their daughter.

The non-dowry property acquired by partition, inheritance or labor is controlled by the woman's husband so long as he lives and then is held in trust to be transmitted to his sons or grandsons after his widow's death. The woman herself cannot freely dispose of it. In contrast her dowry is a woman's personal property and she can freely dispose of at least those parts of it which she has received from her parents and kin.

It is the devolution of a woman's property which most strikingly distinguishes the part of dowry received from parents and kin themselves from the part received, albeit indirectly, from the bridegroom who pays it as brideprice. The part received from parents and kin is inherited by a woman's unmarried daughters, her married daughters, or in default of these by their sons. The part which originated as brideprice is inherited by a woman's brothers, her mother or her father in that order.

These generalizations conceal a variety of differences among the different traditional legal systems of India. They suffice, however, to point up a basic contrast between all of these systems and the Ch'ing code. The Chinese law gives no explicit sanction to inheritance of any part of a woman's property by either her daughters or her brothers. The general expectation underlying the Chinese law seems to have been that a woman's property would be merged with her husband's and sooner or later become the family property of the family begun by their marriage. It would then be inherited in the usual way with her daughters' shares, if any, dependent on the wishes of their brothers, the basic shareholders.

In summary we can say that Chinese law more heavily emphasized the family as a corporate group whose core was composed of agnatically related men. With its greater emphasis on the group of agnates and greater concern for its continuity, the Chinese law more severely restricted the rights of woman than the Indian law. In fact in China women's property rights were generally only customary expectations, permitted by law but not required by law as they were in India. In contrast Indian law gave greater weight to the rights of individuals including, in particular, the rights of individual women.

Goody (1973) has written that he and Tambiah wish to call our attention "to the nature of the property relations between the partners of a marriage and with the parents of each, i.e., to the interrelationship of marriage transactions and the devolution of property." What is striking about this statement is what it omits, the relationships of the bride and groom to their families as groups and relationships between the families as groups. If, as seems to have been the case in China, families were conceived as corporate groups whose existence transcended the personal relationships of their members and, indeed, took precedence over their individual members' private interests, then Goody's approach to the study of dowry is lacking a crucial component. This lack is felt even in cases where individual rights are most pronounced.

WOMEN'S PROPERTY RIGHTS AND DOWRY IN CEYLON

Superficially Sinhalese law would seem to offer an ideal case in support of Goody's interpretation of dowry. At least in the Dry Zone of Ceylon, both men and women were individually owners of private property, and their private property might include land as well as personal effects. The owner of property, whether male or female, was free to dispose of it however he or she saw fit, even to give it or to leave it after their deaths to persons other than their legal heirs (Yalman 1967: 130).

If a parent died intestate, sons and daughters shared equally in their parent's property, regardless of their parent's marital history. Women as well as men retained their rights no matter how often they married, divorced, and married again. Yalman (1967: 134) writes: "the conception of marriage as a powerful, almost indissoluble bond between man and wife, in which their separate properties are united and which clearly defined the heirs to the property as the joint heirs of the couple . . . has no place in the Kandyan way of thinking."

It is against this background that Yalman observes that certain classes of Sinhalese distinguish between virilocal and uxorilocal marriages. Women who marry uxorilocally and their unmarried sisters are entitled to inherit equally with their brothers. Women who marry virilocally with dowry, however, give up their rights to inherit.[3]

Here we have a prima facie case for asserting that dowry replaces rights to inherit after a parent's death and thus that dowry can be seen as a form of premortem inheritance. It can still be argued, however, that dowry and inheritance are essentially different.

Goody (1973: 17) argues that female inheritance and dowry both reflect "a general interest in preserving the status of offspring of both sexes." This interpretation might well apply to the rule of inheritance mentioned above, since daughters inherit equally with sons. There is, however, no rule which requires that a dowry be equal either to the inheritance received by a son or unmarried daughter or to the dowries received by the bride's sisters.

Since bride and groom should contribute equally to their marriage and women are not allowed to marry down, the size of the dowry "depends entirely on the status of the son-in-law" (Yalman 1967: 132). The groom's status is a function partly of inherited rank and partly of wealth, and the higher his rank or the greater his wealth the larger the dowry required to arrange a marriage with him.

In some cases, in order to arrange an especially desirable marriage, "one daughter receives all the cash and even much of the lands owned by her parents" (Yalman 1967: 175). In such a case the daughter's dowry would probably be much larger than her sister's dowry or her brother's or sister's inheritance. The difference between her dowry and the shares of her parents' property received by her brothers or sisters cannot be explained by "a general interest in preserving the status of offspring of both sexes." Her dowry is certainly not simply the share of her parents' property which she would have a right to inherit.

Why dowries are given is a question which the law does not answer. Dowries are legally possible because individuals may dispose of their property as they see fit. They are not, however, legally necessary and thus their causes have to be sought in extralegal circumstances. Yalman (1967: 149) states:

> The lack of a dowry system is associated with egalitarian and immobile villages. Alternatively, dowry—with all that it implies in control over women and solidarity among men as a mark of

status—appears to be a function of diversified communities with at least some mobility.

In China, too, the causes of dowry are extralegal. According to Freedman (1966: 55), a wealthy family provides a dowry for their daughter,

> not because the girl has any specific economic claims on them (she is not a member of the property-owning unit) but because their own status is at stake; a bride-giving family must, in order to assert itself against the family to which it has lost a woman, send her off in the greatest manner they can afford. And it is no accident, therefore, that dowry and trousseau are put on open display; they are not private benefactions to the girl but a public demonstration of the means and standing of her natal family.

The Chinese case also fits the social background and implications of dowry described by Yalman. China has long been a society of diversified communities within which social mobility was not only possible but highly prized, and in China, as well as Ceylon, dowry has been associated with control over women and solidarity among men as a mark of status.

CONCLUSIONS

In China, India, and Ceylon dowry has been associated with women's property rights which have ranged from virtually non-existent to essentially the same as those enjoyed by men. In Ceylon and China, moreover, rights to inherit have been legally defined, while rights to dowry have not. It is clear that at least in these two cases the legal bases of dowry and inheritance were distinct. In neither case were dowry and inheritance simply alternative ways to implement the same basic rights.

It seems clear then that dowry cannot be properly understood as a form of pre-mortem inheritance to the bride. Whether or not it is part of a woman's property complex is a moot point.

In all three societies women could own the same kinds of property as men, but this was at most a necessary but not a sufficient condition for dowry to be given. At least in Ceylon and in China whether or not a dowry was given at all, not to mention the size of the dowry, was up to the men who controlled the family's property.

The conditions which affected whether or not dowries were given were extralegal. Consequently the laws which we have examined do not tell us what they were. It seems likely, however, that dowries are a means of social mobility in stratified societies where men use rights over women, like other property, to compete for higher status.

NOTES

1. In this paper the terms family, clan and lineage are translations of the Chinese terms *chia, tsung,* and *tsu* respectively. The *romanization* is Wade-Giles.
2. Basic shareholders and optional shareholders are translations of the Chinese phrases *chi-pen yu-fen jen* and *cho-kei yu-fen jen* respectively. The *romanization* is Wade-Giles.
3. To speak of a right to inherit might seem inappropriate since parents were free to write wills and dispose of their property however they pleased. A similar objection might be raised for the ideal Chinese case in which a family head was also his heirs' direct ascendant and thus free to dispose of family property as he saw fit. In both the Chinese and Sinhalese cases the rights in question are those which were legally defined when a parent died intestate. In neither case was a right to a dowry prescribed by law.

REFERENCES

Chiu, V.Y. 1966. Marriage Laws and Customs of China. Hong Kong: Chinese University of Hong Kong. New Asia College, Institute of Advanced Chinese Studies and Research.

Ch'u T'ung-tsu. 1961. Law and Society in Traditional China. Paris and The Hague. Mouton.

Derrett, J. Duncan. 1963. Introduction to Modern Hindu Law. Bombay Indian Branch, Oxford University Press.

Freedman, M. 1966. Chinese Lineage and Society: Fukien and Kwangtung. New York.

Goody, J. 1973. Bridewealth and Dowry in Africa and Eurasia. Bridewealth and Dowry, ed., J. Goody and S.J. Tambiah, pp. 1–58. Cambridge.

Lang, O. 1946. Chinese Family and Society. New Haven.

Maine, H.S. 1883. Dissertations on Early Law and Custom. London: J. Murray.

McAleavy, H. 1955. Certain Aspects of Chinese Customary Law in the Light of Japanese Scholarship. Bulletin of the School of Oriental and African Studies 17: pp. 535–547.

Meijer, M.J. 1971. Marriage Law and Policy in the Chinese People's Republic. Hong Kong.

Shiga, S. 1967. Chūgoku Kazokukō no Genri [Principles of Chinese Family Law]. Tokyo.

Taiwan, Governor-General. 1905. Special Taiwanese Customs research group. Taiwan Shihō [Taiwanese Personal Law]. Taipei.

Tai Yen-hui. 1963. Ch'ing Tai Taiwan chih Chia Chih-tu yu Chia Ch'an (Taiwan Family System and Estate in the Ch'ing Dynasty). Taiwan Wen Shian, vol. XIV, No. 3, pp. 1–19. Taipei.

Tambiah, S.J. 1973. Dowry and Bridewealth and the Property Rights of Women in South Asia. Bridewealth and Dowry, ed. J. Goody and S.J. Tambiah, pp. 59–169. Cambridge.

Yalman, N. 1967. Under the Bo Tree: Studies in Caste, Kinship and Marriage in the Interior of Ceylon. Berkeley.

The Legal and Social Transformation of Rural Women in Aegean Turkey

June Starr

INTRODUCTION

This paper links three independent ideas. First, it provides an alternative model to Engels' provocative theory, expounded in *The Origin of the Family, Private Property and the State* (first published in 1884).[1] Engels suggested that women lose out in the historical process at exactly the point in time that capitalist enterprise develops in each society. Not only do women get squeezed out of the right to claim property for themselves and their children, but as marriage systems change from plural spouses to monogamy, women themselves become a kind of property for men. Monogamous marriage, according to

Engels, makes women dependent on men for economic support. Thus men become dominant and women become subordinate and submissive to protect themselves and their young.[2]

Second, it asserts—contrary to much existing theory—that both written and unwritten law is never neutral on the issue of the relationship between the sexes. When law is silent, it supports the dominant power structure and cultural values of a society. The power structure is almost always controlled by adult males (sometimes with a few token women). When written laws specifically promote norms of equality, however, as in the case of Turkey, they provide a useful option for overturning the cultural bias which favours male dominance.

Third, it builds on the Ardeners' suggestive notion that women's models of the world

Reprinted with permission from Renée Hirschon (ed.), *Women and Property: Women As Property* (New York: St. Martin's Press, 1984), pp. 92–116.

may be quite different from men's, because the men have generated the norms for the arenas of *reasoned public argument*. Women thus may not be as good as men at articulating their unverbalised thoughts because they have not been socialised into modes of 'public discourse' which is characteristically male-dominated (S. Ardener, 1975: xi–xvii).

Although Engels foresaw that women would be excluded from owning land as the economic system evolved from transhumance to settled capital intensive agriculture, he foresaw neither how the legal system nor how specific cultural systems would interact with the changing productive and marketing systems. This essay argues that the penetration of capitalist agriculture into the Bodrum region produced a class system which made marriages within a village an advantageous way of consolidating landholdings. Such marriages aid women in two ways. First, it keeps females in close proximity to their mothers, mother's sisters, and own siblings who provide a daily work and supportive group. This prevents young, impressionable brides from being psychologically intimidated into submission by a husband and his kin. Second, a wife's legal right to her share of the patrimony provides a powerful sanction to make a husband treat her well, because the new laws also allow a comparatively easy divorce[3] for mistreatment. I argue that the gradual exposure of females to the law system in Bodrum allows them to learn the necessary forms of behaviour to use the law courts to their advantage. Finally, I suggest that laws providing female access to land, in combination with judicial willingness to enforce these laws, is a powerful mechanism for female emancipation in Aegean Turkey.

BODRUM: A CHANGING REGION

Many feminist scholars consider the modernisation process[4] as always adversely affecting the position of women.[5] Islam, too, is commonly thought to provide a cultural system in which women for the most part are totally subordinate to men, have few legal rights and little or no autonomy.[6] Turkey thus provides a unique situation in which to study problems of development relating to women because ninety per cent of its population are Moslem, and European legal codes were introduced in the 1920s. Furthermore, it is geographically, culturally and historically diverse. This diversity allows female/male relations to be contrasted across temporal, spatial, and cultural dimensions.

The particular focus of this paper is in the southwestern part of Turkey where the region takes its name from the town of Bodrum. In this essay we examine how male and female relationships are mediated by rights to property. In western countries property is identified with valuable resources such as land, houses, jewels and other highly-valued material goods which can be converted into saleable items on the market. In the Turkish region where I lived, orchards, houses, and productive fields were considered valuable property, as were cows, donkeys, camels, bicycles, jeeps, trucks and boats. Because women did not ride bicycles and were not taught to drive other vehicles, jeeps, trucks, bicycles and boats were owned and used only by men and do not figure further in this discussion.

In addition to material property, in Middle Eastern and Mediterranean cultures there is another valued resource, albeit intangible. This is honour. This essay argues that honour or reputation is also a valued possession, that is worth protecting and that it is as valuable to women as to men.[7] Furthermore, how a woman behaves affects the honour of her husband if she is married, and always that of her father and her brothers. This gives males social control over females, lessening women's autonomy. Much of female behaviour in the village intensively studied and in nearby Bodrum town only becomes understandable by knowing that honour and shame play a significant part in daily affairs. Like property, honour or reputation can be accumulated and can be lost.[8] It is a scarce resource.

Questions raised in the paper are: how does access to property and other resources defined as scarce by the society, affect male/female relationships? Under what conditions do women begin to assert their legally granted but customarily withheld rights to land, houses and other inheritance? Does a woman's changing relationship to property facilitate her emergence as an independent person with a growing ability to assert control over certain aspects of her life?

Turkey today is a complex nation-state involved economically with the European Common Market, Nato, and with its eastern neighbours.[9] It has a small but growing industrial sector which was hard hit by the oil crisis of 1973–74. Close to 65 per cent of the country is still agricultural. Poverty and lack of opportunities in rural areas led hundreds of thousands of migrant workers between 1960 and 1974 to seek employment in European countries.[10]

Turkey is divided into sixty-seven different administrative provinces (*il, vilayet*). There are strong class divisions, sharp cleavages between urban and rural dwellers (although migrant workers begin to blur these distinctions among the poor) and at least seven historic, cultural and geographic areas with rich distinctiveness.[11] Differences exist between the two religious groups: the dominant *Sunni* and the minority *Alevi* (or *Shi'ites*, some of them remarkably heterodox). Throughout the 1970s tremendous political instability occurred, caused by violence among rival political groups. In September 1980 a military junta took over in a bloodless coup, ostensibly to restore order and to return to the principles of Atatürk.

Answers to questions concerning gender relationships and property need to be regionally, culturally and historically specific. Within the context of a changing social order this essay examines data collected from a village, Mandalinci, (cf. *mandalina*, 'tangerines') (population 1,000) and a district town, Bodrum (population 5,200) from December 1966 through August 1968.[12]

Bodrum region (*kaza*) is 66,000 hectares[13] of which 22,614 hectares or just over one-third is farmed land. Bodrum town[14] is the administrative centre for the thirty surrounding villages which vary in size from 293 to 2,000 people. In 1966 tangerines were grown in walled irrigated fields in Bodrum and the villages to its west, while animals, tobacco, and wheat were cash crops grown in villages on the Mumcular plateau to Bodrum's east.

Geopolitics and Economics

This section of the essay argues that marriage patterns changed with the changing economic, legal and social order. For centuries the Bodrum coastal region was inhabited by two ethnic groups: Christian Orthodox, Greek-speaking townspeople who inhabited harbour areas and Sunni Moslem, Turkish-speaking *Yörük* sheep herders who practised transhumance (cf. Ramsay, 1917, pp. 31, 83). The Greeks farmed coastal valleys around harbours on the Ottoman mainland and were good sailors. The Turkish transhumants migrated between summer pastures near the sea and winter grazing areas further inland on the Bodrum peninsula.

A second Turkish-speaking ethnic group, remnants of the once powerful Turcoman confederacy,[15] occupied an ecological niche on the higher, inland plain commencing about 25 miles east of Bodrum town. These pastoral nomads had migrated over several centuries down to the region from the Anatolian plateau. They gradually settled into eight villages on the Mumcular plain about 125 years ago.[16] For cultural and religious reasons none of these three groups inter-married.

Between 1900 and 1919 the Greek and Turkish populations were on friendly terms. The Greek population farmed figs, olives, and wheat, and were the craftsmen of the region. They were carpenters, lime-makers, and house builders.[17] The area now known as Mandalinci village was a summer camp ground (*yayla*) for Turkish-speaking *Yörük* transhumants. Their winter quarters (*kisla*) were more protected. The Greek population also was larger in summer than in winter as attested to by ruins of houses and cafes along Mandalinci's deep water harbour (Starr, 1978, pp. 23–4).[18] The population in the entire Bodrum region was in 1912, 8,817 Turkish people and 5,060 Greeks (Soteriadis, 1918, p. 9).[19]

In this period Turkish women from nearby islands were considered the most beautiful and were desired as wives by Turkish-speaking men.[20] Thus marriage practices reveal special socio-economic concerns: far-flung networks, embedded in transhumance, provided pastoral households access to diverse pastures, lands, brides, and information. For women, outward stretching networks meant that after marriage at the age of twelve to fourteen a girl was separated from her natal household for much of the year, because the groom was obligated to give labour to his father who had provided the bridewealth for his marriage. This created a virilocal post-marital residence pattern. But, groups moved with flocks between traditional camp grounds, population pressure was not considerable, land was not scarce, and mostly the Greeks owned private farmlands.

The increasing animosity between the Ottoman homeland and Greece from 1919 onward changed the situation. As news of the fighting between Greek and Turkish peoples in the Izmir area spread southward, Greek-speaking families fled from their Mandalinci seaside farmlands and cafes, abandoning the entire area to Turkish transhumant households. During the population exchanges of 1923 between Greece and Turkey, the Turkish government took an interest in Greek landholdings in the village area. Several elite Turkish households were granted farmlands in Mandalinci for their role in the war of 1919–1922 (Starr, 1978, pp. 23–27). Moslem Turkish-speaking people from Crete were moved into '*Rum*' ward in Bodrum, now called *Kumbahçe* (in Turkish *Rum* means Greek).[21]

In the early 1930s tangerine agriculture was introduced from Rhodes into Betes, a seaside hamlet near Bodrum town.[22] The first orchard of tangerines in Mandalinci dates from 1940. To grow tangerines required a capital investment in three year old trees, as well as in a deep water well or overland cement waterways. It meant that soil had to be checked during dry months of summer (from mid-May until mid-October) to determine when the orchard should be flooded with irrigation water. Such water is raised from ground wells by mechanical lifts or motorised pumps.

Capital for intensive cultivation could be obtained through a bank loan, but to negotiate one, a person needed a *legal* title (*tapu*) and not merely usufruct rights to land. Elite families, of course, already had ties to banking personnel and they obtained much of the best farmland at valley level. Other villagers did obtain legal titles, while others still continued with traditional use rights to grazing lands or fields. There were recognised under village customary law-ways, but they had marginal status under state law until converted through the state legal system into a legally recognised form of ownership.[23] Households owning a tangerine orchard (the only crop raised on irrigated land) tended to invest profits into building a house at the edge of their orchard.

The transformation to single Turkish occupancy of the region and to cash-cropping agriculture led to settled village life. This made privately-owned orchards a prime resource. Marriage between children of orchard-owning families developed, creating both dense kin ties within each seaside village, and an incipient class structure.

The impact of capitalistic agriculture, settled village life and an emergent class structure had profound effects on female/male relations and on females' access to property. But to comprehend fully these changes, we need to consider the third variable, the cultural system.

The Cultural Framework

In this essay culture has an ideological, institutional and behavioural component. It is viewed as the product of specific historical processes. But, cultural codes of behaviour, developed to cope with particular stresses in a certain historic period, may live on into a new era. Thus they can be viewed as transcending one productive system to emerge side-by-side with more adaptive forms of behaviour exhibited by some members of the group.

The value systems of the Turkish ethnic

groups were based on male control of females and a rather loose adherence to Islamic religion. Islamic attitudes toward women had co-mingled for centuries with Hellenistic attitudes in the Bodrum region.[24] Moreover, transhumant populations by and large are not known for their religious ardour.[25] A daughter was under her father's control until marriage. After that her husband had strict control and responsibility for her behaviour. Like most transhumant people in Western Turkey, veiling was not practised. Bride-wealth was given by the fiance to the girl's father in the form of sheep, and some gold coins were given to the girl. Lineages were shallow and blood feuding did not develop. The ideology of honour and shame, however, tended to keep males watchful of female actions.

The transition from transhumance to settled village life did not undercut the ideology of honour and shame, despite the pragmatic views of an emerging entrepreneurial class. Thus the Islamic notions of male dominance/female submission became pitted against the secular notions of the Turkish state which had enacted legislation giving equal rights to women.

Three Types of Marriage. The increase of capitalist agriculture and the involvement with the market prompted marriages to be arranged within the village between orchard-owning households. Marriages within the village consolidated property and focused, mobilised and united resources. The effect for women was to forge dense kin networks within a community. Keeping a young bride near (or in the same village as) the parental household gave her some protection from an aggressive or cruel husband and some leverage against a demanding domineering mother-in-law.

Villagers distinguish three marriage modes: marriage by engagement negotiations, marriage by connivance and marriage by abduction.

Marriages arranged by negotiation (*nikah*) are never handled directly by the boy or girl. A mother first makes casual enquiries of her relatives and friends as to the whereabouts of a suitable mate for her child. Then a series of negotiations is carried out first by the boy's father or father's brother on behalf of the youth, and at a later stage by the boy's father and mother with the father and mother of the bride-to-be.

During these negotiations what is discussed is the amount and kind of land and houses each spouse is due to inherit at the division of the patrimony. Types of land include a house and lot, irrigated orchards, fields and woodlands or grazing pastures. Discussions also include the amount and kinds of gifts the groom will give his bride in the bridewealth.

In Mandalinci the groom gives the gifts to the bride at the time the actual engagement (*nisan*) is celebrated. He cannot go with his parents when they carry his gifts to his fiance. The bridewealth for a middle class agricultural family customarily includes four or more gold bracelets, some gold coins for the girl to wear around her neck or forehead, a watch, head scarves, some cloth for dresses for the bride, her mother and her sisters. Shoes are given to the girl's father, and socks and handkerchiefs to her brothers. The cost of such gifts in 1967 ran from seven hundred to three thousand Turkish lira ($700 to $3,000). In one instance, a 28 year old Mandalinci man and his father mortgaged the first good crop of their newly planted tangerine orchard to the man who lent them money to buy the engagement gifts so the youth could marry.

It is normal to wait at least three months between the giving of engagement gifts and the village wedding (*düğün*). But in Mandalinci the engagement often lasts much longer, because the groom may need to be away for military service, or the girl is not yet ready to leave home, or all the bridewealth has not yet been accumulated and given.

There are two modes of engagement and marriage in Mandalinci—early and later—reflecting economic differences, and especially the difficulties of poor households to accumulate the cash necessary for the bridewealth. The most approved form of marriage (and the only marriage mode available to the wealthy) is for the groom to marry when he is eighteen or nineteen a female of about fourteen or fifteen. The marriage is celebrated and consummated before the groom leaves the village for two years of compulsory military service. In this case the new bride is brought to live at the parental house of the groom where a room or even a house is provided for the couple (the word for bride, *gelin*, also means daughter-in-law and is from *gel*— 'to come').

Most households cannot amass sufficient capital for early male marriages. Youths from impoverished families earn their own bridewealth which means they marry much later, around 26 to 30 years of age. They work in the village as day labourers and tenant-farmers or outside the village as more job opportunities occurred with the expanding Turkish road system of the 1950s. The improved transportation also allowed more production of perishables and with it developed a prosperous fishing trade. Jobs were also available in sponge-diving and boat-building industries of Bodrum town.

The breakdown in obligations across the father/son generation in combination with tangerine agriculture has meant that virilocal residence patterns are giving way towards more neolocal households (compare Stirling, 1974). A newly married couple still may begin with virilocal residence (depending on the marriage mode and who provided the bridewealth), but many develop their own home separate from the groom's family. Ritual and emotional ties to both sets of parents are maintained, however.

A girl who did not wish to accept a proposal or whose parents were arranging a marriage not to her liking needed to convince her parents why that union was unacceptable. She might threaten suicide if they persisted. More usually, however, she found a youth she liked better and persuaded him to elope with her. A boy had many more options for avoiding a marriage not to his liking, thus underlining once again the gender asymmetry of rural Turkish society.

The second type of marriage is by connivance, or elopement, (*kız kaçırma*).

The advantages of elopement is that the groom does not have to give any bridewealth. It also allows both males and females to marry the person of their own choosing. The girl often is the one to suggest it. The usual pattern is for the couple to flee in the night, have sexual relations and then go to the house of a friendly relative who will plead their cause to the girl's parents.

When the girl's parents notice her absence, they immediately report it to the nearest police station. The police will search for the couple. Once apprehended, they bring them back and formal charges are brought against the youth. Or the couple will reappear on their own and plead with the girl's family that they be allowed to marry. Because everyone assumes they have had sexual relations (whether they have or not), the girl is no longer desirable as a local bride, since virginity is a prime requirement. Thus, unless the parents are vindictive they allow them to marry. The fate of a girl who has eloped and not married is a worse shame to a family than a less wealthy bridegroom.

Whether they are apprehended or reappear on their own, a criminal case would be opened against the boy by the Public Prosecutor in Bodrum. Charges would be dropped when they produced a marriage licence for the court to see. The girl's active role in marriage by connivance challenges western stereotypes about submissive Turkish women.

The third marriage type is by abduction (*zorla kız kaçırma*). Turkish villagers and Turkish criminal law distinguish between elopement by mutual consent (*kız kaçırma*) and forcible abduction (*zorla kız kaçırma*). The Bodrum court and written law recognise a number of different actions and degrees of guilt, each carrying more severe penalties. Thus, rape of a virgin who is a minor is more severe than rape of a virgin of legal age to marry. Kidnapping and rape of a married woman also carried severe penalties.

A girl who has been forcibly abducted, kept against her will, and forced to have sexual intercourse, after a time may agree to marry her abductor as the only solution to her future. It is the major way she can be reunited with her family and be re-admitted to local community life, albeit now as a married woman. Because of the norms regarding virginity in a bride (which are supported by the pervasive notions of honour and shame) the girl may realise that if she wishes to marry at all, she must agree to marry her abductor. Here is one victim's story:

> I was on my way to school when he came with two friends and put me into his car and carried me off. He was a driver of a jeep between Milas and Bodrum and had noticed me. I was just a small girl. I didn't know about men. I didn't think about marriage. I was only twelve. He forced me to have sex with him . . . My father didn't open a court case against him because by the time they found us I was pregnant. . . . It was hard at first, but now I am more used to him.[26]

By the summer of 1968, after five years of marriage, they had two small children and had moved to a neighbourhood of Bodrum, near the girl's parents.

In the three year period 1965 through 1967 the Bodrum Middle Criminal Court (*Asliye Ceza*) processed 29 cases ranging from voluntary elopement to forcible abduction and rape (see Table 1). In 17 of these cases the couple married, so charges against the youth were dropped. We can assume that most of these were voluntary elopements on the girl's part. In three cases, each boy was sentenced to large fines and prison which suggests forcible abduction. (We can draw no conclusions from the five cases which had not finished by the time court records were copied, nor from the three cases where charges were dropped for insufficient evidence.) Thus

TABLE 1. Cases Ranging from Voluntary Elopement to Forcible Abduction and Rape (1965–1967 inclusive)

Married	17
Charges dropped	3
Innocent of Charges	1
Unfinished	5
Fine and Prison Sentence	3
Total	29

3 of 20 cases or 15 per cent were clear instances of violence against women.

Two of the five cases I witnessed were noteworthy. In one a girl changed her testimony. At the police station she had said she had gone willingly; in court she said it was under duress. Whether the police forced her to say she was willing to protect the lad, or whether her father forced her in court to say it was by force is unclear. In another case a girl said she loved the youth and they had eloped at her suggestion. When asked if they would marry, she looked downcast while her father stated, 'I have already married her to another'.[27] There was nothing the judge could do to save the ill-starred romance. Paternal control had overpowered female autonomy and independence, and this father had outwitted the legal norms promoting female rights.

Post-Marital Residence and Social Class. Although Bodrum people still affirm the virilocal residence ideal, actual post-marital residence is linked to class, mode of production, resources and bridewealth. By the late 1960s an emerging pattern of class structure had developed, based on intermarriage of landowning households in the village. The strata were:

1. absentee landowning households, which controlled citrus orchards, which were farmed by tenant farmers (*ortakçı*);
2. resident orchard-owning households, who did their own farming, hiring day labourers as needed, or had an *ortakçı*;
3. resident field-owning households with no hired labourers;
4. landless households, whose heads are tenant farmers or day labourers for others.

With capitalist agriculture came absentee landowners and tenant farming. Tenant farmers were provided a small rent-free cottage for their services, which for women from poorer strata meant their own home, separated from their mother-in-law. Wives of day labourers often worked in the fields or orchards for wages themselves in order to add to the household income. In this stratum newly-married couples lived in whatever accommodation could be provided for them by either family.

It was the wealthier households who could demand virilocal residence, because the father had the resources to build a room for the newly-wedded couple adjoining his house, and to provide the bridewealth which obligated the son to work his farmlands. Yet, some wealthier patriarchs chose to set up their older sons in small businesses in Izmir or Aydin. In two cases they married their younger daughters to village men with whom they established tenant farming arrangements. Such a son-in-law is called an *iç güvey* (literally the groom who marries in). This allowed a young girl to stay in close contact with her natal household and provided a father with an assistant who may be more docile than his own sons. It also assured the girl's parents that they could mediate to a great extent the ways their daughter's husband behaved toward her.

Female kin living in adjoining households co-operated in food preparation, fieldwork, childcare, and sometimes in gathering vegetables and cutting tangerines. Mutual cooperation among female kin occurred even when sisters and mothers lived in separate parts of the village. Socialisation of village girls and also Bodrum women de-emphasised female rivalry and emphasised warm, mutually supportive relationships. Most girls thought it was a great advantage to remain near their mothers and sisters after marriage. The most adventurous village girls, however, dreamed of being married to a youth in Izmir or at least in Bodrum.

Mothers were also glad not to be separated from their daughters. Even more important, it meant they would be taken care of in their old age.

The Legal Framework

Islamic Law of the Ottoman Empire. During the 19th century several reforms in Ottoman Law affected the legal and social status of women. The major Ottoman innovation, however, its civil code, affected women only

tangentially. Known as the *Mecelle*, it was simply a modern-looking codification of pure Hanafi law. The committee prepared the code between 1869 and 1888, and published it sequentially between 1870 and 1877. The project was abandoned in 1888 when it proved politically unwise to produce a modern codification of Islamic family law (Onar, 1955, p. 295). Thus it left untouched the *Seriat,* the core of Islamic family law which governed all aspects of family life and personal status including marriage, renunciation of wives, inheritance, and adoption of children.

Other Ottoman reforms affected women directly. For example, the old Ottoman *tax* on brides (*arus resmi*)—of 60 aspers for girls and 40 or 30 for widows and divorcees—was replaced by a *fee* for permission to marry, given to the local Islamic judge (*kadi*). The new fee charged 10 piastres for girls and 5 for widows. Under the old Ottoman tax the amount and destination of payment was determined by the status of a bride's father. For widows' remarriage, however, the tax was paid where she resided or married (B. Lewis, 1960, p. 679). The significance of the new fee was its implicit recognition of a relationship between an unmarried female and the place she lived. Atatürk's secular laws continued the payment of a fee for marriage, which became a fee paid to a secular civil servant for a licence to marry.

Ottoman domestic legislation limited the bridewealth to a maximum of 1,000 piastres and specified that no gifts might be exchanged among the relatives of the bride and groom, nor brought by the wedding guests. The bridal dinner was limited to soup, wedding cake, and five other dishes. The bride was to buy her own cosmetics, but the groom was to pay for her use of the public baths (Young, 1905, vol. II, pp. 209–10).[28]

Attempts to limit the amount of bridewealth and of gifts exchanged among relatives of the bride and groom again appear in the reformist Ottoman Family Laws of 1915 and 1917. But, the importance of the law of 1917, called the Ottoman Law of Family Rights, was its expanded application of the *Seriat.* It allowed whatever school of Islamic law couples wished to use to be applied. This meant that the most flexible rule of any school, *Hanafi*, might be used. It also allowed a woman to have written into her marriage contract her right to annulment should her husband take a second wife. This was a major concession to those Europeanised reformers who were pushing for a monogamous marriage law in Turkey.[29]

The Ottoman Family Law of 1917 gave women rights to divorce on grounds such as impotence, insanity or abandonment. If a woman wished to divorce her husband on grounds of extreme cruelty or incompatibility, the law provided that three male family members must first attempt reconciliation of the couple before divorce was possible. Age limits were set, for the first time in Ottoman history, below which females and males could not marry.[30]

But, inheritance practices continued as they had under the *Seriat*. When a man died his widow had the right to one-eighth of his estate, and the remainder was to be divided among all his children (one-quarter if there were no children); each female share was to be half that of a male's. In practice in rural Turkey women rarely obtained their land in Ottoman times, and in Anatolian and Southeastern Turkey even in the early 1950s and 1960s women were denied access to the patrimony (Stirling, 1965, pp. 121–2; Aswad, 1978, p. 475).[31]

In conclusion, despite the contractual nature of Moslem marriages, women suffered a number of disabilities under Islamic law. Girls moved from control by their father to the authority of their husbands. They had the status of a minor and could not act as independent persons. Women's share of the patrimony was half that of their brothers', and the widow's one-eighth share of the husband's estate was not much reward for a lifetime of service. Furthermore, according to the law, a husband could turn a wife out at will by renouncing her in front of three witnesses; he had rights to the children produced by their marriage, she did not. Culture and circumstances may make this right of males under Islam less absolute

than the law provides, but strict application means children always belong to the agnatic line.

Secular Law Reforms of Atatürk. Under Atatürk's revolutionary vision of the early 1920s, women's rights in Turkey were brought closer to men's. The new Turkish Civil Code, adapted in 1926 from the Swiss Civil Code, abolished male's right to divorce by renunciation and his right to plural wives. Monogamous marriage was established as the only form recognised by the State. A civil certificate, obtainable from a town clerk was the necessary prerequisite for registering a marriage with the state. To obtain a divorce, each party had to apply to the new secular law courts. Polygamy and bigamy were both made punishable by law, and children of polygamous unions were only given legitimate status by a series of separate legislative Acts.[32] Women's rights to their paternal inheritance were now legally recognised as equal to their brothers'. A widow's share was increased to one-fourth the estate, and she got the first choice.

Age limits for marriages were again set; this time males were allowed to marry at eighteen, females at seventeen, and in exceptional cases both could marry at fifteen. The Turkish legislature in 1938 reduced the ages of marriage to seventeen for males and fifteen for females, and in exceptional circumstances with a judge's permission to fourteen for females and fifteen for males (Velidedeoğlu, 1957, p. 63).

Atatürk's policies strongly opposed social and cultural symbols, such as the male *fez* and the female veil (*carsaf*). Turkish friends remember their mothers' stories of walking in city streets in the early 1930s and seeing soldiers rip veils off women. In rural areas of western Turkey, however, agricultural and nomadic women rarely were veiled as it was a hindrance during work in the fields or with animals.

These new policies, codes and legislation promoting equality for women were put in place by a small western-oriented elite. They did not occur in response to demands of a large segment of society, mobilised for action if rights were not granted. In 1934 this small elite even obtained by legislative act the right of Turkish women to vote in all elections (G. Lewis, personal communication).

Sir Henry Maine once remarked that law is always out of step with society; there is always a gap between the legal rules and the existing social reality (Maine, 1861, p. 69). Thus, it is an empirical matter to establish the extent to which cultural practices changed under the impact of the new legislation. The remainder of the paper uses data from fieldwork in 1966 through 1968 to assess the consequences of these new rights for women, especially the ways women's rights to property are changing their relationships to men in rural areas of the Bodrum region.

WOMEN'S ACCESS TO VALUABLES

Earlier we defined property as bridewealth, land, and houses. Reputation is also a valuable resource. It is hoarded in the required virginity of a bride, and in the care with which wives present a modest public demeanour. It is lost through careless and unchaste behaviour of women. A great compliment to a rural Turkish woman is to call her *temiz,* which means clean, virtuous.

Under the new codes a woman can defend her honour and reputation at court in lawsuits against men who attempt to seduce her, who solicit her favours, or who abduct and rape her. She can bring suit against other women and men for spreading rumours and slander about her, and for bearing false witness. She can oppose her husband's attempt to divorce her to marry a new wife and she can sue him if he takes a common-law wife. In other words, she has become a legal person with full adult status to act on her own behalf with legal rights that no Islamic law system ever gave her.

The extent to which she is using these rights is explored, in a preliminary way, below. But, first we discuss tangible property

because it is an implicit premises of this paper that access to self-sufficiency through owning fields, the means of food production, is an important value.

Through Her Life Cycle

Women's access to valuable property in Mandalinci combines both traditional practices and the growing penetration of the market into everyday life. The significant markers in the female life cycle which mediate her access to property are:

(1) engagement, when she is given the bridewealth;
(2) marriage at about fifteen years of age when the moveable trousseau which she prepared is transferred to her new home;
(3) the death of her father, when the patrimony is divided;
(4) widowhood, when the patrimony of her husband is divided, and;
(5) old age (which may occur with (4) above), when she becomes a dependent person in the home usually of a married daughter, but sometimes of a married son.

From the ages of eleven to fourteen a girl will begin to embroider pillow cases, bed sheets, curtains and hand towels in anticipation of her marriage. The sheeting is bought for her by her parents.

During the bridewealth negotiations prior to marriage, she will have learned how much land, houses and family heirlooms (e.g. old pots, kilims, carpets, and some painted pottery) she will inherit when her father dies and his estate is divided. At the celebration of the engagement (*nikah*) she will be given the bridewealth, her fiance's gifts to her. In middle strata households these include gold bracelets, gold coins, perhaps a watch and cloth for dresses.

At the celebration of the village wedding, a bride will be given a small amount of cash by her parents and close relatives at the moment she is ready to leave her parent's house and mount the horse to be carried to the groom's house (or enter the hired jeep to travel to a village further away). Her parents also give her a winter coat, guests bring cooking pots, cooking utensils, towels, plates, cups and other useful household items as gifts.

Bridewealth: Broken Engagements and Divorce.[33] When an engagement is broken, no matter who is at fault all the gold and all the other gifts are returned to the fiance. If the cloth has already been made into dresses then the dresses themselves are returned. The candies and Turkish delights are the only things not returned, because they would no longer be fresh or might already have been eaten.

At divorce, however, none of the gold or presents are returned no matter if the woman is at fault. The bridewealth is considered 'the price of her virginity'. Only if a man married a woman to discover on her wedding night that she is not a virgin can he obtain the return of his bridewealth. But, a provident mother has probably tucked into the bosom of her daughter's wedding dress a handkerchief dipped in chicken blood. Not only is the nuptial room a traumatic occasion for the couple, but they must produce a bloodied handkerchief for the ritual benefit of the groom's sisters waiting outside the door. At divorce all the 'things of the house,' the blankets, quilts, bedding, kilim, rugs, cooking utensils, pottery, heirlooms and sewing machine if there is one, belong to the woman. The house itself belongs to the spouse whose family provided it.

Orchards and Houses. Generally, the first opportunity a village woman has to own land is when her father dies. However, I have documented one situation in which a married woman sued her brother for her share of the patrimony and won rights to a house and grounds while her father was still alive (Starr, 1978, pp. 213–23). This was accomplished with her husband's help. He not only acted as her legal representative (*vekil*) in the lawsuit, but quietened her down during the court's visit to the disputed house and house lot in the village, when she began shouting at her brother (Star, 1978, pp. 216–7). As the angry woman and her husband already owned a house in which they lived, this represents a

clear example of accumulation of property by asserting a woman's rights to her father's estate.

This contrasts sharply with Anatolia in the late 1940s where 'a simple division of land between sons seems to have been the normal customary procedure' (Stirling, 1965, p. 122). It differs also from the Hatay region of southeastern Turkey in 1965, where 'women are also denied access to land through inheritance unless they are brotherless' (Aswad, 1971; 1978, p. 475). In the Bodrum region by the mid-1960s husbands were realising they could markedly increase their household's prosperity by utilising the wife's legal rights to land. Furthermore, during a year's observation of the Bodrum courts I saw numerous cases of division of patrimony in which female siblings actually appeared in court. Inheritance cases (*veraset*) and land division cases (*taksim*) which represented 'routine' (as opposed to disputed) land cases made up the vast majority of the caseload in the High Court in Bodrum (*Asliye Hukuk*).[34]

Land at Divorce. In the three year period 1965 through 1967, 138 divorce cases were heard, and half were brought by wives. The usual grounds were incompatibility and hence most divorces were uncontested. The person who became complainant usually lived nearer the court or desired the divorce more avidly. No stigma was attached to being either defendant or complainant.

Division of land is comparatively easy at divorce, according to the judge interviewed, because each spouse keeps control of her/his orchard during the marriage. If a woman inherited an orchard from her father, the husband merely worked in it. If he bought a motorised pump for the orchard, he could take the pump out of the orchard at divorce. But, if the husband bought the fruit trees while the wife owned the land, the trees belong to the orchard, based on the legal principle 'the person who owns the land owns the trees' (*toprak kimin, ağaç onun*). If the husband built a house on her land, and there was no contract, the house belonged to the person who owned the land. If there was a contract, the person who owned the more expensive thing, would buy the other out. (For a more detailed discussion of divorce cases, cf. Starr, 1983.)

Land at Widowhood. An estate is divided at the death of the patriarch. The legal principle is that the widow gets first choice of one-fourth of the estate, and the remaining parts are divided among all his legitimate heirs equally, regardless of gender. If the wife took the house and remarried, she could live there with her new husband. If the house was given to a child and she remarried , the child could ask her to leave when he/she was of legal age. If a man and woman had no children when he died, the wife still got one-fourth his estate and the rest was divided equally between the dead man's mother and father. But, if there was even one child, the wife still got one-fourth and the child the remainder. His parents then got no part of his estate. Property only went to the deceased's brothers and sisters if he had no children and his parents were not living.

When women were widowed after thirty or forty years of age they may have chosen not to remarry but to live near a married child. They then helped with cooking and childcare, and when they were too old to work they would be looked after by their children till they died.

Women's Use of the Courts

Women's interaction with the Bodrum courts is in part a function of their position in the life cycle and in part a reflection of their growing sophistication in defending their position in society. A young female is slowly socialised into viewing the courts as an institution capable of helping her in a crisis. As a child she may have watched the judge and court recorder come to their village to hold a court hearing to award title to land or to view the place of a serious crime or of a land dispute. Perhaps she had to apply to a judge to have her age raised as her father registered her birth several years after the fact, and without proper age she is too young to marry. Or she may need to waive the required fifteen day period between obtaining a state licence to marry and celebration of the wedding. If she

has eloped, she will have to appear in court to clear her husband of charges of abduction. If she was abducted, her testimony in court will determine his freedom or prison sentence. Later she may be called as a witness to a crime or to a neighbour's application for land title. She and her brothers may need judicial advice about how to divide their father's property. The largest number of civil cases in the Bodrum court concerns land division (*taksim* and *veraset* cases).

Thus in mid-life she is prepared to view the court as a major resource when her husband or brothers fail her.[35] For example, in August 1967, a woman entered the Bodrum judge's office and requested that the judge appoint her as guardian for her mother, who was 'insane'. 'She is giving land to all my brothers and sisters, but not to me' she said. The judge accepted the case and asked that the mother have a doctor's evaluation.[36]

In a different case, Ayse, a fifty year old woman went to the Director of Bodrum (*Kaymakam*) to ask his intervention in a dispute with her neighbour, Hasan. The fifty year old man had built a wall for his orchard on Ayse's field. After viewing the disputed ground, the Director gave a verdict that Hasan must take the wall down from Ayse's land. When he didn't remove the wall, Ayse opened a criminal lawsuit against him in court. She paid for witnesses to appear and eventually she won her case.[37]

In a third case, Zehra, a forty-five year old woman asked the *kaymakam* to prohibit Mehmet's farming of land she had bought. After reviewing the title and the site, the *Kaymakam* made judgment in her favour. But, Mehmet refused to leave. Zehra then opened a lawsuit claiming. 'I just bought this land a year ago, and I find him still farming it.'

Mehmet answered, 'We have been farming this land for thirty years now.'

The judge asked, 'Who has the title?' Zehra responded that she did. 'But', the defendant said, 'It is not her land. She went to the *Kaymakam* and he stopped my farming of it.'

Eventually, Zehra won.[38] Here we see a woman who not only knows about farm titles but actively opposed a man who had usufruct land rights only. This case demonstrates a situation where usufruct was predominant but is now being replaced by notions of private ownership and a woman is able to take advantage of these changing conceptions of property rights.

Women are using the courts not only to gain and keep their property, but also to protect that intangible valuable, reputation.

For example, Hafise, a widow of sixty-five years, had lived in her house for thirty-seven years, raising eight children there. A civil servant inherited (from his mother) the house next door to Hafise. Although Turkish law specifies that windows cannot be put into a side of a house overlooking someone else's walled courtyard, he had built a window in the back of his house, overlooking Hafise's backyard. In making the extension on his home, he had also cut down most of Hafise's almond tree. In the summer of 1968 I went to Hafise's neighbourhood to find out how that case had ended. The following is part of an extended interview I had with Hafise:

Hafise said:

> The cases are not finished and I have been in court for one year and three months now. I have hired a legal representative (*vekil*) so that I don't have to go every week to court. The case about cutting down the tree was decided in his favour, but we sent it to Appeal court in Ankara.

I asked if Hafise had opened a case to gain restitution for the destruction of the tree. Hafise answered:

> No. I sent the dossier to the Appeal Court. I want to wait and see what they will do first. Maybe they will send him to jail. . . . He wanted to buy my wall. Do you remember that 'viewing' the court had of my garden and wall? Well, that 'viewing' determined the wall was mine. I said I'd sell the wall to him for 26,000 Turkish lira, but he offered me only 24,000 T.L. We then opened a different court case to determine the value of the wall. In this 'viewing' the judge only looked at the wall. They established that the wall was worth 1,300 T.L., but they neglected to look at the land it stood on. We are waiting for a viewing of the ground . . . I'll only sell if he pays my price . . . But, I still don't want his window open. Look, I wash in that garden. My toilet is

> there. I bathe there. I am an old lady. Sometimes I go out in my *don* (baggy pants). Can he be always looking at me? I saw apartment buildings in Ankara; they are all open, but this isn't Ankara. Bodrum is a small, old town. We are not so modern here. He should have his window on a street or in his garden. . . .[39]

Thus Hafise used the court to protect her modesty and her property. She had never been to court before this dispute. Nevertheless she pursued the restitution for her almond tree and the issue of his window through three different cases against her male neighbour, and when too many court hearings and postponements taxed her energies, she hired a local legal expert (*vekil*) for legal advice and court appearances.

In a final example, a twenty-two year old married woman, named Sevcihan, from Saz village (to Bodrum's east, adjoining the government forest) brought criminal charges at court. She accused a forest ranger, Mehmet, of molesting her after drinking with her husband while spending the night in their house. In court she told how two other forest rangers had offered her 500 T.L. to drop charges against their friend. Nevertheless, she pursued her grievance through five separate hearings over a five month time period. For each hearing she needed to travel twenty-five miles over rough terrain to court. On at least two occasions she had to bring witnesses and pay their expenses. On three different occasions she had had to retell the events of that night:

> The woman, Sevcihan, in court: That night the forest ranger and my husband came. They had been drinking at the coffee-house. They brought another bottle of *raki* to our house, and my husband told me to make some food ready. And then my husband became drunk and he fell asleep. I went to my husband's father, and I called him. He came to the house for a while and then he left. I went to bed next to my husband. I went to sleep. Someone is touching me and I woke up.
> Judge: How is he touching you? Where is he touching you?
> Sevcihan: He is stroking my neck, my breasts, my arms, my hands. I ran outside. He followed

me. I came back again. I went to the room where my husband was sleeping and I locked the door. He knocked at the window, saying, 'Come. I am waiting for you.' I went again to bed next to my husband.

Mehmet's version: I went home with her husband. We had been drinking at the coffee-house, and we had a bottle of *raki* with us. And then her husband got drunk. He went to sleep. Later his father came and I offered him some *raki*, but he said, 'I do not drink.' When he left I went to the bed they gave me. When I woke up in the morning I went to wash my face. She came to me, and I asked where her husband was. She said, 'He went. He went to the coffee-house.' (He is the proprietor.) She gave me a cup of water. I drank it and then said, 'Say good-bye to your husband for me.'

Judge: Do you go to their house often?

Mehmet: This is the first time.

Lawyer for Mehmet: That girl and her husband made a plan to get 500 T.L. from my client.

Judge: Do you have proof? What kind is it?

Lawyer: Witnesses. Next time I will give a list of witnesses.

Sevcihan: That's not true. The next day two forest rangers came to me by Jeep. They said if you will give up this court case, we will give you 500 T.L.. But, I didn't want to give up this case.

The testimony of the witnesses can be summarised as follows:

One witness had said, 'I drive a jeep for hire. The day after that event I carried two forest rangers to her village, and they went to her house, but I didn't overhear the conversation there.' Another witness had testified that he saw two forest rangers going to her village, and had seen the defendant and her husband drinking in the village coffee-house the night of the alleged event. A third witness, a twenty-three year old woman, testifying for Sevcihan said:

> About a month ago we were stringing tobacco leaves onto thread. This man comes up to Sevcihan and said, 'My dear, Sevcihan, why do you not come to me? Are you angry with me?' She didn't go to him. . . . No, I didn't see him touching her.[40]

Eventually, the charges against the forester were dismissed for insufficient evidence, de-spite the female witness' testimony which im-plied that Mehmet was aggressively pursuing Sevcihan.

From a different perspective Sevcihan can be seen to have won her goal. Her ardent pur-suit of justice through the court made Mehmet's actions public—his co-workers, her villagers, and even her debauched husband must now recognise his lecherous inclinations toward her. After five months of fearing a large fine and jail sentence (which would have meant loss of his job), Mehmet's lusts were probably tempered by prudence. Sevcihan's use of a district level court thus provided her the opportunity to vindicate her honour and safeguard her reputation.

BROADER IMPLICATIONS

In the Bodrum region factors which allowed women to develop more self-sufficient lives were: changing land-use patterns which con-structed the daily work routines for both fe-males and males; a change in post-marital residence in response to the emergence of a new class structure, which occurred as a result of the penetration of capitalist agriculture. And third, the law. Judges' willingness to en-force legislation promoting norms of equality in union with women's growing knowledge of how to activate the official law system were emancipating mechanisms in western Tur-key. In central and eastern Anatolia women's independence is apparently less advanced.[41] I would argue this is due to differences in the agrarian hierarchy, land use patterns, cul-ture, historic conditions, and type of integra-tion into the world market.

An explanation of Bodrum's successful ac-ceptance of the new Civil Code may lie in sev-eral directions. Bodrum has a unique geo-graphic and political position as a frontier of Turkish-Greek contact, and it was early paci-fied by the new Republic of Turkey. With good reason officials in Ankara would have wanted to keep Aegean Turkey pacified, eco-nomically productive and indoctrinated into the values of nation-statehood. Bodrum is much too accessible to the Greek Islands to let it remain a backwater, illustrating the failure of the nation to maintain a western democratic outlook. Furthermore, it is an area of increasing productivity since the 1940s, and since 1968 Bodrum town has had a huge economic boom in summer months due to tourism. The winter population of the town has doubled between 1965 and 1980.[42]

Earlier I suggested that in Aegean Turkey, Hellenistic and Islamic attitudes toward women had long co-existed as Turkish-speaking nomads over a period of several hundred years migrated into and settled in the region now called Bodrum. The ecology of transhumance required far-flung networks for the Yörük sheep herders to gain access to diverse pastures in this multi-ethnic region. Marrying daughters to Turkish-speaking transhumants of different camps within the same ethnic group cemented pastoral relations. The Islamic ideology concerning male dominance and the required submission of females was supported by the institutions of bridewealth, post-marital virilocal residence, divorce by renunciation and the ideology of honour and shame.

Yet, despite the change from pastoral life to settled capitalist agriculture, cultural institutions such as bridewealth and virilocal post-marital residence remained as 'ideal forms'. Writing about European manners and cultural change in the emerging Renaissance Europe, Elias (1939) demonstrated that two or three hundred years may be necessary for ideas, etiquette, and new cultural practices to diffuse throughout a society. Yet, in the Bodrum region, work routines changed rapidly in response to new crops and a new productive system. Marriage patterns changed, too, as cash-cropping agriculture and the transformation of the class structure made marriages within the village a way to consolidate land holdings for middle and upper strata peasants. And third, the norms of sexual equality promoted by the secular legal system through both written law and judicial decisions, provided a way for females to gain control of resources, especially productive land, which for women (as for anyone), are a bridge to autonomous personage.

Thus, Engels', dynamic theory of the process of change from pre-capitalist social formations to capitalist relations neglected the positive role law and culture play. In the region of Bodrum law balanced the disruptive effect that capitalist agriculture and the emergence of private ownership had on women's lives. With increasing scarcity of land for intensive agriculture, the norms of equal division of patrimony had become salient to husbands as a way to increase household land holdings. Elsewhere I noted that tangerine cultivation promotes nuclear households because two adults and two teenage children can provide all the needed labour from within (see Starr, 1978, pp. 38–42). Mastery of the economic processes behind tangerine marketing is information easily accessible to any female who keeps her ears open.

Thus, I can unequivocally state that less than fifty years after the introduction of European Civil and Criminal codes in Turkey, women in the Bodrum region were reaping the benefits of laws of equality. They were able to hold titles to land in their own names. Some women successfully opposed husbands' attempts to usurp their economic resources during marriage and at divorce, and many women went to court to protect their landed interests and their reputations.

Some might argue that under the older system women were protected by fathers, husbands, and brothers; that going to court clearly indicates the breakdown of the older protective system.[43] Didn't women lead better lives, they ask, in a material, social and qualitative sense in the past? I answer, that depends upon your goals for women. Data presented here clearly indicate, I think, that husbands, brothers and fathers do not always look out for a wife's, sister's or daughter's best interests. They may not even know them (even if they wished to) because some women may not be sure what their best interests are, while others may not be able to develop a plan which they can communicate by reasoned argument (cf. S. Ardener, 1975, pp. xi–xviii; E. Ardener, 1975). Given these facts it is better that women have ways to look out for their own interests, that they judge for themselves what these interests are, and that they develop habitual modes of thought and action which allow them to do so.

Therefore, the Bodrum example suggests that several factors need to intersect for women's emergence as more autonomous adults. The implication for policy makers is that legal rights and economic opportunities for women and for men must go hand in hand. The Bodrum study also suggests that we need to take a longer time span than twenty-five years[44] in deciding whether the results of change have improved women's lives. Of course we need to study the processes along the way. But, fifty years after the introduction of new secular codes, and twenty or more years after the gradual emergence of settled village life, we can see ways that women's access to valuables—land, houses, and reputation—are changing their relations to men, allowing them to become fully responsible persons.

NOTES

Acknowledgements. I owe a debt of gratitude to Dr. Geoffrey Lewis, Oriental Institute, Oxford, for taking the time to read critically this manuscript, although I take responsibility for its remaining faults. I also acknowledge with pleasure conversations and careful readings of the essay by Helen Callaway, Shirley Ardener, and especially Renée Hirschon.

1. Engels, of course, was not the only nineteenth century anthropologist to discuss woman's position in society in an evolutionary framework. But, precisely because his writing is the culmination of an anthropological perspective beginning with Maine, and developed by Bachofen, McLennan, Lubbock and Morgan, I choose to confront Engels's theories. Two recent critiques of Engels (1884) are Leacock (1981) and Sacks (1974).

2. See Engels (1981, pp. 120–21, 142–44).

3. Divorce is now easier for women and harder for men than it had been under the previous Islamic law system of the 20th century Ottoman Empire. Divorce was now accessible under the new Civil Code of 1926 by a spouse applying to the nearest secular district court on one of the six grounds: adultery, dishonourable life of the spouse, desertion, mental infirmity, or incompatibility (Ansay and Wallace, 1966, p. 122). For a more detailed discussion Starr (1978).

4. Modernisation is here roughly defined as integration of the group into a nation-state. The linkages between the group and the state may, of course, be imperfectly achieved, e.g., the Kurds in Turkey.

5. See Boserup (1970), Bossen (1975), Papanek (1977), and Nelson (1981).

6. Even those sympathetic to the cultural system of Islam and who advocate reform within Islamic law rather than a complete break, acknowledge Islamic law provides few rights for women and many disabilities when women's rights are compared to men's. See, for example, Coulson and Hinchcliffe (1978) and White (1978, pp. 52–3).

7. The organising force of codes of honour and shame in Mediterranean countries has been argued by Campbell (1964), Davis (1977), Peristiany (1965), Schneider (1971), Schneider and Schneider (1976, p. 2) and others.

8. See Stirling (1955, pp. 98, 168, 230–3); Starr (1978, p. 56); Abel (1979).

9. Approximately half of Turkey's trade in 1982 has been with Islamic countries (*The Guardian,* 12th May, 1982) and in the same year Turkey signed a major Trade Pact with Russia for 600 million lira (*New York Times,* 20th January, 1982, p. a7).

10. In 1960, 22,700 workers left Turkey (Abadan-Unat, 1981, p. 2). The figure continued to rise each year until the oil crisis of 1973–4. In 1980 the combined figure of Turkish residents in France, Germany, the Netherlands, Sweden and Switzerland was 1,762.9 thousand (SOPEMI, 1981, p. 3).

11. Fisher (1963, pp. 293–338) divides Turkey into five geographic regions, the Anatolian plateau, the Black sea coast, eastern Turkey, the Mediterranean, and the Aegean coast, but I suggest six. European Turkey ought to be separated from Aegean and Mediterranean Turkey at the Meander River.

12. The field research between 1966–68 was financed by a United States National Institute of Mental Health Predoctoral Fellowship and Grant and I gratefully acknowledge this support.

13. A hectare is 100 ares or 2.471 acres.

14. For a very interesting study of Bodrum town, see Mansur (1972).

15. Fieldwork revealed cultural differences between villagers on the Bodrum peninsula to Bodrum's west, and those on the Mumcular plain to Bodrum's east which villagers themselves recognise saying 'They are very different from us'. Identifying which villagers were Yurük and which Turcoman was harder and is the topic of current research. But see Field (1881, pp. 62–3), De Planhol (1958, pp. 526, 528, 531) and Ramsay (1897, pp. 100–1; 1917, pp. 31, 83).

16. The transition from pastoralism to settled village life and the identity of these villages was first suggested to me by Osman Nuri Bilgin, Director of the Primary School in Bodrum, and a historian of the Bodrum region.

17. Interview with the Director of Rural Agriculture, Bodrum.

18. In the later 19th century the Turkish population was losing control of the Aegean areas to Greek-speaking farmers and shepherds. (Ramsay, 1897, pp. 130–31, 133). See also Starr (1978, pp. 23–5).

19. The population from the 1965 Census lists Bodrum town as having 5,136 while the surrounding villages are placed at 20,675 (*Genel Nüfus Sayimi* 1965, p. 483).

20. Most women fifty years or older also remember Greek, for they came from islands of Kos and Kalimnos as brides.

21. See note 17.

22. Marketing tangerines only became feasible with the completion of a dirt road linking Bodrum to Milas in 1927, because tangerines ripen between December and March, the period of sudden, violent storms on the Aegean. This makes sea transport particularly precarious at this season.

23. The procedure of converting usufruct rights to a state recognised legal title (*tapu*) involved going to court and applying under Art. 639 of the Turkish Civil Code. 'If the land is not previously registered in the Land Registry and if the person occupies and uses the land as if he were the real owner for 20 years without interruption and dispute, he may request a court to order the registration of the land in his name.' (Letter from Prof. T. Ansay, Dean of Ankara University Law Faculty. 14 December 1980).

24. Cosar (1978, p. 131) astutely observes that as one moves from east to west in Turkey the 'situation of women improves with the general socio-economic situation'.

25. The lack of religious behaviour among Turkish-speaking transhumants has been noted by Barth for the Basseri, (1961, p. 135) and by R.

Tapper for the Shahsevan (1975, pp. 2, 155, 158, 164). But, see Beck for women's religious and ritual practices among the Turkish-speaking *Qashqa'i* (1978, pp. 363–5).

26. Interview with Ayhan A., concerning Bodrum Court Case, B.C. 62. Bodrum *Court Cases File*. Also see Case 11 on film, '*Adliye*: An Ethnography of a Turkish Rural Court,' 1968.

27. Fieldnotes, filed under *Kız Kaçırma* (Elopement) Cases, 1967.

28. This is interesting as an attempt to use legislation to regulate custom and tradition.

29. See Allen (1935, pp. 137–9), Coulson (1964, p. 184), Starr (1978, ftn.2, pp. 1–2).

30. See B. Lewis (1961, pp. 225–6).

31. Maher (1978, p. 102) makes the same point for rural Moroccan women. The male lineage members justify this deprivation of inheritance by saying that if daughters were given their land, it would be transferred to another lineage when they married.

32. The Turkish National Assembly enacted laws legitimising children of irregular marriages in 1932, 1934, 1945, 1950, 1955, 1965 and 1974.

33. The following is a summary of two days of discussions I had in August 1967 with the senior court judge and the Public Prosecutor concerning female and male property rights and bridewealth, at critical times in the life cycle or when engagements were broken or marriages were dissolved.

34. See, Starr and Pool (1974, pp. 552–54) for an analysis of women and men's use of the courts in Bodrum. Also Starr (1983) for women versus men in divorce suits.

35. Additional confirmation of this assertion is available. Female complaints against male defendants as a total of all cases processed in the Bodrum Middle Criminal Court rose from 14 per cent in 1950 to 28 per cent in 1967 (Starr and Pool, 1974, p. 353).

36. Witnessed by me 7 August 1967. Filed under Conversations with Bodrum judges and Public Prosecutor, p. 33, titled, 'Opening a Case, *Sulh Hukuk* (Lower Civil Court).'

37. Bodrum Court Cases, File. *Sulh Ceza* (Lower Criminal Court), B.C. 23, 1967.

38. Bodrum Court Cass, File. *Sulh Hukuk* (Lower Civil Court), B.C. 78.

39. Bodrum Court Cases, File. *Asliye Hukuk* (Higher Civil Court) B.C. 72 and *Asliye Ceza* (Middle Criminal Court) B.C. 85.

40. Bodrum Court Cases, File. *Sulh Ceza* (Lower Criminal Court) B.. 41B.

41. For overviews and comparative statements

about women in Turkey, see Abadan-Unat (1963, 1978 and 1981), Cosar (1978), and Kandiyoti (1977, 1980). For ethnographic accounts of women's position, see Aswad (1967, 1974, 1978).

42. Winter population figures for 1980 were: Bodrum town—10,000 people; Bodrum district (*kaza*) including the town and all the villages had 38,000 people. (Personal communication, Mrs. Emine Cam, Director of Tourism Bureau in Bodrum.

43. Nader (1964, 1965) hypothesized that women in Oaxaca, Mexico used the court only when they did not have a husband, father or brother to protect their interests. In Turkey, however, family structures, law and the market interact so that it is frequently a *brother* or husband who has usurped the women's resources (see Stirling, 1957, p. 27); or a *father* may exploit his daughter for his own financial gain (see Stirling, 1957, p. 31). Even in areas of strong kin group control, 'the "protection" of the lineage which had previously been to the economic advantage of the woman is turning increasingly into dominance and exploitation' (Aswad, 1978, p. 475).

44. Twenty-five years was the time period of the evaluative conference in Istanbul, entitled the 'Reception of Foreign Law in Turkey,' which essentially was pessimistic (see Stirling, 1957, and Velidedeoğlu, 1957).

REFERENCES

Abadan-Unat, Nermin, 1963. *Social Change and Turkish Women*. Publication of the Faculty of Political Science, University of Ankara, No. 17.

———. 1978. The Modernization of Turkish Women. *The Middle East Journal* 32: 291–306.

———. ed. 1981. *Women in Turkish Society*. Leiden: E. J. Brill.

Abel, R. 1979. The Rise of Capitalism and the Transformation of Disputing: From Confrontation over Honor to Competition for Property. *UCLA Law Review* 27(1): 223–255.

Ansay, T. and Wallace, Jr. 1966. *Introduction to Turkish Law*. Ankara: Guzel Instanbul Matbaasi.

Ardener, E. 1975. Belief and the Problem of Women. In J. La Fontaine, ed. *The Interpretation of Ritual*. London: Tavistock Press.

Ardener, S. 1975. Introductory Essay. In S. Ardener, ed. *Perceiving Women*. New York: Halsted.

Aswad, Barbara. 1967. Key and Peripheral Roles of Noblewomen in a Middle Eastern Plains Village. *Anthropological Quarterly* 40: 139–152.

———. 1971. Property Control and Social Strategies: Settlers on a Middle Eastern Plain. *Anthropological Papers No. 44*. Ann Arbor, Michigan: University of Michigan.

———. 1974. Visiting Patterns Among Women of the Elite in a Small Turkish City. *Anthropological Quarterly* 47: 9–27.

———. 1978. Women, Class and Power: Examples from the Hatay, Turkey. In Lois Beck and Nikki Keddie, eds., pp. 473–481. *Women in the Muslim World*. Cambridge: Harvard University Press.

Boserup, Ester. 1970. *Woman's Role in Economic Development*. New York: St. Martin's Press.

Bossen, Laurel. 1975. Women in Modernizing Societies. American *Ethnologist* 2(4): 587–601.

Campbell, John K. 1964. *Honour, Family, and Patronage*. Oxford: Clarendon Press.

Cosar, Fatna Mansur. 1978. Women in Turkish Society. In Lois Beck and Nikki Keddie, eds., pp. 124–140. *Women in the Muslim World*. Cambridge: Harvard University Press.

Coulson, Noel and Doreen Hinchcliffe. 1978. Women and Law Reform in Contemporary Islam. In Lois Beck and Nikki Keddie, eds. *Women in the Muslim World*, pp. 37–52. Cambridge: Harvard University Press.

Davis, John. 1977. *People of the Mediterranean: An Essay in Comparative Social Anthropology*. London: Routledge and Kegan Paul.

Elias, N. 1982. *The Civilizing Process, Vol 1. The History of Manners*. Oxford: Blackwell. Originally published as Uber den Prozess der Zivilisation, 1939.

Engels, F. 1981. *The Origin of the Family, Private Property and the State*. Edited with an introduction by E.B. Leacock. London: Lawrence and Wishart.

Kandiyoti, D. 1977. Sex Roles and Social Change: A Comparative Appraisal of Turkey's Women. *Signs* 3(1): 57–73.

———. ed. 1980. *Major Issues on the Status of Women in Turkey: Approaches and Priorities*. Ankara: Cag Matbaasi.

Leacock, Eleanor B. 1981a. *Myths of Male Dominance*. London: Monthly Review Press.

Leacock, Eleanor B. 1981b. Introduction to Engels' *The Origin of the Family, Private Property and the State*. London: Lawrence and Wishart.

Lewis, B. 1961. Arus Resmi. In *Encyclopedia of Islam*, Vol. 1, p. 697.

Maine, H.S. 1861. *Ancient Law: Its Connection with the Early History of Society and its Relation to Modern Ideas*. London: John Murray.

Nelson, N. 1981. Introduction to African Women in the Development Process. *Journal of Development Studies* 17(3): 1–8.

Onar, S.S. 1955. The Magalla. *Law in the Middle East* 1: 292–308.

Papanek, Helen. 1977. Development Planning for Women. *Signs* 31: 14–22.

Peristiany, John G., ed. 1965. *Honour and Shame: The Values of Mediterranean Society*. London: Weidenfeld and Nicolson.

Ramsay, W. M. 1917. *The Intermixture of Races in Asia Minor, Some of its Causes and Effects. Proceedings of the British Academy*, Vol. 7, pp. 31, 83. London: Oxford University Press.

Sacks, Karen. 1974. Engels Revisited: Women, The Organization of Production and Private Property. In Michelle Rosaldo and Louise Lamphere, eds. *Woman, Culture and Society*, pp. 207–220. Stanford: Stanford University Press.

Soteriadis, G. 1918. *An Ethnological Map Illustrating Hellenism in the Balkans Peninsula and Asia Minor*. London: Edward Stanford.

Schneider, Jane. 1971. Of Vigilance and Virgins: Honor, Shame and Access to Resources in Mediterranean Societies. *Ethnology* 10(1): 1–24.

Schneider, Jane and Peter Schneider. 1976. *Culture and Political Economy in Western Sicily*. New York: Academic Press.

Starr, J. 1978. *Dispute and Settlement in Rural Turkey: An Ethnography of Law*. Leiden: E.J. Brill.

Stirling, Paul. 1957. Land, Marriage and the Law in Turkish Villages. *International Social Science Bulletin* 9: 21–33.

———. 1965. *Turkish Village*. London: Weidenfeld and Nicolson.

———. 1974. Cause, Knowledge and Change: Turkish Village Revisited. In J. Davis, ed. *Choice and Change: Essays in Honour of Lucy Mair*. London: Athlone Press.

Velidedeoğlu, H.V. 1957. The Reception of the Swiss Civil Code in Turkey. *International Social Science Bulletin* 9: 60–65.

Young, G. 1905. *Corps de Droit Ottoman*. Vol. II. Oxford: Clarendon Press.

White, Elizabeth H. 1978. Legal Reform as an Indicator of Women's Status in Muslim Nations. In Lois Beck and Nikki Keddie, eds., *Women in the Muslim World*, pp. 52–68. Cambridge: Harvard University Press.

VIII.
Gender, Household, and Kinship

The study of kinship has been central to cross-cultural research. Marriage customs, systems of descent, and patterns of residence have been described and compared in a range of societies around the world. At the heart of traditional studies of kinship is the opposition between the domestic domain on the one hand and the public, political, and jural domain on the other. Anthropologists, particularly those working in Africa, studied kinship in this latter domain. They delineated large corporate descent groups called lineages that managed property and resources and that were the basic building blocks of political organization (Fortes 1949, 1953). Marriage, for some kinship theorists, is a political transaction, involving the exchange of women between men who wish to form alliances (Lévi-Strauss 1969; see also Ortner, this book). A woman, from this perspective, is a passive pawn with little influence over kinship transactions. She is viewed "in terms of the rights her kin have to her domestic labor, to the property she might acquire, to her children, and to her sexuality"

(Lamphere 1974:98). The dynamic, affective, and even interest-oriented aspects of women's kinship are essentially ignored in an approach that is rooted in androcentric principles: women have the children; men impregnate the women; and men usually exercise control (Fox 1967).

Recent critiques of the traditional study of kinship have pointed out that it is "no longer adequate to view women as bringing to kinship primarily a capacity for bearing children while men bring primarily a capacity for participation in public life" (Collier and Yanagisako 1987:7). A gendered approach to kinship takes a number of different directions but focuses on the status of men and women in different kinship systems and on the power (defined as the ability to make others conform to one's desires and wishes) that accrues to women through their manipulation of social relations. Cross-cultural variations in the status of men and women have been examined in relation to rules of descent and postmarital residence (Martin and Voorhies 1975; Friedl 1975). Among horticulturalists, for example,

women, have higher status in societies characterized by matrilineal descent (descent through
the female line from a common female ancestor) and matrilocal residence (living with the
wife and her kin after marriage) than in societies
characterized by patrilineal descent (descent
through the male line from a common male ancestor) and patrilocal residence (living with the
husband and his kin after marriage). In matrilineal systems descent group membership, social
identity, rights to land, and succession to political office are all inherited through one's mother.

When matrilineality is combined with matrilocal residence, a husband marries into a household in which a long-standing domestic coalition
exists between his wife and her mother, sisters,
and broader kin relations (Friedl 1975). These
women cooperate with one another in work endeavors and provide mutual support. Although a
man retains authority in a matrilineal system
over his sisters and her children, the coalitions
formed by kin-related women can provide them
with power and influence both within and beyond the household (Brown 1970; Lamphere
1974) and also with a degree of sexual freedom.
The important issue for women's status, as
Schlegel (1972:96) has argued, is not the descent system per se but the organization of the
domestic group.

In contrast to matrilineal and matrilocal systems, in patrilineal and patrilocal societies
women do not have their own kin nearby. A
woman enters her husband's household as a
stranger. Separated from her own kin, she cannot forge lateral alliances easily. However, other
opportunities are open to women that enhance
their power and status in patrilineal and patrilocal societies. Taiwanese women, for example,
marry into the household of their husbands
(Wolf 1972). A Taiwanese wife must pay hom-
age to her husband's ancestors, obey her husband and mother-in-law, and bear children for
her husband's patrilineage. According to Wolf
(1972:32). "A woman can and, if she is ever to
have any economic security, must provide the
links in the male chain of descent, but she will
never appear in anyone's genealogy as that all-
important name connecting the past to the future."

After a Taiwanese wife gives birth to a son,
her status in the household begins to change,
and it improves during her life course as she
forges what Wolf calls a uterine family—a family
based on the powerful relationship between
mothers and sons. The subordination of conjugal to intergenerational relationships that is exemplified by the Taiwanese case, as well as the
opportune ways in which women take advantage of filial ties to achieve political power within
and beyond the household, are apparent in
other societies around the world—for example,
in sub-Saharan Africa (Potash 1986).

When a Taiwanese wife becomes a mother-
in-law she achieves the greatest power and status within her husband's household. Wolf
(1972:37) concludes that "the uterine family
has no ideology, no formal structure, and no
public existence. It is built out of sentiments and
loyalties that die with its members, but it is no
less real for all that. The descent lines of men are
born and nourished in the uterine families of
women, and it is here that a male ideology that
excludes women makes its accommodations
with reality." Similarly, Hausa trading women
are able to compensate for an ideology that
keeps them in residential seclusion by depending on their children to distribute their goods,
provide information on the world outside the
household, and help with child-care and cooking (Schildkrout 1983).

Wolf's research on Taiwanese women substantiates Lamphere's (1974:99) observation
that "the distribution of power and authority in
the family, the developmental cycle of the domestic group, and women's strategies are all related." By strategies Lamphere is referring to the
active ways in which women use and manipulate kinship to their own advantage. The strategic use of kinship is a mechanism for economic
survival among the African-American families of
a midwestern town described by Stack (in this
book). The households of these families are flexible and fluid; they are tied together by complex
networks of female kinship and friendship. If the
boundaries of the household are elastic, the ties
that unite kin and friends are long-lasting.
Through these domestic networks, women exchange a range of goods and services including
child care. They rely on one another and
through collective efforts keep one another

afloat. When one member of the network achieves a degree of economic success she can choose to withdraw from kin cooperation to conserve rèsources. However, by reinitiating gift-giving and exchange, at some point she can easily reenter the system. Stack's research shows one example of a strategy pursued by many families in the United States who must cope with urban poverty and the constant threat of unemployment.

A similar approach is shown in research on Afro-Caribbean families, who also live in conditions of economic uncertainty and stress. This research has generated a vigorous debate about a complex of characteristics, including female-headed households, women's control of household earnings and decision making, kinship networks linked through women, and the absence of resident men. This complex of characteristics has been referred to as matrifocality. Drawing on data from her research in Jamaica, Prior (in this book) reviews the concept of matrifocality, a concept first introduced by Raymond Smith in 1956 to describe the central position and power of the mother within the household. Rather than viewing these households as disorganized or pathological results of slavery and colonialism, anthropologists recently have stressed their adaptive advantages (Bolles and Samuels 1989) for women who are both mothers and economic providers. Furthermore, as Prior suggests, the composition of households in the Caribbean is fluid; they can be female-headed at one point in time and nuclear at another. Arguing against a widely held conception within anthropology, Prior suggests that fathers and male partners are by no means marginal to the household.

Prior points out that very little work has been done on the relations between men and women in such households because men were always assumed to be absent. One neglected aspect of male-female household relations is domestic violence. Such violence often emerges because the expectations that women hold for men, whether they are monetary contributions to the household or fidelity, are not fulfilled. The potential for violence that can erupt when women challenge men about these unfulfilled obligations can undercut the power that women otherwise maintain within the household.

Women-centered families like those of African-Americans and Afro-Caribbeans have been described for other parts of the world (Tanner 1974). Cole (in this book) introduces us to Maria, a fisherwoman who lives in a small town on the northern coast of Portugal. Forced into productive activity because her husband emigrated to Brazil and abandoned her for many years, Maria has taken control of her life and her personhood. Like Taiwanese women, she has invested in her relationship with her children rather than in the conjugal tie with her husband, although in this case the significant children are daughters rather than sons. Children, says Cole, are a resource for women. This is most evident in the high rates of illegitimacy that have characterized this town, and northern Portugal in general, until fairly recently. Also characteristic of the region are the significant inheritance of property by women and the tendency for matrilocal residence or neolocal residence near the wife's kin. These women-centered patterns are, as Cole and others (Brettell 1986) stress, closely linked to a long-standing pattern of male emigration. Whether in agriculture or in fishing, many women in northern Portugal must fulfill both male and female roles within the household.

The matrilateral bias in kinship described by Cole for northern Portugal is also apparent among Japanese-American immigrants in the urban United States (Yanagisako 1977). Manifested in women-centered kin networks, this bias influences patterns of coresidence, residential proximity, mutual aid, and affective ties. Rather than stressing the economic reasons for the maintenance of kinship ties, Yanagisako draws attention to the role of women as kin keepers who foster and perpetuate channels of communication and who plan and stage elaborate family rituals.

The social and ritual importance of kinship is precisely what di Leonardo (in this book) focuses on in her discussion of the female world of cards and holidays. The Italian-American women she describes work in the labor market and at home, but they are also engaged in "kin work." Kin work is women's work and involves maintaining contact through all kinds of mechanisms with family members who are deemed important.

Unlike child care and house cleaning, it is a task that has to be carried out by the woman herself. Though it is often burdensome work women undertake kin work, according to di Leonardo, because through it they can set up a chain of valuable and long-term obligations within a wide circle of social relations.

Although di Leonardo identifies other parts of the developed world in which women have greater kin knowledge than men and work hard at maintaining kinship networks (for example, Lomnitz and Perez-Lizaur 1987), several questions are open to further empirical investigation. For example, why in some societies does kin work take on ritual significance, and why is it culturally assigned to women in some contexts and to men in others? Di Leonardo interprets the emergence of gendered kin work in association with a relative decline in importance of the domain of public male kinship that is found, for example, in African societies characterized by a powerful principle of descent. The shift, she suggests, is part of the process of capitalist development. Recently, Enloe (1990) has taken these arguments much further by demonstrating how both global politics and global economics are engendered. Without kin work, for example, Hallmark (the card manufacturer) would be out of business.

Collier and Yanagisako (1987) have recently argued that gender and kinship are mutually constructed and should be brought together into one analytic field. Kinship and gender are closely allied because they are both based in, but not exclusively determined by, biology and because what it means to be a man or a woman is directly linked to the rules of marriage and sexuality that a culture constructs. As Lindenbaum (1987:221) has observed, "Relations of kinship are in certain societies, relations of production. If kinship is understood as a system that organizes the liens we hold on the emotions and labors of others, then it must be studied in relation to gender ideologies that enmesh men and women in diverse relations of productive and reproductive work. The variable constructions of male and female that emerge in different times and places are central to an understanding of the character of kinship."

REFERENCES

Bolles, A. Lynn and Deborah d'Amico-Samuels. 1989 Anthropological Scholarship on Gender in the English-speaking Caribbean. In Sandra Morgen (ed.). *Gender and Anthropology*, pp. 171–188. Washington, DC: American Anthropological Association.

Brettell, Caroline ⅃B. 1986. *Men Who Migrate, Women Who Wait: Population and History in a Portuguese Parish*. Princeton: Princeton University Press.

Brown Judith K. 1970. Economic Organization and the Position of Women Among the Iroquois. *Ethnohistory* 17: 151–167.

Collier, Jane Fishburne and Sylvia Junko Yanagisako. 1987. *Gender and Kinship: Essays Toward a Unified Analysis*. Stanford: Stanford University Press.

Enloe, Cynthia. 1990. *Bananas, Beaches and Bases: Making Feminist Sense of International Politics*. Berkeley: University of California Press.

Fortes, Meyer. 1949. *The Web of Kinship Among the Tallensi*. London: International African Institute, Oxford University Press.

———. 1953. The Structure of Unilineal Descent Groups. *American Anthropologist* 55: 25–39.

Fox, Robin. 1967. *Kinship, and Marriage: An Anthropological Perspective*. Harmondsworth: Penguin.

Friedl, Ernestine. 1975. *Women and Men: An Anthropologist's View*. New York: Holt, Rinehart and Winston.

Lamphere, Louise. 1974. Strategies, Cooperation, and Conflict among Women in Domestic Groups. In Michelle Z. Rosaldo and Louise Lamphere (eds.). *Women, Culture, and Society*, pp. 97–112. Stanford: Stanford University Press.

Lévi-Strauss, Claude. 1969. *The Elementary Structures of Kinship*. Boston: Beacon Press.

Lindenbaum, Shirley. 1987. The Mystification of Female Labors. In Jane Fishburne Collier and Sylvia Junko Yanagisako (eds.). *Gender and Kinship: Essays Toward a Unified Analysis,* Stanford: Stanford University Press.

Lomnitz, Larissa and Marisol Perez-Lizaur. 1987. *A Mexican Elite Family, 1820–1980*. Princeton: Princeton University Press.

Martin, M. Kay and Barbara Voorhies. 1975. *Female of the Species*. New York: Columbia University Press.

Potash, Betty (ed.). 1986. *Widows in African Societies*. Stanford: Stanford University Press.

Schildkrout, Enid. 1983. Dependence and Autonomy: The Economic Activities of Secluded Hausa Women in Kano. In Christine Oppong (ed.). *Fe-*

male and Male in West Africa. Winchester, MA: Allen and Unwin.

Schlegel, Alice. 1972. *Male Dominance and Female Autonomy: Domestic Authority in Matrilineal Societies.* New Haven: Human Relations Area Files.

Tanner, Nancy. 1974. Matrifocality in Indonesia and Africa and Among Black Americans. In Michelle Z. Rosaldo and Louise Lamphere (eds.), *Woman,* *Culture, and Society,* pp. 129–156. Stanford: Stanford University Press.

Wolf, Margery. 1972. *Women and the Family in Rural Taiwan.* Stanford: Stanford University Press.

Yanagisako, Sylvia Junko. 1977. Women-centered Kin Networks in Urban Bilateral Kinship. *American Ethnologist* 2: 207–226.

Domestic Networks: "Those You Count On"

Carol Stack

In The Flats the responsibility for providing food, care, clothing, and shelter and for socializing children within domestic networks may be spread over several households. Which household a given individual belongs to is not a particularly meaningful question, as we have seen that daily domestic organization depends on several things: where people sleep, where they eat, and where they offer their time and money. Although those who eat together and contribute toward the rent are generally considered by Flat's residents to form minimal domestic units, household changes rarely affect the exchanges and daily dependencies of those who take part in common activity.

The residence patterns and cooperative organization of people linked in domestic networks demonstrate the stability and collective power of family life in The Flats. Michael Lee grew up in The Flats and now has a job in Chicago. On a visit to The Flats, Michael described the residence and domestic organiza-

tion of his kin. "Most of my kin in The Flats lived right here on Cricket Street, numbers sixteen, eighteen, and twenty-two, in these three apartment buildings joined together. My mama decided it would be best for me and my three brothers and sister to be on Cricket Street too. My daddy's mother had a small apartment in this building, her sister had one in the basement, and another brother and his family took a larger apartment upstairs. My uncle was really good to us. He got us things we wanted and he controlled us. All the women kept the younger kids together during the day. They cooked together too. It was good living."

Yvonne Diamond, a forty-year-old Chicago woman, moved to The Flats from Chicago with her four children. Soon afterwards they were evicted. "The landlord said he was going to build a parking lot there, but he never did. The old place is still standing and has folks in it today. My husband's mother and father took me and the kids in and watched over them while I had my baby. We stayed on after my husband's mother died, and my husband joined us when he got a job in The Flats."

When families or individuals in The Flats are evicted, other kinsmen usually take them in. Households in The Flats expand or contract with the loss of a job, a death in the family, the beginning or end of a sexual partnership, or the end of a friendship. Welfare workers, researchers, and landlords have long known that the poor must move frequently. What is much less understood is the relationship between residence and domestic organization in the black community.

The spectrum of economic and legal pressures that act upon ghetto residents, requiring them to move—unemployment, welfare requirements, housing shortages, high rents, eviction—are clear-cut examples of external pressures affecting the daily lives of the poor. Flats' residents are evicted from their dwellings by landlords who want to raise rents, tear the building down, or rid themselves of tenants who complain about rats, roaches, and the plumbing. Houses get condemned by the city on landlords' requests so that they can force tenants to move. After an eviction, a landlord can rent to a family in such great need of housing that they will not complain for a while.

Poor housing conditions and unenforced housing standards coupled with overcrowding, unemployment, and poverty produce hazardous living conditions and residence changes. "Our whole family had to move when the gas lines sprung a leak in our apartment and my son set the place on fire by accident," Sam Summer told me. "The place belonged to my sister-in-law's grandfather. We had been living there with my mother, my brother's eight children, and our eight children. My father lived in the basement apartment 'cause he and my mother were separated. After the fire burned the whole place down, we all moved to two places down the street near my cousin's house."

When people are unable to pay their rent because they have been temporarily "cut off aid," because the welfare office is suspicious of their eligibility, because they gave their rent money to a kinsman to help him through a crisis or illness, or because they were laid off from their job, they receive eviction notices almost immediately. Lydia Watson describes a chain of events starting with the welfare office stopping her sister's welfare checks, leading to an eviction, co-residence, overcrowding, and eventually murder. Lydia sadly related the story to me. "My oldest sister was cut off aid the day her husband got out of jail. She and her husband and their three children were evicted from their apartment and they came to live with us. We were in crowded conditions already. I had my son, my other sister was there with her two kids, and my mother was about going crazy. My mother put my sister's husband out 'cause she found out he was a dope addict. He came back one night soon after that and murdered my sister. After my sister's death my mother couldn't face living in Chicago any longer. One of my other sisters who had been adopted and raised by my mother's paternal grandmother visited us and persuaded us to move to The Flats, where she was staying. All of us moved there—my mother, my two sisters and their children, my two baby sisters, and my dead sister's children. My sister who had been staying in The Flats found us a house across the street from her own."

Overcrowded dwellings and the impossibility of finding adequate housing in The Flats have many long-term consequences regarding where and with whom children live. Terence Platt described where and with whom his kin lived when he was a child. "My brother stayed with my aunt, my mother's sister, and her husband until he was ten, 'cause he was the oldest in our family and we didn't have enough room—but he stayed with us most every weekend. Finally my aunt moved into the house behind ours with her husband, her brother, and my brother; my sisters and brothers and I lived up front with my mother and her old man."

KIN-STRUCTURED LOCAL NETWORKS

The material and cultural support needed to absorb, sustain, and socialize community members in The Flats is provided by networks of cooperating kinsmen. Local coalitions formed from these networks of kin and friends are mobilized within domestic networks; domestic organization is diffused over many kin-based households which themselves have elastic boundaries.

People in The Flats are immersed in a domestic web of a large number of kin and friends whom they can count on. From a social viewpoint, relationships within the community are "organized on the model of kin relationships" (Goodenough 1970, p. 49). Kin-constructs such as the perception of parenthood, the culturally determined criteria which affect the shape of personal kindreds, and the idiom of kinship, prescribe kin who can be recruited into domestic networks.

There are similarities in function between domestic networks and domestic groups which Fortes (1962, p. 2) characterizes as "workshops of social reproduction." Both domains include three generations of members linked collaterally or otherwise. Kinship, jural and affectional bonds, and economic factors affect the composition of both domains and residential alignments within them. There are two striking differences between domestic networks and domestic groups. Domestic networks are not visible groups, because they do not have an obvious nucleus or defined boundary. But since a primary focus of domestic networks is child-care arrangements, the cooperation of a cluster of adult females is apparent. Participants in domestic networks are recruited from personal kindreds and friendships, but the personnel changes with fluctuating economic needs, changing life styles, and vacillating personal relationships.

In some loosely and complexly structured cognatic systems, kin-structured local networks (not groups) emerge. Localized coalitions of persons drawn from personal kindreds can be organized as networks of kinsmen. Goodenough (1970, p. 49) correctly points out that anthropologists frequently describe "localized kin groups," but rarely describe kin-structured local groups (Goodenough 1962; Helm 1965). The localized, kin-based, cooperative coalitions of people described in this chapter are organized as kin-structured domestic networks. For brevity, I refer to them as domestic networks.

RESIDENCE AND DOMESTIC ORGANIZATION

The connection between households and domestic life can be illustrated by examples taken from cooperating kinsmen and friends mobilized within domestic networks in The Flats. Domestic networks are, of course, not centered around one individual, but for simplicity the domestic network in the following example is named for the key participants in the network, Magnolia and Calvin Waters. The description is confined to four months between April and July 1969. Even within this short time span, individuals moved and joined other households within the domestic network.

THE DOMESTIC NETWORK OF MAGNOLIA AND CALVIN WATERS

Magnolia Waters is forty-one years old and has eleven children. At sixteen she moved from the South with her parents, four sisters (Augusta, Carrie, Lydia, and Olive), and two brothers (Pennington and Oscar). Soon after this she gave birth to her oldest daughter, Ruby. At twenty-three Ruby Banks had two daughters and a son, each by a different father.

When Magnolia was twenty-five she met Calvin, who was forty-seven years old. They lived together and had six children. Calvin is now sixty-three years old; Calvin and Magnolia plan to marry soon so that Magnolia will receive Calvin's insurance benefits. Calvin has two other daughters, who are thirty-eight and forty, by an early marriage in Mississippi. Calvin still has close ties with his daughters and their mother who all live near one another with their families in Chicago.

Magnolia's oldest sister, Augusta, is childless and has not been married. Augusta has maintained long-term "housekeeping" partnerships with four different men over the past twenty years, and each of them has helped her raise her sisters' children. These men have maintained close, affectional ties with the family over the years. Magnolia's youngest sister, Carrie, married Lazar, twenty-five years her senior, when she was just fifteen. They stayed together for about five years. After they separated Carrie married Kermit, separated from him, and became an alcoholic. She lives with different men from time to time, but in between men, or when things are at loose ends, she stays with Lazar, who has become a participating member of the family. Lazar usually resides near Augusta and Augusta's "old man," and Augusta generally prepares Lazar's meals. Ever since Carrie became ill, Augusta has been raising Carrie's son.

Magnolia's sister Lydia had two daughters, Lottie and Georgia, by two different fathers, before she married Mike and gave birth to his son. After Lydia married Mike, she no longer received AFDC benefits for her children. Lydia and Mike acquired steady jobs, bought a house and furniture, and were doing very well. For at least ten years they purposely removed themselves from the network of kin cooperation, preventing their kin from draining their resources. They refused to participate in the network of exchanges which Lydia had formerly depended upon; whenever possible they refused to trade clothes or lend money, or if they gave something, they did not ask for anything in return. During this period they were not participants in the domestic network. About a year ago Lydia and Mike separated over accusations and gossip that each of them had established another sexual relationship. During the five-month-period when the marriage was ending, Lydia began giving some of her nice clothes away to her sisters and nieces. She gave a couch to her brother and a TV to a niece. Anticipating her coming needs, Lydia attempted to re-obligate her kin by carrying out the pattern which had been a part of her daily life before her marriage. After Lydia separated from her husband, her two younger children once again received AFDC. Lydia's oldest daughter, Lottie, is over eighteen and too old to receive AFDC, but Lottie has a three-year-old daughter who has received AFDC benefits since birth.

Eloise has been Magnolia's closest friend for many years. Eloise is Magnolia's first son's father's sister. This son moved into his father's household by his own choice when he was about twelve years old. Magnolia and Eloise have maintained a close, sisterly friendship. Eloise lives with her husband, her four children, and the infant son of her oldest daughter, who is seventeen. Eloise's husband's brother's daughter, Lily, who is twenty, and her young daughter recently joined the household. Eloise's husband's youngest brother is the father of her sister's child. When the child was an infant, that sister stayed with Eloise and her husband.

Billy Jones lives in the basement in the same apartment house as Augusta, Magnolia's sister. A temperamental woman with three sons, Billy has become Augusta's closest friend. Billy once ran a brothel in The Flats, but she has worked as a cook, has written songs, and has attended college from time to time. Augusta keeps Billy's sons whenever Billy leaves town, has periods of depression, or beats the children too severely.

Another active participant in the network is Willa Mae. Willa Mae's younger brother, James, is Ruby's daughter's father. Even though James does not visit the child and has not assumed any parental duties toward the child, Willa Mae and Ruby, who are the same age, help each other out with their young children.

Calvin's closest friend, Cecil, died several years ago. Cecil was Violet's husband. Violet, Cecil, and Calvin came from the same town in Mississippi and their families have been very close. Calvin boarded with Violet's family for five years or so before he met Magnolia. Violet is now seventy years old. She lives with her daughter, Odessa, who is thirty-seven, her two sons, Josh, who is thirty-five and John, who is forty, and Odessa's three sons and daughter. Odessa's husband was killed in a fight several years ago and ever since then she and her family have shared a household with Violet and her two grown sons. Violet's sons Josh and John are good friends with Magnolia, Ruby, and Augusta and visit them frequently. About five years ago John brought one of his daughters to live with his mother and sister because his family thought that the mother was not taking proper care of the

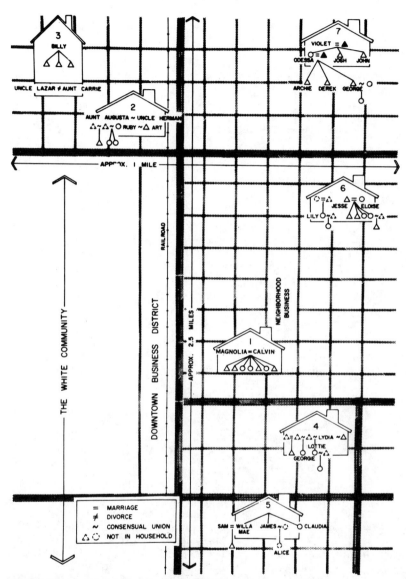

CHART 1. Spatial Relations in Magnolia and Leo's Domestic Network

child; the mother had several other children and did not object. The girl is now ten years old and is an accepted member of the family and the network.

Chart 1 shows the spatial relations of the households in Magnolia and Calvin's domestic network in April 1969. The houses are scattered within The Flats, but none of them is more than three miles apart. Cab fare, up to

two dollars per trip, is spent practically every day, and sometimes twice a day, as individuals visit, trade, and exchange services. Chart 2 shows how individuals are brought into the domestic network.

The following outline shows residential changes which occurred in several of the households within the network between April and June 1969.

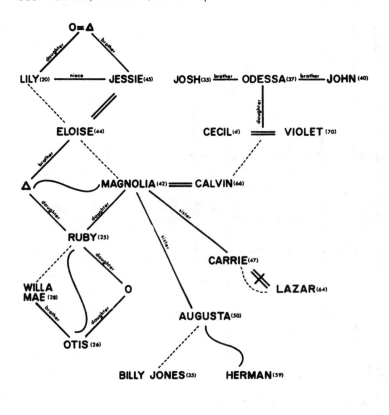

—— kinship	
----- long-term friendship	
= jural couple	**CHART 2.** Kin-structured
∽ consensual couple	Domestic Network
○ △ not in network	

APRIL 1969

Household   Domestic Arrangement

1. Magnolia (38) and Calvin (60) live in a common-law relationship with their eight children (ages 4 to 18).

2. Magnolia's sister Augusta and Augusta's "old man," Herman, share a two-bedroom house with Magnolia's daughter Ruby (22) and Ruby's three children. Augusta and Herman have one bedroom, the three children sleep in the second bedroom, and Ruby sleeps downstairs in the living room. Ruby's boyfriend, Art, stays with Ruby many evenings.

3. Augusta's girlfriend Billy and Billy's three sons live on the first floor of the house. Lazar, Magnolia's and Augusta's ex-brother-in-law, lives in the basement alone, or from time to time, with his ex-wife Carrie. Lazar eats the evening meal, which Augusta prepares for him, at household #2.

4. Magnolia's sister Lydia, Lydia's "old man," Lydia's two daughters, Georgia and Lottie, Lydia's son, and Lottie's three-year-old daughter live in Lydia's house.

5. Willa Mae (26), her husband, her son, her sister Claudia (32), and her brother James (father of Ruby's daughter) share a household.

6. Eloise (37), her husband Jessie, their four children, their oldest daughter's (17) son, and Jessie's brother's daughter Lily (20), and Lily's baby all live together.

7. Violet (70), her two sons, Josh (35) and John (40), her daughter Odessa (37), and Odessa's three sons and one daughter live together. Five years ago John's daughter (10) joined the household.

JUNE 1969

Household	Domestic Arrangement

1. Household composition unchanged.
2. Augusta and Herman moved out after quarreling with Ruby over housekeeping and cooking duties. They joined household #3. Ruby and Art remained in household #2 and began housekeeping with Ruby's children.
3. Billy and her three sons remained on the first floor and Lazar remained in the basement. Augusta and Herman rented a small, one-room apartment upstairs.
4. Lottie and her daughter moved out of Lydia's house to a large apartment down the street, which they shared with Lottie's girl friend and the friend's daughter. Georgia moved into her boyfriend's apartment. Lydia and her son (17) remained in the house with Lydia's "old man."
5. James began housekeeping with a new girl friend who lived with her sister, but he kept most of his clothes at home. His brother moved into his room after returning from the service. Willa Mae, her husband, and son remained in the house.
6. Household composition unchanged.
7. Odessa's son Raymond is the father of Clover's baby. Clover and the baby joined the household which includes Violet, her two sons, her daughter, Odessa, and Odessa's three sons and one daughter and John's daughter.

Typical residential alignments in The Flats are those between adult mothers and sisters, mothers and adult sons and daughters, close adult female relatives, and friends defined as kin within the idiom of kinship. Domestic organization is diffused over these kin-based households.

Residence patterns among the poor in The Flats must be considered in the context of domestic organization. The connection between residence and domestic organization is apparent in examples of a series of domestic and child-care arrangements within Magnolia and Calvin's network a few years ago. Consider the following four kin-based residences among Magnolia and Calvin's kin in 1966.

Household	Domestic Arrangement

1. Magnolia, Calvin, and seven young children.
2. Magnolia's mother, Magnolia's brother, Magnolia's sister and her sister's husband, Magnolia's oldest daughter, Ruby, and Ruby's first child.
3. Magnolia's oldest sister, Augusta, Augusta's "old man," Augusta's sister's (Carrie) son, and Magnolia's twelve-year-old son.
4. Magnolia's oldest son, his father, and the father's "old lady."

Household composition *per se* reveals little about domestic organization even when cooperation between close adult females is assumed. Three of these households (1, 2, 3) were located on one city block. Magnolia's mother rented a rear house behind Magnolia's house, and Magnolia's sister Augusta lived in an apartment down the street. As we have seen, they lived and shared each other's lives. Magnolia, Ruby, and Augusta usually pooled the food stamps they received from the welfare office. The women shopped together and everyone shared the evening meal with their men and children at Magnolia's mother's house or at Magnolia's. The children did not always have a bed of their own or a bed which they were expected to share with another child. They fell asleep and slept through the night wherever the late evening visiting patterns of the adult females took them.

The kinship links which most often are the basis of new or expanded households are those links children have with close adult females such as the child's mother, mother's mother, mother's sister, mother's brother's wife, father's mother, father's sister, and father's brother's wife.

Here are some examples of the flexibility of the Blacks' adaptation to daily, social, and economic problems (Stack 1970, p. 309).

Relational Link	Domestic Arrangement
Mother	Viola's brother married his first wife when he was sixteen. When she left him she kept their daughter.

Mother's mother	Viola's sister Martha was never able to care for her children because of her nerves and high blood. In between husbands, her mother kept her two oldest children, and after Martha's death, her mother kept all three of the children.
Mother's brother	A year after Martha's death, Martha's brother took Martha's oldest daughter, helping his mother out since this left her with only two children to care for.
Mother's mother	Viola's daughter (20) was living at home and gave birth to a son. The daughter and her son remained in the Jackson household until the daughter married and set up a separate household with her husband, leaving her son to be raised by her mother.
Mother's sister	Martha moved to Chicago into her sister's household. The household consisted of the two sisters and four of their children.
Father's mother	Viola's sister Ethel had four daughters and one son. When Ethel had a nervous breakdown, her husband took the three daughters and his son to live with his mother in Arkansas. After his wife's death, the husband took the oldest daughter, to join her siblings in his mother's home in Arkansas.
Father's mother	When Viola's younger sister, Christine, left her husband in order to harvest fruit in Wisconsin, Christine left her two daughters with her husband's mother in Arkansas.
Father's sister	When Viola's brother's wife died, he decided to raise his two sons himself. He kept the two boys and never remarried although he had several girl friends and a child with one. His residence has always been near Viola's and she fed and cared for his sons.

The basis of these cooperative units is mutual aid among siblings of both sexes, the domestic cooperation of close adult females,

and the exchange of goods and services between male and female kin (Stack 1970). R.T. Smith (1970, p. 66) has referred to this pattern and observes that even when lower-class Blacks live in a nuclear family group, what is "most striking is the extent to which lower-class persons continue to be involved with other kin." Nancie Gonzalez (1970, p. 232) suggests that "the fact that individuals have simultaneous loyalties to more than one such grouping may be important in understanding the social structure as a whole."

These co-residential socializing units do indeed show the important role of the black female. But the cooperation between male and female siblings who share the same household or live near one another has been underestimated by those who have considered the female-headed household and the grandmother-headed household (especially the mother's mother) as the most significant domestic units among the urban black poor.

The close cooperation of adults arises from the residential patterns typical of young adults. Due to poverty, young females with or without children do not perceive any choice but to remain living at home with their mother or other adult female relatives. Even if young women are collecting AFDC, they say that their resources go further when they share goods and services. Likewise, jobless males, or those working at part-time or seasonal jobs, often remain living at home with their mother or, if she is dead, with their sisters and brothers. This pattern continues long after men have become fathers and have established a series of sexual partnerships with women, who are living with their own kin, friends, or alone with their children. A result of this pattern is the striking fact that households almost always have men around: male relatives, by birth or marriage, and boyfriends. These men are often intermittent members of the households, boarders, or friends who come and go; men who usually eat, and sometimes sleep, in the households. Children have constant and close contact with these men, and especially in the case of male relatives, these relationships last over the years.

The most predictable residential pattern

in The Flats is that men and women reside in one of the households of their natal kin, or in the households of those who raised them, long into their adult years. Even when persons temporarily move out of the household of their mother or of a close relative, they have the option to return to the residences of their kin if they have to.

GENEROSITY AND POVERTY

The combination of arbitrary and repressive economic forces and social behavior, modified by successive generations of poverty, make it almost impossible for people to break out of poverty. There is no way for those families poor enough to receive welfare to acquire any surplus cash which can be saved for emergencies or for acquiring adequate appliances or a home or a car. In contrast to the middle class, who are pressured to spend and save, the poor are not even permitted to establish an equity.

The following examples from Magnolia and Calvin Waters' life illustrates the ways in which the poor are prohibited from acquiring any surplus which might enable them to change their economic condition or life style.

In 1971 Magnolia's uncle died in Mississippi and left an unexpected inheritance of $1,500 to Magnolia and Calvin Waters. The cash came from a small run-down farm which Magnolia's uncle sold shortly before he died. It was the first time in their lives that Magnolia or Calvin ever had a cash reserve. Their first hope was to buy a home and use the money as a down payment.

Calvin had retired from his job as a seasonal laborer the year before and the family was on welfare. AFDC allotted the family $100 per month for rent. The housing that the family had been able to obtain over the years for their nine children at $100 or less was always small, roach infested, with poor plumbing and heating. The family was frequently evicted. Landlords complained about the noise and often observed an average of ten to fifteen children playing in the household. Magnolia and Calvin never even anticipated that they would be able to buy a home.

Three days after they received the check, news of its arrival spread throughout their domestic network. One niece borrowed $25 from Magnolia so that her phone would not be turned off. Within a week the welfare office knew about the money. Magnolia's children were immediately cut off welfare, including medical coverage and food stamps. Magnolia was told that she would not receive a welfare grant for her children until the money was used up, and she was given a minimum of four months in which to spend the money. The first surplus the family ever acquired was effectively taken from them.

During the weeks following the arrival of the money, Magnolia and Calvin's obligations to the needs of kin remained the same, but their ability to meet these needs had temporarily increased. When another uncle became very ill in the South, Magnolia and her older sister, Augusta, were called to sit by his side. Magnolia bought round-trip train tickets for both of them and for her three youngest children. When the uncle died, Magnolia bought round-trip train tickets so that she and Augusta could attend the funeral. Soon after his death, Augusta's first "old man" died in The Flats and he had no kin to pay for the burial. Augusta asked Magnolia to help pay for digging the grave. Magnolia was unable to refuse. Another sister's rent was two months overdue and Magnolia feared that she would get evicted. This sister was seriously ill and had no source of income. Magnolia paid her rent.

Winter was cold and Magnolia's children and grandchildren began staying home from school because they did not have warm winter coats and adequate shoes or boots. Magnolia and Calvin decided to buy coats, hats, and shoes for all of the children (at least fifteen). Magnolia also bought a winter coat for herself and Calvin bought himself a pair of sturdy shoes.

Within a month and a half, all of the money was gone. The money was channeled into the hands of the same individuals who ordinarily participate in daily domestic exchanges, but the premiums were temporarily higher. All of the money was quickly spent for necessary, compelling reasons.

Thus random fluctuations in the meager flow of available cash and goods tend to be of considerable importance to the poor. A late welfare check, sudden sickness, robbery, and other unexpected losses cannot be overcome with a cash reserve like more well-to-do families hold for emergencies. Increases in cash are either taken quickly from the poor by the welfare agencies or dissipated through the kin network.

Those living in poverty have little or no chance to escape from the economic situation into which they were born. Nor do they have the power to control the expansion or contraction of welfare benefits (Piven and Cloward 1971) or of employment opportunities, both of which have a momentous effect on their daily lives. In times of need, the only predictable resources that can be drawn upon are their own children and parents, and the fund of kin and friends obligated to them.

REFERENCES

Fortes, Meyer. 1962. "Marriage in Tribal Societies." *Cambridge Papers in Social Anthropology*, No. 3. Cambridge: Cambridge University Press.

Gonzalez, Nancie. 1970. "Toward a Definition of Matrifocality." In *Afro-American Anthropology: Contemporary Perspectives*, eds. N. E. Whitten and John F. Szwed. New York: The Free Press.

Goodenough, Ward H. 1962. "Kindred and Hamlet in Lakalai, New Britain." *Ethnology* 1:5–12.

———. 1970. *Description and Comparison in Cultural Anthropology.* Chicago: Aldine Publishing Company.

Helm, June. 1965. "Bilaterality in the Socio-Territorial Organization of the Arctic Drain Age Dene." *Ethnology*, 4:361–385.

Piven, Frances Fox and Richard A. Cloward. 1971. *Regulating the Poor: The Functions of Public Welfare.* New York: Vintage Books.

Smith, Raymond T. 1970. "The Nuclear Family in Afro-American Kinship." *Journal of Comparative Family Studies* 1(1):55–70.

Stack, Carol B. 1970. "The Kindred of Viola Jackson: Residence and Family Organization of an Urban Black American Family." In *Afro-American Anthropology: Contemporary Perspectives*, eds. N. E. Whitten and John F. Szwed. New York: The Free Press, pp. 303–312.

Matrifocality, Power, and Gender Relations in Jamaica

Marsha Prior

Original material prepared for this text.

Anthropologists have long recognized kinship units in which women maintain considerable control over the household earnings and decision making. While numerous studies have provided pertinent data and have contributed to the theory of social organization, the subject of female-focused kinship units has always been controversial, subject to bias, and confusing. The variations in terminology and a preoccupation with the origin of these units is responsible for much of the confusion. In addition, two biases, prevalent throughout the twentieth century, have influenced our understanding and acceptance of female-focused units. One bias has been the predominant view that nuclear families are "normal"; the other bias is the failure to recognize the full extent of female roles in society. The unfortunate result of this is that very little is known about the dynamics within and between female-focused kinship units.

The term *matrifocal*, which is most commonly used to refer to households composed of a key female decision maker, was coined by R.T. Smith in 1956. Recognition of such households precedes the usage of this term, however. As early as the 1930s scholars noted that African-American and African-Caribbean households were not composed of nuclear families as were the majority of middle-class households in the United States and Great Britain. Observers were struck by the authoritative role of women in these households and the limited role of the father in the family. Mothers controlled the earnings brought into the household and made key decisions. Fathers were either absent or did not appear to play a major role in economic contributions and in household decision making. However, attempts to address this situation reveal more the attitudes and biases prevalent at that time—many of which remain with us today—than any real insight as to the nature of such units. These *maternal families*, as they were often called during this early period, were viewed by scholars as deviant structures (Mohammed 1988). The high rate of illegitimacy and instability among mating partners was cited as proof that these families were disorganized and detrimental to the well-being of their members (Henriques 1953; Simey 1946; see also Moynihan 1965).

The bias toward nuclear family organization that dominated early studies stems from nineteenth century evolutionists who viewed the nuclear family as a superior system of kinship organization and from Malinowski who argued that nuclear families are universal (Collier, Rosaldo, and Yanigisako 1982). Thus, societies that exhibited large numbers of non-nuclear households were considered abnormal, and it was essential that their development be explained.

Scholars naturally turned to the common characteristics of these female-focused societies, noting that they were former slave societies from Africa. One explanation, suggested by Frazier (1939), held that maternal families were an adaptive strategy to the slave system

that defined slaves as individual property who could be traded to another plantation at any time. Nuclear families would have been torn apart with frequent trading of adult slaves. Plantation owners were less likely, though, to tear apart mother-child dyads, at least until the child reached adolescence. Thus, the stable unit in a slave system was a household consisting of mothers and their children. The other explanation common during this time period, argued that the maternal family stemmed from the traditional African system that survived in spite of the Africans' forced migration and subsequent integration into the slave system (Herskovits 1941). These two theories enjoyed a lively debate until the mid-1950s when scholars moved away from historical explanations and emphasized the role of present social or economic conditions.

M.G. Smith (1962) argued that family structure in the West Indies was determined by the already existing mating systems that vary somewhat throughout the region. Clarke (1957), R.T. Smith (1956), and Gonzalez (1960) focused more on the effect that the current economic system had on household organization. The prevalent household structure found among African descendants in the United States and the Caribbean was viewed as an adaptive strategy to poverty, unemployment, or male migration. Nuclear families with only two working adults per household are believed by some to be at risk in socioeconomic environments in which poverty conditions exist, unemployment is high, and adult men must migrate to find work (see Durant-Gonzalez 1982; Gonzalez 1970:242). Thus, in such societies we are more likely to see households composed of a mother, a grandparent, and children; a mother and children; adult siblings and their children; or adult siblings, their children, and a grandparent.

The emphasis placed on the socioeconomic environment marked a new trend in matrifocal studies whereby the relationship between men and women took a more prominent position. However, the studies placed more emphasis on the "marginal" or absent man than they did the ever-present woman and were criticized for ignoring the wide range of roles and tasks performed by women. Furthermore, Smith noted (1962:6) specific ethnographic data were used to generalize about matrifocal societies throughout the Caribbean. This proved to be problematic in understanding matrifocal societies theoretically, and it generated confusion as scholars used different terms to refer to similar types of kinship and household organizations.

R.T. Smith used the term *matrifocal* to refer to the type of structure he originally witnessed among lower class British Guianese (1956). Taking a developmental approach, Smith noted that matrifocal households arise with time after a man and woman begin to cohabitate. Early in the cycle the woman is economically dependent on the male partner. Her primary role is to provide care for the children, but as the children grow older and earn money for small tasks and labor it is the mother who controls their earnings. The father, meanwhile, has been unable to make significant contributions to the household economy due to his overall low status within a society that maintains prejudicial hiring policies. Smith's concept of matrifocality focuses on two criteria—the salience of women in their role as mothers and the marginality of men (i.e., their inability to contribute economically to the household) (1956; 1973; 1988).

The study of household structure conducted by Gonzalez on the Garifuna (Black Carib) of Guatemala was not intended, nor originally identified, as a study on matrifocality per se, but Gonzalez did note the effect that male emigration had on household structure (1960). Gonzalez observed that households were comprised of members who were related to each other consanguineally (through blood); no two members of the household were bound by marriage. These consanguineal households developed in response to a socioeconomic environment that encouraged men to migrate as they sought employment (see also Gonzalez 1984 for comments regarding the applicability of dividing households into consanguineal and affinal types).

The terms and definitions for the household structures observed by R.T. Smith and Gonzalez were created to fit specific ethnographic data. They were later applied by various scholars to other societies that exhibited similar structures, which created confusion (see Kunstadter 1963; Randolph 1964; M.G. Smith 1962:6; and R.T. Smith 1973:126) and was exacerbated by the use of other terms to rectify the problem (e.g., the use of matricentric or female headed). Thus, in the literature we see these terms used interchangeably to refer to structures in which women control household earnings and decision making and men are viewed as marginal, though the impetus behind such household formation may differ from one society to the next. The whole concept became so clouded with terms and biases that Gonzalez astutely noted that depending on which scholar one is reading, matrifocality can suggest (1) that women are more important than the observer had expected, (2) that women maintain a good deal of control over money in the household, (3) that women are the primary source of income, or (4) that there is no resident male (1970:231–232).

Recent authors have criticized the emphasis on men's marginality and the focus on women's domestic tasks that arose in the study of matrifocality (Barrow 1988; Mohammed 1988; Tanner 1974). Concentration on women's *domestic* tasks ignores the full extent of women's networks, their access to resources, control over resources, relations with men, and relationship between household and society, all of which are important considerations when discussing matrifocality. Male marginality is problematic in part because the term is difficult to define. Does it mean that the father does not live in the household? Has he migrated out of the community? Does he contribute sporadically, or not at all, to the household economy? Is he not around to make household decisions?

As Tanner has remarked matrifocality should not be defined in "negative terms" (i.e., by the absence of the father). Instead, we should focus on the role of women as mothers, and note that in matrifocal systems mothers have at least some control over economic resources and are involved in decision making. According to Tanner, however, matrifocality goes beyond these two criteria. To be matrifocal a society must culturally value the role of mother—though not necessarily at the expense of fathers. In matrifocal societies the woman's role as mother is central to the kinship structure, but Tanner does not limit this role to domestic tasks. As mothers women may participate in cultivation, petty marketing, wage labor, in rituals, and so forth (1974). This broader definition allows us to recognize matrifocal units within a variety of kinship systems. Matrifocal units can exist in matrilineal or patrilineal societies, within nuclear families, and in bilateral systems. In any society with an emphasis on the mother-child dyad where this unit is culturally valued and where the mother plays an effective role in the economy and decision making of the unit, that unit can be defined as matrifocal (Tanner 1974:131–132).

Tanner's definition finally allows us to avoid some of the problems that previous studies encountered and permits us to further address issues pertinent to matrifocal units. We can examine gender relations within the context of gender hierarchies and the broader socioeconomic environment of which matrifocal households are a part. One area that has received little attention is the relationship between physical violence against women and matrifocality. Violence against women and matrifocality seem to contradict each other due to the assumptions regarding power and the authoritative role of women in matrifocal households.

Women, having access to and control over resources and authority to make household decisions, are viewed as powerful. This view has been particularly evident in studies of women in the Caribbean where a large number of matrifocal households exist (Massiah 1982). Caribbean women are frequently portrayed as powerful, autonomous individuals (Ellis 1986; Powell 1982, 1986; Safa 1986). Although Caribbean women's control and power over resources and decisions is not to be discounted, fieldwork in a low-income community in Jamaica suggests that matrifocality and physical violence against women are not mutually exclusive. To understand the relationship between these two phenomena requires knowledge of sociocultural elements that affect both gender relations and matrifocal household organization.

The community of study is a low-income urban neighborhood approximately 0.05 square miles located in the parish of St. Andrew, Jamaica. During the time at which data were collected, 1987 to 1988, there were an estimated 210 households with a population of 1,300. The majority of the households were of wooden construction, many without electricity, and very few with running water. Some of the wealthier residents maintained houses constructed of concrete. No telephones were present in any household because telephone lines were not available.

Within the community a variety of household organizational units were observed. Nuclear families based on common-law marriage, legal marriage, or coresidency existed. There were also single female-headed households, single male-headed households, and a variety of extended and collateral arrangements. Finally, there were households whose membership included kin and nonkin (i.e., a friend or acquaintance may reside in the household). This range in domestic organization demonstrates that household membership may vary in response to economic and social conditions.

What makes these arrangements more interesting is that the households are subject to change. During the course of the fieldwork households altered their membership; thus, a nuclear arrangement would shift to single female-headed with children as the father moved out, and it might have shifted again if a grandmother or sister moved in. Regardless of the various household arrangements, matrifocality was observed. Women certainly maintained control over the economic resources and were responsible for many household decisions. Women as mothers were structurally central to the kinship units, and mothers were culturally valued as indicated by both male and female informants.

Although Caribbean women are portrayed as powerful and autonomous, male-female relations, as anywhere in the world, are based on some form of interdependence. Within this community social and economic status are intricately tied to gender relations. Both genders support the basic notion that women are to provide sexual services and domestic labor for men, and men are to provide women with money and gifts. However, the relationships are not a simple equation whereby women provide sexual services and domestic labor in exchange for money. Women often spoke of sexual activity as something that they desired and enjoyed, and men felt free to request money from women with whom they have had relations (especially if she is the mother to any of his children). Nevertheless, there is an understanding that if a woman will not provide sexual services or domestic labor or if the man does not provide cash or gifts from time to time, the relationship will end. These expectations played key roles in understanding gender relations and the behavior of men and women.

In addition to these expectations, adult status is primarily attained by the birth of a child. At this socioeconomic level higher educational degrees, prestigious employment, and ownership of cars and houses are out of most community members' reach. Both men and women view the birth of a child as an opportunity to announce their own adult status. Thus, children are normally desired and are a source of pride for both the mother and father.

The instability that marks male-female relationships is recognized by community members and can be related to cultural values as well as to the socioeconomic environment that encourages men and women to seek more resourceful partners. Male and female informants readily acknowledged the shifting allegiances between men and women. Men were known to keep several girlfriends at one time, and marriage, common-law or legal, was no guarantee that monogamy will follow. Women also admitted to keeping an eye out for a better partner and said they would initiate a change if they so desired. Couples tended to set up visiting relationships whereby the couple did not coreside. Children, of course, may be born from these unions. If a Jamaican woman of this socioeconomic class married at all, it was more likely to occur after the age of thirty (see Brody 1981:253–255).

As households were observed and data collected through the course of fieldwork, it became apparent that fathers and male partners were not marginal to the households. Whether or not they resided in the same household as the woman, they could potentially be very influential. It also became clear that in certain situations female control over household issues could be jeopardized. A brief look at some of the households and the gender relations among men and women will demonstrate these points.

MARY'S HOUSEHOLD

Mary is a twenty-seven-year-old mother occupying a one-room wooden house—no electricity or running water—with four children. The two oldest children were fathered by one man; the youngest two were fathered by another. Sexual relations with the first father had ceased several years ago; however, Mary does maintain sexual relations with the younger children's father, though he keeps other girlfriends.

Mary's primary source of income stems from sporadic petty marketing. When Mary has the capital to invest in goods, she sells clothing and shoes in a downtown Kingston stall that is rented by her mother. Mary is very much involved in politics; she attends meetings, distributes literature, and talks to anyone about her party's political candidates and officials. She was able to work for a few months as an enumerator during a national campaign to register voters. Mary depends on contributions from the two fathers of her children. The first father rarely comes to visit, but he is in the National Guard, draws a steady paycheck, and consistently sends money for the children.

The father of her two youngest children, who works as a cook and a driver, is usually good about bringing money but has, on occasion, lapsed. Such lapses can be a severe stress on Mary's limited household budget and was the source of domestic violence on one occasion. Earl, the father of Mary's youngest children, had promised to bring some money. When he showed up at her doorstep she asked for the money, and he told her that he didn't have any. This made her angry so she began yelling at him, and a fight ensued. They began hitting each other with their fists, but the fight escalated when Earl picked up a shovel and hit Mary on the wrist. Mary fought back by taking a cutlass and striking him on the shoulder. Earl then left the premises, and Mary sought medical treatment for the pain in her wrist.

This was the first and only act of violence between the two in a seven-year period. Mary stated that they rarely even quarrel. Though not typical, the violence demonstrates the economic dependence of Mary on the contributions of the fathers and the stress that can surface when she is threatened by the lack of such contributions. Mary admitted that she was extremely angry when he told her that he had no money to give her because he had promised earlier that he would bring her some. She was convinced that he had the money to give but was holding out on her.

DORA'S HOUSEHOLD

Dora, twenty-eight years old, lives under similar circumstances as Mary and has had comparable experience regarding fathers and money. Dora is the mother of three children. Two live with her; one stays with relatives in the country. Dora's one-room house has neither electricity nor running water.

The father of Dora's first two children provides some money to the household. Dora is almost totally dependent on these contributions because she is confined to the house and cannot work due to a crippling disease. Ned, the father of her youngest child, provides nothing to the household, which is a continuous source of grief to Dora. Dora is quiet and normally avoids conflict. Her one attempt to address Ned's negligence resulted in violence, as had Mary's. Dora had decided that because Ned did not provide clothes or money for their son, Michael, he did not deserve to see the child. She packed up Michael's belongings and sent him over to Ned's sister's house for a short while, believing that the sister would feed Michael and buy

him some clothes. When Ned arrived to take Michael for a visit to his own house, he questioned the child's whereabouts and became angry when Dora told him that he had been sent to Ned's sister's house. Ned began hitting Dora. She struck back once but relented when Ned punched her in the side and ran off. She did not see him again for several days. This incident occurred six months prior to our interview, and Dora has not asked Ned for anything since and vows that she never will.

RITA'S HOUSEHOLD

Rita lives in a household consisting of six members, including herself. Two of her four children, a granddaughter, a friend of her daughter, and Rita's boyfriend occupy a three-room apartment without electricity or running water. Rita is thirty nine years old. Her boyfriend, Tom, is 40 and has lived with her for four years. They have no common children.

Rita runs a successful neighborhood bar, giving her control over the major portion of the household budget. She receives some financial contribution from the father of one daughter. Rita and Tom have established a reciprocal relationship regarding money. She does expect him to contribute from his earnings as a taxi driver when he is able, but she may be just as likely to provide Tom with money when he is in need. Rita is aware of Tom's other girlfriends and realizes that a good deal of his earnings go to entertaining these women. With her own successful business Rita is less financially dependent on her male partner than other women. She does look to Tom, however, for companionship and emotional support. The time he spends with other women is reluctantly accepted, though on one occasion his infidelities did result in conflict. One night, as he came home late, Rita began cursing Tom and made derogatory remarks about Tom's other girlfriend. Tom responded by punching Rita. She fought back for a few minutes then they both simply let it go. In the past year Rita has avoided comment on Tom's affairs and is determined to put up with it, for now at least, because she is not ready to end the relationship. Rita's attitude is that most men do this, so there is little point in severing this relationship to find another boyfriend who will do the same.

HANNAH'S HOUSEHOLD

Thirty-six-year-old Hannah is an articulate and ambitious woman. She lives in a two-room house with seven other people (five of her six children live with her along with a friend her age and a friend of one of her daughters). Hannah worked as a domestic but lost her job during my stay in the community. She did have a job lined up, cleaning the office of a dentist.

Hannah's first three children were fathered by one man; her fourth child was fathered by another man; and her last two children were fathered by a third man. The first man to father her children is now sick and unable to work. He does not provide any financial support to Hannah's household. The other two fathers help out every now and then, but the support is not enough for her to rely on. She rarely sees any of her children's fathers now, but Hannah did relate an incident involving the last father, Gerald, that occurred nearly five years prior to our interview. At the time of the incident Hannah and Gerald were still intimately involved but did not coreside. Hannah had grown dissatisfied with the relationship because Gerald provided no support for herself or his children. Thus, she had decided to break off the relationship. When Gerald learned of her decision he became angry and abusive. One night after everyone had gone to bed, he came to her house, began yelling at her, and proceeded to destroy some of her belongings: He broke a lamp and smashed a small table. Another night he came to her window, tore off the screen, and began yelling at her again. He threw a bucket of water on her and the children and threw stones. Hannah, not wanting the children to get hurt, went outside to confront him, and he began physically assaulting her. Hannah managed to grab a broken bot-

tle and cut him with it. Gerald then left the premises, never bothering her much afterwards.

SUMMARY

Although women in matrifocal households often maintain control over resources and decision making within the household, the previous data indicate that the power associated with such control and authority can be compromised. Power, as defined by Adams, is the control over one's environment and the ability to control the environment of others based on access and control of resources that are of value to the other (1975:12). In the cases cited above the interdependence between men and women and the access that men have to certain resources must be addressed to understand female power and domestic violence.

As indicated previously, both genders view women as exercising control over sexual services and domestic labor, and men have access to some (though not all) of the economic resources that women need. At this socioeconomic level men may not be able to contribute significantly to the household economy. Nevertheless, women view men as a source of monetary and material needs and feel they have the right to demand these resources. Though women are constantly seeking ways to earn money and often don't want to rely on contributions from male partners, many, again due to the socioeconomic environment, are dependent on male contributions, no matter how small. The data suggest that while men are dependent on women, they can more easily circumvent the control that female partners have over desired resources than women can circumvent the resources that men control. In this culture it is acceptable for men to have more than one female partner. While women complain of this it is expected and negates the control that individual women can exert. Women, on the other hand, may try to circumvent male control over economic resources, but they are also subjected to an economic system that exploits the lower class for their cheap labor and that offers high unemployment. In addition to this interdependence these women are members of a culture that may value women *as mothers*, but women in general do not necessarily enjoy a high status. In other words the *mother* role is valued, but women are overall subordinate to men (Henry and Wilson 1975). Male informants felt it was their right to physically coerce or punish women as they saw fit, but a man would almost never physically abuse his own mother.

In relating the cases cited previously the intent is not to suggest that the women were weak, powerless, and always dominated by men. Women often fought back and worked to become as independent as possible. These cases are also not intended to promote negative images of men. I recount incidences of abuse to demonstrate the extreme to which men can affect matrifocal households, but I must emphasize that male influence can also be positive and rewarding for members of the household. Fathers were observed visiting their children, taking them to the health clinic, and providing money, food, and clothing.

The data collected from this study remind us that, in spite of a long interest in matrifocality, we still have much to learn. We must rid ourselves of biases that narrow our focus. Just as it was wrong to assume that men are marginal, that women perform only domestic tasks, and that the nuclear family is "normal," we must not assume that women in matrifocal societies are *always* powerful or that they consistently enjoy a high status within that society. The power that women exert must be documented and integrated into the overall cultural context that would also note gender relations, the socioeconomic environment, the political environment, and cultural values. Only then can studies on matrifocality provide us with a better understanding of human behavior.

REFERENCES

Adams, Richard N. 1975. *Energy and Structure: A Theory of Social Power*. Austin: University of Texas Press.

Barrow, Christine. 1988. Anthropology, the Family and Women in the Caribbean. In Patricia Mohammed and Catherine Shepherd (eds.). *Gender in Caribbean Development*, pp. 156–169. Mona, Jamaica: University of West Indies.

Brody, Eugene B. 1981. *Sex, Contraception, and Motherhood in Jamaica*. Cambridge, MA: Harvard University Press.

Clarke, Edith. 1957. *My Mother Who Fathered Me*. London: George Allen & Unwin.

Collier, Jane, Michelle Rosaldo, and Sylvia Yanagisako. 1982. Is There a Family? New Anthropological Views. In Barrie Thorne (ed.). *Rethinking the Family: Some Feminist Questions*, pp. 25–39. New York: Longman.

Durant-Gonzalez, Victoria. 1982. The Realm of Female Familial Responsibility. In Joycelin Massiah (ed). *Women and the Family*, pp. 1–27. Cave Hill, Barbados: University of the West Indies, Institute of Social and Economic Research.

Ellis, Pat. 1986. Introduction: An Overview of Women in Caribbean Society." In Pat Ellis (ed.). *Women of the Caribbean*, pp. 1–24. Kingston: Kingston Publishers.

Frazier, E. Franklin. 1939. *The Negro Family in the United States*. Chicago: Chicago University Press.

Gonzalez, Nancie L. 1960. Household and Family in the Caribbean. *Social and Economic Studies* 9: 101–106.

———. 1970. Toward a Definition of Matrifocality. In Norman E. Whitten, Jr. and John F. Szwed (eds.). *Afro-American Anthropology*, pp. 231–244. New York: The Free Press.

———. 1984. Rethinking the Consanguineal Household and Matrifocality. *Ethnology* 23(1): 1–12.

Henriques, Fernando M. 1953. Family and Colour in Jamaica. London: Eyre and Spottiswoode.

Henry, Frances and Pamela Wilson. 1975. The Status of Women in Caribbean Societies: An Overview of Their Social, Economic and Sexual Roles. *Social and Economic Studies* 24(2): 165–198.

Herskovits, Melville J. 1941. *The Myth of the Negro Past*. New York: Harper & Brothers.

Kunstadter, Peter. 1963. A Survey of the Consanguine or Matrifocal Family. *American Anthropologist* 65: 56–66.

Massiah, Joycelin. 1982. Women Who Head Households. In Joycelin Massiah (ed.). *Women and the Family*, pp. 62–130. Cave Hill, Barbados: University of West Indies, Institute of Social and Economic Research.

Mohammed, Patricia. 1988. The Caribbean Family Revisited. In Patricia Mohammed and Catherine Shepherd (eds.). *Gender in Caribbean Development*, pp. 170–182. Mona, Jamaica: University of West Indies.

Moynihan, Daniel P. 1965. The Negro Family: The Case for National Action. U.S. Department of Labor, Washington, D.C.

Powell, Dorian. 1982. Network Analysis: A Suggested Model for the Study of Women and the Family in the Caribbean. In Joycelin Massiah (ed.). *Women and The Family*, pp. 131–162. Cave Hill, Barbados: University of the West Indies, Institute of Social and Economic Research.

———. 1986. Caribbean Women and Their Response to Familial Experiences. *Social and Economic Studies* 35(2): 83–130.

Randolph, Richard R. 1964. The 'Matrifocal Family' as a Comparative Category. *American Anthropologist* 66: 628–31.

Safa, Helen. 1986. Economic Autonomy and Sexual Equality in Caribbean Society. *Social and Economic Studies* 35(3): 1–21.

Simey, Thomas. 1946. *Welfare Planning in the West Indies*. Oxford: Clarendon Press.

Smith, M.G. 1962. *West Indian Family Structure*. Seattle: University of Washington Press.

Smith, Raymond T. 1956. *The Negro Family in British Guiana: Family Structure and Social Status in the Villages*. London: Routledge and Kegan Paul.

———. 1973. The Matrifocal Family, In Jack Goody (ed.). *The Character of Kinship*, pp. 121–144. London: Cambridge University Press.

———. 1988. *Kinship and Class in the West Indies: A Genealogical Study of Jamaica and Guyana*. New York: Cambridge University Press.

Staples, Robert. 1972. The Matricentric Family System: A Cross-Cultural Examination. *Journal of Marriage and The Family* 34(1): 156–165.

Tanner, Nancy. 1974. Matrifocality in Indonesia and Africa and Among Black Americans. In Michelle Zimbalist Rosaldo and Louise Lamphere (eds.). *Woman, Culture, and Society*, pp. 129–156. Stanford: Stanford University Press.

Maria, A Portuguese Fisherwoman

Sally Cole

Maria lives in the small town of Vila Chã on the north coast of Portugal. She is a retired *pescadeira* (fisherwoman) who still goes to the beach each day to help bait traps or unload fish or just to talk with other fishermen and women. The illegitimate daughter of a poor, landless woman, Maria began fishing when she was only ten years old. And throughout her life she worked both at sea and on land. She fished by net and hand line in one of the small, gaily painted, open wooden boats that, until the 1960s, were powered by oar and sail and were typical in the inshore fishery; on land she, like the other women, harvested

Original material prepared for this text.

and dried seaweed and sold it to local peasant farmers for fertilizer. By the age of thirty-five she was a licensed boat skipper, had bought her own boat and gear, and was fishing daily with crew she hired to work for her. Maria says this was simply the only way she knew how to make a living. She fishes, she tells us, because she was forced to, because her husband emigrated to Brazil abandoning her with three daughters. Nonetheless, she likes her profession and knows she is good at it—as good as any man. Fisherwomen like Maria say they fished "like men," and they mean that not only did women have the skill of fishermen, but at sea they became social men. They stress that women's sexuality was never targeted when they were working with men. "There was more respect (*respeito*) on the sea than there was on the land," some say.

Maria is a large-boned women who dresses in the characteristic manner of rural Portuguese women who were born, raised, and married during the Salazar regime before 1960. She wears her hair pulled into a bun at the back of her head and covered with a head scarf; she wears a dark wool shawl, skirt, socks, and *chinelas* (the mass-produced open-backed flat shoes that have replaced the home-made traditional clogs). Underneath her skirt she wears trousers—unheard of among women of her generation, and she walks with a masculine, lumbering gait and speaks in a deep, quiet authoritative voice.

On one hand Maria found my interest in her life surprising: "There is nothing remarkable about my life," she said. On the other hand, like other women in Vila Chã, Maria tells stories from her every day life in conversations with daughters, neighbors, relatives, and even clients for her fish. Women's daily activities on the beach, on the street, and at the fish auction, provide them with continual opportunities to constitute the female subject and to constitute the self. With this strong sense of self, Maria and other Vila Chã fisherwomen comfortably and skillfully constructed their life stories.

In the following narrative Maria assures us that she only did what she had to do. But we see, in her refusal of her estranged husband's request to take him back and care for him in his old age, how through her life of hard work and economic independence, she has constituted herself as an autonomous person and finds it impossible to do what her husband asks and what he considers to be a wife's duty.

There is nothing remarkable about my life. I am a poor woman. I did what I had to do. I worked hard—all the women here did. I have worked very hard all my life.

I was born in 1926, the third of four children. We had no father. I was raised in Vila Chã by my mother who worked as a *jornaleira* (an agricultural day laborer), harvested seaweed, and sold fish in order to feed us. But often there was no food, and we had to beg from our neighbors.

In my childhood girls used to collect seaweed both from the beach in a hand net and from boats using a type of rake. It was also common for them to accompany relatives fishing. When only ten years old I began to accompany neighbors when they went fishing. When I was fourteen I took out my license, and I continued to fish as a crew member on boats owned by neighbors. These men are all dead now but it was they who taught me this work.

I married when I was only twenty years old, and I think this is too young. My husband was a *pescador* (fisherman) from a neighboring parish. He came to live with me and my mother and my grandmother and took up fishing in Vila Chã. I continued fishing whenever I could, and after my daughters were born I left them in my mother's care so that I could go out on the sea. I also worked on the seaweed harvest often going out alone in the boat to collect seaweed.

From the beginning my husband was selfish. He never helped me with my work but would instead go off to attend to his own affairs (*a vida dele*). I married too young. We had two daughters, and when I was pregnant with the third my husband emigrated to Brazil. He was gone for almost four years, during which time I heard nothing from him, and he sent no money. I decided to go to Brazil to find him. In 1955 I went by ship with my sister-in-law who was going to join her husband, my brother, in Brazil. I found my husband involved in a life of women and drink, and after a few months I returned home alone. I wanted to make my life in Vila Chã, and I missed my daughters. I took up fishing full-time and harvested seaweed when I wasn't fishing, and in this way I supported my mother and my children. In 1961 I bought a boat of my own and took out my skipper's license.

I like my profession, but I fished because I was forced to. My marriage became difficult. My husband went away to Brazil, leaving me in the street with three children, and I had to face life on my own. Fishing was not as productive then as it is now, and the life of a fisherwoman was a hard one. But I had to turn to what I knew. First I fished in a boat belonging to another pescador and then for eighteen years I owned and fished in my own boat "Três Marias." About fourteen years ago I managed to buy this small house, which, little by little, I have fixed up, and this is where I live now.

Although in recent years I have been the only woman skipper, there have been no difficulties for me at all because I know my profession very well—as well as any of my comrades. Men used to like to fish with me because they knew I was strong. C., a member of my crew, used to say that I was stronger than he. Fishing holds no secrets for me, and besides I think that women have the right to face life beside men. What suits men suits women. I am respected by everyone, men and women. I have many friends, and when the weather prohibits fishing we all stay here on the beach working on the nets and enjoying conversation. I have always enjoyed my work on the sea. I was never one who liked to stay at home.

When my daughters were small I used to be at sea day and night—whenever there was fish. They stayed at home with my mother. Later, when they were older and I was fishing, my daughters assisted my mother harvesting seaweed, and in this way they contributed to the maintenance of the household. As soon as I returned from fishing I would start the housework. You see, I was at the same time housewife and fisherman (*Olhe, eu era ao mesmo tempo dona de casa e pescador*).

I retired in 1979. I sold my boat, and I gave my fishing gear to my son-in-law. I sold my boat to a fisherman in Matosinhos because I could not bear to see it anymore here on the beach. In 1982 I bought a piece of land, and two of my daughters are building a duplex on it now. My youngest daughter lives with me in my house along with her husband and three children. I have helped all of my daughters to establish their households. I have been very good to them. And, now that I am old and my heart is not good, they are looking after me. When I returned from Brazil leaving my husband there, I could have found another man to live with. I could have lived with another man. But I never wanted to do that because, if things didn't work out with us, I worried that he would take it out on my daughters because they were nothing to him. I preferred to have my daughters.

Recently, my husband has begun writing to me from Brazil. He wants to return to Portugal, and he wants me to take him back. He needs someone to care for him now in his old age. But I won't take him back. It's not right at all. I liked him once, but that's all over now. The best part of the life of a couple is passed. I'm not interested in his returning. I'm not an object to be put away and then picked up, dusted off, and used again. I am not an object. I am a person. I am human. I have the right to be treated like a person, don't you think? I managed to make a good life for myself and my children here, but he arranged nothing for himself there—nothing. He's got nothing there, but he's also got nothing here. He has never done anything for me or my daughters, and now he wants to come back. Who does he think he is? I'm not crazy. He has no right whatsoever.

Maria describes her life of work in the inshore fishery as it existed in Vila Chã until the 1970s, by which time most households in the community had come to depend primarily on the wages earned by women in factories and men in construction work. This household-based maritime economy had depended on an annual round of diverse activities and on the seasonal availability of natural resources like fish and seaweed. On one hand the unpredictability of resources and weather ensured their poverty; on the other hand maritime production required the participation of all household members (including women and children) and thus created the conditions for the social and economic autonomy of women. The sale of fresh fish and seaweed fertilizer—both commodities that women controlled—enabled women like Maria to support themselves and their children without the assistance of men. Because Vila Chã, like other rural communities in northwestern Portugal, has sustained high rates of male emigration since at least the nineteenth century, the autonomy of women was also strategic.

Maria describes how she invested in property—a house, a boat and gear, and land for her daughters. Perhaps because men were often absent due to either temporary or permanent emigration, property in Vila Chã became identified primarily with women. It was a woman's responsibility to look after the house and garden plot and to look after the boat and gear—either by fishing herself or by hiring others to fish for her. Daughters were favored over sons to inherit property, and younger daughters (or the last to marry) were favored over older daughters. Daughters were favored not only because sons might emigrate but also because parents wanted a daughter to stay on in the house to care for them in old age and to tend their graves after death.

The relationship between women and property also determined residence patterns after marriage. As Maria describes after their marriage her husband came to live with her and her mother and her mother's mother. Maria was the third of four children and the youngest daughter. Maria lived with her mother all her life. Now, her own youngest daughter and her husband and children live with Maria and are caring for her in her old age.

The relations between these four generations of mothers and daughters are typical of relations among blood-related women in Vila Chã. Women's strong ties with their children, especially daughters, may be interpreted as having been among women's multiple strategies to provide for themselves and for their households in the absence of men. Thus, not only did women maximize their economic autonomy through their control of the sale of fresh fish and seaweed fertilizer and by assuming responsibility for the household property, but they also conceived of their children as a resource. Having children gave a woman adult status and the prerogatives (and responsibilities) of managing a household; having children also ensured that a woman—especially an unmarried woman or a deserted wife like Maria—would have someone to care for her in the frailty of her later years.

The importance women placed on having children may be seen in the high rates of illegitimacy that were common in Vila Chã until the 1960s and that are correlated with landlessness and male emigration. Poor, landless women were already limited to finding marriage partners who were of the same low economic position. Male emigration further created a demographic asymmetry, so there were not enough marriageable men to go around. Under these conditions poor women often were less concerned about getting married than they were desirous of having children. Maria's mother and her mother's mother are both women who never married but who had children and managed households. Although Maria herself did marry she tells us directly that her daughters were more important to her than any man could ever be, and for this reason, she says, she chose to live without a male partner when, still a young woman, she was abandoned by her husband. "I preferred to have my daughters," she said.

Finally, Maria describes how gender is negotiated through the relations of daily life and especially through work. Maria negotiated a dual or androgynous gender identity. She spent her entire life working with men in a profession that was locally defined as a masculine pursuit despite the fact that women also fished. This work enabled her to assume masculine roles and prerogatives in other spheres of life and to live without the support of a male companion. At the same time Maria fulfilled a woman's role: she was the mother of three children and the manager of a household. When Maria tells us that she was both "housewife and fisherman" she is telling us that to her children she was both nurturer and economic provider, both mother and father, and in the community she was both woman and man. Now, nearing the end of life, Maria and her husband have reversed positions: Maria once traveled to Brazil to entreat her husband to return and was refused; now her husband is begging her to take him back into her home and she is refusing. Maria, with her life of hard work behind her, cannot even entertain the contradiction. "I am not crazy," she said. "I am not an object. I am a person."

The Female World of Cards and Holidays: Women, Families, and the Work of Kinship[1]

Micaela di Leonardo

> Why is it that the married women of America are supposed to write all the letters and send all the cards to their husbands' families? My old man is a much better writer than I am, yet he expects me to correspond with his whole family. If I asked him to correspond with mine, he would blow a gasket.
>
> Letter to Ann Landers

> Women's place in man's life cycle has been that of nurturer, caretaker, and helpmate, the weaver of those networks of relationships on which she in turn relies.
>
> Carol Gilligan, *In a Different Voice*[2]

Feminist scholars in the past fifteen years have made great strides in formulating new understandings of the relations among gender, kinship, and the larger economy. As a result of this pioneering research, women are newly visible and audible, no longer submerged within their families. We see households as loci of political struggle, inseparable parts of the larger society and economy, rather than as havens from the heartless world of industrial capitalism.[3] And historical and cultural variations in kinship and family forms have become clearer with the maturation of feminist historical and social-scientific scholarship.

Two theoretical trends have been key to this reinterpretation of women's work and family domain. The first is the elevation to visibility of women's nonmarket activities—housework, child care, the servicing of men,

and the care of the elderly—and the definition of all these activities as *labor*, to be enumerated alongside and counted as part of overall social reproduction. The second theoretical trend is the nonpejorative focus on women's domestic or kin-centered networks. We now see them as the products of conscious strategy, as crucial to the functioning of kinship systems, as sources of women's autonomous power and possible primary sites of emotional fulfillment, and, at times, as the vehicles for actual survival and/or political resistance.[4]

Recently, however, a division has developed between feminist interpreters of the "labor" and the "network" perspectives on women's lives. Those who focus on women's work tend to envision women as sentient, goal-oriented actors, while those who concern themselves with women's ties to others tend to perceive women primarily in terms of nurturance, other-orientation—altruism. The most celebrated recent example of this division is the opposing testimony of historians Alice Kessler-Harris and Rosalind Rosenberg in the Equal Employment Opportunity Commission's sex discrimination case against Sears Roebuck and Company. Kessler-Harris argued that American women historically have actively sought higher-paying jobs and have been prevented from gaining them because of sex discrimination by employers. Rosenberg argued that American women in the nineteenth century created among themselves, through their domestic networks, a "women's culture" that emphasized the nurturance of children and others and the maintenance of family life and that discouraged women from competition over or heavy emotional investment in demanding, high-paid employment.[5]

I shall not here address this specific debate but, instead, shall consider its theoretical background and implications. I shall argue that we need to fuse, rather than to oppose, the domestic network and labor perspectives. In what follows, I introduce a new concept, the work of kinship, both to aid empirical feminist research on women, work, and family and to help advance feminist theory in this arena. I believe that the boundary-crossing nature of the concept helps to confound the self-interest/altruism dichotomy, forcing us from an either-or stance to a position that includes both perspectives. I hope in this way to contribute to a more critical feminist vision of women's lives and the meaning of family in the industrial West.

In my recent field research among Italian-Americans in Northern California, I found myself considering the relations between women's kinship and economic lives. As an anthropologist, I was concerned with people's kin lives beyond conventional American nuclear family or household boundaries. To this end, I collected individual and family life histories, asking about all kin and close friends and their activities. I was also very interested in women's labor. As I sat with women and listened to their accounts of their past and present lives, I began to realize that they were involved in three types of work: housework and child care, work in the labor market, and the work of kinship.[6]

By kin work I refer to the conception, maintenance, and ritual celebration of cross-household kin ties, including visits, letters, telephone calls, presents, and cards to kin; the organization of holiday gatherings; the creation and maintenance of quasi-kin relations; decisions to neglect or to intensify particular ties; the mental work of reflection about all these activities; and the creation and communication of altering images of family and kin vis-à-vis the images of others, both folk and mass media. Kin work is a key element that has been missing in the synthesis of the "household labor" and "domestic network" perspectives. In our emphasis on individual women's responsibilities within households and on the job, we reflect the common picture of households as nuclear units, tied perhaps to the larger social and economic system, but not to *each other*. We miss the point of telephone and soft drink advertising, of women's magazines' holiday issues, of commentators' confused nostalgia for the mythical American extended family: it is kinship contact *across households,* as much as women's work within them, that fulfills our cultural expectation of satisfying family life.

Maintaining these contacts, this sense of family, takes time, intention, and skill. We tend to think of human social and kin networks as the epiphenomena of production and reproduction: the social traces created by our material lives. Or, in the neoclassical tradition, we see them as part of leisure activities, outside an economic purview except insofar as they involve consumption behavior. But the creation and maintenance of kin and quasi-kin networks in advanced industrial societies is *work;* and, moreover, it is largely women's work.

The kin-work lens brought into focus new perspectives on my informants' family lives. First, life histories revealed that often the very existence of kin contact and holiday celebration depended on the presence of an adult woman in the household. When couples divorced or mothers died, the work of kinship was left undone; when women entered into sanctioned sexual or marital relationships with men in these situations, they reconstituted the men's kinship networks and organized gatherings and holiday celebrations. Middle-aged businessman Al Bertini, for example, recalled the death of his mother in his early adolescence: "I think that's probably one of the biggest losses in losing a family—yeah, I remember as a child when my Mom was alive . . . the holidays were treated with enthusiasm and love . . . after she died the attempt was there but it just didn't materialize." Later in life, when Al Bertini and his wife separated, his own and his son Jim's participation in extended-family contact decreased rapidly. But when Jim began a relationship with Jane Batemen, she and he moved in with Al, and Jim and Jane began to invite his kin over for holidays. Jane single-handedly planned and cooked the holiday feasts.

Kin work, then, is like housework and child care: men in the aggregate do not do it. It differs from these forms of labor in that it is harder for men to substitute hired labor to accomplish these tasks in the absence of kinswomen. Second, I found that women, as the workers in this arena, generally had much greater kin knowledge than did their husbands, often including more accurate and extensive knowledge of their husbands' families. This was true both of middle-aged and younger couples and surfaced as a phenomenon in my interviews in the form of humorous arguments and in wives' detailed additions to husbands' narratives. Nick Meraviglia, a middle-aged professional, discussed his Italian antecedents in the presence of his wife, Pina:

> *Nick:* My grandfather was a very outspoken man, and it was reported he took off for the hills when he found out that Mussolini was in power.
> *Pina:* And he was a very tall man; he used to have to bow his head to get inside doors.
> *Nick:* No, that was my uncle.
> *Pina:* Your grandfather too, I've heard your mother say.
> *Nick:* My mother has a sister and a brother.
> *Pina:* *Two* sisters!
> *Nick:* Your're right!
> *Pina:* Maria and Angelina.

Women were also much more willing to discuss family feuds and crises and their own roles in them; men tended to repeat formulaic statements asserting family unity and respectability. (This was much less true for younger men.) Joe and Cetta Longhinotti's statements illustrate these tendencies. Joe responded to my question about kin relations: "We all get along. As a rule, relatives, you got nothing but trouble." Cetta, instead, discussed her relations with each of her grown children, their wives, her in-laws, and her own blood kin in detail. She did not hide the fact that relations were strained in several cases; she was eager to discuss the evolution of prob-

lems and to seek my opinions of her actions. Similarly, Pina Meraviglia told the following story of her fight with one of her brothers with hysterical laughter: "There was some biting and hair pulling and choking . . . it was terrible! I shouldn't even tell you. . . . " Nick, meanwhile, was concerned about maintaining an image of family unity and respectability.

Also, men waxed fluent while women were quite inarticulate in discussing their past and present occupations. When asked about their work lives, Joe Longhinotti and Nick Meraviglia, union baker and professional, respectively, gave detailed narratives of their work careers. Cetta Longhinotti and Pina Meraviglia, clerical and former clerical, respectively, offered only short descriptions focusing on factors of ambience, such as the "lovely things" sold by Cetta's firm.

These patterns are not repeated in the younger generation, especially among younger women, such as Jane Batemen, who have managed to acquire training and jobs with some prospect of mobility. These younger women, though, have *added* a professional and detailed interest in their jobs to a felt responsibility for the work of kinship.[7]

Although men rarely took on any kin-work tasks, family histories and accounts of contemporary life revealed that kinswomen often negotiated among themselves, alternating hosting, food-preparation, and gift-buying responsibilities—or sometimes ceding entire task clusters to one woman. Taking on or ceding tasks was clearly related to acquiring or divesting oneself of power within kin networks, but women varied in their interpretation of the meaning of this power. Cetta Longhinotti, for example, relied on the "family Christmas dinner" as a symbol of her central kinship role and was involved in painful negotiations with her daughter-in-law over the issue: "Last year she insisted—this is touchy. She doesn't want to spend the holiday dinner together. So last year we went there. But I still had my dinner the next day . . . I made a big dinner on Christmas Day, regardless of who's coming—candles on the table, the whole routine. I decorate the house myself too . . . well, I just feel that the time will come when maybe

I won't feel like cooking a big dinner—she should take advantage of the fact that I feel like doing it now." Pina Meraviglia, in contrast, was saddened by the centripetal force of the developmental cycle but was unworried about the power dynamics involved in her negotiations with daughters- and mother-in-law over holiday celebrations.

Kin work is not just a matter of power among women but also of the mediation of power represented by household units.[8] Women often choose to minimize status claims in their kin work and to include numbers of households under the rubric of family. Cetta Longhinotti's sister Anna, for example, is married to a professional man whose parents have considerable economic resources, while Joe and Cetta have low incomes and no other well-off kin. Cetta and Anna remain close, talk on the phone several times a week, and assist their adult children, divided by distance and economic status, in remaining united as cousins.

Finally, women perceived housework, child care, market labor, the care of the elderly, and the work of kinship as competing responsibilities. Kin work was a unique category, however, because it was unlabeled and because women felt they could either cede some tasks to kinswomen and/or could cut them back severely. Women variously cited the pressures of market labor, the needs of the elderly, and their own desires for freedom and job enrichment as reasons for cutting back Christmas card lists, organized holiday gatherings, multifamily dinners, letters, visits, and phone calls. They expressed guilt and defensiveness about this cutback process and, particularly, about their failures to keep families close through constant contact and about their failures to create perfect holiday celebrations. Cetta Longhinotti, during the period when she was visiting her elderly mother every weekend in addition to working a full-time job, said of her grown children, "I'd have the whole gang here once a month, but I've been so busy that I haven't done that for about six months." And Pina Meraviglia lamented her insufficient work on family Christmases, "I wish I had really made it tra-

ditional . . . like my sister-in-law has special stories."

Kin work, then, takes place in an arena characterized simultaneously by cooperation and competition, by guilt and gratification. Like housework and child care, it is women's work, with the same lack of clear-cut agreement concerning its proper components: How often should sheets be changed? When should children be toilet trained? Should an aunt send a niece a birthday present? Unlike housework and child care, however, kin work, taking place across the boundaries of normative households, is as yet unlabeled and has no retinue of experts prescribing its correct forms. Neither home economists nor child psychologists have much to say about nieces' birthday presents. Kin work is thus more easily cut back without social interference. On the other hand, the results of kin work—frequent kin contact and feelings of intimacy—are the subject of considerable cultural manipulation as indicators of family happiness. Thus, women in general are subject to the guilt my informants expressed over cutting back kin-work activities.

Although many of my informants referred to the results of women's kin work—cross-household kin contacts and attendant ritual gatherings—as particularly Italian-American, I suggest that in fact his phenomenon is broadly characteristic of American kinship. We think of kin-work tasks such as the preparation of ritual feasts, responsibility for holiday card lists, and gift buying as extensions of women's domestic responsibilities for cooking, consumption, and nurturance. American men in general do not take on these tasks any more than they do housework and child care—and probably less, as these tasks have not yet been the subject of intense public debate. And my informants' gender breakdown in relative articulateness on kinship and workplace themes reflects the still prevalent occupational segregation—most women cannot find jobs that provide enough pay, status, or promotion possibilities to make them worth focusing on—as well as women's perceived power within kinship networks. The common recognition of that power is reflected in Selma Greenberg's book on non-sexist child rearing. Greenberg calls mothers "press agents" who sponsor relations between their own children and other relatives; she advises a mother whose relatives treat her disrespectfully to deny those kin access to her children.[9]

Kin work is a salient concept in other parts of the developed world as well. Larissa Adler Lomnitz and Marisol Pérez Lizaur have found that "centralizing women" are responsible for these tasks and for communicating "family ideology" among upper-class families in Mexico City. Matthews Hamabata, in his study of upper-class families in Japan, has found that women's kin work involves key financial transactions. Sylvia Junko Yanagisako discovered that, among rural Japanese migrants to the United States, the maintenance of kin networks was assigned to women as the migrants adopted the American ideology of the independent nuclear family household. Maila Stivens notes that urban Australian housewives' kin ties and kin ideology "transcend women's isolation in domestic units."[10]

This is not to say that cultural conceptions of appropriate kin work do not vary, even within the United States. Carol B. Stack documents institutionalized fictive kinship and concomitant reciprocity networks among impoverished black American women. Women in populations characterized by intense feelings of ethnic identity may feel bound to emphasize particular occasions—Saint Patrick's or Columbus Day—with organized family feasts. These constructs may be mediated by religious affiliation, as in the differing emphases on Friday or Sunday family dinners among Jews and Christians. Thus the personnel involved and the amount and kind of labor considered necessary for the satisfactory performance of particular kin-work tasks are likely to be culturally constructed.[11] But while the kin and quasi-kin universes and the ritual calendar may vary among women according to race or ethnicity, their general responsibility for maintaining kin links and ritual observances does not.

As kin work is not an ethnic or racial phe-nomenon, neither is it linked only to one social class. Some commentators on American family life still reflect the influence of work done in England in the 1950s and 1960s (by Elizabeth Bott and by Peter Willmott and Michael Young) in their assumption that working-class families are close and extended, while the middle class substitutes friends (or anomie) for family. Others reflect the prevalent family pessimism in their presumption that neither working- nor middle-class families have extended kin contact.[12] Insofar as kin contact depends on residential proximity, the larger economy's shifts will influence particular groups' experiences. Factory workers, close to kin or not, are likely to disperse when plants shut down or relocate. Small businesspeople or independent professionals may, however, remain resident in particular areas—and thus maintain proximity to kin—for generations, while professional employees of large firms relocate at their firms' behest. This pattern obtained among my informants.

In any event, cross-household kin contact can be and is effected at long distance through letters, cards, phone calls, and holiday and vacation visits. The form and functions of contact, however, vary according to economic resources. Stack and Brett Williams offer rich accounts of kin networks among poor blacks and migrant Chicano farmworkers functioning to provide emotional support, labor, commodity, and cash exchange—a funeral visit, help with laundry, the gift of a dress or piece of furniture.[13] Far different in degree are exchanges such as the loan of a vacation home, a multifamily boating trip, or the provision of free professional services—examples from the kin networks of my wealthier informants. The point is that households, as labor- and income-pooling units, whatever their relative wealth, are somewhat porous in relation to others with whose members they share kin or quasi-kin ties. We do not really know how class differences operate in this realm; it is possible that they do so largely in terms of ideology. It may be, as David Schneider and Raymond T. Smith suggest, that the affluent and the very poor are more open in recognizing necessary economic ties to kin than are those who identify themselves as middle class.[14]

Recognizing that kin work is gender rather than class based allows us to see women's kin networks among all groups, not just among working-class and impoverished women in industrialized societies. This recognition in turn clarifies our understanding of the privileges and limits of women's varying access to economic resources. Affluent women can "buy out" of housework, child care—and even some kin-work responsibilities. But they, like all women, are ultimately responsible, and subject to both guilt and blame, as the administrators of home, children, and kin network. Even the wealthiest women must negotiate the timing and venue of holidays and other family rituals with their kinswomen. It may be that kin work is the core women's work category in which all women cooperate, while women's perceptions of the appropriateness of cooperation for housework, child care, and the care of the elderly varies by race, class, region, and generation.

But kin work is not necessarily an appropriate category of labor, much less gendered labor, in all societies. In many small-scale societies, kinship is the major organizing principle of all social life, and all contacts are by definition kin contacts.[15] One cannot, therefore, speak of labor that does not involve kin. In the United States, kin work as a separable category of gendered labor perhaps arose historically in concert with the ideological and material constructs of the moral mother/cult of domesticity and the privatized family during the course of industrialization in the eighteenth and nineteenth centuries. These phenomena are connected to the increase in the ubiquity of productive occupations *for men* that are not organized through kinship. This includes the demise of the family farm with the capitalization of agriculture and rural-urban migration; the decline of family recruitment in factories as firms grew, ended child labor, and began to assert bureaucratized forms of control; the decline of artisanal labor and of small entrepreneurial enter-

prises as large firms took greater and greater shares of the commodity market; the decline of the family firm as corporations—and their managerial work forces—grew beyond the capacities of individual families to provision them; and, finally, the rise of civil service bureaucracies and public pressure against nepotism.[16]

As men increasingly worked alongside of non-kin, and as the ideology of separate spheres was increasingly accepted, perhaps the responsibility for kin maintenance, like that for child rearing, became gender-focused. Ryan points out that "built into the updated family economy . . . was a new measure of voluntarism." This voluntarism, though, "perceived as the shift from patriarchal authority to domestic affection," also signaled the rise of women's moral responsibility for family life. Just as the "idea of fatherhood itself seemed almost to wither away" so did male involvement in the responsibility for kindred lapse.[17]

With postbellum economic growth and geographic movement, women's new kin burden involved increasing amounts of time and labor. The ubiquity of lengthy visits and of frequent letter-writing among nineteenth-century women attests to this. And for visitors and for those who were residentially proximate, the continuing commonalities of women's domestic labor allowed for kinds of work sharing—nursing, childkeeping, cooking, cleaning—that men, with their increasingly differentiated and controlled activities, probably could not maintain. This is not to say that some kin-related male productive work did not continue; my own data, for instance, show kin involvement among small businessmen in the present. It is, instead, to suggest a general trend in material life and a cultural shift that influenced even those whose productive and kin lives remained commingled. Yanagisako has distinguished between the realms of domestic and public kinship in order to draw attention to anthropology's relatively "thin descriptions" of the domestic (female) domain. Using her typology, we might say that kin work as gendered labor comes into existence within the domestic domain with the relative erasure of the domain of public, male kinship.[18]

Whether or not this proposed historical model bears up under further research, the question remains, Why do women do kin work? However material factors may shape activities, they do not determine how individuals may perceive them. And in considering issues of motivation, of intention, of the cultural construction of kin work, we return to the altruism versus self-interest dichotomy in recent feminist theory. Consider the epigraphs to this article. Are women kin workers the nurturant weavers of the Gilligan quotation, or victims, like the fed-up woman who writes to complain to Ann Landers? That is, are we to see kin work as yet another example of "women's culture" that takes the care of others as its primary desideratum? Or are we to see kin work as another way in which men, the economy, and the state extract labor from women without a fair return? And how do women themselves see their kin work and its place in their lives?

As I have indicated above, I believe that it is the creation of the self-interest/altruism dichotomy that is itself the problem here. My women informants, like most American women, accepted their primary responsibility for housework and the care of dependent children. Despite two major waves of feminist activism in this century, the gendering of certain categories of unpaid labor is still largely unaltered. These work responsibilities clearly interfere with some women's labor force commitments at certain life-cycle stages; but, more important, women are simply discriminated against in the labor market and rarely are able to achieve wage and status parity with men of the same age, race, class, and educational background.[19]

Thus for my women informants, as for most American women, the domestic domain is not only an arena in which much unpaid labor must be undertaken but also a realm in which one may attempt to gain human satisfactions—and power—not available in the labor market. Anthropologists Jane Collier and Louise Lamphere have written com-

pellingly on the ways in which varying kinship and economic structures may shape women's competition or cooperation with one another in domestic domains.[20] Feminists considering Western women and families have looked at the issue of power primarily in terms of husband-wife relations or psychological relations between parents and children. If we adopt Collier and Lamphere's broader canvas, though, we see that kin work is not only women's labor from which men and children benefit but also labor that women undertake in order to create obligations in men and children and to gain power over one another. Thus Cetta Longhinotti's struggle with her daughter-in-law over the venue of Christmas dinner is not just about a competition over altruism, it is also about the creation of future obligations. And thus Cetta's and Anna's sponsorship of their children's friendship with each other is both an act of nurturance and a cooperative means of gaining power over those children.

Although this was not a clear-cut distinction, those of my informants who were more explicitly antifeminist tended to be most invested in kin work. Given the overwhelming historical shift toward greater autonomy for younger generations and the withering of children's financial and labor obligations to their parents, this investment was in most cases tragically doomed. Cetta Longhinotti, for example, had repaid her own mother's devotion with extensive home nursing during the mother's last years. Given Cetta's general failure to direct her adult children in work, marital choice, religious worship, or even frequency of visits, she is unlikely to receive such care from them when she is older.

The kin-work lens thus reveals the close relations between altruism and self-interest in women's actions. As economists Nancy Folbre and Heidi Hartmann point out, we have inherited a Western intellectual tradition that both dichotomizes the domestic and public domains and associates them on exclusive axes such that we find it difficult to see self-interest in the home and altruism in the workplace.[21] But why, in fact, have women fought for better jobs if not, in part, to support their children? These dichotomies are Procrustean beds that warp our understanding of women's lives both at home and at work. "Altruism" and "self-interest" are cultural constructions that are not necessarily mutually exclusive, and we forget this to our peril.

The concept of kin work helps to bring into focus a heretofore unacknowledged array of tasks that is culturally assigned to women in industrialized societies. At the same time, this concept, embodying notions of both love and work and crossing the boundaries of households, helps us to reflect on current feminist debates on women's work, family, and community. We newly see both the interrelations of these phenomena and women's roles in creating and maintaining those interrelations. Revealing the actual labor embodied in what we culturally conceive as love and considering the political uses of this labor helps to deconstruct the self-interest/altruism dichotomy and to connect more closely women's domestic and labor-force lives.

The true value of the concept, however, remains to be tested through further historical and contemporary research on gender, kinship, and labor. We need to assess the suggestion that gendered kin work emerges in concert with the capitalist development process; to probe the historical record for women's and men's varying and changing conceptions of it; and to research the current range of its cultural constructions and material realities. We know that household boundaries are more porous than we had thought—but they are undoubtedly differentially porous, and this is what we need to specify. We need, in particular, to assess the relations of changing labor processes, residential patterns, and the use of technology to changing kin work.

Altering the values attached to this particular set of women's tasks will be as difficult as are the housework, child-care, and occupational-segregation struggles. But just as feminist research in these latter areas is complementary and cumulative, so researching kin work should help us to piece together the home, work, and public-life landscape—to see the female world of cards and holidays as it is constructed and lived within the changing political economy. How female that world is to remain, and what it would look like if it were not sex-segregated, are questions we cannot yet answer.

NOTES

Many thanks to Cynthia Costello, Rayna Rapp, Roberta Spalter-Roth, John Willoughby, and Barbara Gelpi, Susan Johnson, and Sylvia Yanagisako of *Signs* for their help with this article. I wish in particular to acknowledge the influence of Rayna Rapp's work on my ideas.

1. Acknowledgment and gratitude to Carroll Smith-Rosenberg for my paraphrase of her title, "The Female World of Love and Ritual: Relations between Women in Nineteenth-Century America," *Signs: Journal of Women in Culture and Society* 1, no. 1 (Autumn 1975): 1–29.

2. Ann Landers letter printed in *Washington Post* (April 15, 1983); Carol Gilligan, *In a Different Voice* (Cambridge, Mass.: Harvard University Press, 1982), 17.

3. Heidi I. Hartmann, "The Family as the Locus of Gender, Class, and Political Struggle: The Example of Housework," *Signs* 6, no. 3 (Spring 1981): 366–94; and Christopher Lasch, *Haven in a Heartless World: The Family Besieged* (New York: Basic Books, 1977).

4. Representative examples of the first trend include Joann Vanek, "Time Spent on Housework," *Scientific American* 231 (November 1974): 116–20; Ruth Schwartz Cowan, "A Case Study of Technological and Social Change: The Washing Machine and the Working Wife," in *Clio's Consciousness Raised*, ed. Mary Hartmann and Lois Banner (New York: Harper & Row, 1974), 245–53; Ann Oakley, *Women's Work: The Housewife, Past and Present* (New York: Vintage, 1974); Hartmann; and Susan Strasser, *Never Done: A History of American Housework* (New York: Pantheon Books, 1982). Key contributions to the second trend include Louise Lamphere, "Strategies, Cooperation and Conflict among Women in Domestic Groups," in *Woman, Culture and Society*, ed. Michelle Zimbalist Rosaldo and Louise Lamphere (Stanford, Calif.: Stanford University Press, 1974), 97–112; Mina Davis Caulfield, "Imperialism, the Family and the Cultures of Resistance," *Social-*

ist Revolution 20 (October 1974): 67–85; Smith-Rosenberg; Sylvia Junko Yanagisako, "Women-centered Kin Networks and Urban Bilateral Kinship," *American Ethnologist* 4, no. 2 (1977): 207–26; Jane Humphries, "The Working Class Family, Women's Liberation and Class Struggle: The Case of Nineteenth Century British History," *Review of Radical Political Economics* 9 (Fall 1977): 25–41; Blanche Weisen Cook, "Female Support Networks and Political Activism: Lillian Wald, Crystal Eastman, Emma Goldman," in *A Heritage of Her Own*, ed. Nancy F. Cott and Elizabeth H. Pleck (New York: Simon & Schuster, 1979); Temma Kaplan, "Female Consciousness and Collective Action: The Case of Barcelona, 1910–1918," *Signs* 7, no. 3 (Spring 1982): 545–66.

5. On this debate, see Jon Weiner, "Women's History on Trial," *Nation* 241, no. 6 (September 7, 1985): 161, 176, 178–80; Karen J. Winkler, "Two Scholars' Conflict in Sears Sex-Bias Case Sets Off War in Women's History," *Chronicle of Higher Education* (February 5, 1986), 1, 8; Rosalind Rosenberg, "What Harms Women in the Workplace," *New York Times* (February 27, 1986); Alice Kessler-Harris, "Equal Employment Opportunity Commission vs. Sears Roebuck and Company: A Personal Account," *Radical History Review* 35 (April 1986): 57–79.

6. Portions of the following analysis are reported in Micaela di Leonardo, *The Varieties of Ethnic Experience: Kinship, Class and Gender among California Italian-Americans* (Ithaca, N.Y.: Cornell University Press, 1984), chap. 6.

7. Clearly, many women do, in fact, discuss their paid labor with willingness and clarity. The point here is that there are opposing gender tendencies in an identical interview situation, tendencies that are explicable in terms of both the material realities and current cultural constructions of gender.

8. Papanek has rightly focused on women's unacknowledged family status production, but what is conceived of as "family" shifts and varies (Hanna Papanek, "Family Status Production: The 'Work' and 'Non-Work' of Women," *Signs* 4, no. 4 [Summer 1979]: 775–81).

9. Selma Greenberg, *Right from the Start: A Guide to Nonsexist Child Rearing* (Boston: Houghton Mifflin Co., 1978), 147. Another example of indirect support for kin work's gendered existence is a recent study of university math students, which found that a major reason for women's failure to pursue careers in mathematics was the pressure of family involvement. Compare David Maines et al., *Social Processes of Sex Differentiation in Mathematics* (Washington, D.C.: National Institute of Education, 1981).

10. Larissa Adler Lomnitz and Marisol Pérez Lizaur, "The History of a Mexican Urban Family," *Journal of Family History* 3, no. 4 (1978): 392–409, esp. 398; Matthews Hamàbata, Crested Kimono Power and Love in the Japanese Business Family (Ithaca, N.Y.: Cornell University Press, 1990); Sylvia Junko Yanagisako, "Two Processes of Change in Japanese-American Kinship," *Journal of Anthropological Research* 31 (1975): 196–224; Maila Stivens, "Women and Their Kin: Kin, Class and Solidarity in a Middle-Class Suburb of Sydney, Australia," in *Women United, Women Divided*, ed. Patricia Caplan and Janet M. Bujra (Bloomington: Indiana University Press, 1979), 157–84.

11. Carol B. Stack, *All Our Kin: Strategies for Survival in a Black Community* (New York: Harper & Row, 1974). These cultural constructions may, however, vary within ethnic/racial populations as well.

12. Elizabeth Bott, *Family and Social Network*, 2d ed. (New York: Free Press, 1971): Michael Young and Peter Willmott, *Family and Kinship in East London* (London: Routledge & Kegan Paul, 1957), and *Family and Class in a London Suburb* (London: Routledge & Kegan Paul, 1960). Classic studies that presume this class difference are Herbert Gans, *The Urban Villagers: Group and Class in the Life of Italian-Americans* (New York: Free Press, 1962); and Mirra Komarovsky, *Blue-Collar Marriage* (New York: Random House, 1962). A recent example is Ilene Philipson, "Heterosexual Antagonisms and the Politics of Mothering," *Socialist Review* 12, no. 6 (November–December 1982): 55–77. Edward Shorter, *The Making of the Modern Family* (New York: Basic Books, 1975), epitomizes the pessimism of the "family sentiments" school. See also Mary Lyndon Shanley. "The History of the Family in Modern England: Review Essay," *Signs* 4, no. 4 (Summer 1979): 740–50.

13. Stack; and Brett Williams, "The Trip Takes Us: Chicano Migrants to the Prairie" (Ph.D. diss., University of Illinois at Urbana-Champaign, 1975).

14. David Schneider and Raymond T. Smith,

Class Differences and Sex Roles in American Kinship and Family Structure (Englewood Cliffs, N.J.: Prentice-Hall, Inc., 1973), esp. 27.

15. See Nelson Graburn, ed., *Readings in Kinship and Social Structure* (New York: Harper & Row, 1971), esp. 3–4.

16. The moral mother/cult of domesticity is analyzed in Barbara Welter, "The Cult of True Womanhood, 1820–1860," *American Quarterly* 18, no. 2 (Summer 1966): 151–74; Nancy Cott, *The Bonds of Womanhood: "Women's Sphere" in New England, 1780–1835* (New Haven, Conn.: Yale University Press, 1977); and Ruth Bloch, "American Feminine Ideals in Transition: The Rise of the Moral Mother, 1785–1815," *Feminist Studies* 4, no. 2 (June 1978): 101–26. The description of the general political-economic shift in the United States is based on Harry Braverman, *Labor and Monopoly Capital: The Degradation of Work in the Twentieth century* (New York: Monthly Review Press, 1974); Peter Dobkin Hall, "Family Structure and Economic Organization: Massachusetts Merchants, 1700–1850," in *Family and Kin in Urban Communities, 1700–1950,* ed. Tamara K. Hareven (New York: New Viewpoints, 1977), 38–61; Michael Anderson, "Family, Household and the Industrial Revolution," in *The American Family in Social-Historical Perspective,* ed. Michael Gordon (New York: St. Martin's Press, 1978), 38–50; Tamara K. Hareven, *Amoskeag: Life and Work in an American Factory City* (New York: Pantheon Books, 1978); Richard Edwards, *Contested Terrain: The Transformation of the Workplace in the Twentieth Century* (New York: Basic Books, 1979); Mary Ryan, *The Cradle of the Middle Class: The Family in Oneida County, New York, 1790–1865* (Cambridge: Cambridge University Press, 1981); Alice Kessler-Harris, *Out to Work: A History of Wage-earning Women in the United States* (New York: Oxford University Press, 1982).

17. Ryan, 231–32.

18. Sylvia Junko Yanagisako, "Family and Household: The Analysis of Domestic Groups," *Annual Review of Anthropology* 8 (1979): 161–205.

19. See Donald J. Treiman and Heidi I. Hartmann, eds., *Women, Work and Wages: Equal Pay for Jobs of Equal Value* (Washington, D.C.: National Academy Press, 1981).

20. Lamphere (n. 4 above); Jane Fishburne Collier, "Women in Politics," in Rosaldo and Lamphere, eds. (n. 4 above), 89–96.

21. Nancy Folbre and Heidi I. Hartmann, "The Rhetoric of Self-Interest: Selfishness, Altruism, and Gender in Economic Theory," in *The Consequences of Economic Rhetoric,* ed. Arjo Klamer and Donald McCloskey (New York: Cambridge University Press, 1988).

IX.
Gender, Ritual, and Religion

In many nonwestern societies women's ritual roles are central and indispensable to community cohesion and well-being. In contrast, in Anglo-European cultures women's religious activities tend to be secondary and marginal because of the preeminence of men in both organizational hierarchies and doctrine. Anthropological research has long recognized that religious systems reflect, support, and carry forward patterns of social organization and central values of a society. What has not been sufficiently recognized is the interrelationships of men and women in the perpetuation of social life through religious activities.

The study of the ritual activities of women has often been embedded in analyses of life cycle events, such as the Nkang'a girl's puberty ritual among the Ndembu of Central Africa (Turner 1968:198) or pregnancy and childbirth rituals in Asia (Jacobson 1989; Laderman 1983). With the exception of this area of research, the study of women and religion has often been neglected, despite the fact that women are prominent in re-

ligious activities. As a result of a renewed interest in gender in various cultures, scholars have begun to explore how the religious experience of women is different from that of men, whether and how women become ritual specialists, what religious functions they perform and the degree to which these are private or public, and, finally, what implications these ritual activities have for female prestige and status.

This has led, in some cultural contexts, to an attempt to formulate a more complete ethnographic picture. For example, in the literature on Australian aborigines, where there is a good deal of debate about gender roles, a number of ethnologists have asserted that the dominance of senior men is sustained by their control of sacred knowledge and that their position is recognized by both men and women in the culture (Warner 1937; White 1975; Bern 1979). This viewpoint has been challenged by Diane Bell (1981), who notes that male anthropologists have underestimated and under-reported the religious life of Australian aboriginal women.

She argues that "both men and women have rituals that are closed to the other, both men and women allow the other limited attendance at certain of their rituals, and, finally, there are ceremonies in which both men and women exchange knowledge and together celebrate their membership in one society and their duty to maintain the law of their ancestors" (1981:319).

Bell focuses in particular on the love rituals of women, rituals that originally were viewed by ethnologists as magic and therefore deviant, unimportant, and marginal to the central decision-making realm of men. In contrast, Bell suggests that in the celebration of these rituals, used by women to establish and maintain marriages of their own choosing, "women clearly perceived themselves as independent operators in a domain where they exercised power and autonomy based on their dreaming affiliations with certain tracts of lands. These rights are recognized and respected by the whole society" (1981:322). The love rituals of Australian aboriginal women are, in short, by no means peripheral to the society. They are underwritten by Dreamtime Law and feared by men who are often unaware that they are being performed and unable to negate their power. Through their rituals some Australian aboriginal women have, as Hamilton (1981) suggests, a mechanism with which to challenge the ideology of male superiority that is expressed in male ritual.

Mathews (in this book) provides us with another example of an important arena of religious activity—the civil-religious hierarchy or cargo system in Mesoamerica—that has long been considered a public and exclusively male arena. If women were mentioned at all in studies of the cargo system, it was for their peripheral roles in food preparation. Based on her research in the state of Oaxaca in Mexico, Mathews begins by pointing out that an application of the domestic-public model (see Part III) to an understanding of these religious ceremonies obscures the significant ritual roles of women because it places the cargo in the public sphere of activity and fails to acknowledge the importance of the household unit. Rather than oppose men and women within a rigid domestic-public model, Mathews emphasizes the parallel and interdependent roles of men and women in the execution of

cargo. Male cargo holders (mayordomos) organize and coordinate the activities of men, and female cargo holders (mayordomas) organize and coordinate the activities of women. Both share in the prestige gained from service at the end of their year of responsibility.

If Oaxacan women have an important and prestige-conferring role within the religious sphere of cargo activity, similar opportunities are denied them within the civil sphere. Thus Mathews explores the impact of the penetration of the state (see Part VII) on the lives of women. A sexual divide-and-rule state policy, she argues, makes men into social adults and women into domestic wards whose dealings with the public sphere becomes restricted. Prestige in local institutions is undermined by its absence in extracommunity institutions, and as civil offices assume increasing importance at the expense of cargo offices, the position of women is eroded.

In contrast with the underestimation of women's religious roles in the literature on Australian aborigines and the Mesoamerican cargo system, studies of sub-Saharan Africa have long recognized that the ritual life of women is both significant and highly elaborated. In this region, women are involved in complex ceremonies of initiation; they are engaged in witchcraft and divination (Mendonsa 1979; Ngubane 1977); they act as spirit mediums and healers (Green 1989; Sargent 1989); they lead and participate in possession cults (Berger 1976); and they form their own secret societies (MacCormack 1979).

In Africa, and elsewhere around the world, female religious practitioners are often conceived of as women apart. They frequently transcend local cultural definitions of womanhood and are recognized as having extraordinary characteristics. Kendall (in this book) notes that Korean women who become shamans (*mansin*) stand above the social and economic constraints generally imposed on a proper Korean wife and mother. The *mansin* occupies an ambiguous status similar to that of other "glamorous but morally dubious female marginals, the actress, the female entertainer, and the prostitute." Though not always accorded respect, the *mansin* wears the costumes and speaks with the authority of the gods. *Mansin* and their rituals are, in Kendall's view, "integral components of Korean family and village religion. Within this religious system, women and shamans perform essential ritual tasks that complement men's ritual tasks" (1985:25).

Women in other cultural contexts use spirit possession and trance as an outlet for the stress that derives from their social and material deprivation and subordination (Broch 1985; Hamer and Hamer 1966; Lewis 1966, 1969; Morsy 1979; Pressel 1973). As Danforth (1989:99) argues with regard to Firewalking (Anastenaria) in northern Greece, "through these rituals women seek to address the discrepancies that characterize the relationship between an official ideology of male dominance and a social reality in which women actually exercise a significant degree of power. Spirit possession . . . provides a context for the resolution of conflict often associated with gender roles and gender identity." However, in Korea, rather than serving as an outlet for stress, possession is the vehicle whereby a *mansin*, as a recognized ritual practitioner, ministers to the needs of other women who are in turn the ritual representatives of their families.

Korean housewives come to the *mansin* for therapeutic answers to a range of personal and household problems, for divinations about the future and prospects for the coming year, and for female solidarity and a "venting of the spleen" (Kendall 1985:25). Women's rituals in Korea, like those in some other parts of the world, are both practical and expressive. As Mernissi (1978) suggests, based on her research in Morocco, female devotional societies provide a tightly knit community of supporters and advisers. The Christian Science movement founded in America by Mary Baker Eddy in the late nineteenth century was a healing religion that also offered middle-class women a "socially acceptable alternative to the stifling Victorian stereotypes then current" (Fox 1989:98).

Mama Lola, the Vodou priestess (*manbo*) described by Brown (in this book) is also a ritual specialist, diviner, and healer working in New York who, when she is possessed, "acts out the social and psychological forces that define and often contain the lives of contemporary Haitian woman." Through ritual, Mama Lola empowers her clients. This phenomenon of psychological empowerment is characteristic of other religious

systems; it is described by Danforth (1989) in his discussion of the New Age Firewalking cult in the United States and by Wadley (1989) in her analysis of the active control over their lives that north Indian village women gain through their ritual activities.

Mama Lola maintains a very personal relationship with two female spirits. To one she stands in the role of child to a spiritual mother and thereby metaphorically expresses an important bond within Haitian culture and society that is manifested in her own relationship with her daughter Maggie. This ritually embedded mother-child metaphor can be found in other parts of the world where women healers meet the physical and emotional needs of their patients just as mothers meet the needs of their children (Wedenoja 1989; Kerewsky-Halpern 1989). If one of Mama Lola's female spirits represents the nurturing side of women in relation to their children, the other represents the romantic side in relation to men.

In Haitian Vodou the diverse roles of women are projected into the religious sphere. This is equally true of other religious traditions. In Catholic cultures values about ideal womanhood are sanctified by the image of the Virgin Mary, who represents submission, humility, serenity, and long suffering (Stevens 1973). In Mexico, for example, Eve and the Virgin Mary are contrasting images that "encode the cycle of reproduction within the domestic group. When a woman is nursing and sexually continent she resembles the Virgin. When she submits to sex, she is more like Eve" (Ingham 1986:76). Hindu goddesses are also multifaceted; they are mothers, mediators, and protectresses.

According to Preston (1985:13), there is a connection "between the role of women in Indian life and the special position of female deities in the Hindu pantheon. Though Indian women are supposed to be absolutely devoted to their husbands who are respected as embodiments of the deity, women may also reign supreme in their own domains as mothers of their children." In Dinaan Hinduism the Great Goddess takes several forms, some good and some evil. Babb (1975:226) suggests that these two aspects reflect an opposition in male and female principles: "When female dominates male, the pair is sinister; when male dominates female the pair is benign."

Of importance, then, to some students of the relationship between gender and religion is the question of how women are portrayed in religious symbolism and doctrine. One of the most intriguing representations of women in religious thought is the Shaker conception of a female God. The Shakers were a millenarian Christian group who arrived on the shores of America in the late eighteenth century. As Procter-Smith (in this book) points out, long before recent feminists began to refer to God as "she," the Shakers believed in God the mother to complement God the father and conceived of their leader, Ann Lee, as a manifestation of the second coming of Christ in female form.

This millenial thinking empowered women and permitted the eradication of women's subordination. Shaker men and women shared spiritual authority and the leadership roles that were specified by this authority. Long before Engels (see Part VII), the Shakers appear to have recognized that property, marriage, and sexuality may undermine the status of women, and they therefore worked to eliminate these phenomena both ideologically and practically from their way of life. They upheld celibacy and the communal ownership of property. Procter-Smith observes, however, that the Shakers were not fully successful in their efforts. A patriarchal and hierarchical model persisted, as did a division of labor that followed broader societal patterns for what men and women do. To this Setta (1989:231) has added the observation that Shaker theology was dominated by men while women were the spirit mediums, a distinction in her view that parallels a frequent human division "between men as scholars and thinkers and women as vehicles for religious experience."

Shakerism in its original form had much in common with some of the female-oriented religious cults described by anthropologists working in other parts of the world. It too was based in spirit possession and other forms of ecstatic behavior. It too was organized around the metaphor of mother who gives birth to, nurtures, and protects her child believers. It too provided an outlet for women who were otherwise constrained by the social institutions of late eigh-

teenth- and nineteenth-century American society.

We have taken the approach in this book that what it means to be male and female (i.e., gender) is learned and shaped within a cultural context. Religious symbols are a powerful mechanism by which culturally appropriate gender messages are transmitted. As Bynum observes, "It is no longer possible to study religious practice or religious symbols without taking gender—that is, the cultural experience of being male or female—into account" (1986:1–2). In addition, through participation and leadership in ritual, women may enhance their social position. Involvement in religious activities may also generate a sense of female or community solidarity through membership in a congregation or participation in ritual functions.

REFERENCES

Babb, Lawrence. 1975. *The Divine Hierarchy*. New York: Columbia University Press.

Bell, Diane. 1981. Women's Business Is Hard Work: Central Australian Aboriginal Women's Love Rituals. *Signs* 7: 314–337.

Berger, Iris. 1976. Rebels or Status-Seekers? Women as Spirit Mediums in East Africa. In Nancy J. Hafkin and Edna G. Bay (eds.). *Women in Africa*, pp. 157–182. Stanford: Stanford University Press.

Bern, J. 1979. Ideology and Domination: Toward a Reconstruction of Australian Aboriginal Social Formation. *Oceania* 50: 118–132.

Broch, Harald Beyer. 1985. "Crazy Women Are Performing in Sombali": A Possession-Trance Ritual on Bonerate, Indonesia. *Ethos* 13: 262–282.

Bynum, Caroline Walker. 1986. Introduction: The Complexity of Symbols. In Caroline Walker Bynum, Steven Harrell and Paula Richman (eds.). *Gender and Religion: On the Complexity of Symbols*, pp. 1–20. Boston: Beacon.

Danforth, Loring M. 1989. *Firewalking and Religious Healing: The Anastenaria of Greece and the American Firewalking Movement*. Princeton: Princeton University Press.

Fox, Margery. 1989. The Socioreligious Role of the Christian Science Practitioner. In Carole Shepherd McClain (ed.). *Women as Healers: Cross-Cultural Perspectives*, pp. 98–114. New Brunswick, NJ: Rutgers University Press.

Green, Edward C. 1989. Mystical Black Power: The

Calling to Diviner-Mediumship in Southern Africa. In Carole Shepherd McClain (ed.). *Women as Healers: Cross-Cultural Perspectives,* pp. 186–200. New Brunswick, NJ: Rutgers University Press.

Hamer, J. and I. Hamer. 1966. Spirit Possession and its Socio-psychological Implications among the Sidamo of Southwest Ethiopia. *Ethnology* 5: 392–408.

Hamilton, Annette. 1981. A Complex Strategical Situation: Gender and Power in Aboriginal Australia. In N. Grieve and P. Grimshaw (eds.). *Australian Women: Feminist Perspectives,* pp. 69–85. Melbourne: Oxford University Press.

Ingham, John. 1986. *Mary, Michael and Lucifer.* Austin: University of Texas Press.

Jacobson, Doranne. 1989. Golden Handprints and Red-Painted Feet: Hindu Childbirth Rituals in Central India. In Nancy Auer Falk and Rita M. Gross (eds.). *Unspoken Worlds: Women's Religious Lives,* pp. 59–71. Belmont, CA: Wadsworth Publishing Co.

Kendall, Laurel. 1985. *Shamans, Housewives, and Other Restless Spirits: Women in Korean Ritual Life.* Honolulu: University of Hawaii Press.

Kerewsky-Halpern, Barbara. 1989. Healing with Mother Metaphors: Serbian Conjurers' Word Magic. In Carole Shepherd McClain (ed.). *Women as Healers: Cross-Cultural Perspectives,* pp. 115–135. New Brunswick, NJ: Rutgers University Press.

Laderman, Carol. 1983. *Wives and Midwives: Childbirth and Nutrition in Rural Malaysia.* Berkeley: University of California Press.

Lewis, I.M. 1966. Spirit Possession and Deprivation Cults. *Man* 1: 307–329.

————. 1969. *Religion in Context: Cults and Charisma.* Cambridge Bennetta: Cambridge University Press.

MacCormack, Carol P. 1979. Sande: The Public Face of a Secret Society. In Bennetta Jules-Rosette (ed.). *New Religions of Africa,* pp. 27–39. Norwood, NJ: Ablex.

Mendonsa, Eugene L. 1979. The Position of Women in the Sisala Divination Cult. In Bennetta Jules-Rosette (ed.). *The New Religions of Africa,* pp. 57–67. Norwood, NJ: Ablex.

Mernissi, Fatima. 1978. Women, Saints and Sanctuaries. *Signs* 3: 101–12.

Morsy, Soheir. 1979. Sex Roles, Power, and Illness. *American Ethnologist* 5: 137–150.

Ngubane, H. 1977. *Body and Mind in Zulu Medicine: An Ethnography of Health and Disease in Nyuswa-Zulu Thought and Practice.* New York: Academic Press.

Pressel, Esther. 1973. Umbanda in São Paulo: Religious Innovations in a Developing Society. In Erika Bourguignon (ed.). *Religion, Altered States of Consciousness and Social Change,* pp. 264–318. Columbus: Ohio State University Press.

Preston, James J. 1985. *Cult of the Goddess: Social and Religious Change in a Hindu Temple.* Prospect Heights, IL: Waveland. (Orig pub. 1980).

Sanday, Peggy. 1974. Female Status in the Public Domain. In Michelle Z. Rosaldo and Louise Lamphere (eds.). *Woman, Culture, and Society,* pp. 189–206. Stanford: Stanford University Press.

Sargent, Carolyn. 1989. Women's Roles and Women Healers in Contemporary Rural and Urban Benin. In Carole Shepherd McClain (ed.). *Women as Healers: Cross-Cultural Perspectives,* pp. 204–218. New Brunswick, NJ: Rutgers University Press.

Setta, Susan M. 1989. When Christ Is a Woman: Theology and Practice in the Shaker Tradition. In Nancy Auer Falk and Rita M. Gross (eds.). *Unspoken Worlds: Women's Religious Lives,* pp. 221–234. Belmont, CA: Wadsworth.

Stevens, Evelyn. 1973. Marianismo: The Other Face of Machismo in Latin America. In Ann Pescatello (ed.). *Female and Male in Latin America,* pp. 89–101. Pittsburgh: University of Pittsburgh Press.

Turner, Victor. 1968. *Drums of Affliction.* Oxford: Clarendon Press.

Wadley, Susan S. 1989. Hindu Women's Family and Household Rites in a North Indian Village. In Nancy Auer Falk and Rita M. Gross (eds.). *Unspoken Worlds: Women's Religious Lives,* pp. 72–81. Belmont, CA: Wadsworth.

Warner, William Lloyd. 1937. *A Black Civilization: A Study of an Australian Tribe.* New York: Harper & Row.

Wedenoja, William. 1989. Mothering and the Practice of "Balm" in Jamaica. In Carole Shepherd McClain (ed.). *Women as Healers: Cross-Cultural Perspectives,* pp. 76–97. New Brunswick, NJ: Rutgers University Press.

White, I. 1975. Sexual Conquest and Submission in the Myths of Central Australia. In L. Hiatt (ed.). *Australian Aboriginal Mythology,* pp. 123–142. Canberra: Australian Institute of Aboriginal Studies.

"We Are Mayordomo": A Reinterpretation of Women's Roles in the Mexican Cargo System

Holly F. Mathews

Nearly two decades have passed since the feminist movement inspired a resurgence of interest in the study of gender roles. Much of the initial research during this period was directed towards overcoming a generation of male bias in anthropological studies by filling in the missing portion of the ethnographic record on women. To analyze this new information on gender, feminist anthropologists formulated a theory of social roles which emphasized a split between the public sphere of male activity and the domestic sphere of female activity. The domestic/public theory as first articulated by Chodorow (1974), Lamphere (1974), Rosaldo (1974), and others holds that (1) familial and extrafamilial realms constitute separate domains cross-culturally; (2) women are universally associated with the family or domestic sphere while men universally control the public or political sphere; (3) and, as a result, women's roles and activities are always subordinate to, or are accorded less value than, the roles and activities of men.

A number of anthropologists (for example, Pearlman 1980; Rosaldo 1980; Sacks 1979) have pointed out the ethnocentric assumptions that underlie the domestic/public model and acknowledged the limitations involved in applying it cross-culturally. As Sacks writes, the domestic/public model projects:

> what is a fairly recent bifurcation of family and society into a universal and natural human con-

Reproduced by permission of the American Anthropological Association from *American Ethnologist* 12:2, May 1985. Not for further reproduction.

dition. In this anthropology has ethnocentrically adopted a basic premise of industrial capitalism [1979:61].

Anthropologists who start with such an ethnocentric premise tend to emphasize the separation between male and female roles and seldom investigate the ways in which such roles interrelate and function within specific sociocultural contexts. Consequently, many anthropological studies fail to capture a sense of the complexity and diversity characteristic of gender roles cross-culturally. Yet without a basic understanding of role diversity, anthropologists cannot begin to assess the differential implications of socioeconomic change for men and women in particular societies. Although some anthropologists (e.g., Collier and Rosaldo 1981; Ortner and Whitehead 1981; Sanday 1981; Sacks 1979) are currently using new models to study gender roles, the empirical consequences of *not* using the domestic/public theory have yet to be explored. Data on the religious ceremonial system known as the *cargo* in the Mexican community of San Miguel are used to illustrate some of these consequences.

Specifically I argue that the use of a domestic/public model led many anthropologists to view cargo service as an exclusively public and hence male domain of activity. A detailed examination of the way in which male and female cargo roles interrelate reveals, however, that cargo service is undertaken not by individual men but by household units on the basis of wealth. Male and female household heads assume parallel roles and responsibilities for ritual, and the participation of each sex is crucial for successful service.

In the newly emerging sphere of civil service, however, male and female roles articulate in a fundamentally different way. Modern civil offices, instituted by the Mexican national government, are held increasingly by individuals elected on the basis of personal skills such as literacy in the Spanish language and experience in interacting with Ladino elites. Women, for reasons outlined in the following sections, usually lack such skills and hence civil offices are dominated by men.

This analysis of role relationships in the religious and civil spheres provides a basis for predicting the likely outcome of socioeconomic changes occurring in San Miguel. To the degree that the ritual cargo system is breaking down, and separate civil offices assuming importance in the administration of community affairs, women are being deprived of opportunities to hold community posts.

THE TRADITIONAL CARGO SYSTEM

Mexico contains hundreds of autonomous Indian communities largely responsible for regulating their own internal affairs. In the past the civil-religious hierarchy or cargo system, instituted in Mexico by Spanish colonial authorities, was the characteristic administrative organization found in these communities. Cancian describes the cargo as "a system in which adult males serve in a series of hierarchically arranged offices devoted to both political and ceremonial aspects of community life" (1967:283).

These offices are ranked in terms of levels of service and authority. An individual begins service in a low-level office before being eligible to serve in a higher ranked one. In the past individuals alternated between civil and religious offices in the course of lifetime service. Since there are more offices at the bottom than at the top, those individuals who complete service at all levels are called elders or *principales*, and community members accord them great respect and prestige (Carrasco 1961:484).

Tenure in cargo offices rotates annually and individuals serve without payment. Elders generally appoint people to cargos, and service involves the officeholders in considerable expense since they must sponsor festivals and banqueting in conjunction with the saints' days and religious holidays celebrated by the Catholic Church. In return for service individuals earn prestige and respect, which sometimes translate into political influence as well.

ANTHROPOLOGICAL INTERPRETATIONS OF MALE AND FEMALE CARGO ROLES

The anthropological literature on the cargo system in Mexico is extensive. Descriptions of the system are varied and often reflect intercommunity variation in cargo organization. In addition, ethnographic reports span a 50-year period during which the cargo system in many communities was undergoing rapid change in response to outside pressures. Consequently, it is often difficult to distinguish differences in cargo interpretation arising from the use of particular theoretical models from those arising out of intercommunity variation and historical change. Nonetheless, certain general trends in the description and analysis of male and female roles can be traced through the various stages of cargo research.

The earliest Mesoamerican ethnographies to include descriptions of the cargo system were produced by a generation of anthropologists (both male and female) who were trained to assume that a description of the male world was an adequate description of the society at large (see Rogers 1978:131). Regarded as the main political and religious actors, men were widely reported to be the only significant participants in cargo service, and cargos were said to rank individual men in terms of relative prestige (Beals 1945; De La Fuente 1949; Foster 1967; Hinton 1964; Lewis 1960; Parsons 1936; Vogt 1969). Few anthropologists of this generation mentioned women's involvement in cargo service, and when they did, women were described as peripheral participants involved primarily in the preparation of food for ritual (Cancian 1965).

These ethnographers did note, however, that a man's chance for a successful cargo career often depended on his ability to raise resources from his kin network. Presumably women, as members of these networks, were important in supporting male cargo careers. This point, however, is often overlooked in many early studies. Cancian (1965), for example, analyzed the importance of labor for cargo service in Zinacantan, Mexico but assumed that only the aid given by brothers and sons was useful to the cargoholder. Consequently, he asked informants to list the reasons why brothers and sons were helpful in cargo service but neglected to ask the corresponding question about sisters and daughters. Cancian's statistical analysis is designed to test if men with more brothers and sons participate to a greater degree in the system than those with fewer. Although his prediction that they would was only weakly confirmed, Cancian made no corresponding attempt to test the effects of greater and lesser numbers of female kin on such participation (1965:103–106).

In summary, although these early ethnographers sometimes acknowledged the ritual roles played by the wives of cargoholders, for the most part they did not see female participation as significant in terms of the larger system.[1] A subsequent generation of anthropologists influenced by the feminist movement began to rectify this situation by focusing more attention on women's cargo roles. Iwanska (1966), for example, found that Mazahua Indians in Mexico did not see men as dominant in the religious system. Rather, the Mazahua referred to husband and wife as joint officeholders saying, "we are *mayordomo*," or "they are *mayordomo*" (1966:78). Such parallel titles to office were extended to men in situations where the women held formal title. As Iwanska writes:

> I was told on one occasion, for instance, that such and such a man was elected to the office of *La Señora* [the lady]—which simply meant in the language of the Mazahua from El Nopal

that his wife was elected to a political-religious group called *Las Señoras* [1966:178–179].

Similarly, Chinas (1973) documents the active role of women in the religious activities of the Isthmus Zapotecs of Oaxaca, Mexico. Chinas found that households were involved in religious participation, and that husbands and wives held joint title to cargo offices. If a single head of household was appointed to a religious office, he or she had to choose a partner of the opposite sex to assist in preparations. Even when the original *mayordoma* was a woman, the prestige accrued for service went to her household and not to the man chosen to assist her (1973:71).

While these feminist-oriented anthropologists succeeded in documenting women's cargo activities, they still tended to conclude that men's cargo roles were more public, formal, and important than women's. Chinas, for example, wrote in her analysis that "where formalized roles occur in complementary pairs by sex, the male role of the pair is normally accorded higher status than the female role" (1973:96).

She later adds: "An examination of the formalized roles in the Isthmus Zapotec public domain makes it clear that men and male roles carry higher status than women and female roles" (1973:99).

Yet apart from the presumed segregation of male and female roles into public and private spheres, Chinas gives no evidence to support this status differential. Her analysis illustrates one of the problems inherent in the use of a domestic/public framework—the framework itself predisposes researchers to view male and female roles as separate and somehow different in kind. The usual interpretation arising from such a view is that female activities, being by definition private and informal, must somehow be less important and prestigious than male activities which are, by definition, public and formal. In reading such accounts, however, it is difficult to determine if community members themselves agree with such an interpretation, or if the interpretation is, instead, an artifact of the theoretical model.

In an update (1983) to her research, Chinas acknowledges this very problem and writes:

> Today I would qualify my former statement regarding the higher status of men's formalized public roles. Although fewer women hold formalized public roles than men, when they do so their status and the respect accorded them seems to be equal to men's [1983:116].

This quotation, however, highlights a second and enduring difficulty that stems from the use of the domestic/public framework. The model assumes that male and female roles can be divided into discrete categories which can then be opposed and compared across all domains of social life. This line of reasoning fails to recognize the variation likely to occur in role relationships across domains of activity.

In this paper I argue that a major consequence of *not* using the domestic/public model is the opportunity to move beyond static, oppositional analyses to look, instead, at the ways in which male and female roles interrelate and function in specific contexts. Such an analysis paves the way for a more sophisticated understanding of the social and cultural factors affecting gender role organization and enables us to assess the potential impact of socioeconomic change on male and female roles in different contexts.

In the following sections of this paper I explore the consequences of moving beyond a domestic/public model in analyzing gender roles in the Mexican community of San Miguel. I use statistical data to demonstrate that religious cargos in San Miguel are held not by individual men but by those household units that possess sufficient economic and labor resources to meet the obligations of service. Qualitative data show that male and female household heads are considered to hold joint title to cargo offices and have parallel roles and duties. The prestige earned in service, moreover, accrues not to individual office-holders but to the household.

I also present statistical data that demonstrate a shift away from household-based service in the newly evolving civil sphere. Political offices were once dominated by individuals from households that had successfully completed service in the religious cargo system. Today, however, this pattern is changing, and individuals are now being elected on the basis of specific skills such as fluency in the Spanish language and experience interacting with outsiders regardless of household wealth. Because women in San Miguel often have difficulty acquiring these specific skills, they are seldom elected to office. Consequently, as the civil sphere assumes increasing importance over the religious in regulating community affairs, women are being deprived of opportunities to hold community posts.

THE RESEARCH COMMUNITY

San Miguel is a community of 2000 people located in the central valley of the state of Oaxaca, Mexico.[2] Inhabitants of the community are of mixed Zapotec and Mixtec descent who now label themselves ethnically as mestizos. The community economy is based on mixed cash and subsistence farming primarily of maize, beans, vegetables, and tobacco. Men and women also engage in a variety of other activities designed to provide supplemental cash income for the household (see Mathews 1982).

The basic social unit in San Miguel is the domestic group or household which consists of co-resident individuals, usually kin, who cooperate in the production and consumption of resources. There are 354 households in San Miguel of which 322, or 91 percent, are headed by men and 32, or 9 percent, are headed by women. Kinship is traced bilaterally and the preferred postmarital residence pattern is patrilocal. In theory the eldest son assumes the headship of the household upon the death of his father. Daughters marry out and go to live in the compounds of their husbands. In practice, however, actual household composition varies as the units move through a developmental cycle and respond to changing economic and social conditions.

When the eldest son marries and brings his wife home the extended network begins as father and son cooperate in farming lands held by individual household members. Over time other sons may marry and bring wives into the compound. After the parents die, the residential groups usually consist of either a single man, his wife and children or a group of brothers, their wives and children. As the children marry, the cycle begins again. If a family has no sons, daughters may bring in husbands to live and work on family lands. Unmarried and widowed daughters are also assured residence in the natal compound and may add to the size of the household unit.

In recent years the increasing birth rate, combined with the limited supply of arable land in San Miguel, has acted to alter slightly the typical pattern of household composition. Many young men have migrated out of the community leading to an increase in the number of unmarried young women remaining at home along with a decrease in the numbers of households consisting of co-resident brothers. Generally it is the eldest son who remains in the community residing with his parents in the household compound.

In San Miguel the majority of households (62 percent) consist of some variant of the extended family described above. Yet a large number of co-resident kin does not necessarily guarantee a household economic success. Household wealth is limited by the amount and quality of land available to household members; access to supplies of irrigation water; ownership of, or access to, plow oxen and agricultural equipment; and the amount of supplemental cash income brought in by household residents.

The Religious Cargo System

The religious cargo system in San Miguel consists of two distinct sets of religious offices known as *cofradías* (sodalities) and *hermandades* (brotherhoods) dedicated to the care of different saints in the Catholic hierarchy.[3] Cofradía and hermandad officeholders, known as *mayordomos*, are chosen each year and must organize and carry out all the rituals and festivities associated with the particular saints in their charge. Cargo service is costly and it often takes household members 10 to 15 years to pay off the debts incurred during

their tenure in office. Although the mayordomo's household bears the brunt of the expense associated with cargo service, much assistance is rendered through the institution of *guelaguetza*, which is a system of reciprocal economic exchange involving both resources and labor.

Because of the time and expense involved, community members once regarded cargo service as a burden, and in the past they often had to be coerced to serve. The town judge or *alcalde* appointed officeholders, and those who refused to serve could be jailed. On a more indirect level community members would use gossip, ridicule, and even ostracism against the members of households that consistently refused to participate in the system.

Over the past 20 years, however, major demographic and economic changes within San Miguel have acted to alter this pattern of participation. An overall increase in population combined with the introduction of cash cropping has created a situation where the demand for service exceeds the number of offices available in the religious sphere. Community members have adopted a "waiting-list" solution similar to the one described by Cancian (1965:174–194) for Zinacantan. Community members now volunteer for religious service, and many offices have long waiting lists. The waiting time currently varies between three and ten years with those offices perceived as more prestigious having longer waiting lists (Mathews 1982:56).

When the civil-religious hierarchy was first instituted in Mexico, Spanish colonial authorities tended to recognize men as official heads of household and often decreed that only men could hold formal title to official civil and religious posts (Nash 1980; Silverblatt 1980). Perhaps, as a consequence, male household heads in San Miguel have been listed traditionally on official cargo rolls as festival sponsors or mayordomos. Community members, however, persist in recognizing male/female couples as joint titleholders to religious office. If the official household head is a man, then he must select a woman (usually but not necessarily his wife) to serve with him as the co-officeholder or *mayordoma*. She not only assumes the companion title but is also charged with the responsibility for administering women's activities during the cargo festival. In the absence of a male household head, the senior woman from a household eligible for service will be officially listed as the officeholder. She, in turn, must select a man, usually a relative, to fulfill the companion obligations of service. In San Miguel no religious office is held by any individual of either sex who cannot provide an appropriate partner of the opposite sex. Thus while community cargo rolls usually list men as "official" mayordomos, service is viewed by community members as a household responsibility, and parallel titles are conferred on male and female representatives of the household.

As a pair, the mayordomos plan the festivities and make decisions about the personnel to be invited to perform important ritual duties. During the festival, the male mayordomo organizes and coordinates the activities of men which may include the preparation and decoration of altars, the arrangement of materials to be used in the rituals, the making of candles and fireworks displays, the roundup and slaughter of animals for feasts, and the performance of music and recitations during ritual. The female mayordoma organizes and coordinates the activities of women, which may include the preparation and cleaning of costumes and adornments for ritual, the making of decorative displays for altars, the preparation of food for feasts, and the performance of songs and recitations during ritual.

Both mayordomos greet guests, record contributions, and receive civil officials, and both are publicly acknowledged as the sponsors of the festival. Upon completion of the religious festivities, the mayordomos share in the prestige accrued for service. Praise for success as well as blame for failure is attributed to the couple, and those men and women who have completed a number of religious cargos are treated with respect by the community as a whole. They are invited as guests, not laborers, to other religious functions and upon arrival are seated first; served ritual drinks and food ahead of others; and are often asked to advise the current mayordomos on ritual procedures.

As one informant who had himself been listed "officially" as the sponsor of five cargos explained it:

> To complete service you need a lot of assistance. The mayordomo has to recruit male helpers and organize their work for the festival. His partner [compañera] must recruit female helpers and organize their work for the festival. Without both—a mayordomo and a mayordoma—you could not have a festival. They work together and without one or the other it would be too much; it would be impossible to complete the obligation. So if there is no man in the home, a woman must look for a kinsman to help her—maybe her brother or her brother-in-law. They work together because they are a pair.

In general, the expense of sponsoring a cargo, both in terms of resources and labor, is so great that only one couple in a household will be active in the religious system. Consequently, in extended family households in San Miguel, the elder generation must make a decision to "retire" or end a career of religious service before a younger couple is free to begin festival sponsorship.

During my three-year study in San Miguel I made a count of all religious posts available and kept records of the individuals officially listed as officeholders on cargo rolls. There are a total of 61 religious offices that must be filled on an annual basis. Of these 61 posts, 25 are filled by people sponsoring religious festivals. Another 36 positions involve people serving as the officers of the religious brotherhoods. In theory tenure in all of these positions rotates annually. In actuality, however, some individuals continued to occupy the same offices throughout the three-year study period. Consequently, over the study period a total of 138 offices were filled by appointment of which 129 were listed on official records as held by men and 9 by women.[4]

The Civil Administration

The civil administration in San Miguel is concerned with public works, the administration of justice, and the maintenance of relations with the outside world. Officers are elected by community members and serve three-year terms. The *presidente municipal* or mayor is the principal authority in the community, and his major responsibility is to handle dealings with the larger governmental system outside the community. The *sindico* or vice-mayor assists the mayor and also handles public works and issues related to social welfare including the recording of births and deaths in the community. There are seven councilmen or *regidores* who are responsible for opening and maintaining the municipal building during the week and who act as heads of municipal committees.

In addition to these elected officials, the presidente also appoints a secretary, a treasurer, and four police chiefs, one for each administrative section of the community. Finally, there is an alcalde or judge and his substitute who are appointed by the presidente to one-year terms of service. The alcalde acts as a justice of the peace and listens to disputes brought before the municipal authorities. The alcalde is empowered to render decisions, assess fines of compensation, and jail those guilty of major offenses.

There are also several permanent committees in San Miguel whose members are appointed by the presidente. These include the committee of the dominant political party in Mexico—the PRI (*Partido Revolucionario Institucional*), the Committee of the Parents of Schoolchildren, the Health Committee, and the Committee for the Celebration of Mexican Independence day. Other temporary committees are formed as needed.

A number of scholars hypothesize that in the cargo system, as first instituted in Mexico, civil officeholding remained dependent upon the successful completion of prior service in the religious sphere. Religious service, in turn, entailed the support and cooperation of household members. This intertwined system of civil and religious service began to change in 1917, however, when the Mexican Constitution decreed that local communities had to elect councils of civil officials who would report directly to state officials (Perez 1968:21). Only men could serve on these councils, since

women in Mexico could not legally vote or hold elective office until 1953 (Elmendorf 1977:158).

The duties of civil officials also changed dramatically as the new system became established. Where officials once had relative autonomy in regulating internal community affairs, they subsequently had to report directly to Ladino elites serving as political officials at the district and state levels (Greenberg 1978; Perez 1968). It became important, therefore, for local officials to be well versed in the dominant Spanish language and have experience in interacting with outsiders. Officials lacking in such skills often had difficulty transacting community business with Ladinos and securing the goods and services needed by their communities. Consequently, over time, good literacy and interactional skills became valued attributes in civil servants, and men possessing these skills began to be elected to office without regard to household wealth or past participation in the religious sphere. The town mayor or presidente summarized it this way:

> The way of doing things has changed since we were young. Before, my father was only a hired worker. He did not have the standing to ask for a mayordomia and his family was too poor to endure the expense. Now, I am still poor, but people respect me. I worked hard. I went to school here and after here I went to the city to learn more. Then I went as a *bracero* to the United States and there I learned what the world is like and how to act. When I came back, people had respect for me, and they asked my advice. I began to work for the town, and the people saw that I worked well with the district officials. And so they elected me presidente.

Just as civil officeholding in San Miguel is no longer dependent on prior religious service, so too the assistance of wives and the availability of household labor is not a prerequisite for service. Men, on the average, spend between eight and ten hours a week in executing the duties of office, and the majority reported no difficulty in reconciling such efforts with the demands of agricultural work. In no instance did any civil official surveyed report the need to call upon the assistance of friends or relatives in discharging the obligations of office.

During my three-year study in San Miguel, I made a count of civil posts in the community and kept lists of the individuals occupying each. There are a total of 31 political offices in San Miguel. Of these, 14 include civil officials elected every three years while the remaining 17 posts are held by individuals appointed on an annual basis by the presidente. Over the study period a total of 61 offices were held by 58 men and 2 women.[5]

DETERMINANTS OF RELIGIOUS AND POLITICAL PARTICIPATION

In contrast to previous studies emphasizing the role of individual men in the cargo, I argue that religious service in San Miguel involves competition between household units. Those households with sufficient resources (here defined to include both wealth and labor) compete for prestige and recognition by volunteering for cargo service. Those households with surplus resources who evince a lack of interest in religious service are often pressured to volunteer by community members in general and family members and friends in particular (see also Walter 1981). In the civil sphere, on the other hand, household wealth is no longer an absolute prerequisite for service. Rather, the basis for service is shifting to emphasize, instead, the possession of certain individual skills, and wealthy, high-status households no longer dominate in the political sphere as they do in the religious.

To measure the extent and nature of household participation in civil and religious offices, I employed two rating scales adapted from the stratification studies of Warner et al. (1960). The Evaluated Participation Scale is used to uncover empirically emic social categories. Informants divided the households of San Miguel into three major social strata and two substrata. I then used an Index of Status Characteristics to obtain a more objective measure of socioeconomic status which I correlated with the assignment of households to

strata by informants. The result was an overall socioeconomic ranking for the 354 households in San Miguel. For ease of presentation, I have collapsed the two substrata into the three larger categories and compared rates of political and civil participation for households in each of these categories (see Table 1).[6]

Religious Service

In the religious sphere cargo rolls listed 129 men and 9 women from 138 different households as the official holders of the religious posts filled during the three-year study period. The data presented in Table 1 show the distribution of participating households by category of socioeconomic status. Of the 92 households in the highest stratum, 68, or 74 percent, are active participants in the religious sphere. Similarly, of the 84 households in the middle stratum, 60, or 71 percent, are active participants. Since membership in these two strata is dependent upon the possession of economic resources, these households would be expected to participate to a significantly greater degree than those in the lowest stratum. This is, in fact, the case since only 10, or 6 percent, of the 178 low-stratum households are active in the religious domain.

If religious service is dependent on socioeconomic status, then a higher percentage of low-status households can be expected not to undertake religious service. The data in

TABLE 1.   Frequency Distribution of Active and Inactive Households in the Religious Cargo System According to Socioeconomic Status

Stratum	Total		Active		Inactive	
	n	$\%$	n	$\%$	n	$\%$
High	92	26	68	74	24	26
Medium	84	24	60	71	24	29
Low	178	50	10	6	168	94
Total	354	100				

$\chi^2 = 165$

$p < .001$

Table 1 show that of the 178 households in the lowest stratum, 168, or 94 percent, were inactive in the religious sphere. Conversely, of the 92 households in the highest stratum, 24, or 26 percent, were inactive, and of the 84 households in the middle stratum, 24, or 29 percent, were inactive. The numbers of inactive households in the two top strata are surprisingly close and seem somewhat higher than might be expected if religious service was completely dependent upon the possession of financial resources.

A closer examination of the circumstances of the 48 inactive households in the upper and middle strata show that in 14 cases households had held religious posts during the ten-year period immediately preceding this study. Since households must "rest" after completing religious service in order to pay off debts and accumulate the resources necessary for future participation, these 14 households can be considered "involved" in religious service although none was currently holding a religious office. An additional 13 of the 48 inactive households were registered on official waiting lists for future religious posts and consequently could also be considered "involved" although not currently active in the religious sphere.

Individuals in an additional 9 of the 48 inactive households were holding civil posts during the study period. When interviewed, those individuals unanimously agreed that the requirements of civil service did not allow them to take on additional obligations in the religious domain. Thus, although they may have had the resources necessary for religious service, these individuals were reluctant to assume dual commitments.

This leaves 12 of the 48 inactive, high-status households to be considered. When interviewed, members in 3 of these 12 households indicated some interest in future religious service. The remaining nine, however, did not participate and indicated no desire to do so. One reason for the inactivity of these households, lack of available labor, will be discussed below.

The data presented thus far suggest that religious service is dominated by households of higher socioeconomic standing in the community. A Chi Square test, moreover, indicates that the level of participation of high-status households is statistically significant (see Table 1). Community members, however, suggest another factor that may be crucial for the successful completion of religious service—the ability to mobilize adult laborers of both sexes. As one informant states:

> To have the cofradía is much work—it is work for a year before with all the visits and planning; then it is work during the year having all the fiestas and making sure everything is right. I could not do it without Micaila [mother-in-law] to help cook the meals and watch the children while I am gone. I could also not have done it without my father-in-law because he has helped a lot with the farm work and seeing that the sharecroppers did not cheat us this year.

That the labor of both sexes is vital is further explained by this informant because:

> The cofradias are divided—there is the work of women and the work of men. You cannot have a festival without rituals. The men, they do the heavy work of building the altar and collecting the plants. They decorate the Church and the house and prepare for ritual. The women get the food ready. They dress the animals, toast the chilies, and cook the meals. They also get the clothes ready for the Saints and repair the costumes and decorations. Then they make sure everything runs smoothly on the day of the festival when the men are drinking. Everybody has their job to do. Women are not good at men's jobs and men do not know anything about food. But all must eat and all must have an altar to pray under. So I direct the men in their activities, and my wife, she has charge of the women.

I investigated the importance of labor resources in religious participation by comparing the numbers of adults (both male and female) present in the households of San Miguel with rates of religious participation. The number of adults in active households averaged 2.9 while the number of adults in inactive households averaged 2.0. A finer breakdown of activity rates relative to the number of adults present in the household is presented in Table 2. The data demonstrate that rates of religious participation increase in accordance with the number of adults present in the household. A statistical test indicates, moreover, that the association between activity level and number of adults is such that those households with three or more adult laborers are significantly more likely to be active in the system than those with two or fewer.

A subsequent comparison of religious activity according to the sex composition of households in San Miguel is recorded in Table 3. The households of San Miguel are grouped into five categories. "Equal" households are those having equal numbers of male and female adult members. This category is subdivided in the table according to whether the members number one male and one female or more than one male and more than one female. The "male predominant" households are those with more male than female adult members. Conversely, the "female predominant" households have more female than male adult members. Finally, the "single-sex" households have only a single male or a single female adult member.

The data show significant differences in activity levels by sex composition of the household. Those "equal" households with two or more male and female members and the "female predominant" households participate more than would be expected if sex composi-

tion made no difference in religious service. It appears that an adequate number of adult members of both sexes are necessary for festival sponsorship, and that those households with two or more adult members of both sexes are significantly more likely to participate than those with fewer. Hence, those households having only one adult member of each sex, and those households with only one adult member of either sex, are significantly less likely to participate in religious service than would be expected if the sex and number of adult members present made no difference in religious participation.

The extent to which labor availability acts as a mitigating factor affecting the participation of wealthy households can be explored by returning to a consideration of the 12 higher status households whose lack of religious activity remained unexplained in the preceding section. Of these 12 households, 8 have only 2 adult members available while the remaining 3 households have only 3 adult members. This finding corresponds to the median number of 2.5 adults found in inactive households in San Miguel and contrasts with the median number of 4 adults found in active ones. These findings suggest that the availability of adult labor is an important factor in cargo service that may militate against participation in households that have sufficient wealth but lack personnel.

Civil Service

I suggest that the pattern of high-status household participation characteristic of religious service is beginning to shift, in the civil sphere, to one based on the possession of individual skills. If this hypothesis is valid, then rates of civil participation should be distributed more evenly across households in all three social strata. The figures in Table 4 show that of the 92 households in the highest stratum, only 17, or 18 percent, are active in the civil sphere. Similarly, 23, or 27 percent, of the 84 middle-stratum households are active, and 21, or 12 percent, of the 178 low-status households are active.

TABLE 2. A Comparison of Religious Activity in Terms of Numbers of Adult Members Present in the Household

Number of Adult Members	Number of Active Households	Number of Inactive Households
0–2	7	97
3–5	115	116
6–8	16	3
Total	138	216

$\chi^2 = 75$

$p < .001$

TABLE 3. Frequency Distribution of Rates of Religious Activity According to Sex
Composition of Households

	Equal		Female	Male	Single	
	1 Male	> 1 Male	Female	Male	Single	
	1 Female	> 1 Female	Predominant	Predominant	Sex	Total
Active	5	61	25	44	3	138
Inactive	81	30	59	27	19	216
						354

$\chi^2 = 88.77$

$p < .001$

A comparison of the rates of religious and civil participation for households in each stratum (see Tables 1 and 4) shows some clear differences. While 74 percent of the high-stratum households and 71 percent of the middle-stratum households are religious participants, only 17 and 27 percent of the households in these strata are active in the civil sphere. Conversely, 6 percent of the low-stratum households are religious participants while double that percentage are active in the civil sphere. Rates of civil participation by strata are still not what would be expected if wealth had no influence on officeholding. I suggest, however, that these figures point toward a trend for the increasing participation of low-status households in civil service and indicate that wealth is no longer an absolute prerequisite for civil officeholding.

CHANGING PATTERNS OF WOMEN'S RELIGIOUS AND POLITICAL PARTICIPATION

The data presented thus far indicate that socioeconomic status is the single overwhelming determinant of religious participation in San Miguel. Consequently, it is not surprising to find that households with surplus resources participate in religious activity regardless of the sex of the head of household. The use of a domestic/public model emphasizing the separation between public and private spheres tends to obscure the fact that in religious cargo service, the domestic unit is the unit involved in public service. The two spheres are, in this case, one and the same. Households, not individual men, compete for prestige through service involving the expenditure of

TABLE 4. Frequency Distribution of Active and Inactive Households in the Civil System According
to Socio-economic Status

Stratum	Total		Active		Inactive	
	n	%	n	%	n	%
High	92	26	17	18	75	82
Medium	84	24	23	27	61	73
Low	178	50	21	12	157	88
Total	354	100				

$\chi^2 = 8.74$

$p < .05$

surplus resources. The labor of both male and female household members is vital in accomplishing this goal, and the prestige earned through service is shared equally by the members of the household unit.

Women, as integral members of such units, served and continue to serve in all aspects of the religious system. They contribute labor needed in accumulating surplus resources and in discharging the obligations of office. Consequently, when male heads of household hold official title to office, they must appoint a female partner as co-sponsor of the cargo and vice versa. The two mayordomos share responsibilities for discharging the ritual obligations of office with each having parallel duties to perform. In the religious sphere both female and male members of wealthy, high-status households are able to participate on a parallel basis in cargo service.

Women, however, do not have similar opportunities for participation in the civil sphere in San Miguel. During the study period, women held only 2 of the 61 civil posts available and both were appointive, as no woman in San Miguel has ever been elected to civil office. I suggest that women's exclusion from civil office is tied directly to the changing bases for service in San Miguel. Election to office is no longer absolutely dependent on past success in the religious system. Rather, individual skills including literacy in the Spanish language and the ability to interact with outsiders have become valued attributes in civil officeholders. Men in San Miguel possess these kinds of skills to a greater degree than do women because traditionally they traveled more widely and made more contacts with outside officials. In addition, men in San Miguel had, and continue to have, greater access to formal schooling than women and hence have been better able to improve their Spanish literacy skills.

Bossen (1975) and Boserup (1970) suggest that the greater development of interactional and literacy skills on the part of men is an established pattern in modernizing nations. Men are often recruited by the state to serve in the armed forces or provide labor in areas far distant from their homes. As men travel,

they are exposed to outside people and customs leading to the development of these skills. In Guatemala, for example, Bossen (1975) found that Indian men were frequently recruited to labor on lowland coffee plantations and conscripted to serve in the national armed forces. These Indian men traveled more extensively than women who had to remain behind to care for households in the highlands. As a result of their experiences, these Indian men learned the dominant Spanish language, often acquired formal schooling, and gained valuable experience interacting with Ladinos.

The situation described by Bossen for Guatemala parallels that occurring in San Miguel today. As official heads of households, men in San Miguel have always been responsible for regulating interaction between the household and outside authorities. In recent years, moreover, large numbers of men have left the community to work stints as agricultural laborers in the U.S. and to serve in the Mexican military to earn additional cash. In the process, men's literacy skills in Spanish improved as did their ability to interact with outsiders. Today, as parents in San Miguel perceive the importance of education for improving the quality of life, young men are often sent to secondary school in Oaxaca City where these skills are further developed.

Even though women now have the legal right to hold civil posts in San Miguel, they seldom achieve them because they often lack the particular skills valued in officeholders. The only two women to hold civil posts in San Miguel are ones who, through a combination of unusual circumstances, did have the opportunity to acquire some of these valued skills. The circumstances of their cases illustrate the processes now at work in the assumption of civil offices.

One woman, Hermelinda, was appointed as a member of the local committee of the dominant political party in Mexico (PRI). Another woman, Elena, is currently serving in the civil system as a member of the Committee of the Parents of Schoolchildren. Both women are single heads of household in the upper socioeconomic stratum designated in

Table 1. Interviews with Hermelinda and Elena reveal that in each instance the appointment to political office was predicated on somewhat unusual circumstances.

Hermelinda, for example, first got involved with civil officials after her husband murdered a fellow townsman in a drunken brawl. She hid her husband at a neighbor's house and later smuggled him out to Mexico City. He has not returned to San Miguel since, although it is rumored that he sometimes visits Hermelinda in secrecy. After her husband fled, Hermelinda was questioned at great length by civil authorities who pressed her to reveal his whereabouts. She refused to answer their questions and began, instead, to ask town officials about what would happen to her husband and about why he was being held responsible for a crime of passion committed in a drunken state. The local officials became annoyed and refused to answer her questions. Consequently, Hermelinda pursued these issues with civil officials in the district capital. These officials promised to look into her husband's case and even hinted to Hermelinda that her husband might be the innocent victim of persecution by an unscrupulous official in San Miguel. Hermelinda was grateful for the assistance of the district officials and invited them to stop for beer at her store any time they visited San Miguel. Thus even though the district officials never helped solve her husband's case, Hermelinda did make and maintain valuable political contacts.

About five years ago, according to Hermelinda, the state branch of the PRI party issued a directive encouraging districts to appoint women to local PRI committees. One of the district officials, who had met Hermelinda, convinced her to serve on the committee by suggesting that in so doing she might meet people who could assist in solving her husband's case.

The other woman to hold office in San Miguel, Elena, is one of three members of the Committee of the Parents of Schoolchildren. Committee members are responsible for handling the money raised by the school cooperative and negotiate requests for repairs and services made by the teachers. Twice a year the committee meets with all the parents to announce projects for the school and discuss problems arising between parents and teachers.

The presidente municipal appoints the members of the committee who have, in the past, been men. Women are active, however, in auxiliary roles relating to fundraising, planning school festivals, and maintaining school facilities. In addition, as parents of schoolchildren, women have always attended the twice annual meetings held by the committee. Elena's appointment to office stemmed from her public protest at one of these meetings. The protest occurred because the teachers had convinced committee members that mothers should work two days a year at the school cleaning the bathrooms and sweeping the floors. Mothers who refused to work, they argued, should be fined. The plan was protested vociferously, and Elena took the floor to argue this point with the president of the committee. She said:

> If we have the money, then why do you not use it to pay a girl to come to the school in the mornings to clean up? There are many young girls who need the money. Why do you expect the mothers to spend their time cleaning up like servants? We have to care for our own homes and children first.

Other women shouted their agreement, and the president said he would consider the idea. In the meantime, Elena canvassed the community and urged mothers not to go to the school when it was their turn to clean. Many of the women Elena visited in turn convinced their husbands that the work being asked of them was demeaning. As a result both men and women started to oppose the plan. The president of the committee had to call another meeting and at that time suggested that Elena join the committee to devise a plan for cleaning the school. The parents agreed, and Elena set up a plan whereby all the parents came to the school collectively twice a year in alternating groups to do a general cleaning of the facility. For the remainder of the year

Elena hired two local girls to clean on a daily basis. The plan satisfied everyone, and Elena continues to serve on the committee.

These two cases represent very different but equally unusual paths to civil service. Even though women can legally hold civil posts in San Miguel they find it difficult to do so since they often lack the skills valued in civil servants. The only two women to hold civil office in San Miguel are women who, through a combination of unusual circumstances, did acquire some of these valued skills.

Yet, because women are active participants in the religious system we cannot assume that their exclusion from civil service represents a lack of interest or ability, nor can we assume it results from confinement to a domestic sphere. Rather, women's exclusion from civil service is the complex outcome of a number of specific political and historical developments both within and outside the community. Spanish colonial authorities and later the Mexican national government created an administrative domain where men were favored for service. Additional socioeconomic changes led to conditions favoring men's travel outside the community and promoted their greater access to formal educational systems. As these skills obtained by men became increasingly important for election to civil office, they began to dominate in these posts. From a community-wide perspective, the implication for women is apparent. To the extent that the civil sphere is assuming increasing importance over the religious in regulating community affairs, women are being deprived of opportunities to hold community posts.

CONCLUSION

The data presented in this paper indicate that what appears on the surface to be a division in San Miguel between the domestic roles of women and the public roles of men is, instead, a manifestation of a more complex division emerging between the community-oriented religious sphere and the ex-

tracommunity-oriented political sphere. Because men dominate in the extra-community sphere, it often seems they control all the public roles of importance in San Miguel. Yet obviously they do not. I would argue that many ethnographic descriptions of a domestic/public division in postcontact societies may actually depict this more complex split in orientation between community and extracommunity institutions brought about by the penetration of state-level systems into formerly autonomous or semi-autonomous areas.

The penetration of the state, as anthropologists like Reiter (1975) and Sacks (1974, 1976, 1979) document, is accompanied by major political and economic transformations within local communities. State officials usually recruit men for public works projects and military service because of their greater mobility and physical strength, and because they are more easily exploited than women who must care for children. In the absence of men, the duties of domestic work and local subsistence fall to women. This division between women's production for family use, and men's corresponding involvement in social production, provides the basis for a sexual divide-and-rule policy in state-level systems (Sacks 1974:221). The effect of this policy, according to Sacks, has been to convert the productive role differences between men and women into a system of differential worth such that men become social adults while women are seen as domestic wards (Sacks 1974:221). As domestic wards, women's dealings with the public sphere are necessarily restricted, and they must depend on men to mediate for them with the larger extradomestic system of authority. Thus, although women in many state-level systems may exercise considerable amounts of power within the community, states are still prone to deny women's authority by excluding them from formal positions of importance in dealing with extracommunity officials. While the policies of the state have acted in general to promote the ties between men and state officials, this pattern of participation is by no means universal. Klein's (1980) work with the

Tlingit of Alaska shows how specific historical conditions act, in some situations, to provide women with the opportunities to accrue the skills and positions necessary for extra-community service.

The tendency of many anthropologists to assume that differential patterns of male and female participation necessarily reflect a domestic/public division is misplaced. Such reasoning fails to recognize the amount of variation that exists in the roles associated with both local and extracommunity institutions. Only by moving beyond the domestic/public model can researchers begin to focus on role relationships in order to specify both the determinants behind, and consequences of, particular patterns of sexual participation.

NOTES

Acknowledgments. This is a revised version of a paper originally presented in a symposium entitled, "Problems of Bias in Feminist Fieldwork," organized by Mari Clark and Nancy Scheper-Hughes for the 81st Annual Meeting of the American Anthropological Association in Washington, DC, December 1982. The funding for the collection of these data was provided by the Shell Foundation. I thank the people of San Miguel for their cooperation. I am indebted to Naomi Quinn for her encouragement and advice in all phases of the research. I would also like to thank Ernestine Friedl, Jim Mitchell, Bonnie Nardi, Jean O'Barr, Karen Sacks, Carol Stack, Carol Smith, and seven anonymous reviewers for comments on earlier versions of this material. I acknowledge, however, that their ideas may not agree with my own as presented herein.

1. See the work of Reina (1966) on the religious system in a Guatemalan community for an exception to this general trend.
2. The research community is located in the Valley of Oaxaca, Mexico. In accordance with anthropological precedent, the name of the community has been changed to protect informant confidentiality. Similarly, informant names have been changed in order to guarantee their anonymity.
3. The religious cargo system in San Miguel today conforms in structure to what De Walt (1975) labels the "faded" type and what Smith (1977) labels the "truncated" type. A more detailed description of cargo organization can be found in Mathews (1982).
4. Theoretically, all these 61 religious posts are filled annually, which would lead to a total of 183 offices over the three-year study period. In actuality, however, 38 were filled annually while another 24 were only filled once over the course of the study. Consequently, there were 138 religious posts filled over the three-year period.
5. In the civil sphere, 14 offices were filled only once, by election, during the three-year study period. Another 15 were filled three separate times by annual appointment. In two additional cases, the offices were not appointed annually, but rather the same two individuals held these posts throughout the three-year study period. Thus the total number of posts to be filled over three years was 61.
6. I used two rating scales, the Evaluated Participation Scale (EP) and the Index of Status Characteristics (ISC), to assess the socioeconomic status of households in San Miguel. The methodology is adapted from Warner et al. (1960). The goal of the EP technique is the empirical discovery of what people mean by the descriptive terms they use when talking about different social strata (Warner et al. 1960:35). I used open-ended interviews with 20 informants to elicit relevant terms and phrases for social class. Community members talked about three major strata and two substrata based on household standing in the community or *categoria*. In the interview context, informants often cited households as examples for each of the social categories. After constructing a model of the social system, I asked a panel of five informants to sort index cards with the names of all community households into the relevant categories. I tested this model with data from an identical task done by a separate panel of five informants.

   After completing this work, I next constructed an Index of Status Characteristics designed to yield an objective assessment of socioeconomic status that enables the analyst to determine what is meant in socioeconomic terms by community-derived categories of status. I used four status characteristics including occupation of household head, household landholdings, house type, and location of household. I had a panel of informants rate each household in the community on each characteristic, using a scale from an excellent rating of 1 to a poor rating of 7. Each score was then weighted to reflect the relative importance of each characteristic in the determination of status by community members. The composite rating score was then matched to the previous placements of households into emically derived status categories by informants to produce an overall picture of socioeconomic status in the community (see Mathews 1982 for a more detailed account of methodology).

REFERENCES

Beals, Ralph. 1945. Ethnology of the Western Mixie. University of California Publications in American Archaeology and Ethnography 42:1–176.

Boserup, Ester. 1970. Women's Role in Economic Development. London: George Allen Unwin, Ltd.

Bossen, Laurel. 1975. Women in Modernizing Societies. American Ethnologist 2(4):587–601.

Cancian, Frank. 1965. Economics and Prestige in a Maya Community. Stanford: Stanford University Press.

———. 1967. Political and Religious Organization. In Handbook of Middle American Indians. Manning Nash and R. Wauchope, eds. pp. 283–298. Vol. 6. Austin: University of Texas Press.

Carrasco, Pedro. 1961. The Civil-Religious Hierarchy in Mesoamerican Communities: Pre-Spanish Background and Colonial Development. American Anthropologist 63:483–497.

Chinas, Beverly L. 1973. The Isthmus Zapotecs. New York: Holt, Rinehart & Winston.

———. 1983. The Isthmus Zapotecs. 2nd edition. Prospect Heights, IL: Waveland Press.

Chodorow, Nancy. 1974. Family Structure and Feminine Personality. In Woman, Culture and Society. M. Rosaldo and L. Lamphere, eds. pp. 43–66. Stanford: Stanford University Press.

Collier, Jane F., and Michelle Z. Rosaldo 1981. Politics and Gender in Simple Societies. In Sexual Meanings. Sherry B. Ortner and Harriet Whitehead, eds. pp. 275–329. Cambridge: Cambridge University Press.

De La Fuente, Julio. 1949. Yalalag: Una Villa Zapoteca Serrana. Serie Cientifica 1. Mexico: Museo Nacional de Antropologia.

De Walt, Billie R. 1975. Changes in the Cargo System of Mesoamerica. Anthropological Quarterly 48:87–105.

Elmendorf, Mary. 1977. Mexico: The Many Worlds of Women. In Women: Roles and Status in Eight Countries. Janet Giele and Audrey Smock, eds. pp. 129–172. New York: John Wiley and Sons.

Foster, George. 1967. Tzintzuntzan: Mexican Peasants in a Changing World. Boston: Little, Brown.

Greenberg, James Brian. 1978. Santiago's Sword: Adaptation to Exploitation among the Chatino of Oaxaca, Mexico. Ph.D. dissertation. University of Michigan.

Hinton, Thomas. 1964. The Cora Village; a Civil Religious Hierarchy in Northern Mexico. In Essays in Memory of Olive Ruth Barker and George C. Barker. Ralph Beals, ed. Berkeley and Los Angeles: California Press.

Iwanska, Alicja. 1966. Division of Labor among Men and Women in a Mazahua Village of Central Mexico. Sociologus 16(2):173–186.

Klein, Laura F. 1980. Contending with Colonization: Tlingit Men and Women in Change. In Women and Colonization. M. Etienne and E. Leacock, eds. pp. 88–108. New York: J.F. Bergin, Inc.

Lamphere, Louise. 1974. Strategies, Cooperation and Conflict among Women in Domestic Groups. In Woman, Culture and Society. M. Rosaldo and L. Lamphere, eds. pp. 97–112. Stanford: Stanford University Press.

Lewis, Oscar. 1960. Tepoztlan: Village in Mexico. New York: Holt, Rinehart & Winston.

Mathews, Holly F. 1982. Sexual Status in Oaxaca, Mexico: An Analysis of the Relationship between Extradomestic Participation and Ideological Constructs of Gender. Ph.D. dissertation. Duke University.

Nash, June. 1980. Aztec Women. The Transition from Status to Class in Empire and Colony. In Women and Colonization. Mona Etienne and Eleanor Leacock, eds. pp. 134–148. New York: Praeger.

Ortner, Sherry B., and Harriet Whitehead. 1981. Introduction: Accounting for Sexual Meanings. In Sexual Meanings. Sherry B. Ortner and Harriet Whitehead, eds. pp. 1–28. Cambridge: Cambridge University Press.

Parsons, Elsie Clews. 1936. Mitla: Town of Souls. Chicago: University of Chicago.

Pearlman, Cynthia. 1980. In and Out of Focus: Gender and Social Domains. Paper Presented to the 79th Annual Meeting of the American Anthropological Association. Cincinnati, OH. December 7, 1980.

Perez, Jimenez Gustavo. 1968. La Institucion del Municipio Libre en Oaxaca: Prontuario de

Legislacion Organica Municipal. Mexico City: Mexican National Archives.

Reina, Ruben E. 1966. The Law of the Saints. Indianapolis and New York: The Bobbs-Merrill Co., Inc.

Reiter, Reina R. 1975. Men and Women in the South of France: Public and Private Domains. *In* Toward an Anthropology of Women. R. Reiter, ed. pp. 252–282. New York: Monthly Review Press.

Rogers, Susan Carol. 1978. Woman's Place: A Critical Review of Anthropological Theory. Comparative Studies in Society and History 20(1):123–162.

Rosaldo, Michelle Zimbalist. 1974. Woman, Culture and Society: A Theoretical Overview. *In* Woman, Culture and Society. M. Rosaldo and L. Lamphere, eds. pp. 17–42. Stanford: Stanford University Press.

———. 1980. The Use and Abuse of Anthropology: Reflections on Feminism and Cross-Cultural Understanding. Signs 5(3):389–417.

Sacks, Karen. 1974. Engels Revisited: Women, the Organization of Production, and Private Property. *In* Woman, Culture and Society. M. Rosaldo and L. Lamphere, eds. pp. 207–222. Stanford: Stanford University Press.

———. 1976. State Bias and Women's Status. American Anthropologist 78:565–569.

———. 1979. Sisters and Wives: The Past and Future of Sexual Equality. Westport, CT: Greenwood Press.

Sanday, Peggy Reeves. 1981. Female Power and Male Dominance: On the Origins of Sexual Inequality. Cambridge: Cambridge University Press.

Silverblatt, Irene. 1980. "The Universe Has Turned Inside Out . . . There Is No Justice For Us Here": Andean Women under Spanish Rule. *In* Women and Colonization. Mona Etienne and Eleanor Leacock, eds. pp. 149–185. New York: Praeger.

Smith, Waldemar R. 1977. The Fiesta System and Economic Change. New York: Columbia University Press.

Vogt, Evon A. 1969. Zinacantan: A Maya Community in the Highlands of Chiapas. Cambridge, MA: Harvard University Press.

Walter, Lynn. 1981. Social Strategies and the Fiesta Complex in an Otavaleno Community. American Ethnologist 8(1):172–185.

Warner, W. Lloyd with Marcia Meeker and Kenneth Eells. 1960. Social Class in America: A Manual of Procedures for the Measurement of Social Status. New York: Harper & Row.

Divine Connections: The *Mansin* and Her Clients

Laurel Kendall

> This order is recruited from among hysterical and silly girls as well as from women who go into it for a livelihood or for baser reasons.
>
> —H. N. Allen, *Some Korean Customs*

Excerpted with permission from Laurel Kendall, *Shamans, Housewives, and Other Restless Spirits: Women in Korean Ritual Life* (Honolulu: University of Hawaii Press, 1985), pp. 54–85.

> The magistrate said, "Alas! I thought *mutangs* were a brood of liars, but now I know that there are true *mutangs* as well as false." He gave her rich rewards, sent her away in safety, recalled his order against witches, and refrained from any matters pertaining to them for ever after.
>
> —Im Bang, from "The Honest Witch"

The *mansin's* house is much like any other country residence. She hangs no sign outside.

Women seek out the *mansin's* house by word of mouth or on the recommendation of kinswomen or neighbors. Once inside, a client makes herself comfortable, sitting on the heated floor. She should feel at home in the *mansin's* inner room, for the place resembles her own. The room where Yongsu's Mother divines could be the main room of any prosperous village home, crammed with the stuff of everyday life. Here are cabinets full of clothes and dishes, a dressing table with a neatly arranged collection of bottled cosmetics, an electric rice warmer, and a television set decorated with an assortment of rubber dolls and pink furry puppies.

THE GODS AND THEIR SHRINE

Yongsu's Mother's shrine, tucked away behind the sliding doors of the one spare room, resembles a rural temple. Gilt-plaster Buddha statues sit on the front altar. Bright printed portraits of Yongsu's Mother's gods hang on the walls. Incense burners, brass candleholders, aluminum fruit plates, water bowls, and stemmed offering vessels clutter the main and side altars. Each utensil and the three brass bells above the altar all bear the engraved phrase "Grant the wish of," followed by the name of the client. These are clients' gifts. The *mansin* advises a client to secure a particular god's good offices with appropriate tribute. One incense burner and water bowl bear my name. Yongsu's Mother told me, with some embarrassment, that the Buddhist Sage and the Mountain God requested gifts since I was doing my research through their will. She told a soldier's wife worried about her husband's fidelity and a young wife worried about her husband's job prospects to dedicate brass bells. She told another young wife to dedicate a water bowl because the Mountain God has helped her husband. Other clients gave the *mansin* her drum and battle trident, her cymbals and knives, her robes and hats, all the equipment she uses to perform *kut* [the most elaborate Shaman ritual]. She stores this equipment out of sight under the altar. Like the shrine fittings, each

of these accoutrements bears a client's name. A shrine littered with bells, water vessels, and incense pots advertises a successful *mansin*. In the early morning the *mansin* burns incense, lights candles, and offers cold water inside the shrine. Clients leave incense and candles, and the *mansin* echoes their requests in her own prayers.

A *mansin's* shrine is called a god hall (*sindang*) or hall of the law (*pŏptang*), a Buddhist term. In casual conversation Yongsu's Mother calls her shrine the grandfather's room (*harabŏjiŭi pang*). When I first visited her, I mistook the unmarked plural and thought she was renting a spare room to an older man. "Grandmother" and "grandfather" are honorific, but not excessively formal, terms. In Korea all old men and all old women, by virtue of the status white hair confers, are politely addressed as grandfather and grandmother. Gods also carry a faint connotation of kinship. Although both power and position set gods (*sillyŏng*) above ancestors (*chosang*), some gods, like the Chŏns' Great Spirit Grandmother, are also known ancestors. They are grandfathers and grandmothers writ large. Whether venerable distant kin or generalized venerable elders, Yongsu's Mother owes her gods respect and good treatment. Her gods are not distant, awesome beings; with a common term of address, she brings them close. She dreads their anger and anticipates their will, but she also expects them to help her, as a Korean child looks to a grandparent for small indulgences.

Standing before the gods in her shrine, Yongsu's Mother assumes the self-consciously comic pose of a young child, head slightly bowed, eyes wide with pleading. Speaking in a high, soft voice, she says, "Grandfather, please give me some money. I'm going to the market." She takes a bill from the altar and stuffs it into her coin purse. "I'll be right back," and she brings her hands together and nods her head in a quick bow.

Yongsu's Mother originally kept her gods in a narrow storage alcove off the porch and rented her spare room. She began to suspect that the gods disliked the alcove when she, her son, and her roomers' child were all sick at the same time in the middle of winter. One night her dead husband appeared in a dream. He boldly marched into the spare room while its occupants were in Seoul. Yongsu's Mother yelled at him, "You can't go in there when people are away. They'll think you're going to take something." Her husband answered, "This is my room. I'll give you the rent money." Yongsu's Mother continued to quarrel with her husband until she woke up.

The very next day, her roomers announced that they were moving to Seoul. Someone else wanted to rent the room immediately, but Yongsu's Mother said that she would have to think about it. That night she dreamed that all of the grandmothers and grandfathers in her shrine left the alcove and followed Yongsu's Father into the spare room, calling as they passed, "We'll give you the rent money, we'll give you the rent money."

She told her dream to the Chatterbox Mansin who agreed that Yongsu's Mother must make the spare room into a shrine. Thereafter, she prospered as a *mansin*. Her grandmothers and grandfathers gave her the rent money.

This incident is typical of Yongsu's Mother's ongoing tug-of-war with her grandmothers and grandfathers. Her gods do well by her, but they are even more demanding than her clients' gods. She intended to give a *kut* every three years for their pleasure, but after a prosperous early spring, they made her ill to let her know that they wanted an annual *kut*. The next year, in the fall, she gave the grandmothers and grandfathers special feast food (*yŏt'am*) before her stepdaughter's wedding. The gods were angry because she hit the hourglass drum and roused them but did not give them a *kut*. Her luck was bad for several months. She purchased fabric to make new robes for the General and the Warrior, and gave another *kut* the following spring.

Like many children from Enduring Pine Village, her son Yongsu goes to the private Christian middle school in Righteous Town. The fees at the school are minimal and admissions relatively open, but pressure to convert is high. The gods in the shrine do not like Yongsu's daily brush with Christianity. They make his thoughts wander in school. He says he feels an urge to rush home. Yongsu's Mother told the principal that Yongsu's family had "honored Buddha from long ago," and asked him to understand that Yongsu cannot become a Christian. Then she went to her shrine, hit the cymbals, and implored her grandmothers and grandfathers: "Please understand, please forgive. Yongsu has to get an education. Let him go to that place until he's gotten his education."

THE DESCENT OF THE GODS

A *mansin* engages in a battle of wills with the gods from the very beginning of her career. A woman is expected to resist her calling and struggle against the inevitable, but village women say that those who resist the will of the gods to the very end die raving lunatics. Strange, wild behavior marks a destined *mansin*. Yongsu's Mother describes the struggle:

> They don't know what they're doing. They yell, "Let's go, let's go!" and go running out somewhere. They snatch food from the kitchen and run out into the road with it. God-descended people swipe things and run away. They strike at people and shout insults.
>
> If I were a god-descended person and my husband were hitting me and calling me crazy woman, I'd shout back at him, "You bastard! Don't you know who I am, you bastard?" That's what the Clear Spring Mansin did. Then she sat beside the road talking to the chickens. So funny!

The destined *mansin,* or god-descended person (*naerin saram*), can experience a variety of symptoms. According to Yongsu's Mother,

> It's very difficult for them. They're sick and they stay sick, even though they take medicine. And there are people who get better even without taking medicine. There are some who can't eat the least bit of food; they just go hungry. There are some who sleep with their eyes open, and

some who can't sleep at all. They're very weak but they get well as soon as the gods descend in the initiation *Kut*. For some people the gods descend gently, but for others the gods don't descend gently at all. So they run around like crazy women.

Although the destined *mansin* acts like a "crazy woman," Yongsu's Mother makes a distinction between the god-descended person (*naerin saram*) and someone struck temporarily insane (*mich'ida*) by angry household gods or ancestors. "You just have to see them to tell the difference. Insane people look like they're in pain somewhere. The god-descended person wanders here and there singing out, 'I'm this god, I'm that god.'" The *mansin* exorcise insane people as swiftly as possible in a healing *kut* for fear that the possessing spirits will torment their victims to death. The *mansin* flourish knives and flaming torches, threatening, cajoling, and pleading with the offending spirits, urging them to depart (Kendall 1977a). In the initiation *kut* for a god-descended person (*naerim kut*), the initiating *mansin* invites the gods to complete their descent and allow their chosen one to dance and sing as a *mansin*.

A woman often endures considerable anguish before her initiation. The Chatterbox Mansin's story is typical. She was a young matron when the gods descended, a first son's wife living with her mother-in-law. She had already produced two healthy sons. Her husband was away in the air force when she began to exhibit bizarre behavior. She would wander about, talking in a distracted fashion. Worried, her mother-in-law sent for Chatterbox's sister, but when the sister arrived, Chatterbox was sitting in the main room, calmly sewing. She said that every night an old woman—a grandmother—came and asked her to go wandering about with her.

Her sister thought that if Chatterbox was normal enough in the daytime and only behaved strangely at night, she would be all right soon enough. But a few days later, Chatterbox came back to her natal home, clapping her hands together and shrieking like a lunatic. She looked like a beggar woman in torn clothes. Her hair was a tangled mass down her back and her face was filthy. When her mother-in-law came to take her back home, she just sat on the porch and screamed. They tried to pull her up, but her legs stuck fast to the wooden boards of the porch. She asked for some water and poured it all over her body. That night she wandered away. She went into a house and stole a Buddha statue. When her family asked her why she did this, she said, "I was told to do it." For two weeks she went about clapping her hands and pilfering small objects. Then she disappeared completely.

Her family thought she was dead. Much later they heard that she had become the apprentice spirit daughter of the Boil-face Mansin, a great shaman (*k'ŭn mudang*) in the next county. The Boil-face Mansin had taken her in, initiated her, and was training her to perform *kut*. Over the years she learned chants, dances, and ritual lore.

During Chatterbox's distracted wanderings her mother-in-law began divorce proceedings. The woman never lived with her husband again and was forbidden to see her children. But when sorrow overwhelmed her, she would go to the school and, from a safe distance, watch her sons playing in the school yard. A quarrel with his stepmother prompted the oldest son to search out Chatterbox in the countryside. After the boy's flight her sons visited her every summer.

Chatterbox prospered as a *mansin* and built up her own clientele. She broke with her spirit mother after a bitter fight, claiming the shaman overworked and underpaid her. Today, some twenty years after the gods' initial descent, no trace of the haunted young matron remains. Well dressed in Western-style clothing, Chatterbox walks through the streets of the county seat where she has just purchased a new house. Today people in the area consider her a "great shaman" and her own spirit daughter accuses her of stinginess.

By her own admission, Yongsu's Mother had an easy experience as a god-descended person. Widowed after only two years of marriage, she was left with two stepchildren and her own small son. She worked as a peddler, one of a limited number of occupations open to a woman who must support a family. At the end of the mourning period, she went to a *kut* at Chatterbox's shrine.

During an interlude in the *kut*, women danced the *mugam* in the Chatterbox Mansin's costumes to amuse their personal guardian gods and bring luck to their families. The Chatterbox Mansin told Yongsu's Mother to use the *mugam* and dance for success in her precarious business ventures. As Yongsu's Mother remembers it,

> I said, "What do you mean 'use the *mugam?*' It's shameful for me to dance like that." But the Chatterbox Mansin kept saying, "It'll give you luck. You'll be lucky if you dance." So I put on the clothes and right away began to dance wildly. I ran into the shrine, still dancing, and grabbed the Spirit Warrior's flags. I started shouting, "I'm the Spirit Warrior of the Five Directions," and demanded money. All of the women gave me money. I ran all the way home. My heart was thumping wildly. I just wanted to die like a crazy woman. We talked about it this way and that way and decided there was no way out. So the next year I was initiated as a *mansin*.

Although Yongsu's Mother's possession was sudden and unique in its relative painlessness, there had been suggestions throughout her life that she would become a *mansin*.[1] In her early teens during the Korean War, she was fingered as a member of a right-wing youth organization and arrested by North Korean soldiers just before their retreat. Taken on the march north, she made a bold escape on the same night that the Mountain God appeared to her in a dream and said, "It's already getting late."

In late adolescence she had frightening hallucinations. The little Buddha statue a friend brought her from Japan burst into flames in the middle of the room. She watched her mother's face turn into a tiger's face. She wandered about at night, drawn to the stone Buddha near a neighborhood temple. Her mother held a healing *kut*. During the *kut* the girl fell asleep. A white-haired couple appeared and gave her a bowl of medicinal water to drink. When she woke up, she

told her dream to the *mansin*, who was pleased. The *mansin* asked her to become her spirit daughter and be initiated as a *mansin*, but she and her mother refused.

Years later, on her wedding night, her sister-in-law dreamed that the new bride was sitting in the inner room hitting a drum. Overhead, on a rope line, hung all of the gods' clothes, as if a *kut* were in progress. Later, when her husband was fatally ill, Yongsu's Mother went to a *mansin's* shrine for an exorcism. She set out her offerings and the *mansin* began to chant, but when Yongsu's Mother went to raise her arms over her head and bow to ground, her arms stuck to her sides as if someone were holding them down. She could not budge them. It was destined that her husband would die and she would become a *mansin*. There was nothing she could do about it.

Yongsu's Mother was a young widow awash in economic difficulties when the gods descended. The Chatterbox Mansin was separated from her husband but living with her mother-in-law, the woman who would later insist on divorce. I am reluctant to speculate on the two initiates' subconscious motivations, but Harvey (1979, 1980) suggests that severe role stress propels women like the Chatterbox Mansin and Yongsu's Mother into god-descended behavior. It is true that, as *mansin*, such women stand above the social and economic constraints imposed on a proper Korean wife, and as *mansin*, they wear the gods' costumes and speak with the gods' authority. But whatever personal and economic gratification she enjoys, the *mansin* and her family pay a price. Shamans were listed, under the occupational classification system of the Yi dynasty, among the despised "mean people" (*ch'ŏnmin*) along with butchers, fortune-tellers, roving players, monks, and female entertainers. According to one early missionary, "Sometimes the daughter of a genteel family may become a Mootang, though this is rare, as her people would rather kill her than have her madness take this form" (Allen 1896, 164).

Like the female entertainer, the *kisaeng*, the shaman engages in public display, singing and dancing. An element of ambiguous sexuality wafts about the *mansin's* performance. In folklore and literature *mudang* are portrayed as "lewd women," and so they are often perceived (Wilson 1983). The *mansin* Cho Yŏng-ja told Ch'oe and Chang that the county chief had come to her home on the pretext of having his fortune told and had then insisted on sleeping with her. Disgusted, she contrived an escape. Thereafter all was coldness between the *mansin* and the county chief (Ch'oe and Chang 1967, 32–33).

The *mansin* play to their female audience, but when the supernatural Official sells "lucky wine," the costumed *mansin* roams through the house seeking male customers. The men have been drinking by themselves in a corner of the house, as far removed from the *kut* as possible. Now they emerge, red faced, and the bolder of their company dance a few steps on the porch. Men buy the Official's wine and tease the *mansin*, flourishing their bills in front of her face before securing the money in her chestband. An audacious man may try to tweak the *mansin's* breast as he secures his bill.

The *mansin* is caught at cross purposes. By her coy, flirtatious performance, she encourages the men to spend more money on wine. But as a woman alone, she must defend herself from harassment and protect her reputation. Yongsu's Mother was resourceful.

> It doesn't happen so much anymore, but when I first started going to *kut*, men would bother me. We were doing a *kut* at a house way out in the country, and I was going around selling the Official's wine. Some son-of-a-bitch grabbed my breast. I put out my hand so the drummer would go faster, then brought my arms up quick to start dancing. I knocked that guy against the wall. Afterwards, he asked me, "What did you mean by that?" I said, "Oh, that wasn't me, it was the honorable Official who did that." Other times, I'd be drumming and some guy would say, "Auntie, where is Uncle? What is Uncle doing now?" and go on like that. I'd reach out to beat the drum faster and slap the guy with the drumstick.

At the *kut* for the dead, performed outside the house gate, men gather off to the side. They gaze at the *mansin* garbed like a princess

who sings the long ballad tale of Princess Pari, rapping the drum with elegant flicks of her wrist. My landlady told me of a famous *mansin,* now aged, who was once a beauty. "When she did the *kut* for the dead, it would take forever. This one would carry her off on his back, and that one would embrace her."

To the exemplar of Confucian virtue, the *mansin* offends simply because she dances in public. When an officer from the district police station tried to stop a *kut* in Enduring Pine Village, he threatened to arrest the *mansin* because "they were dancing to drum music and students were watching." The moral education of the young was thereby imperiled. An envelope of "cigarette money" finally silenced this paragon.

It would be a distortion to paint the *mansin* I knew in northern Kyŏnggi Province as social pariahs. Since she has no husband, Yongsu's Mother's house is a favorite gathering place for village women. In their leisure moments they drop by to chat about the latest school fee, the inept village watch system, the new neighborhood loan association, or simply to gossip. Even the wife of the progressive village chief, though she disdains "superstition," seeks out the company of the articulate, loquacious *mansin*. Yongsu's Mother is a favorite guest at birthday parties. She gets the singing started and makes people laugh. She can sometimes be persuaded to bring her drum so the women can dance.

But Yongsu's Mother lives under the shadow of potential insult. Village people say, "Not so many years ago, even a child could use blunt speech [*panmal*] to a shaman.[2] Although this is no longer true, when tempers flare Yongsu's Mother's occupation is still flung in her face. Yongsu's Mother and the widowed Mr. Yun were great friends. Village gossips expected them to marry. Mr. Yun's daughter-in-law rankled at the possibility. She finally exploded in a fit of rage, shrieking at Yongsu's Mother, "Don't come into my house! I don't want a shaman to come into my house! It's bad luck if a shaman comes into your house." Pride wounded to the quick, Yongsu's Mother avoided the Yun family and there was no more talk of marriage.

After her stepdaughter's marriage Yongsu's Mother was anxious lest the groom discover her occupation. She did only one hasty New Year Rite for a client on the second day of the New Year since she expected a visit from the newlyweds on that day. She dreaded the thought of them walking in and catching her banging her cymbals in the shrine.

The Chatterbox Mansin's sister-in-law found her own children dancing in time to the drum rhythm during a *kut.* She slapped them soundly, then howled at her miserable fortune to have married into a shaman's house. Since this was all in the family, and the Chatterbox mansin is never at a loss for words, whatever the circumstance, she snapped back, "Well then, you knew this was a shaman's house. You didn't have to marry my brother and come to live here."

The *mansin* shares in the ambiguous status of other glamorous but morally dubious female marginals, the actress, the female entertainer, and the prostitute. Like the others, she makes a living, often a comfortable living, by public performance in a society where so-called good women stay home. But the *mansin* is neither an actress nor a courtesan. She is the ritual specialist of housewives. The good women who stay home need her. She came from their midst, lives like them, and speaks to their anxieties and hopes.

The gods who have claimed a woman as a *mansin* leave her one lingering shred of respectability. It is well known that only by virtue of divine calling is she a shaman, and that is a compulsion fatal to resist.[3] Her neighbors assume that she did not want to become a *mansin.* She tells her story to clients, describes how she resisted the call with the last ounce of her strength and succumbed only after considerable suffering and in fear for her very life. . . .

WOMEN WHO COME TO THE MANSIN'S HOUSE

A shaman's divination (*mugŏri*) is the first step in any ritual therapy. Women like Grandmother Chŏn come to the *mansin's* house when they suspect that malevolent forces lurk behind a sudden or persistent illness or do-

mestic strife. In Yongsu's Mother's shrine I heard reports of inflamed lungs, an infected leg, fits of possession "craziness," alcoholism, and dreamy, wandering states of mind. One woman, afflicted with this last complaint, feared that she was god-descended, but Yongsu's Mother laughed off her worries and divined more commonplace godly displeasure as the source of her problems. Other women who came to the shrine worried about their husbands' or sons' career prospects, or about sudden financial reverses. Should the husband switch jobs? Would the son receive his security clearance to work in Saudi Arabia? Thieves had broken into the family rice shop, what did that presage? Other women were anxious that adulterous husbands might abandon them. Some had only the vaguest suspicion that their spouses had "smoked the wind," but one young woman was certain that her husband took the grain his mother sent up from the country and shared it with his mistress. One woman, caught in a compromising position by her enraged spouse, had fled to the *mansin* in fear of life and limb. And still other women asked about wayward children, stepchildren, or grandchildren whose transgressions ranged from mild rebelliousness to Christian zealotry, petty theft, and delinquency. A mother-in-law asked how she should deal with a runaway daughter-in-law. A daughter-in-law who had fled home asked if she should divorce her husband. An older woman wondered if she should join a married son's household. . . .

The *mansin* chats with the women before fetching the divination tray. Sometimes the women begin to discuss their anxieties before the actual divination, but these are usually long-standing clients. Clients who come to the *mansin* for the first time tend to hold back and see how much the *mansin* can uncover in the divination.

The *mansin* brings in the divination tray, an ordinary low tray of the sort used for meals in any Korean home. The tray bears a mound or rice grains, a handful of brass coins (imitations of old Chinese money), and the brass bell rattle a *mansin* uses to summon up her visions.

"Well now, let's see," says the *mansin*, settling down to a kneeling posture behind her tray. The client places a bill under the pile of grain on the tray. At Yongsu's Mother's shrine in 1977 and 1978, this fee was usually five-hundred or a thousand won. Now the *mansin* shakes the brass bells beside her own ear and chants, asking the gods to send "the correct message." She receives a message for each member of the client's family, beginning with the client's husband if he is alive. She announces each subject's name and age to the gods, tosses her coins on the tray, and spills handfuls of rice grains until the Great Spirit Grandmother speaks and sends visions.

Coin and rice configurations hint at the client's concerns. A broad spread of coins bespeaks quarrels between husband and wife or parent and child, or betrays financial loss. A long line of coins broken by one or two solitary coins at the end tells of someone leaving home, a change of employment, a death, or the inauspicious influence of an ancestor who died far from home. A few grains spilled on the floor caution financial prudence; the client should postpone switching jobs or buying a house.

The *mansin* describes a situation and asks for confirmation. "Your husband has a cold or something, is that it?" "Your thirteen-year-old daughter doesn't get along with her father, is that right?" The *mansin* develops the theme, weaving her visions together with her client's information. With more tosses of coins and grain, the Great Spirit Grandmother sends more specific visions. "I see a steep embankment. Is there something like that near your house?" The woman and her neighbor nod affirmation. "Be careful of that place." To another woman, "Your daughter has two suitors. One is quite handsome. The other is extremely clever but also very meticulous. Since your daughter isn't especially clever herself, she'll have a better life if she marries the second suitor, but she must watch her step and scrupulously manage her house."

Sometimes she sights the discontented gods and ancestors of her clients' households. "Is there a distant grandfather in your family who carried a sword and served inside the palace?" "Did someone in your family die far

from home and dripping blood?" She circles in on the supernatural source of her client's problems and suggests an appropriate ritual to mollify a greedy god's demands or send a miserable and consequently dangerous soul "away to a good place."

For a housewife to evaluate the skill of an individual *mansin* and trust her diagnosis, she must know the supernatural history of her husband's family and of her own kin. And if the *mansin* is convinced that there was "a grandmother who worshiped Buddha," or "a bride who died in childbirth," she tells her client, "Go home and ask the old people, they know about these things. . . ."

SEEING THE YEAR'S LUCK

During the first two weeks of the lunar year, women crowd the *mansin's* house to "see the year's luck" (*illyŏn sinsurŭl poda*). The New Year marks a fresh, auspicious start for each household. A woman therefore gets a prognosis on each member of her family. If noxious influences threaten someone in her charge, she can "make them clean" by performing simple rituals under the first full moon.

This is the peasants' winter slack season and the women are in a holiday mood when they come to the *mansin's* house. Most arrive in groups. Waiting their turn, they bunch together in the hot-floor inner room. If the wait is long, they play cards, doze, or listen to other divinations. They sigh sympathetically for the woman whose divination reveals an adulterous husband, unruly child, or pitiable ghost. They coach the young matron who does not yet know the vocabulary of women's rituals. Not for them, the confidential atmosphere of the Western doctor's or analyst's office. The confessional's anonymity is missing here. The women enjoy each other's stories and accept each other's sympathy.

A woman, as a matter of course, receives divinations for her husband, herself, living parents-in-law, sons, unmarried daughters, sons' wives, and sons' children. Many women, however, pay an extra hundred or two hundred won for the fortunes of those whose ties stretch outside the woman's "family," the family she enters at marriage and represents in the *mansin's* shrine. Some women ask about a married daughter, her husband, and their children, or about other natal kin. During New Year divinations in 1978, one woman asked about her own mother, brother, and brother's wife, another about her own elder sister. Yongsu's Mother teased, "What do you want to know about them for?" but provided the divinations. Women acknowledge their concern for mothers, married daughters, and siblings, but it costs more, an extra coin or two.

In the New Year divination the *mansin* predicts dangerous and advantageous months, warns against potentially dangerous activities, and suggests preventive ritual action. The following condensation of Yongsu's Mothers New Year divination for a seventy-year-old widow is an example.

> My seventy-year-old lady, you shouldn't go on long trips; you must be careful now. Your children will receive succor; someone will come with aid in the seventh or eighth month. You will have some good news in the third or fourth month.
>
> Your thirty-nine-year-old son should not visit anyone who is sick [since in this horoscope year, he is vulnerable to noxious influences]. His thirty-five-year-old wife should be heedful of things other people say about her. Their twelve-year-old son should be exorcised with five-grain rice left at the crossroads and by casting out a scarecrow stuffed with his name [because he has acquired an accretion of noxious influences and his year fate is bad]. The eight-year-old daughter will be lucky but you should burn a string of pine nuts, one for each year of her life, and address the moon on the night of the first full moon.
>
> Your thirty-five-year-old son is troubled with sorrow and regret, but his luck is changing. There is no trouble between husband and wife, nothing to worry about there. Their seven-year-old child has a cold or something. This is a dangerous time for him so they must guard him carefully. Your unmarried thirty-year-old son doesn't even have a girl friend, but next year his prospects will improve. He should marry when he's thirty-two. He'll succeed in life when he's thirty-five or thirty-seven.

The scarecrow, five-grain rice left at the crossroads, and pine nuts burned under the moon are minor rituals performed on the fifteenth day of the lunar year. The first full moon marks the end of the New Year holidays, a time when women immunize a threatened family member, usually a child, against noxious influences lurking in the year's fortune. When the *mansin's* visions reveal a swarm of noxious influences on the road, a growing splotch of red, she tells the child's mother or grandmother to leave five-grain rice at a crossroads, then wave it over the child's head and cast it out. A mother must warn her child to be especially mindful of traffic. When the *mansin* sees swimming fish, she tells the woman to write the child's name, age, and birthdate on a slip of paper and wrap the paper around a lump of breakfast rice on the morning of the fifteenth. The woman throws the packet into a well or stream saying, "Take it, fish!" She substitutes the rice for a child with a drowning fate.

The *mansin* also cautions that children should not swim, go fishing, or climb mountains in certain months. Here the women sigh, "How can I do that?" The *mansin* tells the housewife which family members, according to the particular vulnerability of their year horoscope, must disdain funerals, feasts, or visits to sick friends. She advises switching a sixty-first birthday celebration to a more auspicious month. She predicts the compatibility of a son's or daughter's lover or a matchmaker's candidate. She determines when "the ancestors are hungry and the gods want to play," and advises these families to hold *kut* early in the new year. The early spring is a busy season for the *mansin*. . . .

A woman goes to the *mansin* with some ambivalence. She assumes the *mansin* will discern a supernatural problem and suggest ritual action. Rituals, be it an inexpensive exorcism or an elaborate *kut*, require cash. Hangil's Mother told me, "I don't go to the *mansin's* house anymore. They always tell you to do things that cost money, and I can't afford to do that. I'm just like a Christian now, only I don't believe in Jesus." Though some women are cynical, Hangil's Mother is not. She advised me on the rituals I should perform for my own spirits and was almost invariably among the women watching a *kut* in Yongsu's Mother's shrine. A divination is the essential first step in a *mansin's* treatment, but the whole process may stop here. Whenever Yongsu's Mother counseled a woman to dedicate a brass bell or sponsor a ritual, the client would almost always say, "I'll have to talk it over with my husband," or "I'll have to see what the old people say." At home she weighs the potential benefits against the household budget. A woman told me, "They say we ought to do a *kut* because a grandmother of this house was a great shaman, but it takes too much money." Some women decide to wait and see if their problems will improve over time. There was, for example, the woman who said,

Years ago, I went to a *mansin* in Righteous Town. Someone told me she was good, so I went to her by myself. My husband was losing money and I felt uneasy. The *mansin* said, "Do a *kut*," but I didn't.

Others are satisfied with the *mansin's* actions on their behalf:

I was sick last year. I felt exhausted and my whole body ached. I went to the hospital for treatment and that took a lot of money. . . . After the exorcism I got better.

or:

We did a *kut* two years ago for my eldest son. He drank too much and had pains in his chest. He took Western medicine, but that didn't work. The Brass Mirror Mansin did a *kut* and he got better, so he didn't have to go to the hospital.

Some of the women were reluctant to attribute a successful cure directly and exclusively to the *mansin's* efforts. "The *mansin* did an exorcism and my daughter took medicine; she recovered." There are also clients who claim total dissatisfaction with the *mansin's* cure. Everyone in the Song family's immediate neighborhood knew that the entire household of the minor line became Christian when their

healing *kut* did not cure the son's acute headaches. He recovered slowly over the next few months. Another woman said that she stopped believing when she learned that she had cancer of the womb. On the other side of the ledger was a young woman who, years ago, had prayed to the Christian god to spare her ailing parents. They died and she stopped believing. Now she was sponsoring a *kut*. Other women wonder if the *kut* the *mansin* advised might have saved an afflicted family member:

Three years ago, I went to a *mansin* I'd heard was good. I went for my husband who was paralyzed. The *mansin* did an exorcism and told us to do a *kut*. We didn't do the *kut*, and my husband died.

or:

My son died when he was sixteen years old. We should have gone to a *mansin*, but we didn't. There was something wrong with his thigh. It seemed fine from the outside. We couldn't see anything wrong and neither did the hospital. We went to the Western hospital and the hospital for Chinese medicine. . . .

HOUSEHOLD TRADITIONS AND WOMEN'S WORK

Women go to *mansin's* shrines and to Buddhist temples as the ritual representatives of their families and households. They sponsor *kut* in the shrine and in their own homes, but never in other houses. Other houses have their own house gods. A bond like an electrical connection links the *mansin's* house to the housewife's own dwelling. When clients leave after making offerings in the shrine or sponsoring a *kut* there, they give no farewell salutation. The *mansin* carefully reminds new clients of this necessary breach of etiquette, and tells the women to go straight home. A woman brings blessings from the shrine directly to her own house lest they be lost along the way. The woman leaves the shrine without a farewell and enters her own home without a greeting. Salutations mark boundaries and transitions; they are inappropriate here.

Any woman, old or young, married or single, can visit the *mansin's* house and receive a divination, but the *tan'gol* [regular customer] who make seasonal offerings in the shrine and sponsor *kut* are female househeads, the senior women in their households. Commensurate with their temporal responsibilities, they come to the shrine on behalf of husbands, children, and retired parents-in-law. Some *tan'gol* are young matrons, but others are grandmothers whose concerns stretch beyond their own households to their married sons' households. They pray on behalf of sons, daughters-in-law, and grandchildren. Sometimes a worried mother brings her own daughter to the *mansin*. Occasionally mothers press their married daughters to hold a *kut* or perform a clandestine conception ritual, and mothers often pay an extra fee to include a married daughter's household in their divinations. A mother's concern for her own daughter might suggest pity for the suffering shared by all women, but it also suggests a mother's assumed ability to aid all of her children, even those who have left the ritual family she represents in the shrine. . . .

In the ideal flow of tradition, a daughter-in-law continues her mother-in-law's relationship with a particular *mansin*. The *mansin's* spirit daughter inherits the shrine and the old *mansin's* clients or her clients' daughters-in-law. In practice, the relationship is far more flexible. The daughter-in-law sometimes favors a *mansin* close to her own age over the white-haired *mansin* her mother-in-law patronized. A spirit daughter may not enjoy the rapport her spirit mother had with clients. Some women switch *mansin* when they are dissatisfied with a diagnosis and cure. Other clients, like the Songs who converted to Christianity, stop visiting *mansin* altogether out of disappointment or because of diminishing returns. Other women said they stopped going to the *mansin's* shrine because their present lives were "free of anxiety" (*uhwani ŏptta*). Yongsu's Mother said, "When things are fine, people don't do anything. When someone is sick, when they lose money, or when there's

trouble with the police, then they do things like exorcisms and *kut*."

Yongsu's Mother acknowledges her role as a specialist. The women who seek her services share with her a rich lore of belief and practice aimed at securing the health, harmony, and prosperity of households. At the new year or in time of crisis, she helps them order their world. Across her divination table, ordinary women's concerns and stories mingle with the painful tales of a shaman's destiny.

NOTES

1. Pyongyang-mansin, one of Harvey's informants, reports a similar experience (Harvey 1979:109).
2. Like the Japanese language, spoken Korean sentence endings are shorter or longer depending on the relative status of the speaker and the addressee. Adults use blunt endings, *panmal*, when addressing children, and children use them when addressing dogs.
3. There are hereditary *mundang* families in the southernmost provinces. Whether by birth or divine will, the point is the same: The female religious practitioner does not voluntarily assume her role.

REFERENCES

Allen, H. N. 1896. Some Korean Customs: The Mootang. *Korean Repository* 3: 163–168.

Ch'oe, Kil-sŏng, and Chang Chu-gŭn. 1967. *Kyŏ-nggido Chiyŏk Musok (Shaman Practices of Kyŏnggi Province)*. Seoul: Ministry of Culture.

Harvey, Youngsook Kim. 1979. *Six Korean Women: The Socialization of Shamans*. St. Paul: West Publishing Company.

———. 1980. Possession Sickness and Women Shamans in Korea. In N. Falk and R. Gross (eds.). *Unspoken Worlds: Women's Religious Lives in Non-Western Cultures*, pp. 41–52. New York: Harper and Row.

Kendall, Laurel. 1977. Caught Between Ancestors and Spirits: A Korean Mansin's Healing Kut. *Korea Journal* 17(8): 8–23.

Wilson, Brian. 1983. The Korean Shaman: Image and Reality. In L. Kendall and M. Peterson (eds.). *Korean Women: View from the Inner Room*, pp. 113–128. New Haven: East Rock Press.

Mama Lola and the Ezilis: Themes of Mothering and Loving in Haitian Vodou

Karen McCarthy Brown

Mama Lola is a Haitian woman in her mid-fifties who lives in Brooklyn, where she works as a Vodou priestess. This essay concerns her relationship with two female *lwa*, Vodou spirits whom she "serves." By means of trance states, these spirits periodically speak and act through her during community ceremonies and private healing sessions. Mama Lola's story will serve as a case study of how the Vodou spirits closely reflect the lives of those who honor them. While women and men routinely and meaningfully serve both male and female spirits in Vodou, I will focus here on only one strand of the complex web of relations between the "living" and the Vodou spirits, the strand that connects women and female spirits. Specifically I will demonstrate how female spirits, in their iconography and possession-performance, mirror the lives of contemporary Haitian women with remarkable specificity. Some general discussion of Haiti and of Vodou is necessary before moving to the specifics of Mama Lola's story.

Vodou is the religion of 80% of the population of Haiti. It arose during the eighteenth century on the giant sugar plantations of the French colony of Saint Domingue, then known as the Pearl of the Antilles. The latter name was earned through the colony's veneer of French culture, the reknowned beauty of its Creole women, and most of all, the productivity of its huge slave plantations. Haiti is

Reprinted with permission from Nancy Falk and Rita Gross (eds.), *Unspoken Worlds: Women's Religious Lives* (Belmont, Calif.: Wadsworth Publishing Co.), pp. 235–245. The main ideas in this article are developed further in a chapter of *Mama Lola: Vodou Priestess in Brooklyn* (Berkeley: University of California Press, 1991).

now a different place (it is the poorest country in the Western hemisphere) and Vodou, undoubtedly, a different religion from the one or ones practiced by the predominantly Dahomean, Yoruba, and Kongo slaves originally brought there. The only shared language among these different groups of slaves was French Creole, yet they managed before the end of the eighteenth century to band together (most likely through religious means) to launch the only successful slave revolution during this immoral epoch. As contemporary Haitian history has made amply clear, a successful revolution did not lead to a free and humane life for the Haitian people. Slave masters were quickly replaced by a succession of dictators from both the mulatto and black populations.

Haitians started coming to the United States in large numbers after François Duvalier took control of the country in the late 1950s. The first wave of immigrants was made up of educated, professional people. These were followed by the urban poor and, most recently, the rural poor. All were fleeing dead-end lives in a society drenched in corruption, violence, poverty, and disease. There are now well over one-half million Haitians living in the U.S.

Alourdes, the name by which I usually address Mama Lola, came to New York in 1963 from Port-au-Prince, the capital of Haiti and a city of squalor and hopelessness where she had at times resorted to prostitution to feed three small children. Today, twenty-five years later, Alourdes owns her own home, a three-story rowhouse in the Fort Greene section of Brooklyn. There she and her daughter Maggie run a complex and lively household that varies in size from six people (the core family, consisting of Alourdes, Maggie, and both their children) to as many as a dozen. The final tally depends on how many others are living with them at any given time. These may be recent arrivals from Haiti, down-on-their-luck friends and members of the extended family, or clients and members of the extended family, or clients of Alourdes's Vodou healing practice.

Maggie, now in her thirties, has been in the United States since early adolescence and consequently is much more Americanized than her mother. She is the adult in the family who deals with the outside world. Maggie does the paperwork which life in New York requires and negotiates with teachers, plumbers, electricians, and an array of creditors. She has a degree from a community college and currently works as a nurse's aide at a New York hospital.

Most of the time Alourdes stays at home where she cares for the small children and carries on her practice as a *manbo,* a Vodou priestess. Many Haitians and a few others such as Trinidadians, Jamaicans, and Dominicans come to her with work, health, family, and love problems. For diagnostic purposes, Alourdes first "reads the cards." Then she carries out healing "work" appropriate to the nature and severity of the problem. This may include: counseling the client, a process in which she calls on her own life experience and the shared values of the Haitian community as well as intuitive skills bordering on extrasensory perception; administering baths and other herbal treatments; manufacturing talismans; and summoning the Vodou spirits to "ride" her through trance-possession in order that spiritual insight and wisdom may be brought to bear on the problem.

Vodou spirits (Haitians never call them gods or goddesses) are quite different from deities, or even saints, in the way that we in North America usually use those terms. They are not moral exemplars, nor are their stories characterized by deeds of cosmic or even heroic proportion. Their scale (what makes them larger than life though not other than

it) comes, on the one hand, from the key existential paradoxes they contain and, on the other, from the caricature-like clarity with which they portray those pressure points in life. The *lwa* are full-blown personalities who preside over some particular social arena, and the roles they exemplify contain, as they do for the living who must fill them, both positive and negative possibilities.

Trance-possession within Vodou is somewhat like improvisational theater.[1] It is a delicate balancing act between traditional words and gestures which make the spirits recognizable and innovations which make them relevant. In other words, while the character types of the *lwa* are ancient and familiar, the specific things they say or do in a Vodou ritual unfold in response to the people who call them. Because the Vodou spirits are so flexible and responsive, the same spirit will manifest in different ways in the north and in the south of Haiti, in the countryside and in the cities, in Haiti and among the immigrants in New York. There are even significant differences from family to family. Here we are considering two female spirits as they manifest through a heterosexual Haitian woman who has lived in an urban context all her life and who has resided outside of Haiti for a quarter of a century. While most of what is said about these spirits would apply wherever Vodou is practiced, some of the emphases and details are peculiar to this woman and her location.

Vodou is a combination of several distinct African religious traditions. Also, from the beginning, the slaves included Catholicism in the religious blend they used to cope with their difficult lives. Among the most obvious borrowings were the identifications of African spirits with Catholic saints. The reasons why African slaves took on Catholicism are complex. On one level it was a matter of habit. The African cultures from which the slaves were drawn had traditionally been open to the religious systems they encountered through trade and war and had routinely borrowed from them. On another level it was a matter of strategy. A Catholic veneer placed over their own religious practices was a convenient cover for the perpetuation of these frequently outlawed rites. Yet this often cited and too often politicized explanation points to only one level of the strategic value of Catholicism. There was something deep in the slaves' religious traditions that very likely shaped their response to Catholicism. The Africans in Haiti took on the religion of the slave master, brought it into their holy places, incorporated its rites into theirs, adopted the images of Catholic saints as pictures of their own traditional spirits and the Catholic calendar as descriptive of the year's holy rhythms, and in general practiced a kind of cultural judo with Catholicism. They did this because, in the African ethos, imitation is not the sincerest form of flattery but the most efficient and direct way to gain understanding and leverage.

This epistemological style, exercised also on secular colonial culture, was clearly illustrated when I attended Vodou secret society[2] ceremonies in the interior of Haiti during the 1983 Christmas season. A long night of thoroughly African drumming and dancing included a surprising episode in which the drums went silent, home-made fiddles and brass instruments emerged, and a male and female dancer in eighteenth-century costume performed a slow and fastidious *contradans.* So eighteenth-century slaves in well-hidden places on the vast sugar plantations must have incorporated mimicry of their masters into their traditional worship as a way of appropriating the masters' power.

I want to suggest that this impulse toward imitation lies behind the adoption of Catholicism by African slaves. Yet I do not want to reduce sacred imitation to a political maneuver. On a broader canvas this way of getting to know the powers that be by imitating them is a pervasive and general characteristic of all the African-based religions in the New World. Grasping this important aspect of the way Vodou relates to the world will provide a key for understanding the nature of the relationship between Alourdes and her female spirits. When possessed by her woman spirits, Alourdes acts out the social and psychological forces that define, and often confine, the lives of contemporary Haitian women. She appro-

priates these forces through imitation. In the drama of possession-performance, she clarifies the lives of women and thereby empowers them to make the best of the choices and roles available to them.

Sacred imitation is a technique drawn from the African homeland, but the kinds of powers subject to imitation shifted as a result of the experience of slavery. The African religions that fed into Haitian Vodou addressed a full array of cosmic, natural, and social forces. Among the African spirits were those primarily defined by association with natural phenomena such as wind, lightning, and thunder. As a result of the shock of slavery, the lens of African religious wisdom narrowed to focus in exquisite detail on the crucial arena of social interaction. Thunder and lightning, drought and pestilence became pale, second-order threats compared with those posed by human beings. During the nearly 200 years since their liberation from slavery, circumstances in Haiti have forced Haitians to stay focused on the social arena. As a result, the Vodou spirits have also retained the strong social emphasis gained during the colonial period. Keeping these points in view, I now turn to Alourdes and two female Vodou spirits she serves. They both go by the name Ezili.

The Haitian Ezili's African roots are multiple.[3] Among them is Mammy Water, a powerful mother of the waters whose shrines are found throughout West Africa. Like moving water, Ezili can be sudden, fickle, and violent, but she is also deep, beautiful, moving, creative, nurturing, and powerful. In Haiti Ezili was recognized in images of the Virgin Mary and subsequently conflated with her. The various manifestations of the Virgin pictured in the inexpensive and colorful lithographs available throughout the Catholic world eventually provided receptacles for several different Ezilis as the spirit subdivided in the New World in order to articulate the different directions in which women's power flowed.

Alourdes, like all Vodou priests or priestesses, has a small number of spirits who manifest routinely through her. This spiritual coterie, which differs from person to person, both defines the character of the healer and sets the tone of his or her "temple." Ezili Dantor is Alourdes's major female spirit, and she is conflated with Mater Salvatoris, a black Virgin pictured holding the Christ child. The child that Dantor holds (Haitians usually identify it as a daughter!) is her most important iconographic detail, for Ezili Dantor is above all else the woman who bears children, the mother par excellence.

Haitians say that Ezili Dantor fought fiercely beside her "children" in the slave revolution. She was wounded, they say, and they point to the parallel scars that appear on the right cheek of the Mater Salvatoris image as evidence for this. Details of Ezili Dantor's possession-performance extend the story. Ezili Dantor also lost her tongue during the revolution. Thus Dantor does not speak when she possesses someone. The only sound the spirit can utter is a uniform "de-de-de." In a Vodou ceremony, Dantor's mute "de-de-de" becomes articulate only through her body language and the interpretive efforts of the gathered community. Her appearances are thus reminiscent of a somber game of charades. Ezili Dantor's fighting spirit is reinforced by her identification as a member of the Petro pantheon of Vodou spirits, and as such she is associated with what is hot, fiery, and strong. As a Petro spirit Dantor is handled with care. Fear and caution are always somewhere in the mix of attitudes that people hold toward the various Petro spirits.

Those, such as Alourdes, who serve Ezili Dantor become her children and, like children in the traditional Haitian family, they owe their mother high respect and unfailing loyalty. In return, this spiritual mother, like the ideal human mother, will exhaust her strength and resources to care for her children. It is important to note here that the sacrifice of a mother for her children will never be seen by Haitians in purely sentimental or altruistic terms. For Haitian women, even for those now living in New York, children represent the main hope for an economically viable household and the closest thing there is to a guarantee of care in old age. The mother-child relationship among Haitians is thus strong, essential, and in a not unrelated way,

potentially volatile. In the countryside, children's labor is necessary for family survival. Children begin to work at an early age, and physical punishment is often swift and severe if they are irresponsible or disrespectful. Although in the cities children stay in school longer and begin to contribute to the welfare of the family at a later age, similar attitudes toward childrearing prevail.

In woman-headed households, the bond between mother and daughter is the most charged and the most enduring. Women and their children form three- and sometimes four-generation networks in which gifts and services circulate according to the needs and abilities of each. These tight family relationships create a safety net in a society where hunger is a common experience for the majority of people. The strength of the mother-daughter bond explains why Haitians identify the child in Ezili Dantor's arms as a daughter. And the importance and precariousness of that bond explain Dantor's fighting spirit and fiery temper.

In possession-performance, Ezili Dantor explores the full range of possibilities inherent in the mother-child bond. Should Dantor's "children" betray her or trifle with her dignity, the spirit's anger can be sudden, fierce, and uncompromising. In such situations her characteristic "de-de-de" becomes a powerful rendering of women's mute but devastating rage. A gentle rainfall during the festivities at Saut d'Eau, a mountainous pilgrimage site for Dantor, is readily interpreted as a sign of her presence but so is a sudden deluge resulting in mudslides and traffic accidents. Ezili's African water roots thus flow into the most essential of social bonds, that between mother and child, where they carve out a web of channels through which can flow a mother's rage as well as her love.

Alourdes, like Ezili Dantor, is a proud and hard-working woman who will not tolerate disrespect or indolence in her children. While her anger is never directed at Maggie, who is now an adult and Alourdes' partner in running the household, it can sometimes sweep the smaller children off their feet. I have never seen Alourdes strike a child, but her wrath can be sudden and the punishments meted out severe. Although the suffering is different in kind, there is a good measure of it in both Haiti and New York, and the lessons have carried from one to the other. Once, after Alourdes disciplined her ten-year-old, she turned to me and said: "The world is evil. . . . You got to make them tough!"

Ezili Dantor is not only Alourdes's main female spirit, she is also the spirit who first called Alourdes to her role as priestess. One of the central functions of Vodou in Haiti, and among Haitian emigrants, is that of reinforcing social bonds. Because obligations to the Vodou spirits are inherited within families, Alourdes's decision to take on the heavy responsibility of serving the spirits was also a decision to opt for her extended family (and her Haitian identity) as her main survival strategy.

It was not always clear that this was the decision she would make. Before Alourdes came to the United States, she had shown little interest in her mother's religious practice, even though an appearance by Ezili Dantor at a family ceremony had marked her for the priesthood when she was only five or six years old. By the time Alourdes left Haiti she was in her late twenties and the memory of that message from Dantor had either disappeared or ceased to feel relevant. When Alourdes left Haiti, she felt she was leaving the spirits behind along with a life marked by struggle and suffering. But the spirits sought her out in New York. Messages from Ezili and other spirits came in the form of a debilitating illness that prevented her from working. It was only after she returned to Haiti for initiation into the priesthood and thus acknowledged the spirits' claim on her that Alourdes's life in the U.S. began to run smoothly.

Over the ten years I have known this family, I have watched a similar process at work with her daughter Maggie. Choosing the life of a Vodou priestess in New York is much more difficult for Maggie than it was for her mother. To this day, I have yet to see Maggie move all the way into a trance state. Possession threatens and Maggie struggles mightily; her body falls to the floor as if paralyzed, but she fights off the descending darkness that marks the onset of trance. Afterwards, she is angry and afraid. Yet these feelings finally did not prohibit Maggie from making a commitment to the *manbo's* role. She was initiated to the priesthood in the summer of 1982 in a small temple on the outskirts of Port-au-Prince. Alourdes presided at these rituals. Maggie's commitment to Vodou came after disturbing dreams and a mysterious illness not unlike the one that plagued Alourdes shortly after she came to the United States. The accelerated harassment of the spirits also started around the time when a love affair brought Maggie face to face with the choice of living with someone other than her mother. Within a short period of time, the love affair ended, the illness arrived, and Maggie had a portentous dream in which the spirits threatened to block her life path until she promised to undergo initiation. Now it is widely acknowledged that Maggie is the heir to Alourdes's successful healing practice.

Yet this spiritual bond between Alourdes and Maggie cannot be separated from the social, economic, and emotional forces that hold them together. It is clear that Alourdes and Maggie depend on one another in myriad ways. Without the child care Alourdes provides, Maggie could not work. Without the check Maggie brings in every week, Alourdes would have only the modest and erratic income she brings in from her healing work. These practical issues were also at stake in Maggie's decision about the Vodou priesthood, for a decision to become a *manbo* was also a decision to cast her lot with her mother. This should not be interpreted to mean that Alourdes uses religion to hold Maggie against her will. The affection between them is genuine and strong. Alourdes and Maggie are each other's best friend and most trusted ally. In Maggie's own words: "We have a beautiful relationship . . . it's more than a twin, it's like a Siamese twin. . . . She is my soul." And in Alourdes's: "If she not near me, I feel something inside me disconnected."

Maggie reports that when she has problems, Ezili Dantor often appears to her in dreams. Once, shortly after her arrival in the

United States, Maggie had a waking vision of Dantor. The spirit, clearly recognizable in her gold-edged blue veil, drifted into her bedroom window. Her new classmates were cruelly teasing her, and the twelve-year-old Maggie was in despair. Dantor gave her a maternal backrub and drifted out the window, where the spirit's glow was soon lost in that of a corner streetlamp. These days, when she is in trouble and Dantor does not appear of her own accord, Maggie goes seeking the spirit. "She don't have to talk to me in my dream. Sometime I go inside the altar, just look at her statue . . . she says a few things to me." The image with which Maggie converses is, of course, Mater Salvatoris, the black virgin, holding in her arms her favored girl child, Anaise.

It is not only in her relationship with her daughter that Alourdes finds her life mirrored in the image of Ezili Dantor. Ezili Dantor is also the mother raising children on her own, the woman who will take lovers but will not marry. In many ways, it is this aspect of Dantor's story that most clearly mirrors and maps the lives of Haitian women.

In former days (and still in some rural areas) the patriarchal, multigenerational extended family held sway in Haiti. In these families men could form unions with more than one woman. Each woman had her own household in which she bore and raised the children from that union. The men moved from household to household, often continuing to rely on their mothers as well as their women to feed and lodge them. When the big extended families began to break up under the combined pressures of depleted soil, overpopulation, and corrupt politics, large numbers of rural people moved to the cities.

Generally speaking, Haitian women fared better than men in the shift from rural to urban life. In the cities the family shrank to the size of the individual household unit, an arena in which women had traditionally been in charge. Furthermore, their skill at small-scale commerce, an aptitude passed on through generations of rural market women, allowed them to adapt to life in urban Haiti, where the income of a household must often be patched together from several small and sporadic sources. Urban women sell bread, candy, and herbal teas which they make themselves. They also buy and re-sell food, clothing, and household goods. Often their entire inventory is balanced on their heads or spread on outstretched arms as they roam through the streets seeking customers. When desperate enough, women also sell sex. They jokingly refer to their genitals as their "land." The employment situation in urban Haiti, meager though it is, also favors women. Foreign companies tend to prefer them for the piecework that accounts for a large percentage of the jobs available to the poor urban majority.

By contrast, unemployment among young urban males may well be as high as 80%. Many men in the city circulate among the households of their girlfriends and mothers. In this way they are usually fed, enjoy some intimacy, and get their laundry done. But life is hard and resources scarce. With the land gone, it is no longer so clear that men are essential to the survival of women and children. As a result, relationships between urban men and women have become brittle and often violent. And this is so in spite of a romantic ideology not found in the countryside. Men are caught in a double bind. They are still reared to expect to have power and to exercise authority, and yet they have few resources to do so. Consequently, when their expectations run up against a wall of social impossibility, they often veer off in unproductive directions. The least harmful of these is manifest in a national preoccupation with soccer; the most damaging is the military, the domestic police force of Haiti, which provides the one open road toward upward social mobility for poor young men. Somewhere in the middle of this spectrum lie the drinking and gambling engaged in by large numbers of poor men.

Ezili Dantor's lover is Ogou, a soldier spirit sometimes pictured as a hero, a breathtakingly handsome and dedicated soldier. But just as often Ogou is portrayed as vain and swaggering, untrustworthy and self-destructive. In one of his manifestations Ogou is a drunk. This is the man Ezili Dantor will take into her bed but would never depend on. Their relationship thus takes up and comments on much of the actual life experience of poor urban women.

Ezili Dantor also mirrors many of the specifics of Alourdes's own life. Gran Philo, Alourdes's mother, was the first of her family to live in the city. She worked there as a *manbo*. Although she bore four children, she never formed a long-term union with a man. She lived in Santo Domingo, in the Dominican Republic, for the first years of her adult life. There she had her first two babies. But her lover proved irrational, jealous, and possessive. Since she was working as hard or harder than he, Philo soon decided to leave him. Back in Port-au-Prince, she had two more children, but in neither case did the father participate in the rearing of the children. Alourdes, who is the youngest, did not know who her father was until she was grown. And when she found out, it still took time for him to acknowledge paternity.

In her late teens, Alourdes's fine singing voice won her a coveted position with the Troupe Folklorique, a song and dance group that drew much of its repertoire from Vodou. During that period Alourdes attracted the attention of an older man who had a secure job with the Bureau of Taxation. During their brief marriage Alourdes lived a life that was the dream of most poor Haitian women. She had a house and two servants. She did not have to work. But this husband, like the first man in Philo's life, needed to control her every move. His jealousy was so great that Alourdes was not even allowed to visit her mother without supervision. (The man should have known better than to threaten that vital bond!) Alourdes and her husband fought often and, after less than two years, she left. In the years that followed, there were times when Alourdes had no food and times when she could not pay her modest rent but, with pride like Ezili Dantor's, Alourdes never returned to her husband and never asked him for money. During one especially difficult period Alourdes began to operate as a Marie-Jacques, a prostitute, although not the kind who hawk their wares on the street. Each day

she would dress up and go from business to business in downtown Port-au-Prince looking for someone who would ask her for a "date." When the date was over she would take what these men offered (everyone knew the rules), but she never asked for money. Alourdes had three children in Haiti, by three different men. She fed them and provided shelter by juggling several income sources. Her mother helped when she could. So did friends when they heard she was in need. For a while, Alourdes held a job as a tobacco inspector for the government. And she also dressed up and went out looking for dates.

Maggie, like Alourdes, was married once. Her husband drank too much and one evening, he hit her. Once was enough. Maggie packed up her infant son and returned to her mother's house. She never looked back. When Maggie talks about this marriage, now over for nearly a decade, she says he was a good man but alcohol changed him. "When he drink, forget it!" She would not take the chance that he might hit her again or, worse, take his anger and frustration out on their son.

Ezili Dantor is the mother—fierce, proud, hard-working, and independent. As a religious figure, Dantor's honest portrayal of the ambivalent emotions a woman can feel toward her lovers and a mother can feel toward her children stands in striking contrast to the idealized attitude of calm, nurture, and acceptance represented by more standard interpretations of the Holy Mother Mary, a woman for whom rage would be unthinkable. Through her iconography and possession-performances, Ezili Dantor works in subtle ways with the concrete life circumstances of Haitian women such as Alourdes and Maggie. She takes up their lives, clarifies the issues at stake in them, and gives them permission to follow the sanest and most humane paths. Both Alourdes and Maggie refer to Ezili Dantor as "my mother."

Vodou is a religion born of slavery, of wrenching change and deep pain. Its genius can be traced to long experience in using the first (change) to deal with the second (pain). Vodou is a religion in motion, one without canon, creed, or pope. In Vodou the ancient African wisdom is preserved by undergoing constant transformation in response to specific life circumstances. One of the things which keeps Vodou agile is its plethora of spirits. Each person who serves the spirits has his or her own coterie of favorites. And no single spirit within that group can take over and lay down the law for the one who serves. There are always other spirits to consult, other spirit energies to take into account. Along with Ezili Dantor, Alourdes also serves her sister, Ezili Freda.

Ezili Freda is a white spirit from the Rada pantheon, a group characterized by sweetness and even tempers. Where Dantor acts out women's sexuality in its childbearing mode, Freda, the flirt, concerns herself with love and romance. Like the famous Creole mistresses who lent charm and glamour to colonial Haiti, Ezili Freda takes her identity and worth from her relationship with men. Like the mulatto elite in contemporary Haiti who are the heirs of those Creole women, Freda loves fine clothes and jewelry. In her possession-performances, Freda is decked out in satin and lace. She is given powder and perfume, sweet smelling soaps and rich creams. The one possessed by her moves through the gathered community, embracing one and then another and then another. Something in her searches and is never satisfied. Her visits often end in tears and frustration.[4]

Different stories are told about Freda and children. Some say she is barren. Others say she has a child but wishes to hide that fact in order to appear fresher, younger, and more desirable to men. Those who hold the latter view are fond of pointing out the portrait of a young boy that is tucked behind the left elbow of the crowned Virgin in the image of Maria Dolorosa with whom Freda is conflated. In this intimate biographical detail, Freda picks up a fragment from Alourdes's life that hints at larger connections between the two. When Alourdes was married she already had two children by two different men. She wanted a church wedding and a respectable life, so she hid the children from her prospective in-laws. It was only at the wedding itself, when they asked about the little boy and girl seated in the front row, that they found out the woman standing before the altar with their son already had children.

Alourdes does not have her life all sewn up in neat packages. She does not have all the questions answered and all the tensions resolved. Most of the time when she tells the story of her marriage, Alourdes says flatly: "He too jealous. That man crazy!" But on at least one occasion she said: "I was too young. If I was with Antoine now, I never going to leave him!" When Alourdes married Antoine Lovinsky she was a poor teenager living in Port-au-Prince, a city where less than 10% of the people are not alarmingly poor. Women of the elite class nevertheless structure the dreams of poor young women. These are the light-skinned women, who marry in white dresses in big Catholic churches and return to homes that have bedroom sets and dining room furniture and servants. These are the women who never have to work. They spend their days resting and visiting with friends and emerge at night on the arms of their men dressed like elegant peacocks and affecting an air of haughty boredom. Although Alourdes's tax collector could not be said to be a member of the elite, he provided her with a facsimile of the dream. It stifled her and confined her, but she has still not entirely let go of the fantasy. She still loves jewelry and clothes and, in her home, manages to create the impression, if not the fact, of wealth by piling together satin furniture, velvet paintings, and endless bric-a-brac.

Alourdes also has times when she is very lonely and she longs for male companionship. She gets tired of living at the edge of poverty and being the one in charge of such a big and ungainly household. She feels the pull of the images of domesticity and nuclear family life that she sees everyday on the television in New York. Twice since I have known her, Alourdes has fallen in love. She is a deeply sensual woman and this comes strongly to the fore during these times. She dresses up, becomes coquettish, and caters to her man. Yet when describing his lovable traits, she always says first: "He help me so much. Every month, he pay the electric bill," and so forth. Once again the practical and the emotional issues cannot be separated. In a way, this is just another version of the poor woman selling her "land." And in another way it is not, for here the finances of love are wound round and round with longing and dreams.

Poor Haitian women, Alourdes included, are a delight to listen to when their ironic wit turns on what we would label as the racism, sexism, and colonial pretense of the upper-class women Freda mirrors. Yet these are the values with power behind them both in Haiti and in New York, and poor women are not immune to the attraction of such a vision. Ezili Freda is thus an image poor Haitian women live toward. She picks up their dreams and gives them shape, but these women are mostly too experienced to think they can live on or in dreams. Alourdes is not atypical. She serves Freda but much less frequently than Dantor. Ezili Dantor is the one for whom she lights a candle every day; she is the one Alourdes turns to when there is real trouble. She is, in Alourdes' words, "my mother." Yet I think it is fair to say that it is the tension between Dantor and Freda that keeps both relevant to the lives of Haitian women.

There is a story about conflict between the two Ezilis. Most people, most of the time, will say that the scars on Ezili Dantor's cheek come from war wounds, but there is an alternative explanation. Sometimes it is said that because Dantor was sleeping with her man, Maria Dolorosa took the sword from her heart and slashed the cheek of her rival.

A flesh and blood woman, living in the real world, cannot make a final choice between Ezili Dantor and Ezili Freda. It is only when reality is spiced with dreams, when survival skills are larded with sensuality and play, that life moves forward. Dreams and play alone lead to endless and fruitless searching. And a whole life geared toward survival becomes brittle and threatened by inner rage. Alourdes lives at the nexus of several spirit energies. Freda and Dantor are only two of them, the two who help her most to see herself clearly as a woman.

To summarize the above discussion: The Vodou spirits are not idealized beings removed from the complexity and particularity of life. On the contrary, the responsive and flexible nature of Vodou allows the spirits to change over space and time in order to mirror people's life circumstances in considerable detail. Vodou spirits are transparent to their African origins and yet they are other than African spirits. Ancient nature connections have been buried deep in their iconographies while social domains have risen to the top, where they have developed in direct response to the history and social circumstances of the Haitian people. The Vodou spirits make sense of the powers that shape and control life by imitating them. They act out both the dangers and the possibilities inherent in problematic life situations. Thus, the moral pull of Vodou comes from clarification. The Vodou spirits do not tell the people what should be; they illustrate what is.

Perhaps Vodou has these qualities because it is a religion of an oppressed people. Whether or not that is true, it seems to be a type of spirituality with some advantages for women. The openness and flexibility of the religion, the multiplicity of its spirits, and the detail in which those spirits mirror the lives of the faithful makes women's lives visible in ways they are not in the so-called great religious traditions. This visibility can give women a way of working realistically and creatively with the forces that define and confine them.

NOTES

1. I use terms such as possession-performance and theater analogies in order to point to certain aspects of the spirits' self-presentation and interaction with devotees. The terms should not be taken as indicating that priestesses and priests simply pretend to be spirits during Vodou ceremonies. The trance states they enter are genuine, and they themselves will condemn the occasional imposter among them.

2. In an otherwise flawed book, E. Wade Davis does a very good job of uncovering and de-

scribing the nature and function of the Vodou secret societies. See *The Serpent and the Rainbow* (New York: Simon and Schuster, 1985).

3. Robert Farris Thompson traces Ezili to a Dahomean "goddess of lovers." *Flash of the Spirit: African and Afro-American Art and Philosophy* (New York: Random House, 1983), p. 191.

4. Maya Deren has drawn a powerful portrait of this aspect of Ezili Freda in *The Divine Horsemen: The Living Gods of Haiti* (New Paltz, N.Y.: Documentext, McPherson and Co., 1983), pp. 137–45.

FURTHER READINGS

Brown, Karen McCarthy. "The Center and the Edges: God and Person in Haitian Vodou." *The Journal of the Interdenominational Theological Center* 7, no. 1 (Fall 1979).

———. "Olina and Erzulie: A Woman and a Goddess in Haitian Vodou." *Anima,* Spring 1979.

———. "Systematic Forgetting, Systematic Remembering: Ogou in Haiti." In *Africa's Ogun: Old World and New.* ed. by Sandra T. Barnes. Bloomington, Ind.: University of Indiana Press, 1988.

———. "Alourdes: A Case Study of Moral Leadership in Haitian Vodou." In *Saints and Virtues,* ed. by John S. Hawley. Berkeley, Calif.: University of California Press, 1987.

———. "Afro-Caribbean Spirituality." In *Caring and Curing: Health and Medicine in the Western Religious Traditions,* ed. by Lawrence Eugene Sullivan. New York: Macmillan Press, 1988.

———. "The Power to Heal: Reflections on Women, Religion and Medicine." In *Shaping New Vision: Gender and Values in American Culture.* Ann Arbor, Mich.: UMI Press, 1987.

Deren, Maya. *Divine Horsemen: The Living Gods of Haiti.* New Paltz, N.Y.: Documentext, McPherson and Co., 1983.

Metraux, Alfred. *Voodoo in Haiti.* New York: Schocken Books, 1972.

Thompson, Robert Farris. *Flash of the Spirit: African and Afro-American Art and Philosophy.* New York: Random House, 1983.

Blessed Mother Ann, Holy Mother Wisdom: Gender and Divinity in Shaker Life and Belief

Marjorie Procter-Smith

Can Christians speak of God the Creator and God the Savior in any terms but male? "I believe in God, the Father Almighty, maker of heaven and earth; and in Jesus Christ his only Son, our Lord." "Glory be to the Father and to the Son and to the Holy Ghost." These phrases, recited or sung by generations of Christians, make it clear that the traditional Christian emphasis rests on a male God and

Original material prepared for this text.

his divine male son. Centuries of Christian doctrine, ritual, prayer, and song have repeated and developed the Father-Son imagery so thoroughly that it is difficult for many to imagine Christianity using any other language. When some contemporary feminists propose calling God Mother or imagining a woman Christ, they are often ridiculed or accused of abandoning the Christian tradition.

But in fact 200 years ago a Christian sect known as the Shakers spoke of God as Mother and believed that their founder, Ann Lee, was the second coming of Christ in female form. This essay discusses who the Shakers were, why they used female language for God, and how that language related to the roles and lives of women in the community.

WHO ARE THE SHAKERS?

In 1774, nine English passengers disembarked at New York harbor after a seventy-nine-day voyage from Liverpool. The passengers were Ann Lee, a prophetess and religious leader from Manchester in England, and her eight followers (six men and two women). These voyagers had been members of a group known in England as "Shaking Quakers." One of many small sects who prophesied the imminent end of the world and return of Christ to earth, the Shaking Quakers were chiefly known in England for disrupting church services with their ecstatic speech, singing, and prophesying.

When Ann Lee joined the group, they were guided by a charismatic woman, Jane Wardley. However, sometime around 1770, Ann Lee had an extraordinary religious experience, which propelled her into prominence among them. She later described this experience in language borrowed from her own experience of childbirth:

> Thus I labored, in strong cries and groans to God, day and night, till my flesh wasted away, and I became like a skeleton, and a kind of down came upon my skin, until my soul broke forth to God; which I felt as sensibly as ever a woman did a child, when she was delivered of it.[1]

As a result of this experience of new birth, Lee was favored with ecstatic visions of God and Jesus, Heaven and Hell. In the course of these visions, it was revealed to Lee by Jesus Christ that the "sin which is the root of all evil" is sexual intercourse, even within lawful marriage. Ann Lee's witness against "the doleful works of the flesh," an insistence on absolute celibacy, became one of the central tenets of

Shaker faith and a foundation for the development of Shaker community life.

Armed with these powerful heavenly visions, Lee claimed authority as leader of the group and convinced her followers of the necessity of resettling in America, where new missionary fields lay open to them. Once in America, Ann Lee and her small group settled in the wilderness of New York state in a village called Niskeyuna (now Watervliet, New York, near Albany) and began to gather new believers in Lee's message.

Lee taught that perfection was possible in this life, provided one "took up a full cross," which meant, practically speaking, willingness to confess all known sins to a Shaker leader (either Mother Ann or someone designated by her); to accept a celibate life, regardless of marital status; and to live a sinless life after the manner of Christ.

The term "Shaker" was a derisive one, given by non-Shakers who observed the ecstatic religious behavior of Ann Lee and her followers. Typical Shaker worship included shouting, leaping, dancing, whirling about, singing in unknown tongues, and falling into trances. Prophetic announcements and gestures were common, and Shaker worshippers thereby gained access to the spiritual world.

Lee's visions, however, were exceptional. To the observer, she appeared strange, otherworldly, and perhaps a bit frightening. One early follower remembered seeing Lee

> sit in her chair, from early in the morning, until afternoon, under great operations and power of God. She sung in unknown tongues, the whole of the time; and seemed to be wholly divested of any attraction to material things. All her sensations appeared to be engaged in the spiritual world.[2]

Lee reported that her visions during such periods included face-to-face conversations with God and with Jesus, visions of Heaven and the saints, and harrowing views of the suffering of the damned in Hell. In particular she described her relationship with Jesus as especially intimate:

I have been walking in fine valleys with Christ, as with a lover. . . . Christ is ever with me, both in sitting down and rising up; in going out and coming in. If I walk in groves and valleys, there he is, with me; and I converse with him as one friend converses with another, face to face.[3]

She also referred to Christ as her husband, her "Lord and Head," who preempts the authority of any human man. Lee's earthly husband, who had accompanied her to America, had not found Shaker doctrine and life satisfactory and apparently left the group early on.

At first Lee and the other leaders of the group advised new converts to return to their families and live in peace and holiness with them, an evangelical strategy that often seemed to work, because many of the first converts to Shakerism in America were members of a few large New England families. However, by 1782 or so necessity was conspiring with religious disposition to encourage the development of communal living, at least in a rather informal way. Clusters of Believers (as Shakers preferred to call themselves) began pooling their financial resources to provide support for poorer families and to provide food and lodging for traveling Shaker missionaries and visitors who gathered to hear the Shaker message.

When Ann Lee died in 1784 the remaining leaders recognized that for their movement to survive they needed to establish a more formal order and structure for living the Shaker life. Lee's successor, James Whittaker, began the process of organizing Believers into communities on the basis of common ownership of property and goods, or "joint interest." This process of "gathering into order" was continued by Whittaker's successor, Joseph Meacham, and his associate and successor, Lucy Wright.

Shaker communities, organized into units called "families," were constructed in part to replace the natural families that celibate Shakers were required to give up. All members were called "brother" or "sister," with those in leadership designated as "elders" and "eldresses." Each family had two elders

and two eldresses who held spiritual authority over the brothers and sisters; two deacons and two deaconesses who were responsible for the material well-being of the family (providing for food, clothing, upkeep of buildings and grounds, and so forth); and several trustees, who handled all business dealings with the "World," as non-Shakers were called.[4]

Overall, there have been eighteen major Shaker communities and several smaller and short-lived ones. During the middle of the nineteenth century the Shakers reached their peak membership of perhaps as many as 6,000.[5] Membership began to decline soon after this, however, and now only a very few individuals remain.[6]

SHAKER RELIGIOUS LANGUAGE

Shakerism grew in a religious environment in which many Christians believed in the imminent return of Jesus Christ to earth. This millennialism, as it is called, predisposed people to expect miraculous signs of various kinds. For example, on May 19, 1780, settlers clearing land in New England burned off brush and trees, and the resulting smoke hid the sun, making the day as dark as night. Terrified New Englanders, seeing birds and farm animals go to sleep as if it were night and remembering apocalyptic Biblical prophecy about the sun becoming "black as sackcloth," cried, "The day of judgment is come!" During Ann Lee's missionary journey through New England between 1781 and 1783 she and some of her followers saw a particularly spectacular display of the Northern Lights. One commented that the lights were "a sign of the coming of the Son of Man in the clouds of heaven." Although Ann Lee rejected this interpretation, clearly Shakers shared the general disposition of people to look for "signs and portents."

Likewise, millennialist expectations predisposed people to look for prophets and visionists. In such a milieu, then, Ann Lee's extraordinary visions and prophecies, her singing in unknown tongues, and astonishing messages about sin and perfection aroused intense interest. The extravagant singing and dancing in Shaker gatherings and the charismatic presence of Ann Lee combined to convince many New Englanders that the Second Coming was upon them.

In this religious context, believers concluded that Ann Lee had been the instrument of initiating the millennial church and had opened to the world the possibility of a life of Gospel perfection. The official name of the Shakers was the United Society of Believers in Christ's Second Appearing, also sometimes called the Millennial Church.

Some of the earliest Shaker theological works are explicit that Ann Lee herself is the one "in whom Christ did visibly make his second appearance."[7] Ann Lee and Jesus Christ are described in parallel terms as embodiments of the Christ-Spirit:

> The man who was called Jesus and the woman who was called Ann, are verily the two foundation pillars of the Church of Christ.[8]

Fundamental to this interpretation of Ann Lee as parallel to Jesus is Lee's own claim to have been married to Christ.

Another important element in the development of Shaker religious language is the title by which most Believers addressed Ann Lee during her life and remembered her after her death: "Mother" Ann. Perhaps because Lee was older than many of her American converts and because of the emotional attachment Believers felt for Ann Lee, the title of "Mother" became synonymous with Ann Lee, and Shaker documents routinely assume that the reader will know that any reference to "Mother" is a reference to Ann Lee.

Although Lee is often remembered as a rather stern mother who chastised her errant children and spoke sharply to them, she is represented predominantly as a loving mother who gave birth to her children in the faith, who labored over them and for them, and who guided them in the faith. A Shaker hymn expresses this idea:

> Born by our Mother, we were led,
> By her our infant souls were fed;

> And by her suff'rings and her toils
> She brought salvation to our souls.[9]

Thus, Jesus and Mother Ann were Believers' "Gospel Parents," as described in this hymn:

> Our Father and our Mother
> Have borne us in the birth,
> Their union is together,
> Redeemed from the earth:
> We children born, are not forlorn,
> But like our Parents dear,
> We've overcome the wicked one,
> And reign in Zion here.[10]

Having worked out the theological significance of Ann Lee as Mother and as Second appearing of Christ, Shakers turned their thoughts to the question of God. Unlike the theological development of an understanding of Ann Lee, which was based on personal experience of her as their spiritual mother, the Shaker doctrine of God was largely based on intellectual conviction.

The reasoning went something like this: If Ann Lee is our Mother and she is the female embodiment of the Christ-Spirit, then she holds a parallel position to Jesus as the first and male embodiment of the Christ-Spirit. If Jesus as the Christ reveals God the Father to humankind, then Mother Ann must also reveal God, and the God she reveals must necessarily be God the Mother. A major Shaker theological work puts it this way:

> The first appearing of Christ, in the simplest terms of language, is the Revelation of the Father, and the second appearing of Christ is the Revelation of the Mother; but for the subject under consideration we have preferred the title, "The Revelation of the Holy Ghost," as the most forcible and striking of all other scripture terms.[11]

This Mother-Holy Ghost God whom Ann Lee was said to reveal was later called Holy Mother Wisdom, who was said to reign with God the Father in heaven, as described in this hymn:

Long ere this fleeting world began
Or dust was fashioned into man,
There *Power* and *Wisdom* we can view,
Names of the *Everlasting Two*.

The Father's high eternal throne
Was never fill'd by one alone:
There Wisdom holds the Mother's seat
And is the Father's helper-meet.[12]

Shaker theologians regarded their dual Father-Mother God as logically superior to the trinitarian God of more traditional Christian theology. "As every individual on the world sprang from a father and a mother, the conclusion is self-evident, that the whole sprang from one joint parentage," argued Shaker theologian Benjamin Seth Youngs in 1808. It makes more sense, he reasoned, to talk about a God who is male and female than a God who is all male. Ridiculing "defective" trinitarian doctrine, Youngs wrote:

First the Father, second the Son, and third the Holy Ghost; He proceeding from Father and Son . . . without the attribute of either Mother or Daughter . . . and [they] finally look for the mystery of God to be finished in the odd number of three males. . . . Where then is the correspondent cause of the woman's existence?[13]

The cause of woman's existence, Shakers believed, had been revealed by Mother Ann, a Mother God, who shared God the Father's throne and represented "wisdom" to God the Father's "power."

Beginning in the 1830s a period of intense internal revival affected all the Shaker communities and brought the image of God the Mother into prominence in Shaker experience. Beginning with trance-like experiences similar to the ecstatic worship of the earliest days of Shakerism, the revival swept through all of the communities and lasted for more than ten years. Believers once again sang heavenly songs in unknown tongues, leaped and whirled about uncontrollably, and fell into trances in which they saw and spoke to long-dead Shaker leaders, including Mother Ann, Father William Lee (Ann Lee's brother),

Father Joseph (Meacham), and others. This period became known as "Mother Ann's Work," because it was believed that Mother Ann, seeing the loss of vitality in the faith of her children, had sent them this revival.

Most notably, certain Believers claimed to have been chosen as "instruments" of various heavenly beings, usually angels, who delivered messages from Mother Ann and other heavenly denizens to Believers. For the most part these claims were accepted by the leadership and by the members, and their messages were received with great respect and awe.[14] A disproportionate number of these instruments were women.

During the height of the revival, between 1840 and 1843, Holy Mother Wisdom made a series of visits to the communities in the person of a female instrument. Sometimes the visits lasted several days and included individual interviews by Holy Mother Wisdom of each member of the community. These visits were carefully prepared for by periods of fasting, prayer, confessions of sin, and intensive cleaning of the grounds and buildings. The visit normally concluded with Holy Mother Wisdom bestowing her "mark" on the forehead of each Believer or granting them some similar spiritual blessing. One contemporary observer remembered Holy Mother Wisdom concluding the visit with these words: "Around thy head I place a golden band. On it is written the name of me, Holy Mother Wisdom! the Great Jehovah! the Eternal God! Touch not mine anointed!"[15]

SHAKER WOMEN

Shaker women had before them the example of Ann Lee. On the one hand, she was extraordinarily gifted: prophetess, visionary, bride, and companion of Christ; teacher; judge; and loving but strict spiritual mother. On the other hand she shared the experiences of many of the women who were drawn to Shakerism: She was poor and illiterate; she had been married to a man she described as "very kind, according to nature," and had given birth to four children and had seen them all die in infancy; she had suffered persecution for her religious beliefs; and she had struggled to make a living and survive in a new land. Lee's exceptional ability to infuse with religious meaning her own struggles and sufferings as a woman provided a rich resource to her female followers who shared many of her experiences.

Later theological speculation interpreted Ann Lee as the Second Christ, an object not only of loving memory but also a figure of cosmic significance: one of the two "foundation pillars" of the Church, the Daughter of God, the Mother of All Living, the Revelation of God the Mother. Shaker women had not only the memory of a spiritually powerful woman who was like them in many ways, but they also had access to a positive, powerful female Christ and a loving Mother God.

The loving Mother God came to be known as Holy Mother Wisdom and was presented to them materially in the form of a woman visionist. During the visitations of Holy Mother Wisdom each woman and man in the community received at the hands of a woman a gift directly from God, the mark of Holy Mother Wisdom, and heard from the mouth of a woman words of judgment or blessing. Although female instruments did not always speak only in the name of Holy Mother Wisdom or Mother Ann, the strength of the communities' belief in these figures legitimated women's exercise of their prophetic gifts in general.

Shaker women's more temporal gifts were also legitimated by Shaker community structures. The development of a centralized and tightly structured leadership after the "gathering into order" might have excluded women, after the pattern of many other religious movements founded by women. Indeed leadership did not automatically pass to other women on Ann Lee's death. On the contrary Lee was succeeded by two men before a pattern of female leadership was established with the appointment by Joseph Meacham of Lucy Wright as "Mother" of the entire sect alongside himself as "Father."

At first there was considerable resistance to Mother Lucy's leadership from male Shakers who were offended by the idea of a woman in a position of religious authority over them, and many people left the community in protest. However, the pattern of dual male and female leadership was established and remained the norm for all Shaker communities. This requirement gave Shaker women greater access to positions of religious leadership than women in most other Christian groups. Appointment to eldress of a community meant the opportunity to exercise temporal and spiritual leadership, greater responsibility, and chances to travel to other communities.

At the same time along with the advantages of the Shaker theological and communal system for woman came some disadvantages. The theological interpretation of Holy Mother Wisdom, for example, depended a great deal on popular nineteenth-century views of "women's sphere" and the "cult of True Womanhood."[16] Holy Mother Wisdom was described by one Shaker writer as "endless love, truth, meekness, long forbearance, and loving kindness ... the Mother of all Godliness, meekness, purity, peace, sincerity, virtue, and chastity."[17] Although in theory such virtues were to apply to all Shakers, in fact they were associated with women primarily, even divine women.

The Shaker communal system provided opportunities for leadership for women, but it did so in the context of a strictly hierarchical system in which leaders were not elected but appointed by their superiors, and virtually absolute obedience to the leaders was expected. Work in the communities was rigidly divided, with women largely confined to traditional "women's work": food preparation, clothing manufacture and maintenance, and household maintenance. This pragmatic division of labor was interpreted as being of divine origin, and Shaker women were advised that true freedom for them lay in remaining within "woman's sphere."

CONCLUSIONS

It is striking how many contemporary feminist religious issues are found in the history of Shakerism. Contemporary feminists have challenged mainstream religious groups to expand women's opportunities for religious leadership, to reconsider the use of exclusively male language about God and Christ, and to develop religious language that draws on women's experience. From an examination of Shaker history we may see a Christian group that struggled to preserve women's religious leadership, that worshipped God as Mother as well as Father, and that drew some of its central religious terms from women's traditional childbearing and household work.

Most radical of the Shakers' ideas about women and religion, and most startlingly contemporary, is their grasp of the connection between an exclusively male representation of God and a male-dominated society. Antoinette Doolittle, editor of the Shaker journal *Shaker and Shakeress* from 1873 to 1875, observed, "As long as we have all male Gods in the heavens we shall have all male rulers on the earth."[18] They also insisted that the recognition of the female in deity was essential to women's social and religious emancipation, and they were unflinching in their criticism of male-centered theology and church.

However, their answer to their critique of male-centered religion was a highly dualistic system based on the fundamental difference between men and women. In this oppositional system women's "sphere" was diametrically opposed to that of men, and it left women in the same place reserved for them by conventional wisdom. Although redeemed Shaker women were spiritually superior to all unredeemed women and men, women by nature were understood to be more sinful than men. Indeed, this greater sinfulness of women necessitated, in part, the Second Coming of Christ in female form. A Shaker hymn says,

> As disobedience first began
> In Eve, the second part of man
> The second trumpet could not sound
> Til second Eve her Lord had found.[19]

"Second Eve" here refers to Ann Lee, whose Lord is Christ.

The questions these limitations of the Shaker system raise are several and are now being dealt with in contemporary feminist critiques of religion. First, there is the question of valorizing women's traditional experience. Such valorization recognizes that the work women have done for eons—care of children, care of households, concern for maintenance of human relationships—is the work of world-construction and world-maintenance, and as such it is religious work. The risk of such valorization, as the Shaker history shows, is that it reinforces the cultural notion that such work is women's sole work and that it is solely women's work. Such a view restricts women's access to other kinds of work and suggests that men need not concern themselves with such work, a bifurcation that feminism has taken some pains to correct.

Second, the Shaker story raises questions about essentialism. Is there some essential female character or virtue? Some Shaker theologians assumed that there was such a thing and that they knew what it was. Both arguments that female character is essentially flawed or sinful and that female character is essentially nurturant, loving, and caring claim such knowledge, and both views can be found not only in Shakerism but in other religions as well. Some contemporary feminists have challenged such claims about women, insisting instead that while women share some oppressions in common as women, women's experiences are diverse and complex and cannot be simplified into claims of innate evil or innate goodness.

Third, the Shakers demonstrate both the difficulties of preserving and perpetuating strong female leadership and the value of having the example of a female founder as a living memory in the community's life. The Shaker's most effective method of ensuring the continuation of female leadership, however, was their ideological system, which demanded equal leadership by men and women and recruited and developed strong women for leadership positions. Without such structural demands even the memory of Ann Lee would not have sufficed to preserve women's religious leadership.

NOTES

1. *Testimonies of the Life, Character, Revelations and Doctrines of our Ever Blessed Mother Ann Lee, and the Elders With Her* (Hancock, MA: J. Talcott and J. Deming, Junrs., 1816), p. 47.
2. Ibid., p. 200.
3. Ibid., p. 211.
4. For further information on the Shakers' business dealings, see Edward Deming Andrews, *The Community Industries of the Shakers* (University of the State of New York, 1933; New York State Museum Handbook No. 15).
5. The actual peak population of Shaker communities is disputed. Compare Edward Deming Andrews, *The People Called Shakers* (New York: Dover Publications, 1953), p. 224; Priscilla J. Brewer, *Shaker Communities, Shaker Lives* (Hanover, NH: University Press of New England, 1986), p. 156; and William Sims Bainbridge, "Shaker Demographics 1840–1900: An Example of the Use of U.S. Census Enumeration Schedule," *Journal For the Scientific Study of Religion* 21 (1982), p. 355.
6. At present the Shaker communities of Sabbathday Lake, Maine, and Canterbury, New Hampshire, are the only occupied communities.
7. *Testimonies* (1816), p. 2.
8. Benjamin Seth Youngs, *The Testimony of Christ's Second Appearing* (Albany: The United Society, 1810, Second Edition), p. 440.
9. Seth Y. Wells, compiler, *Millennial Praises* (Hancock, MA: Josiah Talcott, 1813), p. 105.
10. Ibid., p. 35.
11. Youngs, p. 537.
12. Wells, p. 1.
13. Youngs, p. 454.
14. Shaker manuscript collections such as those found at the Western Reserve Historical Society, the Shaker Museum at Old Chatham, New York, and the Archives and Manuscript Division of the New York Public Library have large numbers of recorded gift drawings and messages from this period, most of them by women.
15. David R. Lamson, *Two Years' Experience Among the Shakers* (West Boylston, MA: Published by the Author, 1848), p. 95.
16. See Barbara Welter, "The Cult of True Womanhood," *American Quarterly* 18 (1966), pp. 151–174.
17. Paulina Bates, *The Divine Book of Holy Wisdom* (Canterbury, NH: n.p., 1849), p. 661.
18. "Address of Antoinette Doolittle, Troy, NY, March 24, 1872," *The Shaker* 2.6 (June 1872), p. 43.
19. Wells, p. 250.

REFERENCES

Andrews, Edward Deming. 1953. *The People Called Shakers.* New York: Dover Publications.

Foster, Lawrence. 1984. *Religion and Sexuality: The Shakers, the Mormons, and the Oneida Community.* Urbana: University of Illinois Press.

Garrett, Clarke. 1989. *Spirit Possession and Popular Religion: From the Camisards to the Shakers.* Baltimore: Johns Hopkins.

Humez, Jean. 1981. *Gifts of Power: The Writings of Rebecca Jackson, Black visionary, Shaker Eldress.* Amherst: University of Massachusetts Press.

Mercadante, Linda. 1990. *Gender, Doctrine, and God: The Shakers and Contemporary Theology.* Nashville: Abingdon Press.

Patterson, Daniel W. 1979. *The Shaker Spiritual.* Princeton: Princeton University Press.

Procter-Smith, Marjorie. 1985. *Women in Shaker Community and Worship.* Lewiston, NY: Edwin Mellen Press.

Sasson, Diane. 1983. *The Shaker Spiritual Narrative.* Knoxville: University of Tennessee.

X.
Gender, Politics, and Reproduction

All human reproductive behavior is culturally patterned. This cultural patterning includes menstrual beliefs and practices; restrictions on the circumstances in which sexual activity may occur; beliefs and practices surrounding pregnancy, labor, and the postpartum period; understandings and treatment of infertility; and the significance of the menopause. While research on human biological reproduction has been dominated by medical concerns such as normal and abnormal physiological processes, an increasing anthropological literature addresses reproduction as a sociocultural process. Biological reproduction refers to the production of human beings, but this process is always a social activity, leading to the perpetuation of social systems and social relations. The ways in which societies structure human reproductive behavior reflect core social values and principles, informed by changing political and economic conditions (Browner and Sargent 1990:215).

Much of the available anthropological data on reproduction prior to 1970 is to be found within ethnographies devoted to other subjects. For example, Montagu analyzed concepts of conception and fetal development among Australian aborigines, and Malinowski wrote about reproductive concepts and practices among the Trobriand Islanders (Montagu 1949; Malinowski 1932). Several surveys of ethnographic data on reproduction were compiled, such as Ford's (1964) study of customs surrounding the reproductive cycle or Spencer's (1949–1950) list of reproductive practices around the world.

In the past twenty years anthropologists have sought to use cross-cultural data from preindustrial societies to help resolve women's health problems in the industrialized world (Oakley 1977; Jordan 1978). For example, comparative research on birth practices has raised questions regarding the medicalization of childbirth in the United States. Anthropologists have also involved themselves in international public health efforts to improve maternal and child health around the world. In addition, anthropological research has helped to clarify the relationship between population growth and poverty. While some analysts have held the view that overpopulation is a determinant of poverty and the poor must control their fertility to overcome impoverishment, others argue the reverse: people have many children *because* they are poor (Rubinstein and Lane 1991:386).

Concern with population growth has often focused on women as the potential users of contraceptives, although women's personal desires to limit fertility may not be translated into action because of opposition from husbands, female relations, or others with influence or decision-making power. In this area of research anthropologists have an important contribution to make in examining such factors as cultural concepts regarding fertility and family size, the value of children, dynamics of decision making within the family and community, and the relationship between women's reproductive and productive roles.

Since the 1970s anthropological interest has turned to the linkages between cultural constructions of gender, the cultural shaping of motherhood, and reproductive beliefs and practices. In many societies throughout the world the relationship between women's status and maternity is clear: a woman attains adult status by childbearing, and her prestige may be greatly enhanced by bearing numerous male children (Browner and Sargent 1990:218). Thus, in the Middle East a woman is "raised for marriage and procreation [and] acquires her own social status only by fecundity" (Vieille 1978:456), while in parts of Africa pressures to be prolific weigh heavily on women (Sargent 1982).

In much of the world infertility is dreaded by men and women alike but is a particular burden to women (Browner and Sargent 1990:219). Such pressure to reproduce is especially intense in agrarian societies, which have a high demand for labor. However, in many hunter-gatherer and horticultural societies, motherhood and reproduction are less emphasized. As Collier and Rosaldo observe, "Contrary to our expectation that motherhood provides women everywhere with a natural source of emotional satisfaction and cultural value, we found that neither women nor men in very simple societies celebrate women as nurturers or women's unique capacity to give life" (1981:275).

Just as beliefs and practices regarding fertility are culturally patterned, birth itself is a cultural production (Jordan 1978). As Romalis notes, "The act of giving birth to a child is never simply a physiological act but rather a performance defined by and enacted within a cultural context" (Romalis 1981:6). Even in advanced industrial societies such as the United States, childbirth experiences are molded by cultural, political, and economic processes (Oakley 1980; Martin 1987; Michaelson et al. 1988). Studying the cultural patterning of birth practices can illuminate the nature of domestic power relations and the roles of women as reproductive health specialists, and it can increase our understanding of the relations between men and women cross-culturally.

While reproduction is culturally patterned, not all individuals in a society share reproductive goals. As Browner (this book) points out, reproductive behavior is influenced by the interests of a woman's kin, neighbors, and other members of the community, and these interests may conflict. Government policies regarding the size and distribution of population may differ from the interests of reproducing women. Women's goals in turn may not be shared by their partners or other individuals and groups in the society. Browner examines the ways in which access to power in a society determines how conflicts concerning reproduction are carried out and dealt with by analyzing population practices in a Chinantec-Spanish-speaking township in Oaxaca, Mexico.

In this community the government's policy to encourage fertility reduction was imposed on a preexisting conflict between the local community as a whole, which encouraged increased fertility, and women of the community, who sought to limit family size. Women and men manifested very different attitudes concerning fertility desires: women sought much smaller families than men. As children increasingly attend school their economic benefits appeared slight to their mothers. Further, women viewed pregnancy as stressful and debilitating. Yet despite these negative views, women felt they could not ignore pressures to reproduce.

Such pressure came from community men, who valued a large community for the interests of the defense and well-being of the collectivity, and from other women, who, while not desiring more children themselves, wanted other women to bear children in the interests of the group. In spite of the ease of obtaining government contraceptives, women rejected their use. Some felt that state policy promoting family planning was in fact cultural genocide, designed to eliminate indigenous Indian populations. In this cultural, political, and economic context, local women experienced conflict between personal desires to have few children and local pressures to be prolific.

Ginsburg (in this book) also discusses reproduction as a contested domain, using the example of abortion in American culture. She suggests that the focus of this conflict of interests is the relationship between reproduction, nurturance, sex, and gender. Using life histories of prolife and prochoice activists in Fargo, North Dakota, she reveals how different historical conditions affect reproductive decisions. The activist protesters in Fargo vie for the power to define womanhood in light of a basic American cultural script, in which pregnancy results in childbirth and motherhood in the context of marriage. Ginsburg argues that the struggle over abortion rights is a contest for control over the meanings attached to reproduction in America and suggests that "female social activism in the American context operates to mediate the construction of self and gender with larger social, political, and cultural processes."

Similarly, Whitbeck argues that controversy over abortion rights in the United States must be understood in relation to a cultural context that neglects women's experiences and the status of women as "moral individuals." Rather, American culture regards women and women's bodies as "property to be bartered, bestowed, and used by men" (Whitbeck 1983:259). Concern with restricting access to abortions derives from the interest of the state or others in power to control women's bodies and their reproductive capacity (Whitbeck 1983:260).

Ginsburg's research shows that prochoice activists in Fargo cluster in a group born in the 1940s and influenced by the social movements of the 1960s and 1970s. These movements offered a new vision of a world defined not only by reproduction and motherhood, but filled with broader possibilities. Right-to-life women comprised one cohort born in the 1920s and a second cohort born in the 1950s. Many of these women experienced their commitment to the right-to-life movement as a sort of conversion, occurring at the time they moved out of the paid work force to stay home with children. Women's life histories indicate that embracing a prolife or prochoice position "emerges specifically out of a confluence of reproductive and generational experiences." Reproduction, often defined in American culture as a biological domain, takes on meaning within a historically specific set of cultural conditions.

While Ginsburg discusses how abortion activists seek to define American womanhood in relation to cultural ideals of motherhood and nurturance, Gruenbaum (this book) shows that cultural expectations of marriage and motherhood in Sudan form the context for the deeply embedded practice of female circumcision. Female circumcision is reported to exist in at least twenty-six countries, and estimates of the number of women of all ages who have been circumcised in Africa reach 80 million; other estimates suggest that as many as 5 million children are operated on each year (Kouba and Muasher 1985; Sargent 1991). The various forms of female circumcision present serious risks, such as infection and hemorrhage at the time of the procedure and future risks to childbearing; therefore, social scientists, feminists, and public health organizations have opposed the practices. However, as Gruenbaum observes, female circumcision "forms part of a complex sociocultural arrangement of female subjugation in a strongly patrilineal, patriarchal society" and continues to be most strongly defended by women, who carry out the practice.

Women in Sudan derive status and security as wives and mothers. Virginity is a prerequisite for marriage, and in this context clitoridectomy and infibulation, the major forms of circumcision, are perceived as protecting morality. Thus, these practices persist because they are linked to the important goal of maintaining the reputation and marriageability of daughters. Forty years of policy formulated by the Sudanese government and by international health organizations emphasizing the physically dangerous dimensions of female circumcision and prohibiting the most extensive forms of the practice have not resulted in its elimination.

As Gruenbaum notes, clitoridectomy and infibulation are considered by Sudanese men and women to enhance a woman's ability to please her husband sexually, while attenuating inappropriate sexual desire outside marriage. Insofar as women are dependent on husbands for social and economic support and have few opportunities for educational advancement or viable employment, female circumcision is unlikely to be eradicated on medical grounds.

Miller's discussion of female infanticide and child neglect in North India (this book) is also set in a strongly patrilineal, patriarchal society and dramatically illustrates the links between gender ideology, reproduction, and health. In North India family survival depends on the reproduction of sons for the rural labor force, and preference for male children is evident in substantial ethnographic data documenting discrimination against girls. In this region preferences for male children result in celebrations at the birth of a boy, while a girl's birth goes unremarked. Sex-selective child care and female infanticide also indicate cultural favoring of male children.

Reports of female infanticide in India have occurred since the eighteenth century. There is evidence that a few villages in North India had never raised one daughter. In spite of legislation prohibiting female infanticide, the practice has not totally disappeared, although Miller argues that direct female infanticide has been replaced by indirect infanticide or neglect of female children. Indirect female infanticide is accomplished by nutritional and health-care deprivation of female children, a phenomenon also discussed by Charlton (see Part XI). Miller argues that the strong preference for sons in rural North India is related to the economic and social functions of sons.

The preference for male children has important repercussions in the increasing demand for abortion of female fetuses following amniocentesis. For example, in one clinic in North India 95% of female fetuses were aborted following prenatal sex determination. Thus, new reproductive technologies such as amniocentesis are

seen to be manipulated in patriarchal interests. Miller suggests that, ultimately, understanding the patriarchal culture of north India may help promote more effective health care and enhanced survival chances for female children.

The readings in this part illustrate the ways in which human reproductive behavior is socially constructed and influenced by economic and political processes. Rather than perceiving reproductive health in a narrow biological or purely personal framework, cross-cultural research suggests that women's health needs should be addressed in the context of their multifaceted productive, reproductive, and social roles. Consequently, decisions about such reproductive health issues as family size and composition are never left to the individual woman, but are influenced by kin, community, and state interests. These interests are often contested with the introduction of new reproductive technologies enabling sophisticated prenatal testing, treatment for infertility, and surrogate mothering. As these technologies increasingly spread throughout the world, their availability will raise important questions regarding cultural definitions of parenting, concepts of personhood, and gender roles and relations.

REFERENCES

Browner, Carole and Carolyn Sargent. 1990. Anthropology and Studies of Human Reproduction. In Thomas M. Johnson and Carolyn Sargent (eds.). *Medical Anthropology: Contemporary Theory and Method*, pp. 215–229. New York: Praeger Publishers.

Collier, Jane F. and Michelle Z. Rosaldo. 1981. Politics and Gender in Simple Societies. In Sherry B. Ortner and Harriet Whitehead (eds.). *Sexual Meanings: The Cultural Construction of Gender and Sexuality*. Cambridge: Cambridge University Press.

Ford, Clellan Stearns. 1964. *A Comparative Study of Human Reproduction*. Yale University Publications in Anthropology No. 32: Human Relations Area Files Press.

Jordan, Brigitte. 1978. *Birth in Four Cultures*. Montreal: Eden Press Women's Publications.

Kouba, Leonard J. and Judith Muasher. 1985. Female Circumcision in Africa: An Overview. *African Studies Review* 28(1): 95–110.

Malinowski, Bronislaw. 1932. *The Sexual Life of Savages in Northwestern Melanesia.* London: Routledge and Kegan Paul.

Martin, Emily. 1987. *The Woman in the Body: A Cultural Analysis of Reproduction.* Boston: Beacon Press.

Michaelson, Karen, et al. 1988. *Childbirth in America: Anthropological Perspectives.* South Hadley, MA: Bergin and Garvey.

Montagu, M. F. Ashley. 1949. Embryology from Antiquity to the End of the 18th Century. *Ciba Foundation Symposium* 10(4): 994–1008.

Oakley, Ann. 1977. Cross-cultural Practices. In Tim Chard and Martin Richards (eds.). *Benefits and Hazards of the New Obstetrics.* London: William Heinemann Medical Books.

———. 1980. *Women Confined: Towards a Sociology of Childbirth.* New York: Schocken Books.

Rubinstein, Robert A. and Sandra D. Lane. 1991. International Health and Development. In Thomas M. Johnson and Carolyn Sargent (eds.). *Medical Anthropology: Contemporary Theory and Method,* pp. 367–391. New York: Praeger Publishers.

Romalis, Shelly (ed.). 1981. *Childbirth: Alternatives to Medical Control.* Austin: University of Texas Press.

Sargent, Carolyn. 1982. *The Cultural Context of Therapeutic Choice.* Dordrecht, Holland: D. Reidel Publishing Company.

———. 1991. Confronting Patriarchy: The Potential for Advocacy in Medical Anthropology. *Medical Anthropology Quarterly* 5(1): 24–25.

Spencer, Robert. 1949–1950. Introduction to Primitive Obstetrics. *Ciba Foundation Symposium* 11(3): 1158–88.

Vieille, Paul. 1978. Iranian Women in Family Alliance and Sexual Politics. In Lois Beck and Nikki Keddie (eds.). *Women in the Muslim World,* pp. 451–472. Cambridge: Harvard University Press.

Whitbeck, Caroline. 1983. The Moral Implications of Regarding Women as People": New Perspectives on Pregnancy and Personhood. In William B. Bondeson et al. (eds.). *Abortion and the Status of the Fetus,* pp. 247–272. Dordrecht, Holland: D. Reidel Publishing.

The Politics of Reproduction in a Mexican Village

Carole H. Browner

Although women in all societies bear children in private, or with only a select few present, human reproduction is never entirely a personal affair. Kin, neighbors, and other members of the larger collectives of which women are a part seek to influence reproductive behavior in their groups. Their concerns, however, about who reproduces, how often, and when frequently conflict quite sharply with the desires of the reproducers themselves.[1] At

Reprinted with permission of The University of Chicago Press from *Signs* 11(4):710–724, 1986. ©1986 by The University of Chicago. All rights reserved.

the state level, governments develop policies with which they try to shape the size, composition, and distribution of their populations. These policies inevitably seek to influence the reproductive activities of individuals. They may be directed toward the fertility of the whole society or selectively imposed on particular classes, subcultures, or other internal groups,[2] but they are usually promoted without much consideration for the individual women who bear and raise the children, and, as a result, they may not be embraced by their target groups. Further, state-initiated population policies are sometimes challenged by internal groups whose objectives differ from those of the state.[3]

It is surprising that conflicts between the reproductive desires of a society's fecund women and the demographic interests of other individuals, groups, and political entities are rarely explored. After a comprehensive review of research in demography, population studies, and the anthropology and sociology of reproduction, Rosalind Pollack Petchesky reports, "Utterly lacking [in these fields] is any sense that the methods and goals of reproduction, and control over them, may themselves be a contested area within [a] culture."[4] Also absent from this research is the recognition that differential access to a society's sources of power determines how conflicts over reproduction are conducted and resolved, and even whether resolution ever occurs.

The following account analyzes the relationship between the population practices in one indigenous community in Mexico and the Mexican government's recent effort to reduce population growth. It shows that the government's fertility-reducing policy was superimposed on a long-standing local conflict between this community's women, who wished to limit the size of their own families, and the community as a whole, which wanted all of its female members to reproduce abundantly. Despite their apparent concordance with the goals of the state, the women refused the government's contraceptive services. They continued to have many children instead. The discussion will consider both why these indigenous rural women did not act on the fertility desires they expressed and why the demographic policies of Mexico have met uncertain success; for the two are outcomes of the same phenomenon: an overriding cultural prohibition in that community against any kind of fertility control.

BACKGROUND

The data presented here were collected in 1980–81 in a community I will call San Francisco, a Chinantec-Spanish-speaking *munici-* *pio* (township) located five hours by bus from the capital of the state of Oaxaca. The *municipio* was made up of a *cabecera* (head town) and a number of *ranchos* (hamlets) spread over a fifty-kilometer range. A year's participant observation was combined with interviews from a sample selected from the 336 adult women who lived in San Francisco. This sample consisted of 180 women selected to represent the age, residence, and linguistic background of the women. The husbands of the married women were also interviewed, a total of 126 men.

Historically, an important element in women's attempts to control their fertility was the use of medicinal plants. In addition to learning the respondents' reproductive desires and attitudes toward childbearing and child rearing, one aim of the interviews was to determine how the knowledge and use of such plants for management of reproduction and the maintenance of reproductive health were distributed and what might be the social implications of this distribution of knowledge before and after the Mexican government's introduction of modern birth control techniques. Demographic, economic, and health data were also obtained.

The *municipio* consisted of just over three hundred families of subsistence farmers who lived dispersed over its 18,300 hectares. Nearly two-thirds of the households (65 percent) cultivated the community's abundant communal landholdings in the tropical lowlands thirty miles east of the *cabecera*, or three hours from there by bus. The remainder used private plots located either in the *cabecera* or in the highland territory that individual Franciscanos purchased in 1930 from a neighboring *municipio*, or they farmed in both places. About a third of the families (32 percent) lived permanently on lowland ranches while most of the rest divided their time between the town center and the lowlands. Although only 5 percent of the households worked solely for wages, another 80 percent reported cash income from at least occasional wage labor.

Most full-time *rancho* residents had regular contact with the *cabecera*. Men made the trip several times each year to attend mandatory town assemblies. Men were also required to reside in the head town during their terms of civil and/or religious community service (*cargos*), which required several years of full-time commitment over the course of their lifetimes. Women had no formal reason for regular visits to the *cabecera*, but they sometimes went during holidays. In addition, they were expected to help their husbands carry out *cargo* responsibilities and often moved with them to the *cabecera* during their husbands' terms of office.

Until about 1965, the *municipio* fit the model of a closed corporate peasant community,[5] maintaining only sporadic contact with the world outside. Since that time, San Francisco's isolation had been sharply reduced by mandatory primary education, the construction of the Oaxaca-Tuxtepec highway and a feeder road connecting the *cabecera* in it, and a growing stream of migrants leaving the area for Oaxaca City, Mexico City, and the United States. Nevertheless, for many residents, daily life was much as it had always been: 42 percent of the women interviewed and 16 percent of the men had never been more than a few miles outside the community.

WOMEN'S ATTITUDES TOWARD PREGNANCY AND CHILDREN

Women in San Francisco expressed sharply negative attitudes about childbearing and child rearing, an unexpected finding that is contrary to the results of most other studies of peasants' attitudes toward fertility in Latin America.[6] While most research has suggested that peasant women want fewer children than they actually have, it has also suggested that, among these women, three to five children is considered the ideal family size and childlessness is considered a great misfortune. In San Francisco, a very different picture emerged. Among my study population, it was not unusual for women to volunteer that they would have preferred to remain childless or to have far smaller families than they did have. (Sixty

of the 180 women interviewed had five or more children.) Sixty-three percent believed that there were women in their community who would choose childlessness if they could. As one informant explained, "The women without children, they're the smart ones"; and yet, as we shall see, choosing childlessness was socially very problematic.[7]

The differences in fertility desires between women and men in San Francisco underscored the women's negative attitudes. Respondents were asked whether they wanted to have more children. The majority of both sexes who still considered themselves of childbearing age said they wanted no more (see Table 1), but women were satisfied with far smaller families than were men. The overwhelming majority of the women (80 percent) who had at least one living child said they were content with their present family size. Moreover, of the small number of childless women ($N = 9$), one-third indicated that they were satisfied to remain so. However, most of the men who were satisfied with family size had at least four children (60 percent), and of the childless men ($N = 6$), none indicated that he was satisfied.

Women with large families said they resented the demands of child care and the limitations it placed on them. Many saw children as a burden. They considered them too much work, too hard to raise, a source of problems, "war," and domestic strife. They viewed children as pesky disturbances who kept them tied to the house. One woman told me, "[The people of the community] want us to have many children. That's fine for them to say. They don't have to take care of them and keep them clean. My husband sleeps peacefully through the night, but I have to get up when the children need something. I'm the one the baby urinates on; sometimes I have to get out of bed in the cold and change both our clothes. They wake me when they're sick or thirsty, my husband sleeps through it all."

This resentment was balanced to some extent by the women's perception of advantages associated with children. They particularly valued the physical and emotional companionship of their children, in part because the

TABLE 1. Fertility Goals of Adults in a Mexican Municipio, 1980

Living Children (N)	Women				Men			
	No	Yes	Total	Yes (%)	No	Yes	Total	Yes (%)
0	3	6	9	67	0	6	6	100
1	7	4	11	36	3	3	6	50
2	9	4	13	31	5	5	10	50
3	16	7	23	30	10	13	23	57
4	11	3	14	21	13	2	15	13
5	11	3	14	21	6	4	10	40
6+	31	1	32	3	23	1	24	4
Totals	88	28	116	24	60	34	94	36

NOTE—Number of responses to the question. "Do you want more children?" by number of living children. The remaining responses among women and men are: Women (N = 180): too old, 47; no husband, 8; ambiguous, 3; missing data, 6. Men (N = 126): too old, 25; ambiguous, 3; missing data, 4. (The response "no wife" was not possible since all men in the sample were the husbands of women interviewed.)

women were extremely reluctant to be at home alone, especially at night. They feared ghosts, phantoms, and spirits and worried about drunks reputed to harass solitary women. Women also tried to avoid going alone on errands out of town, for they feared wild animals and unknown men. They always sought out a child—their own or someone else's—if no other companion could be found.

Overall, however, most Franciscanas did not perceive much practical advantage in rearing large families. There was little economic benefit seen, for the women considered their offspring lazy or too busy with other activities to be of much help. Since mandatory school attendance was strictly enforced in San Francisco, and children were encouraged by school authorities to attend frequent after-school activities, mothers often felt saddled with chores that their children should have done. Although women hoped their offspring would care for them in their old age, the expectation that they would actually do so was changing as children left the village to find employment elsewhere. Interestingly, mothers expressed greater support for their children's migration than did fathers.[8] Nevertheless, the women felt disappointed when they realized that they had been forgotten at home.

In addition to resenting the hard work of raising children and the frustrations of its uncertain rewards, the women in this sample saw frequent pregnancies as physically stressful and even debilitating. In their view, much of a women's blood supply during pregnancy was devoted to nourishing the developing fetus. This left their own bodies unbalanced and susceptible to the large number of disorders that could be caused by penetration of cold and *aire* (air, winds). They also saw parturition as a threat to their health, believing that, during childbirth, the womb—and the rest of the body—must "open" to expel the newborn and that this process increased the body's already heightened vulnerability to *aire*.

Postpartum complications were common among Franciscanas. Of the 180 interviewed, two-thirds reported at least one. They ranged from conditions the women considered relatively minor, such as facial swelling and backaches, to such serious conditions as uterine prolapsis and uncontrolled bleeding. Emotional complications were sometimes mentioned as well. For instance, one woman reported that, after the birth of her second child, she was unable to tolerate criticism from her husband's relatives, with whom she and her family then lived. "I wanted to get up and run and run, I had no idea to where," she told me. In addition to the complications of pregnancy per se, women also feared that frequent childbirth and short birth intervals caused menstrual hemorrhaging, exhaustion, and early death. There are no reliable data on postpartum mortality for this particular population, but examples existed in the memories of all women interviewed.

The women's illness experiences that were not related to pregnancy reinforced their understanding that frequent pregnancies harmed their general health. Those who had had four or more pregnancies were significantly more likely than the rest to report at least one serious illness ($\chi^2 = 7.06, P < .001$). Even when age was controlled for, this pattern occurred. Women with four or more pregnancies were also significantly more likely to report a greater number of minor health problems overall, including headaches, backaches, breast problems, and *coraje* (anger sickness; $\chi^2 = 6.38, P < .025$). Again with age controlled for, women who had had four or more pregnancies were less healthy overall than women who had had fewer pregnancies.

THE CASE FOR LARGE FAMILIES

Despite the desires of many Franciscanas to have few (or no) children, they did not think that they could actually do so. The pressures on them to reproduce were simply too great to ignore. These pressures came most often and overtly from the community's men, who argued that a populous community was vital to the defense of the collectivity and its interests. Women were another source of pressure. Although most wanted few children themselves, they felt that other women were obligated by the needs of the collectivity to bear many children.

Maintaining a sufficient population base was a constant source of concern. San Francisco was surrounded by communities that coveted its comparatively large landholdings. It needed a sizable male population to defend its borders in case of armed attack by neighboring enemy communities who still threatened the *municipio*. One particularly bloody battle in the 1950s claimed the lives of thirteen Franciscanos. Residents also felt threatened by indications that the federal government might resettle members of other communities or ethnic groups onto San Francisco's lands or allocate territory to other *municipios* that were litigating for it because, unlike many rural *municipios*, San Francisco had more land than its population required. Residents were also concerned about the regional government's proposals to consolidate San Francisco with neighboring *municipios* because it was considered far too small to remain independent. The most likely of these plans would combine San Francisco with its most hated and feared enemy.

A number of endogenous factors also threatened the community's population base. Despite the presence in the *cabecera* of two government health centers, disease continued to take a significant toll. The rate of infant mortality in the state was one of Mexico's highest. On average, deaths from all causes in San Francisco had not declined during the past fifteen years.[9] Migration from the community to the state and national capitals and to the United States was also taking increasing numbers of the most able-bodied women and men. In the past two decades, the state of Oaxaca had experienced Mexico's highest rate of out-migration, suffering a net population loss of 290,000 between 1960 and 1970 alone. Because this trend had continued, Oaxaca's population had grown more slowly than that of any other Mexican state.[10] San Francisco had been acutely affected by these broader demographic trends. Of the women interviewed whose children were grown, nearly two-thirds reported having at least one child who resided outside the *municipio*, and more than one-fourth reported that all their grown children lived elsewhere.

Half of San Francisco's adult population was now over forty years old. As a result of this aging trend, an increasing proportion of the population were experiencing declining physical strength and productivity, which residents felt boded ill for the community's future. One concrete and very important manifestation of these difficulties was the inability of the *municipio* to find enough men to fill the annual eighteen-man quota for civil and religious *cargo* positions. Moreover, there had been increasing pressure for independence from San Francisco on the part of some of the lowland *rancho* subcommunities (*agencias*); two had already won semiautonomous status from the regional government, and at least one of these was continuing to press for even greater independence.[11] All of these trends led residents of San Francisco to worry about the collectivity's future and to seek ways to diminish the impact of depopulation.

THE BIRTH CONTROL TREE

Although some of the reasons for the depopulation of San Francisco were new, concern about the size and strength of the collectivity was not. The conflict between the collective desire for a large and populous community and individual women's wishes to have few children had had a long, dramatic history in the *municipio*.

On many occasions during my fieldwork, men told me how, some twenty years before, they had cut down a tree whose bark was used by women as a contraceptive. They needed to eliminate the tree, they said, because so many women were refusing to bear children. This is the story the men told: Not far from the town center and just off a popular path to the lowland hamlets was a tree without a name. Its bark turned red when stripped from its trunk and was said to prevent conception. The large old tree was the only one of its kind known to the people of San Francisco. "Who knows where the seed came from," said one elderly resident; "strange it was the only one." Women who wished to avoid pregnancy brewed tea from the bark and drank it prior to intercourse. This would "burn" their wombs and render them temporarily sterile. This tea was dangerous and powerful, "like poison," some said. It could kill an incautious user. Women who drank the tea several times grew emaciated and weak. Even if they subsequently wished to bear children, as many as eight years might pass before a pregnancy.

Some said the users went secretly at night to get bark from the tree. Others thought that itinerant peddler women from an enemy town secretly sold Franciscanas strips of the dried bark along with other wares. Said one man, "It was they who deceived our women into not wanting children because they didn't want our town to grow."

A group of San Francisco's men were at work one day cutting back brush from the path that passed near the tree. They could see it from where they worked, almost stripped of its bark from frequent use. "Let's get rid of it," one of them said quietly; "we must have more children in this town." The others quickly agreed. "So," explained one who had been there, "we cut down the tree and tore its roots right out." They used the trunk to restore a nearby bridge in disrepair and returned home tired but satisfied with their work. (In an alternate version of the story, the men saw the tree, were angered, and stripped it entirely of its bark, causing it to die.)

I asked some of the men who said they were responsible for the act why they had killed the tree. "We were angry," one told me. "The women weren't having babies. They were lazy and didn't want to produce children." Another said that the women "had stopped making children. We were working hard with our men's work, but they weren't doing any of their women's work." One who said he remembered the incident explained that "the town was small and we wanted it to grow. We wanted a big town and we needed more people. But the women wouldn't cooperate." A woman I interviewed saw the men's motives differently. "The men depended on the women," she said. "They couldn't have their children by themselves. But the women were walking free. The men pulled out the tree to control the women so they'd have children for them."

My research in San Francisco led me to ask often about the birth control tree. Every man I asked had heard of it although none could tell me its name or show me one like it. These days, they explained, people seldom passed the spot where it had grown because a better road to the lowlands had been built. After weeks of asking, I nearly concluded that the tree was only a myth. Persistence finally led me to a woman who said her husband could show me the tree. He was more than reluctant to comply. "What if people found out that it has grown back?" he said. "What if they began to use it again? Then what would happen to the town?"

I continued to press him. Finally, he said he would not show me the tree but would take my field assistant's nine-year-old son to see it. The boy could later lead me to the spot. During the same period, one of the men who said he had participated in the destruction of the tree agreed to see if it had possibly regenerated. During different weeks, each of the two informants independently led me to the same clump of *Styrax argenteus*. As the second man showed me the abundant young growth, he expressed surprise that several had grown where only one had been.

The women I asked about the tree were consistently less informative than the men. While all the men knew of the birth control tree, the majority of women said they had never even heard of it, let alone used it to avoid pregnancy. The men did not believe the women were as ignorant as they claimed. I asked one man how the men had learned of the tree if the women had used it only in secret. He replied, "Of course the women think they have their secrets. But we men were able to find out. They have no secrets from us."

THE WOMEN'S RESPONSES TO PRESSURES TO REPRODUCE

There are several morals to this story, but the inevitability of negative reactions to behaviors that place individual interests above those of the collectivity is a very important one. In San Francisco, married women with few or no children were seen as selfish and socially negligent regardless of whether their low fertility was natural or willfully induced. Such women were particularly vulnerable to gossip, much of which centered on their fertility behavior. They were sharply and repeatedly criticized for causing miscarriages and using contraceptives. Some were even accused of infanticide. All of their acts were carefully monitored by relatives and other interested parties to detect any efforts to avoid pregnancy. For example, lemon juice was widely regarded as a contraceptive and an abortifacient.[12] After failing to conceive during her first year of marriage, one woman fell subject to her mother-in-law's constant gossip and criticism for avoiding her reproductive responsibilities by eating too much of the fruit. Another woman determinedly broke her young daughter of the habit of enjoying lemons, for she feared that they would damage her daughter's fertility.

Women with small families were susceptible to gossip about marital infidelity, which diminished the social status of their husbands as well. As a middle-aged mother of six explained, "The women who are most likely to go with other men are the ones who don't have much work to do. They have time for sex. But if you have a lot of kids like I do, you have to work very hard all the time. The tiredness takes over at the end of the day and you don't have time to think about the husbands of other women. You don't have time to go out looking for men." The targets of such gossip attributed it to envy of the relative wealth and freedom they enjoyed as a result of having small families—and they adamantly denied that their low fertility was due to contraceptives.

Contraceptives were, however, readily available at the town's two government-run health centers; one even provided the services free of charge. The Mexican government's interest in lowering its national birth rate had led it since 1972 to promote family planning aggressively.[13] The walls of both clinics were decorated almost exclusively with posters demonstrating the benefits of small families and *paternidad responsable* (responsible parenthood).[14] They were written in simple language with humorous illustrations. The text of a typical one read: "What will happen when we are more? We will have less money . . . less food . . . less education . . . less space . . . less clothing . . . less peace. You can avoid these problems if you plan your family. Now planning is easier! Consult the family doctor at the Social Security Clinic although you may not be insured. *The consultation is free.*"[15] Each clinic assigned its staff monthly inscription quotas for new contraceptive users. Health center personnel were expected to undertake house-to-house campaigns to introduce fecund women to modern birth control techniques.

Overwhelmingly, Franciscanas rejected these government services. For the period between January 1980 and February 1981, records from the two clinics indicated that thirteen Franciscanas initiated contraceptive use—only 7 percent of women between the ages of eighteen and forty-five. These women used contraceptives for an average of just 3.5 months before stopping, and only one continued using contraceptives for longer than six months.

When I asked several who said they wanted no more children why they did not seek the means to avoid pregnancy, they revealed an extreme reluctance to engage in socially disapproved behavior. Some indicated they would never consider obtaining birth control from government clinics because they would be ashamed to be publicly "registered" as a user of contraceptives. This same fear of community censure led women to avoid other means of fertility control and even the kinds of behavior that could be construed as attempts at fertility limitation. When I naively asked one of the town midwives if she had ever been asked to perform an abortion, she looked at me and said, "They wouldn't dare." Similarly, a Franciscana suffering from menstrual delay was afraid to inquire locally for a remedy. Even though she was convinced that she was not pregnant, she was sure she would be accused of abortion if she took a remedy to induce menstrual bleeding.

The women responded to these pressures to reproduce not simply by refusing to use contraceptives but also by denying they knew anything whatsoever about ways to limit fertility. It seemed they felt that merely possessing information would be interpreted as evidence of their malevolent intentions. When I asked women the direct question, "Do you know of any herbs or other remedies that can be used

to avoid pregnancy?" only 11 percent mentioned specific techniques such as the infamous birth control tree. Another 6 percent said they believed that ways existed but knew of none themselves. The remaining 83 percent said they believed there were no traditional ways to avoid getting pregnant. An even larger proportion (86 percent) said they knew no ways to induce an abortion. Even Franciscanas who considered themselves authorities on a great many subjects pleaded ignorance when it came to birth limitation.

Denial, however, did not necessarily imply ignorance. Probes revealed that 60 percent who had initially said they knew no ways to limit births had at least heard of the existence of techniques for fertility limitation. The vast majority of these respondents named modern rather than traditional methods and the responses were often quite oblique. For example, to the questions, "Is there *anything* that can be done to not have children if one doesn't want to have them? If so, what things?" typical responses were: "Yes, in the health center"; "I know the doctor has some"; "They say there are pills, medicines." Other replies explicitly identified the government as the source of contraceptives, shifting the question away from indigenous techniques for birth limitation to methods made available from outside the community. For example, "These days the government doesn't allow people to have so many children. It gives them medicines so they won't"; and "There used to be lots of herbs. Now, the government sends us doctors."

Yet none of the affirmative responses to the questions about knowledge of birth control could be interpreted as endorsements of contraceptive use. No respondent seemed to regard the available fertility-limiting techniques as liberating or as helping them to achieve their expressed goals of having small families. In fact, when responding affirmatively to the probe concerning their knowledge of contraceptives, the women would frequently volunteer a disclaimer in an apparent effort to dissociate themselves even further from the information, even though the probe did not concern their own experiences with contraceptives. For instance; "Well, yes, I have heard that there are medicines available, but I haven't tried them"; "Yes, there are remedies in the health center, but I haven't looked into it"; and, "They say there are medicines in the health center, but I myself haven't used any." Even most of those few in my study population (four out of six women) whose health center records revealed a history of contraceptive use strenuously denied use when directly asked during interviews.

Others told me with extreme caution what they knew about contraception. Some who during interviews had denied all knowledge of contraceptive methods subsequently came to my house to tell me about plants or other techniques that had previously "escaped" their memories. Even knowledge that seemed to me benign was very reluctantly conveyed if it pertained to birth limitation. For example, after initially denying she knew any remedies to induce an abortion, one woman reconsidered and whispered, "I don't know if this would really work, but some say that it can: carrying heavy loads, carrying heavy tumplines of firewood every day, doing a lot of laundry. It's said this can make one abort." Although this idea might be inferred from the circumstances under which miscarriages were observed to have occurred, women carefully guarded even this much knowledge, for they feared it would be incriminating.

IMPLICATIONS OF THE RESEARCH

These data shed light on the context in which a national population planning program was experienced in a rural indigenous community. The context was political, economic, civic, and cultural. On the part of the Mexican government, the decision to promote family planning among indigenous populations was politically delicate, for many Mexican nationalists regard the preservation of their Indian cultural heritage as fundamental to their cultural identity as Mexicans, and aggressive programs to limit the growth of indigenous groups may be perceived as cultural geno-

cide.[16] However, because economic development could not keep pace, the need to check population growth proved more pressing than the state's concerns with the politics of ethnic preservation. Terry L. McCoy has shown, moreover, that the recognition that the government could be destabilized by unchecked growth among less than fully loyal social classes and cultural groups provided significant impetus for the Mexican population policy.[17] In Mexico, as in other developing countries, such policies are used to further state consolidation.

A reduction in San Francisco's rate of population growth was, as we have seen, the last thing the male guardians of the collectivity wanted. While appreciating the value of birth control for the nation in the abstract, and in some cases even wishing for relatively small families themselves, the men unambivalently rejected family planning for the people of San Francisco. In contrast, the women were caught between their desires to have very few children and inexorable local social pressures to be prolific. Because of this pressure, government family planning services could not help the women achieve their own fertility goals. In fact, the existence of these services may have made it even more difficult for the women to practice covert fertility limitation: with the availability of modern contraceptives in the community, women fell under even more suspicion than before.

It has all too often been assumed that women's reproductive goals could be understood by analyzing those of the larger collectivities of which they are a part. However, when collectivities have specific fertility goals, it is reasonable to expect that these goals will conflict with the reproductive desires of at least some of the female members of the group. The extent to which women successfully implement their individual fertility goals depends on a number of factors that vary according to the characteristics of the particular society in which they live. These include the nature of the gender-based power relations and the extent to which women feel they can support one another in controversy. In stratified societies, issues related to social class and ethnicity also play a part, and women may be torn by conflicting sets of interests.[18] Studies that fail to consider *both* these broad sociopolitical conditions and the interests and desires of individual women will understate the complexity, misrepresent the realities, and yield questionable conclusions about reproductive policy and reproductive behavior.

NOTES

Support for this research was generously provided by grants from the National Science Foundation (BNS-8016431), National Institute for Child Health Development (HD-04612), and the Wenner-Gren Foundation for Anthropological Research (3387). Arthur J. Rubel provided truly valuable assistance during all phases of this research, including the production of this report. Judith Friedlander's suggestions also contributed importantly to the manuscript.

1. Burton Benedict, "Social Regulation of Fertility," in *The Structure of Human Populations,* ed. G. A. Harrison and A. J. Boyce (Oxford: Clarendon Press, 1972), 73–89; Carole Browner, "Abortion Decision Making: Some Findings from Colombia," *Studies in Family Planning* 10, no. 3 (1979): 96–106; Thomas K. Burch and Murray Gendall, "Extended Family Structure and Fertility: Some Conceptual and Methodological Issues," in *Culture and Population: A Collection of Current Studies,* ed. Steven Polgar (Cambridge, Mass.: Schenkman Publishing Co.; Chapel Hill, N.C.: Carolina Population Center, 1971), 87–104; Ronald Freedman, "The Sociology of Human Fertility: A Trend Report and Bibliography," *Current Sociology* 10/11, no. 2 (1961–62): 35–121; Frank Lorimer, *Culture and Human Fertility: A Study of the Relation of Cultural Conditions to Fertility in Nonindustrial and Transitional Societies* (Paris: Unesco, 1958); John F. Marshall, Susan Morris, and Steven Polgar, "Culture and Natality: A Preliminary Classified Bibliography," *Current Anthropology* 13, no. 2 (April 1972): 268–78; Moni Nag, *Factors Affecting Human Fertility in Nonindustrial Societies: A Cross-cultural Study* (New Haven, Conn.: Human Relations Area Files Press, 1976); Steven Polgar, "Population History and Population Policies from an Anthropological Perspective." *Current Anthropology* 13, no. 2 (April 1972): 203–11.

2. Bernard Berelson, *Population Policy in Developed Countries* (New York: McGraw-Hill Book Co., 1974); J. C. Caldwell, "Population Policy: A Survey of Commonwealth Africa," in *The Population of Tropical Africa,* ed. John C. Caldwell and Chukuka Okonjo (New York: Columbia University Press, 1968), 368–75; Leslie Corsa and Deborah Oakley, *Population Planning* (Ann Arbor: University of Michigan Press, 1979), chap. 5, 155–94; William L. Langer, "Checks on Population Growth, 1750–1850," *Scientific American* 226, no. 2 (1972): 92–99; Benjamin White, "Demand for Labor and Population Growth in Colonial Java," *Human Ecology* 1, no. 3 (1973): 217–39.

3. Ad Hoc Women's Studies Committee against Sterilization Abuse, *Workbook on Sterilization and Sterilization Abuse* (Bronxville, N.Y.: Sarah Lawrence College, 1978); Toni Cade, "The Pill: Genocide or Liberation?" in *The Black Woman,* ed. Toni Cade (New York: New American Library, 1970), 162–69; Lucinda Cisler, "Unfinished Business: Birth Control and Women's Liberation," in *Sisterhood Is Powerful: An Anthology of Writings from the Women's Liberation Movement,* ed. Robin Morgan (New York: Vintage Books, 1970), 245–89; Sally Covington, "Is 'Broader' Better? Reproductive Rights and Elections '84," *Taking Control: The Magazine of the Reproductive Rights National Network* 1, no. 1 (1984): 6–8; Boston Women's Health Book Collective, *Our Bodies, Ourselves: A Book by and for Women* (New York: Simon & Schuster, 1971); Reproductive Rights National Network, "Caught in the Crossfire: Third World Women and Reproductive Rights," *Reproductive Rights Newsletter* 5, no. 3 (Autumn 1983): 1–13; Helen Rodriguez-Trias, *Sterilization Abuse* (New York: Barnard College, Women's Center, 1978).

4. Rosalind Pollack Petchesky, *Abortion and Woman's Choice: The State, Sexuality, and Reproduction Freedom* (New York and London: Longman, Inc., 1984), esp. 10.

5. Eric R. Wolf, "Types of Latin American Peasantry: A Preliminary Discussion," *American Anthropologist* 57 (1955): 452–71, and "Closed Corporate Peasant Communities in Mesoamerica and Central Java," *Southwestern Journal of Anthropology* 13 (1957): 1–18.

6. Clifford R. Barnett, Jean Jackson, and Howard M. Cann, "Childspacing in a Highland Guatemala Community," in Polgar, ed. (n. 1 above), 139–48; Paula H. Hass, "Contracep-

tive Choices for Latin American Women," *Populi* 3 (1976): 14–24; Jenifer Oberg, "Natality in a Rural Village in Northern Chile," in Polgar, ed., 124–38; Michele Goldzieher Shedlin and Paula E. Hollerbach, "Modern and Traditional Fertility Regulation in a Mexican Community: The Process of Decision-Making," *Studies in Family Planning* 12, no. 6/7 (1981): 278–96. John Mayone Stycos, *Ideology, Faith, and Family Planning in Latin America: Studies in Public and Private Opinion on Fertility Control* (New York: McGraw-Hill Book Co., 1971).

7. It should be noted that the women's professed negative attitudes toward childbearing and child rearing generally were not apparent in their behavior toward their children.

8. C. H. Browner, "Gender Roles and Social Change: A Mexican Case," *Ethnology* 25, no. 2 (April 1986): 89–106.

9. Arthur J. Rubel, "Some Unexpected Health Consequences of Political Relations in Mexico" (paper presented at the eighty-second annual meeting of the American Anthropological Association, Chicago, 1983).

10. Consejo Nacional de Población México (CONAPO), *México Demográfico: Breviario* (Mexico City: CONAPO, 1979), 52, 78. More recent statistics on out-migration are not available.

11. Anselmo Hernandez Lopez, personal communication, Oaxaca, Mexico, 1981.

12. C. H. Browner and Bernard Ortiz de Montellano, "Herbal Emmenagogues Used by Women in Columbia and Mexico," in *Plants Used in Indigenous Medicine: A Biocultural Approach*, ed. Nina Etkin (New York: Docent Publishers, 1986), 32–47.

13. Victor Urquidi et al., *La explosión humana* (Mexico City: Litoarte, 1974); Frederick C. Turner, *Responsible Parenthood: The Politics of Mexico's New Population Policies* (Washington, D.C.: American Enterprise Institute for Public Policy Research, 1974).

14. This official slogan of the government's population control program was chosen to emphasize the concrete advantages of small families to individual couples rather than the macrodemographic benefits of a reduced national birth rate (Terry L. McCoy, "A Paradigmatic Analysis of Mexican Population Policy," in *The Dynamics of Population Policy in Latin America*, ed. Terry L. McCoy [Cambridge, Mass.: Ballinger Publishing Co., 1974], 377–408, esp. 397).

15. Mexico City: Instituto Mexicano de Seguro Social (IMSS); italics in original. In the mid-1960s, the government's Social Solidarity Program (*Solidaridad Social*) extended the social security health system to cover the health needs of some rural areas. Family planning services were part of the coverage.

16. [Gonzalo] Aquirre Beltrán, *Obra polémica* (Mexico City: Instituto Nacional de Antropología e Historia, 1976); Luis Leñero Otero, *Valores ideológicos y las políticas de población en México* (Mexico City: Editorial Edicol, 1979), 115–17.

17. McCoy, 377–408.

18. Floya Anthias and Nira Yuval-Davis, "Contextualizing Feminism: Gender, Ethnic and Class Divisions," *Feminist Review* 15 (Winter 1983): 62–75, esp. 70–71.

Procreation Stories: Reproduction, Nurturance, and Procreation in Life Narratives of Abortion Activists

Faye Ginsburg

The residents of Fargo, North Dakota—a small metropolitan center providing commercial and service industries for the surrounding rural area—pride themselves on their clean air, regular church attendance, rich topsoil, and their actual and metaphorical distance from places like New York City. The orderly pace of Fargo's daily life was disrupted in the fall of 1981 when the Fargo Woman's Health Center—the first free-standing facility in the state to publicly offer abortions—opened for business. A right-to-life[1] coalition against the clinic formed immediately. Soon after, a pro-choice group emerged to respond to the antiabortion activities. Each side asked for support by presenting itself as under attack, yet simultaneously claimed to represent the "true" interests of the community. The groups have evolved and fissioned. There are approximately 1000 potentially active supporters on each side and a hard core of 10 to 20 activists.

Broadly sketched, two positions emerged. For the pro-life movement in Fargo, the availability of abortion in their own community represented the intrusion of secularism, narcissism, materialism, and anomie, and the reshaping of women into structural men. Pro-choice activists reacted to right-to-life protesters as the forces of narrow-minded intolerance who would deny women access to a choice that is seen as fundamental to women's freedom and ability to overcome sexual discrimination.

When pro-life forces failed to close the clinic through conventional political tactics,[2] they shifted their strategy. They currently are engaged in a battle for the clinic's clientele. Competition is focused increasingly on winning the minds, bodies, and power to define the women who might choose to violate a basic cultural script—the dominant American procreation story—in which pregnancy necessarily results in childbirth and motherhood, preferably within marriage.

The local controversy over the clinic opening in Fargo revealed at close range how the struggle over abortion rights has become a contested domain for control over the constellation of meanings attached to reproduction in America. In the course of fieldwork,[3] it became clear to me that this conflict does not indicate two fixed and irreconcilable positions. Rather, the social movements organized around abortion provide arenas for innovation where cultural and social definitions of gender are in the process of material and semiotic reorganization.

In each movement, then, a particular understanding of reproduction is demonstrated through abortion activism. This was especially apparent in life stories[4]—narratively shaped fragments of more comprehensive life histories—I collected with female abortion activists.[5] Such narratives, which I am calling procreation stories, reveal the way in which women use their activism to frame and interpret their experiences—both historical and biographical. The stories create provisional solutions to disruptions in a coherent cultural model for the place of reproduction and motherhood in the female life course in contemporary America. They illuminate how those dimensions of experience considered "private" in American culture intersect with particular social and historical conditions that distinguish the memberships of each group. In the ways that the rhetoric and action of abortion activism are incorporated into life stories, one can see how cultural definitions of the female life course, and the social consequences implied, are selected, rejected, reordered, and reproduced in new form.

This paper is based on my own fieldwork with local women activists engaged in the Fargo abortion controversy from 1981 to 1983. I chose subjects who were most prominent in local activity at the time and who reflected, in my estimation, the range of diversity encompassed in the active memberships of both pro-life and pro-choice groups in terms of age, socioeconomic status, religious affiliation, household and marriage arrangements, style of activism, and the like. Altogether I collected 21 life stories from right-to-life activists and 14 from pro-choice activists. While most of these people are still active, each side continues to undergo rapid permutations both locally and nationally. Thus, the benefits of in-depth participant observation research must be balanced against the debits of a small sample bound by the conditions of a particular time and setting. In addition, because of space limitations, I can present only a few cases, which are illustrative of themes that are prominent in the narratives more generally. However, my conclusions are confirmed in other qualitative studies of abortion activists (for example, Luker 1984), which also find abortion activism linked to a more general integrative process. For example, in an article discussing the role abortion seems to play in activists' lives, authors Callahan and Callahan write:

> The general debate has seen an effort, on all sides, to make abortion fit into some overall coherent scheme of values, one that can combine personal convictions and consistency with more broadly held social values. Abortion poses a supreme test in trying to achieve that coherence. It stands at the juncture of a number of value

systems, which continually joust with each other for dominance, but none of which by itself can do full justice to all the values that, with varying degrees of insistence and historical rootedness, clamor for attention and respect [1984:219].

On the basis of such findings, it seems appropriate to use life stories as texts in which abortion is a key symbol around which activists are interpreting and reorienting their lives. More generally, this suggests a model for understanding how female social activism in the American context operates to mediate the construction of self and gender with larger social, political, and cultural processes.

REPRODUCTION, GENERATION, AND NURTURANCE

Surveys of representative samples of pro-life and pro-choice activists have not established any clear correlations between such activity and conventional social categories. Activists span and divide religious, ethnic, and occupational lines. The core of membership on both sides is primarily white, middle class,[6] and female[7] (Granberg 1981). Ideologically, the connections drawn between abortion activism and other social issues are diverse (Ginsburg 1986:76–81). Of the life stories I collected from abortion activists in Fargo, in almost all cases, pro-choice and pro-life alike, women described a coming to consciousness regarding abortion in relation to some critical realignment of personal and social identity, usually related to reproduction. Initially, this recognition only seemed to confound the problem of trying to understand the differences between the women on opposite sides of the issue. From accounts of the early histories of Fargo activists, up to the age of 18 or so, it would be hard to predict whether women would end up pro-choice or pro-life in their views. Devout Catholics became ardent feminists; middle-class, college-educated, liberal Protestants became staunch pro-lifers. As I puzzled over the seeming convergences in catalyzing experiences, social backgrounds, and even sentiments—most see themselves as working toward the reform of society as a whole—and I began to notice a generational distinction.

The pro-choice activists cluster in a group born in the 1940s. For the most part, they had reached adulthood—which generally meant marriage and children—in the late 1960s and early 1970s. Their life stories indicate that contact with the social movements of that period, particularly the second wave of feminism, was a central experience for nearly all of them. They describe their encounter with these movements as a kind of awakening or passage from a world defined by motherhood into one seen as filled with broader possibilities. For most of these women, feminism offered new resources with which to understand and frame their lives; it provided an analysis, a community of others, and a means for engaging in social change that legitimated their own experience.

By contrast, the right-to-life women cluster in two groups. Those born in the 1920s were most active in pro-life work in the early 1970s. A second cohort, the one currently most active, was born in the 1950s. Typically, this latter group was made up of women who had worked prior to having children and left wage labor when they became mothers. This transition occurred in the late 1970s or even more recently, a period when feminism was on the wane as an active social movement and pro-life and anti-ERA activity were on the rise. This latter group claims to have been or even be feminist in many respects (that is, on issues such as comparable worth). Many describe their commitment to the right-to-life movement as a kind of conversion; it occurs most frequently around the birth of a first or second child when many women of this group decided to move out of the paid work force to stay home and raise children.

Let me clarify that I am not arguing that all abortion activists fall neatly into one or another historical cohort. As is the case in most anthropological studies in complex societies, my study is small and local, allowing for fine-grained, long-term study that can reveal new understandings but not necessarily support broad generalizations. In this case, the appearance of a generational shift, even in this small sample, is intended less as an explanation and more as a reminder of the importance of temporal factors in the dialectics of social movements. In other words, social activists may hold different positions due not only to social and ideological differences. Differing views may also be produced by historical changes, which include their experience of the opposition at different points over the life course. On the basis of my research, I would argue that this might be particularly relevant in conflicts tied so closely to life cycle events. In the narratives, *all* the women are struggling to come to terms with problematic life-cycle transitions, but in each group, the way they experience those as problematic is associated with very particular historical situations. Abortion activism seems to mediate between these two domains, as a frame for action and interpretation of the self in relation to the world. For most of these women, their procreation stories create harmonious narrative out of the dissonance of history, both personal and generational.

In his classic essay "The Problem of Generations," Karl Mannheim underscores the importance of this nexus between the individual life cycle and rapidly changing historical conditions in understanding generational shifts in the formation of political consciousness and social movements:

> in the case of generations, the "fresh contact" with the social and cultural heritage is determined not by mere social change but by fundamental biological factors. We can accordingly differentiate between two types of "fresh contact": one based on a shift in social relations, and the other in vital factors [1952:383].

> The *sociological* problem of generations . . . begins at that point where the sociological relevance of these biological factors is discovered [1952:381].

To use Mannheim's suggestion, one must consider the intersection of two unfolding processes in order to understand what attracts women to opposing movements in the abortion controversy. One is the "biological factors," the trajectory of a woman's sexual and reproductive experiences over her life course and her interpretation of those events. The second is the historical moment shaping the culture when these key transitional points occur. It is this moment of "fresh contact" that creates the conditions of "a changed relationship" and a "novel approach" to the culture that ensures its continual reorganization. Such "fresh contact" is manifest in the self-definition and social actions of women engaged in the abortion controversy, some of whose life stories are analyzed below. Their narratives reveal how the embracing of a pro-life or pro-choice position emerges specifically out of a confluence of reproductive and generational experiences. In the negotiation of critical moments in the female life course with an ever-shifting social environment, the contours of their own biographies and the larger cultural and historical landscape are measured, reformulated, and given new meaning.

Such reconstructing is most marked at critical transitional points in the life course. In situations of rapid change when the normative rules for an assumed life trajectory are in question, these life-cycle shifts are experienced as crises, revealing contention over cultural definitions. In other words, when the interpretation of a particular life event—abortion or more generally the transition to motherhood, for example—becomes the object of political struggle, it indicates a larger disruption occurring in the social order as well. What emerges in the biographical narratives of these women is an apparent dissonance between cultural codes, social process, and individual transformation in the life course. Analytically, then, life stories can be seen as the effort of individuals to create continuity between subjective and social experience, the past and current action and belief.

These orientations provide a useful framework for interpreting the narratives of abortion activists in relation to the social movements that engage them. The battles they fight are loci for potential cultural and social transformation; in life stories, change is incorporated, ordered, and assigned meaning by and for the individual. This process is cen-

tral to the "changed relationships" of many women to American culture that have generated struggles over conflicting views of the interpretation of gender in the last two decades. Thus, in the case of abortion, two mutually exclusive interpretations and arenas of action are formulated, which give the narrator symbolic control over problematic transitions in the female life cycle.

I am arguing that these transitions constitute life crises for women at this moment in American history because of the gap between experiences of discontinuous changes in their own biographies and the available cultural models for marking them, both cognitively and socially. As increasing numbers of women are entering the wage labor market and traditional marriage and familial arrangements seem to be in disarray, it is hardly surprising that the relationship of women to reproduction, and mothering in particular, has been thrown open to reinterpretation.

In the United States, where the culture and economy are underwritten by an ideal of individual autonomy and achievement and the separation of workplace and home, the fact of dependency over the life course has been hidden in the household. Assigned to the "private realm"—the domain of unpaid labor performed by women serving as emotional and often material providers for infants, children, the sick, the elderly—nurturance thus escapes consideration as a larger cultural concern. Rather, the general social problem of caring for dependent human beings is linked to biological reproduction and childrearing in heterosexually organized families, all of which are conflated with the category female.[8] When women vote with their bodies to eschew the imperatives of American domesticity by remaining single, childless, and/or entering wage labor in large numbers, both the conditions and native understandings of nurturance and reproduction necessarily change.

Such changes are central themes in the procreation stories of abortion activists. While their "life scripts" are cast against each other, both provide ways for managing the structural opposition in America between work and parenthood that still shapes the lives of most women and men in this culture. Because contrasting definitions of the cultural and personal meaning of reproduction are being created in a contested domain, they are shaped dialectically. Each side attempts to both incorporate and repudiate the claims to truth of their opposition, casting as unnatural, immoral, or false other possible formulations. In the abortion debate, both positions serve to "naturalize" constructions regarding women's work, sexuality, and motherhood, and the relationships among them, thus claiming a particular view of American culture and the place of men and women in it in a way that accommodates discontinuities and contradictions.

The location of and responsibility for nurturance in relationship to biological reproduction is of critical concern, the salient value and contradiction for women on both sides of the debate. Nurturance is claimed by activists as a source of moral authority for female action. Yet, it is also understood as the culturally assigned attribute that puts women at a disadvantage socially, economically, and politically, confining them to the unappreciated tasks of caring for dependent people. These two views of the "proper" place of reproduction and nurturance in the female life course are the poles around which activists' life stories are constituted.

Activists' views on abortion are linked to a very diverse range of moral, ethical, and religious question, which I discuss in more detail elsewhere (Ginsburg 1986).[9] In this paper, however, I have confined my analysis to the issues that emerge in their life stories. My goal here is an effort to understand how abortion activism and abstract notions tied to it mediate between historical experience, construction of self, and social action. What I think is striking about the emergence of nurturance as a central theme in these narratives is that it ties female life-cycle transitions to the central philosophical questions of each side: the pro-life concern with the protection of nascent life, and the pro-choice concern with the rights and obligations of women, those to whom the care of that nascent life is culturally assigned.

THE LIFE STORIES

The Pro-Choice Narratives

The pro-choice narratives were drawn from women activists who organized to defend the Fargo abortion clinic; most were born between 1942–52. They represent a range of backgrounds in terms of their natal families, yet all were influenced as young adults by the social unrest of the late 1960s and early 1970s, and by the women's movement in particular. While their current household, conjugal, and work arrangements differ, for almost all, the strong commitment to pro-choice activism was connected to specific life-cycle events, generally having to do with experiences and choices around sexuality, pregnancy, and childbearing, including the choice not to have children.

A central figure of the current controversy in Fargo is Kay Bellevue, an abortion rights activist since 1972. Kay grew up in the Midwest, the oldest of seven children. Her father was a Baptist minister; her mother worked as a homemaker and part-time public school teacher. In her senior year of college, Kay got pregnant and married. Like almost *all* of the women activists, regardless of their position on abortion, Kay's transition to motherhood was surrounded by ambivalence.

> "I enjoyed being home, but I could never stay home all the time. I have never done that in my life. After being home one year and taking care of a kid, I felt my mind was a wasteland. And [my husband and I] were so poor we could almost never go out together."

Although her *behavior* was not that different from that of many right-to-life women—that is, as a young mother she became involved in community associations—Kay's interpretation of her actions stresses the limitations of motherhood; by contrast, pro-life women faced with the same dilemma emphasize the drawbacks of the workplace. Not surprisingly, for both groups of women, voluntary work for a "cause" was an acceptable and satisfying way of managing to balance the pleasures and duties of motherhood with the structural isolation of that work as it is organized in America. La Leche League, for example, is a group where one stands an equal chance of running into a pro-life or pro-choice women. In her early 20s, Kay became active in a local chapter of that organization, an international group promoting breast-feeding and natural childbirth. She marks this as a key event.

"My first child had not been a pleasant birth experience so I went [to a La Leche meeting] and I was really intrigued. There were people talking about this childbirth experience like it was the most fantastic thing you'd ever been through. I certainly didn't feel that way. I had a very long labor. I screamed, I moaned, my husband thought I was dying. So . . . this group introduced me to a whole different conception of childbirth and my second experience was so different I couldn't believe it.

And the way I came to feminism was that through all of this, I became acutely aware of how little physicians actually knew about women's bodies . . . So I became a real advocate for women to stand up for their rights, starting with breastfeeding."

Surprisingly, the concerns Kay voices are not so different from those articulated by her neighbors and fellow citizens who so vehemently oppose her work.

In 1972, Kay moved to Fargo; she remembers this transition as a time of crisis. Her parents were divorcing, one of her children was having problems, and Kay became pregnant for the fifth time.

"Then I ended up having an abortion myself. My youngest was 18 months old and I accidentally got pregnant. We had four small kids at the time and we decided if we were going to make it as a family unit, we had all the stress we could tolerate if we were going to survive."

In her more public role, as was the case in these personal decisions regarding abortion, Kay always linked her activism to a strong commitment to maintain family ties. As such, she was responding to accusations made by right-to-life opponents that abortion advocacy means an oppositional stance toward marriage, children, and community.

"I think it's easy for them to stereotype us as having values very different than theirs and that's not the case at all. Many of the people who get abortions have values very similar to the anti-abortion people. The Right-to-lifers don't know how deeply I care for my own family and how involved I am, since I have four children and spent the early years of my life working for a breast-feeding organization."

Kay particularly resents the casting of pro-choice activists by right-to-lifers as not only "antifamily" but "godless" as well. Although she stopped attending church services when she got married—something she feels could stigmatize her in a community noted for its church attendance—Kay nonetheless connects her activism to religious principles of social justice learned in her natal family.

"I have always acted on what to me are Judeo-Christian principles. The Ten Commandments, plus love thy neighbor. I was raised by my family to have a very strong sense of ethics and it's still with me. I have a strong concern about people and social issues. I've had a tough time stomaching what goes on in the churches in the name of Christianity. I've found my sense of community elsewhere. I think pro-choice people have a very strong basis in theology for their loving, caring perspective. . . . It's very distressing to me that, particularly the people opposed to abortion will attempt to say their moral beliefs are the only correct ones."

Such stereotypes, to which most of the pro-choice women in Fargo were extremely sensitive, are addressed implicitly or explicitly in the repeated connections these activists made between abortion rights and a larger claim to the cultural values of nurturance which, in their view, women represent.

These concerns are prominent, for example, in the narratives of other abortion rights advocates. Janice Sundstrom, like most of the pro-choice activists in Fargo, frames her story by emphasizing her differentiation from, rather than integration with, her childhood milieu.

"In 1945, shortly after I was born, my mom and dad moved here and brought me along and left all the other children with relations back in Illinois. I think I'm different from the rest of them because I had the experience of being the only child at a time when they had far too many children to deal with."

While the transformations Janice eventually experienced are cast, in her story, as almost predictable, they hardly seem the inevitable outcome of her youth and adolescence: 12 years in Catholic parochial school and marriage to her high-school sweetheart a year after graduation, followed immediately by two pregnancies.

"We were both 19 then and I didn't want to have another child. We were both in school and working and there we were with this kid. But I didn't have any choice. There was no option for me about birth control because I was still strongly committed to the Church's teaching. And then, three months later, I was pregnant again. After Jodie was born I started taking pills and that's what ended the Church for me."

For Janice, ambivalent encounters with reproduction—in this case the problem of birth control that made her question her church—are key events in her story. In this way, her interpretation of her experiences resembles the way that pregnancy and pro-life activism are linked in the right-to-life narratives discussed later on. It is a central pivoting moment in her life, which turned her toward alternative cultural models.

"Up to that time, I felt very strongly about abortion as my church had taught me to think and somehow between 1968 and 1971—those years were crucial to the political development of a lot of people in my generation—I came to have different feelings about abortion. My feeling toward abortion grew out of my personal experiences with friends who had abortions and a sensitivity to the place of women in this society."

What is striking in the connections Janice goes on to make to her abortion rights position is not its *difference* from that of her opponents, but its similarities. She is disturbed by

cultural currents that promote, in her view, narcissistic attitudes toward sexuality and personal fulfillment in which the individual denies any responsibility to kin, community, and the larger social order. Several pro-choice women referred to this constellation of concerns as "midwestern feminism." They are described as natural attributes possessed and represented by women. In Janice's words,

"It's important that we remember our place, that we remember we are the caregivers, that we remember that nurturing is important, that we maintain the value system that has been given to us and that has resided in us and that we bring it with us into that new structure. . . . It's important that we bring to that world the recognition that 80-hour work weeks aren't healthy for anyone—that children suffer if they miss relationships with their fathers and that fathers suffer from missing relationships with their children. This society has got to begin recognizing its responsibility for caring for its children."

Such concerns are emblematic of a broader goal of pro-choice women to improve conditions in a less than perfect world. More generally, the agenda of women on the pro-choice side is to use legal and political means to extend the boundaries of the domain of nurturance into the culture as a whole. They are attempting to reformulate the requirements of human reproduction and dependency as conditions to be met collectively. Their narratives reveal both an embracing of nurturance as a valued quality natural to women and the basis of their cultural authority, and their rejecting of it as an attribute that assigns women to childbearing, caretaking, and domesticity. These themes emerge in pro-choice stories as well as in action. In their view, nurturance is broadly defined. It includes the stated and actual preference for nonhierarchical relationships and group organization, and an insistence that their activism is not for personal gain or individual indulgence but in the interests of women and social justice. This utopian subtext of their position is rooted in their historical encounter with feminism. More directly, it is expressed as a desire to create a society more hospitable to the qualities and tasks they identify as female: the reproduction of generative, compassionate, or at least tolerant relationships between family, friends, members of the community, people in the workplace, and even the nation as a whole. In the narratives they construct, their desire to control their own reproduction is linked to a larger goal of (re)producing cultural values of nurturance on a large social scale.

The Right-to-Life Narratives

Right-to-life activists express a similar concern for the preservation of female nurturance. While it is linked directly to biological reproduction, nurturance in their narratives is not natural but achieved. In all the stories of pregnancy and birth told by right-to-life women, the ambivalence of the mother towards that condition—either through reference to the storyteller's own mother or children, or experience of motherhood herself—is invoked and then overcome through a narrative strategy that stresses continuities between generations, as the following quote illustrates. The speaker is Shirley, a 63-year-old widow, part-time nurse, mother of six, and a well-known member of Fargo's comfortable middle class.

"Our Senator, he's not pro-life, sent me a congratulations letter when [my son] John got a teacher of the year award in 1980. I wanted to take the letter back to him and say, "It was very inconvenient to have this son. My husband was in school and I was working. We thought we needed other things besides a child. And had abortion been available to me, I might have aborted the boy who was teacher of the year.' What a loss to society that would have been. What losses are we having in society now?"

The first wave of right-to-life activity in Fargo received much of its support from women of Shirley's cohort, many of whom had recently been widowed and were facing the loss of children from their immediate lives as well. At a moment in their life cycles when the household and kin context for a lifelong vocation of motherhood was diminishing, pro-life work provided an arena for extending that work beyond the boundaries of home and family.

Another woman of that cohort, Helen, also drew cross-generational connections through her right-to-life commitment. Raised in one of Fargo's elite Lutheran families, Helen fulfilled her mother's dream by attending an eastern "seven sisters' school" and going on for a master's degree in social work. After World War II, she married, returned to Fargo, and had three children. There, she has led the life appropriate for the wife of a local retail magnate. She was, until recently, a pro-choice advocate, a position of which her mother disapproved.

"Years ago, as a social worker, even though I reverenced life, I can still see some of those families and how they lived. I was pro-choice because I thought of those little children and how they lived. And I remember my mother saying 'Helena,' (she always called me Helena when it was serious) 'That's murder . . . ' And I said, 'Better those children were never born, mother. They live a hell on earth . . . ' and she never talked about it to me after that but I'm sure it hurt."

When the clinic opened in 1981, Helen was asked by a member of one of her prayer groups to join the pro-life coalition against the clinic, which she did. She saw her "conversion" to the right-to-life movement as a repudiation of a prior sense of self that had separated her from her mother, who recently died. She links all of these to the circumstances of her own birth.

"I had a sister killed in a car accident before I was born and . . . I don't know if I ever would have been if she hadn't died . . . My mother was so sick when she was pregnant with me because she was still grieving. They wanted to abort her and she said, 'No way.'

So when she died last year and all these checks came in, I gave them to LIFE Coalition and as a thank you note to people, I told them about her story . . . It brought life to me that at her death this could go on.

You know there is one scripture in Isaiah 44 that I especially pray for my family and that says

'I knew you before you were formed in your mother's womb. Fear not, for you are my witness.'

In this fragment, Helen establishes metaphorical continuity between her pro-life conviction and the opening story of her narrative, in which she reconstucts her own sojourn in her mother's womb, identifying herself simultaneously with her earliest moments of existence and with her mother's trauma as well. As in Shirley's story, the denial and acceptance of mother and child of each other's lives are merged, and then given larger significance as reproductive events are linked figuratively and materially to the right-to-life movement and given new meaning.

The connections of the right-to-life position with overcoming ambivalence toward pregnancy, and the merging of divergent generational identities in the act of recollection are present, though less prominent, in the procreation stories of younger pro-life women as well. Sally Nordsen is part of a cohort of women born between 1952–62 who make up the majority and most dedicated members of Fargo's antiabortion activists. Like most of the other pro-life women of this group, Sally went to college and married soon after her graduation; she worked for seven years as a social worker. In her late 20s, she got pregnant and decided to leave the work force in order to raise her children. Sally regards this decision as a positive one; nonetheless, it was marked by ambivalence.

"I had two days left of work before my resignation was official but Dick was born earlier than expected. So I left the work on my desk and never went back to it. There were so many things that were abrupt. When I went into the hospital it was raining, and when I came out it was snowing. A change of seasons, a change of work habits, a new baby in my life. It was hard. I was so anxious to get home and show this baby off. And when I walked in the door, it was like the weight of the world and I thought, 'What am I going to do with him now?' Well, these fears faded.

So it was a change. When Ken would come home, I would practically meet him at the door

with my coat and purse cause I wanted to get out of there. I couldn't stand it, you know. And that's still the case sometimes. But the joys outweigh the desire to go back to work."

For Sally and the other pro-life activists her age, the move from wage labor to motherhood occurred in the late 1970s or more recently. Feminism was identified, more often than not, with its distorted reconstruction in the popular media. Women like Sally, who have decided to leave the work force for a "reproductive phase" of their life cycle, are keenly aware that the choices they have made are at odds with the images they see in the popular media of young, single, upwardly mobile corporate women. Sally's colleague, Roberta makes the case succinctly.

"They paint the job world as so glamorous, as if women are all in executive positions. But really, what is the average woman doing? Mostly office work, secretarial stuff. When you watch TV, there aren't women being pictured working at grocery store check-outs."

For Roberta, her decision to leave the workplace represents a critique of what she considers to be the materialism of the dominant culture. For example, she sees in abortion a reevaluation of biological reproduction in the cost-benefit language and mores of the marketplace, and an extension of a more pervasive condition, the increasing commercialization of human relations, especially those involving dependents.

"You know, reasons given for most abortions is how much kids cost. How much work kids are, how much they can change your lifestyle, how they interrupt the timing of your goals. What is ten years out of a 70-year life span? . . . If you don't have your family, if you don't have your values, then what's money, you know?"

In this view, legal abortion represents the loss of a locus of unconditional nurturance in the social order and the steady penetration of the forces of the market. In concrete terms, the threat is constituted in the public endorsement of sexuality disengaged from motherhood. From the right-to-life perspective, this situation serves to weaken social pressure on men to take responsibility for the reproductive consequences of intercourse. Pro-life women are fully cognizant of the fragility of traditional marriage arrangements and recognize as well the lack of other social forms that might ensure the emotional and material support of women with children or other dependents. Nonetheless, the movement's supporters continue to be stereotyped as reactionary right-wing housewives unaware of alternative possibilities. Almost all of the Fargo pro-life activists were aware of these representations and addressed them in a dialectical fashion, using them to confirm their own position. As Roberta explained,

> "The image that's presented of us as having a lot of kids hanging around and that's all you do at home and you don't get anything else done, that's really untrue. In fact, when we do mailings here, my little one stands between my legs and I use her tongue as a sponge. She loves it and that's the heart of grassroots involvement. That's the bottom. That's the stuff and the substance that makes it all worth it. Kids are what it boils down to. My husband and I really prize them; they are our future and that is what we feel is the root of the whole pro-life thing."

The collective portrait that emerges from these stories, then, is much more complex than the media portrayals of right-to-life women as housewives and others passed by in the sweep of social change. It is not that they discovered an ideology that "fit" some prior sociological category (see notes 6 and 7). Their sense of identification evolves from their own changing experiences with motherhood and wage labor, and in the very process of voicing their views against abortion. In their narratives and the regular performance of their activism, they are, simultaneously, transforming themselves, projecting their vision of the culture onto their own past and future, both pragmatically and symbolically. Sally, for example, describes her former "liberated" ideas about sexuality as a repression of her true self:

> "You're looking at somebody who used to think the opposite. I used to think that sex outside of marriage was fine. I think there was part of me that never fully agreed. It wasn't a complete turnaround. It was kind of like inside you know it's not right but you make yourself think it's OK."

Rather than simply defining themselves in opposition to what they understand feminist ideology and practice to be, many of the younger right-to-life women claim to have held that position and to have transcended it. For example, a popular lecture in Fargo in 1984 was entitled, "I Was A Pro-choice Feminist But Now I'm Pro-Life." Much in the same way that pro-choice women embraced feminism, right-to-life women find in *their* movement a particular symbolic frame that integrates their experiences of work, reproduction, and marriage with shifting ideas of gender and politics that they encounter around them.

In the pro-life view of the world, to subvert the fertile union of men and women, either by denying procreative sex or the differentiation of male and female character, is to destroy the bases of biological, cultural, and social reproduction. This chain of associations to reproductive, heterosexual sex is central to the organization of meaning in pro-life discourse. For most right-to-lifers, abortion is not simply the termination of an individual potential life, or even that act multiplied a million-fold. It represents an active denial of the reproductive consequences of sex and a rejection of female nurturance, and thus sets forth the possibility of women structurally becoming men. This prospect threatens the union of opposites on which the continuity of the social whole is presumed to rest. In the words of a national pro-life leader

> "Abortion is of crucial importance because it negates the one irrefutable difference between men and women. It symbolically destroys the precious essence of womanliness—nurturance. . . . Pro-abortion feminists open themselves to charges of crass hypocrisy by indulging in the very same behavior for which they condemn men: the unethical use of power to usurp the rights of the less powerful."

For pro-life women, then, their work is a gesture against what they see as the final triumph of self-interest. In their image of the unborn child ripped from the womb, they have symbolized the final penetration and destruction of the last arena of women's domain thought to be exempt from the truncated relations identified with both male sexuality and commercial exchange: reproduction and motherhood. At a time when wombs can be rented and zygotes are commodities, abortion is understood by right-to-lifers as an emblematic symbol for the increasing commercialization of human dependency. Their perception of their opponents' gender identity as culturally male—sexual pleasure and individual ambition separated from procreation and nurturant social bonds—is set against their own identification of "true femininity" with the self-sacrificing traits our culture conflates with motherhood. The interpretation of gender that underpins pro-life arguments, however, is based not on a woman's possession of but in her *stance toward* her reproductive capacities. Nurturance is achieved rather than natural, as illustrated in the procreation stories in which the point of the narrative is to show that pregnancy and motherhood are accepted *despite* the ambivalent feelings they produce. In their view, a woman who endorses abortion stresses the other side of the ambivalence and thus is "like a man," regardless of the shape of her body. Conversely, pro-life men encourage and take on a nurturant stance culturally identified as female, often at the urging of their activist wives.

CONCLUSION

This paper examines how American concepts of gender are being redefined by female activists in life story narratives and collective movements. While the analysis is specific to the abortion controversy as it developed in one locale, it is part of two interrelated areas of research: the cultural and social meanings of gender, reproduction, and sexuality; and

arenas of conflict in contemporary American culture.[10] The common theoretical assumption of such work (cf. Colen 1986; Harding 1981; Martin 1986; Rapp 1986; Vance 1986) is that understandings of gender and its attendant meanings in American culture are not unified but multiple, and most clearly visible in moments of social and cultural discord. Methodologically, those interested in such dialectical processes focus on contested domains in America in which the definitions and control of procreation, sexuality, family, and nurturance are in contention.

At such moments of reformulation of cultural definitions, models from other societies offer instructive (or deconstructive) counterpoints to our own arrangements. New Guinea and Australia provide notable cases in which a high valuation is placed on nurturance and reproduction, broadly defined, and the role of men as well as women in "growing up" the next generation. Writing on the Trobriand Islanders, Annette Weiner points out.

> all societies make commitments to the reproduction of their most valued resources, i.e. resources that encompass human reproduction as well as the regeneration of social, material, and cosmological phenomena. In our Western tradition, however, the cyclical process of the generation of elements is not of central concern. Even the value of biological reproduction remains a secondary order of events in terms of power and immortality achieved through male domains. Yet in other societies, reproduction, in its most inclusive form, may be a basic principle through which other major societal structures are linked [Weiner 1979].

Similarly, the abortion struggle demonstrates how reproduction, so frequently reified in American categorizations as a biological domain of activity, is always given meaning and value within a historically specific set of cultural conditions. Looked at in this way, the conflict over abortion, regardless of its particular substance, presents a paradox. The claims of opponents to each represent "the truth" about women are at odds with the fact of the controversy. The very existence of the contest that they have created draws attention to reproduction as an "open" signifier in contemporary America. Yet, both pro-life and pro-choice women are trying, in their activism and procreation stories, to "naturalize" their proposed solutions to the problems created by the differential consequences of biological reproduction for men and women in American culture.

Activists, as narrators of their life stories, create symbolic continuity between discontinuous transitions in the female life cycle, particularly between motherhood and wage work, that, for larger reasons, are particularly problematic for specific cohorts in ways that mark them as "generations." In the procreation stories, abortion not only provides a framework for organizing "disorderly" life transitions and extending a newly articulated sense of self in both space and time, it also provides narrators a means of symbolically controlling their opposition. The narratives show how these activists require the "other" in order to exist. This is what gives these stories their dialectical quality; in them the two sides are, by definition, in dialogue with each other, and thus must address the position of their opposition in constituting their own identities.

The signification attached to abortion provides each position with opposed but interrelated paradigms which reconstitute and claim a possible vision of being female. Reformulated to mesh with different historical and biographical experiences, the authority of nurturance remains prominent in both positions. As historian Linda Gordon points out

> contemporary feminism, like feminism a century ago, contains an ambivalence between individualism and its critique. [Right-to-lifers] fear a completely individualized society with all services based on cash nexus relationships, without the influence of nurturing women counteracting the completely egoistic principles of the economy, and without any forms in which children can learn about lasting human commitments to other people. Many feminists have the same fear [1982:50–51].

Grassroots pro-life and pro-choice women alike envision their work as a full-scale social crusade to enhance rather than diminish women's position in American culture. While their solutions differ, both sides share a critique of a society that increasingly stresses materialism and self-enhancement while denying the value of dependents and those who care for them. These conditions are faced by all parties to the debate. Nonetheless, the abortion issue persists as a contested domain in which the struggle over the place and meaning of work, reproduction, and nurturance, and their relationship to the category female, are being reorganized in oppositional terms. By casting two possible interpretations of this situation in opposition, the abortion debate masks their common roots in, and circumvents effective resistance to, problematic conditions engendered by a central contradiction for women living in a system in which motherhood and wage labor are continually placed in conflict.

The procreation stories told by women on each side—spun from the uneven threads of women's daily experience and woven into life stories—give compelling shape to the reproductive experiences of different generations, which stress one side of the contradiction. It is not surprising that the abortion contest arouses such passion. Its effects, played out on women's bodies and lives in particular, are the evidence and substance on which activists draw. Their verbal and political performances are created to fix with irreversible meaning events in the female life course that are inherently contingent, variable, and liminal. Yet, the narrative and political actions of activists are intended to close off other possible interpretations, as each side claims to speak the truth regarding contemporary as well as past and future generations of American women.

NOTES

Acknowledgments. I gratefully acknowledge research support from the following sources: American Association for University Women Dissertation Fellowship; a Newcombe Fellowship for Studies in Ethics and Values; the David Spitz Distinguished Dissertation Award, CUNY; and a Sigma Xi research grant. I would also like to thank the women in Fargo with whom I worked, who were so generous with their time and insights. They shall remain anonymous, as was agreed. This paper is a longer version of a talk delivered at the 1986 meetings of the American Ethnological Society. It has improved, I hope, from the many helpful comments I received in the discussion there as well as from the thoughtful critiques of the anonymous reviewers of the first draft of this paper. In addition, I would like to thank Susan Harding, Fred Myers, and Rayna Rapp for their invaluable intellectual support.

1. There is considerable argument in the debate over abortion regarding the proper name for each position. Those advocating abortion rights prefer to call their opposition "anti-choice" while those opposed to legal abortion refer to their opponents as "pro-abortion." Following Malinowski's axiom that the anthropologist's task is, in part, to represent the world from the native's point of view, I have used the appellation each group chooses for itself.

2. For a description and analysis of the "social drama" that took place over the clinic opening, see Faye Ginsburg (1984), "The Body Politic: The Defense of Sexual Restriction by Anti-Abortion Activists," in *Pleasure and Danger*, C. Vance, ed.; and Part III of *Reconstructing Gender in America: Self-Definition and Social Action Among Abortion Activists* (1986).

3. I carried out research in Fargo during 1981–82, as a producer for WCCD-TV Minneapolis, for a documentary on the clinic conflict, "Prairie Storm," broadcast in 1982. I am grateful to Joan Arnow, the George Gund Foundation, Michael Meyer, and the Money for Women Fund for their financial assistance; and to Jan Olsen, Greg Pratt, and Mike Sullivan with whom I worked on that project. I returned for another eight months of participant observation fieldwork in 1983.

4. In a 1984 review article on life histories in the *Annual Review of Sociology*, Daniel Bertaux and Martin Kohli use the term "life story" to distinguish such oral autobiographical fragments from more comprehensive, fully developed narrative texts that would more properly be called life histories, such as Vincent Crapanzano's *Tuhami* (Chicago: University of Chicago Press, 1980); Sidney Mintz's *Worker in the Cane* (New York: Norton, 1974); or Marjorie Shostak's *Nisa* (New York: Vintage, 1983). See Daniel Bertaux and Martin Kohli, "The Life Story Approach: A Continental View." *Annual Review of Sociology* 10:215–237, 1984.

5. In order to better understand the connections activists made between their sense of personal identity and the engagement in a social movement, I asked them to work with me in creating "life stories." People were already well known to me. I interviewed them (using a tape recorder) for four to five hours, sometimes twice, at a location of their choice where we knew we would not be interrupted. Simply put, I asked people to tell me how they saw their lives in relation to their current activism on the abortion issue. I explained that my interests were to understand why women were so divided on the abortion issue, and to provide a more accurate portrayal of grassroots abortion activists since they tend to be overlooked or misrepresented in both popular and scholarly discussions of the issue. In general, the activists shared these concerns. I chose subjects who had taken during 1981–83, the period of my fieldwork, the most prominent roles in local activity and who reflected, in my estimation, the range of diversity encompassed in the active memberships of each group in terms of age, socioeconomic status, religious affiliation, household and marriage arrangements, style of activism, and the like. While most of these people continue to be active, each side continues to undergo rapid permutations both locally and nationally. Most of my interviews were with women since the membership of both groups is primarily female, as is the case throughout the country. The men I worked with were either husbands of activists or pro-life clergy. Altogether, I collected 21 life stories from right-to-life activists and 14 life stories from pro-choice activists. In the presentation of the data in the thesis I have changed names and obvious identifying features as I agreed to do at the time of the interview.

6. As Rayna Rapp notes in her essay "Family and Class in Contemporary America" (1982),

If ever a concept carried a heavy weight of ideology, it is the concept of class in American social science. We have a huge and muddled literature that attempts to reconcile objective and subjective criteria, to sort people into lowers, uppers, and middles, to argue about the relation of consciousness to material reality. . . . "Social class" is a short-hand for a process, not a thing . . . by which different social relations to the means of production are inherited and reproduced under capitalism. . . . there are shifting frontiers which separate poverty, stable wage-earning, affluent salaries, and inherited wealth [170–171].

Recognizing this, as well as the complicated questions raised by the sticky question of the relationship of "class" to women's unpaid domestic labor, I use Rapp's definitions for middle-class families and households.

Households among the middle class are obviously based on a stable resource base that allows for some amount of luxury and discretionary spending . . . Middle-class households probably are able to rely on commodity forms rather than kinship processes to ease both economic and geographic transitions.

The families that organize such households are commonly thought to be characterized by egalitarian marriages [p. 181].

(For egalitarian marriages, see Schneider and Smith 1973.) This definition is consistent with those used in the studies I cite (see note 7) as evidence for the middle-class basis for the abortion movement as a whole. It offers a good general description of the households and families of activists I worked with in Fargo. I do not mean to dismiss class but rather want to underscore the point that the opposing positions on abortion are not isomorphic with distinctive groups of people situated differently in the social relations of production. I use the life histories in particular to show how much more complicated the process is, and the multiple settings from which identity is drawn.

7. See, for example, Daniel Granberg 1981; Harding 1981; and Tatalovich and Daynes 1981: 116–137. Granberg's random sample survey of members of the National Abortion Rights Action League (NARAL) and National Right to Life Committee (NRLC), which is the most thorough of all research to date, gives a breakdown of selected demographic and social status characteristics (see Granberg 1981, Table 1, p. 158).

8. In an article on new anthropological views of the family, authors Collier, Rosaldo, and Yanagisako write:

One of the central notions in the modern American construct of The Family is that of nurturance . . . a relationship that entails affection and love, that is based on cooperation as opposed to competition, that is enduring rather than temporary, that is noncontingent rather than contingent upon performance, and that is governed by feeling and morality instead of law and contract. . . . a symbolic opposition to the market relations of capitalism [1982:34].

9. In assessing the way that abortion opponents view the world in relation to their ideology, authors Callahan and Callahan write:

Both sides are prepared to argue that abortion is undesirable, a crude solution to problems that would better be solved by other means. The crucial difference, however is that those on the pro-choice side believe that the world must be acknowledged as it is and not just as it ought to be.

By contrast, the pro-life group believes that a better future cannot be achieved . . . unless we are prepared to make present sacrifices toward future goals and unless aggression toward the fetus is denied, however high the individual cost of denying it. The dichotomies are experienced in our ordinary language when "idealists" are contrasted with "realists." [1984:221].

10. Several sessions at professional anthropology meetings in 1986 were indicative of this trend. A panel organized by the author and Linda Girdner entitled "Contested Domains of Reproduction, Sexuality, Family and Gender in America" was held at the American Ethnological Society meetings in April. At the December meetings of the American Anthropological Association, a session entitled "Speaking Women: Representations of Contemporary American Femininity" was organized by Joyce Canaan; at the same event, Susan Harding organized a panel on "Ethnographic America." Specific research presented at these sessions included Rayna Rapp's study of amniocentesis, Carole Vance's investigation of the pornography debates, Susan Harding's research on the Moral Majority, Shellee Colen's work on domestic childcare workers, Emily Martin's study of conflicting metaphors for birth and the female body, Joyce Canaan's work on adolescent sexuality in America, Linda Girdner's

study of contested child custody disputes, and Judy Modell's research on adoption.

REFERENCES

Callahan, Daniel, and Sidney Callahan. 1984. Abortion: Understanding Differences. Family Planning Perspectives 16(5):219–220.

Colen, Shellee. 1986. Stratified Reproduction: The Case of Domestic Workers in America. Paper presented at the American Ethnological Society Meetings, Wrightsville Beach, NC.

Collier, Jane, Michelle Rosaldo, and Sylvia Yanagisako. 1982. Is There A Family? New Anthropological Views. *In* Rethinking the Family. B. Thorne and M. Yalom, eds. New York: Longman.

Ginsburg, Faye. 1984. The Body Politic: The Defense of Sexual Restriction by Anti-Abortion Activists. *In* Pleasure and Danger: Exploring Female Sexuality. C. Vance, ed. Boston: Routledge and Kegan Paul.

———. 1986. Reconstructing Gender in America. Self-Definition and Social Action Among Abortion Activists. Ph.D. dissertation. City University of New York.

Gordon, Linda. 1982. Why Nineteenth-Century Feminists Did Not Support "Birth Control" and Twentieth Century Feminists Do: Feminism, Reproduction and the Family. *In* Rethinking the Family. B. Thorne and M. Yalom, eds. New York: Longman.

Granberg, Daniel. 1981. The Abortion Activists. Family Planning Perspectives 13(4).

Harding, Susan. 1981. Family Reform Movements: Recent Feminism and Its Opposition. Feminist Studies 7(1).

Luker, Kristin. 1984. Abortion and the Politics of Motherhood. Berkeley: University of California Press.

Mannheim, Karl. 1952. The Problem of Generations. *In* Essays on the Sociology of Knowledge. P. Kecskemeti, ed. New York: Oxford University Press.

Martin, Emily. 1986. Mind, Body and Machine. Paper presented at the American Anthropological Association Meetings, Philadelphia, PA.

Rapp, Rayna. 1982. Family and Class in Contemporary America. *In* Rethinking the Family. B. Thorne and M. Yalom, eds. New York: Longman.

———. 1986. Constructing Amniocentesis: Medical and Maternal Voices. Paper presented at the American Anthropological Association Meetings, Philadelphia, PA.

Schneider, David M., and R. T. Smith. 1973. Class Differences and Sex Roles in American Kinship and Family Structure. Englewood Cliffs, NJ: Prentice-Hall.

Tatalovich, Raymond, and Byron W. Daynes. 1981. The Politics of Abortion. New York: Praeger.

Vance, Carole S. 1986. Of Sex and Women, Meese and Men: The 1986 Attorney General's Commission on Pornography. Paper presented at the American Ethnological Society Meetings, Wrightsville Beach, NC.

Weiner, Annette. 1979. Trobriand Kinship From Another View: The Reproductive Power of Women and Men. Man 14(2): 328–348.

The Movement Against Clitoridectomy and Infibulation in Sudan: Public Health Policy and the Women's Movement

Ellen Gruenbaum

Sudan is one of the countries where the most severe form of female circumcision persists and is practiced widely among both Muslims and Coptic Christians, in both urban and rural communities. Only the largely non-Muslim Southern Region is free of the practice, except among people of northern origin.

The most common form of the operation is referred to as pharaonic circumcision, consisting of the removal of all external genitalia—the clitoris, the clitoral prepuce, the labia minora and all or part of the labia majora—and infibulation (stitching together of the opening), so as to occlude the vaginal opening and urethra. Only a tiny opening is left for the passage of urine and menses. A modified version, Sunna circumcision, is less common, and consists of excision of the prepuce of the clitoris, generally also with partial or total excision of the clitoris itself (clitoridectomy), but without infibulation.

The operations customarily are performed by traditional or government-trained midwives on girls in the 5–7 year age range; the girls, however, may be older or younger, since it is common to circumcise two or three sisters at the same time. These occasions are ones of celebration, with new dresses, bracelets, and gifts for the girls. An animal may be slaughtered and a special meal prepared for the many guests and well-wishers who are expected to drop in. In wealthy families, musical entertainment is often arranged for an evening party. The girls themselves, though they

Reproduced by permission of the American Anthropological Association from *Medical Anthropology Newsletter* 13:2, February 1982. Not for further reproduction.

may be fearful of the operation, look forward to the first occasion at which they will be treated as important people.

The origin of the practice is unknown, though its existence in the ancient civilizations of the Nile Valley in Egypt and Sudan has been documented. The practice survived the spread of Christianity to the ruling groups of the Nile Valley kingdoms in Sudan in the 6th century. Waves of Arab migration, intermarriage with the indigenous people, and the influence of Islamic teachers resulted in Islam's becoming the dominant religion of northern Sudan by about 1500. Pharaonic circumcision, along with other non-Islamic beliefs such as veneration of ancestors or saints and spirit possession cults, was successfully incorporated into the Sudanese Islamic belief system. The practice is deeply embedded in Sudanese cultures; and it should be recognized that the symbolic significance and cultural concomitants of female circumcision undoubtedly play important roles in individual repetition of the custom, as the work of Janice Boddy (1979) has shown.

Still, to say that it is a "custom" is not a sufficient explanation for the persistence of this damaging practice. Numerous physically harmful effects have been documented in the medical literature (Verzin 1975, Cook 1976, Shandall 1967). At the time of circumcision, girls may suffer from hemorrhage, infections, septicemia, retention of urine, or shock; deaths may result from these complications. The infibulated state may also result in retention of menses or difficulties in urination (due to scar tissue), and may be related to an apparently high prevalence of urinary tract and other chronic pelvic infections (Boddy 1979, Toubia 1981). At first intercourse, infibulation presents a barrier which is painfully torn unless cut open by husband, midwife, or doctor. Childbirth is complicated by the inelastic scar tissue of infibulation, which must be cut open by the birth attendant and restitched after delivery. Vasicovaginal fistulae, which can result from such obstructed labor, are by no means rare in Sudan. Such a fistula—a passage between the urinary bladder and the vagina created by damage to tissue between the two organs—results in a most embarrassing condition for the woman, who cannot retain her urine and therefore leaks constantly (Toubia 1981).

Why, then, in light of these physically harmful, even life-threatening, consequences, do women continue to perform these operations on their daughters? Much of the literature has gone no further than the observation that it is "customary," or as one Sudanese writer has put it, "the implicit and explicit message being that it is something we inherited from an untraceable past which has no rational meaning and lies within the realm of untouchable sensitivity of traditional people" (Toubia 1981:4).

Social scientists and feminists writing on the subject have pointed out that female circumcision forms part of a complex sociocultural arrangement of female subjugation in a strongly patrilineal, patriarchal society (*cf.*, Assaad 1980, Hayes 1975, El Saadawi 1980). The fact that it is women who carry out the practice, and who are its strongest defenders, must be analyzed in terms of their weaker social position.

Women in Sudan generally must derive their social status and economic security from their roles as wives and mothers. Among most cultural groups in northern Sudan, female virginity at marriage is considered so important that even rumors questioning a girl's morality may be enough to besmirch the family honor and to bar her from the possibility of marriage. In this context, clitoridectomy and infibulation serve as a guarantee of morality. Sudanese women hold that clitoridectomy helps to attenuate a girl's sexual desire so that she is less likely to seek premarital sex; infibulation presents a barrier to penetration. Any girl known to have been "properly" circumcised in the pharaonic manner can be assumed to be a virgin and therefore marriageable, while doubts can be raised about those who are not circumcised or have had only the modified Sunna circumcision.

Attempts to formulate policies against the practice have seldom recognized the significance of the linkage between the operations and the social goal of maintaining the reputations and marriageability of daughters in a strongly patriarchal society. In addition, the economic and social status of midwives, the group chiefly responsible for performing the operations, has seldom been seriously considered. Instead, government policies have tended to emphasize simple legal prohibitions; propaganda against the apparent ideological supports of the practice; spreading information on some of the physically harmful aspects of female circumcision; and tacit acceptance of a compromise policy of modification and "modernization" of the practice.

Some policies resulting from these emphases are undoubtedly useful. Certainly the recommendations of the 1979 Khartoum Conference (Seminar on Traditional Practices Affecting the Health of Women, sponsored by the Eastern Mediterranean Regional Office of the World Health Organization) are to be commended and supported. These recommendations included a call for clear national policies for the abolition of the practice in the countries where it persists; the passage of legislation in support of such policies; the intensification of general education on the dangers and undesirability of the practice; and intensification of educational programs for birth attendants and other practitioners to enlist their support. Because there is such strong social motivation for continuing the practice in Sudan, however, I would argue that the proposed public health education approach would have only a weak or slow effect. Policy on female circumcision requires rethinking.

In the following sections, I draw upon my experience in Sudan, where I carried out research on rural health services and lectured at the University of Khartoum. My goal here is twofold: to consider the reasons for failure of past anticircumcision policies, and to provide a critique of current policy efforts. In addition, I hope to provide insights into what is necessary for the development of viable policies.

ABOLITION EFFORTS IN SUDAN

The first efforts to eliminate the practice of clitoridectomy and infibulation in Sudan came during the British colonial period (1898–1956). When a British midwife was brought in to organize a midwifery training school in 1920, efforts were made to dissuade the traditional midwives enrolled in the training program from continuing the practice. But persuasion and example apparently had little effect.

In 1946, an edict was promulgated prohibiting pharaonic circumcision. This attempt to impose the colonialists' values on the culture of a subject people by force of law also failed completely, and was even met with violent resistance. Residents of the town of Rufa'a still talk about "our Revolution"—the day in 1946 when they tore the government prison to the ground to free a midwife who had been arrested for circumcising a girl. Government troops fired on the crowd, and injured some; yet even this failed to stem popular resistance to the British and to their attempts to outlaw the entrenched custom.

Resistance to the government ban did not require rebellion. Since the activity took place outside the purview of the foreign government, the practice simply continued as before. In fact, historically, the government seldom attempted the sort of enforcement that led to the Rufa'a "Revolution."

Another approach used by the British against the practice was propaganda. In 1945, the Sudan Medical Service issued and circulated a pamphlet, written in both English and Arabic, that condemned pharaonic circumcision and urged the Sudanese to abandon the practice. It was signed by the highest ranking British and Sudanese doctors, and was endorsed by Sudanese religious leaders. The Mufti of Sudan provided an authoritative Islamic legal opinion stating that female circumcision was not obligatory under Islam; and another endorsing religious leader advocated the substitution of Sunna circumcision (clitoridectomy). Thus, while the backing of the religious leaders was something less than total opposition to female circumcision, their opposition to the pharaonic form is important. (Few Sudanese queried in villages where I worked, however, were aware that the religious leaders had ever spoken against female circumcision.)

During this same period, the mid-1940s, several educated Sudanese women—teachers and midwives—undertook speaking tours in the provinces to publicize the bad effects of pharaonic circumcision. An Arabic poster used during the campaign declared that the Sunna circumcision came from the Prophet Mohammed, and should therefore replace the pharaonic form, ascribed to "Pharaoh the enemy of God" (Hall and Ismail 1981:93–95).

Today, after three decades of illegality, pharaonic circumcision of girls continues to be widely performed in both rural and urban areas. It is openly celebrated, with feasting and gift-giving. Midwives speak freely of their participation in the perpetuation of the practice. To my knowledge there have been no government efforts in recent years to enforce the legal prohibition.

There has, however, been some change in the methods used in performing the operations, although this has not been uniform. The dangerously unhygienic traditional methods, such as performing the operation over a hole in the ground, using knives for cutting, thorns and leg binding for infibulation, and plain water for cleansing, have been supplanted by the availability of better equipment and knowledge of more hygienic methods. The government-trained village midwife whose practice I observed did the operations on a wood and rope bed covered with a plastic sheet. She used xylocaine injections for local anesthesia, new razor blades, suture needles, dissolving sutures when available, and prophylactic antibiotic powder. Her equipment was sterilized with boiling water before use. After this initial use, however, she returned the instruments to the same bowl of previously boiled water, and did not resterilize them before using them in a second girl's operation. The midwife purchases most of the necessary supplies and medications out of her earnings; some of the basic equipment necessary for childbirth attendance is provided by the government, however, and some supplies are obtained informally through the local government health center.

CURRENT POLICY EFFORTS

In more recent years, opponents—ordinarily resorting to medical and psychological arguments against pharaonic circumcision—have recognized that complete eradication of the practice is an unrealistic short-term objective. While continuing to advocate eventual eradication, policymakers have tended to attempt to mitigate the effects by substituting the less drastic Sunna form of circumcision. This opinion, held unofficially by the government health service's leaders and many medical doctors with whom I spoke in the late 1970s, has meant that many doctors are willing to perform such operations themselves. They assume that, in terms of medical safety, it is better for them to perform clitoridectomies in their offices.[1]

As policy positions, both the eradication goal and the "modification" compromise are problematic. The view that the practice should or could be "eradicated," as if it were a disease, is a particularly medical view. While it is reasonable that arguments against circumcision stress physical risks, the problem nevertheless is one that is not necessarily amenable to medical solutions. The medical view implies not only that the practice is "pathological," but that its solution might lie in some sort of campaign-style attack on the problem. Social customs, however, are not "pathologies"; and such a view is a poor starting point for change, since it is not one necessarily shared by the people whose customs are under attack. While these people may be

open to the view that a practice such as this may be harmful in some ways, to approach it as an evil or pathological situation is to insult those who believe strongly in it and consider it a means of promoting cleanliness and purity, and is unlikely to foster consideration of change. Furthermore, the decades of emphasis on medical reasons for discontinuing the practice have not in fact resulted in its abandonment. For example, in a study of medical records of 2526 women in Khartoum and Wad Medani, Mudawi (1977a) found only seven to be uncircumcised; 12 had been clitoridectomised only, and the remainder had been infibulated.[2] A questionnaire sample survey of about 10,000 women in Sudan found that 82% were infibulated (El Dareer 1979).

Another problem with the strategy of promoting a modified form of circumcision as a transitional program relates to the unfortunate ideological linkage of the modified type. Among Sudanese who practice pharaonic circumcision, it is widely believed that the practice is commanded by Islam. While this interpretation is disavowed by many Islamic scholars, the belief that both male and female circumcision were commanded by the Prophet Mohammed persists.[3] This widespread belief serves as strong ideological support for a practice known to predate Islam (Diaz and Mudawi 1977) and which is perpetuated largely because of its important social functions.

The use of the term "Sunna circumcision" for the less drastic operation, which many reformers are encouraging as the most feasible short-term alternative, has unfortunately reinforced the ideological linkage with Islam. To describe a practice as "Sunna" is to consider it religious law.[4] Since Sudanese Muslims are adherents of the Sunni branch of Islam (i.e., "those who follow the Sunna"), they do not want to say their practice is incongruent with Sunni tradition. The linguistic root of the words Sunni and Sunna is the same, and although "Sunna circumcision" does not literally imply linkage to Sunni Islam, they are commonly associated. Indeed, the ideological linkage between the term

"Sunna circumcision" and the religion has been reinforced even by an eminent Sudanese gynecologist, Dr. Suliman Mudawi, who writes that, "The Sunna circumcision, or clitoridectomy, is the legal operation recommended by Islam, consisting of the excision of the glans clitoris and sometimes a small portion of the clitoris itself" (Mudawi 1977b).

Thus, now that the term "Sunna circumcision" is widely known, many people profess to practice it—since they wish to be regarded as faithful Sunnites—even when the operation is performed as before with infibulation after removal of clitoris and labia. Reform efforts advocating a modified operation, therefore, may have resulted in a change in nomenclature, rather than widespread change in the operations. Thus, reports that pharaonic circumcision with infibulation is gradually being abandoned in Sudan, which are based on questionnaire interviews or anecdotal material (e.g., Clark and Diaz 1977, Cook 1976), may be misleading, since some of those who say they have adopted the Sunna form simply may have begun calling pharaonic circumcision by another name.

In spite of the importance of ideological supports, it would not be sufficient to attack the presumed religious reasons. Change efforts must take into consideration the socioeconomic relations in which Sudanese women are enmeshed, and the social dilemmas to which families that try to change the practice would be exposed. After all, where a most significant aspect of marriage is control of female reproductive capacity, and where circumcision has come to be the mechanism for guaranteeing the perfect condition of that capacity, to dispense with circumcision is to violate a basic condition of an essential social relation. Thus, a religious scholar's testimony that female circumcision is not necessary for religious reasons would not be sufficient for a mother to risk her daughter's marriageability. Similarly, awareness of medical and psychological[5] hazards may be only weakly deterrent; a daughter's marriageability would scarcely be risked because of a psychological notion that she may suffer bad dreams or never experience orgasm. Marriage and children are more vital, closer to the meaning of life and to a woman's economic survival, than transitory emotional feelings.

While most women are economically active, either in subsistence production, wage employment, trade, or production of commodities, economic well-being—indeed, survival in many of the harsher rural areas—requires large family production units. A husband and children are necessary to a woman's economic security; not only do children contribute their labor at an early age to the family's economic production—especially in rural areas—but also they are security for old age. Commonly, women are to some degree dependent on their husbands for access to land or domestic animals, their labors, and/or their wages. A husband dissatisfied with his wife—either personally or because of reproductive inadequacy—is considered more likely to take a second wife. Although polygyny frequently enhances the prestige and wealth of the husband, it commonly weakens the individual woman's economic position and, if the other wife or wives bear children, lessens her own children's inheritance. Under Islamic law,[6] a divorced woman has no right to child custody after the age of seven for boys and the age of nine for girls, regardless of the reasons for divorce or on whose initiative the marriage was ended. Men have the right to unilateral divorce, but women do not. With these constraints it is not surprising that most women put considerable effort into pleasing their husbands and protecting their reputations, so as to safeguard their marriages.

Efforts to please husbands and safeguard virtue take many forms. Beautification methods, while pleasurable for a woman herself and usually done in pleasant camaraderie with other women, are primarily directed toward husbands, with the most sensuous techniques being reserved for married women. Even poor rural women spend considerable time and effort on the arts of decorative henna staining of hands and feet, removal of body hair, sauna-like incensing of the body, careful selection of clothing and ornaments, and decorative hair plaiting. They also prepare special scented substances for massaging their husbands.

Beyond these, the enhancement of a woman's ability to please her husband is considered to be most importantly achieved by clitoridectomy and infibulation. One midwife I spoke with claimed that clitoridectomy allowed for longer intercourse, pleasing to the man. This belief presupposes that a woman experiencing more sexual stimulation would be less patient, and can hardly be credited as a major factor in perpetuating clitoridectomy. On the other hand, the attenuation of *inappropriate* sexual desire, before marriage and extramaritally, should be considered one of the major goals of the practice.

It is infibulation, and especially reinfibulation, that is alleged to contribute most significantly to the sexual pleasure of men. Following childbirth, the midwife restitches the long incision made for the delivery of the baby. A tighter reinfibulation is expected to result in greater pleasure for the husband when intercourse is resumed following the customary 40-day postpartum recovery period. One reinfibulation I witnessed, performed by a government-trained midwife following a woman's thirteenth childbirth, left a completely smooth vulva, the urethral opening completely concealed, and only a pin-sized opening to the vagina. A number of women told me that such tight reinfibulation gives husbands greater sexual pleasure, the tightness lasting approximately three months after resumption of sexual intercourse. They claimed that husbands were more generous in their gifts (clothes, jewelry, perfumes) when the reinfibulation is very tight. It was clear, too, that such marital sexual satisfaction is considered important in avoiding the possibility of the husband exercising his legally guaranteed rights to unilateral divorce or polygynous marriage.

The attitudes of women toward the practice of clitoridectomy and infibulation are often contradictory. Occasionally, I encountered Sudanese women who were surprised to learn that American and European women are not circumcised. Others realized that Europeans did not circumcise women, but believed that all Muslims did. Although they found it hard to believe that Saudi Arabian women are not circumcised, such information did nothing to undermine their faith in the importance of the practice. To my comment that American women are left "natural," they replied, "But circumcision *is* natural for us."

There was, however, recurrent ambivalence expressed in many of the conversations I had on this topic. Without questioning the necessity of circumcision, a woman might sigh and say, "Isn't it difficult?" When discussing repeated reinfibulation with one small group of urban women (which included a new mother who had just been reinfibulated a few days before), I was urged, "Be sure and put all this in your report, about how difficult it is for us."

DEVELOPING VIABLE POLICY ALTERNATIVES

That women perpetuate practices painful and dangerous to themselves and their daughters and that inhibit their own sexual gratification must be understood in the context of their social and economic vulnerability in a strongly patriarchal society. Public health policymakers must allow for the fact that the circumcision of girls is a deeply rooted social custom. Even among urban-dwelling, educated families, there are those who would take their daughters back to the relatives in a rural village for circumcision, to ensure a traditional, thorough operation.

Although harmful sequelae have brought female circumcision to the attention of medical professionals, it is argued here that medical opinion can have little relevance in changing the situation. While more research into the psychological and medical hazards of circumcision could be useful for convincing influential educated people to back efforts toward change, the medical model and the efforts of the medical services system are limited in terms of policy development. Effective change can only come in the context of a women's movement oriented toward the basic social problems affecting women, particularly their economic dependency, educational disadvantages, and obstacles to employment (e.g., the dearth of child day-care facilities for urban workers). To improve women's social and economic security, marital customs must be challenged, and new civil laws are needed to offer additional protection to married and divorced women concerning child custody, rights in marital property, and financial support, going beyond the present provisions of Islamic and customary law. Further, general health conditions are very poor and must be improved. With an infant mortality rate conservatively estimated at 140 per 1000 (Sudan, Ministry of Health, 1975:6), and with a high prevalence of numerous disabling and life-threatening illnesses, especially dangerous to children, it is not surprising that Sudanese women—particularly in rural areas—seek to give birth to large numbers of children. The crude birth rate is approximately 49 per 1000 (Sudan, Ministry of Health 1975:5). Thus, basic health issues are important concerns of women.

The implications of reducing women's dependency through improvement of their economic opportunities are far-reaching. Any policy that would threaten the form or importance of the family and its functions would obviously excite widespread reaction. At the same time, Sudan's current laws and social values already offer some advantages to women in promising productive roles. Educated women are expected to hold full-time jobs and to have the right to the same pay and benefits as men in comparable jobs, although there are social barriers to women's participation in certain occupations. While many struggles remain to be fought on this front, the fact that wide networks of people benefit from each person employed in a stable job means that families generally back the educated woman who wants to work. Frequently, child care can be provided by relatives during working hours, and there is a general acceptance of the principle of equal pay for equal work. In addition, the government (the largest employer of the educated) gives eight weeks' paid maternity leave, often additional unpaid leave with position held, and makes special allowances for the needs of nursing mothers.

While these offer a good basis for developing women's position, many problems prevent women from taking full advantage of the opportunities that do exist. Working women complain (or, more often, do not complain, but simply carry on) that they must still perform all the usual housework after coming home, and are still expected to make time for all the traditional visiting and hospitality. Women college students find their neighbors and relatives consider them snobbish if they do not take the time for such visiting, regardless of the demands of their studies. This is especially hard on women medical students who must keep odd hours, and often spend the night at the hospital during their clinical training.

The family continues to be an extremely important factor, however, in the lives of even the most advantaged, educated, employed women. Since childbearing is expected to begin immediately after marriage, the employed woman most commonly depends on her mother or another female relative to provide child care. Family members become dependent on her income, and she may find herself locked into the necessity of working even when other social obligations make it difficult. Should her marriage falter and her husband divorce her, she may not only lose his support but custody of her children as well. Clearly, additional social services would help overcome these problems. For example, while government-sponsored child care centers presently exist in some towns, many women workers find them unavailable or too costly. Some form of social security benefits could reduce women's vulnerability to divorce and loss of support and child custody. But state subsidy of such services outside the family currently is neither a feasible nor a desired alternative in Sudan, where government policy favors investment in economic development over expansion of social service expenditures.

A full discussion of development strategies and their implications for women's position in the society would be outside the scope of this paper. It is important to realize, however, that while women share in the desire for economic development in their poor country, just as they desire increased incomes for their families and themselves, current development policies offer little to women. Sudan's development has been of the peripheral capitalist pattern of uneven development (O'Brien 1980). Investment has gravitated toward the center of the country in the most highly productive centers of primary products for export or import substitution. All too frequently, foreign investments have been self-serving, emphasizing high technology that the developed countries want to sell, or the production of products that the investors want to import. The high technology emphasis, which appeals to scheme managers and government officials seeking to "modernize," results in jobs for men rather than women, and sometimes even undercuts existing productive roles of women (see Sørbø 1977).

Sudanese and other Middle Eastern women have demonstrated their interest in changing their lot by the formation of women's organizations such as the Sudanese Women's Union. The Union has a history of militant action, as when Sudanese women took to the streets in the popular uprising that overthrew the military regime in 1964. While the issues such women's groups have chosen to address have long included modifying or abolishing circumcision, they have addressed themselves more urgently to other problems. In the 1950s and 1960s for example, the women's organization in Sudan was concerned with nationalist issues: the achievement of national independence, avoidance of control by U.S. imperialist interests, and the development of democratic government. In the early 1970s, the women's union was restructured under the ruling party (under Nimeiri's government, which came to power in a coup d'etat in 1969), and most of the communist and other politically radical women were purged or barred from leadership. Since then, the thrust of the organization has also changed somewhat. In the urban and "modern" sector rural areas (such as the

Gezira Irrigation Scheme), the primary activities of the Union as they touch the lives of the ordinary women center on cultural and educational activities—embroidery classes, crafts shows, and the like and support for the ruling party; eradication of circumcision has not been a high priority.

The majority of women in the country, who live outside the towns and agricultural schemes or in the poor neighborhoods and rural villages in those areas, have not by and large been recruited into such organizations. Yet these women, too, have a number of very basic concerns: improved incomes, education for their children, clean water, and basic health services. Organizing these rural women, however, has proven difficult. In a prosperous village in the Gezira Irrigated Scheme, for example, the membership of the local branch of the Women's Union has not met in two years. One divorced woman, a Union member, tried to organize women in that village to take an active part in improving village sanitation. She was unable to mobilize support, however, even though a fully staffed health center (which should share responsibility for public health) is located in the village. Further, though this woman is part of the mandated one-third female membership of the village People's Council, she and the other women members are not ordinarily informed of meetings. Her participation as an individual in development is also blocked. Although she is literate, she is not highly enough educated to qualify for a white-collar job; and her brother has opposed her working in agriculture, a position that would threaten the prestige of the family.

This is not to say that women's organizations and programs are everywhere ineffective. In fact there is much enthusiasm in Gezira villages for the literacy campaigns and home economics courses offered by the Gezira Scheme's Social Development Department. But if the woman just mentioned must face such obstacles even in a relatively well off village that has resources to devote to local projects, the problems of the more remote and poorer villages, where literacy campaigns and women's organizations have not penetrated at all, are far greater.

Since, as history demonstrates, circumcisions can continue with or without governmental sanction, it is impossible to conceive of any efforts to change the custom having an effect unless they are supported by women themselves. These changes will come only as the result of many other societal changes, especially those that enable women to be less economically dependent on men and thus less oriented toward pleasing husbands.

POLICY CONTRIBUTIONS

To assert that changes in female circumcision must come from the women themselves and their social movement is not to say that policymakers have nothing to contribute. Indeed, there are several key areas where public policy and specifically health policy could contribute significantly.

First, further research is appropriate. Much of the writing thus far has been based on case studies, anecdotal material, or haphazard sampling (e.g., Assaad 1980, Hayes 1975). It would be useful to relate the place of circumcision and its celebration to the social position of women in societies where the practice is common. Studies should focus particularly on the significance of marriage, the importance of virginity and its relation to the maintenance of family "honor" (e.g., segregation of sexes, chaperoning, infibulation, manner of dress), and the economic participation of women and form of economic organization (especially whether the organization of production continues to emphasize family production units). Whether more clinical medical articles, describing the operations and their sequelae, would add anything to arguments against the practice is uncertain, although more information on the treatment of complications could be useful. Epidemiological studies of the apparently high rates of urinary and vaginal infections associated with circumcision also would be in order. Although I am aware of no data on a relationship between the operations and infertility or low fertility, such a relationship has nevertheless been suggested (*cf.*, Hosken 1980; Hayes 1975); Hayes (1975), in fact, considered lowered fertility a "latent function" of female circumcision. Certainly infertility might be expected in cases of obstructed intercourse (Sudan Medical Service 1945), and in association with the medical complications of circumcision. The existence of a demonstrable relationship between circumcision and infertility could provide a powerful argument against the operations in countries such as Sudan with strong pronatalist values.

Second, policies that promote the opportunities of women in education and employment could be beneficial in two ways. First, reducing women's dependence on marriage and motherhood as the only economically viable social roles could separate circumcision from basic economic survival and thus weaken support for it. Second, education and employment could be expected to enhance women's ability to act as a group by enabling them to become more involved in shaping their own destiny through access to political and economic power and greater opportunities for organizing themselves. Women then would be better able to influence and implement policies according to their own priorities. The realization of such opportunities may require not only that additional social security and other support services be provided but, in addition, that economic development policies be challenged. The high technology strategies which have so often resulted in skilled jobs for men while undermining women's traditional productive roles and ignoring the possibility of their involvement in new areas, may need to be revised.

The Role of Midwives

A particularly important locus of policy concerns should be the role of midwives, since they are the principal practitioners of circumcision. It is not enough to recommend that they be educated as to its harmful effects; it must also be recognized that fees, together with gifts such as soap, perfume, meat from the celebration slaughter and other foods, constitute important elements of a midwife's income. Government-trained midwives, if they are paid at all, receive only a very small monthly retainer fee from the local government. This is not paid in all areas and is too small to be considered even a meager salary. Untrained, traditional midwives receive no benefits from the government at all; even basic equipment for childbirth attendance is supplied only to the trained midwives, and both groups must purchase their own drugs and supplies, unless acquired informally through local health services facilities of the government. The fee-for-service payment system means that the midwife's income is directly dependent on the number of births attended and circumcision performed.

The current drive for the development of Primary Health Care for the achievement of WHO's goal of "Health for All by the Year 2000" could very usefully seek out midwives to be Community Health Workers. The additional training would benefit their midwifery practices, and whatever status individual midwives already have achieved as respected community members concerned with health could enhance their influence as health care providers. Further, since barriers to the effective health care of women by male health care providers now prevent women from receiving needed care, more female providers would fill a real need.[7]

Providing midwives with a wider role and some other income might help them heed educational efforts against circumcision by reducing the conflicts of interest with respect to income. Difficulties inherent in the training of midwives (involving a full year's study away from family, especially hard for married women and mothers) have been overcome. The same could be expected for Community Health Workers, whose training period is shorter. Such a strategy could help to achieve primary health care goals while improving midwifery at less cost than training and supporting two separate specialized individuals. Since midwives, as women, have access to women and children even in the most tradi-

tional communities, they could be expected to be very effective in promoting maternal and child health goals.

PERSPECTIVES ON INTERNATIONAL POLICYMAKING

Such recommendations should be considered in the context of the social dynamics of an underdeveloped country. The dependency relations between a country such as Sudan and the more powerful capitalist financial centers has surely played as much a part in molding priorities in social and health policy as have religion and cultural tradition.

Social scientists who seek to design rational, sensible, and culturally sensitive public health policies, must ask themselves several questions. What would be necessary to ensure the adoption of their proposals? What are the interests of the social classes with access to the most political power in a country? What image of their country do the relevant national ministries, organizations, and occupational groups wish to portray? What sort of research or program priorities might they want to block? Which would they prefer to support?

Similarly, international organizations and the aid missions of developed countries are limited by their own hidden agendas.[8] For example, USAID projects ordinarily must be demonstrated to have some beneficial effect on U.S. trade, U.S. geopolitical strategies, or other U.S. interests; beneficial effects on the people or the economies of the developing countries are desirable, but secondary. To suppose that an aid mission might withhold support from such programs as primary health care until serious work against female circumcision is undertaken is to pretend that aid missions are moral entities instead of international political and economic tools. For aid to be accepted by the host government, its terms ordinarily must be beneficial to the interests of ruling groups or to governmental stability. Aid must not, therefore, make the nation or the government appear backward, discriminatory, or as having anything less than the best interests of the entire populace at heart.

While international bodies such as the United Nations organizations are less likely to have such strongly political agendas, and can be assumed to be genuinely oriented to abstract goals such as peace and health, they, too, suffer from an inability to be critical of host governments. Programs must be invited and collaborative, although these organizations' apparently neutral political position gives them somewhat more leeway to provide guidance without seeming offensively imperialistic.

I believe it is a mistake to insist, as some outspoken critics do, that aid missions, international organizations, and even nongovernmental and church groups take firm stands "to prevent the operations" (Hosken 1980). Such agencies and organizations would have no political interest in taking such a controversial stand except where host governments might ask them to do so as part of an indigenous movement against the practice. But even if the necessary forces could be mobilized in the developed countries to force the adoption of such a policy and such agencies and organizations *did* adopt this stance, a "backlash" phenomenon would all too likely follow. Heavy-handedness on the part of the developed countries is generally unwelcome in fiercely nationalistic underdeveloped countries such as Sudan. Thus, while its external relationships may be those of dependency and its economic system capitalist (including some state-capitalist structures and some use of "socialist" ideology), there is no loyalty to a particular power which extends beyond national interests or economic constraints. Even Saudi Arabia, with its stranglehold control of the supply of much of Sudan's energy and investment capital and its influential role in religious leadership of the Islamic countries, has thus far been able to impose only temporary or partial social programs—such as the crackdown on prostitution in Khartoum in 1976–77. The Nimeiri government, however, has stalled on such issues as the abolition of alcohol or imposition of an Islamic constitution, which might prove either widely unpopular or which might jeopardize the government's control over the largely non-Muslim south.

Policy research must be placed in this context. It is clear that the movement against clitoridectomy and infibulation must receive its primary momentum for national movements in which women themselves play a leading role. Thus, policy researchers should keep in mind that it is not appropriate merely to expose practices and make recommendations to outside organizations. Wherever possible, indigenous women and women's organizations should be involved in all stages of the research, from formulation of the problem to development of policy. Only in this way will such indigenous movements be sure to benefit from the research.

NOTES

1. In support of this point, one Sudanese doctor recently stated that before the Khartoum Conference in 1979, the medical profession's official policy "was not total abolition of female circumcision, but the promotion of clitoridectomy under more hygienic circumstances as a substitute for infibulation" (Toubia 1981).

2. It is ironic that this same author, a senior Sudanese gynecologist, has said, "Although the habit is still practised in some parts of the Sudan it is gratifying to note that it is gradually dying out." He is further quoted as saying, "The most effective line of attack was a medical one" (quoted in Toubia 1981:3).

3. The sayings attributed to the Prophet Mohammed on this subject do not, however, endorse infibulation. "Reduce but do not destroy," is often quoted by reformers. Another saying, handed down by Um Attiya, is, "Circumcise but do not go deep, this is more illuminating to the face and more enjoyable to the husband" (Sudanese Medical Service 1945, in Foreword by the Mufti of the Sudan).

4. While "Sunna" may be translated as "rule" or "tradition," the Islamic ideology asserts that Islam is not simply a religion, but a "way of life." Hence, it is not uncommon for Sudanese Muslims to assume linkages between cultural traditions and religious beliefs, and to assume that their shared beliefs and practices are

rooted in formal Islamic doctrine. In his statement against pharaonic circumcision in 1945,
the Mufti of Sudan cited a religious authority
who believed that "male circumcision was a
Sunna and female circumcision was merely
preferable" (Sudanese Medical Service 1945).
This usage implies a greater obligation for
that which is termed "Sunna." Therefore, to
attach the term "Sunna" to female circumcision is to imply that *some* form of circumcision
is expected by religious law.

5. The psychological effects of female circumcision have only recently received any systematic attention in Sudan (*see*, e.g., Baashar et al.
1979).

6. All matters concerning marriage, divorce,
custody and inheritance in Sudan are governed by customary rather than civil law. A
system of *shari'a* courts exists for the administration of Islamic law for cases where the individuals involved are Muslims.

7. It is interesting to note that in Sudan, where
the great majority of primary health care
workers at all levels are male, government statistics show males outnumbering females in 89
out of the 93 categories of treated illnesses
that are not female-specific conditions
(Sudan, Ministry of Health 1975a).

8. Dr. Nawal el Saadawi, an Egyptian physician
and novelist who has written extensively on
women in Arab societies, has criticized the
"'them' helping 'us'" approach of some foreign groups: "That kind of help, which they
think of as solidarity, is another type of colonialism in disguise. So we must deal with female circumcision ourselves. It is our culture,
we understand it, when to fight against it and
how, because this is the process of liberation"
(El Saadawi 1980a).

REFERENCES

Assaad, Marie Bassili. 1980. Female Circumcision
in Egypt: Social Implications, Current Research, and Prospects for Change. Studies in
Family Planning 11(1):3–16.

Baashar, T. A., et al. 1979. Psycho-social Aspects of
Female Circumcision. Seminar on Traditional
Practices Affecting the Health of Women.
World Health Organization, Regional Office
for the Eastern Mediterranean.

Boddy, Janice. 1979. Personal Communication.
[Based on her PhD research, University of British Columbia.]

Clark, Isobel and Christina Diaz. 1977. Circumcision: A Slow Change in Attitudes. Sudanow
(March 1977):43–45.

Cook, R. 1976. Damage to Physical Health from
Pharaonic Circumcision (Infibulation) of Females: A Review of the Medical Literature.
World Health Organization, September 30,
1976.

Diaz, Christina and Suliman Mudawi. 1977. Circumcision: The Social Background. Sudanow
(March 1977):45.

El Dareer, Asma. 1979. Female Circumcision and
Its Consequences for Mother and Child. Con-
tributions to the ILO African Symposium on the
World of Work and the Protection of the Child.
Yaoundé, Cameroun.

El Saadawi, Nawal. 1980a. Creative Women in
Changing Societies: A Personal Reflection.
Race and Class 22(2):159–182.

———. 1980b. The Hidden Face of Eve: Women
in the Arab World. London: Zed Press.

Hall, Marjorie and Bakhita Amin Ismail. 1981. Sisters Under the Sun: The Story of Sudanese
Women. London: Longmans.

Hayes, Rose Oldfield. 1975. Female Genital Mutilation. Fertility Control. Women's Roles and the
Patrilineage in Modern Sudan. American Ethnologist 2(4):617–633.

Hosken, Fran P. 1980. Female Sexual Mutilations:
The Facts and Proposals for Action. Lexington,
MA: Women's International Network News.

Mudawi, Suliman. 1977a. Circumcision: The Operation. Sudanow (March 1977):43–44.

———. 1977b. The Impact of Social and Eco-
nomic Changes on Female Circumcision.
Sudan Medical Association Congress Series,
No. 2.

O'Brien, John J. 1980. Agricultural Labor and Development in Sudan. PhD dissertation, University of Connecticut.

Shandall, A. A. 1967. Circumcision and Infibulation of Females. Sudan Medical Journal 5:178–
212.

Sørbø, Gunnar M. 1977. How to Survive Development: The Story of New Halfa. Khartoum: Development Studies and Research Centre Monograph Series No. 6.

Sudan Medical Services. 1945. Female Circumcision in the Anglo-Egyptian Sudan. Khartoum:
Sudan Medical Service, March 1, 1945.

Sudan Ministry of Health. 1975a. Annual Statistical Report. Khartoum: Ministry of Health.

———. 1975b. National Health Programme
1977/78–1983/84. Khartoum: Ministry of
Health.

Toubia, Nahid F. 1981. The Social and Political Implications of Female Circumcision: The Case of Sudan. MSc Proposal, University of College of Swansea, Wales.

Verzin, J. A. 1975. Sequelae of Female Circumcision. Tropical Doctor (Oct., 1975).

Female Infanticide and Child Neglect in Rural North India

Barbara D. Miller

INTRODUCTION

Sitting in the hospital canteen for lunch every day, I can see families bringing their children into the hospital. So far, after watching for five days, I have seen only boys being carried in for treatment, no girls (author's field notes, Ludhiana Christian Medical College, November 1983).

When the hospital was built, equal-sized words for boys and girls were constructed. The boys' ward is always full but the girls' ward is under-utilized (comment of a hospital administrator, Ludhiana Christian Medical College, November 1983).

In one village, I went into the house to examine a young girl and I found that she had an advanced case of tuberculosis. I asked the mother why she hadn't done something sooner about the girl's condition because now, at this stage, the treatment would be very expensive. The mother replied, "then let her die, I have another daughter." At the time, the two daughters sat nearby listening, one with tears streaming down her face (report by a public health physician, Ludhiana Christian Medical College, November 1983).

From Nancy Scheper-Hughes (ed.), *Child Survival* (Dordrecth: D. Reidel Publishing Co., 1987), pp. 95–112. Reprinted by permission of Kluwer Academic Publishers.

When a third, fourth, or fifth daughter is born to a family, no matter what its economic status, we increase our home visits because that child is at high risk (statement made by a public health physician, Ludhiana Christian Medical College, November 1983).

These quotations, taken from field notes made during a 1983 trip to Ludhiana, the Punjab, India are indicative of the nature and degree of sex-selectivity in health care of children there. Ethnographic evidence gleaned from the work of other anthropologists corroborates that intrahousehold discrimination against girls is a fact of life in much of the northern plains region of India (Miller 1981: 83–106). The strong preference for sons compared to daughters is marked from the moment of birth. Celebration at the birth of a son, particularly a first son, has been documented repeatedly in the ethnographic literature (Lewis 1965: 49; Freed and Freed 1976: 123, 206; Jacobson 1970: 307–309; Madan 1965: 63; and Aggarwal 1971: 114). But when a daughter is born, the event goes unheralded and anthropologists have documented the unconcealed disappointment in families which already have a daughter or two (Luschinsky 1962: 82; Madan 1965: 77–78; Minturn and Hitchcock 1966: 101–102). The extreme disappointment of a mother who greatly desires a son, but bears a daughter instead, could affect her ability to breastfeed successfully; "bonding" certainly would not be automatically assured between the mother and the child; and the mother's disappointed in-laws would be far less supportive than if the newborn were a son (Miller, 1986).

A thorough review of the ethnographic literature provides diverse but strongly suggestive evidence of preferential feeding of boys in North Indian villages (Miller 1981: 93–94), as well as preferential allocation of medical care to boys. Sex ratios of admissions to northern hospitals are often two or more boys to every one girl. This imbalance is not due to more frequent illness of boys, rather to sex-selective parental investment patterns.

The practice of sex-selective child care in northern India confronts us with a particularly disturbing dilemma that involves the incongruity between Western values that insist on equal life chances for all, even in the face of our universal failure to achieve that goal, versus North Indian culture which places strong value on the survival of sons rather than daughters. Public health programs in North India operate under the guidance of the national goal of "equal health care for all by the year 2000" which was declared by many developing nations at the Alma Ata conference in 1978. Yet the families with whom they are concerned operate with a different set of goals less concerned with the survival of any one individual than with the survival of the family. In rural North India the economic survival of the family, for sociocultural reasons, is dependent on the reproduction of strong sons and the control of the number of daughters who are financial burdens in many ways.

The chapter examines a variety of data and information sources on the dimensions and social context of female infanticide and daughter neglect in rural North India, an area where gender preferences regarding offspring are particularly strong. I review what is known about outright female infanticide in earlier centuries and discuss the situation in North India today, examining the empirical evidence and current theoretical approaches

to the understanding of son preference and daughter disfavor. The next section considers the role of a public health program in the Punjab. In conclusion I address the issue of humanist values concerning equal life chances for all versus North Indian patriarchal values promoting better life chances for boys than girls, and the challenge to anthropological research of finding an appropriate theoretical approach to the study of children's health and survival.

INFANTICIDE: BACKGROUND

I consider infanticide to fall under the general category of child abuse and neglect which encompasses a range of behaviors. As I have written elsewhere:

> . . . it is helpful to distinguish forms of neglect from those of abuse . . . abuse is more "active" in the way it is inflicted; it is abuse when something is actually *done* to harm the child. In the case of neglect, harm comes to the child because something is *not done* which should have been. Thus, sexual molestation of a child is abusive, whereas depriving a child of adequate food and exercise is neglectful. One similarity between abuse and neglect is that both, if carried far enough, can be fatal (Miller 1981: 44–45).

Infanticide, most strictly defined, is the killing of a child under one year of age. Infanticide would be placed at one extreme of the continuum of effects of child abuse and neglect—it is fatal. At the opposite end of the continuum are forms of child abuse that result in delayed learning, slowed physical growth and development patterns, and disturbed social adjustment. Outright infanticide can be distinguished from indirect or "passive" infanticide (Harris 1977); in the former the means, such as a fatal beating, are direct and immediate, while in the latter, the means, such as sustained nutritional deprivation, are indirect.

Infanticide is further delineated with respect to the ages of the children involved. Most broadly defined, infanticide applies to the killing of children under the age of twelve months (deaths after that age would generally be classified as child *homicide,* although the definition and, hence, duration of childhood is culturally variable). *Neonaticide* usually pertains to the killing of a newborn up to twenty-four hours after birth and is sometimes given a separate analysis (Wilkey *et al.* 1982). The induced *abortion* of a fetus is sometimes categorized as a pre-natal form of infanticide that has been termed *"feticide"* in the literature.[1]

The discussion in this chapter encompasses both infanticide and child homicide, that is non-accidental deaths to minors from the time of birth up to the age of about fifteen or sixteen when they would become adults in the rural Indian context. For convenience, I will use the term infanticide to apply to the entire age range.

I have asserted (1981: 44) that where infanticide is systematically sex-selective, it will be selective against females rather than males. There are few cases of systematic male-selective infanticide in the literature that I reviewed. Some more recent work on the subject, however, has begun to reveal a variety of patterns. For example, a study conducted on several villages in a delta region of Japan using data from the Tokugawa era (1600–1868) reveals the existence of systematic infanticide which was sex-selective, but selective against males almost as frequently as females, depending on the particular household composition and dynamics (Skinner 1984).

Obviously all household strategies concerning the survival of offspring are not based solely on gender considerations, and it is doubtful that we can ever come close to a good estimation of just "how much" gender-based selective differential in the treatment of children exists, and how much of this is biased against females. Nevertheless, one part of the world where female-selective infanticide is particularly apparent is in North India, and across India's northwestern border through Pakistan . . . to the Near East, and perhaps in a diminished form also in North Africa. Looking toward the East from India, it seems that Southeast Asia is largely free of the son preference/daughter disfavor syndrome, as opposed to China where one result of the one-child policy. . . was the death of thousands of female infants.

FEMALE INFANTICIDE IN PRE-TWENTIETH CENTURY INDIA

The British discovery of infanticide in India occurred in 1789 among a clan of Rajputs in the eastern part of Uttar Pradesh, a northern state.[2] All of the infanticide reported by British district officers and other observers was direct female infanticide. A lengthy quotation from a mid-nineteenth century description by a British magistrate in the Northwest Provinces of India demonstrates how open was the knowledge of the practice of female infanticide at that time:

There is at Mynpoorie an old fortress, which looks far over the valley of the Eesun river. This has been for centuries the stronghold of the Rajahs of Mynpoorie, Chohans whose ancient blood, descending from the great Pirthee Raj and the regal stem of Neem-rana, represents *la crème de la crème* of Rajpoot aristocracy. Here when a son, a nephew, a grandson, was born to the reigning chief, the event was announced to the neighboring city by the loud discharge of wall-pieces and matchlocks; but centuries had passed away, and no infant daughter had been known to smile within those walls.

In 1845, however, thanks to the vigilance of Mr. Unwin [the district collector], a little granddaughter was preserved by the Rajah of that day. The fact was duly notified to the Government, and a letter of congratulations and a dress of honour were at once dispatched from head-quarters to the Rajah.

We have called this incident, the giving of a robe of honour to a man because he did not destroy his grand-daughter a *grotesque* one; but it is very far from being a ridiculous incident. When the people see that the highest authorities in the land take an interest in their social or domestic reforms, those reforms can give an impetus which no lesser influences can give them. The very next year after the investiture of the Rajah, the number of female infants preserved in the district was *trebled!* Fifty-seven had been saved in 1845; in 1846, one hundred and eighty were preserved; and the number has gone on steadily increasing ever since (Raikes 1852: 20–21).

A review of the secondary literature on female infanticide in British India reveals its practice mainly in the Northwest, and among upper castes and tribes. Not all groups practiced female infanticide, but there are grim reports that a few entire villages in the northwestern plains had never raised one daughter.[3] On the basis of juvenile (under ten years of age) sex ratios for districts in the Northwest Provinces, 1871, I have estimated crudely that for nineteenth-century Northwest India it would not be unreasonable to assume that one-fourth of the population preserved only half the daughters born to them, while the other three-fourths of the population had balanced sex ratios among their offspring (Miller 1981: 62). This assumption yields a juvenile sex ratio of 118 (males per 100 females) in the model population, which is comparable to current juvenile sex ratios in several districts of northwestern Indian and Pakistan (Miller 1981, 1984). It seems clear that female infanticide in British India was widespread in the Northwest rather than of limited occurrence.

The British investigated the extent and causes of female infanticide, and in 1870 passed a law against its practice. Other policy measures, based on their assessment of the causes of the practice, included subsidizing the dowries of daughters that were "preserved" by prominent families, and organizing conferences in order to enlighten local leaders and their followers about the need to prevent infanticide (Cave Browne 1857).

There are two areas of ignorance about the wider context of the historic practice of female infanticide in India. First, we know little about the apparent and gradual transition from direct to indirect infanticide. It appears that either deep-seated social change and/or British policy against the practice of female infanticide succeeded in bringing about the near-end of direct female infanticide by the beginning of this century. In the twentieth century we hear little about female infanticide in census reports, district gazetteers, or anthropological descriptions of rural life. What is needed is a careful tracing of the situation from roughly 1870 when the practice was outlawed to the present time in order to plot the dynamics of change from outright to indirect infanticide. Second, we need to know much more about the sociocultural determinants of female infanticide in British India. The British pointed to two causal factors—"pride and purse." The pride of upper castes and tribes is said to have pushed them to murder female infants rather than give them away as tribute to a more dominant group, or even as brides which is viewed as demeaning in rural North India today. By "purse" is meant dowry, and most groups that practiced infanticide did have the custom of giving large dowries with daughters.[4] But there is some contradictory evidence. In the undivided Punjab, it has been documented for the early twentieth century that dowry was not widely given among the rural Jats, a caste which nonetheless exhibited very high sex ratios (i.e., males over females) among its juvenile population. In fact, the Jats, a landed peasant caste, often secured brides through brideprice, which should have provided an economic incentive for parents to preserve daughters (Darling 1929; see also the discussion in Miller 1984). Further exploration of archival materials for the nineteenth century would help illuminate this matter.

FEMALE INFANTICIDE AND NEGLECT: THE CURRENT CONTEXT

It is beyond doubt that systematic indirect female infanticide exists today in North India. It is possible that outright infanticide of neonates is also practiced, though nearly impossible to document due to the extreme privacy of the birth event and the great ease with which a neonate's life may be terminated.[5] This section of the paper is concerned with indirect female infanticide, which is accomplished by nutritional and health-care deprivation of children, and which results in higher mortality rates of daughters than sons.[6]

There is a strong preference for sons in rural North India and there are several strong sociocultural reasons for this preference. Sons are economic assets: they are needed for farming, and for income through remittances if they leave the village. Sons play important roles in local power struggles over rights to land and water. Sons stay with the family after their marriage and thus maintain the parents in their old age; daughters marry out and cannot contribute to the maintenance of their natal households. Sons bring in dowries with their brides; daughters drain family wealth with their required dowries and the constant flow of gifts to their family of marriage after the wedding. Sons, among Hindus, are also needed to perform rituals which protect the family after the death of the father; daughters cannot perform such rituals.

Elsewhere I have argued that extreme son preference is more prevalent in North India than in the South and East, and that it is more prevalent among upper castes and classes than lower castes and classes (Miller 1981). By extension, daughter neglect would follow the same pattern. Some of the key research questions include: how extensive is daughter disfavor in different regions and among various social strata in India? How serious are its consequences in terms of mortality and in health status of the survivors (not to mention more difficult to diagnose conditions such as emotional and cognitive development)? Are these patterns changing through time? At this point, scattered studies help illuminate some aspects of these questions, but there is no study that addresses them all systematically either for one locale or for India as a whole.

First, let us consider the question of the extent of the practice in India. In a recent publication, Lipton (1983) suggests that fatal discrimination against daughters in India is a very localized, and thus minor, problem. But my all-India analysis (1981), using juvenile sex ratios as a surrogate measure of child mortality, shows that while the most afflicted area encompasses only two or three states of India, there are seriously unbalanced sex ra-

tios among children in one-third of India's 326 rural districts, an area spanning the entire northwestern plains.[7] Simmons *et al.* (1982) provide results from survey data on 2064 couples in the Kanpur region of Uttar Pradesh (a state in northern India) which reveal that reported infant and child mortality rates for girls aged one month up to three years of age are much higher than the rates for boys. This finding is similar to, though less astonishing than, Cowan and Dhanoa's (1983) report that in a large sub-population carefully monitored in Ludhiana district, the Punjab, 85 percent of all deaths to children aged 7–36 months were female. Another dependable database that has been carefully analyzed by Behrman (1984) and Behrman and Deolalikar (1985) concerns an area of India where juvenile sex ratios are not notably unbalanced, south-central India in the area between Andhra Pradesh and Maharashtra. The authors have found that there is a noticeable nutrient bias in favor of boys in the intrahousehold allocation of food. This unequal distribution has a seasonal dimension: in the lean season boys are more favored over girls in the distribution of food in the family, while in the surplus season distribution appears quite equal.

Class/caste variations in juvenile sex ratios are also important. Simmons *et al.* (1982) unfortunately do not present findings on class or caste patterns. They mention that education of the parents is a positive influence on child survival in the first year of life, less so in the second and third. If parental education can be used as a crude indicator of class status, then it would seem that survival for both boys and girls would be more assured in better-off families. Demographic data from the Ludhiana area of Punjab state have been analyzed for class differences by Cowan and Dhanoa (1983). Among upper class, landed families (termed "privileged" by Cowan and Dhanoa), there is a large disparity between survival rates for male and female children and also in the nutritional status of those surviving (Table 1). These disparities are mirrored, though less severe, in the lower class, landless population. Cowan and Dhanoa found that

TABLE 1. Prevalence of 2nd/3rd Degree Malnutrition in 911 Children in Second and Third Year of Life, Ludhiana, the Punjab

	Number	Sex Ratio[a]	With 2nd/3rd Degree Malnutrition[b]	Ratio of male to Female Malnourished
Privileged males	231	111.0	2	1:6.5
Privileged females	208		13	
Under-privileged males	244	102.5	11	1:2.6
Under-privileged females	228		29	
TOTAL	911	106.5	55	1:3.2

[a]Sex ratio refers to the number of males per hundred females.

[b]The numbers in this column were read from a graph and may be off by a small margin

Source: Cowan and Dhanoa (1983: 352).

birth order strongly affects the survival and status of daughters. Second-born and third-born daughters are classified by health care personnel as "high risk" infants, as are high birth order children of both sexes born to very large families, regardless of socioeconomic status. The extent of fatal daughter disfavor in this relatively affluent state of India is severe, and it contributes to Punjab's having infant (up to one year of age) mortality rates higher that those of poorer states where daughter discrimination is less severe (Miller 1985).

Caldwell's data on a cluster of villages in Karnataka (southern-central-India), with a total population of more than 5000, revealed "surprisingly small" differences in infant and child mortality by economic status, father's occupation and religion (1983:197). (This area of the country is characterized by balanced juvenile sex ratios at the district level.) The authors do not mention whether there are any sex differentials in child survival and health. Infant mortality rates are, however, much lower in households with an educated mother than those where the mother has little education. Girls tend to receive less food than boys, and family variables are mentioned as being involved in this matter.

Another report from a region with balanced juvenile sex ratios, a two-village study in West Bengal reported on by Sen and Sengupta (1983), produced some provocative findings. The authors did not look at mortal-

ity but rather at levels of undernourishment in children below five years of age according to caste and land ownership status of the household. Results were surprising: the village with a more vigorous land redistribution program had a greater nutritional sex bias, even among children in families who had benefited from the redistribution. In the second village, children in poor families had higher nutritional standards and a lower male-female differential than their counterparts in the first village.

Rosenzweig and Schultz (1982) used a subsample of rural households in India, presumably nationwide, and found that boys have significantly higher survival rates relative to girls in landless rather than in landed households. Horowitz and Keshwar report that survey data from a Punjab village (northern India) demonstrate more pronounced son preference among the propertied peasant castes, although the phenomenon is "nearly" as strong among agricultural laborers (1982: 12); they do not provide health or survival statistics, but use data on stated preferences of parents.

The above review indicates that, while we do not possess an ideal picture of the extent and nature of daughter disfavor, there is evidence that its practice does exist widely in India and does tend to exhibit class/caste patterns—though the exact nature of these is in dispute. We know very little about the question of change through time since few good sources of longitudinal data exist, and those that do exist have not been examined for sex disparity information as yet.

SEX-SELECTIVE ABORTION

Several years ago a Jain woman in her sixth month of pregnancy came to Ludhiana Christian Medical Hospital for an amniocentesis test. The results of the test showed that genetic defects such as Down's syndrome or spina bifida were not present in the fetus. The test indicated that the fetus was female. The woman requested an abortion and was refused. She went to a clinic in Amritsar, another major city in the Punjab, and had the abortion done (report by a physician, Ludhiana, November 1983).

This anecdote was told to me at Ludhiana Christian Medical College as an explanation why Ludhiana CMC no longer performs amniocentesis. There were so many requests for abortion of female fetuses following amniocentesis that the hospital made a policy decision not to provide such services.[8] Today a person with intent to abort a female fetus in Ludhiana must take the train about 90 miles to Amritsar where the service is available. An especially poignant aspect of the anecdote is the information that the woman was a Jain. Jainism supports nonviolence toward all life forms. Orthodox Jains sometimes wear cloths over their mouths so as not to swallow a fly, and Jains do not plow the earth for fear of inadvertently cutting in half a worm. But the Jain woman in the anecdote was willing to abort a female fetus in the sixth month of gestation, so strong was the cultural disfavor toward the birth of daughters.

At this time I do not have access to data on the number of female fetuses aborted each year in India, nor to data on the social characteristics of those people who seek to abort their female fetuses. Nonetheless, several considerations are important: how can we estimate the extent of the practice? What are the social and economic characteristics of those families seeking to abort female fetuses? What are the demographic characteristics of the families seeking sex-selective abortion? There are some clues.

In 1980 an article published in *Social Science and Medicine* provided some evidence of the extent of the phenomenon based on clinic records in a large city of western India (Ramanamma and Bambawale 1980). In one hospital, from June 1976 to June 1977, 700 individuals sought prenatal sex determination. Of these fetuses, 250 were determined to be male and 450 were female.[9] While all of the male fetuses were kept to term, fully 430 of the 450 female fetuses were terminated. This figure is even more disturbing in light of the fact that western India is characterized by a less extreme son preference than the Northwest.

There is an eager market in India for sex-selective abortion, although the cost of the service may make it prohibitive for the poorest villagers. A report in *Manushi* (1982) states that the service is available in Chandigarh, the Punjab, for only 500 rupees.[10] Another report mentions that the charge was 600 rupees at a clinic in Amritsar, the Punjab (*Washington Post* 1982). A recent visitor to Ahmedabad, Gujarat, reports a charge of only 50 rupees in a clinic there (Everett 1984). Whether the charge is 50 rupees or 500 rupees, the cost is minor compared to the benefits reaped from the possibility of having a son conceived at the next pregnancy, or compared to the money that would have been needed to provide a dowry for the girl were she to survive.

DETERMINANTS OF SON PREFERENCE AND DAUGHTER DISFAVOR

Why does son preference exist, and why does it often exist in tandem with the practices of sex-selective abortion, female infanticide, and female neglect? Anthropologists have proposed "explanations" for the practice of female infanticide in simple societies, but less work has been done for complex civilizations. Recent problems in China, provoked by the one-child policy, have attracted attention to the subject, but little scholarly thinking, with few exceptions. . . . A range of hypothesized causal factors has been suggested to account for female infanticide in the past few years. They can be divided into ecologic/economic determinants, social structural determinants and sociobiological determinants.

From the broadest population ecology perspective, Harris (1977) proposes that female infanticide, and by extension sex-selective abortion, will most likely occur when a society has reached a crisis level in its population/resources ratio, or right after that crisis when the society has moved into a necessarily expendable portion of the population in relation to resources. This theory has explanatory power for some cases, but we might bear in mind that infanticide is only one of many possible strategies for ameliorating a high population/resources ratio. Other options include migration, and the reduction of natural population growth through delayed marriage, abstinence, abortion, and other forms of birth control both traditional and modern.

My interpretation, based on the case of North India, gives more emphasis to economic demand factors. I have hypothesized that labor requirements for males versus females (themselves ecologically, agriculturally and culturally defined) are key in determining households' desires regarding number and sex of offspring (Miller 1981, 1984). Although I take the sexual division of labor as primary, I view it as creating a secondary and very powerful determinant in the domestic marriage economy. In the case of India, the contrast between dowry marriages and bridewealth marriages illustrates the "mirroring" of the sexual division of labor in marriage costs: generally where few females are employed in the agricultural sector, large dowries prevail, but where female labor is in high demand, smaller dowries or even bridewealth are the main form of marriage transfers.

Other more orthodox economic approaches stress rational decision-making on the part of the family based on perceived "market opportunities" of offspring (Rosenzweig and Schultz 1982) or intrafamily resource allocation systems (Simmons *et al.*

1982). Sen and Sengupta propose that land distribution patterns are an important determinant of sex differentials in children's nutritional status (1983).

The major exponents of a social structural theory are Dyson and Moore (1983). They identify the patriarchal nature of North Indian society as the basis for the neglect of daughters and other manifestations of low female status. They do not seek to explain why society in North India is strongly patriarchal—that is simply a given.

Dickemann, who studied female infanticide cross-culturally and particularly in stratified societies such as traditional northern India and China, provides a sociobiological interpretation for female infanticide (1979, 1984). Her early observation of the connection between hypergynous marriage systems and female infanticide was a particularly important contribution (1979). Dickemann views sex ratio manipulation among offspring as one reproductive strategy that will, under alternate resource conditions, result in maximum reproductive success for the family. She has recently stated that:

> Like other acts of reproductive management, infanticide-pedicide seems to be best understood at present, in all species, as one parameter of interindividual and interfamilial competition for the proportional increase in genes in the next generation . . . (1984: 436).

In terms of the explanatory power of evolutionary models with respect to the cause of violent mistreatment of human offspring, however, Hrdy and Hausfater (1984: xxxi) agree with Lenington (1981) that "only a portion of such cases" will be thus explained.

PUBLIC HEALTH AND PATRIARCHY

Ten years ago when I began my research on fatal neglect of daughters in rural India the problem was not widely accepted by scholars in the West or in India as a serious one.[11] Today the practice of fatal daughter disfavor is more widely recognized by scholars as a serious social issue. Current concern in India about the growing recourse to sex-selective abortion, using information on sex of the fetus derived from amniocentesis, adds a new and important dimension to problems of female survival and the ethics of abortion (Ramanamma and Bambawale 1980; Kumar 1983).

Operating within such a patriarchal system, could any health care program seeking to provide equal health care for all have any success? There is controversy concerning the impact of health care programs in alleviating sex differences in child survival in patriarchal cultures, particularly North India. Some writers suggest that a simple increase in health care services will improve the situation for girls (Minturn 1984). Others have found evidence that increased services will be diverted to priority children, most often boys, and that only secondarily will low priority children, most often girls, benefit.[12] Finally, the introduction of new medical technologies—such as amniocentesis—can be manipulated to advance patriarchal priorities (Miller 1986).

Focus on the Punjab

The Punjab, India's wealthiest state, is located in the northwestern plains region adjacent to Pakistan. Its economy is agricultural with wheat the major food crop, but there is a well-developed industrial sector also. Within the Punjab, Ludhiana district is usually recognized as the most "developed" district. Ludhiana district also stands out because it houses one of the best medical colleges and community health programs in India, Ludhiana Christian Medical College. Ludhiana, and the Punjab district, are squarely in the area in northwestern India where juvenile sex ratios are the most masculine and excess female child mortality the greatest (Miller 1985).

Since the early 1970s, Ludhiana CMC has been monitoring the reproductive and health status of the surrounding population—first as a pilot project in three rural locations and one urban location, and later in the entire block of Sahnewal (an administrative subdivision of the district), with a population of about 85,000. The monitoring is part of a decentralized, comprehensive basic health care program that focuses on the welfare of mothers and children and includes both health care delivery at village centers and home-based educational programs. For each of the nearly 14,000 families in Sahnewal block, the CMC Ludhiana program maintains family folders containing information on all family members and their health status. Mortalities are carefully recorded in each folder and also in Master Registers kept in 49 village centers throughout the block. Some analysis of these data has been performed (Cowan and Dhanoa 1983) which provides startling figures on sex differentials of mortality for children aged 7–36 months in which female deaths constituted 85 percent of the total (1983: 341).

Cowan and Dhanoa note that one important result of their intensive home-based visiting approach in the rural Punjab is a reduction in the percentage of female child deaths (1983: 354). There is no doubt that their approach can be effective for saving the lives of high-risk children, though it requires great effort and entails much surveillance of private life. Two questions arise from this finding: a related result of increased survival for girls is an increase in the percentage of malnourished girls—girls' lives have been saved, but the quality of those lives may not be at all equal to that of males. Would even more intensive home visiting help alleviate this problem? Furthermore, some would argue that the death of unwanted children might be preferable to their extended mistreatment and suffering (Kumar 1983. . .).

We have not estimated the unit health care costs by sex and priority of the child, but the cost of saving the life of a low priority female child must far outweigh the cost of saving and improving the life of a high priority male. It is not unthinkable that the time will arrive when, with fiscal stringency the watchword of the day, the cost of intensive health care and survival monitoring for girls becomes a barrier to programs such as the one at Ludhiana CMC. Two arguments can be developed to counter policies which would limit special efforts to equalize life chances between boys and girls. First, one might look to the broader social costs of a society in which the sex ratio is seriously unbalanced. It cannot be proven that unbalanced sex ratios invariably lead to social disturbances, but there is much cross-cultural evidence to support this (Divale and Harris 1976). A balanced sex ratio does not guarantee social tranquility, but it could minimize some sources of social tension. Second, in a strongly son-preferential culture, women bear many children in the attempt to produce several sons. The pattern of selective care which promotes son survival to the detriment of daughter survival is built on "over-reproduction" and much child wastage. Mothers bear a physical burden in this system. The Ludhiana program seeks to keep children alive and wanted, and to promote family planning after a certain number and sex composition of children have been born in a household; this goal should reduce the physical burden on mothers created by extended childbearing.

HUMANISTIC VALUES, PATRIARCHAL VALUES AND ANTHROPOLOGY

This chapter discusses an extreme form of sex-selective child care, one which is not universally found throughout the world though it is not limited to rural North India. Strong preference for sons which results in life-endangering deprivation of daughters is "culturally" acceptable in much of rural North India with its patriarchal foundation. It is not acceptable from a Western humanistic or altruistic perspective . . . nor from that of an emergent, international feminist "world view." But, how can anthropological research, with its commitment to nonethnocentric reporting of cultural behavior, contribute to an amelioration of the "worldview conflicts" that create inappropriate public health programs targeted at high-risk children, that sometimes only prolong the suffering of these disvalued ones?

. . . [P]erhaps positivistic anthropology and Western altruism can work together. First, let me hasten to soften the hard edges of the "conflict" in world views that Cassidy has constructed: there is no such thing as purely objective and nonethnocentric anthropological research and there is, increasingly, less and less culturally uninformed altruism being foisted on the Third World. All anthropologists, as Schneider so clearly states (1984), have their own unavoidable, culturally-influenced presuppositions and biases through which they choose subjects for research and through which they analyze their data. The best an anthropologist can do is state the nature of his/her presuppositions at the outset: mine, influenced by my white, middle class, American upbringing, are based on the precept that human life, its duration and quality, is something to which all persons should have equal access, although I am fully aware of the fact that scarcity (real or culturally defined) results in priorities about the quality of life that certain groups will receive. Thus I define female infanticide and skewed sex ratios as a social "problem." As an applied anthropologist I believe that socio-behavioral data can provide the key to successful public programs which seek to ameliorate the "problem."

My experience, though too brief, in working with Dr. Betty Cowan and Dr. Jasbir Dhanoa (two "altruists") in Ludhiana convinced me that there is hope for a realistic solution to the conflict between altruism and, in this case, extreme patriarchy, in the sensitive applications of social science knowledge and research. The public health program at Ludhiana is perhaps never going to dilute the force of Indian patriarchy, but knowledge about the patriarchal culture can help promote more effective health care. For instance, the Ludhiana hospital built equal-sized wards for boys and girls, on the Western model. But families bring their boys in for health care in much greater numbers than their girls; the girls' ward is relatively empty while the boys' ward is overflowing. Health care practitioners thus realized the need for very decentralized health care rather than only hospital-based services, including frequent home visiting, if health care was to reach girls.

Anthropologists can provide important information to health care intervenors which will allow those intervenors to be more effective in delivering their services. The most important issue in the Ludhiana area still to be resolved is the impact of class and caste stratification on female survival. Health care practitioners see daughter disfavor largely as a result of poverty. My own research would question poverty as the principal determinant in Ludhiana because there is a marked disparity in survival of boys and girls in the propertied class as well as in the unpropertied class. Although the larger picture is unclear because of lack of data across North India, it is obvious that policy implications differ greatly depending on class/caste dimensions of village life. If health care programs are to be targeted to "high-risk" groups, anthropologists can help by providing data on the nature of these groups and the potential implications of intervention in their lives.

NOTES

Much of my recent research on this subject has been supported by grants from the Wenner-Gren Foundation for Anthropological Research. I am grateful for the Foundation's support which enabled me to visit two hospitals in India during November 1983 in order to learn about their community health programs: Ludhiana Christian Medical College in the Punjab and Vellore Christian Medical College in Tamil Nadu. While in India, I received help from many people, but I especially want to thank Dr. Betty Cowan, Principal of Ludhiana CMC, and Dr. P.S. Sundar Rao, Chief of the Biostatics Department at Vellore CMC. An earlier version of this chapter was presented at a seminar sponsored by the Department of Anthropology and the Asian Studies Program at the University of Pittsburgh in March 1985, and I am grateful for the comments I received from those who attended. Finally, I must thank The Metropolitan Studies Program, The Maxwell School, Syracuse University, for support of my work.

1. A discussion of abortion and infanticide from a Western philosophical view is provided in Tooley (1983); compare his presentation with Potter's description of the Chinese view (this volume).

2. We know very little about the practice of female infanticide in India before the British era. The discussion that follows is extracted in large part from Miller (1981: 49–67).

3. Critics are quick to point out that without daughters, villages will not "survive." But in the case of North India, marriage is village exogamous, particularly for Hindus; that is, brides must come from a village other than the groom's. Villages without daughters would "survive" because they would bring in daughters-in-law. More anecdotally, the Community Health Program at Ludhiana CMC was started by a woman physician who was the third daughter of the Grewal lineage to be preserved; even without daughters, the Grewal lineage has "survived" for centuries.

4. Another effect, largely urban and upper-class, of the dowry system in North India is the murder of young wives by their in-laws in order to procure a second bride with her dowry (Sharma 1983).

5. Knowledgeable physicians who have worked with the community health care program in the rural areas surrounding Ludhiana, the Punjab, know that there is a preponderance of female neonatal deaths as compared to those of males. They are averse to labelling this as due to infanticide since an autopsy may well not reveal an intentional death as opposed to a stillbirth or an unintentional death. The physicians do know that neonatal deaths constitute a serious problem, and one that is the hardest for them to deal with due to the secrecy surrounding births in rural India.

6. A detailed discussion of the dynamics of son preference in India can be found in Miller (1981), and a comparison between Pakistan and Bangladesh in Miller (1984).

7. This pattern in Northwest India extends over the Indian border into Pakistan . . . .

8. The central government of India has banned prenatal sex determination tests in government hospitals throughout the country for the same reason.

9. The preponderance of females in the sample is probably due to sheer accident.

10. In 1984–85, one dollar equalled approximately twelve rupees.

11. There are some notable exceptions to this generalization (Bardhan 1974; Chandrasekhar 1972; Dandekar 1975; Visaria 1961), although none of these scholars emphasized the major role of sex-differential survival of children in creating the preponderance of males over females.

12. Srilatha (1983) reports that in a large study

area in Tamil Nadu, South India, infant and child mortality rates have declined significantly in the last ten years, but the decline was dramatic for boys and only slight for girls. The implication is that improved health services may be differentially allocated to boys and girls in this area of India.

REFERENCES

Aggarwal, Partap C. 1971. Caste, Religion and Power. An Indian Case Study. New Delhi: Shri Ram Centre for Industrial Relations.

Bardhan, Pranab K. 1974. 'On Life and Death Questions.' Economic and Political Weekly 10(32–34): 1293–1303.

Behrman, Jere R. 1984. 'Intrahousehold Allocation of Nutrients in Rural India: Are Boys Favored? Do Parents Exhibit Inequality Aversion?' Unpublished manuscript, University of Pennsylvania, Department of Economics. (Revised 1985.)

Behrman, Jere R. and Anil B. Deolalikar. 1985. 'How Do Food and Product Prices Affect Nutrient Intakes, Health and Labor Force Behavior for Different Family Numbers in Rural India?' Paper presented at the 1985 Meetings of the Population Association of America, Boston.

Caldwell, J.C., P.H. Reddy, and Pat Caldwell. 1983. 'The Social Component of Mortality Decline: An Investigation in South India Employing Alternative Methodologies.' Population Studies 37: 185–205.

Cave Browne, John. 1857. Indian Infanticide: Its Origin, Progress, and Suppression. London: W.H. Allen.

Chandrasekhar, S. 1972. Infant Mortality, Population Growth and Family Planning in India. Chapel Hill, NC: University of North Carolina Press.

Cowan, Betty and Jasbir Dhanoa. 1983. 'The Prevention of Toddler Malnutrition by Home-based Nutrition Education.' In Nutrition in the Community: A Critical Look at Nutrition Policy, Planning, and Programmes. D.S. McLaren (ed.), pp. 339–356. New York/London: John Wiley and Sons.

Dandekar, Kumudini. 1975. 'Why Has the Proportion of Women in India's Population Been Declining?' Economic and Political Weekly 10(42): 1663–1667.

Darling, Malcolm Lyall. 1929. Rusticus Loquitur or the Old Light and the New in the Punjab Village. London: Oxford University Press.

Dickemann, Mildred. 1979. 'Female Infanticide, Reproductive Strategies, and Social Stratification: A Preliminary Model.' In Evolutionary Biology and Human Social Behavior: An Anthropological Perspective. N.A. Chagnon and W. Irons (eds.), pp. 321–367. North Scituate, MA: Duxbury Press.

———. 1984. Concepts and Classification in the Study of Human Infanticide: Sectional Introduction and Some Cautionary Notes 'In Infanticide: Comparative and Evolutionary Perspectives. Glenn Hausfater and Sarah Blàffer Hrdy (eds.), pp. 427–439. New York: Aldine Publishing Company.

Divale, William and Marvin Harris. 1976. 'Population, Warfare, and the Male Supremacist Complex.' American Anthropologist 78: 521–538.

Dyson, Tim and Mick Moore. 1983. 'Gender Relations, Female Autonomy and Demographic Behavior: Regional Contrasts within India.' Population and Development Review 9(1): 35–60.

Everett, Jana. 1984. Personal communication. (Dr. Everett is a political scientist at the University of Colorado, Denver.)

Freed, Stanley A. and Ruth S. Freed. 1976. Shanti Nagar: The Effects of Urbanization in a Village in North India: 1. Social Organization. Anthropological Papers of the American Museum of National History. Vol. 53: Part 1. New York: The American Museum of Natural History.

Harris, Marvin. 1977. Cannibals and Kings: The Origins of Cultures. New York: Random House.

Horowitz, B. and Madhu Keshwar. 1982. 'Family Life—The Unequal Deal.' Manushi 11: 2–18.

Hrdy, Sarah Blaffer and Glenn Hausfater. 1984. 'Comparative and Evolutionary Perspectives on Infanticide: Introduction and Overview' In Infanticide: Comparative and Evolutionary Perspectives. Glenn Hausfater and Sarah Blaffer Hrdy (eds.), pp. xii–xxxv. Aldine Publishing Company.

Jacobson, Doranne. 1970. 'Hidden Faces: Hindu and Muslim Purdah in a Central Indian Village.' Unpublished doctoral dissertation, Columbia University.

Kumar, Dharma. 1983. 'Male Utopias or Nightmares?' Economic and Political Weekly, January 15: 61–64.

Lenington, S. 1981. 'Child Abuse: The Limits of Sociobiology.' Ethnology and Sociobiology 2: 17–29.

Lewis, Oscar. 1965. Village Life in Northern India: Studies in a Delhi Village. New York: Random House.

Lipton, Michael. 1983. Demography and Poverty. World Bank Staff Working Papers, Number 623. Washington, DC: The World Bank.

Luschinsky, Mildred S. 1962. 'The Life of Women in a Village of North India: A Study of Role and Status.' Unpublished doctoral dissertation, Cornell University.

Madan, T.N. 1965. Family and Kinship: A Study of the Pandits of Rural Kashmir. New York: Asia Publishing House.

Manushi. 1982. 'A New Form of Female Infanticide.' 12: 21.

Miller, Barbara D. 1981. The Endangered Sex: Neglect of Female Children in Rural North India. Ithaca, NY: Cornell University Press.

———. 1984. 'Daughter Neglect, Women's Work and Marriage: Pakistan and Bangladesh Compared.' Medical Anthropology 8(2): 109–126.

———. 1985. 'The Unwanted Girls: A Study of Infant Mortality Rates.' Manushi 29: 18–20.

———. 1986. 'Prenatal and Postnatal Sex-Selection in India: The Patriarchal Context, Ethical Questions and Public Policy.' Working Paper No. 107 on Women in International Development (East Lansing, MI: Office of Women in International Development, Michigan State University).

Minturn, Leigh. 1984. 'Changes in the Differential Treatment of Rajput Girls in Khalapur: 1955–1975.' Medical Anthropology 8(2): 127–132.

Minturn, Leigh and John T. Hitchcock. 1966. The Rajputs of Khalapur, India. Six Cultures Series, Volume III. New York: John Wiley and Sons.

Raikes, Charles. 1852. Notes on the North-Western Provinces of India. London: Chapman and Hall.

Ramanamma, A. and Usha Bambawale. 1980. 'The Mania for Sons: An Analysis of Social Values in South Asia.' Social Science and Medicine 14B: 107–110.

Rosenzweig, Mark R. and T. Paul Schultz. 1982. 'Market Opportunities, Genetic Endowments, and Intrafamily Resource Distribution: Child Survival in Rural India.' American Economic Review 72(4): 803–815.

Schneider, David M. 1984. A Critique of the Study of Kinship. Ann Arbor, MI: The University of Michigan Press.

Sen, Amartya and Sunil Sengupta. 1983. 'Malnutrition of Children and the Rural Sex Bias.' Economic and Political Weekly Annual Number, May: 855–864.

Sharma, Ursula. 1983. 'Dowry in North India: Its Consequences for Women.' In Women and Property, Women as Property. Renee Hirschon (ed.), pp. 62–74. London: Croom Helm.

Simmons, George B., Celeste Smucker, Stan Bernstein, and Eric Jensen. 1982. 'Post Neo-Natal Mortality in Rural India: Implications of an Economic Model.' Demography 19(3): 371–389.

Skinner, G. William. 1984. 'Infanticide as Family Planning in Tokugawa Japan.' Paper prepared for the Stanford-Berkeley Colloquium in Historical Demography, San Francisco.

Srilatha, K.V. 1983. Personal communication. (Dr. Srilatha is an epidemiologist, Senior Training and Research Officer, Rural Unit for Health and Social Assistance, Vellore Christian Medical College, Tamil Nadu, India).

Tooley, Michael. 1983. Abortion and Infanticide. Oxford: Oxford University Press.

Visaria, Pravin M. 1961. The Sex Ratio of the Population of India. Census of India 1961. Vol. 1. Monograph No. 10. New Delhi: Office of the Registrar General.

Washington Post. August 25. 1982. 'Birth Test Said to Help Indians Abort Females.'

Wasserstrom, Jeffrey. 1984. 'Resistance to the One-Child Family.' Modern China 10(3): 345–374.

Wilkey, Ian, John Pearn, Gwynneth Petrie, and James Nixon. 1982. 'Neonaticide, Infanticide and Child Homicide.' Medicine, Science and the Law 22(1): 31–34.

XI.
Colonialism and Development

We live today in a global world based on complex political and economic relationships. There are few places that remain untouched by international markets, the mass media, geopolitics, or economic aid. However, the global world, particularly the global economy, is not a new phenomenon. It has its roots in the sixteenth century, when the powerful countries of western Europe began to colonize populations in Asia, Africa, and the Americas. Part of this process involved the extraction of raw materials such as gold, sugar, rubber, and coffee and the exploitation of the labor of indigenous populations for the profit of the colonizing nations.

Although most of the colonized world achieved independence by the 1960s, the economic domination of the capitalist world system that was initiated during the colonial period has not been significantly altered. In the late twentieth century an imbalanced relationship between the countries of the industrial, or "developed," world and the developing, or Third World, remains. How have the men and women of the developing world experienced the continuing impact of the penetration of capitalism and the integration of their societies into the global economy?

This question has been addressed in particular with regard to women, and two opposing views have been formulated. Chaney and Schmink (1980), in a review of studies on women and modernization, describe a minority position suggesting that women in the Third World are downtrodden and that capitalist development can help them improve their situation. Those who hold this opinion emphasize that women's economic and social status can be enhanced by an increase in female labor force participation. Another perspective, stimulated by Ester Boserup's argument that in the course of economic development women experience a decline in their relative status within agriculture (1970:53), suggests that colonialism and development have introduced "a structure and ideology of male domination" (Leacock 1979:131). In many parts of the world, originally egalitarian gender relationships have been replaced by more hierarchical ones, and women have consequently been marginalized, removed from the positions of economic and political decision making that they held in the precolonial period.

Researchers have demonstrated the negative effects of colonialism and capitalist penetration in a number of different historical contexts. Silverblatt (1980:160), for example, portrays the Spanish conquest of the Andes as a "history of the struggle between colonial forces which attempted to break down indigenous social relations and reorient them toward a market economy and the resistance of the indigenous people to these disintegrating forces." Her focus is on the impact of this struggle on the lives of Andean women in particular.

In the pre-Inca and Inca periods Andean women had status and power that were manifested in their customary usufruct rights to land and in their ability to organize labor. After the conquest Spanish law came up against Andean custom with regard to the property rights of women. In addition, "the Spanish system . . . ignored the deeply embedded Andean conception of the household—embodying the necessary complementarity of male and female labor" (Silverblatt 1980:168). The result of Spanish colonialism in the Andes was the strengthening of patrilineal and patrilocal ties at the expense of matrilineal and matrilocal ties. Women became both politically and religiously disenfranchised. Indeed, women who continued to practice traditional religion were persecuted. Despite this persecution, the religious practices survived and became a very important mechanism of cultural resistance and defense (Silverblatt 1980:179).

The Spanish conquest of the Americas was a religious enterprise as much as a political and economic enterprise. In other parts of the world this religious dimension was also present. Grimshaw (in this book) presents a historical analysis of the efforts of Christian missionary wives to introduce native Hawaiian women to western notions of femininity, particularly the values of piety, purity, submissiveness, and domesticity that were given new meaning with the rise of the "cult of true womanhood" in nineteenth-century America. Missionary wives were horrified by the lack of education and relaxed

sexuality of their Hawaiian female counterparts and set out to teach them a set of new ideas about marriage, child care, family, and religion. All these were founded in the gendered division of labor and society that predominated in their own cultural tradition. In the process, in Grimshaw's view, they attacked several aspects of traditional Hawaiian culture that gave women some measure of autonomy.

The work of these missionary wives was by no means easy because they faced a kinship system that emphasized relationships among a wide network of kin rather than the exclusive relationship between husband and wife. Though the education that was provided to Hawaiian women helped them adjust to the world into which they were progressively integrated, Grimshaw notes that many other aspects of Hawaiian society—especially the notions of masculinity and femininity—were ultimately resistent to change in an economic system that could not be easily transformed into a carbon copy of that in the American continent. As she argues, "The male breadwinner, the independent artisan, the small farmer, the wage earner, supporting a wife and family in modest but independent comfort, was a dream that faded before it could emerge."

Van Allen (in this book) also deals with the impact of Christianity on native populations, in her discussion of Igbo gender relations in Nigeria, from the late nineteenth century to the 1970s. Here too an ideology of male domination was inculcated in mission schools. This ideology in turn sustained new economic and political structures that were introduced as part of the colonial system of government. In the traditional dual-sex political system of the Igbo, both men and women had access to political participation and public status, though the opportunities for wealth and power were always greater for men. For women group solidarity and associations provided a basis for their power and activity in what were clearly public decision-making processes. When the British arrived they immediately attempted to alter a system that was characterized by "diffuse authority, fluid and informal leadership, shared rights of enforcement, and a more or less stable balance of male and female power."

Operating with their own set of cultural assumptions about the appropriate roles for men and women, the British established a political structure in which women could not easily participate. The ultimate result, says Van Allen, was a social system that concentrated national political power in the hands of a small, educated, wealthy male elite. This eventually culminated in the "Aba Riots" (in British terms) or "Women's War" (in the Igbo language) of 1929. In this action Igbo women were using a traditional mechanism to express their frustrations, but the British interpreted their actions as instigated by men and failed to recognize that the roots of the women's demonstration lay in Igbo political structures that gave equal voice to men and women.

While the Igbo were ultimately not very successful in their protest efforts, Etienne and Leacock (1980) suggest that in other historical contexts women resisted colonization and acted to defend themselves. This was true, for example, of Seneca women in Pennsylvania and New York who withstood the attempts of Quakers to put agricultural production in the hands of men, to individualize land tenure, and to deny them political participation (Rothenberg 1980). A similar resistance to change has been documented for several other North American Indian groups (Grumet 1980). According to Weiner (1980:43), the colonial period did not diminish the economic power of women in the Trobriand islands in Melanesia "because no one ever knew that banana leaves had economic value." Women's wealth withstood a number of western incursions and, as a result, "served to integrate new kinds of Western wealth, as well as individual economic growth, into the traditional system."

The impact of culture contact and colonialism on the lives of women in the developing world has not been uniform. Indeed, Silverblatt (1980) stresses class distinctions—elite Inca women had different experiences from peasant women. However, it is evident that one aspect of colonialism was the imposition of European and American ideas about the appropriate roles of men and women. Programs designed to stimulate economic development in Third World societies continue to perpetuate culturally rooted assumptions about gender and the division of labor, particularly the definition of men as breadwinners and women as homemakers (Charlton, this book).

Based on these assumptions, development planners, often with the support of local elites, direct their efforts at providing new skills and technology to men, even when women are the ones involved in subsistence production and trade (Chaney and Schmink 1980). As Schrijvers (1979:111–112) has observed, "If women got any attention, it was as mothers and housekeepers in family-planning projects and in training programs for home economics. . . . Male-centered development programs often resulted in new divisions of labor between the sexes, by which the dependency of women on men greatly increased." In Charlton's view this dependency is partly the result of the replacement of complementary and cooperative economic structures by those in which each individual is a unit of labor.

Greater female dependency on men has also resulted from the process of urbanization, from the shift from household to factory industry, and from the introduction of cash crops. In some societies women have lost their traditional rights to land (Okeyo 1980) and men, "though continuing to rely on women's traditional assistance, claim the entire income from the cash-producing export crops for themselves. . . . As for women, they keep their old domain, that of family food growing; but family food growing, deprived of all monetary prestige, becomes the negative pole of the family economy" (Bissilliat and Fieloux 1987:30). The result, as Charlton astutely notes, is the increased polarization of sex roles.

Framed as a critique of international development programs for women that are directed toward non–income-producing skills, Wilson-Moore (in this book) explores the viability of homestead gardening as an economic strategy for women in developing countries. In Bangladesh both men and women are involved in gardening, but they use different methods and cultivate different crops. Women's gardens can be an effective foundation for the nutritional well-being of family members and do not necessarily have to compete with those of men. Development, in Wilson-Moore's view, is as much about feeding as it is about profit, and any program that is introduced should take into account the importance of subsistence as well as cash cropping in the context of the complementary gender roles in the local social system. Wilson-Moore and Charlton appear to concur that when the traditional roles of women are considered, development can have a positive impact on their lives.

In contrast, Arizpe and Aranda (in this book) argue that strawberry agribusiness, although a major employer for women in Zamora, Mexico, does not enhance women's status or create viable new opportunities for women. These researchers examine why women comprise such a high proportion of the employees in this business and cite cultural factors that constrain opportunities for women and continue to define women's work as temporary and supplementary. Employers take advantage of these constraints—it permits them to keep wages low and work schedules flexible. Arizpe and Aranda's conclusions support those of other researchers who point to a range of phenomena that make a female labor force attractive to multinational business and industry. "Women's socialization, training in needlework, embroidery and other domestic crafts, and supposedly 'natural' aptitude for detailed handiwork, gives them an advantage over men in tasks requiring high levels of manual dexterity and accuracy; women are also supposedly more passive—willing to accept authority and less likely to become involved in labour conflicts. Finally, women have the added advantage of 'natural disposability'— when they leave to get married or have children, a factory temporarily cutting back on production simply freezes their post" (Brydon and Chant 1988:172). Arizpe and Aranda do not view the strawberry agribusiness as a way for women to get ahead. Nor do they view it as a mechanism for regional development; it has certainly not solved the problem of male unemployment.

As with agribusiness, the internationalization of capitalist production has led to the relocation in developing countries of many labor-intensive and export-oriented manufacturing and processing plants owned by multinational corporations. Many of these have provided new oppor-

tunities for employment, primarily for women. For example, in some electronics factories in Southeast Asis, women make up 80% to 90% of the labor force (Brydon and Chant 1988). However, just as with the assessment of the impact of development schemes on the lives of women in the developing world, there are two opposing views about the effect of multinationals. Some emphasize the benefits of jobs that provide women with greater financial stability (Lim 1983), while others see multinationals perpetuating or even creating new forms of inequality as they introduce young women to a new set of individualist and consumerist values. The sexually segregated work force remains in place within paternalistic industrial contexts that encourage turnover and offer no opportunities for advancement (Nash and Fernandez-Kelly 1983). In a study of the assembly plants (called *maquiladoras)* that have been set up along the U.S.-Mexican border, Fernandez-Kelly (1983) describes companies that test women for pregnancy when they are recruited because they want to avoid paying for maternity leave.

In the final analysis, much of the work on women in development tends to support Leacock's (1979) rather pessimistic assessment. Real development, from her perspective, "would mean bringing an end to the system whereby the multinational corporations continue to 'underdevelop' Third World nations by consuming huge proportions of their resources and grossly underpaying their workers" (1979:131). For Arizpe and Aranda this will require a truly international effort. The gendered approach to colonialism and development has demonstrated the close relationship between capitalist penetration, patriarchal gender ideologies, and the sexual division of labor. This relationship has been present since the early days of the Spanish conquest and has been perpetuated by a global economy that has created an international division of labor often oppressing both men and women, but especially women. As Chaney and Schmink (1980:176) put it, development policies and programs frequently lead "not only to the degradation of the physical environment but also of the social environment, as various groups are systematically excluded from the tools of progress and their benefits."

REFERENCES

Bisilliat, Jeanne and Michele Fieloux. 1987. *Women of the Third World: Work and Daily Life.* London: Associated University Press.

Boserup, Ester. 1970. *Woman's Role in Economic Development.* New York: St. Martin's Press.

Brydon, Lynne and Sylvia Chant. 1988. *Women in the Third World: Gender Issues in Rural and Urban Areas.* New Brunswick, NJ: Rutgers University Press.

Chaney, Elsa M. and Marianne Schmink. 1980. Women and Modernization: Access to Tools. In June Nash and Helen I. Safa (eds.), *Sex and Class in Latin America,* pp. 160–182. South Hadley, MA: J. F. Bergin Publishers.

Etienne, Mona and Eleanor Leacock. 1980. Introduction. In Mona Etienne and Eleanor Leacock (eds.), *Women and Colonization: Anthropological Perspectives,* pp. 1–24. New York: Praeger.

Fernandez-Kelly, Maria Patricia. 1983. Mexican Border Industrialization, Female Labor Force Participation, and Migration. In June Nash and Maria Patricia Fernandez-Kelly (eds.), *Women, Men and the International Division of Labor,* pp. 205–223. Albany: State University of New York.

Grumet, Robert Steven. 1980. Sunksquaws, Shamans, and Tradeswomen: Middle Atlantic Coastal Algonkian Women During the 17th and 18th Centuries. In Mona Etienne and Eleanor Leacock (eds.), *Women and Colonization: Anthropological Perspectives,* pp. 43–62. New York: Praeger.

Leacock, Eleanor. 1979. Women, Development, and Anthropological Facts and Fictions. In Gerrit Huizer and Bruce Mannheim (eds.), *The Politics of Anthropology: From Colonialism and Sexism Toward a View from Below,* pp. 131–142. The Hague: Mouton.

Lim, Linda Y. C. 1983. Capitalism, Imperialism, and Patriarchy: The Dilemma of Third-World Women Workers in Multinational Factories. In June Nash and Maria Patricia Fernandez-Kelly (eds.), *Women, Men and the International Division of Labor,* pp. 70–91. Albany: State University of New York.

Nash, June and Maria Patricia Fernandez-Kelly (eds.). 1983. *Women, Men and the International Division of Labor.* Albany: State University of New York.

Okeyo, Achola Pala. 1980. Daughters of the Lakes and Rivers: Colonization and the Land Rights of Luo Women. In Mona Etienne and Eleanor Leacock (eds.), *Women and Colonization: Anthropological Perspectives,* pp. 186–213. New York: Praeger.

Rothenberg, Diane. 1980. The Mothers of the Nation: Seneca Resistance to Quaker Intervention. In Mona Etienne and Eleanor Leacock (eds.), *Women and Colonization: Anthropological Perspectives,* pp. 63–87. New York: Praeger.

Schrijvers, Joke. 1979. Viricentrism and Anthropology. In Gerrit Huizer and Bruce Mannheim (eds.), *The Politics of Anthropology: From Colonialism and Sexism Toward a View from Below,* pp. 97–115. The Hague: Mouton.

Silverblatt, Irene. 1980. Andean Women Under Spanish Rule. In Mona Etienne and Eleanor Leacock (eds.), *Women and Colonization: Anthropological Perspectives,* pp. 149–185. New York: Praeger.

Weiner, Annette. 1980. Stability in Banana Leaves: Colonization and Women in Kiriwina, Trobriand Islands. In Mona Etienne and Eleanor Leacock (eds.), *Women and Colonization: Anthropological Perspectives,* pp. 270–293. New York: Praeger.

New England Missionary Wives, Hawaiian Women and 'The Cult of True Womanhood'

Patricia Grimshaw

One Sunday morning in early November 1825, Kaahumanu, awe-inspiring queen regent of the Hawaiian Islands, widow of the great warrior chief Kamehameha, was carried into the Christian mission chapel at Waimea for the morning service. The preacher was Samuel Whitney, his wife Mercy Partridge Whitney, New England Protestant missionaries supported by the American Board of Commissioners for Foreign Missions. The Whitneys had arrived with the first contingent of missionaries in 1820 and had laboured for four years, with their growing young family, on this unusual frontier. On this particular morning, Kaahumanu's bearers seated their chief's chair at the front of the chapel level with the preacher and, like him, facing the congregation (M. Whitney, Journal, 16 November 1825).

To the joy of the mission band, this powerful queen had already submitted to instruction in reading and writing and at a Honolulu school examination earlier in the year had written on her slate, 'This is my word and hand. I am making myself strong. I declare in the presence of God, I repent of my sin, and believe God to be our Father' (*Missionary Herald*, July 1825). This impressive matriarch, so enormous in size that Laura Judd, wife of the mission doctor, reported that 'she could hold any of us in her lap, as she would a little child, which she often takes the liberty of doing' (Carter 1899:26), had allotted tenancy rights

From Margaret Jolly and Martha Macintyre (eds.), *Family and Gender in the Pacific: Domestic Contradictions and the Colonial Impact* (Cambridge: Cambridge University Press, 1989), pp. 19–44. Reprinted with the permission of Cambridge University Press.

for mission land and had expressed the encouraging belief that a ruler belonging to Christ's family should not only serve God personally but persuade her people to follow suit.

On this particular Sunday, however, Samuel and Mercy Whitney were not satisfied with Kaahumanu's behaviour. This proud chief had placed herself symbolically on the same level as the preacher, God's representative. Moreover, it was essential that the minister face the entire congregation if play and disturbance were to be avoided. The missionary pair chided the queen who, her haughty and disdainful airs apparently a thing of the past, responded in a humble fashion. Kaahumanu admitted her ignorance, and 'begged them to tell her how to conduct herself at home, at church, in the house, eating and drinking, lying down or rising up' (M. Whitney, Journal, 16 November 1825).

Mercy Whitney, who recorded this incident in her daily journal, expressed special approbation for Kaahumanu's clear perception of the degree of changed behaviour now required of her. For acceptance into the full favour of the American missionaries Hawaiians could not simply attend church and mission school faithfully. To be recognised as good Christians they needed not only to regulate public and private behaviour according to the new moral laws of the fledgling state, but must also mediate every single aspect of their daily habits, trivial though these changes might seem, but all of which were evidence of the new heart, the reformed consciousness, that genuine conversion to Christ entailed.

The missionary general meeting in 1832 spelled out some of the mission's aims:

Resolved, that while it is our main business to publish the word of God, we will discountenance the use and cultivation of tobacco; encourage improvements in agriculture and manufacture; habits of industry in the nation; neatness in the habits and dress of the inhabitants; punctuality in all engagements, especially in the payment of debts; justice and temperance in the rulers in the execution of the law, and loyalty, order and peace among their subjects, in all the relations and duties of life. (Sandwich Islands Mission 1832:133–4)

The women of the mission took as their special portion of this ambitious brief the 'transformation' of Hawaiian notions of femininity. Kaahumanu had at least realised the magnitude of the task they undertook and clearly saw adherence to mission ways to be ultimately in her own best political interests. The majority of Hawaiian women remained ignorant of or baffled by the essentially changed order that the American women sought to create. The story of three decades of intercultural contact in Hawaii—one of frustration for the mission women, and evasion by the Hawaiians— was fraught with considerable tension and unhappiness for both groups of women. Neither side could triumph: by the late 1840s, stalemate was reached. . . .

Mercy Whitney was one of the nearly eight women, predominantly from New England or the west of New York State, who left America for Hawaii (the 'Sandwich Islands') in the three decades from 1819 onwards. They were for the most part energetic, intelligent and well-educated women, daughters of farmers or small-business men, whose youthful ambition to serve on a mission field led them to marry departing missionaries. In the decades following the War of Independence, Protestant missionary outreach shifted from the native American Indians of their own west to encompass non-Christian peoples of the new lands opened to the imagination by explorers and travellers. Captain James Cook had visited and named the Sandwich Islands in 1778, on his third and last great Pacific expedition. Yankee traders had brought Hawaiian youths to New England port towns; some had

displayed an interest in Christianity. The churches planned and prayed for the conversion of this 'interesting' people, and sent successive contingents of missionaries to accomplish this purpose (Andrew 1976).

It was no accident that young women were found to dedicate their lives to this missionary work. Women were centrally involved in the religious revivals which swept the northeast during the early decades of the century, the so-called 'second great awakening', which had provided metaphysical justification for a range of religious and charitable activity undertaken by women. Women were prominent in efforts to teach the young, reform slum dwellers, persuade men to temperance, rescue prostitutes and, increasingly, to free Southern slaves. To quit home and family in order to bring the strongly upheld benefits of Christian civilisation to non-believers on a distant, exotic frontier was an uncommon but nevertheless strongly valorised choice of reform endeavour (Grimshaw 1983). As Catherine Beecher wrote in her *Treatise on Domestic Economy* in 1842, 'To American women, more than to any others on earth, is committed the exalted privilege of extending over the world those blessed influences, which are to renovate degraded man, and "to clothe all climes with beauty"' (Hunter 1984:xiii).

Women's involvement in mission work was linked in an intricately complex fashion with the economic changes arising from early industrialisation in the northeast and a particular elaboration of notions of the family, and of femininity, that accompanied changes in material life. An appreciation of this social change makes more comprehensible the agenda which underwrote the mission women's activities in Hawaii. As the integrated household economy of small farms and independent artisanal industry began to break down with the introduction of mills and factories, a family structure involving the man as the sole breadwinner involved in paid, public employment, with the wife as the housekeeper removed from most productive labour, became dominant in growing urban areas. Married, middle-class women were portrayed in much prescriptive literature as the essential focus of an intimate, personal circle whose relationships contrasted radically with the alienated marketplace of male endeavour. Good family life would prove the catalyst for rejuvenation and reform in the fast-changing and potentially corrupt new social order. The articulation of proper femininity needed to fit women to their part in this haven of domesticity. Puritan traditions had sustained a significant role for women in the God-fearing family. The ante-bellum period saw an enhanced elaboration of 'the cult of true womenhood', in Barbara Welter's definition, involving piety, purity, submissiveness and domesticity (Cott 1977; Ryan 1981; Welter 1966; Sklar 1973; Smith-Rosenberg 1971).

The elevation of women's nature inherent in these fresh definitions of femininity contained within it the seeds of change in women's social and political roles. Women's supposed moral and spiritual value was used to stress a new competency for women in the public arena, initially within the orbit of social reform. Hence arose the decision of this particular group of American women to Christianise and raise the status of Hawaiian women to their own presumed level. Emerging from their own small worlds, sustained by both religious and national enthusiasm, they were innocent of notions of cultural relativism and prepared to designate every deviance from their own moral values as sinful, abroad no less than at home. When they reached their Polynesian destination it was inevitable that they would interpret what they saw within the set of cultural beliefs so deeply a part of their own identities.

The various contingents of American missionaries established themselves first in the port towns and eventually spread to the most dense centres of population in the five main islands. The Hawaiian society on the fringes of which they lived was in the process of change as a result of decades of intercultural contact with explorers, traders, beachcombers and, finally, the missionaries. Some months before the first missionaries arrived the religious system, the *kapu* laws, had been overthrown on the initiative of powerful chiefs, the islands' political leaders. Much of the social organisation of traditional Hawaiian culture persisted, however, changing shape radically in some aspects, minimally in others, from 1820 to 1850. For most of this time a chiefly elite, the landowners, dominated much of the daily life of the commoners, the *maka'ainana,* in a style reminiscent of feudal society. Commoners laboured as tenants on the chiefs' land, and surrendered much of the fruits of their labour to their superiors. The labour of commoners was not usually especially onerous since the land and sea provided plentiful nutritious food, but at times the acquisitiveness of chiefs, impressed by Western skills and goods, could drive the population to sustained and often excessive stints of labour. It appeared that pockets of impoverishment, physical deterioration and the neglect of the care of the young were the result, exacerbated by the acceptability of alcohol and nicotine to men, women and children. European diseases, too, took their toll, particularly the venereal diseases that were all too often the undesired result of Hawaiian women's sexual relationships with foreign visitors and which caused suffering and sterility.

The social status of Hawaiian women was closely intertwined with their class position and their place in the life cycle. Chiefly women wielded enormous power. As one missionary observed of the *konohiki,* or headmen of his district, 'some, by the way, are women, for Paul's injunctions are not observed on the Sandwich Islands. Women often usurp the reigns of government over large districts'. Before the ending of *kapu* such women had been subject to definitions of the female sex as profane or dangerous which were inherent in the Polynesian dichotomy of male and female qualities, and which had kept the sexes separate in both religious ritual and in such mundane areas as eating meals (Hanson 1982). . . . Chiefly women now were freed from such restrictions.

The lot of non-chiefly women was similarly relieved by the ending of *kapu,* but they still shared with their menfolk restrictions on their autonomy arising from their inferior social status as a group. Subject to some extent to male physical domination, their social position was not, however, noticeably inferior to that of non-chiefly men. Except when chiefs drove commoners to unaccustomed toil, women were if anything advantaged by the usual division of labour which persisted through the mission period. Men undertook the bulk of heavy labour in building, fishing and agriculture, and also cooked the meals. Women made mats and barkcloth, collected shellfish, and were more closely involved than men in the care of young children. Descent was traced through both the male and female lines, but although patrilocal residence was the norm, women's families of origin remained their significant point of reference. Sexual relations were little restrained in early youth, and marriages were easily terminated; chiefly men and women often had several spouses at the same time. Fertility was controlled by abortion and infanticide, and babies were often adopted among the extended kinship network which sustained significant material support systems (Goldman 1970; Sahlins 1958). Hawaiian women's share in productive labour, then, was not onerous; their sexuality was not heavily constrained; means of fertility control were normative; and the task of child socialisation was shared with kin.

It was not a figment of the American imagination, however, that the lives of Hawaiian women were not idyllic in precontact times, nor without tensions in the decades after 1820. Nothing in the Hawaiians' situation, however, appeared even remotely acceptable to the self-appointed evangelists who saw Hawaiian women as their life-long cause. The men of the mission automatically undertook the dominant roles as preachers and teachers of men, delegating to women a share in the teaching of children and a special obligation to female adults. Hiram Bingham, the foremost missionary in Honolulu, explained the strategy in this way. Separating Hawaiian women for instruction gave the mission women a full opportunity to read scripture, pray and 'conveniently to give sisterly and maternal counsel to multitudes of their own

sex'. (Conventionally, mission women would have had to cede priority to men in a mixed gathering.) The separation similarly gave more scope for 'the awakened native talent and zeal' of Hawaiian women as well as men in church work. The separate instruction also produced 'a more perfect system of mutual watchfulness over the different members, and a more feasible mode of discipline' (Bingham 1981:365). The American missionary women's active participation in direct mission work was, in practice, heavily curtailed by their decision to segregate their own children from Hawaiian influence, and at various stages of their life cycle they participated only peripherally in formal teaching (Grimshaw 1983). The mission women's influence, however, emerged from all the various ways in which they transmitted their cultural prescriptions.

Arriving as they did at a critical period of Hawaiian cultural change, the American missionaries made rapid headway in persuading chiefs to a sympathetic interest in their religious system, and the adherence of Kaahumanu and other chiefs to church attendance and support of the mission effected a swift conversion of the population, remarkable when compared with the situation facing missionaries in the east. Granted that Western incursion was already setting in motion great change, the Christian chiefs undoubtedly believed that by welcoming the new religion and becoming leaders in the fledgling church their own political hegemony would be best preserved (Howe 1984; Daws 1974). Commoners began attending church because the chiefs commanded them to do so. As the Hilo missionaries told the home mission board in 1833, church attendance had not been voluntary, but in obedience to the commands of their chiefs. Hawaiians had 'put on the profession of true religion and engaged in the performance of its external duties', but all that had been secured was 'a prompt though thoughtless, servile and sycophantic audience' (Dibble *et al.* to ABCFM, 14 October 1833). Hawaiians were listless at meetings, according to Mary Parker, and could be moved neither to fear or anger. 'They submit wholly to what you say, ever having been accustomed to it.' If a chief told them to go to meeting, they immediately complied, but they simply did not know enough to become Christians (Parker, Journal (A), [?] June 1833). Meanwhile, despite new laws governing theft, murder and adultery, old ways of living, condemned over and over again by the missionaries, persisted.

The problem of how to bring about the genuine, deep-seated change in the hearts, minds and consciences of Hawaiians preoccupied mission thinking. In the last analysis, their strategy for reform came to rest on that institution so stressed in their own culture: the family. Family relationships on Hawaii appeared chaotic so that neither children, the citizens of tomorrow, nor adults could find reinforcement for decent behaviour in the one place where, as the missionaries saw it, altruistic and uplifting relationships were essential. 'It is impossible to conjecture who are husbands and wives, parents and children from their appearance assembled on the sabbath or at any other time', one missionary wrote. 'Nothing of that courtesy and attention is shown to each other by persons most intimately related as in the Christian population' (Dibble [c. 1831]). 'Where', asked Fidelia Coan, 'were the dutiful sons, virtuous daughters, chaste wives and faithful husbands of home?' (Mother's Magazine, 1837). Here, said a missionary at Waimea, was 'none of that mother's fondness of her darling child and that child's attachment to its affectionate mother which is seen in enlightened America' (Lyons to ABCFM, 6 September 1833).

Rather than in state, church or school, a reform endeavour should be shaped around the family life of Hawaiians and it was the mission women who spearheaded this effort. Above all, the women singled out the Hawaiian wife and mother as the agent for 'regeneration'. Hawaiian women were presented with the model of American femininity, the full force of the American's material wealth, skills, and the missionaries' undeniable altruism and forceful personal attributes. Hawaiian women

should be rendered genuinely pious, sexually pure, dutifully submissive and domestically oriented as housewives and mothers. Then, as the centre of a better-ordered family, their influence would ripple outwards, redeeming not only wayward children and errant husbands, but the whole kingdom for godly living.

The foremost goal of the American mission women was to convert Hawaiian women to a genuine piety, the mainspring as they saw it of all worthy moral behaviour. The Americans led Hawaiian women in sex-segregated prayer meetings, held classes for women after the Sunday Services, or made time available in their own homes to hear Hawaiians 'tell their thoughts' on religious matters. Charlotte Baldwin, for example, during a period of increased religious interest, set apart a room in her house where, 'when not engaged in personal conversation, she could resort with pious females for prayer; and when she was not able to be with them, they prayed there by themselves' (Alexander 1952:91). One newly arrived single missionary, Maria Patton (later Chamberlain), found the American women's efforts impressive. At Lahaina in 1828 she witnessed Clarissa Richards 'sitting in the midst of 200 females addressing them on divine truths', women who sat with solemn expressions and 'big tears stealing down their cheeks' (Patton to sister, 19 May 1828). A determined effort was mounted for the souls of Hawaiian women. The souls of the heathen, they often told themselves, were of 'incalculable worth'.

For Hawaiian women to reach a direct and vital relationship with their Maker, however, wider instruction was needed than the bare elements of the Christian faith. Hawaiian women needed a formal Western education so that they could read the Bible and other spiritually uplifting literature and attain the spiritual refinement of sensibility and understanding gained through a liberal education. Most of the American women themselves had felt the benefits of an education in the new female seminaries of the northeast in their youth, and some had fought hard to attain this higher education. Hawaiian women, too, not just young children, would be offered the fruits of this learning.

And so, in daily or weekly sessions, the American mission women taught Hawaiians to read and write and count, and for the more forward scholars the curriculum included geography, geometry and philosophy. The Americans, devoid of customary teaching aids beyond the simple readers put out by the mission press, devised ingenious ways of matching the needs of the situation. Hawaiian women brought seeds to school for counting lessons, wrote on smooth sand with sticks and used home-made maps and globes which the mission women sat up at night to construct. Charlotte Baldwin at Waimea in the early 1830s daily held a school for female teachers (women who would in turn teach other Hawaiians), and on two days a week a school for three hundred women, as well as working with children (Baldwin, Report, 1832:2). Such onerous work loads were undertaken by brides until babies appeared, by the childless or by those whose children had been sent away to school.

Despite the distractions of infants in arms, Hawaiian women showed interest in acquiring basic literacy. Indeed they showed an aptitude which compared well with that of Americans in the opinion of Mercy Whitney, which was surprising considering 'their habits of sloth and indolence, being unaccustomed from infancy, to apply their minds to anything which required thought or the exercise of their mental faculties' (M. Whitney, Journal, 30 September 1834). The link between such pursuits and piety was frequently stressed. Sarah Joiner Lyman's attitudes in her educational work at Hilo was common. Many women in her school for females aged eight to sixty years might not be expected to make remarkable progress, but the school at least brought scholars more regularly under the means of grace (Lyman Journal, 24 January 1837).

When Maria Ogden first joined the mission station at Waimea in 1829, she wrote approvingly of the schoolroom for Hawaiian women. 'Their seats and writing tables are chiefly made of those boards, on which the natives used to spend much of their time, sporting in the surf' (Gulick to ABCFM, 27 April 1829). The use of surfboards in such an enterprise was both practical and symbolic. If women were to be pious they must be weaned away from pastimes that were far from moral and what better way to do so than by offering the substitute of education for their customary games and amusements? Hawaiians did not appear to the missionaries to have enough work to do, and some missionaries felt it valueless to urge them to greater labour while an autocratic government prevented the people from personal accumulation. Their free time was spent in swimming and surfing, in cardplaying, boxing matches, games, cockfights, hulas and other traditional games of skill or chance. Not only were these games seen as a useless waste of time, but they were inextricably mingled with such sins as gambling and with sexuality of an overt kind which appeared subversive of Christian morals.

The women, whose labour appeared even less onerous than the men's, seemed particularly in need of those alternative pursuits which Christian education could offer: Bible-reading groups, church meetings, school examinations, Sunday school picnics and tea meetings, as well as formal classroom instruction. Choir work in particular attracted the American women's interest, since they so much missed the good music of their home congregations. Maria Patton described such a choir rehearsal at Lahaina where 'twenty-four genteely dressed Hawaiian ladies sat opposite the same number of gentlemen with an elegant table sporting three glass lamps placed between them' (Patton to sister, 20 August 1828).

With choirs, as in so many pursuits, American hopes were often thwarted. Mary Parker told a friend that she could hardly keep herself from laughing sometimes, the Hawaiians sang so laboriously. 'Nature seems not to have designed them for the best of singers' (M. Parker to Mrs Frisbie, April 1836). Her reaction to singing mirrored a deep-seated skepticism about the depth of genuine piety that the mission women's activity had really achieved. Newly arrived women could be impressed at the sight of a large group of Hawaiian women led in prayer by one of their number in a style not too far removed from expected forms. Those American women who had been years in the field however felt increasingly that the manifestation of piety was superficial. When a religious revival which swept the largest island and rapidly increased church membership (as opposed to mere attendance), many mission women were unmoved by the local missionaries' elation. 'We tremble, yet know not what to say, nor scarcely what to think', Sybil Bingham told a mission friend, musing on the 'fickleness' of the Hawaiian character (S. Bingham to N. Ruggles, 16 August 1838).

The essential thrust of the American women's strategy was to substitute piety for the sexuality which seemed to be the dominant drive in Hawaiian women's activities. The effort to induce notions of sexual purity extended far beyond prohibitions on 'promiscuous' bathing and sexually suggestive dances. While the American women saw monogamous marriage as the sole legitimate avenue for the expression of physical sex, their own notions of purity clearly accepted such sexuality in a relatively positive way. However to be confronted with a society in which matters concerning the body were explicitly, publicly and unselfconsciously presented was shocking. Nudity, urination, defecation and, above all, intimate sexual relations appeared scarcely subject to even minimal regulation, insensitive as they were to the cultural bases of Hawaiian sexual behaviour.

The Kailua missionaries complained in 1831 that 'the sin of uncleanness' clung to Hawaiians like leprosy, even to church members, despite the two-year probation period the ministers imposed. There was little concern or watchfulness over one another. Hawaiians congregated together in the same small house, and slept together on the one mat. Missionaries blamed 'the unceremonious manner of intercourse between the sexes, without any forms of reserve or any delicacy

of thought and conversation—The idle habits of all, especially the women, and their fondness for visiting from home at night—and the force of long established habits' (*Missionary Herald*, July 1832). 'The degradation of the *females* in this spot deeply affects my heart', wrote Clarissa Richards. 'On this subject I could *write* much—but delicacy forbids' (C. Richards, Journal, 1822–3:40). The missionaries sought to establish and sustain monogamous marriage, acting wherever possible to stamp out premarital and extramarital sexuality and encouraging Hawaiians to cover nude bodies with decent clothing in Western style.

Instruction on the married state was spelled out clearly in a pamphlet *A Word Relating to Marriage*, prepared for mission purposes. Marriage meant one partner, in a relationship lasting for life. Prostitution, adultery and 'male and female impersonations' were sins of the flesh. Marriages forbidden by God, such as those between close blood relatives, were prohibited. Couples should not marry too young, but wait until their bodies grew stronger and their characters more developed. Partners should be close in age so that they shared many interests; they should know each other well, understand each other's commitments and love each other. They should have joint residence, and own all property together (Clark 1844). Divorce was sanctioned only in the case of adultery or wilful desertion where mediation had failed.

Missionaries did not require couples married Hawaiian style to submit to a Christian service lest every married person in the islands should feel perfectly free to consider their current relationships null and void, and to swap partners at will, but they insisted that all future liaisons be blessed by the church. Female and male chiefs, however, who had more than one spouse, were to choose one and relinquish the rest. One chiefly woman of Kailua claimed to have had no fewer than forty spouses, usually several at the same time (*Missionary Herald*, October 1829), and a male chief seven. Samuel Whitney asked him whether so many wives did not give rise to some anxiety. 'Yes, much', replied the chief. 'I can not sleep for fear some other man will get them!' (S. Whitney, Journal, 30 April 1826). Such irregularities were insupportable in the political leaders of the country. They were encouraged to introduce stringent punishments for bigamy and adultery; by the late 1820s in Lahaina, errant subjects were being forced to pay for their sins by making roads (men), or confinement in irons (women) (*Missionary Herald*, February 1829).

'Marriage is honorable in all, and the bed undefiled, but whoremongers and adulterers God will judge', thundered preachers from a favourite Hebrew text. It was easier to get Hawaiians to the altar, alas, than to restrain 'whoremongers and adulterers' thereafter. The most clearcut case of irregularity that the mission could bring under some degree of surveillance was the sexual trafficking between Hawaiian women and foreign sailors off visiting ships. Initially such exchange of sexual favours for material goods was welcomed by Hawaiian girls, who may even have hoped to absorb *mana* (sanctity or divine strength) from the god-like white men (Sahlins 1981b:40). As well as material goods, however, the exchange often entailed unwanted pregnancies, uncontrollable venereal disease, jealous male violence and, where a Hawaiian woman had been abandoned after several months of cohabitation, penury. Whatever the subtleties of sexual politics in this interchange, the mission women viewed it within the model of their own society as sheer exploitative prostitution. They wept when, a fresh ship in port, their young female scholars turned a deaf ear to instruction and went off in the boats with pleasurable excitement (Ogden to M. Chamberlain, n.d.). They were in the forefront of pressure on chiefs to try to prevent this trade, with an anger made more intense by their daily contact with girls whose bodies were covered with syphilitic sores and with women rendered sterile from venereal disease.

Hawaiian brides decked themselves out with clothes for weddings and prayer meetings. The rule that the body, particularly the breasts, ought to be clothed at all times, was one held without conviction, while the myriad rules governing appropriate dress to match

various occasions was hardly won. One of Maria Chamberlain's first actions after acquiring some of the Hawaiian language was to exhort women at Waikiki, in faltering tongue, 'to be modest, to tell their neighbours it was a shame to go exposed and without kapa as we had recently seen some of them' (M. Chamberlain, Journal, 8 December 1829). Mary Parker's first sight of Hawaiians inspired a chill of disappointment: 'naked, rude and disgusting to every feeling' (M. Parker, Journal (A), 31 March 1833). The American women pressed clothes on to their parishioners, sewing early and late for chiefs and teaching the skill to as many women as would heed them. Their first success was to persuade women, at least in the sight of Westerners, to wear a cotton shift with a skirt of Hawaiian cloth wound around their waists, and eventually a style of dress patterned on their own nightgowns became common usage. Frequently clothes were removed for work or for bathing, and women would sit wet through in church services if they had been caught in rain, although they customarily removed wet clothing when they were outside.

At times success seemed imminent. At a school examination at Waimea in 1829, the women decked themselves out in silk gowns, black with white headdresses or green with yellow headdresses (Guilick to ABCFM, 27 April 1829). The high chief Kapiolani, defier of the goddess Pele, won acclaim, as was described by a mission daughter in this way:

> Her hair was becomingly arranged with side puffs, and a high tortoise shell comb, which was the admiration of our childish eyes. Her feet were always clad in stockings and shoes . . . on public occasions, or when visiting away from home, she wore a tight fitting dress, not even adopting the *'holuku'* (or 'Mother Hubbard') which afterwards became the national style. Silk and satin of the gayest colors were the chosen dress of the chiefs, but she preferred grave and quiet shades. (Taylor 1897:6)

Yet for the most part the women were pained at the sight of inappropriate dress, even among the chiefs: rich satin dresses with bare feet, expensive mantles over cotton shifts. Other Hawaiian women showed a tendency to see clothes as ornamentation rather than to cover nakedness. When straw hats were introduced to replace flower wreaths, women loaded them with bows of dyed kapa ribbon and extended the brims to enormous proportions. Leg of mutton sleeves, padded with cloth, ballooned out voluminously.

The proper balance in dress was a rare achievement indeed, as rare as the reordering of sexuality they had tried to impose. Marriage was no security against the sin of adultery, mourned Clarissa Armstrong in 1838. No less than nine quite young girls who attended meetings regularly and heard religious instruction every day had been guilty of adultery (Armstrong, Journal, 4 February 1838). Unless some honest way was laid out 'for the people to supply their new and clamorous wants', wrote Laura Judd from Honolulu in 1841, 'wives and daughters will continue to barter virtue for gain' just as the other sex resorted to extortion and theft (L. Judd to Mrs. R. Anderson, August 1841).

The American missionaries always looked askance at the marriage of Christian believers and non-believers, but particularly so when the non-believer was the wife. The problem involved in this case was the proper submission that a wife owed to husbandly authority: 'in the marriage contract', the mission asserted, 'the woman surrenders herself to the authority and control of the husband in a sense materially different from the surrender of the husband to the wife (though the husband's authority cannot contravene the authority of Christ which is always paramount)' (Sandwich Islands Mission 1837:13–14). It was this consideration that led them also to oppose older chiefly women's marriages to youths where there was a great disparity in rank, age or influence, 'for the wife would probably surrender her superiority reluctantly if at all; or the youth might exercise his authority in an unseemly manner'. If the older partner were a male chief, the tension would not be as severe. 'There is not the same danger of unwelcome usurpation, or competition for supremacy', as there was of discontent and unfaithfulness *(ibid.)*.

The concept of submissiveness as a feature of feminine behaviour and personality was not unproblematic for the mission women themselves, as the reminder that the Christian conscience was the ultimate arbiter of authority hinted. Most certainly the women did not equate 'submission' with any notion of passivity, weakness or ineffectualness. Courage, determination in a rightful cause, moderate assertiveness, were all qualities the American women often displayed and certainly valorised. Indeed such attributes were essential if women were to engage, as seemed essential, in charitable and religious concerns in the community. As daughters they had shown deference to their parents' opinions, and as wives they were undoubtedly prepared, should an irreconcilable difference arise, to yield to a husband's judgment, just as they assumed that a husband's interests preceded their own. Yet, partly because the gender division of labour was clearly spelt out in the marriage, and partly because much of their activism was conducted in a sex-segregated style, submissive behaviour in the conventional sense seemed rarely to be called for. The notion of women's moral leadership in the marriage offered in any case a countervailing source of power to that given the man by right.

The mission treatise on marriage instructed Hawaiians that the husband was head of the wife and should love, nurture and care for her. Wives, in turn, should reside in proper conduct under their husbands, and, through the fine example they set in living without sin and in the fear of the Lord, would influence their husbands to the good (Clark 1844:4). One reason that the mission women waged their campaign against Hawaiian women's customary amusements was the need to encourage those personal qualities of gentility that matched the submissive wife's role. 'The females, too, at the other end of the village are assembled for female fights, that is, *pulling hair, scratching* and *biting*', wrote two missionaries about the boxing craze among their community (Spaulding and Richards 1831). Women used alcohol and smoked to excess, in both cases inducing indelicate, hoydenish behaviour. Involving women in the organisational and educational work of the church—teaching, leading prayer groups, preparing parish functions—not only offered women alternative occupations but pointed them in the path of an effective community activism which could be reconciled with deference to the dominant sex.

Hawaiian women were begged to change their ways, and in particular wives were urged to combine their interests more closely with their husbands. 'The property of a husband and wife are perfectly separate', one missionary complained. '*Hoapili* [a chief] and his wife have two perfectly distinct establishments, they rarely eat together. No man ever uses his wife's book and vice versa and so of a slate and other property, each must have one of his own' (Andrews to ABCFM, 2 December 1835). When Hukona, one of Clarissa Richard's servants, was guilty of 'delinquency' while assisting Fanny Gulick, another mission wife, Clarissa insisted that the woman should remain with Fanny 'and that she live quietly with her husband and submit herself cheerfully to his authority and theirs'. She could return to visit the Armstrongs and her relations after Fanny's confinement, but Clarissa did not want Hukona to feel that her services were indispensable, 'if she does not love her husband, nobody wants her' (C. Richards to F. Gulick, April [1834]).

It was the kinship network, the 'relations', that many missionaries realised was the stumbling block to much submissive wifely behaviour. Their own culture upheld dutiful deference of young unmarried daughters to the authority of parents. Hawaiian women, however, sustained links with their family of origin which superseded their ties with their husbands throughout their lives. Their roles as sisters, daughters, nieces took precedence over the marriage bond and represented the reference point for status. American women expected a married woman to have status conferred by the husband. Hawaiian women were involved in strong bonds of reciprocity with their kin for material, emotional and physical support, and such demands frequently drew wives from the marital home. Increasingly, as European diseases ravaged the population, they were called upon to nurse sick relatives some distance from their homes. Maria Chamberlain articulated common exasperation with the strength of kinship ties. 'If we should give the natives in our family a whole hog or goat they would boil it up and share it with their friends and then perhaps go without any meat for 2 or 3 days' (M. Chamberlain to sister, 11 March 1830). The functional value of such behaviour escaped the missionaries.

However it was not merely the force of the kinship network which the Americans saw as undermining proper lines of authority. They abhorred the continuing power of the chiefs over the lives of individual members of the family except where this influence was exercised on behalf of the church. Mary Ives described such an incident that epitomised chiefly tyranny at Hana. A young girl had brought Mary two eggs to exchange for a needle. A chief, observing the transaction, seized the eggs and angrily told the girl she had no right to sell eggs without asking him. As the girl fled in shame, Mary recalled her, gave her a needle and remonstrated with the chief—who did not take her advice in good spirit (M. Ives to aunt, 21 January 1838). If a chief detained a Hawaiian in some place distant from his home and family, wrote Sarah Lyman, the man did not even express a wish to return, even if he was detained six months or a year. 'Such veneration they still have for chiefs' (Lyman, Journal, 4 January 1835). For women to be dutiful wives, continuity in cohabitation and regularity in material subsistence was essential, and the Americans looked forward to the time when the despotism of chiefs would be ended, while they expressed regret at individual chiefly acts in the meantime.

The teaching of submissiveness, then, was intimately related to the encouragement of women to lead a domestic-oriented existence based on a gender division of labour in the American mode. Mission teaching was explicit on this point. 'It is the husband's role to work out-doors—he farms and builds the home and prepares that which concerns the welfare of the body. The role of the wife is to maintain the house and all that is within. It is her responsibility to look after the husband's clothing and the food—the household chores—setting in place the sleeping quarters and all else that is within' (Clark 1844). The wife was advised against deficiency in this area. 'It is wrong to neglect work and to leave the husband to keep the household. It is right to remain within the house and to work without daydreaming, providing food, clothing and all that is essential for life together' *(ibid., 5).* And by such domestic devotion, the wife would foster the husband's love for the children. The married couple should guide children, as Solomon said, on the correct path. If husband and wife loved each other, their love for their children would be great and the children would not abandon their parents in later life.

The reality of Hawaiian domestic life was far from the ideal projected by the Americans. When Abigail Smith arrived at Kaluaaha in 1833, she was driven to distraction by Hawaiian women coming to observe her performance of domestic chores. She begged them to go home to their household duties and the care of their children so she could get on with her own tasks undisturbed. They asserted cheerfully that they had no duties, and continued unabashed to occupy her yard and doorway (Frear 1934:71). On several occasions when Hawaiian women saw the Americans ironing they said, with heartfelt sympathy, 'I pity you'.

The simply constructed Hawaiian houses with their sparse furnishings, together with the plainness of diet and dress, militated against the mission plan. The Waimea missionaries tried to persuade the people 'to live like human beings', Lyons said, to put away dogs, give up tobacco, build better houses, make tables, seats, use separate dishes and eating utensils, make fences around their houses and cultivate the soil more extensively (Lyons, Report on Waimea Station, 1837:1). The chiefs built Western-style houses, and eventually a few of the better-off church families lived in Western style with thatched mud-walled cottages sporting separate sleeping places for children, a shelf of books, an engraved map on the wall, home-built furniture and wooden bowls and spoons *(Mother's Mag-*

azine, February 1839). But for the most part the Americans considered the Hawaiians' homes and diet totally unconducive to the performance of a day's domestic work by Hawaiian women. When the mission women went house-to-house visiting it was usually only the sick, the lame, the blind, the maimed or the old that they found at home—not a busy and welcoming Hawaiian housewife.

It seemed to the Americans that vast material improvement among commoners was dependent on breaking the hegemony of the chiefs. In the meantime, as they sought a cash crop which might give Hawaiian men employment and livelihood, they also looked for an avenue of household production for the women. One proposal was to induce Hawaiian women to spend more time sewing and knitting, since this not only afforded domestic occupation but provided the clothing so sorely needed by the whole population, and the clothes would generate occupation in mending, laundering, ironing and storing. The most concerted effort was the attempt to initiate clothmaking in the homes, that old skill of American women which was swiftly being overtaken by factory production back home. In 1834 a middle-aged spinster, Miss Lydia Brown, was sent to the islands to spearhead this enterprise. The mission board justified the appointment of Lydia, 'a woman of superior mind and character', in these terms. 'It is certainly of the utmost importance to make employment, and to create a necessity for it, for the people of the Islands. And it is very desirable to exert every influence on them that will be likely to produce among them industrious, orderly families.' The Hawaiians, therefore, should be trained in the domestic manufacture of cloth (Wisner to Missionaries, 23 June 1834). A number of Hawaiian women were intrigued by the process and keen to try it until they saw how coarse was the cloth of their own manufacture, and until more and more imported cottons made home spinning and weaving superfluous for the same reason as in America.

Persuading Hawaiian women to devote more time to childcare was similarly a frustrating task. 'In our opinion', stated the

Lahaina mission report in 1833, 'all that ever has been written on the subject of a mother's influence, has come far short of giving it the high rank which it really holds. Could the influence of a pious mother be brought to bear upon the children of Hawaii, then these islands might be transformed . . . Otherwise it will be the work of ages to change the character of the nation's children' (*Missionary Herald*, September 1834). The children, all the missionaries agree, were growing up like wild goats in the field. The only way to get them to school was to seek them out and bribe them with books in exchange for attendance. To keep them in school, the teachers had to sustain the children's interest constantly, no small task considering that the knowledge which Hawaiian children attained appeared to bear no relevance for their future employment. If made the objects of anger or corporal punishment, the children deserted in decisive fashion. One missionary described their activities. 'From morning to night, ungoverned by their parents, almost naked, ranging the fields in companies of both sexes, sporting on the sand-beach, bathing promiscuously in the surf, or following the wake of some drunken sailors' (Dibble 1909:267). Something had to be done.

That something involved the formation of Maternal Associations on each station devoted to the task of explaining to Hawaiian women the serious business of rearing godly children. On occasions, with caution, a mission wife brought in one of her own offspring for brief display.

Instruction began with a sharp and anguished attack on abortion and infanticide. Abortions, 'base and inhuman practices' (Lyons to ABCFM, n.d. [*c.* 1836]), were suspected to be common but difficult to detect. Mercy Whitney, reporting that she had seen a child with an eye put out by his mother 'in endeavouring to kill him' before his birth, commented also on the common practice of former years, infanticide: 'They seemed to think but little more of killing a child, than they would an animal' (M. Whitney, Journal, 24 October 1828). Most mission women reported that the incidence of infanticide de-

clined swiftly, however. This was very likely due to the high infant mortality rate from introduced diseases if for no other reason.

The mission publication *A Few Words of Advice for Parents* (Sandwich Islands Mission 1842) cautioned mothers against leaving their infants to cry in another's care while they went off wherever they wished. Infants should be fed only breast milk, not fish, or *poi*, or sugarcane juice. But beyond everything else, infants should not be given away to relatives, but reared by their biological parents in the one home. This common practice was seen not just as the chief cause of the high infant mortality, but the reason for the entire lack of discipline over older children. Sarah Lyman expressed the usual exasperation at this practice when, at a Maternal Association meeting at Hilo, she failed dismally to compile a neat list of mothers and children. Thirty women attended, but it proved impossible to discover exactly how many children they had as 'their *real* mother, grandmother, aunt, nurse and perhaps someone else' would all claim the one child (Lyman, Journal, 17 January 1837).

Consequently, as the children grew more independent, it proved impossible for parents to exert strong control over them. As one Hawaiian mother after another explained, if they were nasty to their children, the children simply rolled up their mats under their arms and moved on to be welcomed by a related household. One Hawaiian mother described how she had tried to hit her disobedient child with the rod—the child spat in her face, bit and scratched her, tore her clothes, and then ran away for several days (*Mother's Magazine*, October 1837). If Hawaiian mothers had been accustomed to govern their children instead of being governed by them, it might have been a simple matter to substitute alternative advice. But, said Fidelia Coan, 'The most simple directions we can give, presuppose, in many cases, more knowledge, more skill, more advancement in the art of governing a family than they have attained' (*ibid.*).

It was arguable, from observing non-Christian mothers, that good church members were a little less likely to give up their infants for adoption and attempted to control their children a little more firmly. Certainly where the wife was an unbeliever, and a Christian father exerted parental authority, his efforts were clearly undermined; the wife would intervene if he tried to whip a child and set up a fearful wailing. 'It is true here, as in civilized lands', wrote one missionary, 'that the female fills an important sphere and may be the means of doing *much* mischief or *much* good' (Forbes to ABCFM, 23 July 1836). For the most part, however, even Christian women resigned themselves to a continuation of usual practices. We hear your advice, but we forget it quickly, Hawaiians goodnaturedly told the mission wives. Anyway, they were convinced that American children were born different: it was inconceivable that Hawaiian children could be so well-behaved.

On occasions Hawaiian women could express gratitude to American wives for their unswerving reform efforts. Maria Chamberlain had that experience one pleasant day in May, 1831. As an Hawaiian woman sat by Maria's baby's cradle brushing the flies off his face, she said to Maria that Hawaiians were fortunate that the missionaries had come with wives to the islands. Formerly, she said, Hawaiians had known nothing of taking care of children; gave newborn babies to others; knew nothing of domestic happiness. 'Husbands and wives quarrelled, committed adultery, drank, lied, stole ... Now we wish to obey the word of God, to live together with love, to take care of our children and have them wear clothes as the children of the missionaries' (M. Chamberlain, Journal, 11 May 1831). Such praise was a rare treat and one which the mission women in any case came to regard with some skepticism. Penetrating the Hawaiian mind was a baffling task. 'It is exceedingly difficult to ascertain the true character of this people', wrote Nancy Ruggles after thirteen years in the islands. 'The expression of the lips merely, is no sure indication of the state of the heart' (N. Ruggles to Rev. and Mrs. S. Bartlett, 27 June 1833). Another missionary spelled out one of the major problems of communication. 'Unless every trifling particular is named they rarely have the judgement to carry out the principle themselves. They suppose they

have complied when they observe the particular act forbidden' (Forbes to ABCFM, 10 October 1836). Scholars in the schools learned to pronounce the words, but that was all. They did not understand the essential *meaning*.

By the time the second decade of mission work was nearing its end without the reformation they craved becoming visible, many missionary women began to express the discouragement that had never, in any case, been far beneath the surface. They had God on their side; they had sacrificed a good deal to come to Hawaii; they felt exhausted in the cause; the population was ostensibly Christian and some change in women's behaviour had taken place. All Hawaiian women, however, fell far short of the desired model of true womanhood that they had tried so hard to impose. 'What in me hinders their salvation?' Lucia Smith plaintively asked her friend Juliette Cooke, as she watched women drift away from her instruction (L. Smith to J. Cooke, 5 May [1838]). Many another mission sister echoed her painful self-assessment.

Forceful and efficient fresh male missionaries who arrived in Hawaii in the 1830s were horrified by what they saw as the slow progress of the mission's work and began to question the decision of earlier missionaries to devote so much of the effort to the reformation of adults. Many felt a renewed onslaught should be made on the character formation of Hawaiian children. Lorrin Andrews, principal of the Lahainaluna Seminary which was founded on Maui in 1831 to offer advanced education to young Hawaiian men, was one who came to this opinion. '*We must begin with* children or the *most* of our labour must be lost as far as civilization and mental improvement are concerned', he told fellow missionaries with some vehemence (Andrews to ABCFM, 2 December 1835). He and his co-workers became disillusioned with their work with young men when they encountered sexual immorality both within the Seminary and among some graduate teachers in the community who used their new status to gain sexual favours from female pupils (Andrews *et al.* to ABCFM, 1836–37).

While others agreed about renewed emphasis on children, the teachers of day schools felt their task an impossible one. Children, said one missionary, lost the salutary effects of religious instruction by 'mingling with their vicious parents and others and observing all their heathenish and polluting habits and practices' (L. Lyons to ABCFM, Report, 1836). No sooner, reiterated another, did one alert children to their 'filthy and indecent appearance' and to the evils of quarrelling and lying than they returned to the 'beastly indifference' to the conventions of good behaviour, or even the sneers, of those with whom they associated back home. The solution seemed difficult, but obvious. The mission must educate children, but in sex-segregated boarding schools where they could be removed from their parents' influence (Hitchcock to ABCFM, April 1836). The missionaries on Hawaii knew that their fellow missionaries in Ceylon were finding this a constructive approach. The graduates of the girls' and boys' boarding schools in Ceylon were marrying and then re-entering their former communities as Christian leaders (Wisner to missionaries, 23 June 1834). A beginning on this policy was made. Lahainaluna was converted to a high school for young boys in 1837, and the Wailuku Girls' Seminary, for girls aged six to ten years, was opened at a discreet geographical distance.

At Wailuku, under the principal Miss Maria Ogden, Hawaiian girls received the training in true womanhood that the female missionaries had tried to offer adult women. Their daily schedule revealed much. Girls rose before dawn for prayers, set the tables, cleaned their rooms, washed, combed their hair and came down to breakfast at the sound of the bell. Some girls were rostered to wait at each meal. The girls sewed from 7:30 a.m. to 9:00 a.m., studied till midday, and again after lunch from 2:00 p.m. to 4:00 p.m. Another hour's sewing preceded supper at 5:00 p.m., followed by a scripture reading and prayer. On Saturdays the scholars scoured the dining room, schoolroom, tables, basins, aprons, plates, knives and forks; they washed and ironed their clothes, neat uniforms of sensible cottons. They learned at the school the basic elements of a formal education combined with an apprenticeship in female arts and crafts (Ogden to M. Chamberlain 27 June [?1837]). By 1839, however, Dr. Judd recommended some improvement not only in the quality of their diet but in the time allotted for physical exercise, when serious illness, resulting in deaths, occurred at the school. It seemed impossible, the missionaries concluded, 'to restrain them from rude and romping behaviour, and to confine them to those exercises deemed more proper for females without serious injury to health' (Dibble 1909:284; Judd 1960:95).

The 1840s saw a slow period of disengagement in active involvement in the mission by many missionary wives, which they lamented in an increasingly hopeless fashion. It was impracticable for most children to be confined for years in boarding schools—the one area where a small group of women remained involved. Their efforts with the Hawaiian women appeared to bear little fruit, and the Americans faced the gloomy experience of watching many of their most precious converts dying prematurely during the epidemics which swept the islands. 'Surely this people are melting away like dew . . . What we do for them must be done quickly', wrote Sarah Lyman (Lyman, Journal, 22 January 1838). Another missionary wrote, 'We bless the Lord and take courage but, oh, what a dying people this is. They drop down on all sides of us and it seems that the nation must speedily become extinct' (Gulick 1918:159). The mission women's nursing skills seemed more in demand than any other offering they could make. By the 1850s, there was often little to distinguish the mission women's daily round and preoccupations from many of their sisters' lives back home, the exotic character of their environment notwithstanding.

A young American, staying in the Hawaiian islands for his health in the 1830s, described his missionary aunt's activities, and the Hawaiian response, in an ironical yet sympathetic fashion:

My aunt could work, scold, preach, wash, bake, pray, catechize, make dresses, plant, pluck, drive stray pigs out the garden. There was nothing useful in this wilderness which she could not do. She exercised an influence from her energy and practical virtue which bordered on absolute authority. As I walked with her through the village, her presence operated as a civilizing tonic. True, the effect in many cases was transient. But the natives knew what she expected. As she appeared, tobacco pipes disappeared, idle games or gambling were slyly put by. Bible and hymn books brought conspicuously forward and the young girls hastily donned their chastest dresses and looks. (Restarick 1924:50–1)

His characterisation of this intercultural relationship nicely captures both the single-minded effort of missionary women and the apparent conformity, but essentially evasive, response of Hawaiians. It also exemplifies the style of much outsiders' writing about mission women, the tendency to stress a comic element in the encounter. In truth, however, although the endeavour of the American missionary women could easily be described as comedy, it more nearly approaches tragedy.

The American women attempted what was, given the circumstances, a constructive role in the process of social change in Hawaii which it is easy to overlook. Hawaiian culture was being subjected to intense pressure to adapt to the rapid incursion of foreigners into their community. The missionaries were only one element in these first decades, and from an immediate economic perspective the least exploitative element in this capitalist and colonialist invasion. Granted that change in Hawaiian culture was inevitable, what in fact the American missionaries offered Hawaiian girls and women was initiation into that range of skills and behaviour that would ensure some successful negotiation of the new order. Kaahumanu, the queen regent, was astute enough to recognise this fact.

The constructive nature of the American women's enterprise has been overlooked partly by the tendency of historians, themselves products of the same work-oriented society, to envy, and to enjoy vicariously, the lives of those Polynesian island dwellers who were innocent of puritanical drives. Yet there seems little basis in fact for describing Hawaiian women's lives as romantic or idyllic, either in their pre-contact world or in the period of

change of the nineteenth century. This tendency to denigrate the missionary women's efforts is intensified by the trappings of Victorian gentility which necessarily surrounded their agenda, particularly with respect to sexuality. Yet the formal and informal education in Western forms which the mission women, alone of their sex, were prepared to offer would enable Hawaiian women to make out in a world increasingly dominated by this alien culture. Such Hawaiian women who were 'successful' in nineteenth-century Hawaii served an apprenticeship in the American mission programme.

Yet ultimately the American women's activities would prove of only marginal value to the vast majority of those Hawaiians who survived the ravages of imported diseases. Clearly a wide range of cultural beliefs and practices were bound to persist, and among these notions of masculinity, femininity and personal familial relationships would prove the most persistent. Moreover, the American prescriptions of femininity were based on an economic organisation which it proved impossible to replicate for indigenous Hawaiians. The male breadwinner, the independent artisan, the small farmer, the wage earner, supporting a wife and family in modest but independent comfort, was a dream that faded before it could emerge (Grimshaw 1986). Eventually large plantations and businesses headed by foreign capitalists dominated, employing non-Hawaiian labour for the most part. The bulk of Hawaiians remained excluded from the prosperity of this new Hawaii. The relative affluence of Hawaiian families and the Western gender division of labour desired by the Americans remained elusive goals. It was no wonder that their cultural constructs of gender characteristics proved unattainable.

The experience of American and Hawaiian cultural contact was an ironic one. The Americans sacrificed much personal comfort, suffered home-sickness, ill-health and heartache in their effort to transform Hawaiian lives. Yet they tended to attack, along with destructive elements in the processes of foreign incursion, many of the very aspects of Hawaiian culture which afforded Hawaiian women some measure of autonomy within their own social system. Meanwhile the Americans were powerless to reproduce for their protégés the framework which afforded American women informal power within American society.

REFERENCES

Alexander, M. C. 1952. *Baldwin of Lahaina.* Stanford, Stanford University Press.

Andrew, J. A. III. 1976. *Rebuilding the Christian Commonwealth: New England Congregationalists and Foreign Missions 1800–1830.* Lexington, University of Kentucky Press.

Andrews, L. Letter to ABCFM, 2 December 1835. ABCFM—Hawaii Papers, Missionary Letters.

Andrews, L., E. Clark and S. Dibble. Letter to ABCFM, 1836–1837. ABCFM—Hawaii Papers, Missionary Letters.

Armstrong, C. Journal, 1831–1838. Journal Collection, HMCS.

Baldwin, D. Report of Waimea Station, June 1832. Mission Station Reports. HMCS.

Bingham, H. 1981 [1848]. *A Residence of Twenty–one Years in the Sandwich Islands.* Rutland, Vermont, Charles E. Tuttle.

Bingham, S. Letter to N. Ruggles, 16 August 1936. Missionary Letters. HMCS.

Carter, H. A. P. 1899. *Kaahumanu.* Honolulu, R. Grieve.

Chamberlain, M. Journal, 1825–1849. Journal Collection, HMCS.

———. Letter to sister, 11 March 1830. Missionary Letters. HMCS.

Clark, E. 1844. *A Word Relating to Marriage,* translated by Carol Silva. Honolulu; Mission Press.

Cott, N. 1977. *The Bonds of Womanhood: 'Women's Sphere' in New England, 1780–1835.* New Haven, Yale University Press.

Daws, G. 1974 [1968]. *Shoal of Time: A History of the Hawaiian Islands.* Honolulu, University of Hawaii Press.

Dibble, S. 1909 [1834]. *A History of the Sandwich Islands.* Honolulu: Thomas G. Thrum.

———. Review of "A Visit to the South Seas" by Rev. C. S. Stewart [n.d.] [c. 1831]. ABCFM—Hawaii Papers, Missionary Letters.

Forbes, C. Letters to ABCFM, 23 July 1836 and 10 October 1836. ABCFM—Hawaii Papers, Missionary Letters.

Frear, M. D. 1934. *Lowell and Abigail: A Realistic Idyll.* New Haven, privately published.

Goldman, I. 1970. *Ancient Polynesian Society.* Chicago, University of Chicago Press.

Grimshaw, P. 1983. Christian woman, pious wife, faithful mother, devoted missionary: conflicts in roles of American missionary women in nineteenth–century Hawaii. *Feminist Studies,* 9:489–522.

———. 1986. Paths of duty: American missionary wives in early nineteenth–century Hawaii. Unpublished Ph.D. thesis, University of Melbourne, Australia.

Gulick, O. and A. Gulick. 1918. *The Pilgrims of Hawaii.* New York, Fleming H. Revell Company.

Gulick, P. Letter to ABCFM, 27 April 1829. ABCFM—Hawaii Papers, Missionary Letters.

Hanson, F. A. 1982. Female Pollution in Polynesia. *JPS* 91:335–381.

Hanson, F. A. and L. Hanson. 1983. *Counterpoint in Maori Culture.* London, RKP.

Hitchcock, H. Letter to ABCFM: [?] April 1836. ABCFM—Hawaii Papers. Missionary Letters.

Howe, K. R. 1984. *Where the Waves Fall.* Sydney, Allen & Unwin.

Hunter, J. 1984. *The Gospel of Gentility: American Women Missionaries in Turn of the Century China.* New Haven, Yale University Press.

Ives, M. Letter to aunt, 21 January 1838. Missionary Letters. HMCS.

Judd, G. P. IV. 1960. *Dr. Judd: Hawaii's Friend.* Honolulu, University of Hawaii Press.

Judd, L. Letter to Mrs. R. Anderson, [?] August 1841. Missionary Letters. HMCS.

Lyman, S. Journal 1830–1863. Journal Collection. HMCS.

Lyons, L. Letter to ABCFM, 6 September 1833. ABCFM—Hawaii Papers, Missionary Letters.

———. Letter to ABCFM, n.d. [c.1836]. ABCFM—Hawaii Papers, Missionary Letters.

———. Report on Waimea Station. 1837 (typescript). Mission Station Reports. HMCS.

Missionary Harold. ABCFM Boston, 1821–1834.

Mother's Magazine. New York, 1836–1845.

Ogden, M. Letter to Maria Chamberlain, 27 June [?1837], Missionary Letters. HMCS.

Parker, M. Letter to Mrs. L. Frisbie, [?] April 1836. Missionary Letters. HMCS.

———. Journal (A): Voyages to Hawaii and Marquesas 1823–1833. Journal Collection. HMCS.

Patton (Chamberlain) M. Letters to sister, 19 May 1828 and 20 August 1828. Missionary Letters. HMCS.

Restarick, H. 1924. *Hawaii 1778–1920: From the Viewpoint of a Bishop.* Honolulu, Paradise of the Pacific.

Richards, C. Journal en route to Hawaii 1822–1823. Journal Collection. HMCS.

————. Letter to Fanny Gulick, April [?1834]. Missionary Letters. HMCS.

Ruggles, N. Letter to Reverend and Mrs. S. Bartlett, 27 June 1833. Missionary Letters. HMCS.

Ryan, M. P. 1981. *Cradle of the Middle-Class: The Family in Oneida County, New York, 1790–1865*. Cambridge, Cambridge University Press.

Sahlins, M. 1958. *Social Stratification in Polynesia*. Seattle, University of Washington Press.

————. 1981. *Historical Metaphors and Mythical Realities: Structure in the Early History of the Sandwich Islands Kingdom*. Ann Arbor, University of Michigan Press.

Sandwich Islands Mission. 1832. *Extracts from the Minutes of a General Meeting of the Sandwich Islands Mission*, June 1832. Oahu, Mission Press.

————. 1837. *Extracts from the Records of the Hawaiian Association from 1832 to 1836*. Honolulu, Mission Press.

————. 1842. *A Few Words (of Advice) for Parents*. Lahainaluna, Lahainaluna High School Press.

Sklar, K. K. 1973. *Catherine Beecher: A Study in American Domesticity*. New Haven, Yale University Press.

Smith, L. Letter to Juliette Cooke, 5 May [1838]. Missionary Letters. HMCS.

Smith-Rosenberg, C. 1971. Beauty, the beast, and the militant woman: a case study of sex roles and social stress in Jacksonian America. *American Quarterly*, 23:562–584.

Spaulding, E. and W. Richards. 1831. A Brief History of Temperance for Twelve Years at the Sandwich Islands . . . , written 15 December 1831. ABCFM—Hawaii Papers, Missionary Letters.

Taylor, P. G. 1897. *Kapiolani*. Honolulu, Robert Grieve.

Welter, B. 1966. The culture of true womanhood, 1820–1860. *American Quarterly*, 18:151–174.

Whitney, S. Journal at Kauai 2 April–1 June 1826. ABCFM— Hawaii Papers, Missionary Letters.

Whitney, M. Journal, 1821–1860. Journal Collection. HMCS.

Wisner, B. Letter to missionaries at the Sandwich Islands, 23 June 1834. ABDFM–HEA Papers: Letters to missionaries.

"Aba Riots" or Igbo "Women's War"? Ideology, Stratification, and the Invisibility of Women

Judith Van Allen

The events that occurred in Calabar and Owerri provinces in southeastern Nigeria in November and December of 1929, and that have come to be known in Western social-science literature as the "Aba Riots," are a natural focus for an investigation of the impact of

Reprinted from *Women in Africa: Studies in Social and Economic Change*, edited by Nancy J. Hafkin and Edna G. Bay with the permission of the publisher, Stanford University Press. © 1976 by the Board of Trustees of the Leland Stanford Junior University.

colonialism on Igbo women.[1] In the development and results of that crisis can be found all the elements of the system that has weakened women's position in Igboland—and in much of the rest of Africa as well.[2] The "Aba Riots" are also a nice symbol of the "invisibility" of women: "Aba Riots" is the name adopted by the British; the Igbo called it *Ogu Umunwanyi*, the "Women's War" (Uchendu 1965: 5; Okonjo 1974: 25, n. 40). This is more than a word game. In politics, the control of language means the control of history. The dominant group and the subordinate group almost always give different names to their conflicts, and where the dominant group alone writes history, its choice of terminology will be perpetuated. Examples of this manipulation of language abound in American history, as any examination of standard textbooks will reveal.

Calabar and Owerri provinces covered roughly the southeast and southwest quarters of Igboland, the traditional home of the Igbo peoples. In November of 1929, thousands of Igbo women from these provinces converged on the Native Administration centers— settlements that generally included the headquarters and residence of the British colonial officer for the district, a Native Court building and a jail, and a bank or white trader's store (if such existed in the district).[3] The women chanted, danced, sang songs of ridicule, and demanded the caps of office (the official insignia) of the Warrant Chiefs, the Igbo chosen from each village by the British to sit as members of the Native Court. At a few locations the women broke into prisons and released prisoners. Sixteen Native Courts were attacked, and most of these were broken up or burned. The "disturbed area" covered about 6,000 square miles and contained about two million people. It is not known how many women were involved, but the figure was in the tens of thousands. On two occasions, British District Officers called in police and troops, who fired on the women and left a total of more than 50 dead and 50 wounded. No one on the other side was seriously injured.[4]

The British "won," and they have imposed their terminology on history; only a very few scholars have recorded that the Igbo called this the "Women's War." And in most histories of Nigeria today one looks in vain for any mention that women were even involved. "Riots," the term used by the British, conveys a picture of uncontrolled, irrational action, involving violence to property or persons, or both. It serves to justify the "necessary action to restore order," and it accords with the British picture of the outpouring of Igbo from their villages as some sort of spontaneous

frenzy, explained by the general "excitability" of these "least disciplined" of African peoples (Perham 1937:219). "Aba Riots," in addition, neatly removes women from the picture. What we are left with is "some riots at Aba"— not by women, not involving complex organization, and not ranging over most of southeastern Nigeria.

To the British Commissions of Enquiry established to investigate the events, the Igbo as a whole were felt to be dissatisfied with the general system of administration. The women simply were seen as expressing this underlying general dissatisfaction. The British explanation for the fact that women rather than men "rioted" was twofold: the women were aroused by a rumor that they would be taxed at a time of declining profits from the palm products trade; and they believed themselves to be immune from danger because they thought British soldiers would not fire on women (Perham 1937:213–217). The possibility that women might have acted because as women they were particularly distressed by the Native Administration system does not seem to have been taken any more seriously by the Commissions than women's demands in testimony that they be included in the Native Courts (Leith-Ross 1939:165).

The term "Women's War," in contrast to "Aba Riots," retains both the presence and the significance of the women, for the word "war" in this context derived from the pidgin English expression "making war," an institutionalized form of punishment employed by Igbo women and also known as "sitting on a man." To "sit on" or "make war on" a man involved gathering at his compound at a previously agreed-upon time, dancing, singing scurrilous songs detailing the women's grievances against him (and often insulting him along the way by calling his manhood into question), banging on his hut with the pestles used for pounding yams, and, in extreme cases, tearing up his hut (which usually meant pulling the roof off). This might be done to a man who particularly mistreated his wife, who violated the women's market rules, or who persistently let his cows eat the women's crops. The women would stay at his hut all night and day, if necessary, until he repented and promised to mend his ways (Leith-Ross 1939: 109; Harris 1940: 146–48).[5]

"Women's War" thus conveys an action by women that is also an extension of their traditional method for settling grievances with men who had acted badly toward them. Understood from the Igbo perspective, this term confirms the existence of Igbo women's traditional institutions, for "making war" was the ultimate sanction available to women for enforcing their judgments. The use of the word "war" in this specifically Igbo sense directs attention to the existence of those female political and economic institutions that were never taken into account by the British, and that still have not been sufficiently recognized by contemporary social scientists writing about the development of nationalist movements.

Conventionally, Western influence has been seen as "emancipating" African women through (1) the weakening of kinship bonds; (2) the provision of "free choice" in Christian monogamous marriage; (3) the suppression of "barbarous" practices (female circumcision, ostracism of mothers of twins, slavery); (4) the opening of schools; and (5) the introduction of modern medicine, hygiene, and (sometimes) female suffrage. What has not been seen by Westerners is that for some African women—and Igbo women are a striking example—actual or potential autonomy, economic independence, and political power did not grow out of Western influences but existed already in traditional "tribal" life. To the extent that Igbo women have participated in any political action—whether anticolonial or nationalist struggles, local community development, or the Biafran war—it has been not so much because of the influence of Western values as despite that influence.

TRADITIONAL IGBO POLITICAL INSTITUTIONS

In traditional Igbo society, women did not have a political role equal to that of men. But they did have a role—or more accurately, a

series of roles—despite the patrilineal organization of Igbo society. Their possibilities of participating in traditional politics must be examined in terms of both structures and values. Also involved is a consideration of what it means to talk about "politics" and "political roles" in a society that has no differentiated, centralized governmental institutions.

Fallers (1963) suggests that for such societies, it is necessary to view "the polity or political system . . . not as a concretely distinct part of the social system, but rather as a functional aspect of the whole social system: that aspect concerned with making and carrying out decisions regarding public policy, by whatever institutional means." Fallers's definition is preferable to several other functionalist definitions because it attempts to give some content to the category "political." Examples will make this clear. Let us take a society that has no set of differentiated political institutions to which we can ascribe Weber's "monopoly of the legitimate use of physical force within a given territory," and yet that holds together in reasonable order; we ask the question, What are the mechanisms of social control? To this may be added a second question, based on the notion that a basic governmental function is "authoritative allocation": What are the mechanisms that authoritatively allocate goods and services? A third common notion of politics is concerned with power relationships, and so we also ask, Who has power (or influence) over whom?

The problem with all of these approaches is that they are at the same time too broad and too narrow. If everything in a society that promotes order, resolves conflicts, allocates goods, or involves the power of one person over another is "political," then we have hardly succeeded in distinguishing the "political" as a special kind of activity or area or relationship. Igbo women certainly played a role in promoting order and resolving conflicts (Green 1947: 178–216; Leith-Ross 1939: 97, 106–9), but that does not make them political actors. In response to each of those broad definitions, we can still ask, Is this mechanism of social control or allocation, or this power relationship, a *political* mechanism or relationship? In answering that question, Fallers provides some help. It is their relationship to public policy that makes mechanisms, relationships, or activities "political."

There are many different concepts of "public" in Western thought. We will consider only two, chosen because we can possibly apply them to Igbo politics without producing a distorted picture. There seem to be actions taken, and distinctions made, in Igbo politics and language that make it not quite so ethnocentric to try to use these Western concepts. One notion of "public" relates it to issues that are of concern to the whole community; ends served by "political functions" are beneficial to the community as a whole. Although different individuals or groups may seek different resolutions of problems or disputes, the "political" can nevertheless be seen as encompassing all those human concerns and problems that are common to all the members of the community, or at least to large numbers of them. "Political" problems are shared problems that are appropriately dealt with through group action— their resolutions are collective, not individual. This separates them from "purely personal" problems. The second notion of "public" is that which is distinguished from "secret," that is, open to everyone's view, accessible to all members of the community. The settling of questions that concern the welfare of the community in a "public" way necessitates the sharing of "political knowledge"— the knowledge needed for participation in political discussion and decision. A system in which public policy is made publicly and the relevant knowledge is shared widely contrasts sharply with those systems in which a privileged few possess the relevant knowledge—whether priestly mysteries or bureaucratic expertise— and therefore control policy decisions.

Traditional Igbo society was predominantly patrilineal and segmental. People lived in "villages" composed of the scattered compounds of relatively close patrilineal kinsmen; and related villages formed what are usually referred to as "village groups," the largest functional political unit. Forde and Jones (1950: 9, 39) found between 4,000 and 5,000 village groups, ranging in population from several hundred to several thousand persons. Political power was diffuse, and leadership was fluid and informal. Community decisions were made and disputes settled through a variety of gatherings (villagewide assemblies; women's meetings; age grades; secret and title societies; contribution clubs; lineage groups; and congregations at funerals, markets, or annual rituals) as well as through appeals to oracles and diviners (Afigbo 1972: 13–36).[6] Decisions were made by discussion until mutual agreement was reached. Any adult present who had something to say on the matter under discussion was entitled to speak, so long as he or she said something that the others considered worth listening to; as the Igbo say, "A case forbids no one." Leaders were those who had "mouth"; age was respected, but did not confer leadership unless accompanied by wisdom and the ability to speak well. In village assemblies, after much discussion, a small group of elders retired for "consultation" and then offered a decision for the approval of the assembly (Uchendu 1965: 41–44; Green 1947: chaps. 7–11; Harris 1940: 142–43).

In some areas, the assemblies are said to have been of all adult males; in other areas, women reportedly participated in the assemblies, but were less likely to speak unless involved in the dispute and less likely to take part in "consultation." Women may have been among the "arbitrators" that disputants invited to settle particular cases; however, if one party to the dispute appealed to the village as a whole, male elders would have been more likely to offer the final settlement (Green 1947: 107, 112–13, 116–29, 169, 199). Age grades existed in most Igbo communities, but their functions varied; the predominant pattern seems to have been for young men's age grades to carry out decisions of the village assembly with regard to such matters as clearing paths, building bridges, or collecting fines (Uchendu 1965: 43). There was thus no distinction among what we call executive, legislative, and judicial activities, and no political authority to issue commands. The settling of a dispute could merge into a discussion of a new "rule," and acceptance by the disputants and the group hearing the dispute was necessary for the settlement of anything. Only within a family compound could an individual demand obedience to orders; there the compound head offered guidance, aid, and protection to members of his family, and in return received respect, obedience, and material tokens of good will. Neither was there any distinction between the religious and the political: rituals and "political" discussions were interwoven in patterns of action to promote the good of the community; and rituals, too, were performed by various groups of women, men, and women and men together (Afigbo 1972; Meek 1957: 98–99, 105; Uchendu 1965: 39–40).

Matters dealt with in the village assembly were those of common concern to all. They could be general problems for which collective action was appropriate (for example, discussion might center on how to make the village market bigger than those of neighboring villages); or they could be conflicts that threatened the unity of the village (for example, a dispute between members of different families, or between the men and the women) (Harris 1940: 142–43; Uchendu 1965: 34, 42–43). It is clear, then, that the assembly dealt with public policy publicly. The mode of discourse made much use of proverbs, parables, and metaphors drawn from the body of Igbo tradition and familiar to all Igbo from childhood. Influential speech involved the creative and skillful use of this tradition to provide counsel and justification—to assure others that a certain course of action was both a wise thing to do and a right thing to do. The accessibility (the "public" nature) of this knowledge is itself indicated by an Igbo proverb: "If you tell a proverb to a fool, he will ask you its meaning." Fools were excluded from the political community, but women were not.[7]

Women as well as men thus had access to political participation; for women as well as for men, public status was to a great extent achieved, not ascribed. A woman's status was determined more by her own achievements than by those of her husband. The resources available to men were greater, however; thus, although a woman might rank higher among women than her husband did among men, very few women could afford the fees and feasts involved in taking the highest titles, a major source of prestige (Meek 1957: 203). Men "owned" the most profitable crops and received the bulk of the money from bridewealth. Moreover, if they were compound heads, they received presents from compound members. Through the patrilineage, they controlled the land. After providing farms for their wives, they could lease excess land for a good profit. Men also did more of the long-distance trading, which had a higher rate of profit than did local and regional trading, which was almost entirely in women's hands (Green 1947: 32–42).

Women were entitled to sell the surplus of their own crops. They also received the palm kernels as their share of the palm produce (they processed the palm oil for the men to sell). They might also sell prepared foods, or the products of women's special skills (processed salt, pots, baskets). All the profits were theirs to keep (Leith-Ross 1939: 90–92, 138–39, 143). But these increments of profit were relatively low. Since the higher titles commonly needed to ensure respect for village leaders required increasingly higher fees and expenses, women's low profits restricted their access to villagewide leadership. Almost all of those who took the higher titles were men, and most of the leaders in villagewide discussions and decisions were men (Green 1947: 169; Uchendu 1965: 41). Women, therefore, came out as second-class citizens. Though status and the political influence it could bring were "achieved," and though there were no formal limits to women's political power, men by their ascriptive status (membership in the patrilineage) acquired wealth that gave them a head start and a lifelong advantage over women. The Igbo say that "a child who washes his hands clean deserves to eat with his elders" (Uchendu 1965: 19).

What they do not say is that at birth some children are given water and some are not.

WOMEN'S POLITICAL INSTITUTIONS

Though women's associations are best described for the south—the area of the Women's War—their existence is reported for most other areas of Igboland, and Forde and Jones made the general observation that "women's associations express their disapproval and secure their demands by collective public demonstrations, including ridicule, satirical singing and dancing, and group strikes" (1950: 21).

Two sorts of women's associations are relevant politically: those of the *inyemedi* (wives of a lineage) and of the *umuada* (daughters of a lineage). Since traditional Igbo society was predominantly patrilocal and exogamous, almost all adult women in a village would be wives (there would also probably be some divorced or widowed "daughters" who had returned home to live). Women of the same natal village or village group (and therefore of the same lineage) might marry far and wide, but they would come together periodically in meetings often called *ogbo* (an Igbo word for "gathering"). The *umuada's* most important ritual function was at funerals of lineage members, since no one could have a proper funeral without their voluntary ritual participation—a fact that gave women a significant measure of power. The *umuada* invoked this power in helping to settle intralineage disputes among their "brothers," as well as disputes between their natal and marital lineages. Since these gatherings were held in rotation among the villages into which members had married, they formed an important part of the communication network of Igbo women (Okonjo 1974: 25; Olisa 1971: 24–27; Green 1947: 217–29).

The companion grouping to the *umuada* was the *inyemedi*, the wives of the lineage, who came together in villagewide gatherings that during the colonial period came to be called *mikiri* or *mitiri* (the Igbo version of the English "meeting"). *Mikiri* were thus gatherings of women based on common residence rather than on common birth, as in the case of *ogbo*. The *mikiri* appears to have performed the major role in daily self-rule among women and to have articulated women's interests as opposed to those of men. *Mikiri* provided women with a forum in which to develop their political talents and with a means for protecting their interests as traders, farmers, wives, and mothers (Green 1947; Leith-Ross 1939; Harris 1940; Okonjo 1974). In *mikiri*, women made rules about markets' crops, and livestock that applied to men as well as women; and they exerted pressure to maintain moral norms among women. They heard complaints from wives about mistreatment by husbands, and discussed how to deal with problems they were having with "the men" as a whole. They also made decisions about the rituals addressed to the female aspect of the village's guardian spirit, and about rituals for the protection of the fruitfulness of women and of their farms. If fines for violations or if repeated requests to husbands and elders were ignored, women might "sit on" an offender or go on strike. The latter might involve refusing to cook, to take care of small children, or to have sexual relations with their husbands. Men regarded the *mikiri* as legitimate; and the use of the more extreme sanctions—though rare—was well remembered.

Though both *ogbo* and *mikiri* served to articulate and protect women's interests, it is probably more accurate to see these groups as sharing in diffused political authority than to see them as acting only as pressure groups for women's interests. Okonjo [1976] argues . . . that traditional Igbo society had a "dual-sex political system"; that is, there was a dual system of male and female political-religious institutions, each sex having both its own autonomous sphere of authority and an area of shared responsibilities. Thus, women settled disputes among women, but also made decisions and rules affecting men. They had the right to enforce their decisions and rules by using forms of group ostracism similar to those used by men. In a society of such diffuse political authority, it would be misleading to call only a village assembly of men a "public" gathering, as most Western observers unquestioningly do; among the Igbo, a gathering of adult women must also be accepted as a public gathering.

COLONIAL "PENETRATION"

Into this system of diffuse authority, fluid and informal leadership, shared rights of enforcement, and a more or less stable balance of male and female power, the British tried to introduce ideas of "native administration" derived from colonial experience with chiefs and emirs in northern Nigeria. Southern Nigeria was declared a protectorate in 1900, but ten years passed before the conquest was effective. As colonial power was established in what the British perceived as a situation of "ordered anarchy," Igboland was divided into Native Court Areas that violated the autonomy of villages by lumping together many unrelated villages. British District Officers were to preside over the courts, but they were not always present because there were more courts than officers. The Igbo membership was formed by choosing from each village a "representative" who was given a warrant of office. These Warrant Chiefs also constituted what was called the Native Authority. The Warrant Chiefs were required to see that the orders of the District Officers were executed in their own villages, and they were the only link between the colonial power and the people (Afigbo 1972: 13–36, 207–48).

In the first place, it was a violation of Igbo concepts to have one man represent the village; and it was even more of a violation that he should give orders to everyone else. The people obeyed the Warrant Chief when they had to, since British power backed him up. In some places Warrant Chiefs were lineage heads or wealthy men who were already leaders in the village. But in many places they were simply ambitious, opportunistic young men who put themselves forward as friends of the conquerors. Even where the Warrant

Chief was not corrupt, he was still, more than anything else, an agent of the British. The people avoided using Native Courts when they could do so, but Warrant Chiefs could force cases into the Native Courts and fine people for infractions of rules. Because he had the ear of the British, the Warrant Chief himself could violate traditions and even British rules and get away with it (Anene 1967: 259; Meek 1957: 328–30).

Women suffered particularly under the arbitrary rule of Warrant Chiefs, who reportedly took women to marry without allowing them the customary right to refuse a particular suitor. They also helped themselves to the women's agricultural produce and domestic animals (Onwuteaka 1965: 274). Recommendations for reform of the system were made almost from its inception both by junior officers in the field and by senior officers sent out from headquarters to investigate. But no real improvements were made. An attempt by the British in 1918 to make the Native Courts more "native" by abolishing the District Officers' role as presiding court officials had little effect, and that mostly bad. Removing the District Officers from the courts simply left more power in the hands of corrupt Warrant Chiefs and the increasingly powerful Court Clerks. The latter, intended to be "servants of the court," were able in some cases to dominate the courts because of their monopoly of expertise—namely, literacy (Meek 1957: 329; Gailey 1970: 66–74).

THE WOMEN'S WAR

In 1925, the British decided to introduce direct taxation in order to create the Native Treasury, which was supposed to pay for improvements in the Native Administration, in accordance with the British imperial philosophy that the colonized should pay the costs of colonization. Prices in the palm trade were high, and the tax— on adult males—was set accordingly. Taxes were collected without widespread trouble, although there were "tax riots" in Warri Province (west of the Niger) in 1927.

In 1929, a zealous Assistant District Officer in Bende division of Owerri Province, apparently acting on his own initiative, decided to "tighten up" the census registers by recounting households and property. He told the Chiefs that there was no plan to increase taxes or to tax women. But the counting of women and their property raised fears that women were to be taxed, particularly because the Bende District Officer had lied earlier when the men were counted and had told the men that they were not going to be taxed. The women, therefore, naturally did not believe these reassurances. The taxation rumor spread quickly through the women's communication networks, and meetings of women took place in various market squares, which were the common places for women to have large meetings. In the Oloko Native Court Area—one of the areas of deception about the men's tax—the women leaders, Ikonnia, Nwannedie, and Nwugo, called a general meeting at Orie market. Here it was decided that as long as only men were approached in a compound and asked for information the women would do nothing. If any woman was approached, she was to raise the alarm; then the women would meet again to decide what to do. But they wanted clear evidence that women were to be taxed (Afigbo 1972; Gailey 1970: 107–8).

On November 23, an agent of the Oloko Warrant Chief, Okugo, entered a compound and told one of the married women, Nwanyeruwa, to count her goats and sheep. She replied angrily, "Was your mother counted?" at which "they closed, seizing each other by the throat" (Perham 1937: 207). Nwanyeruwa's report to the Oloko women convinced them that they were to be taxed. Messengers were sent to neighboring areas, and women streamed into Oloko from all over Owerri Province. They "sat on" Okugo and demanded his cap of office. They massed in protest at the District Office and succeeded in getting written assurances that they were not to be taxed. After several days of mass protest meetings, they also succeeded in get-

ting Okugo arrested, tried, and convicted of "spreading news likely to cause alarm" and of physical assault on the women. He was sentenced to two years' imprisonment (Gailey 1970: 108–13).

News of this victory spread rapidly through the market-*mikiri-ogbo* network, and women in many areas then attempted to get rid of their Warrant Chiefs and the Native Administration itself. Nwanyeruwa became something of a heroine as reports of her resistance spread. Money poured in from grateful women from villages scattered over a wide area but linked by kinship to Nwanyeruwa's marital village. Nwanyeruwa herself, however, was "content to allow" leadership in her area to be exercised by someone else. The money collected was used not for her but for delegates going to meetings of women throughout southern Igboland to coordinate the Women's War.

The British ended the rebellion only by using large numbers of police and soldiers—and, on one occasion, Boy Scouts. Although the shootings in mid-December and the growing numbers of police and soldiers in the area led the women to halt most of their activities, disturbances continued into 1930. The "disaffected areas"—all of Owerri and Calabar provinces—were occupied by government forces. Punitive expeditions burned or demolished compounds, took provisions from the villages to feed the troops, and confiscated property in payment of fines levied arbitrarily against villages in retribution for damages (Gailey 1970: 135–37).

During the investigations that followed the Women's War, the British discovered the communication network that had been used to spread the rumor of taxation. But that did not lead them to inquire further into how it came to pass that Igbo women had engaged in concerted action under grassroots leadership, had agreed on demands, and had materialized by the thousands at Native Administration centers dressed and adorned in the same unusual way—all wearing short loincloths, all carrying sticks wreathed with palm fronds, and all having their faces smeared with charcoal or ashes and their heads bound with young ferns. Unbeknown to the British, this was the dress and adornment signifying "war," the sticks being used to invoke the power of the female ancestors (Harris 1940: 143–45, 147–48; Perham 1937: 207ff; Meek 1957: ix).

The report of the Commission of Enquiry exonerating the soldiers who fired on the women cited the "savage passions" of the "mobs"; and one military officer told the Commission that "he had never seen crowds in such a state of frenzy." Yet these "frenzied mobs" injured no one seriously, which the British found "surprising"; but then the British did not understand that the women were engaged in a traditional practice with traditional rules and limitations, only carried out in this instance on a much larger scale than in precolonial times.[8]

REFORMS—BUT NOT FOR WOMEN

The British failure to recognize the Women's War as a collective response to the abrogation of rights resulted in a failure to ask whether women might have had a role in the traditional political system that should be incorporated into the institutions of colonial government. Because the women—and the men—regarded the investigations as attempts to discover whom to punish, they volunteered no information about women's organizations. But would the British have understood those organizations if they had? The discovery of the market network had suggested no further lines of inquiry. The majority of District Officers thought that the men had organized the women's actions and were secretly directing them. The women's demands that the Native Courts no longer hear cases and that "all white men should go to their own country"—or at least that women should serve on the Native Courts and a woman be appointed a District Officer—were in line with the power of women in traditional Igbo society but were regarded by the British as irrational and ridiculous (Gailey 1970: 130ff; Leith-Ross 1939: 165; Perham 1937: 165ff).

The reforms instituted in 1933 therefore ignored the women's traditional political role, though they did make some adjustments to traditional Igbo male and male-dominated political forms. The number of Native Court Areas was greatly increased, and their boundaries were arranged to conform roughly to traditional divisions. Warrant Chiefs were replaced by "massed benches," which allowed large numbers of judges to sit at one time. In most cases it was left up to the villages to decide whom and how many to send. Though this benefitted the women by eliminating the corruption of the Warrant Chiefs, and thus made their persons and property more secure, it provided no outlet for collective action, their real base of power (Perham 1937: 365ff).

In 1901 the British had declared all jural institutions except the Native Courts illegitimate, but it was only in the years following the 1933 reforms that Native Administration local government became effective enough to make that declaration at all meaningful. The British had also outlawed "self-help"—the use of force by anyone but the government to punish wrongdoers. And the increasingly effective enforcement of this ban eliminated the women's ultimate weapon: "sitting on a man." In attempting to create specialized political institutions on the Western model, with participation on the basis of individual achievement, the British created a system in which there was no place for group solidarity, no possibility of dispersed and shared political authority or power of enforcement, and thus very little place for women (Leith-Ross 1939: 109–10, 163, 214). As in the village assemblies, women could not compete with men for leadership in the reformed Native Administration because they lacked the requisite resources. This imbalance in resources was increased by other facets of British colonialism—economic "penetration" and missionary influence. All three—colonial government, foreign investment, and the church—contributed to the growth of a system of political and economic stratification that made community decision-making less "public" in both senses we have discussed and that led to the current concentration of national political power in the hands of a small, educated, wealthy, male elite. For though we are here focusing on the political results of colonialism, they must be seen as part of the whole system of imposed class and sex stratification.

MISSIONARY INFLUENCE

Christian missions were established in Igboland in the late nineteenth century. They had few converts at first, but by the 1930's their influence was significant, though generally limited to the young (Leith-Ross 1939: 109–18; Meek 1957: xv). A majority of Igbo eventually "became Christians," for they had to profess Christianity in order to attend mission schools. Regardless of how nominal their membership was, they had to obey the rules to remain in good standing, and one rule was to avoid "pagan" rituals. Women were discouraged from attending meetings where traditional rituals were performed or where money was collected for the rituals, which in effect meant all *mikiri, ogbo,* and many other types of gatherings (Ajayi 1965: 108–9).

Probably more significant, since *mikiri* were losing some of their political functions anyway, was mission education. The Igbo came to see English and Western education as increasingly necessary for political leadership—needed to deal with the British and their law—and women had less access to this new knowledge than men had. Boys were more often sent to school than girls, for a variety of reasons generally related to their favored position in the patrilineage, including the fact that they, not their sisters, would be expected to support their parents in their old age. But even when girls did go, they tended not to receive the same type of education. In mission schools, and increasingly in special "training homes" that dispensed with most academic courses, the girls were taught European domestic skills and the Bible, often in the vernacular. The missionaries' avowed purpose in educating girls was to train them for Christian marriage and motherhood, not for jobs or for citizenship. Missionaries were not necessarily against women's participation

in politics; clergy in England, as in America, could be found supporting women's suffrage. But in Africa their concern was the church, and for the church they needed Christian families. Therefore, Christian wives and mothers, not female political leaders, were the missions' aim. As Mary Slessor, the influential Calabar missionary, said: "God-like motherhood is the finest sphere for women, and the way to the redemption of the world."[9] As the English language and other knowledge of "book" became necessary to political life, women were increasingly cut out and policy-making became less public.

ECONOMIC COLONIALISM

The traditional Igbo division of labor—in which women owned their surplus crops and their market profits, while men controlled the more valuable yams and palm products and did more long-distance trading—was based on a subsistence economy. Small surpluses could be accumulated, but these were generally not used for continued capital investment. Rather, in accord with traditional values, the surplus was used for social rather than economic gain: it was returned to the community through fees and feasts for rituals for title-taking, weddings, funerals, and other ceremonies, or through projects to help the community "get up." One became a "big man" or a "big woman" not by hoarding one's wealth but by spending it on others in prestige-winning ways (Uchendu 1965: 34; Meek 1957: 111).

Before the Pax Britannica, Igbo women had been active traders in all but a few areas (one such was Afikpo, where women farmed but did not trade).[10] The ties of exogamous marriage among patrilineages, the cross-cutting networks of women providing channels for communication and conciliation, and the ritual power of female members of patrilineages all enabled the traditional system to deal with conflicts with relatively little warfare (Anene 1967: 214ff; Green 1947: 91, 152, 177, 230–32). Conflict also took the nonviolent form of mutual insults in obscene and satirical songs (Nwoga 1971: 33–35, 40–42); and even warfare itself was conducted within limits, with weapons and actions increasing in seriousness in inverse proportion to the closeness of kinship ties. Women from mutually hostile village groups who had married into the same patrilineage could if necessary act as "protectors" for each other so that they could trade in "stranger" markets (Green 1947: 151). Women also protected themselves by carrying the stout sticks they used as pestles for pounding yams (the same ones carried in the Women's War). Even after European slave-trading led to an increase in danger from slave-hunters (as well as from headhunters), Igbo women went by themselves to their farms and with other women to market, with their pestles as weapons for physical protection (Esike 1965: 13).

The Pax increased the safety of short- and especially of long-distance trading for Igbo women as for women in other parts of Africa. But the Pax also made it possible for European firms to dominate the market economy. Onwuteaka argues that one cause of the Women's War was Igbo women's resentment of the monopoly British firms had on buying, a monopoly that allowed them to fix prices and adopt methods of buying that increased their own profits at the women's expense (1965: 278). Women's petty trading grew to include European products, but for many women the accumulated surplus remained small, often providing only subsistence and a few years' school fees for some of their children—the preference for sending boys to school further disadvantaging the next generation of women (Mintz 1971: 251–68; Boserup 1970: 92–95). A few women have become "big traders," dealing in £1000 lots of European goods, but women traders remain for the most part close to subsistence level. Little is open to West African women in towns except trading, brewing, or prostitution, unless they are among the tiny number who have special vocational or professional training (for example, as dressmakers, nurses, or teachers) (Boserup 1970: 85–101, 106–38). The "modern" economic sector, like the "modern" political sector, is dominated by

men, women's access being limited "by their low level of literacy and by the general tendency to give priority to men in employment recruitment to the modern sector" (Boserup 1970: 99).

Women outside urban areas—the great majority of women—find themselves feeding their children by farming with their traditional digging sticks while men are moving into cash-cropping (with tools and training from "agricultural development programs"), migrant wage-labor, and trading with Europeans (Boserup 1970: 53–61, 87–99; Mintz 1971: 248–51). Thus, as Mintz suggests, "while the economic growth advanced by Westernization has doubtless increased opportunities for (at least some) female traders, it may also and simultaneously limit the range of their activities, as economic changes outside the internal market system continue to multiply" (p. 265). To the extent that economic opportunities for Africans in the "modern" sector continue to grow, women will become relatively more dependent economically on men and will be unlikely to "catch up" for a very long time, even if we accept education as the key. The relative stagnation of African economic "growth," however, suggests that the traditional markets will not disappear or even noticeably shrink, but will continue to be needed by the large numbers of urban migrants living economically marginal lives. Women can thus continue to subsist by petty trading, though they cannot achieve real economic independence from men or gain access to the resources needed for equal participation in community life.

It seems reasonable to see the traditional Igbo division of labor in production as interwoven with the traditional Igbo dispersal of political authority into a dual or "dual-sex" system. It seems equally reasonable to see the disruptions of colonialism as producing a new, similarly interwoven economic-political pattern—but one with stronger male domination of the cash economy and of political life.

To see this relationship, however, is not to explain it. Even if the exclusion of women from the colonial Native Administration and from nationalist politics could be shown to derive from their exclusion from the "modern" economic sector, we would still need to ask why it was men who were offered agricultural training and new tools for cash-cropping, and who are hired in factories and shops in preference to women with the same education. And we would still need to ask why it was chiefly boys who were sent to school, and why their education differed from that provided for girls.

VICTORIANISM AND WOMEN'S INVISIBILITY

At least part of the answer must lie in the values of the colonialists, values that led the British to assume that girls and boys, women and men, should be treated and should behave as people supposedly did in "civilized" Victorian England. Strong male domination was imposed on Igbo society both indirectly, by new economic structures, and directly, by the recruitment of only men into the Native Administration. In addition, the new economic and political structures were supported by the inculcation of sexist ideology in the mission schools.

Not all capitalist, colonialist societies are equally sexist (or racist); but the Victorian society from which the conquerors of Igboland came was one in which the ideology that a woman's place is in the home had hardened into the most rigid form it has taken in recent Western history. Although attacked by feminists, that ideology remained dominant throughout the colonial period and is far from dead today. The ideal of Victorian womanhood—attainable, of course, only by the middle and upper classes, but widely believed in throughout society—was of a sensitive, morally superior being who was the hearthside guardian of Christian virtues and sentiments absent in the outside world. Her mind was not strong enough for the appropriately "masculine" subjects: science, business, and politics.[11] A woman who showed talent in these areas did not challenge any ideas about typical women: the exceptional woman simply had "the brain of a man," as Sir George Goldie said of Mary Kingsley (Gwynn 1932: 252).[12] A thorough investigation of the diaries, journals, reports, and letters of colonial officers and missionaries would be needed to prove that most of them held these Victorian values. But a preliminary reading of biographies, autobiographies, journals, and "reminiscences," plus the evidence of statements about Igbo women at the time of the Women's War, strongly suggests that the colonialists were deflected from any attempt to discover or protect Igbo women's political and economic roles by their assumption that politics and business were not proper, normal places for women.[13]

When Igbo women forced the colonial administrators to recognize their presence during the Women's War, their brief "visibility" was insufficient to shake these assumptions. Their behavior was simply seen as aberrant and inexplicable. When they returned to "normal," they were once again invisible. This inability to "see" what is before one's eyes is strikingly illustrated by an account of a visit by the High Commissioner, Sir Ralph Moor, to Aro Chukwu after the British had destroyed (temporarily) the powerful oracle there: "To Sir Ralph's astonishment, the women of Aro Chukwu solicited his permission to reestablish the Long Juju, which the women intended to control themselves" (Anene 1967: 234). Would Sir Ralph have been "astonished" if, for example, the older men had controlled the oracle before its destruction and the younger men had wanted to take it over?

The feminist movement in England during the colonial era did not succeed in making the absence of women from public life noted as a problem that required a remedy. The movement did not succeed in creating a "feminist" consciousness in any but a few "deviants," and such a consciousness is far from widespread today; for to have a "feminist" consciousness means that one notices the "invisibility" of women. One wonders where the women are—in life and in print. That we have not wondered is an indication of our own ideological bondage to a system of sex and class stratification. What we can see, if we look, is that Igbo men have come to dominate women economically and politically: individual women have become economic auxiliaries to their husbands, and women's groups have become political auxiliaries to nationalist parties. Wives supplement their husbands' incomes but remain economically dependent; women's "branches" have provided votes, money, and participants in street demonstrations for political parties but remain dependent on male leaders for policymaking. Market women's associations were a vital base of support for the early National Council for Nigeria and the Cameroons (NCNC), the party that eventually was to become dominant in Igbo regions (although it began as a truly national party). And though a few market-women leaders were ultimately rewarded for their loyalty to the NCNC by appointment to party or legislative positions, market women's associations never attained a share in policymaking that approached their contribution to NCNC electoral success (Bretton 1966: 61; MacIntosh 1966: 299, 304–9; Sklar 1963: 41–83, 251, 402). The NCNC at first had urged female suffrage throughout the country, an idea opposed by the Northern People's Congress (NPC), dominated by Moslem emirs. Soon, however, the male NCNC leadership gave up pushing for female suffrage in the north (where women have never yet voted) in order to make peace with the NPC and the British and thus insure for themselves a share of power in the postindependence government. During the period between independence in 1960 and the 1966 military coups that ended party rule, some progress was made in education for girls. By 1966, consequently, female literacy in the East was more than 50 percent in some urban areas and at least 15 percent overall—high for Africa, where the overall average is about 10 percent and the rural average may be as low as 2 percent (MacIntosh 1966: 17–37; *West African Pilot*, April 29, 1959; Pool 1972: 238; UNESCO 1968).

Exhortations to greater female participation in "modern life" appeared frequently in the newspapers owned by the NCNC leader, Nnamdi Azikiwe, and a leadership training course for women was begun in 1959 at the Man O' War Bay Training Centre, to be "run on exactly the same lines as the courses for men, with slight modifications," as the *Pilot* put it. The motto of the first class of 22 women was, "What the men can do, the women can" (Van Allen 1974b: 17–20). But there was more rhetoric than reality in these programs for female emancipation. During the period of party politics, no women were elected to regional or national legislatures; those few who were appointed gained favor by supporting "party first," not "women first." Perhaps none of this should be surprising, given the corruption that had come to dominate national party politics (MacIntosh 1966: 299, 612–14; Sklar 1963: 402; Van Allen 1974b: 19–22).

BIAFRA AND BEYOND

On January 15, 1966, a military coup ended the Igbos' relationship with the NCNC: all political parties, and therefore their women's branches, were outlawed. A year and a half later—after the massacres of more than 30,000 Easterners in the North, the flight of more than a million refugees back to the East, a countercoup, and the division of the Igbo-dominated Eastern Region into three states—Biafra declared herself an independent state. In January 1970 she surrendered; the remaining Igbo are now landlocked, oilless, and under military occupation by a Northern-dominated military government.[14] Igbo women demonstrated in the streets to protest the massacres, to urge secession, and, later, to protest Soviet involvement in the war (Ojukwu 1969: 91, 143, 145–46, 245). During the war, the women's market network and other women's organizations maintained a distribution system for what food there was and provided channels for the passage of food and information to the army (Uzoma 1974: 8ff; Akpan 1971: 65–67, 89, 98–99,

128–30). Women joined local civilian-defense militia units and in May 1969 formed a "Women's Front" and called on the Biafran leadership to allow them to enlist in the infantry (Uzoma 1974: 5–8; Ojukwu 1969: 386).

During and after the war, local civilian government continued to exist more or less in the form that evolved under the "reformed" Native Administration. The decentralization produced by the war has by some reports strengthened these local councils, and the absence of many men has strengthened female participation (Peters 1971: 102–3; Adler 1969: 112; Uzoma 1974: 10–12). Thus, at tragic human cost, the war may have made possible a resurgence of female political activity. If this is so, women's participation again stems much more from Igbo tradition than from Western innovation.

It remains to be seen whether Igbo women, or any African women, can gain real political power without the creation of a "modern" version of the traditional "dual-sex" system (which is what Okonjo argues is needed) or without a drastic change in economic structures so that economic equality could support political equality for all women and men, just as economic stratification now supports male domination and female dependence. What seems clear from women's experiences— whether under capitalism, colonialism, or revolutionary socialism—is that formal political and economic equality are not enough. Unless the male members of a liberation movement, a ruling party, or a government themselves develop a feminist consciousness and a commitment to male-female equality, women will end up where they have always been: invisible, except when men, for their own purposes personal or political, look for female bodies.

NOTES

1. This paper is a revised version of papers presented at the 1971 African Studies Association meeting and at the 1974 UCLA African Studies Center Colloquium on "Women and Change in Africa: 1870–1970." I am grateful to Terrence O. Ranger, who organized the UCLA colloquium, and to the other participants (particularly Agnes Aidoo, Jim Brain, Cynthia Brantley, Temma Kaplan, and Margaret Strobel) for their encouragement, useful criticisms, and suggestions.

2. Today the Igbo, numbering about 8.7 million, live mainly in the East-Central State of Nigeria, with some half million in the neighboring Mid-Western State. The area in which they live corresponds approximately to Igboland at the time of the colonial conquest.

3. A number of Ibibio women from Calabar were also drawn into the rebellion, but the mass of the participants were Igbo.

4. Perham 1937: 202–12. Afigbo 1972 and Gailey 1970 give more detailed accounts of the Women's War than does Perham; all three, however, base their descriptions on the reports of the two Commissions of Enquiry, issued as Sessional Papers of the Nigerian Legislative Council (Nos. 12 and 28 of 1930), on the Minutes of Evidence issued with No. 28, and on intelligence reports made in the early 1930's by political officers. Afigbo, an Igbo scholar, provides the most extensive and authoritative account of the three, and he is particularly good on traditional Igbo society.

5. Similar tactics were also used against women for serious offenses (see Leith-Ross 1939: 97).

6. Though there is variation among the Igbo, the general patterns described here apply fairly well to the southern Igbo, those involved in the Women's War. The chief exceptions to the above description occur among the western and riverain Igbo, who have what Afigbo terms a "constitutional village monarchy" system, and among the Afikpo of the Cross River, who have a double-descent system and low female participation in economic and political life (P. Ottenberg 1959 and 1965). The former are more hierarchically organized than other Igbo but are not stratified by sex, having a women's hierarchy parallel to that of the men (Nzirimo 1972); the latter are strongly stratified by sex, with the senior men's age grade dominating community decision-making. Afikpo women's age grades are weak; there is no *mikiri* or, because of the double-descent system, *ogbo* (these terms are defined later in this paper . . . Afikpo women have not traditionally been active in trade; and female status among the Afikpo is generally very low. Afikpo Igbo, unlike almost all other Igbo, have a men's secret society that has "keeping

women in their place" as a major purpose (P. Ottenberg 1959 and 1965).

7. I rely here chiefly on Uchendu 1965 and personal conversations with an Igbo born in Umu-Domi village of Onicha clan, Afikpo division. Some of the ideas about leadership were suggested by Schaar 1970. His discussion of what "humanly meaningful authority" would look like is very suggestive for studies of leadership in "developing" societies.

8. A few older men criticized the women for "flinging sand at their chiefs," but Igbo men generally supported the women though they nonetheless considered it "their fight" against the British. It is also reported that both women and men shared the mistaken belief that the women would not be fired upon because they had observed certain rituals and were carrying the palm-wrapped sticks that invoked the power of the female ancestors. The men had no illusions of immunity for themselves, having vivid memories of the slaughter of Igbo men during the conquest (Perham 1937: 212ff; Anene 1967: 207–24; Esike 1965: 11; Meek 1957: x).

9. For the missionaries' views and purposes, see Ajayi 1965, Basden 1927, Bulifant 1950, Maxwell 1926, and Livingstone n.d.

10. It is an unfortunate accident that the Afikpo Igbo, with their strong sexual stratification, have been used as examples of "the Igbo" or of "the effect of colonialism on women" in widely read articles. Simon Ottenberg's "Ibo Receptivity to Change" is particularly misleading, since it is about "all" Igbo. There is one specific mention of women: "The social and economic independence of women is much greater in some areas than in others." True, but the social and economic independence of women is much greater in virtually *all* other Igbo groups than it is in Afikpo, where the Ottenbergs did fieldwork. There are said to be "a variety of judicial techniques" used, but all the examples given are of men's activities. There is a list of non-kinship organizations, but no women's organizations are listed. Sanday's otherwise useful and thought-provoking article (1973) both takes the Afikpo as "the" Igbo and exaggerates the amount of change in female status that female trading brought about. Phoebe Ottenberg, Sanday's ultimate source on Afikpo women, described the change in female status as existing "chiefly on the domestic rather than the general level," with the "men's position of religious,

moral, and legal authority . . . in no way threatened" (1959: 223). For examples of precolonial female trading in Igboland and elsewhere, see Little 1973 (particularly p. 46, n. 32); Uchendu 1965; Van Allen 1974b: 5–9; Dike 1956; and Jones 1963.

11. The fact that Englishwomen of the "lower classes" had to work in the fields, in the mills, in the mines, or on the street did not stop the colonialists from carrying their ideal to Africa, or from condemning urban prostitution there (just as they did at home) without acknowledging their contribution to its origin or continuation.

12. Mary Kingsley, along with other elite female "exceptions" who influenced African colonial policy (e.g., Flora Shaw Lugard and Margery Perham), held the same values that men did, at least in regard to women's roles. They did not expect ordinary women to have political power any more than men expected them to, and they showed no particular concern for African women.

13. For examples of this attitude among those who were not missionaries, see Anene 1967: 222–34; Crocker 1936; Meek 1957; Kingsley 1897; Perham 1960; and Wood 1960.

14. The attitude of the Northern emirs who now again dominate the Nigerian government is perhaps indicated by their order in June 1973 that single women get married or leave Northern Nigeria because Moslem religious authorities had decided that the North African drought was caused by prostitution and immorality. Landlords were ordered not to let rooms to single women, and many unmarried women were reported to have fled their home areas (*Agence France-Presse*, as reported in *The San Francisco Chronicle*, June 23, 1973). In late 1975 the military government appointed a 50-man body to draft a constitution for Nigeria's return to civilian rule. As of this writing women's protests have produced no changes in its membership.

REFERENCES

Adler, Renate. 1969. "Letter from Biafra," *The New Yorker*, Oct. 4.

Afigbo, A. E. 1972. The Warrant Chiefs: Indirect Rule in South-Eastern Nigeria, 1891–1929. London.

Ajayi, J. F. Ade. 1965. Christian Missions in Nigeria, 1841–1891: The Making of a New Elite. Evanston, Ill.

Akpan, Ntieyong U. 1971. The Struggle for Secession, 1966–1970. London.

Anene, J. C. 1967. Southern Nigeria in Transition, 1885–1906. New York.

Basden, G. T. 1927. Edith Warner of the Niger. London.

Boserup, Ester. 1970. Woman's Role in Economic Development. New York.

Bretton, Henry L. 1966. "Political Influence in Southern Nigeria," in Herbert J. Spiro, ed., Africa: The Primacy of Politics. New York.

Bulifant, Josephine C. 1950. Forty Years in the African Bush. Grand Rapids, Mich.

Crocker, W. R. 1936. Nigeria: A Critique of British Colonial Administration. London.

Dike, K. Onwuka. 1956. Trade and Politics in the Niger Delta, 1830–1885. London.

Esike, S. O. 1965. "The Aba Riots of 1929." *African Historian* (Ibadan), 1, no. 3.

Fallers, Lloyd Ashton. 1963. "Political Sociology and the Anthropological Study of African Politics," *Archives Européennes de Sociologie.*

Forde, Daryll, and G. I. Jones. 1950. The Ibo- and Ibibio- Speaking Peoples of South-Eastern Nigeria. London.

Gailey, Harry A. 1970. The Road to Aba, New York.

Green, M. M. 1947. Igbo Village Affairs. London.

Gwynn, Stephen. 1932. The Life of Mary Kingsley. London.

Harris, J. S. 1940. "The Position of Women in a Nigerian Society," *Transactions of the New York Academy of Sciences.* New York.

Jones, G. I. 1963. The Trading States of the Oil Rivers. London.

Kingsley, Mary H. 1897. Travels in West Africa. London.

Leith-Ross, Sylvia. 1939. African Women: A Study of the Ibo of Nigeria. London.

Little, Kenneth. 1973. African Women in Towns. London.

Livingstone, W. P. n.d. Mary Slessor of Calabar. New York.

MacIntosh, John P., ed. 1966. Nigerian Government and Politics. London.

Maxwell, J. Lowry. 1926. Nigeria: The Land, the People and Christian Progress. London.

Meek, C. K. 1957. Law and Authority in a Nigerian Tribe. London.

Mintz, Sidney W. 1971. "Men, Women, and Trade," *Comparative Studies in Society and History,* 13.

Nwoga, D. I. 1971. "The Concept and Practice of Satire among the Igbo," *Conch,* 3, no. 2.

Nzirimo, Ikenna. 1972. Studies in Ibo Political Systems: Chieftaincy and Politics in Four Niger States. Berkeley, Calif.

Ojukwu, C. Odumegwu. 1969. Biafra. New York.

Okonjo, Kamene, 1974. "Political Systems with Bisexual Functional Roles—The Case of Women's Participation in Politics in Nigeria." Paper presented at the Annual Meeting of the American Political Science Association, Chicago.

———. 1976. "The Dual-Sex Political System in Operation: Igbo Women and Community Politics in Midwestern Nigeria," In Nancy J. Hafkin, and Edna Bay, eds., Women in Africa: Studies in Social and Economic Change. Stanford.

Olisa, Michael S. O. 1971. "Political Culture and Political Stability in Traditional Igbo Society," *Conch, 3, no. 2.*

Onwuteaka, J. C. 1965. "The Aba Riot of 1929 and Its Relation to the System of 'Indirect Rule,'" *The Nigerian Journal of Economic and Social Studies,* November.

Ottenberg, Phoebe V. 1959. "The Changing Economic Position of Women Among the Afikpo Ibo," in W. R. Bascom and M. J. Herskovits, eds., Continuity and Change in African Cultures. Chicago.

———. 1965. "The Afikpo Ibo of Eastern Nigeria," in James L. Gibbs, Jr., ed., Peoples of Africa. New York.

Ottenberg, Simon. 1959. "Ibo Receptivity to Change," in W. R. Bascom and M. J. Herskovits, eds., Continuity and Change in African Cultures. Chicago.

Perham, Margery. 1937. Native Administration in Nigeria. London.

———. 1960. Lugard: The Years of Authority, 1898–1945. London.

Peters, Helen. 1971. "Reflections on the Preservation of Igbo Folk Literature," *Conch, 3, no. 2.*

Pool, Janet E. 1972. "A Cross-Comparative Study of Aspects of Conjugal Behavior Among Women of Three West African Countries," *Canadian Journal of African Studies, 6, no. 2.*

Sanday, Peggy R. 1973. "Toward a Theory of the Status of Women," *American Anthropologist, 75, no. 5.*

Schaar, John H. 1970. "Legitimacy in the Modern State," in Philip Green and Sanford Levinson, eds., Power and Community. New York.

Sklar, Richard. 1963. Nigerian Political Parties. Princeton, N.J.

Uchendu, Victor C. 1965. The Igbo of Southeast Nigeria. New York.

United Nations Economic and Social Council (UNESCO). 1968. "Problems of Plan Implementation: Development Planning and Economic Integration in Africa."

Uzoma, Chinwe. 1974. "The Role of Women in the Nigerian/Biafran Civil War as Seen Through My Experiences Then." Unpublished personal communication to Judith Van Allen.

Van Allen, Judith. 1972. "'Sitting on a Man': Colonialism and the Lost Political Institutions of Igbo Women," *Canadian Journal of African Studies*, 6, no. 2.

————. 1974a. "African Women—Modernizing into Dependence?" Paper presented at the conference on "Social and Political Change: The Role of Women," sponsored by the University of California, Santa Barbara, and the Center for the Study of Democratic Institutions.

————. 1974b. "From Aba to Biafra: Women's Associations and Political Power in Eastern Nigeria." Paper presented at the UCLA African Studies Center Colloquium on Women and Change in Africa, 1870–1970.

————. 1974c. *"Memsahib, Militante, Femme Libre: Political and Apolitical Styles of African Women,"* in Jane Jaquette, ed., Women in Politics. New York.

Wood, A. H. St. John. 1960. "Nigeria: Fifty Years of Political Development among the Ibos," in Raymond Apthorpe, ed., From Tribal Rule to Modern Government. Lusaka, Northern Rhodesia.

Debating the Impact of Development on Women

Sue Ellen M. Charlton

Since 1970, a debate has been under way concerning the effects of change in developing countries on the well-being of women. In the study that marked a turning point in the thinking about women in Third World countries, Ester Boserup argued that a single technological change in farming could entail a "radical shift in sex roles in agriculture." For example, in areas where the old methods of cultivation have been replaced by plow cultivation, men have taken over the plowing, and men rather than women now operate the main farming equipment. If men are subsequently taught new methods of cultivation, or if they receive credit, new seed varieties, or tools to increase their agricultural productivity, the gap between the productivity—and income—of men and women widens.

Reprinted with permission from Sue Ellen M. Charlton, *Women in Third World Development* (Boulder: Westview Press, 1984), pp. 32–38.

Such a development has the unavoidable effect of enhancing the prestige of men and of lowering the status of women. It is the men who do the modern things. They handle industrial inputs while women perform the degrading manual jobs; men often have the task of spreading fertilizer in the fields, while women spread manure; men ride the bicycle and drive the lorry, while women carry headloads, as did their grandmothers. In short, men represent modern farming in the village, women represent the old drudgery.[1]

Much of the negative impact of development may be due to changes it provokes in family structures. The less complex the level of development, the more agricultural production and distribution are directly linked to the family—women and children as well as men are viewed as a source of labor. Since public services typically are very limited or absent, all members of the family participate in providing a wide range of social services, such as old-age "insurance" or child care.

Economic growth and industrialization may encourage women to direct their productive efforts away from the home; they may also reduce the relative value of the economic contributions of women if the women lack the education and skills that are essential to employment in the secondary and tertiary sectors. . . . This situation may be one of the costs of increased specialization. If there is competition between family members for jobs, the women tend to lose out. The Committee on the Status of Women in India summarized the process this way:

> In agrarian societies the family is the unit of production. The place of work being close to the home, women and children all participate in the production process. As a society moves from the traditional agricultural and household industry to organised industry and services, from rural to urban areas, the traditional division of labour ceases to operate, and the complementary relationship of the family is substituted by the competitive one between units of labour. The scarcer the jobs, the sharper is the competition. Technological changes in the process of production call for acquisition of new skills and specializations which are very different from the traditional division of labour. Women, handicapped by lack of opportunities for acquisition of these new skills, find their traditional productive skills unwanted by the new economy.[2]

One consequence of the altered family roles and, in particular, the loss of economic complementarity between husband and wife, is that the family itself becomes both smaller (reduced from an extended to a nuclear family) and it is often less stable.[3] If one member of the family migrates to find work, the family is further altered; often the women find that their work load is increased but that their resources are more limited. One does not have to idealize the family as the basic unit of social organization to recognize that in the absence of viable alternatives, the family remains the primary source of security and well-being for the vast majority of Third World women.

Some authors have pointed out that social and economic changes may not overturn relationships between the sexes to the disadvantage of women but simply intensify a preexisting asymmetry. In Turkey and other Middle Eastern countries, for example, women traditionally have never controlled the products of their labor, so compared to women in Africa, the women in Muslim countries have suffered proportionately less erosion in their status.[4] This fact should not imply, however, that women in the Islamic world are necessarily better off. When women are confined by law and/or custom to the family, they may fall further and further behind as development accelerates.

> The exclusion of women from extrafamilial activities was not particularly important in the traditional society that was not concerned with progress, but it is an anachronism in a society that professes to wish to change and is actually investing both capital and effort in bringing about change and development. To confine women to the family structure is to keep them at a subsistence level at a time when entire sectors of the economy are moving toward a money base.[5]

The spread of educational opportunities, a normal part of development, may have the effect of further polarizing sex roles that were previously established by differences in labor productivity, traditional religious or cultural practices, or family organization. When education is a scarce resource, as it continues to be in most rural areas, the tendency is to educate boys before, and longer than, girls. This fact is the reason that worldwide, perhaps two-thirds of the illiterate people are female.

Urbanization, another major factor in social and economic change, also affects women in numerous ways. Some of the effects may be considered beneficial, but many are detrimental. What Elise Boulding has described as the "enclosure movement" for women has always been associated with urbanism.[6] When women are secluded—because of some form of purdah (female seclusion) or feminine mystique—the effect is the same: They are removed from active and effective participation in all the affairs of society. At the same time, urban centers can facilitate the creation of networks among women, and in the nineteenth and twentieth centuries, urban centers have meant a greater access to education and more diverse job opportunities for women. This effect occurred as early as the late eighteenth century in Western Europe and occurs today in much of the Third World. The cost of these opportunities, however, may be that women continue to occupy a marginal position in the economy as they are concentrated in the underpaid, intermittent informal labor sector.[7]

The declining status of women that often accompanies modernization is more than an intellectual assertion of scholars and activists as it is also reflected in statistics on mortality, morbidity, employment, and literacy. India is an unfortunate case in point.

AN INDIAN CASE STUDY

One of the most severe indictments of the impact of development on women emerged in the 1974 report of the Committee on the Status of Women in India. Since 1901, the male population of India has grown at a faster rate than the female population except in the period 1941–1951 (see Table 1). Since India modernized along numerous dimensions from 1901 to 1971 (despite persistent and widespread poverty), the continued higher mortality rates among the female population suggest that development has not benefitted women and men equally. Consequently, the life expectancy at birth is lower for females than for males.

Indian demographers have proposed several hypotheses to explain the declining sex ratio, and five of these suggest important contributory factors.

1. Females are underenumerated in the Indian census.
2. The general mortality rate of females is higher than that of males.
3. Indian families prefer sons, and female infants are consequently neglected.
4. Frequent and excessive childbearing has an adverse effect on the health of women.
5. Certain diseases have a higher incidence in women.[8]

In the absence of more reliable data, it is impossible to say which of these factors might be the most important, but each, including the underenumeration of women in a census, suggests at least an inequitable involvement of women in Indian society or the fact that females do not enjoy the same status or facilities as males. The authors of the Indian report stressed the importance of this last factor.

> The explanation [of the declining sex ratio] which seems to have received general acceptance is that due to improvement of health services in the last few decades the reduction in mortality has been greater for males than females. The differential improvement in health conditions must have contributed substantially to the decline in sex ratio. This raises the whole question of the attitudes towards females and the role of women in Indian society.[9]

TABLE 1. Growth of Female Population in India, 1901–1971

Year	Total Population (millions)	Male Population (millions)	Female Population (millions)	Females per 1000 Males
1901	238	121	117	972
1911	252	128	124	964
1921	251	128	123	955
1931	279	143	136	950
1941	319	164	155	945
1951	361	186	175	946
1961	439	226	213	941
1971	548	284	264	930

Source: Government of India, Department of Social Welfare, Ministry of Education and Social Welfare, *Towards Equality, Report of the Committee on the Status of Women in India* (New Delhi, 1974), p. 10.

In an important study of neglect of female children in northern India, Barbara D. Miller reinforces the explanations of the Indian Committee on the Status of Women. Neglect and starvation were routinely used in some areas during the eighteenth and nineteenth centuries to rid a family of female infants, and British observers reported that some villages had no female children.[10] Miller used census data from the nineteenth and twentieth centuries to trace the preponderance of males reflected in the sex ratios. One of the important contributions to her study is that she examined several reasons for the cultural preference for sons, such as the high cost of marrying daughters (because of dowries). She also suggests that the higher demand for female agricultural labor in southern India works against male preference there and contributes to more equitable sex ratios in that region.

It is hard to avoid the conclusion that a preference for boys lies at the heart of the inferior status of women and girls in India and many other countries. Equally disturbing are the increasing indications that when public services—ranging from medical and health facilities to agricultural extension projects—are provided in the course of development efforts, they may either reinforce the traditional male biases or diminish the status that women enjoyed in the traditional society. For example, in field studies conducted in 1971, the Indian Council of Medical Research found that girls outnumbered boys among children with kwashiorkor, a disease resulting from severe malnutrition, but among children hospitalized with kwashiorkor, boys outnumbered girls.[11] If a family must choose between children in deciding who will receive food or medical care, boys will be given preference. The provision of a public service thus may exacerbate the differential treatment of boys and girls that begins at birth.

The use of neglect or, in extreme cases, of infanticide to limit the number of female children may acquire a sinister twist with improved medical technology. Where amniocentesis was available in private urban clinics in India, nearly all women who had the test in the early 1980s had abortions when the fetus was female. A similar preference for sons has also undermined China's family planning program.[12]

Considerable alarm has also been sounded over the decline in the number of women who are a part of the paid work force in India. Census data have shown a decline both in proportion of female workers to the total population and in the percentage of women in the total labor force. Even allowing for statistical inaccuracies and changes in census procedures, which exaggerate differences, census data from 1961 and 1971 show a decline both in absolute numbers and in percentages.[13]

Three researchers at the Indian Council of Social Science Research conducted a detailed study based on the 1961 census. They examined female participation in several major categories of household and nonhousehold industry in rural and urban areas. They looked carefully at employment in household manufacturing (such as in cottage industries) because traditionally, this type of work has been regarded as the stronghold of female workers, even though at the time of the 1961 census, it accounted for only 21 percent of all nonagricultural workers. The researchers found that the proportion of women employed in household industry was less than 50 percent that of men in half of the major employment categories studies, such as in the production of tobacco products, woolen textiles, and jute textiles.[14] The participation of women in nonhousehold industries was even lower.

A different study covering a later period shows a drop in the proportion of female to total workers in factories employing more than twenty people (a drop from 10.4 percent to 8.7 percent from 1963 to 1972).[15] Since employment in industry is frequently taken as an indicator of economic development, the declining participation of women in this sector is another disturbing suggestion of the effects of modernization on women. The situation is urgent because the alternative for these women is not household leisure but unemployment, underemployment, or menial agricultural labor.

An examination of macrolevel data published in 1981 suggests that the employment trends might not be as discouraging as the earlier studies had concluded. The director of India's Central Statistical Organisation has argued that noncensus surveys, such as the annual survey of industries, conducted during the 1960s and 1970s suggest that female labor force participation rates did not undergo major changes in those two decades.[16] These contradictions may be resolved by ongoing analyses of the 1981 Indian census; until such analyses are made, they stand as a frustrating illustration of the data problems discussed in the next section.

All of the studies cited above offer three reasons for the decline in female employment when it has occurred along with industrialization. One factor is the decline in household industry in general, a decline that began under British colonialism and accelerated after 1947.[17] Since household industries constituted the largest traditional nonagricultural source of women's employment, women were the greatest victims of that economic transformation. A second factor is that within the category of household industry, those activities performed by women—such as some kinds of hand weaving, oil pressing, rice pounding, and tobacco processing—faced especially stiff competition from factory production. Finally, technological changes reduced the demand for unskilled labor, and since the majority of the women in the industrial sector were unskilled, they were the main victims of this change also.[18] To this last factor might be added the observation that as long as women are considered secondary in the home, they will be considered secondary in the formal labor market.[19]

CHANGING ROLES
IN CHANGING SOCIETIES

Detailed studies make it clear that generalizing about the impact of social and economic changes must be done with caution, because to date, research has only complicated the picture of the impact of development on women. Agricultural development projects do not inevitably increase female work loads,[20] and changes in the rural economy under colonial rule or in response to production for cash and/or export may not be the primary factors in dichotomizing the sex roles.[21] A new road into a village may open up new opportunities for women traders in remote communities,[22] or modernization and technological advances may create more jobs for women in public services and in the tertiary sector in general.[23]

In those cases in which change has not had an adverse impact on women, it appears as if one of two situations has been present. Either the traditional roles of women have been reshaped in ways that are compatible with broader social changes, or the women have developed viable new roles. By definition, avoiding change is not an option in a non-static society. The questions are where, how, and when change comes. In the presence of this reality, the people who have the power to make choices about development must come to grips with the indictment so forcefully articulated by Irene Tinker: "In virtually all countries and among all classes, women have lost ground relative to men; development, by widening the gap between the incomes of men and women, has not helped improve women's lives, but rather has had an adverse effect upon them."[24]

The process of "coming to grips" with this fact is difficult, for ultimately, that means considering the issues raised by discussions of female political dependency. What are the relationships between women's reproductive and productive roles and their secondary status? How do macrolevel political and economic trends—such as expanded state control—affect women? Answers to these kinds of questions demand that research continue even as the subject of the research changes constantly.

NOTES

1. Ester Boserup, *Woman's Role in Economic Development* (New York: St. Martin's Press, 1970), p. 56.
2. India, Ministry of Education and Social Welfare, Department of Social Welfare, *Towards*

Equality: Report of the Committee on the Status of Women in India (New Delhi, 1974), p. 149.

3. Fredricka Pickford Santos, "The Role of Women in the Development Process: Market Integration or Family Disintegration?" *Journal of International Affairs 30* (Fall/Winter 1976–1977):173–174, and Nadia H. Youssef, "Women in Development: Urban Life and Labor," in Irene Tinker and Michèle Bo Bramsen, eds., *Women and World Development* (Washington, D.C.: Overseas Development Council, 1976), pp. 71–72.

4. Deniz Kandiyoti, "Sex Roles and Social Change: A Comparative Appraisal of Turkey's Women," in Wellesley Editorial Committee, ed., *Women and National Development: The Complexities of Change* (Chicago and London: University of Chicago Press, 1977), and Nadia H. Youssef, *Women and Work in Developing Societies* (Westport, Conn.: Greenwood Press, 1976), pp. 3–4, 19ff.

5. Fatima Mernissi, "The Moslem World: Women Excluded from Development," in Tinker and Bramsen, eds., *Women and World Development*, p. 36.

6. Elise Boulding, *Women in the Twentieth-Century World* (New York: John Wiley and Sons, for Sage Publications, 1977), pp. 41–42.

7. Lourdes Arizpe, "Women in the Informal Labor Sector: The Case of Mexico City," in Wellesley Editorial Committee, ed., *Women and National Development*, pp. 25–37, and Kenneth Little, "Women in African Towns South of the Sahara: The Urbanization Dilemma," in Tinker and Bramsen, eds., *Women and World Development*, pp. 78–87.

8. India, *Towards Equality*, p. 11.

9. Ibid.

10. Barbara D. Miller, *The Endangered Sex: Neglect of Female Children in Rural North India* (Ithaca: Cornell University Press, 1981), p. 51. See also Maureen Norton's commentary on Miller's research and related work, "Death at an Early Age: Culture, Sex Discrimination, and Mortality in South Asia," *Horizons 2* (May 1983):37–39.

11. Kathleen Newland, *The Sisterhood of Man* (New York: W. W. Norton and Company, for the Worldwatch Institute, 1979), p. 47. On differences in male-female medical care, see Miller, *Endangered Sex*, pp. 98–102 and Table 6, pp. 93–97.

12. *Christian Science Monitor*, April 11, 1983. In China, an experiment with early sex-determination techniques to permit selective abortion in early pregnancy demonstrated the limited impact of the Communist revolution on traditional gender preferences. In one trial, of thirty women who chose to have abortions, twenty-nine aborted females (see Newland, *Sisterhood of Man*, p. 180).

13. India, *Towards Equality*, p. 153.

14. Asok Mitra, Adhir K. Srimany, and Lalit P. Pathak, *The Status of Women: Household and Non-household Economic Activity* (Bombay and New Delhi: Allied Publishers, for the Indian Council of Social Science Research, 1979), pp. 2–14.

15. Swapna Mukhopadhyay, "Women Workers of India: A Case of Market Segmentation," in International Labour Office (ILO), *Women in the Indian Labour Force* (Bangkok: Asian Employment Programme, International Labour Organisation, 1981), pp. 96, 114.

16. K. C. Seal, "Women in the Labour Force in India: A Macro-level Statistical Profile," in ILO, *Women in the Indian Labour Force*, pp. 24–29.

17. For a case study of the effects of colonialism on women in agriculture and handicrafts, see Manoshi Mitra, "Women in Colonial Agriculture: Bihar in the Late 18th and the 19th Century," *Development and Change* 12 (January 1981):29–53.

18. India, *Towards Equality*, p. 153; Mitra, Srimany, and Pathak, *Status of Women*, p. 13; and ILO, *Women in the Indian Labour Force*, pp. 13–14.

19. ILO, *Women in the Indian Labour Force*, p. 11.

20. Dunstan S. C. Spencer, *African Women in Agricultural Development: A Case Study in Sierre Leone*, OLC Paper no. 9 (Washington, D.C.: American Council on Education, Overseas Liaison Committee, 1976).

21. Ann Stoller, "Class Structure and Female Autonomy in Rural Java," in Wellesley Editorial Committee, ed., *Women and National Development*, pp. 74–89.

22. Mary Elmendorf, "The Dilemma of Peasant Women: A View from a Village in Yucatan," in Tinker and Bramsen, eds., *Women and World Development*, pp. 88–94.

23. India, *Towards Equality*, p. 151.

24. Irene Tinker, "The Adverse Impact of Development on Women," in Tinker and Bramsen, eds., *Women and World Development*, p. 22. See also the summary of a debate at the seminar on women in development held in Mexico City during International Women's Year (June 1975) in ibid., pp. 141–146.

Doing Their Homework: The Dilemma of Planning Women's Garden Programs in Bangladesh

Margot Wilson-Moore

Recently a number of development agencies in Bangladesh (for example, CARE, CIDA, Helen Keller International, the Mennonite Central Committee, Save the Children, UNICEF, USAID) have planned and implemented independent projects or program components directed specifically toward homestead gardening as an alternative to field crop production. For the growing cadre of marginal and landless farmers with little or no cultivable land outside of the household, homestead gardening constitutes a subsistence strategy with considerable potential for improving family nutrition and cash generation.

Traditionally a complement to field crop production, homestead gardens provide a much-needed supply of nutritious, interesting, and vitamin-rich foods for home consumption. Additionally, the sale of homestead garden produce makes substantial amounts of cash available for rural farm families. The discussion that follows considers homestead gardening within the broad context of international development in Bangladesh and more particularly in relation to the burgeoning literature on the role of women in development. This discussion focuses specifically on homestead gardening as a viable development strategy for rural women.

International development aid constitutes a major influence for change today. In Bangladesh millions of foreign aid dollars comprise a large proportion of the national budget. Since 1974 to 1975, Bangladesh has

received not less than $700 million from the United States each year in international aid, and these donations represent two to three and one-half times the total revenue budget generated in-country. However, the results in terms of quantifiable improvements are relatively few, and despite these substantial foreign aid contributions Bangladesh continues to demonstrate a negative balance of payments (greater than $5 million in 1984 to 1985) and a negative balance of trade ($135 million US in 1984 to 1985).

Environmental stress, population pressure, illiteracy, and historical explanations such as exploitation and isolation have been espoused as general causes for the persistent poverty in Bangladesh. Similarly, behavioral causes, such as a closely structured hierarchy and system of patronage, rugged individualism, and failure of Bangladeshis to "trust" one another and work cooperatively, have been offered as causes of the destitution and privation that characterize daily life in Bangladesh (Maloney 1986).

Whatever the causes, pervasive poverty and widespread destitution are commonplace, and in terms of standard "development" criteria, such as per capita income, literacy rate, mortality and fertility rates, economic diversification, and physical and social infrastructure, Bangladesh can only be termed a development failure. Historically, vast transfers of resources out of the area have significantly depleted the resource base while more recent problems of overpopulation, land fragmentation, and environmental disasters have drawn the attention of the international aid community.

Original material prepared for this text.

Women's issues have received considerable attention from the international donor community in recent years, but to understand the "state of the art" of women and development research[1] in Bangladesh, it is necessary to trace its roots in broader issues of development theory and feminism. Early development theory tended to overlook the special needs of women, anticipating perhaps a "trickle-down" of benefits from men toward whom most programs are directed. Feminist critiques of development theory revolve primarily around this issue—the failure of development theory to address the problems of women directly. Women are either categorized with men or ignored altogether. Women are routinely subsumed within the rubric of more general development processes that are expected to address the issues of both men and women.

A variety of critiques of development theory exist (for an in-depth discussion see Jaquette 1982; Barnes-McConnell and Lodwick 1983; Wilson-Moore 1990), and the ongoing dialogue among these critiques has generated a vast and critical literature addressing the issue of women and development in the Third World. The feminist critique of development theory is firmly grounded in feminist thought, and the theoretical perspectives that have emerged in feminist development theory clearly reflect theoretical underpinnings in feminist theory. Feminist theoretical models predict relationships between various spheres of women's lives[2] and generate research questions and information useful, indeed imperative, for appropriate development planning for women.

Too often, however, women and development researchers fail to incorporate feminist theory into their research designs or neglect to articulate the underlying feminist assumptions that influence their work. Theorizing is, in large part, left to feminist academicians who usually rely on ethnographic (rather than development) literature for constructing and testing their models. As a result feminist theory, women, and development research have progressed, in recent years, along separate and divergent paths. Despite the actuating influence of feminist theory on women and development research and their common concerns with the situation of women, discourse between these two bodies of literature is remarkably scant.

Women and development research tends to be of a highly practical nature, concentrating on the immediate and pragmatic problems faced by women in developing nations. Resources and institutional support are then directed toward these identified needs. A women's component may be incorporated into existing development programs, or alternatively projects may be designed specifically and solely for women. Often, however, development programs do not meet the needs of the women for whom they are designed. Many focus on "individual solutions," such as education to improve women's opportunities for urban wage employment, increase their access to innovative technology, or improve their subsistence production skills. Too often the systemic constraints on Third World people in general and on women in particular, such as high rates of unemployment and lack of child-care facilities, are overlooked.

The role of women in socioeconomic development has been the subject of much interest in Bangladesh (cf. Hossain, Sharif, and Huq 1977; Islam 1986) and has focused the attention of the aid community on those development issues particular to women, especially those at the lowest economic levels who are often the poorest of the poor. Khan et al. (1981) have shown that in 1981 326 government and nongovernment programs for women were registered with the Ministry of Women's Affairs. The majority provide training in knitting, sewing, embroidery, handicrafts, and garment-making. Unfortunately, however, although directed toward poor and destitute women, the income-generating potential of these skills is minimal (Khan et al. 1981:24) and the emphasis on low payment and domestic-like work only serves to perpetuate women's subordinate status and economic circumstance.

In 1986 Schaffer found that the focus of more than 100 development projects directed specifically toward women had expanded to include self-help and income generation, family planning and health, education and literacy, agriculture development projects, rural employment and industry, and female leadership training. The majority of these projects focus on integrating women into existing programs, although a few "women only" projects exist. Most donor agencies philosophically support development activities for women (Schaffer 1986:4); however, a number of cultural attitudes toward women constrain them. The view of women's work as minimal and unimportant is compounded by the women's own perception of their work as noneconomic and therefore without value.

Beyond this, religious proscriptions that predicate family honor on women's virtue and legislate women's appropriate place as inside the household necessitate development on an outreach basis (providing inputs and training to women in their own homes), while effectively preventing agencies from recruiting female staff to provide that outreach service.

Initially, little specific information was available about women in Bangladesh, and the resulting imperative for more and better data regarding women's roles, statuses, and activities generated a predominantly descriptive focus in the early research. This is especially true in the rural areas where early village studies (cf. Raper 1970; Zaidi 1970) provided only brief references to women's activities. Other village studies followed (cf. Arens and Van Beurden 1980; BRAC 1983; Chowdhury 1978; Hartmann and Boyce 1983; Mukherjee 1971), but still little direct reference was made to women.

More recently a number of authors have commented on the "invisibility" of women's economic contribution in Bangladesh (cf. Chen 1986; Huq 1979; Islam 1986; Smock 1977; Wallace et al. 1987). Women's labor routinely includes postharvest processing of field crops, such as rice, jute, mustard seed, lentils and millet; care of animals; homestead gardening; and minor household maintenance, to name only a few. Because the labor of rural women takes place primarily inside the household, it often goes unnoticed. Nev-

ertheless, their economic contribution is substantial (Chen 1986; Wallace et al. 1987). The importance of these kinds of studies is in shifting the focus away from the view of women as dependent and helpless. Instead, they are recognized as actors, engaged in economic pursuits in both rural and urban areas. As such they cease to be "welfare cases" and become instead an appropriate target for "mainstream" development processes.

In addition to their traditional domestic roles increasing numbers of women from landless and marginal families are being forced by economic circumstance to leave their homes to seek wage labor. At the same time technology, especially mechanized rice processing, is displacing rural women from their traditional roles in postharvest processing of field crops (Begum 1989). Cooperative programs are encouraging and supporting female entrepreneurs, but the success of these schemes often accrues from their constituting an extension of existing female roles that do not "encroach upon the traditional domain of men . . . [and are] not conceived as a threat to men's interests" (Begum 1989: 527).

Homestead gardening as a development strategy for women fits easily within these dictates because it neither encroaches on nor threatens men's traditional subsistence activities. Homestead gardening is an integral part of women's work in Bangladesh (cf. Chen 1983; Hannan 1986; Hassan 1978; Huq 1979; Hussain and Banu 1986; Scott and Carr 1985) and provides an opportunity for women to make sizable contributions to the rural farm family in terms of nutritious food for consumption as well as income generated from the sale of excess produce.

Homestead gardening is *not* the exclusive purview of women, although much of the research to date suggests that it is (Chen 1986; Huq 1979). This misconception is likely a result of research bias toward women. In Bangladesh women's issues have become a primary concern of development planners, and as a result women's roles are often considered without reference to other members of the community and to men in particular.

The result is a misrepresentation of women as the principle, even exclusive, actors in certain sectors of the subsistence economy; in this case as the cultivators of homestead gardens. By contrast data from my own research (Wilson-Moore 1989, 1990) show that both men and women are involved in vegetable cultivation, although some clear differences exist between what men and women do in the garden.

Men and women grow different crop varieties at different times of the year—men in winter, women in summer. The fact that the crops grown by women tend to be more indigenous in nature and those cultivated by men more likely to be imported varieties may be an artifact of men's more active participation in the public sphere. Because men are active in the marketplace, they may simply be exposed to new varieties of vegetables most often and are therefore more predisposed to experimentation. In a similar vein it may be argued that women are in some sense a reservoir of traditional information and cultivation patterns, reflective of a time before imported varieties and development inputs were available.

A clear distinction also exists between male and female patterns of vegetable cultivation in which men's patterns are reminiscent of field crop production patterns characterized by monocropping and the rows and beds of European gardens. Women's gardens, by contrast, have a jumbled appearance and may represent the indigenous patterns commonly in practice prior to outside influence (for a discussion of cross-cultural gardening traditions see Brownrigg 1985).

Women's gardens are found inside or immediately adjacent to the household. Requirements for housing, cooking, stabling of animals, and postharvest processing and storage of field crops necessitate that individual plants or small clusters of plants be scattered throughout the homestead, dotted around the central courtyard and household structures. Small plots may be located around the periphery of larger homesteads, usually immediately outside of the circle of infacing buildings.

Gourds are encouraged to grow over trellises, along the walls, and across the roofs of buildings. Other climbing plants may be trained to grow up the trunks of nearby trees. Shade-loving plants are grown under the cover of fruit and fuelwood trees, and those more tolerant of direct sun are planted in the clear places.

Plant species are highly diverse. Because there are no beds or rows, tall and medium height trees, smaller bushy shrubs, upright plants, creepers, and root crops form the horizontal layers characteristic of this type of garden. Weeding is infrequent, and it is often difficult to differentiate the homestead garden from the surrounding undergrowth. In fact an untrained observer might not recognize this type of homestead garden at all.

Husbands often fail to recognize the gardening efforts of their wives, even when the proof was crawling across the roofs and walls of the homestead and into the cooking pot at meal times. That men fail to acknowledge women's productive labor in gardens may lie partially in more general societal attitudes toward women as producers (they are not seen as such) but also in the scattered appearance of their homestead gardens, which prevents their immediate recognition by uninterested, or uninitiated, observers, be they husband, anthropologist, or development worker.

Women cultivate vegetable varieties that spring up readily, can be produced from seed preserved from the previous year, and are well-adapted to the seasonal vagaries of the climate, flourishing inside and around the homestead with a minimum of care or input. Women often stagger the planting times so that everything does not mature at once. In fact related women in separate households may coordinate their planting times, as well as the varieties planted, to maximize their production through sharing.

Vegetable gardens cultivated by women tend to have a high diversity of plant species but a small number of plants of any particular type. Accordingly, the quantities are smaller yet more varied, and they are intended for family consumption. High diversity and low volume production is the predominant characteristic of women's gardening patterns in Bangladesh and throughout Asia, a strategy well-suited to fulfilling family consumption needs.

It is no coincidence that the vegetables grown most commonly in homestead gardens are the ones villagers prefer to eat. These vegetables can be eaten on a daily basis without becoming unappetizing. Alternatively the diversity of vegetables produced in the homestead garden also helps to offset the boredom of eating the same food every day. In fact villagers prefer to have a variety of foods, even if that means eating something that they dislike from time to time.

In this way the garden acts as a living larder, providing fresh produce on a daily basis. As individual plants become ripe the women harvest them and prepare them for consumption. If more vegetables become ripe than can be consumed within the household at one time, they may be given away, traded with neighbors, or sent to the market for sale.

Homestead gardening as a development strategy for women is predicated on a view of women's production as valuable and essential to the nutritional and economic welfare of the rural farm family. Furthermore, the minimal overlap between men's and women's gardening patterns ensures that as a development strategy homestead gardening also does not compete with men's traditional activities in field crop cultivation or vegetable production. Thus, homestead gardening conforms to two primary stipulations (Begum 1989; Schaffer 1986) for success and would seem an ideal development strategy for women.

Unfortunately, these stipulations do not necessarily guarantee a positive result, and outcomes of garden programming may prove surprising if the planners have not "done their homework" prior to implementation. In this regard Brownrigg has (1985) emphasized the necessity of in-depth locally based research and observes that when such research is omitted or conducted in a cursory manner programs often fail to meet the needs of the target population. Barnett (1953) has argued that acceptance of innovation is based on the ability of recipient populations to analyze new

ideas and technologies and to identify some similarity with existing culture traits. Accordingly, the more identifiable an innovation is, the more easily it can be matched with a trait already existing in the cultural lexicon, and the more readily it will be adopted.

Social science, and anthropology in particular, has much to contribute. Participant observation is a field methodology well-suited to producing detailed information about existing indigenous practices; information often not available through any other means; and information appropriate, perhaps imperative, for planners who wish to build on and enhance those existing practices. By focusing on extant patterns planners can effectively determine which goals are attainable and which populations are most appropriately targeted.

In the context of Bangladesh, for example, homestead garden programs intended to improve family nutrition and increase consumption of vitamin-rich vegetables are most appropriately directed toward women because their production is intended, in the first instance, for home consumption. If, on the other hand, program goals include increasing family income through sale of garden produce, men may constitute a more appropriate target group because their vegetable production is traditionally intended for the market. Finally, a program goal of increased access to cash for women requires careful consideration because women's limited access to the market and ramifications of cash generation on family nutrition are two important, potentially negative, dimensions of income-generating schemes for women.

Women routinely remain secluded within the household in Bangladesh. As a result, marketing of women's garden produce constitutes something of a dilemma. Produce must be transported and sold by a male family member or neighbor. Women are able to retain control over the cash generated in this way by providing a shopping list (for household essentials such as oil or kerosene) when they turn over the produce for sale. Accordingly, the money is recycled back into the family budget on a daily basis and does not accumulate. It fails to be assigned a "value" by men or women and as a result goes unrecognized. That this particular economic contribution fails to affect women's status in any appreciable way has been discussed elsewhere (Wilson-Moore 1989).

Beyond the lack of recognition that greets women's economic enterprise in the garden, Boserup (1970) has shown that when women's economic activities become profitable (especially in terms of cash generation), men tend to take them over (see also Chaney and Schmink 1976). Male takeovers of the income-generating component of women's homestead gardening and the displacement of women from their traditional roles in vegetable production necessitates only a small shift in production activities. However, the ramifications in terms of family nutritional well-being may be far reaching. Rural farm families depend on women's homestead production for a ready supply of varied and vitamin-rich vegetable foods, a complement nutritionally and aesthetically to the *masebhate* (rice and fish) mainstays of the Bangladeshi diet.

Redirecting women's vegetable production toward the market would necessitate a change in production technique, disrupting the traditional patterns of women's homestead garden production and interfering with that ready supply of vegetable foods. The traditional pattern that produces small quantities of diverse vegetable foods intended for consumption within the homestead would have to be replaced by high-output, low-diversity cropping. Furthermore, there is little evidence to suggest that rural families would use the cash earned in this way to "buy back" or replace vegetable foods in the diet. Rather, high-status processed foods such as tea, white sugar, white flour, and bread are more apt to make an appearance when cash becomes available for their purchase.

Maintaining a balance between growing vegetable crops in large volume for sale and in sufficient variety for home consumption represents a problem in terms of the space and time constraints of homestead production. However, the existing, complementary yet rarely overlapping patterns of men's and women's traditional vegetable production seems well-suited to the respective cash generation and consumption needs of the family. Accordingly, planners concerned with pervasive poverty and widespread nutritional deficiency diseases in Bangladesh may wish to consider the benefits of developing each of these gardening strategies as they mutually, yet independently, support the rural farm family.

NOTES

1. Throughout this paper the terminology women and development has been used as a generic term for women's development in an effort to avoid more specific references such as women in development (WID) or development for women. These advocate, in the first case, the incorporation of a women's component into existing programs and, in the second, separate programming by women for women (see Jaquette 1982; Barnes-McConnell and Lockwick 1983; Wilson-Moore 1990 for a more comprehensive discussion of these terms).

2. For example, see Boserup (1970), Friedl (1975), and Sanday (1973, 1974) for models that predicate women's status on women's participation in the work force and their economic contribution to the family.

REFERENCES

Arens, Jenneke and Jos Van Beurden. 1980. *Jhagrapur: Poor Peasants and Women in a Village in Bangladesh*. Calcutta: Orient Longman.

Barnes-McConnell, Pat and Dora G. Lodwick. 1983. *Working with International Development Projects: A Guide for Women–in–Development*. East Lansing: Michigan State University, Office of Women in International Development.

Barnett, Homer. 1953. *Innovation: The Basis of Culture Change*. New York: McGraw-Hill.

Begum, Kohinoor. 1989. Participation of Rural Women in Income-Earning Activities: A Case Study of a Bangladesh Village. *Women's Studies International Forum* 12(5):519–528.

Boserup, Ester. 1970. *Women's Role in Economic Development*. New York: St. Martin's Press.

BRAC (Bangladesh Rural Advancement Committee). 1983. *Who Gets What and Why: Resource Allocation in a Bangladesh Village*. Dhaka: BRAC Publication.

Brownrigg, Leslie. 1985. *Home Gardening in International Development: What the Literature Shows*. Washington, DC: League for International Food Education.

Chaney, Elsa and Marianne Schmink. 1976. Women and Modernization: Access to Tools. In June Nash and Helen Safa (eds.). *Sex and Class in Latin America*. New York: Praeger.

Chen, Martha Alter. 1986. *A Quiet Revolution: Women in Transition in Rural Bangladesh*. Cambridge: Schenkman Publishing.

Chowdhury, Anwarullah. 1978. *A Bangladesh Village: A Study of Social Stratification*. Dhaka: Centre for Social Studies.

Friedl, Ernestine. 1975. *Women and Men: An Anthropologist's View*. New York: Holt, Rinehart and Winston.

Hannan, Ferdouse H. 1986. *Past, Present and Future Activities of Women's Desk*. Comilla: Bangladesh Academy for Rural Development.

Hartmann, Betsy and James K. Boyce. 1983. *A Quiet Violence: Views from a Bangladesh Village*. London: Oxford University Press.

Hassan, Nazmul. 1978. *Spare Time of Rural Women: A Case Study*. Dhaka: University of Dacca, Institute of Nutrition and Food Science.

Hossain, Monowar, Raihan Sharif, and Jahanara Huq (eds.). 1977. *Role of Women in Socio-Economic Development in Bangladesh*. Dhaka: ABCO Press.

Huq, Jahanara. 1979. Economic Activities of Women in Bangladesh: The Rural Situation. In Women for Women (eds.). *The Situation of Women in Bangladesh*, pp. 139–182. Dhaka: BRAC Printers.

Hussain, S. and S. Banu. 1986. *BARD Experiences in Organization of Women in their Involvement in Agricultural Related Activities*. Comilla: Bangladesh Academy for Rural Development.

Islam, Shamima. 1986. Work of Rural Women in Bangladesh: An Overview of Research. Paper presented at workshop on women in agriculture. Comilla: Bangladesh Academy for Rural Development.

Jaquette, Jane S. 1982. Women and Modernization Theory: A Decade of Feminist Criticism. *World Politics* 34(2):267–284.

Khan, Salma, Jowshan Rahman, Shamima Islam, and Meherunnessa Islam. 1981. *Inventory for Women's Organizations in Bangladesh*. Dhaka: UNICEF.

Maloney, Clarence. 1986. *Behavior and Poverty in Bangladesh*. Dhaka: University Press Limited.

Mukherjee, Ramkrishna. 1971. *Six Villages of Bengal*. Bambay: Popular Prakashan.

Raper, Arthur. 1970. *Rural Development in Action: The Comprehensive Experiment at Comilla, East Pakistan*. Ithaca: Cornell University Press.

Sanday, Peggy. 1973. Toward a Theory of the Status of Women. *American Anthropologist* 75(5): 1682–1700.

———. 1974. Female Status in the Public Domain. In Michelle Z. Rosaldo and Louise Lamphere (eds.). *Woman, Culture, and Society*, pp. 189–206. Stanford, CA: Stanford University Press.

Sattar, Ellen. 1979. Demographic Features of Bangladesh with Reference to Women and Children. In Women for Women (eds.), *The Situation of Women in Bangladesh*, pp. 1–22. Dhaka: BRAC Printers.

Schaffer, Teresita C. 1986. *Survey of Development Project and Activities for Women in Bangladesh*. Dhaka: Provatee Printers.

Scott, Gloria L. and Marilyn Carr. 1985. *The Impact of Technology Choice on Rural Women in Bangladesh: Problems and Opportunities*. Washington, DC: World Bank Working Paper No 731.

Smock, Audrey Chapman. 1977. Bangladesh: A Struggle with Tradition and Poverty. In Janet Z. Giele and Audrey C. Smock (eds.). *Women: Roles and Status in Eight Countries*, pp. 83–126. New York: John Wiley and Sons.

Wallace, Ben J., Rosie M. Ahsan, Shahnazz H. Hussain, and Ekramul Ahsan. 1987. *The Invisible Resource: Women and Work in Rural Bangladesh*. Boulder: Westview Press.

Wilson-Moore, Margot. 1989. Women's Work in Homestead Gardens: Subsistence, Patriarchy, and Status in Northwest Bangladesh. *Urban Anthropology* 18(203):281–297.

———. 1990. Subsistence, Patriarchy, and Status: Women's Work in Homestead Gardens in Northwest Bangladesh. Ph.D. dissertation, Southern Methodist University, Dallas, Texas.

Zaidi, S. M. Hafeez. 1970. *The Village Culture in Transition: A Study of East Pakistan Rural Society*. Honolulu: East-West Press.

The "Comparative Advantages" of Women's Disadvantages: Women Workers in the Strawberry Export Agribusiness in Mexico

Lourdes Arizpe and Josefina Aranda

In recent years, the women's movement the world over has stressed the need to provide women with increased access to salaried employment in order to improve their living conditions. In some industrialized countries, however, the recession and long-term economic trends are making it more difficult for women to get adequate employment, because, among other reasons, many of the jobs traditionally held by women in industries—particularly in textiles, garment manufacturing, and electronics—are being relocated in developing countries.[1] For several decades, many of the labor-intensive agricultural activities in which women worked as wage laborers have also been shifting to developing regions. In these regions, where male and female unemployment has been perennial, most governments welcome capital investments that will create employment and bring in foreign currency through exports. For example, many jobs formerly held by women in the northern cities and in the southern rural areas of the United States have moved south to Mexico and to other Latin American and Caribbean countries.

Behind this movement lie both the market pressures that force companies into a constant search for lower production costs, and the rationale of "comparative advantages," according to which different economies are advised to specialize in those products that they can sell profitably in the international market. But it so happens that such "advan-tages" are closely linked to the cheap labor costs that come from women's social and economic "disadvantages"; a woman's loss in one country may be some woman's gain in another country. Thus, it could be said that women in developing countries are gaining the jobs that have been redeployed from industrial countries. In fact, companies are using women's liberation slogans in deprived areas to justify giving jobs to eager young women rather than to older women or men who also desperately need jobs.[2]

The main issue raised by these events—whether the fluidity of the international labor market has become more of a zero-sum game for women than for men—cannot be fully discussed in this paper, but some light can be shed on it by examining the extent to which such a "gain" for women in a developing country actually improves their status and living conditions. A survey through interviews of young Mexican peasant women who have recently entered salaried employment in the strawberry-export packing plants of Zamora in the State of Michoacán helps us to understand the changes created by salaried work in their consciousness, their living conditions, and their situation within family and community.

AGROINDUSTRY AND RURAL EMPLOYMENT IN DEVELOPING COUNTRIES

Worldwide, the optimism generated in the 1950s by the projects for rural community development and after that by the increase in agricultural production due to the Green Revolution came to an end in the 1970s. Meanwhile, in the last three decades rural unemployment, movement of peasants toward the cities, demographic growth, and the marginalization of rural women from the technological and economic benefits of development have increased rapidly in many countries of Latin America, Africa, and Asia.

Import-substitution policies as a strategy for development in such countries led to rising foreign debts due to the high costs of technology and of capital goods imported from the industrialized countries.[3] The governments of developing countries, in order to acquire foreign exchange to improve their balance of payments, have encouraged export-oriented agriculture, which in many African, Latin American, and Asian rural areas has led to food scarcity.[4] Attempts to compensate for this scarcity by purchasing food from abroad have only perpetuated the vicious circle of dependency and poverty.[5]

The use of technological improvements from the Green Revolution increased yields and efficiency in rural production, but also led to higher concentration of agricultural resources in the hands of capitalist entrepreneurs.[6] In many countries this concentration has displaced small family producers who have become agricultural laborers or migrants surviving precariously in the outskirts of overpopulated cities.[7] The expansion of this surplus population in rural and urban areas is being attacked through massive family planning campaigns, even though it is clear that population growth is closely linked to the conditions of extreme poverty and insecurity that prevail on the land. Another solution now being proposed to stop the rural exodus lies in the creation of rural employment through agroindustries, a policy sponsored both by national governments and by multinationals who have found a fertile field for investment.

Following this trend, in Latin America the per capita production of subsistence crops decreased by 10 percent between 1964 and 1974, while that of agricultural products for export increased by 27 percent.[8] During this same period U.S. capital investments in agriculture for export in this region increased considerably, since investments in the food industry provide a 16.7 percent profit abroad, compared to an 11.5 percent return within the United States.[9] Since World War II, food processing companies have invested more in Mexico than in any other country of the Third World. An example of this type of investment is the strawberry industry in Zamora, which since 1970 has provided employment for approximately 10,000 young peasant women in its packing plants. Significantly, as in the textile and electronics industries that are also redeploying their production units abroad, the employment of women rather than men is clearly preferred in these agroindustries.[10] Why are young women preferred? Is it sufficient to say, as do the managers of such plants, that it is because they are "more dexterous" and "less restless"?

PEASANT WOMEN AND RURAL DEVELOPMENT IN LATIN AMERICA

According to recent census statistics in Latin America, women's agricultural work shows a relative decrease in all countries and an absolute decrease in many.[11] This may be due, partly, to inadequate census registration of rural women's activities, but it also reflects increased female migration from rural areas, as well as the shift to other self-employment (especially petty trade) and intermittent domestic service—occupations that fall between the borders of organized economic activities and unpaid female domestic and community work.[12] Another important shift in rural women's activities has been reported among small family producers, where the agricultural labor of household women is intensified in order to increase or maintain productivity in deteriorating market conditions.[13] Finally, a fourth trend in which poor, rural women enter wage labor in agricultural and livestock production or in agroindustrial activities is also becoming widespread.[14]

These four trends appear separately or in combination in different countries and regions. But all of them stem from the same process: the economic crisis of small peasant family production in rural areas in Latin America. Discussion of the causes of this crisis go beyond the scope of this paper, but the major trends in the status and employment of poor rural women in Latin America must be understood in the context of strategies these households use to survive in an increasingly difficult environment. There are also, of course, large numbers of women who have broken completely with their parents' or their husbands' households and who live and make decisions on their own. We find them, for example, along the Mexico-U.S. border or in the shantytowns of all the major Latin American and Caribbean cities.[15] Their choice of economic activity and lifestyle constitutes an individual decision-making process that should be analyzed as such within the narrow limits set by widespread unemployment and underemployment, cramped housing, and strict social pressures.

But in agrarian societies, there is little room for individualistic response. Especially in the case of young peasant women, the decision to work or to migrate is either made by the family patriarch or through permission granted by him. In any case, even more than sons, daughters are bound to their parents' households by the religious and social norms that prescribe absolute obedience, docility, and service toward others. In fact, this paper will argue that it is precisely these qualities that make the young women so attractive as a work force. The data that follow should make this abundantly clear.

STRAWBERRY PACKING AND FREEZING PLANTS IN ZAMORA

The strawberry agribusiness in Zamora began to expand in the mid-1960s, first through U.S. capital and later through Mexican capital. Its competitiveness in the international market comes from the fact that Mexican strawberries are cultivated in the winter and that their transport and especially their labor costs are very low.[16] Production is completely dependent on U.S. companies: the seedlings are imported from California; the export

trade is handled entirely by six U.S. commercial brokers who have stopped attempts by Mexican plants to sell directly to the European market; and the strawberry prices are dictated by conditions in the U.S. market, especially by the success of the California strawberry harvest.

Eighteen packing and freezing plants for strawberries functioned during the 1979–80 cycle in Zamora and in Jacona, a neighboring village. Among them the hiring characteristics and working conditions for women, as well as male personnel, vary little: for example, some pay $14.70 (US¢66) per hour of work on the conveyor belts and others $14.00 (US¢63), but the lower wage is counterbalanced by payment of bus tickets and by better treatment for the workers. As Marta Rodriguez put it: "X is the packing plant where women workers are treated the worst, and that is why they have many problems in hiring people. Even though they pay more there, the girls prefer better treatment, such as they get at Bonfil, where no overtime or commissions are paid. At X the bosses are almost Nazis. . . . " It is interesting to note that firm X is the one that consistently shows the highest productivity and efficiency; it is the only one, for example, that has devices under the roofing to prevent swallows from nesting there. In most of the plants there is a minimum investment in installations: they are prefabricated metal structures that can be easily dismantled. Everything reflects short-term investment.

Fifty percent of production for export in the 1978–79 cycle, which produced 88 million pounds of frozen strawberries (though the official figure given for exports was lower, 72.7 million pounds), was handled by the six companies we studied. Of these, three hire as many as 900 women workers at the height of the season, one hires 650, and two hire up to 350. One of the worst conditions of work women face in these plants is the acute annual fluctuation in labor demand according to changing conditions in cropping and in the price of sugar (sugar is added to the frozen strawberries). . . . Except in special conditions, all plants are closed from four to six months each year and have a peak season for hiring from March to May. Later on we shall see how the hiring is organized and how the women workers adjust their working lives to such conditions.

THE SITUATION
OF WOMEN WORKERS
IN THE STRAWBERRY PLANTS

Approximately 10 percent of the personnel in the plants do administrative work; of these usually all managers and accountants are men, and the secretaries are young, single women from the town of Zamora. In production work, except for the young men who unload the strawberry crates from the trucks and those in charge of the refrigerators, the great majority of workers are young peasant women who live in outlying villages of the Zamora valley and the region.

The 300 women workers interviewed were selected at random from each of the six plants. On the average, between 5 and 10 percent of the total female workers in each plant were interviewed, with the exception of El Duero, where 18.3 percent of the women were surveyed. Interviewed in proportional numbers, they perform the different tasks described below:

1. Stem Removers. Women who remove the stems of the strawberries do piecework, that is, they are paid $5.00 (US¢23) per crate of strawberries, each weighing seven kilograms. A worker with magic hands is able to remove the stems of up to thirty-five crates of strawberries per day; one with slow hands can barely manage five crates per day. But the number of crates available to work on varies from week to week. For example, on February 4, 1980, the 400 workers at Frutas Refrigeradas were assigned only one crate of strawberries each, because it rained the previous week and very few strawberries were harvested. On days like this the expenses of the workers for transportation and food are the same, but they earn only according to the number of crates they finish. On average, 80 percent of the women workers in the plants do this type of work; in the sample taken for the survey, they represent 75 percent of those interviewed.

2. Supervisors. These women are chosen by the head of personnel, or by the union leader, to check whether the strawberries tossed into the canals have had the stem properly removed. They represent 4 percent of those interviewed, which is equivalent to the proportion of women working as supervisors in most plants.

3. Selectors. Once the stem is removed, strawberries float along canals filled with water and disinfectant until they reach the conveyor belts, where the selectors pick out defective or rotten strawberries. As in the case of the supervisors, the selectors are chosen by the head of personnel or by the union leader, both of whom frequently show favoritism toward their friends or toward women from their own villages. This type of work is done by about 15 percent of the women workers in the plants and by 18 percent of those surveyed.

4. Tray Workers. From the conveyor belts the strawberries are put in tins or small boxes to be frozen, the best being placed on trays and frozen individually. This is also done by women who are selected in the manner described for those performing the two previous tasks. The women who performed the last three tasks mentioned were paid hourly, at the rate of $14.00 (US¢66) per hour during the 1979–80 cycle. Though a stem remover who works with amazing dexterity might earn a higher wage than women engaged in the other tasks, normally supervisors, selectors, and tray workers earn more. Those who work on an hourly wage enjoy greater prestige because they earn more and are closer to the higher-level employees. Many of the stem removers would prefer to work on the conveyor belts, especially those who, because of their age, are no longer able to work at high speed. But seniority normally is not taken into account for either promotion in tasks or other

fringe benefits. The younger workers sometimes resent the favoritism, not so much for
personal reasons, but rather because of loyalty to their villages: "See here—why aren't
there more from Tinguincharo on the conveyor belts?" But others say that it is a tiring
job. For instance, Berta Olivares prefers
working as a stem remover because, "We can
at least go and walk around a little when we go
get a crate for strawberries to de-stem . . . but
those on the conveyor belts are damned uncomfortable, they don't even let them move,
they can hardly even sigh. We can even sing."

Now that the scene of their work has been
described, the first questions to be answered
are: Who are these women? Did they work before? If so, what jobs did they hold?

Occupational Background of the Workers

Of the women surveyed, 61 percent stated
that they had never worked before. It must be
noted that these included those who, because
they are very young, had not yet entered the
work force. Those who had worked before
going into the packing and freezing plants
(41.3 percent) performed the types of jobs indicated in Tables 1 and 2. More than half
worked in agriculture previously, and a third
passed through paid domestic service. Their
agricultural wage labor in the region has been
replaced by immigrant labor, but this is not
the case in paid domestic work, since housewives in Zamora repeatedly complained that

TABLE 1. Workers' Previous Employment
by Sector

Sector	Cases (N)	%
Agriculture	69	55.7
Services	38	30.7
Industry	7	5.8
Trade	7	5.8
Agroindustry	2	1.7
Handicrafts	1	0.3
Total	124	100.0

TABLE 2. Workers' Previous Occupations

Position	Cases (N)	%
Agricultural laborer	52	41.9
Servant	25	20.2
Unpaid family worker in Agriculture	17	13.7
Office or shop employee	13	10.5
Factory worker	11	8.9
Trader	2	1.6
Others	4	3.2
Total	124	100.0

"you just can't find servants around here anymore."

Table 2 shows that of the formerly wage-
earning women whom the strawberry agroindustry has attracted most have been servants and agricultural laborers. We can now
ask: Why have they taken jobs in the strawberry plants? Most of the female employees
prefer to work in these plants rather than as
servants because, as Irma Cortes said, "We
are not subject to the will of *la patrona* [the
employer] and we can live in our own homes
in the village where we have friends." Some of
them like working in agriculture, but they
find the work harsh. One of them said she
preferred work in the fields "because we are
out in the air, and not under the discipline of
the factory, even though it is much more tiring work; for example, pulling out the weeds
growing in the fields is awful hard work, and
one ends up with one's back real tired."

Did they change jobs because of wage differentials? The income of 76.6 percent of
those interviewed increased with their employment in the plants, while that of 7.6 percent remained the same. The high percentage of those who earned lower incomes (16.6
percent) can be partly explained by the fact
that many of these had only recently joined
the plants and had not yet acquired the necessary skills, while others attended work irregu-
larly. Of those who previously held jobs, 66.1
percent worked in their own community, 28.2
percent in the region, and only 0.7 percent in

another state, in Mexico City, or in the United States. Clearly, the strawberry companies have not brought back women working outside the region, nor have they attracted migrants from outlying regions, for the recruitment system precludes doing so. In fact, only 6.7 percent of the female workers were born in Zamora and Jacona, or in Ecuandureo, a neighboring municipality. The rest come from other municipalities in the same region.

None of the women workers live by themselves or with friends. With one exception—a woman who was adopted by the family with whom she lives—they all live with family or kin. The fact that they still live with their families is due to a very deeply rooted social rule that forbids a young woman's leaving her father's home unless it be through marriage. But their choice of residence is also directly enforced by the acute housing scarcity in Zamora and Jacona and by the fact that the wages they earn are clearly insufficient to permit living in a boardinghouse, the only socially acceptable form of habitation for single women living away from home.

Age, Marriage, and Schooling

Most of the workers, 68.7 percent of the sample, are between fifteen and twenty-four years of age (Table 3). Managers of the plants stated that they prefer to hire young women because of their higher productivity, and because they are "very quick with their hands" and "concentrate better than the men." In

TABLE 3. Ages of Female Workers

Age	Cases (N)	%
12–14	30	10.0
15–19	141	47.1
20–24	65	21.6
25–29	16	5.3
30–50	39	13.0
51–80	9	3.0
Total	300	100.0

fact, the younger women's manual dexterity is crucial in the task of removing the stems, but it is of only secondary importance in selecting and packing the strawberries; older women could do the latter tasks just as well. In only two of the plants, however, were older women predominantly chosen for these. Additional factors that influence the preference for hiring young women are analyzed in the next sections.

Girls usually begin to work in the plants when they are twelve to fifteen years old, and they work until they marry, normally between the ages of seventeen and twenty-one. As one of them put it, "The women marry before they are twenty because at that age the men say we have already missed the last boat." Those who do not marry continue working, and a few young married women return to work in the plants.

Of the female workers interviewed, 85.3 percent are single, 9.0 percent are married, 3.0 percent are divorced or abandoned, and 2.7 percent are widows. Almost all workers over the age of thirty are widowed, divorced, or separated from their husbands. Most of them support their children and perhaps their parents or siblings. The few married women workers state that their husbands do not send back enough money from the United States where they are working.

One older woman told us that in the early times of the packing plants women stood in long lines outside of the plants hoping to be hired: "There were little girls, young girls and adults, even old women." But, at present, the increase in the number of plants has led to a relative scarcity of women workers, particularly during the peak time of the season. At this busy time, plants hire women of all ages, including twelve-year-olds and older women. Then, as strawberries begin to come in at a slower rate, the management begins to eliminate workers: "First the little girls, then the lazy ones, then others begin to drop out by themselves when they see that there is very little working time left," one worker told us.

Sixteen percent, mostly the older workers, have not been to school at all, while 31 percent attended primary school up to the third grade. This low average in schooling can be explained by conditions in their communities, but it is significant to note that 3.7 percent have reached the high school or preparatory school level, since in theory their education should have given them access to jobs with higher incomes and prestige. But the fact is that very few such jobs are available in Zamora, and, besides, these women explained that they earn more money working at a fast pace in the plants than they would working in a shop or an office.

Although they seem to recognize this, the great majority of the women are convinced that their low degree of schooling prevents them from getting other jobs, and they complain bitterly that their parents, especially their fathers, did not allow them to go on studying: "Women are not allowed to finish [school] because our parents say it does not pay for itself because we then go and get married, and it has only been a waste." "If I were to study," said another, "I could be a secretary, and I would stop doing this very tiring job." The mythical nature of this hope becomes clear if we realize that, as has happened in other developing countries, an increase in levels of education would lead to an increase in job entrance requirements, and consequently, the same proportion of less qualified women—even if their educational level were higher in absolute terms—would continue filling the lower-level jobs.

This hypothesis is further strengthened if we compare the plant workers surveyed in Zamora with a group of female agricultural laborers, surveyed in the state of Aguascalientes north of Michoacán, who pick grapes seasonally.[17] The profile of marital status among the grape pickers resembles that of the workers in the strawberry plants: 80 percent are single, 8 percent are married, 3 percent are divorced or separated, and 9 percent are widowed.[18] In ages and schooling, the percentage distribution is also similar, but there are significant differences.

The similarities in both age structure and schooling indicate that roughly the same social group of women enter either of those jobs (Tables 4 and 5). But more women with

TABLE 4. Ages of Female Agricultural Laborers in Aguascalientes and Women Workers in Agroindustry in Zamora

Age	Women Workers in Zamora (%)	Women Laborers in Aguascalientes (%)
12–19	57.0	52
20–29	27.0	21
30–39	7.7	10
40 or over	8.3	17
Total	100.0	100

Source:—For the Aguascalientes: Lucia Diaz Ronner and Maria Elena Munoz, "La Mujer Asalariada en el sector agricola," *America indigena* 38 (April–June 1978): 327–34. Other statistics from authors' research.

higher schooling between the ages of twelve and nineteen enter strawberry-factory work in Zamora. The foregoing suggests that many young, single girls enter agroindustry who otherwise would not work for wages and, second, that strawberry-plant work attracts women whose higher educational levels make it unlikely that they would accept work in agriculture. However, additional data not included in the surveys on the educational levels in the communities would be necessary to confirm the latter hypothesis.

TABLE 5. Schooling of Female Agricultural Workers in Aguascalientes and Women Workers in Agroindustry in Zamora

Education	Wormen Workers in Zamora (%)	Women Laborers in Aguascalientes (%)
None	16.0	32
1st–3rd grade, primary	31.0	28
4th–6th grade, primary	49.3	40
Secondary or preparatory	3.7	. . .
Total	100.0	100

Source.—See Table 4.

Social Attitudes toward Women's Work in the Factories

When the strawberry industry first began, it was very difficult for the plant managers to recruit enough women workers. They could get those who were already working in other jobs but were unable to attract young women whose families were not in dire need of additional income. The women's reluctance to enter paid employment was due to the very real fear, confirmed by women's experiences, that unaccompanied young women in public places would be "stolen." Carmen Garcia summarizes it neatly: "Previously, it was really rotten for the girls, because they were frequently stolen when they were going to fetch water, or to wash clothes or to bring the *nixtamal* [maize dough]. . . . They were even stolen with the help of a gun or a machete. They were taken into the woods and then the men would come to ask their parents for the girl [in marriage]. Most of the girls did marry them, even if they did not want to, and here divorce is out of the question. If they don't get on together, the woman just puts up with it. Here it is customary for the husbands to beat the women when they are drunk, they say that blows make women love them more. . . . " Yet, as it happens, the fact that the young girls are no longer "stolen" as often in the peasant villages of the region as they were in the past is attributed mainly to their working in the strawberry plants, although no one ever explains exactly why this is so.

At first, the fathers flatly refused their daughters permission to work in the factories. One woman told us: "The parents are not used to one's working and in the village people gossip a lot, they say that the women who go out to work go with many men." Not long ago it was still forbidden for men and women in the villages to address one another on the street. What the parents most feared, did occasionally happen. An experienced worker, Ines Gomez, explained: "When it [work in the plants] began, it turned out that many of the girls got pregnant because they did not know how to look out for themselves, and as we move in an environment of 'machismo' and paternalism, it happened frequently. . . . but now the girls know how to handle themselves, now they even want to study and improve themselves." The young women workers see their situation in a different way and complain bitterly: "All they do is spread rumors about us. Many boys say they won't marry those who work in the plants, and all the girls from the village work there, but of course later they themselves are after us. They spread many untrue stories about us. Some of our nieces even went around saying that we were pregnant, and that we had left the children at the Social Security."

The young women workers' situation is further complicated by the migration of most of the marriageable men: "The girls don't go North [to the United States] because people talk badly about them. Even if we just go to Zamora they talk badly, we can never go anywhere. . . . The boys are allowed to go North and they come back real proud, some of them shack up with the American girls over there. They say they are very loose, that they even go after the boys. Others do return here to get married."

Initially the local priests were opposed to the women's factory work too. One incident illustrates the situation very clearly. The strawberry plants in Jacona were unable to get female workers because every Sunday the local priest thundered that women would go to hell if they sinned by going out to work in the factories. It is said that the problem was solved when the owners of the plant spoke with the priest and offered to pay for the cost of a new altar for the parish church. Since that day, the local priest has exalted the dignity of work.

Wages and Expenditures

As has been noted, the workers' wages are subject to the rate at which the plants buy strawberries during the year and to their own level of skill. The monthly average wage among workers surveyed is $1,126 (US$51.18). Eleven percent earn an average of $1,750 (US$79.51), 26 percent earn an average of $750 (US$34.09) per month, while 8 percent earn an average of $350 (US$15.90).

These wage levels are very far below the legal minimum wage, which amounted to $4,260 (US$193.63) for that region in 1980. Since a single person, let alone a family with children, cannot survive on this income, such low wages can only be considered as complementary to the main income of a family.

Worse still is the fact that the wages these women get vary enormously on a day-by-day and week-by-week basis. The season begins in November or December and lasts until July or August. However, during that period there are "bad months," as the women call them— November, December, January, February, August, September—in which they earn an average of less than $500 (US$22.72) per month. During the good months they may earn as much as $2,200 (US$90.90) per month. Most of the women are not hired at the plants for the whole year; 56 percent work from seven to nine months; 5 percent work from ten to twelve months; 16 percent from four to six months; 11.6 percent from one to three; and 11.3 percent do not get to work even one month per year. Many of those in this latter group work only on the Saturdays during the peak season, or they are younger sisters of the workers who tag along a few days per week.

During the months when there is no work in the plants, 75.3 percent remain at home helping with the domestic work; some do embroidering or knit pieces for sale. The surprisingly large number of women who follow this pattern indicates that these families do not urgently require a constant income from the women workers. In some cases— as, for example, one where the daughter supports herself and her mother—the income earned in the plant in the months of seasonal work is sufficient to keep them during the three months without work. Among the 24.3 percent of the workers who do work during these months, 7 percent work as servants, 11 percent go harvesting in the fields as day laborers, 1.0 percent work in offices, and 0.3 percent migrate to the United States. The remainder work in the informal sector in a variety of ways.

To what extent do these predominantly peasant families depend on the women workers' income? The majority (61.6 percent) answered that their work only partially supports their families, 20.7 percent replied that they give no financial help to their families, and 17.7 percent stated that they offer major support. It is usual for one of the younger girls to hand over the entire weekly wage to her father or mother, who then little by little lets her have whatever money she requires for her expenses. Table 6 shows that the correlation between the amount a worker gives her parents and the amount she earns is not significant.

How are their wages spent? What the workers keep for themselves, they spend on fashionable clothes, costume jewelry, romantic comics and stories, and beauty products. But the larger part of their wage, handled by their parents, goes into buying household consumer goods. This has been a boom for shops selling furniture and electric appliances. Some of the consumer goods purchased in the poorer households are basic items such as gas stoves, beds, wardrobes, and sewing machines; in other households the goods may be televisions, radios, blenders, and record players. Only a few households buy luxury items such as enormous consoles, fancy furniture, porcelain figurines, wine glasses, and so on.

TABLE 6. Workers' Monthly Wages by Proportion Given to Parents (%)

Monthly Wages (Pesos)	All	Almost All	One-Half	A Little	Nothing
200–1,000	36.9	15.7	23.8	10.5	13.1
1,001–2,000	30.1	25.3	27.4	12.4	4.8
2,001–3,000	38.2	27.4	25.4	7.2	1.8
Over 3,000	11.2	44.4	11.1	22.2	11.1
All wage categories*	31.0	24.0	25.7	11.0	5.7

*2.6% of workers surveyed did not answer this question..

The survey indicates, however, that the parents buy these items not only for prestige but also because they can sell or pawn them when times get hard. It must be noted that the commercial boom in Zamora is due only in part to the women workers' income; it is mainly a result of the income in dollars sent back by the male migrants working in the United States. Even so, the pattern of consumption is the same in both cases.

Recruitment of Workers for the Plants

Women workers are recruited each season through social networks in the communities. In the plants that have unions, the union secretary chooses women delegates in each village or hamlet; in plants that don't have a union, the head of personnel chooses these delegates. Once the word is sent to them that they should begin recruiting, these delegates go around the village letting everyone know that they are hiring. They list the names of those women who want to go to work, purportedly giving preference to experienced workers. But Antonieta Castro complained that previous experience matters little: "Some of the new ones are given preference by the bosses, because they give them *gollete* [some present]. We don't get angry about this, we only feel hurt." The "loyalty" that a worker has shown toward the general secretary of the union or the company is also taken into account during compilation of the lists, as are personal preferences and group rivalries within the community. In hiring, the company follows the list made by the delegate, moving through it progressively as the season advances. The recruiter in the village, usually an older woman, is socially responsible for the young girls she recruits as workers. Parents sometimes allow their daughters to go only if they trust the recruiter. This responsibility also gives the latter the power to decide who will work in the plant.

Conditions of Work

Hiring conditions and benefits in most plants are clearly below legal requirements stated in Mexican law. In the first place there are no contracts or permanent jobs for the workers. (According to the law the companies should pay the minimum wage, establish fixed working schedules, and hire the workers permanently during the entire year.) In the second place, fringe benefits are nonexistent: plant workers have no Social Security, nor do they have adequate medical services. More mothers could work if the plants had nurseries, and by law factories must provide one whenever there are more than thirty permanent women workers. When the women ask for a nursery, however, they are turned down. One manager said: "We saw that the nursery was not really necessary because only two or three children come along with their mothers, and that is why we did not put one in."

Women's Perception of Their Work in the Plants

Although these conditions persist, and in spite of the fact that many of the women employed in the plant consider the work to be tiring and oppressive, they prefer it because their only alternative would be to remain shut in their homes doing domestic work or to work in jobs that are even more underpaid. Of the workers surveyed, 65 percent said that they prefer to work outside their home. As Amalia Vega put it: "We like so much to go out and work in the packing plant that when we return to our village in the evening we skip along the road dancing and singing. We don't mind about being tired [after a working day of eight to eleven hours]; because we have earned our few pennies and have left the little ranch for a while, we are very happy. In the village you get bored by seeing the same faces all day long and listening to the same gossip. By working we entertain ourselves." This is, in fact, a very fair assessment of the situation. When asked what type of work they like best, 59 percent answered that they prefer to work in a strawberry plant; only 4.5 percent prefer to work on the land, and 36.5 percent would prefer to be employed in an office.

Although four out of every five workers interviewed said they wanted improvements in their working conditions, particularly in wages and in the treatment they receive from their bosses, there are no real channels for protest. Only half of them belonged to a union, but this was due to the fact that only four of the six plants had a union. However, less than half of the workers (46.7 percent) thought that unionization could help them get better working conditions. This distrust reflects the fact that the existing unions closely collaborate with management. The pragmatic attitude of the union leaders, some of them women, is evident in the statement of one woman leader. Asked how she and other leaders got along with management, she said: "Fortunately there has always been a good relationship. People get to understand each other by talking. Also, we are interested in the company not having a loss, otherwise, we don't get *utilidades* [a profit-sharing government scheme]." In actual fact, workers rarely receive *utilidades*, which are sometimes used to pay for the annual fiesta and Mass in the plant. As a result, workers hardly participate in union activities: "We get bored going to the meetings," one worker told us. "We don't understand anything and we get nothing out of it. We just waste our time."

Almost all the younger workers consider their job in the agroindustry as a stage in their life that allows them to get out of the daily routine of the village. More than half (58 percent) answered that they do not plan to go on working once they get married. In so many words, they were saying: "Why, that's what I'm getting married for, to stop working!" Of those who say they may continue to work, most believe they will marry a bum and will end up having to support their household.

CONCLUSIONS

Why does the strawberry agroindustry predominantly employ women? It is true that the jobs of removing stems and selecting strawberries require a manual dexterity that men do not usually achieve, but this is not the main reason that the industry employs women. In the region of Zamora, agroindustry cannot compete with the wages paid in the United States in order to attract and retain migrant male labor. At the same time there is a large population of young women who have very few alternatives for work. The strawberry plants do not have to compete with urban wages for women workers, since the emigration of women from the region is not frequent; male emigration largely covers the deficit in the budget of most peasant families. Moreover, the great majority of young women in peasant families have access only to paid domestic work or to wage labor on the land, both of them unrewarding jobs.

Therefore, the main reason for employing women is that they can be paid much lower wages than those stipulated by law, and can be asked to accept conditions in which there is a constant fluctuation in schedules and days of work. Here it seems to us that the companies take advantage of the traditional idea that any income earned by a daughter, wife, or mother is an "extra" over and above the main income of the father, husband, or son. If such wages were paid to male workers, the low income and the instability of the job would be untenable in the long run; workers would either move to other jobs or organize and strike to get higher wages.

Other results of the analysis support this view. That the percentage of women household-heads in the packing and refrigerating plants is very low—5.7 percent as compared to 12 percent in the region as a whole—suggests that the wages paid by the plants cannot constitute the central income of a household. In a circular fashion, of course, it also reflects the factories' preference for young, unmarried workers.

Thus, the plants attract many young women—approximately one-half of the women workers—who normally would not enter wage-earning jobs if the plants did not exist. So it seems, at least, from a comparison made with a group of agricultural laborers from Aguascalientes and from the fact that 42.4 percent of the workers surveyed gave only half or less than half of their wages to their households. Further support for this hypothesis is found in the large majority of women workers who do not seek alternative work during the months they are not employed in the plants. Another advantage for the plants is the constant turnover among women workers. This impermanence allows a company considerable savings in wage increases due to seniority as well as in payments for maternity, disease, or disablement and in old-age pensions. It also prevents the workers from accumulating information and experience that would lead them to organize and to demand improvements in hiring and working conditions. Meanwhile, the traditional culture itself assures continuous instability by making marriage the only aspiration for women.

Clearly, the strawberry agroindustry in Zamora can exist only thanks to particular conditions by which cheap female labor is readily available. This conclusion coincides with that reached by Ernst Feder, who points to the low cost of labor as one of the most important factors in making the Mexican strawberry industry competitive internationally.[19] Thus, the "comparative advantages" of this industry in the international market are closely associated with the "comparative disadvantages" of young, inexperienced, rural women who suffer social, legal, and economic discrimination. From a sociological point of view, what the agribusiness capitals have done is to make use of certain social and cultural characteristics of the region, that is, the high demographic growth, the traditional cultural values that assign a subordinate role to women, the family structure of the communities, and the local patterns of consumption. The key question to be asked is whether this way of using resources will improve the living conditions of the women and of their communities.

Have conditions for women changed with their entry into salaried industrial work? This study shows that they have changed very little. The great majority of workers continue to live in their parents' homes; a very few go to live with other relatives in Zamora, but always under the same conditions of subordination and restriction they experienced in their own homes. About half of them hand over the greater part of their wages to their parents or use their earnings to support their own families. Thus they have only slightly increased their personal consumption. Their families, of course, have an improved standard of living, at least temporarily.

Although the women have more freedom when working outside of their homes, they are harassed by the men in the streets and are not free to move around the town or the villages on their own. Even when traveling to and from the plants the young women are closely supervised by the recruiters and the union leaders. There have been some changes: the young girls are not "stolen" as frequently as before, and apparently they have a more decisive voice as to whom they will marry. Also, some have become eager to study and to get ahead.

But work in this agroindustry, for the majority of women, is certainly no way to get ahead. There are no promotions; the workers get no encouragement or help to acquire skills or education; and the instability and low wages of the jobs, as mentioned previously, do not offer any prospects for improvement in the future. Predictably, under these conditions no significant cultural change is taking place. On the contrary, the lack of prospects for promotion in the agroindustry, the low wages, and the high level of unemployment only push the workers back into the traditional hope of marriage as the only road toward a better future. Only a few of the young women, mostly those who have not married, have acquired new aspirations about employment possibilities and lifestyles. For these too, however, it will be very difficult to find employment once the strawberry industry declines. The strawberry companies take advantage of the traditional values and conditions that subordinate women and end up reinforcing this traditional order. In fact, it is in their interest to oppose any initiatives to change the passive, submissive role of women in Zamora. In this sense, no "modernization" of women's roles is evident in the region.

What has been the impact of the strawberry agroindustry on the communities of the region? In the short run the industry has provided a better standard of living for rural families. The majority use the women's incomes to improve their housing and, particularly, to purchase household goods—furniture and electric appliances—which also serve as a form of saving. The workers' wages, then, flow rapidly through the merchants of Zamora toward the urban industries that manufacture these consumer goods.

But while the market for consumer goods has expanded, the poorer groups in the region have not been brought into the market. Because of the hiring practices in the plants, work is not given to women heads of households, nor to the poorer male and female laborers—those who most require an income. Rather, since the survey shows that the majority of the workers do not support themselves, it would seem that jobs are given mostly to young women of the middle-level peasant families, whose wages serve to improve their families' standard of living. Although such a gain is not to be underestimated, it benefits only minimally those households whose economic survival depends entirely or partially on women's wages. As a result, older women who are heads of households are pushed back into the strenuous, harsh, and even more poorly paid job of strawberry picking in the fields.

The strawberry agroindustry is not creating conditions for the future development of the region. It is not training workers, nor is it promoting or improving the social services. It does not serve to stem emigration of men to the United States. The cultivation of strawberries, on the contrary, tends toward the concentration of land and capital while it displaces and undermines production in small landholdings.

Thus, it seems to us that the strawberry agroindustry has provided some short-term improvements, but in the long run—aside from the profits that flow mainly to U.S. agribusiness concerns and to affluent local entrepreneurs—it will leave behind nothing but ashes when it collapses. The collapse is expected, according to two plant managers, in about three to five years. It is difficult to refrain from apocalyptic forecasts when we can see that the decline of this agroindustry will plunge the region back into underdevelopment: peasant household incomes will fall, massive unemployment will force countless women and families to migrate, and the hopes for a better life that have been raised among women will, once again, be destroyed. Basically, nothing will have changed for women. Since the strawberry industry requires female workers whose income is not essential for the household, it bypasses the needy and predominantly employs women from middle-income groups. Since it requires submissive and docile workers, it reinforces patriarchal and authoritarian structures. Since it benefits from a constant turnover of workers, it does not oppose the machismo that confines women to home and marriage.

The basic dilemma emerges very clearly under a feminist analysis. Much of the data—for instance, Amalia Vega's touching description of the joy she and other women feel at being allowed to leave the narrow horizons of their villages—shows that the plants improve the lives of women and therefore from a feminist point of view should be defended. At the same time, salaries and working conditions at these plants are dismally exploitative, comparing unfavorably both to the norms set down by Mexican law and to actual situations elsewhere in Mexican industry; for this reason they should be denounced and opposed.

An even more painful dilemma faced by women's movements in situations such as this is that women whose consciousness has been raised by a temporary prosperity will be left stranded when economic and social survival again becomes difficult if not impossible, while industries that were once a source of hope move to regions populated by another group of docile and disadvantaged women. Thus, by the time the strawberry agribusiness—or the U.S. assembly plants along the Mexican border, for that matter—move to other countries that offer lower production costs, the jobs Mexican women had temporarily gained from the loss experienced by their U.S. counterparts will also be lost to them. The jobs will then become a temporary gain for, perhaps, Haitian or Honduran women.

In this way, women's "comparative disadvantages" in the labor market in any given country can, at some point in time, be translated into "comparative advantages" for companies, capitals, and governments in the international markets. When disadvantaged women organize to get even minimal improvements in wages and working conditions, the "comparative advantages" are lost, and investments go elsewhere. Clearly, all women lose along this chain. This being the case, one can only conclude that discrimination against women in employment, reflecting as it does the disadvantages women suffer from attitudes about gender, from social customs, and from their lack of political power, cannot be fought effectively in one place or country unless an appropriate international perspective is developed.

NOTES

1. Helen I. Safa, "Runaway Shops and Female Employment: The Search for Cheap Labor," in this issue; United Nations Industrial Development Office (UNIDO), "Women in the Redeployment of Manufacturing Industry to Developing Countries" (UNIDO Working Paper, no. 3, United Nations, 1980).

2. Linda Lim, *Women Workers in Multinational Corporations: The Case of the Electronics Industry in Malaysia and Singapore*, Michigan Occasional Papers, no. 9 (Ann Arbor: University of Michigan, 1978).

3. Michael Todaro, *Economics for a Developing World* (London: Longman Group Ltd., 1977).

4. Francis Moore Lappe et al., *Food First: Beyond the Myth of Scarcity* (Boston: Houghton Mifflin Co., 1977).

5. Susan George, *How the Other Half Dies* (Montclair, N.J.: Allanheld, Osmun & Co., 1977).

6. Ingrid Palmer, "Rural Poverty in Indonesia," in *Poverty and Landlessness in Rural Asia* (Geneva: International Labour Office, 1977); Cynthia Hewitt de Alcantara, *La modernizacion de la agricultura Mexicana* (Mexico: Siglo XXI Editores, S.A., 1978).

7. Lourdes Arizpe, *Migracion, etnicismo y cambio economico* (Mexico: Colegio de México, 1978).

8. R. Burbach and P. Flynn, "Agribusiness Targets Latin America," *NACLA Report on the Americas* 12(January–February 1978):5.

9. Ernst Feder, *El imperialismo fresa* (Mexico: Ed. Campesina, 1977).

10. Lim; and George.

11. International Labour Office (ILO), *Women in the Economic Activities of the World: A Statistical Analysis* (Geneva: ILO, 1980).

12. United Nations Development Program (UNDP), "Rural Women's Participation in Development," UNDP Evaluation Study, no. 3 (Geneva: United Nations, 1980); and Jocelyn Massiah, "Family Structure and the Status of Women in the Caribbean, with Particular Reference to Women Who Head Households," UNESCO, SS-80/Conf.627/COL.34 (paper delivered at the Conference on Women, Development and Population Trends, Paris, 1980).

13. Carmen Diana Deere and Magdalena León de Leal, "Peasant Production, Proletarianization, and the Sexual Division of Labor in the Andes," in this issue; and Cheywa Spindel, "Capital Oligopólico e a produçao rural de base familiar paper socio-economico da mulher" (unpublished research paper for the Rural Employment Policies Branch, ILO, Geneva, 1980).

14. Lucila Diaz Ronner and Maria Elena Munoz, "La Mujer asalariada en el sector agricola," *America indigena* 38 (April–June 1978): 327–34; Alicia E. Silva de Rojas and Consuelo Corredor de Prieto, "La explotacion de la mano de obra femenina en la industria de las flores: Un estudio de caso en Colombia" (unpublished research paper for the Rural Employment Policies Branch, ILO, Geneva, 1980); Diana Medrano, "El caso de las obreras de los cultivos de flores de los municipios de Chia, Cajica y Tabio en la sabana de Bogota, Colombia" (unpublished research paper for the Rural Employment Policies Branch, ILO, Geneva, 1980); and Marta Roldan, "Trabajo asalariado y condicion de la mujer rural en un cultivo de exportacion: El caso de las trabajadoras del tomate en el estado de Sinaloa, Mexico" (unpublished research paper for the Rural Employment Policies Branch, ILO, Geneva, 1980).

15. Maria Patricia Fernández Kelly, "Mexican Border Industrialization, Female Labour Force Participation and Migration," International Migration Review, In Press.

16. Feder.

17. Ronner, p. 331.

18. Ibid.

19. Feder.

Film List

BIOLOGY, GENDER, AND HUMAN EVOLUTION

Jane Goodall Studies of the Chimpanzee. "Tool Using." National Geographic Society. 1978. 24 minutes. Describes how young chimpanzees play with objects and how this play prepares them for making and using tools as adults.

Among the Wild Chimpanzees. National Geographic Society. 1984. 59 minutes. Features Jane Goodall as researcher and examines infant chimpanzee development and behavior, male-female dominance, and hunting.

Ax Fight. Penn State. 1971. 30 minutes. Portrays conflict between hosts and visitors among the Yanomamo.

The Two Brains. PBS Brain Series. 1984. 60 minutes. Examines the unique functions of each hemisphere of the human brain and the possible effects of culture on the brain. Describes differences between male and female brains that seem to result from sex hormones and shows how some brain abnormalities may chemically affect the brain.

Sex and Money. Filmakers Library. 1989. 50 minutes. Focuses on transsexual individuals in the United States and the Netherlands. Dr. John Money addresses differences between gender identity and gender roles. Contains explicit sexual material.

Argument About a Marriage. DER. 1966. 18 minutes. Views a conflict that arises between two !Kung bands concerning the legitimacy of a marriage, discusses a charge of infidelity, and illustrates use of verbal aggression among the !Kung.

DOMESTIC WORLDS AND PUBLIC WORLDS

Kypseli: Women and Men Apart—A Divided Reality. University of California, Berkeley. 1976. 40 minutes. Examines gender roles in a Greek peasant village.

Afghan Women. University of California, Berkeley. 1975. 17 minutes. Examines the role of women in a rural community in northern Afghanistan.

Some Women of Marrakech. Granada Disappearing World Series. Thomas Howe Associates. 1976. 55 minutes. Re-edited for Odyssey, 1981. Discusses the importance of marriage and family for women in Morocco and shows the impact of religion and class on women's lives.

Women, Work and Babies. NBC production. 1985. 60 minutes. Discusses gender ideology in the United States and problems of working mothers.

The Double Day. IWFP. Cinema Guild. 1975. 54 minutes. Discusses burdens of working women in Latin America.

Clotheslines. Filmakers Library. 1981. 32 minutes. Shows the love-hate relationship that women have with cleaning the family clothes.

THE CULTURAL CONSTRUCTION OF GENDER AND PERSONHOOD

A Man, When He is a Man. Women Make Movies. 1982. 66 minutes. Set in Costa Rica, this film illuminates the social climate and cultural traditions that nurture machismo and allow the domination of women to flourish in Latin America.

Small Happiness. Women of a Chinese Village. New Day Films. VHS video cassette. 1984. 58 minutes. Provides historical perspective on marriage, birth control, work, and daily life.

The Women's Olamal: The Organization of a Maasai Fertility Ceremony. Documentary Educational Resources. 1984. 115 minutes. Presents a picture of women's lives in the male-dominated society of the Maasai in Kenya.

Maasai Manhood. ISHI. 1983. 53 Minutes. Describes a male initiation ritual among pastoral Maasai of Kenya.

Rivers of Sand. University of California, Berkeley. 1975. 83 minutes. Portrays male supremacy among the Hamar of Ethiopia, including male initiation.

Killing Us Softly. Cambridge Documentary Films. 1979. 30 minutes. Details psychological and sexual themes in American advertising.

Men's Lives. New Day Films. 1974. 43 minutes.

*An asterisk indicates that the film was previewed by the editors.

500

Discusses American concepts of masculinity and links gender ideology, power, and capitalism.

Beyond Macho. Films for the Humanities and Sciences. 1985. 26 minutes. Explores roles for men that have evolved in response to feminism and economic changes in the United States through an examination of the lives of two men, one a nurse and the other a "househusband."

Men and Masculinity. OASIS. 1990. 30 minutes. Covers the thirteenth National Conference on Men and Masculinity and discusses a broad range of men's movement issues in the United States, including antipornography activism, challenges to homophobia, and domestic violence.

Stale Roles and Tight Buns. OASIS. 1988. 29 minutes. Uses advertising images to show how men are stereotyped in the media and how myths develop that limit men's and women's roles.

Becoming a Woman in Okrika. Filmakers Library. 1990. 27 minutes. A coming of age ritual in a village in the Niger Delta.

Surname Viet Given Name Nam. Women Make Movies. 1989. 108 minutes. Explores the multiplicity of identities of Vietnamese women in Vietnam and in California.

Faces of Change: Andean Women. University of California, Berkeley. 1975. 19 minutes. Describes cultural ideals of female subservience among Aymara.

Dear Lisa: A Letter to My Sister. New Day Films. 1990. 45 minutes. Based on interviews with 13 women and girls from various backgrounds, the film explores women's roles in the United States in relation to childhood, play, work, parenting, and family culture. It also touches on questions of body image, the "second shift," self esteem, and sexual assault.

CULTURE AND SEXUALITY

Women Like Us. Women Make Movies. 1990. 49 minutes. Portrays older lesbian women in Great Britain, their feelings and lifestyles, and discusses the implications of sexual orientation for family and work relations.

On Being Gay. TRB Productions. 1986. 80 minutes. Through monologue by Brian McNaught, this film addresses myths about homosexuality and such topics as growing up gay in a straight world, Bible-based bigotry, stereotypes, transvestitism, transsexualism, and AIDS.

Metamorphosis: Man Into Woman. Filmakers Library. 1990. 58 minutes. Features a transsexual confronting gender stereotypes in society.

Man Oh Man—Growing Up Male in America. New Day Films, Inc. 1987. 19 minutes. Focuses on being a man in contemporary American society, with an emphasis on the difficulties of living up to cultural ideals of manhood.

Choosing Children. Cambridge Documentary. Explores three situations in which lesbians have had children.

Masai Manhood. Films Incorporated Video. 1983. 52 minutes. Focuses on the lives of Masai men and the Eunoto ceremony that marks their transition from warrior to elder.

EQUALITY AND INEQUALITY: THE SEXUAL DIVISION OF LABOR AND GENDER STRATIFICATION

Hunters and Gatherers

N!ai: The Story of a !Kung Woman. Penn State University. 1980. 59 minutes. Features the biography of a !Kung woman from early childhood to middle age and the impact of colonial penetration on her life.

The Warao. University of California, Berkeley. 1978. 57 minutes. Ethnographic account of division of labor among the Warao of the Orinoco River delta in Venezuela.

Horticulturalists

Seasons of the Navajo. PBS Video, Peace River Films. 1984. 60 minutes. Presents one family's kinship with the earth through seasons, touching briefly on Navajo matriliny and women's work and craft responsibilities.

Summer of Loucheux: A Portrait of a Northern Indian Family. New Day Films. 28 minutes. 1983. Portrays a young woman who joins her family at their summer fishing camp.

Agriculturalists

Luisa Torres. Chip Taylor Communications. 1980. 28 minutes. The recollections of a Hispanic woman in northern New Mexico; discusses division of labor, marriage, use of medicinal plants, and other aspects of daily life.

Kheturni Bayo: North Indian Farm Women. Penn State. 1980. 19 minutes. Examines the roles and the duties of the women in a typical extended family of land-owning peasants in Gujarat, India.

Pastoralists

Masai Women. Thomas Howe Associates. 1983. 52 minutes. Examines the role of women among pastoralists in Kenya.

Women of the Toubou. University of California, Berkeley. 1974. 25 minutes. Examines gender roles among nomads of the Sahara.

Boran Women. University of California, Berkeley. 1975. 18 minutes. Shows women's daily work in Kenyan society, including caring for cattle, milk storage, and child-care.

Deep Hearts. University of California, Berkeley. 1980. 53 minutes. Documentary on the Bororo Fulani in Niger, Africa. Focuses on ritual dances in which men compete in a beauty contest.

Miscellaneous

Asante Market Women. Penn State. 1983. 52 minutes. Power of Ghanaian market women from a matrilineal and polygynous society.

From the Shore. Indiana University. 1989. Explores the formation of a fishing cooperative among women in the coastal village of Shimoni, Kenya, in defiance of the traditional roles of women.

With These Hands. Filmakers Library. 1987. 33 minutes. Shows how African women are overworked, how cash crops interfere with their food production, and how their political empowerment might overcome constraints to agricultural production.

Shunka's Story. University of California, Berkeley. 1977. 20 minutes. Portrait of a Tzotzil Maya woman in Mexico, conveying her thoughts about her life, culture, and children.

Maids and Madams. Filmakers Library. 1985. 52 minutes. Describes the plight of Black female domestic servants in South Africa and analyzes the relationship between gender, class, and apartheid.

The Trobriand Islanders of Papua New Guinea. Films Incorporated Video. 1990. 52 minutes. Focuses on the distribution of women's wealth after a death, and the month of celebration following the yam harvest.

A Kiss on the Mouth. Women Make Movies. 1987. 30 minutes. Examines female prostitution in urban Brazil.

GENDER, PROPERTY, AND THE STATE

Who Will Cast the First Stone? Cinema Guild, Inc. 1988. 52 minutes. Examines the impact of Islamization on women in Pakistan, in particular the Hudood Ordinances under which adultery, rape, or extramarital sex are considered a crime against the state, punishable by stoning to death.

No Longer Silent. International Film Bureau. 1986. 57 minutes. Analyzes dowry deaths in India, as well as the cultural preference for boys and female infanticide.

Modern Brides. South Asian Area Center, University of Wisconsin. 1985. 30 minutes. Features two young women, one with an arranged marriage and one with a "love match," and discusses the bride's capacity to work as a substitute for dowry.

Las Madres. The Mothers of Plaza de Mayo. Direct Cinema Ltd. 1986. 64 minutes. Focuses on Argentinean mothers who, beginning in 1977, defy laws against civil demonstrations to protest the disappearance of their children under the military dictatorship.

Donna: Women in Revolt. Women Make Movies. 1980. 65 minutes. An examination of the history and development of Italian feminism through the personal stories of women involved in the women's rights movement at the turn of the century, the resistance during World War II, and of present day feminists.

Weaving the Future: Women of Guatemala. Women Make Movies. 1988. 28 minutes. A perspective on women in Guatemala's liberation struggle, exploring the pivotal role of women in building a just society amid political strife and poverty.

Gabriella. Women Make Movies. 1988. 67 minutes. Examines the work of a mass organization of diverse women's groups in the Philippines.

GENDER, HOUSEHOLD, AND KINSHIP

Dadi's Family. Odyssey. 1981. 58 minutes. Describes family tensions in a patrilineal joint household in northern India.

A Wife Among Wives. University of California, Berkeley. 1981. 70 minutes. Turkana women discuss polygyny.

The Vanishing Family: Crisis in Black America. University of California, Berkeley. 1986. 64 minutes. CBS News production with Bill Moyers that examines the disintegration of the black family in America, emphasizing individual responsibility rather than the structural conditions affecting employment rates and use of welfare.

Tobelo Marriage. University of California, Berkeley. 1990. 106 minutes. Chronicles a marriage ritual in Eastern Indonesia, including exchange of valuables, negotiations, and preparatory activities.

Asian Heart. Filmakers Library. 1987. 38 minutes. Deals with marriage brokering between clients from Denmark and Filipino "mail order brides."

A Village in Baltimore. Doreen Moses. 1730 21st St. N.W. Washington, DC 20009. 1981. 63 minutes. Conveys the problems and conflicts of changing identities and traditions among Greek immigrants in the United States, focusing on dowry, marriage, and other social events.

A Family To Me. New Day. 1986. 28 minutes. Portrays four nonstereotypical American families, their philosophies of childrearing, and family organization.

GENDER, RITUAL, AND RELIGION

Out of Order. Icarus Films. 1983. 88 minutes. Presents personal narratives of six women in various stages of convent life.

Behind the Veil: Nuns. Wombat Productions. 1984. 115 minutes. Examines the history of women in the Christian Church.

The Living Goddess. University of California, Berkeley. 1979. 30 minutes. Studies the Newar of Nepal, focusing on a ritual cult in which young virgin girls are thought to embody the spirits of goddesses.

The Shakers. University of California, Berkeley. 1974. 29 minutes. Traces the growth and decline of the Shaker community.

A Sense of Honor. Films Incorporated. 1984. 55 minutes. Made by an Egyptian anthropologist, the film describes the impact of Islamic fundamentalism on the lives of women in Egypt.

Rastafari: Conversations Concerning Women. Eye in I Filmworks. 1984. 60 minutes. Examines the roles and relations of men and women in the Jamaican Rastafarian movement.

A Veiled Revolution. Icarus. 1982. 27 minutes. Attempts to discern the reasons behind the movement in Egypt by young, educated women to resume wearing traditional Islamic garb.

Saints and Spirits. Disappearing World Series. 1978. 25 minutes. Explores the religious life of Muslim women in Marrakech, Morocco, including domestic rituals and pilgrimage to a mountain shrine.

An Initiation Kut for a Korean Shaman. Laurel Kendall and Diana Lee and the Center for Visual Anthropology. University of Hawaii Press. 1991. 36 minutes. Portrays the initiation of Chini, a young Korean woman, demonstrating her ability to perform as a shaman and shouting out the spirits' oracles.

GENDER, POLITICS, AND REPRODUCTION

No Longer Silent. International Film Bureau. 1986. 57 minutes. Discusses dowry deaths in India, as well as the cultural preference for boys and female infanticide.

Blood of the Condor. Penn State. 1969. 70 minutes. Describes U.S.-imposed sterilization of Quechua Indian women.

Rites. Filmakers Library. 1990. 52 minutes. Considers three major contexts in which female "genital mutilation" occurs: cosmetic, punitive, and rite of passage. Particularly emphasizes the health risks and psychological consequences of female circumcision.

China's One-Child Policy. Nova Special. 1985. 60 minutes. A documentary on China's population policy, its implementation, unpopularity, and its relation to gender ideology.

Nyamakuta—the One Who Receives: An African Midwife. Filmakers Library. 1989. 32 minutes. Portrays a traditional African midwife who incorporates pharmaceuticals with local practices to improve health standards in her village.

Kutambura, Struggling People. Films, Inc. 1987. 30 minutes. Focuses on women's efforts to ensure economic opportunity for their families in Zimbabwe. Family planning is emphasized as the key to raising women's self esteem and standard of living.

COLONIALISM AND DEVELOPMENT

The Four Seasons in Lenape Indian Life. 1983. Spoken Arts Inc. Treatment of experiences of women and men under colonialism through stories of Old Elm Bark Woman. Film Strip.

Women in a Changing World. University of California, Berkeley. 1975. 48 minutes. Impact of modernization on women in Bolivia, Kenya, Afghanistan, and Hong Kong.

Women in the Third World. PBS Video. 30 minutes. Examines living conditions of women in the developing world, emphasizing their central economic roles.

Women at Risk. Filmakers Library. 1991. 56 minutes. Presents portraits of women refugees in Asia, Africa, and Latin America.

The Global Assembly Line. New Day Films. 1986. 58 minutes. A portrayal of the lives of working women and men in the "free trade zones" of developing countries and North America. Focuses on Mexico and the Philippines.

Bringing It All Back Home. Women Make Movies. 1987. 48 minutes. Analyzes how the patterns of international capital investment and the exploitation of Third World women workers in free trade zones are being brought home to the First World, as Britain's declining industrial regions have been designated "enterprise zones" to attract the multinationals.

The Price of Change. Icarus. 1982. 27 minutes. A picture of changing attitude of and toward women in Egyptian society, focusing particularly on work outside the home.

Sweet Sugar Rage. Third World Newsreel. Illustrates the harsh conditions under which women live and work and the efforts of the Sistren theatre collective to change these conditions in a creative way.

Smile Orange. Portrays the tourist industry from the perspective of Jamaican male workers.

Women Under Siege. Icarus. 1982. 26 minutes. Illustrates women's lives and political goals in a Palestinian refugee camp near the Israeli border.

A State of Danger. Women Make Movies. 1989. 28 minutes. Offers a perspective on the Intifada, presenting women's testimonies on their experiences with the Israeli military.

The Price of Change. Icarus. 1982. 26 minutes. Shows the effect of economic change on women in Egypt.

Hell to Pay. Women Make Movies. 1988. 52 minutes. Presents an analysis of the international debt situation through the eyes of the women of Bolivia.

Holding Our Ground. International Film Bureau, Inc. 1988. 51 minutes. Features women and children in the Philippines who pressure the government for land reform, establish their own money lending system, and build shelters for street children.

South Africa Belongs to Us. University of California, Berkeley. 1980. 35 minutes. Describes economic and emotional burdens borne by black women in South Africa.

Maria's Story. Filmakers Library. 1990. 53 minutes. Portrays an FMLN guerilla, Maria Serrano, who has been living in the countryside for eleven years. Discusses her role in the revolution as well as the impact of the revolution on her family.

Reassemblage. Women Make Movies. 1982. 40 minutes. A study of the women of rural Senegal that addresses issues of the ethnographic representation of cultures.

Time of Women. Women Make Movies. 1988. 20 minutes. A portrait of the life of women in an Ecuadorian village where men are absent as migrants. The film looks at the impact of national economic policies on these rural women.

Fair Trade. Indiana University. 1989. Profiles Tanzanian women and their struggle to become small entrepreneurs and looks at the impact of development organizations and the aid that they extend to women through capital loans.

Where Credit Is Due. Indiana University. 1989. Features the problem that Kenyan women have with the banking system, which generally refuses loans to women, and describes the Kenya Women's Finance Trust as an example of a credit cooperative for women borrowed from rural traditions of women's support groups.